Digital Assets and the Law

This book delves into the intricacies of digital assets. With the increasing reliance on crypto and the potential adoption of digital currencies by central banks, our monetary system is at a critical point. The importance of taking the next step has become even more stringent, as evidenced by this systematic scientific reconstruction.

Divided into five concentric parts, the book starts with a historical, technical, and financial introduction to digital assets. It then explores the changing role of central banking and monetary economics in the upcoming era. Finally, it focuses on the broad legal issues arising from the new digital landscape, not shying away from exploring forward-thinking solutions and policies for the future.

With the contributions of prominent international experts in the field, this collection supplies a transdisciplinary analysis based on the belief that complex phenomena can only be handled by complex solutions. This groundbreaking work aims to be more than just an academic treatise; it is a must-read for students, scholars, financial professionals, and all those who want to understand the emerging digital currency reality that many have yet to fully recognise.

Filippo Zatti is an associate professor in economic law at the University of Florence. He leads a working group called BABEL, which focuses on blockchains and artificial intelligence for business, economics, and law.

Rosa Giovanna Barresi is a lawyer focusing on corporate and financial law. She teaches at the University of Florence's School of Economics and Management as an adjunct professor for the Lab in Cryptoassets.

Digital Assets and the Law

Fiat Money in the Era of Digital Currency

Edited by Filippo Zatti and Rosa Giovanna Barresi

Finanziato dall'Unione europea NextGenerationEU | Ministero dell'Università e della Ricerca | Italiadomani | Università degli Studi Firenze

This publication is funded by the EU Recovery and Resilience Plan (PNRR), as part of the Department of Economics and Management's Research Project of National Interest (PRIN) at the University of Florence.

Routledge
Taylor & Francis Group
LONDON AND NEW YORK

G. Giappichelli Editore

First published 2024
by Routledge
4 Park Square, Milton Park, Abingdon, Oxon OX14 4RN

and by Routledge
605 Third Avenue, New York, NY 10158

Routledge is an imprint of the Taylor & Francis Group, an informa business

British Library Cataloguing-in-Publication Data
A catalogue record for this book is available from the British Library

ISBN: 978-1-032-19227-7 (hbk)
ISBN: 978-1-032-19235-2 (pbk)
ISBN: 978-1-003-25826-1 (ebk)
ISBN: 979-12-211-0380-9 (Giappichelli)

DOI: 10.4324/9781003258261

Typeset in Galliard
by Deanta Global Publishing Services, Chennai, India

To Vincenzo Atripaldi,

My only 'Master,'
Forever grateful for having
shown me the Way

Contents

List of figures and tables

Figures

Tables

Acronyms and abbreviations

ACH	Automated Clearing House
AML	Anti Money Laundering
BIS	Bank for International Settlements
BoE	Bank of England
CFT	Countering the Financing of Terrorism
DAO	Decentralised Autonomous Organisation
DvP	Delivery Versus Payment
ECB	European Central Bank
ESCB	European System of Central Banks
ESMA	European Securities and Markets Authority
Fed	Federal Reserve
FSB	Financial Stability Board
FMI	Financial Market Infrastructure
CBDC	Central Bank Digital Currency
CBoB	Central Bank of The Bahamas
CPMI	Committee on Payment and Market Infrastructure
CPSS	Committee on Payment and Settlement Systems
DeFi	Decentralised Finance
DLT	Distributed Ledger Technology
EMIR	European Market for Infrastructure Regulation
GDP	Gross Domestic Product
GFC	Global Financial Crisis
GSC	Global Stablecoin
ICO	Initial Coin Offering
IMF	International Monetary Fund
IOSCO	International Organization of Securities Commissions
IoT	Internet of Things
KYC	Know Your Customer
LVTS	Large Value Transfer System
MiCA	Markets in Crypto-Assets Regulation
MIFID	Markets in Financial Instruments Directive
MIFIR	Markets in Financial Instruments Regulation
OCC	Office of the Comptroller of the Currency

PSP	Payment Service Provider
PBoC	People's Bank of China
PoS	Proof of Stake
PoW	Proof of Work
RBI	Reserve Bank of India
RTGS	Real-Time Gross Settlement
SEC	Securities and Exchange Commission
SEPA	Single Euro Payments Area
SFD	Settlement Finality Directive
SME	Small-Medium Enterprise
SVP	Special Purpose Vehicle
TFEU	Treaty on the Functioning of the European Union
TIPS	TARGET Instant Payment Settlement
UCC	Uniform Commercial Code
UNCITRAL	United Nations Commission on International Trade Law
UNIDROIT	International Institute for the Unification of Private Law
USC	Utility Settlement Coin
ZKP	Zero-Knowledge Proof

Editors and Authors

Editors

Filippo Zatti, PhD (Univ. Sapienza Rome), is an associate professor in economic law at the University of Florence. He leads a working group called BABEL, which focuses on blockchains and artificial intelligence for business, economics, and law. He has held numerous positions, including fellow academic member of the European Banking Institute (EBI), individual fellow of the European Law Institute (ELI), research associate at the University College London Centre of Blockchain Technology (UCL CBT), expert at the Digital Euro Association (DEA), and academic advisory member of the International Association for Trusted Blockchain Applications (INATBA).

Rosa Giovanna Barresi, LLM (FU), is a lawyer focusing on corporate and financial law. She teaches at the University of Florence's School of Economics and Management as an adjunct professor for the Lab in Cryptoassets. She is also affiliated with BABEL and the DEA as an associate member and expert, respectively. She is part of the Digital Asset Task Force, a global coalition against financial crime. She is also the founder of Amerigo for Law.

Authors

Roman Avdeev, BSc (FSFM), is a partner at J3L Capital, leading risk at a top 10 Ethereum Mainnet DAO.

María Cecilia del Barrio Arleo, PhD (Univ. Trento), is a supervisor at ECB Banking Supervision and an EBI associate researchers' group (ARG) member.

Aurelia Philine Birne, Dr iur, is a research fellow at the Institute for Law and Regulation of Digitalization at the University of Marburg.

Andrea Bracciali, PhD (Univ. Pisa), is a SICSA lecturer at the Department of Computing Science and Mathematics of the University of Stirling and a UCL CBT research associate.

Sangita Gazi, LLM (DU) and LLM (UW), is a PhD candidate at the University of Hong Kong, a senior research fellow at Rutgers Law School and a UCL CBT research associate.

Gabriella Gimigliano, PhD (Univ. Siena), is a lecturer in economic law at the University of Siena.

Jonas Gross, PhD (U UBT), is the DEA chairman and COO at etonec GmbH.

Caroline Kleiner is a full private international law and banking law professor at the University Paris Cité (formerly Paris V, René Descartes).

Shuji Kobayakawa, DPhil (OU), is a professor at the School of Political Science and Economics of Meiji University.

Ilona Larionova, JD (OHLS), is legal counsel at the Ontario Securities Commission.

Eugenia Macchiavello, PhD (Univ. Genoa) and LLM (NYU), is a tenure-track professor in economic law at the University of Genoa and an EBI research associate.

Francesca Mattassoglio, PhD (Univ. Milan), is an associate professor in economic law at the Bicocca University of Milan.

Franklin Noll, PhD (UMD), is the former President and Chief Historian at Noll Historical Consulting, LLC and now Lead Payments Specialist at the Federal Reserve Bank of Kansas City.

Sebastian Omlor, Dr iur, LLM (NYU), LLM Eur (UdS), is a full professor and director of the Institute for Law and Regulation of Digitalization at the University of Marburg.

Reyes Palá Laguna, PhD (UZ), is a tenure-track professor in business law at the University of Zaragoza.

Christian Pfister is a lecturer at Sciences Po (Paris) and a senior consultant in digital currencies.

Poonam Puri, LLM (HU) and LLB (U of T) is a full professor of corporate law, corporate governance and securities regulation at Osgoode Hall Law School, York University in Toronto.

Deyan Radev, PhD (GSEFM), is a fintech and banking associate professor at the Faculty of Economics and Business Administration of Sofia University St. Kliment Ohridski.

Arthur Rossi is a financial regulation lead at the Saudi Central Bank.

Philipp Sandner, PhD (LMU), is a professor in business and IT at the Frankfurt School of Finance and Management and head of the Frankfurt School Blockchain Centre.

David Tercero-Lucas, PhD (UAB), is teaching at the Comillas Pontifical University—ICADE and is a DEA associate team member.

Vincenzo Vespri is a full professor in mathematics at the Department of Mathematics and Informatics of the University of Florence.

Acknowledgements

In December 2020, during the Covid-19 pandemic, BABEL, a research team of the Department of Economics and Management of the University of Florence, organised a webinar with the unusual title (for an academic conference) of 'What do fiat currencies still are for?' Speakers included Francisco Rivadeneyra, Zighuo He, Bitange Ndemo, and Reyes Palá Laguna. In November of that year, we participated in a webinar organised by the Italian Embassy in the United States and the Amerigo Association. The topic of discussion was 'Digital Dollar & Digital Euro: An International Perspective' and featured guest speakers Christopher Giancarlo and Daniel Gorfine, who are advocates of the 'Digital Dollar Project,' as well as Tommaso Mancini-Griffoli of the IMF. The webinars led to a research project that created the book. After that, we had many meetings, discussions, and research tasks. It would not be easy to list them all because we had the chance to meet with numerous scholars, institutions, and organisations. We want to thank the Digital Euro Association (DEA) for extending the call for chapters to their members. We also appreciate Flaviano de Fusco for his behind-the-scenes contributions, especially in clarifying the technical aspects of how the digital currency works during the custody phase.

The digital euro project has eliminated concerns about the legality of a digital currency as legal tender. However, unforeseen circumstances could still hinder its development. Our book explores the creation of fiat currency and legal tender in the digital era for all readers, regardless of background.

Currency is a complex concept, especially with the advancements in DLT. Legal experts struggle to define sovereignty's role, making setting boundaries for the monetary phenomenon difficult.

We are currently observing the emergence of the third wave of currency—digital money. This comes after the use of paper money and electronic money. Electronic money only impacts the payment system, whereas digital money has the potential to replace both electronic and traditional currency. It is a novel form of currency with distinctive features that have the potential to revolutionise the concept of money and the way we carry out transactions. Money's legal concept is evolving, affecting possession and custody.

A comprehensive analysis that includes legal, economic, and technical factors is required to fully grasp digital currency's potential. We have gathered scholars from various regions of the world who possess diverse, yet complementary skill sets in developing digital money solutions. The manuscript's printing was stalled until late Spring 2023 due to the project's ambitious nature.[1]

As we move towards a more digitally oriented economy, there may be changes in how monetary policy and central banking are approached. The final part of this book delves into the legal implications of this shift, with a focus on the digital euro project as a case study. Looking ahead, we will need to develop new policies and solutions to adapt to this new digital landscape. We hope that readers will appreciate the originality of this path and will be able to use these insights to inform their own strategies moving forward.

Before we conclude, we would like to express our gratitude to all the authors who contributed to this book. Each author's unique perspectives, talents, and roles have created rich and valuable content for the readers. Our gratitude also goes to Miguel Fernández-Ordõnez, the former Governor of the Bank of Spain, for writing the preface to our book. Additionally, we thank Professor Iris Chiu for her supportive words that facilitated the acceptance of our project as a publication. At last, with a heavy heart, we extend our gratitude to Professor Lloyd Blenman. Unfortunately, he passed away during the book's processing. We want to honour his memory by sharing the words he wrote about the project and his desire for the research findings to be published:

> This proposed book will be a standard reference for years to come. We are on the cusp of a major revolution in what is defined as money, how it can be used, created, and how monetary policy is conducted. It means that we will now be able to reach many of the people who do not have traditional bank accounts via e-wallets.
>
> These changes will also have significant implications for settlements in almost real-time as well as the finality of payments. They will cause major privacy issues as well as bring increased benefits. It is, therefore, no understatement to say the coming changes will have the most significant multivariate impacts on banking, monetary policy, payment systems and, most importantly, cross-border cash flows since the Bretton Woods agreements were put in place.

Dear Professor Blenman, we genuinely hope we have met all your expectations. May God bless you.

Filippo Zatti and Rosa Giovanna Barresi

1 Kindly note that the book endeavours to provide a broad perspective that transcends short-term goals and delves into the underlying principles of legal and financial systems. Additionally, we would like to apprise you that the manuscript underwent minimal modifications during its production cycle after its submission to the publisher.

It is worth noting that this book was written prior to the releases of the "Payments Package" and the "Digital Euro Package" by the European Commission, as well as the agreement between the Council and the European Parliament regarding the instant payment proposal and the European Digital Identity Wallets.

Please, moreover note that the authors are solely responsible for any errors present in this manuscript. The editors have taken all reasonable measures to ensure the accuracy of what is contained in each manuscript. However, the editors cannot assume responsibility for any errors that may have inadvertently crept in.

Preface

We are amid a Big Bang, an impressive explosion of new concepts and initiatives regarding money, payments, and finance. How do we grasp this incredible number of ideas and ventures? Its diversity and complexity require an approach to it from different perspectives, and this book is a solid illustration of how to apply different viewpoints and disciplines. I leave it to the reader to delve into the soul of each reflection, interpretation, and proposal about what is happening through the economic and legal literature views. I hope to ignite the reader's interest in providing the thoughts of a former central banker.

One interesting perspective is analysing what is happening in the payment system as a case of liberalisation. This is the most crucial liberalisation process after introducing competition in China and the other planned economies. There are many lessons from past liberalisation processes of different economic sectors that can be applied to the current disruption of the monetary system. Let me explain.

I Seventy years of structural reforms

The legacy of the first half of the 20th century was disastrous from the perspective of economic regulation. In some countries, the temptation of the centrally planned economy implemented systems where the State has a dominant role in the functioning of the economy. Communism, fascism, war, and even post-war governments gave the State excessive power that stifled competition and deeply worsened the prosperity of all of us. Since then, and over the last seven decades, the roles of the State and the Market have been reassigned through numerous structural reforms that have had spectacular effects in increasing the welfare of most citizens worldwide.

The first and most important of these regulatory changes was the GATT's liberalisation of international trade. Further, the list of regulatory changes is extensive: the privatisation of public companies; the liberalisation of regulated or monopolised sectors such as telecommunications and transport; the introduction of 'flexicurity' in labour markets; the creation of the internal market in the European Union; and capital flows liberalisation, to name the more relevant. No one should ignore the great transformation at the end of the

20th century in most former communist countries, as they introduced market mechanisms for producing goods and services. All these structural reforms have introduced freedom and competition to the economic decisions of citizens and companies by devoting to the State the adoption of policies restricted to general interest objectives not fully served by the Market. Governments of diverse ideologies have adopted these structural reforms, such as the conservative Margaret Thatcher or the socialist party in Spain. In the United States, Republicans defended deregulation, and Democrats initiated several sector liberalisations. In recent decades, the most crucial Market reform has been led by the Chinese Communist Party. All these governments were not guided by dogmatism but by pragmatism. They did not defend the Market and the State for ideological reasons but just decided to leave to the Market what it knows best and exit the State from what it knows worst.

Nowadays, reassigning the roles of the State and the Market in money, payments, and other financial activities is opening. Indeed, the State has heavily intervened in activities such as payments and financing. And the creation of money, which should be public, is in private companies' hands. The fragility of private means of payment has been the primary source of financial instability over the last centuries. The State had to intensely protect and regulate banking activities to avoid continuous and severe episodes of instability. This accumulation of protections and privileges has turned activities such as payments into a regulated monopoly. And, paradoxically, regarding money creation, the State has lost space. Physical money is public, but the only digital money accessible to all citizens is bank deposits which are private money. Digital public money—central bank reserves—can only be used by the banks themselves.

This bizarre distribution of roles between the State and the Market has lasted a long time because there were no alternatives to bank deposits. However, over the last decade, new technologies have arisen so that we can reassign the role of the State and the Market in money and payments regulation. Today there are alternatives. We do not need to use fragile financial assets, such as bank deposits, as a means of payment.

Three proposals for digital money aside from bank deposits have appeared in recent years. In chronological order, we find the self-styled cryptocurrencies, the digital currencies issued by central banks (CBDC), and the most recent proposal is 'stablecoins.' We are in the middle of a debate, and it would be pretentious to predict what the role of these currencies will be in the future. Still, we can suggest what would be the most reasonable lines of structural reform of money, payments, and other banking activities.

II Structural reform characteristics

Let us, therefore, examine the changes in the regulation of money and payments as if they were one more episode of the structural reforms of recent decades that have reassigned the roles of the State and the market in sectors that the State strongly regulates. Each of these economic sectors is different from the others, and undoubtedly, the financial industry is different. However, it shares some characteristics that can be used to reform money and payments.

The most important feature of structural reforms is known as *unbundling*. To introduce competition in regulated sectors, we must distinguish monopolistic activities from those performed with the competition. Monopolistic activities must be regulated and separated from those supplied in competition by different private companies. Examples of 'unbundling' in the telecommunications reform are the separation between networks and services; the air transportation reform separates airport management from airlines.

A second tool is to *maximise competition in liberalised activities.* To achieve this, we must remove all privileges from the current companies and the rules regulating their economic conduct. For this reason, it is common to speak of *deregulation*. However, it would be better to talk of *reregulation*. Although the State ceases to intervene in the economic conduct of economic actors, its regulatory action is even more necessary to maintain the integrity and functioning of markets, protect users, prosecute cartels, prevent the formation of monopolies, protect data, defend privacy, and so on. With competition, goods and services prices fall, increasing in quality. The main virtue of competition is, nevertheless, innovation. The most valuable thing about competition is that private initiative strives to create goods and services that do not still exist but will become highly appealing to consumers and users. When the telecom sector was liberalised, no one would have imagined the positive impact of smartphones.

Finally, the third characteristic of a structural reform that tries to eliminate protections and privileges to get competition is *to find an adequate transition formula* to go from a heavily intervened system to a system where the free market works.

Below we will examine the structural change that we are experiencing as an episode of liberalisation like those that have occurred in recent decades in other sectors of the economy. We will highlight the necessary unbundling of activities, the complete competition dismantling of all protections and monopolistic privileges, and the design of an adequate transition from the current to the new system.

III Stability and competition

On the one hand, we have a financial instability problem in our current monetary and banking system. That is a consequence of the means of payment we use—bank deposits—which are a risky asset. On the other hand, there is a lack of competition in payment services due to the privileges, protections, and intrusive regulations necessary to avoid the stability problems created by that unsafe money. These problems—instability and lack of competition—are intimately related to the current system. It is impossible to introduce competition in the services banks provide because this would immediately damage their profitability and solvency, leading to bankruptcy and a collapse of money flows. But while the current monetary system has not changed, most means of payment continue to be assets—bank deposits—with credit and liquidity risk. The existing corpus of protections, privileges, and intrusive regulation is fully justified. Those barriers to competition are indispensable to avoid crises in a system with no alternatives to bank deposits. This accumulation of protections for banks makes it impossible to open competition in payment services to any company other than banks. It has been necessary to avoid money crises. However, the new technologies allow us to unbundle activities such as money, payment services, and other financial services. If we unbundle these activities, we can have safe money, not fragile with no need for protection and privileges, such as 'lender of last resort,' the guarantee of deposits, the rescue of banks with taxpayers' money, or the vast collection of prudential regulations. That is why the structural change in money and payments will be a double reform. On the one hand, we will achieve safe money and, on the other, a liberalisation of banking activities.

A reform was adopted in the 19th century with physical money and banknotes. Indeed, in the first half of that century, in many countries, most banknotes were issued by private banks, and because the banks were not so protected, they were perpetually in crisis. At first, it may seem paradoxical that having public money would be an indispensable condition for competition in payment services and other banking activities, but this is not the case. Sovereign money has characteristics that make it necessary to compete in payment services. In the first place, central bank money does not need State protections or privileges; therefore, all service providers compete on a level playing field. That is important to make the competition happen. Second, the State facilitates the functioning of the market by deciding on a unit of measurement. When the State chooses the units of weight measurement, this is also observed in the goods market. Leaving the units of measurement to private competition does not favour and harm the operation of the market. If there are different private means of payment, citizens are forced to study the solidity of the various issuers. One characteristic of money is ***uniformity***.

Of course, there is a way to make various private currencies look uniform. It can be achieved if the State ensures and protects those different means of payment so citizens perceive them as single public money. That happened regarding bank deposits, which, as private means of payments with varying solvency levels, are definitively considered uniform and public money. For centuries, the State needed to protect banks and grant them privileges to make deposits appear equally safe. The new technologies' advantage is that they separate money from payment services. The State ensures that money is unique and safe without giving privileges to anyone, and the Market provides many competitors in activities that should be purely private, such as payment services.

Money creation is wholly separated from the provision of payment services when unbundling money from payment services. As in other sectors that have been liberalised, this unbundling is essential for competition to occur. And collapses in payments disappear. Instead of instability and lack of competition, we will have stability and competition simultaneously.

IV Competition and innovation

It is necessary to remove all the protections and privileges that regulated companies had and the regulations that constrained their activity to maximise competition in previously regulated sectors. It is essential to *level the playing field* so new competitors and incumbents can compete on equal terms without State support. In the case of banking activities, it would be necessary to eliminate the many privileges that banks enjoy, such as those of lender of last resort, privileged access to digital money issued by central banks, deposit guarantees, or bailing out the banks with taxpayer money. Likewise, all prudential regulations may be repealed because they would no longer be necessary since the money would be a safe asset. The competition will reduce the prices of transactions and their unfounded slowness in a digitised world. But the most positive effect of competition, likewise in other sectors such as telecommunications, will be the creation of innovative products and services. For sure, the innovation will not arise exclusively in the payment system but also in other financial activities that will emerge when the banking monopoly ends. One of the difficulties in convincing public opinion of structural reforms for the competition is that the most important benefits are unknown. We can talk about what exists but not what still needs to exist: innovation. We are still determining what will produce innovation; we only know that if there is competition, there will be innovation.

V The transition to competition

The third essential element in all liberalisation policies is the design of an adequate transition bridge from a protected and strongly regulated system to a system based on free-market rules. No liberalisation policy, no method of introducing competition, is carried out without giving protected companies time to transform to provide their services subject to market discipline, without state support. For example, in international trade liberalisation agreements, the transition was done through gradual calendars to progressively dismantle national producers' protections and privileges. In other sectors, various categories of aid or subsidies were transitorily provided to the old companies so that they could transform and compete in the new system or shut down their businesses in an orderly manner. The transition is a critical phase of any liberalisation policy because introducing competition reallocates productive resources. Capital, human resources, and management capacity to provide low-quality, high-priced services must be employed to offer better and even new services that those companies did not previously present. New and vested private interests do not help design adequate transitions in money and payments.

On the one hand, the new entrants have no interest in a transition phase. They want immediate liberalisation because they are perfectly equipped to provide users with their highest quality and lowest priced services. On the other hand, the incumbents are interested in delaying the transition or approving regulations that put all kinds of difficulties on the new entrants. But these two ways to go from the old to the new system are unacceptable.

The first procedure, having no transition process, letting the free market allow the new businesses to succeed and the old ones to go bankrupt, is an economic waste regardless of the social effects. Much of their capital resources, management capacity, and workers would be lost by not allowing the incumbents to transform themselves and use those resources to offer their services in competition. The second transition method, delaying the change or hindering new competitors, is unacceptable because users need to obtain the advantages of the best services. The banks are not encouraged to transform themselves to provide those services with the whole competition. Unfortunately, some central banks are considering limiting transactions with digital public money so that commercial banks are not harmed. This kind of transition of abusing the new digital money is a daydream of wanting to liberalise a sector and introduce competition but do it without dismantling the monopoly. It is unrealistic because it will be challenging for public opinion to tolerate governments maintaining the privileges and protections for commercial banks when people see safer money possibilities that only need some of those privileges. It is not reasonable to reform the current system without addressing transition problems. But neither does it make sense to harm the use of public digital money to avoid problems for banks. The essential piece of a well-designed transition is helping commercial banks transform. They must be temporarily enabled to compete with new competitors in different banking activities (payments and loans) without the need for perpetual state support or privileges.

VI Hope

It is fair to recognise that the current debate on structural changes in money, payments, and banking started in the so-called 'crypto world.' They presented technological changes that could improve the efficiency of the financial system. They announced a radical change in the role of the State and individual decisions, as well as in the functions of central banks and intermediaries. Those cryptos were wrong to exaggerate, say that the State would disappear, that intermediaries would no longer be necessary, and that there would no longer be inflation problems because the central banks would not be able to increase the quantity of money. But certainly, we need to reach this millenarian vision to see a substantial change in the role of the State and individual decisions in the financial system. We must recognise that we will continue to have some of the problems that we currently have with the fragility of money, the inefficiency of monetary policy, and the lack of competition in designing a sound system of money, payments, and financial activities. Economic policies are more than just the result of correctly assessing the problems and benefits of the different regulations and choosing the most appropriate ones. The private interests many have in adopting the regulatory changes also count. But let's hope that progress will be made in more stability and competition because payments and the financial system play a vital role in the economy. A good reform could significantly increase productivity, output, and state revenues. Today there is a broad consensus that the essential policies fight climate change and correct inequalities. These policies are critical to the economy's growth in the long term, but in the short term, they reduce private income growth and require many public resources. For this reason, the reform of money and banking activities is a complementary policy with these two, to the extent that competition increases productivity and output in the short term and provides an increase in public resources that could be used to subsidise those policies without increasing deficits or public debt.

Let's hope so.

Miguel Fernández-Ordóñez

Part I

Overview

1 A History of Central Bank Digital Currency and the Money Monopoly

Franklin Noll[1]

1.1 CBDCs defined

What do we mean when we talk about a CBDC? Here, we run into an imprecision in the definition. The term first appeared in 2015,[2] even though the idea had been discussed for years before. As early as 1985, James Tobin talked about something he called 'deposited currency.' This currency would be electronic 'store-of-value embodiments of a monetary unit of account...supplied by the central government' either directly or through traditional bank accounts.[3] Around the same time (the late 1980s), Finland experimented with electronic money and smart payment cards. In 1991, the Bank of Finland rolled out a central bank 'e-money system' for retail payments. This e-money would be deployed via a stored-value card. It was a central bank token distributed by commercial banks.[4] During the 1990s and early 2000s, the idea that would become a CBDC ranged from legal tender e-cash to government-issued e-money.[5] Basically, these were forms of electronic currency that would act the same way as hard currency. The model was a banknote in digital format. As the 2010s arrived, ideas became refined. People began to talk about coins and tokens and Bitcoin.[6] Then, the Bank of England spoke about a 'CBDC,'

1 I finished writing this chapter before I started working at the Federal Reserve Bank of Kansas City. It is important to note that the thoughts expressed in this chapter are my own and may not match the opinions of my colleagues at the Bank.

2 Bank of England, 'One Bank Research Agenda', February 2015, 6, https://www.bankofengland.co.uk/-/media/boe/files/research/one-bank-research-agenda---summary.pdf?la=en&hash=B2C820FBF6A960C4A625C2DAB5B5B6CE4FEDF120.

3 James Tobin, 'Financial Innovation and Deregulation in Perspective', *BoJ Monetary and Economic Studies*, September 1985, 22, 25.

4 Aleksi Grym, 'Lessons Learned from the World's First CBDC', BoF Economics Review (Helsinki: Bank of Finland, 2020), 2, 3, 5, 14-15, http://hdl.handle.net/10419/224448.

5 Joshua B Konvisser, 'Coins, Notes, and Bits: The Case for Legal Tender on the Internet', *Harvard Journal of Law & Technology* 10, no. 2 (Winter 1997): 32.

6 JP Koning, 'Moneyness: Why the Fed Is More Likely to Adopt Bitcoin Technology than Kill It Off', *Moneyness* (blog), 14 April 2013, https://jpkoning.blogspot.com/2013/04/why-fed-is-more-likely-to-adopt-bitcoin.html; Simon Scorer, 'Central Bank Digital Currency: DLT, or Not DLT? That Is the Question', Bank Underground, 5 June 2017, https://bankunderground.co.uk/2017/06/05/central-bank-digital-currency-dlt-or-not-dlt-that-is-the-question/.

DOI: 10.4324/9781003258261-2

meaning a government currency using blockchain and cryptographic technologies. By the late 2010s and early 2020s, there was no official definition of a CBDC. However, there was a general agreement that a CBDC had the following attributes: it is a central bank liability on par with cash and reserves, giving the CBDC user a claim on the central bank; it is digital, being based on a form of the electronic ledger; it is denominated in the national currency; and it is intended to be used to make payments and be a store of value.[7]

1.2 The evolution of CBDCs

1.2.1 The e-money threat

As we have seen, the idea of a CBDC has been discussed for a while. Nevertheless, what first prompted the investigation into a digital currency issued by a central bank?

Suppose we start with Tobin's article in 1985. In that case, we see that the pursuit of central bank digital currencies arose out of a need to meet the potentially destabilising monetary forces of the new e-money.

From the 1980s to the early 2000s, electronic money was seen as a revolutionary phenomenon, threatening to upset the monetary world and make central banks obsolete.[8] E-money was developing so fast that its definition changed over time.

At first, electronic money meant reloadable smartcards (electronic purses) and programs that used the internet to make payments (digital cash).[9] Later, e-money included products that allowed users or their agents to access their bank accounts to transfer money (credit and debit cards).[10]

In 1985, Tobin saw the rise of computing power and electronic payments as threatening the dominance and efficiency of government money: 'Electronic payments networks are making possible instantaneous payments via computer from one account to another.' He saw the idea that private monies and 'free market principles' could supply an economy's money as a challenge to 'the exception which assigns government the responsibility to limit the supply of money.' Tobin believed that his 'deposit currency' would allow the central bank to 'still have effective monetary control in the new system.'[11]

7 Grym, 'Lessons Learned from the World's First CBDC', 11–12; 'Central Bank Digital Currency', Banque de France, 4 February 2020, 2, https://publications.banque-france.fr/en/central-bank-digital-currency.

8 Grym, 'Lessons Learned from the World's First CBDC', 4.

9 Bank for international settlements, ed., *Implications for Central Banks of the Development of Electronic Money* (Basle [Paris]: Bank for international settlements [diff. Banque de France], 1996), 1.

10 Marco Arnone and Luca Bandiera, 'Monetary Policy, Monetary Areas, and Financial Development with Electronic Money', *IMF Working Papers* 04, no. 122 (2004): 4, https://doi.org/10.5089/9781451854527.001.

11 Tobin, 'Financial Innovation and Deregulation in Perspective', 20,21,28.

At the same time, in Finland, the central bank thought that it was its responsibility to avoid inefficiencies in payments arising from 'a situation where multiple, incompatible systems would be competing in a fragmented market.'[12] It was feared (and not just at the Bank of Finland) that this new e-money would create a private issuers system that would issue their own electronic alternative to cash.[13] Also, the bank saw it as its mandate to provide an electronic equivalent to cash, although it need not be considered a legal tender.[14]

During the 1990s and 2000s, the threat of e-money replacing central bank cash worried central banks the most. There were fears of monetary and financial chaos as private issuers competed to supplant cash as a payment vehicle.[15] The widespread acceptance of e-money as a substitute for physical money could also shrink a central bank's balance sheet, impacting open market operations and the ability of the bank to affect monetary policy.[16] There might also be a decline in central bank seigniorage because of the decline in asset holdings and interest earned on these assets.[17] The decline in seigniorage was especially troubling, and it was seen as part of a long-term decline that could threaten central banks' ability to fund themselves.[18]

The way for a central bank to counter these threats was for it to either impose reserve requirements on e-money issuers or for it to issue its own form of e-money held on its balance sheet.[19] After all, it was argued that if a central bank had a monopoly on cash, it was only logical for it to have one on its electronic alternative, e-money. This would allow for economies of scale, security in transactions, and the provision of an electronic legal tender.[20] By the middle

12 Grym, 'Lessons Learned from the World's First CBDC', 4.

13 Konvisser, 'Coins, Notes, and Bits: The Case for Legal Tender on the Internet', 334.

14 Grym, 'Lessons Learned from the World's First CBDC', 5.

15 Yuksel Gormez and Forrest Capie, *Surveys on Electronic Money*, Bank of Finland Discussion Papers 7/2000 (Helsinki: Bank of Finland, 2000), 7.

16 Arnone and Bandiera, 'Monetary Policy, Monetary Areas, and Financial Development with Electronic Money', 3.

17 Bank for international settlements, *Implications for Central Banks of the Development of Electronic Money*, 7; Johannes M Groeneveld and Ad Visser, 'Seigniorage, Electronic Money and Financial Independence of Central Banks', *Banca Nazionale Del Lavoro Quarterly Review*, n.d., 82–83; Bank for international settlements, 'Survey of Electronic Money Developments', 14 November 2001, https://www.bis.org/cpmi/publ/d48.htm.

18 Groeneveld and Visser, 'Seigniorage, Electronic Money and Financial Independence of Central Banks', 80–85; Konvisser, 'Coins, Notes, and Bits: The Case for Legal Tender on the Internet', 343.

19 Bank for international settlements, *Implications for Central Banks of the Development of Electronic Money*, 10; Groeneveld and Visser, 'Seigniorage, Electronic Money and Financial Independence of Central Banks', 86; Arnone and Bandiera, 'Monetary Policy, Monetary Areas, and Financial Development with Electronic Money', 9, 14–15.

20 Groeneveld and Visser, 'Seigniorage, Electronic Money and Financial Independence of Central Banks', 86; Konvisser, 'Coins, Notes, and Bits: The Case for Legal Tender on the Internet', 321–52.

of the 2000s, the idea of a CBDC was present and current. All that was lacking was the name.

1.2.2 The cryptocurrency threat

Over the next decade, the threat of the e-money revolution faded, and the idea of a CBDC largely slept. Moreover, by the middle of the 2010s, the need for a central bank to issue its own e-money was being dismissed.[21] Nevertheless, during this time, a new phenomenon arose —cryptocurrency.

Bitcoin, launched in January 2009, was largely unknown outside its own community. However, by the 2010s, some commentators in central bank circles were referring to 'digital currency.' One Bank of England blogger said:

> Digital currency is no longer the preserve of cypherpunks and crypto-anarchists.[22]

Private digital currencies were the potential new threat to central bank operations.[23]

In 2009, Facebook announced a new digital currency called Facebook Credits, which some foresaw becoming a global currency.

This and the growth of PayPal prompted new central bank investigations into creating their own 'digitisation of state-issued currencies.'[24] Then, in a 2013 blog, JP Koning applied the Bitcoin model to United States payments, primarily Fedwire, arguing that the Fed should adopt distributed ledger technology.[25] From here, it was a short jump to the idea of a *Fedcoin*, which would be a cryptocurrency issued by the Fed and be convertible at a rate of 1:1 with the Fed's physical currency and its electronic reserves.[26] The idea was already in

21 Ben Fung, Miguel Molico, and Gerald Stuber, 'Electronic Money and Payments: Recent Developments and Issues', *Bank of Canada Discussion Paper*, no. 2 (April 2014), https://doi.org/10.34989/SDP-2014-2.

22 Marylin Tolle, 'Central Bank Digital Currency: The End of Monetary Policy as We Know It?', *Bank Underground* (blog), 25 July 2016, https://bankunderground.co.uk/2016/07/25/central-bank-digital-currency-the-end-of-monetary-policy-as-we-know-it/.

23 CPMI, 'Digital Currencies', BIS Report (Basel: Bank for International Settlements, 2015), 3, https://www.bis.org/cpmi/publ/d137.pdf.

24 Joshua S Gans and Hanna Halaburda, 'Some Economics of Private Digital Currency', in *Economic Analysis of the Digital Economy*, ed. Avi Goldfarb, Shane M Greenstein, and Catherine E Tucker (University of Chicago Press, 2015), 257, 260–61, https://doi.org/10.7208/9780226206981-012; M Shoaib, M Ilyas, and M S Hayat Khiyal, 'Official Digital Currency', in *Eighth International Conference on Digital Information Management (ICDIM 2013)*, 2013, 346–52, https://doi.org/10.1109/ICDIM.2013.6693982.

25 Koning, 'Moneyness', 14 April 2013.

26 JP Koning, 'Moneyness: Fedcoin', *Moneyness* (blog), 19 October 2014, https://jpkoning.blogspot.com/2014/10/fedcoin.html. Koning fully developed his ideas in JP Koning, 'Fedcoin: A Central Bank- Issued Cryptocurrency', R3 Reports, 15 November 2016, https://www.r3.com/wp-content/uploads/2017/06/fedcoin_central-bank_R3.pdf.

the air as Sina Motamedi had contemporaneously raised the idea of a *BitDollar* along the same lines as Koning.[27]

Indeed, as 2014 became 2015, the Bank of England recognised that the new digital currencies were raising 'fundamental questions for financial regulation, money demand generally and central bank money in particular.' For example, might central banks issue digital currencies...?'[28] The agenda was now set to study the future of a CBDC. Moreover, there were studies of 'government cryptocurrency' and 'centrally banked cryptocurrencies' involving the search for 'a scalable cryptocurrency' whose supply and deployment could be controlled by a central bank.[29] Such a move would meet 'the threat of Bitcoin' to a central bank's control over monetary policy, financial stability, and other elements of its sovereignty in such matters.[30]

1.2.3 The cooptation of cryptocurrency technology

The new concept of a CBDC was now applied to the old fears first raised by the rise of e-money in the 1990s. Central banks explored how a CBDC could help meet the replacement of cash by private digital currencies, how it could help a central bank maintain sufficient seigniorage to continue operating, and how it could enable a central bank to execute monetary policy effectively in this new digital age.[31] So, some central banks began experimenting with digital currencies to execute interbank settlements.[32] Furthermore, in 2017, Sweden

27 Sina Montemedi, 'Will Bitcoins Ever Become Money? A Path to Decentralized Central Banking', *Tannu Tuva Initiative* (blog), 21 July 2014, https://tannutuva.org/2014/will-bitcoins-ever-become-money-a-path-to-decentralized-central-banking/.

28 This is considered the first use of the term 'central bank digital currency': Bank of England, 'One Bank Research Agenda', 6.

29 George Danezis and Sarah Meiklejohn, 'Centrally Banked Cryptocurrencies', 2015, 2, https://doi.org/10.48550/ARXIV.1505.06895; David Andolfatto, 'MacroMania: Fedcoin: On the Desirability of a Government Cryptocurrency', *MacroMania* (blog), 3 February 2015, https://andolfatto.blogspot.com/2015/02/fedcoin-on-desirability-of-government.html.

30 David Andolfatto, 'MacroMania: Bitcoin and Central Banking', *MacroMania* (blog), 12 November 2015, https://andolfatto.blogspot.com/2015/11/bitcoin-and-central-banking.html.

31 For example, see European Central Bank, 'More than an intellectual game: exploring the monetary policy and financial stability implications of central bank digital currencies', 8 April 2022, https://www.ecb.europa.eu/press/key/date/2022/html/ecb.sp220408~980e39957b.nl.html; Michael Bordo and Andrew Levin, 'Central Bank Digital Currency and the Future of Monetary Policy' (Cambridge, MA: National Bureau of Economic Research, August 2017), https://doi.org/10.3386/w23711; Walter Engert and Ben S C Fung, 'Central Bank Digital Currency: Motivations and Implications', 2017, https://doi.org/10.34989/SDP-2017-16.

32 See, for example, Rod Garratt, 'CAD-Coin versus Fedcoin', R3 Reports, 15 November 2016, https://www.r3.com/wp-content/uploads/2017/06/cadcoin-versus-fedcoin_R3.pdf; Monetary Authority of Singapore, 'MAS, R3 and Financial Institutions Experimenting with Blockchain Technology', 16 November 2016, https://www.mas.gov.sg/news/media-releases/2016/mas-experimenting-with-blockchain-technology.

launched the e-krona project to offset the country's declining cash use, which threatened to hand the payment market to private payment services.[33]

However, by this time, countries were seeing what else CBDCs might do. One idea was financial inclusion. A CBDC could allow everyone to have an account directly with the central bank. No one would be left unbanked.[34] Such accounts would also allow for speedy, paperless government payments. Further, smaller countries, such as the Bahamas, Ecuador, Senegal, and Uruguay, believed that a CBDC would be a low-cost means of payment as compared with cash, saving the central bank money and extending access to central bank money to a wider segment of the population.[35] These ideas and others, like the remuneration of CBDCs (including negative interest rates to break the zero lower bound) and their uses in maintaining price stability, dealing with criminal activities, and providing helicopter money, were also being explored in 2018.[36]

Discussions about the technical aspects of central bank digital currencies also became more sophisticated. Debates coalesced around two points: how to distribute CBDCs and what form they would take. The two basic ways to distribute a CBDC were laid out by Tobin in 1985.[37] By 2017, these had various labels but are currently referred to as the retail and wholesale methods. The retail approach—sometimes referred to as the 'general' or the 'direct' approach[38]—argued that a CBDC would be best distributed by having all users hold accounts with the central bank. Users would then have direct access to the digital currency. The wholesale or 'indirect' approach was more decentralised. A central bank would issue its CBDC to banks, distributing it, like cash,

33 Sveriges Riksbank, 'The Riksbank's e-Krona Project', September 2017, 39.

34 Aleksander Berentsen and Fabian Schar, 'The Case for Central Bank Electronic Money and the Non-Case for Central Bank Cryptocurrencies', *Review* 100, no. 2 (2018): 101–2, https://doi.org/10.20955/r.2018.97-106.

35 Tommaso Mancini-Griffoli et al., 'Casting Light on Central Bank Digital Currencies', IMF Staff Discussion Note, 18, no. 08 (November 2018): 16, 27–28, https://www.imf.org/-/media/Files/Publications/SDN/2018/SDN1808.ashx.

36 For example, see Nuño Barrau, 'Monetary Policy Implications of Central Bank-Issued Digital Currency'; Berentsen and Schar, 'The Case for Central Bank Electronic Money and the Non-Case for Central Bank Cryptocurrencies'; JP Koning, 'Approaches to a Central Bank Digital Currency in Brazil', R3 Reports, 15 October 2018, https://www.r3.com/wp-content/uploads/2018/11/CBDC_Brazil_R3.pdf.

37 Tobin, 'Financial Innovation and Deregulation in Perspective', 25–26.

38 Codruta Boar, Henry Holden, and Amber Wadsworth, 'Impending Arrival – a Sequel to the Survey on Central Bank Digital Currency', *BIS Papers* 107 (January 2020): 1–5, https://www.bis.org/publ/bppdf/bispap107.pdf.

via accounts held by individuals and businesses.[39] (In some cases, a wholesale CBDC was to be limited to use in interbank settlements.)[40]

The discussion about what form a CBDC would take involved systems based on accounts or tokens and how payments would be settled. An account-based CBDC would execute payments by transferring claims between accounts in a centralised system. Meanwhile, in a token-based system, a digital token would be transferred through a more decentralised arrangement. Researchers debated which system was best given the inherent counterparty risks, varying degrees of access by the public, and differing losses of anonymity in transactions in each approach. On the latter point, it was noted that in an account-based system, the account holder had to be identified.

Nevertheless, only the token's authenticity had to be identified in a token-based system.[41]

The years 2018 and 2019 saw the accelerated expansion of CBDC studies. While in 2014, there were approximately six published studies relating to central bank digital currencies and one pilot project underway, in 2019, around 45 studies were released, and 16 new pilots were undertaken. The accelerant was the recent cryptocurrency boom.

By the middle of 2019, the monetary world had passed through the ICO boom, seen Bitcoin run through two great bull markets, and heard the announcement by Facebook of a new global stablecoin known as Libra.

As investigations into central bank digital currencies jumped into high gear in 2020 and 2021, ideas arose about hybrid and programmable CBDCs. A hybrid CBDC distribution model is a rough combination of the retail or direct and wholesale or indirect models. Under the retail model, consumers perform transactions with the central bank's digital currency. Moreover, under the wholesale model, banks manage the use of the CBDC. However, in the hybrid model, users do not have an account with the central bank or direct access to the CBDC. Neither do the banks generate their own form of CBDC (being their liability) for distribution. Instead, banks act as a passthrough for the central bank's digital currency, acting as distribution channels for the central bank's liability.[42]

39 For example, see Ben Dyson and Graham Hodgson, 'Why Central Banks Should Start Issuing Electronic Money', Positive Money, January 2016, 15–19; Engert and Fung, 'Central Bank Digital Currency', 1; Michael Kumhof and Clare Noone, 'Central Bank Digital Currencies – Design Principles and Balance Sheet Implications', *Bank of England*, Staff Working Paper, no. 7 (May 2018): 18–29, https://doi.org/10.2139/ssrn.3180713.

40 Morten Bech and Rodney Garratt, 'Central Bank Cryptocurrencies', BIS Quarterly Review, September 2017, 66–67.

41 Mancini-Griffoli et al., *Casting Light on Central Bank Digital Currencies*, 4; Charles Kahn, Francisco Rivadeneyra, and Tsz-Nga Wong, 'Should the Central Bank Issue E-Money?', Federal Reserve Bank of St. Louis Working Paper, no. 2019–003 (2019): 8–11, https://doi.org/10.20955/wp.2019.003.

42 Raphael Auer and Rainer Boehme, 'The Technology of Retail Central Bank Digital Currency', *BIS Quarterly Review*, March 2020, 88–91. The hybrid model was also known as a two-tiered

Meanwhile, the promise of building smart contracts into a CBDC caught the imagination. Smart contracts are lines of code inserted into a blockchain-based cryptocurrency that prompt a certain action when the correct conditions are met. So, a cryptocurrency could be programmed.[43] Such smart contracts could be inserted into a CBDC, and the result would be the ability of the central government to adjust the value of the currency under certain predetermined conditions. A currency smart contract could be used for any number of purposes. They could be used to stop the funding of defined illegal activities or as a targeted stimulus and create an incentive for consumers.[44]

By the end of 2021 and the writing of this chapter, concerns over CBDCs were clustering around three topics: anonymity, inclusion, and cross-border settlements. These areas of concern have been around almost since thinking about central bank digital currencies began.

The concern over privacy in transactions arises from the fact that a CBDC may allow the central bank to monitor individual transactions and perhaps have knowledge of the identities of those involved. Ways to ensure anonymity stretch back to the 1980s. The use of hardware-based e-purses that could be loaded with value and used in transactions dates back to the Mondex system of the 1990s.[45] Another idea, dating back to the 1980s and revived in 2021, was using blind-signature cryptography in issuing CBDCs.[46] Ideas also arose of erasing transaction records after a set time or not recording transactions occurring beneath a certain value threshold.[47] However, the use of zero-knowledge proofs to secure anonymous transactions, first mentioned in 2018, seems to have garnered the most attention.[48]

CBDC, Centre for the Fourth Industrial Revolution, 'Central Bank Digital Currency Policy-Maker Toolkit' (World Economic Forum, January 2020), 9, https://www3.weforum.org/docs/WEF_CBDC_Policymaker_Toolkit.pdf.

43 Jonas Gross, 'The Digital, Programmable Euro: Statement by the FinTech Council of the German Federal Ministry Of...', *Medium* (blog), 30 December 2020, https://jonasgross.medium.com/the-digital-programmable-euro-statement-by-the-fintech-council-of-the-german-federal-ministry-of-14b85a951218.

44 Kristin Boggiano and Franklin Noll, 'Central Bank Digital Currencies Have the Power to Upend Global Finance', Cointelegraph, 26 October 2020, https://cointelegraph.com/news/central-bank-digital-currencies-have-the-power-to-upend-global-finance.

45 Franklin Noll, 'Three Ways to Have Anonymous CBDCs', *New Money Review* (blog), 10 March 2021, https://newmoneyreview.com/index.php/2021/03/10/three-ways-to-have-anonymous-cbdcs/.

46 David Chaum, Christian Grothoff, and Thomas Moser, 'How to Issue a Central Bank Digital Currency', *SSRN Electronic Journal*, SNB Working Papers, no. 3 (2021), https://doi.org/10.2139/ssrn.3965032.

47 Noll, 'Three Ways to Have Anonymous CBDCs'.

48 Koning, 'Approaches to a Central Bank Digital Currency in Brazil', 18–20; Jonas Gross et al., 'Designing a Central Bank Digital Currency with Support for Cash-Like Privacy', SSRN Scholarly Paper (Rochester, NY: Social Science Research Network, 22 July 2021), https://doi.org/10.2139/ssrn.3891121.

Debates around CBDCs and financial inclusion revolve around the use of the retail distribution model over the wholesale one. We have already reviewed the differences in these approaches that arose around 2017. Nevertheless, despite fears of disintermediation of the banking industry,[49] the retail model retains its popularity in some circles. In 2021, the idea of FedAccounts was being entertained at the highest levels of the United States Government, being introduced into Congressional bills. Basically, FedAccounts calls for the Fed to allow anyone to hold accounts with the Fed, not just select banks.[50] These interest-bearing accounts would give everyone access to all the Fed services currently limited to banks. Retail services would be handled through post offices with specially trained postal clerks.[51]

Indeed, retail distribution models were the ones put into actual practice, beginning with the e-krona project of the Bank of Sweden. By 2020, the most advanced CBDC projects were based on direct access. The digital Chinese yuan of the PBoC saw its deployment in several cities. Added to this notable project were the Sand Dollar of CBoB (launched October 2020) and the DCash of the Eastern Caribbean Central Bank (launched March 2021). Combined with those of Ecuador, Ukraine, and Uruguay, these efforts make the retail CBDC model the most popular one to date.[52] However, pilots solely between banks also gained new attention recently.

Stretching back to the origins of central bank digital currencies was the idea of interbank settlements, as reviewed earlier in this chapter. Lately added was the idea of cross-border settlement between banks and concerns of interoperability between different CBDCs. While these concerns were touched upon in 2016,[53] they have recently garnered serious attention with projects in the

49 See, for example, Engert and Fung, 'Central Bank Digital Currency', 20–21; Mancini-Griffoli et al., *Casting Light on Central Bank Digital Currencies*, 21–25; Jonas Gross and Jonathan Schiller, 'A Model for Central Bank Digital Currencies: Do CBDCs Disrupt the Financial Sector?', *SSRN Electronic Journal*, 2020, https://doi.org/10.2139/ssrn.3721965.

50 Rosa Giovanna Barresi and Filippo Zatti, 'The Importance of Where Central Bank Digital Currencies Are Custodied: Exploring the Need of a Universal Access Device', SSRN Scholarly Paper (Rochester, NY: Social Science Research Network, 11 September 2020), 4–5, https://doi.org/10.2139/ssrn.3691263.

51 John Crawford, Lev Menand, and Morgan Ricks, 'FedAccounts: Digital Dollars', *The George Washington Law Review* 89, no. 1 (January 2021). The Fed acknowledges the problem of inclusion but avoids the idea of Fed accounts. See, for example, Jesse Leigh Maniff, 'Inclusion by Design: Crafting a Central Bank Digital Currency to Reach All Americans', *Federal Reserve Bank of Kansas City*, KC Fed Payments System Research Briefing, 2 December 2020, 5.

52 For a focus see here Chapter 5: Sangita Farzana Gazi, Capitalizing Existing Digital Infrastructure: Unlocking the Potential of Central Bank Digital Currencies for Unbanked Communities in Developing Countries; Raphael Auer et al., 'Central Bank Digital Currencies: Motives, Economic Implications and the Research Frontier', *SSRN Electronic Journal*, 2021, 5–6, https://doi.org/10.2139/ssrn.3922836.

53 Danezis and Meiklejohn, 'Centrally Banked Cryptocurrencies'.

Far East.[54] The study of mCBDCs or multiple CBDCs seeks to overcome the problems that could be encountered when central banks seek to perform cross-border settlements using their own central bank digital currencies. Ideas to solve potential problems include setting standards for building compatible CBDCs, creating interlinked systems, and making one universal CBDC that all banks could access.[55]

1.3 The money monopoly

So, we have reached the end of our journey of the history of central bank digital currencies. We have seen how the rise of computers gave rise to ideas about central bank electronic money and how the subsequent rise of cryptocurrencies gave rise to further thoughts about central bank cryptographic currency. We have explored remuneration, anonymity, financial inclusion, retail and wholesale models, tokens and account-based models, and programmable money. Nevertheless, we need not be blinded by all these details, all these tangents in thought. For at the base of this varied theorisation and debate is the basic impetus behind all of it: central banks have a monetary monopoly that they seek to maintain. Without this monopoly, central banks are just banks, and none of this discussion would have occurred.

Put simply, a money monopoly is the ability of a central government, usually through a central bank, to produce and control the only legal tender available within its borders. It means centralised control, which is a primary political goal for any sovereign state. However, the primary reason for a money monopoly is economic. Controlling the value of money, its nature, supply, and movement are crucial for internal economic development and foreign trade.

1.3.1 Legal tender and definitions of money

As mentioned, at the base of this monopolistic power is the concept of legal tender or the official definition of what is and is not money. Legal tender has varying meanings around the world. In some cases, transactions are required to be conducted in a nation's legal tender to be enforceable. In the United States, transactions can be conducted in any medium that both parties agree upon, but legal tender must be used in any transaction with the Federal Government. What all views of legal tender have in common is that it is the official currency of a country, and its value is managed and safeguarded by the

54 Project Inthanon-LionRock began between the Hong Kong Monetary Authority and the Bank of Thailand in May 2019. See BIS Innovation Hub Hong Kong SAR Centre, 'Inthanon-LionRock to MBridge: Building a Multi CBDC Platform for International Payments', September 2021, 72.

55 Raphael Auer, Philipp Haene, and Henry Holden, 'Multi-CBDC Arrangements and the Future of Cross-Border Payments', *BIS Papers*, no. 115 (March 2021), https://www.bis.org/publ/bppdf/bispap115.pdf.

government. This tends to make legal tender the favoured currency for use in all cases.

Central banks exist and operate under systems with legal tender laws that compel (or at least impel) the usage of their money. This gives them a monopoly over money. Without this legal monopoly, users could eschew the official currency and use whatever form of money they wished. Stripped of its monopoly power, a central bank would be just another bank or currency provider competing on the open market. As a result, central bank policy would be driven by user demand and wishes rather than by policy goals set by the bank or the government. In effect, the central bank would just be part of a free banking system.[56] An illustration of the development of a money monopoly is seen in the history of the United States.

1.3.2 The evolution of the money monopoly in the United States

From winning independence in 1776 until the Civil War period, 1861–1865, the United States had a government operating in a free banking system through the Department of the Treasury. (The United States did not have a central bank until the founding of the Federal Reserve in 1913.) Indeed, the early nineteenth century saw a decentralised currency system that accommodated a myriad of currencies that had different values and purposes. At this time, the money of the United States consisted of coins produced by the United States Mint, diverse foreign coins, and banknotes issued by private banks.

These private banks were part of the Free Banking system.[57] This was a system of independent banks that all issued their own currency. All that was needed to set up a bank was some initial capital and registration with the state in which you were to operate. There were no United States Government regulations regarding banking. If you wanted to issue currency, you had to deposit bonds with your state's banking authority and hire a printer to produce the banknotes.

The existence of so many kinds of currency created several practical problems for the US Treasury and individuals.[58] The main problem was figuring out the values of different currencies. In daily transactions, merchants and customers could readily determine the value of US coins or Spanish Reals,

56 Max Raskin and David Yermack, 'Digital Currencies, Decentralized Ledgers, and the Future of Central Banking' (Cambridge, MA: National Bureau of Economic Research, May 2016), 7, https://doi.org/10.3386/w22238.

57 On Free Banking see, for example, 'Wildcat Banking, Banking Panics, and Free Banking in the United States', *Economic Review (Federal Reserve Bank of Atlanta)* 81, no. 3 (December 1996); Joshua R Greenberg, *Bank Notes and Shinplasters: The Rage for Paper Money in the Early Republic*, American Business, Politics, and Society (Philadelphia: University of Pennsylvania Press, 2020).

58 Jane Ellen Knodell, The Second Bank of the United States: 'Central' Banker in an Era of Nation-Building, 1816-1836. (London: Routledge, 2019).

which were widely circulated in the early nineteenth century, by condition and weight of the silver and, sometimes, gold. However, banknotes were a different problem. There were thousands of different banknotes issued by private banks. Not surprisingly, the different banknotes had different values.

Few banknotes were worth face value. Most banknotes traded at a discount from 1 to 25 per cent of face value, depending on the financial strength and location of the bank. To determine the value of a piece of currency, a shopkeeper or consumer needed a bank note reporter. This weekly journal published entries for each banknote issued by various state-chartered banks nationwide. It listed which notes were being counterfeited and how to spot a fake note. Imagine running a shop where customers pay with many different bank notes. How long would it take to inspect all the notes, look up their various values (and ensure they were not counterfeit), and then tally them?

At the heart of the multiplicity of currencies, the problem was the question of what, legally, was money. For example, Congress could declare various instruments legal tender. In 1827, it was the Spanish Real. In 1862, it was US Demand Notes. However, legal tenders co-circulating with a myriad of other widely used currencies did not give the US Treasury any real control over the money supply or help it stabilise the value of the dollar. To create a money monopoly, the government had to define what money was and what it was not. In the United States, this came down to defining 'current' or 'lawful' money.[59]

In 1814, the US Treasury held its money in various private banks. Furthermore, given that there were multiple currencies at the time and no US dollar bill, the Treasury had multiple accounts segregated by types of currency/asset: cash or local currency (current money), Treasury notes bearing interest, small Treasury notes not bearing interest, and special deposits (banknotes from suspended state banks). Here, current money meant 'money that was valued at par,' as cash meant coins and local currency referred to banknotes issued by local banks that could be readily redeemed in specie. This term became embedded in US law.

Indeed, an 1864 law states:

> [No one] shall utter or pass...any coins of gold or silver, or other metals or alloys of metals, intended for the use and purpose of current money, whether in the resemblance of coins of the United States or of foreign countries, or of original design.[60]

59 How these definitions of money impact stablecoin development is explored in Franklin Noll, 'How the Civil War Shapes the Future of Stablecoins', 8 June 2021, https://www.coindesk.com/business/2021/06/08/how-the-civil-war-shapes-the-future-of-stablecoins/.

60 An Act to punish and prevent the Counterfeiting of Coin of the United States, 13 Stat. 120 of June 8, 1864.

Meanwhile, an 1862 law used the term lawful money, which appears to refer to official money:

> no private corporation, banking association, firm, or individual shall make, issue, circulate, or pay any note, check, memorandum, token, or other obligation, for a less sum than one dollar, intended to circulate as money or to be received or used in lieu of lawful money of the United States.[61]

It seems that current money was being conflated with lawful money.

By the twentieth century, the two terms were synonymous, and the courts had to define what they actually meant. This was done in 1906 in the case *State v. Quackenbush*, 108 N.W. 953 (Minn. 1906). Here current money was defined:

> Whatever is lawfully and actually current in buying and selling, of the value and as the equivalent of coin. Current money means money which passes from hand to hand and from person to person and circulates through the community. It is synonymous with lawful money. Whatever is intended to, and does actually, circulate as money... Current money, that which is generally used as a medium of exchange.

While the United States was defining that the only official money was legal money issued by the government and banning private money, especially coins, it also established a monopoly on banknote issuance. This started with the Legal Tender Act of 1862, setting up the US Note (the original Greenback).[62] This was the first fiat currency in the United States, backed by nothing but the declaration that the notes were 'lawful money and legal tender in payment of all debts, public and private.' This opened the door to the Treasury issuing its own paper currency and reinterpreting Article I, Section 8, Clause 5 of the United States Constitution (the coinage power) to include banknotes. This new money monopoly was tested and confirmed in the Legal Tender Cases that went before the US Supreme Court after the Civil War.[63] These cases decided that the government could determine what money was, what form it would take, and what value it would have. The money monopoly of the United States, exercised by the Department of the Treasury, was now complete.

61 An Act to authorize Payments in Stamps, and to prohibit Circulation of Notes of less Denomination than One Dollar, 12 Stat. 592 of July 17, 1862.

62 An Act to authorize the Issue of United States Notes, and for the Redemption or Funding thereof, and for Funding the Floating Debt of the United States, 12 Stat. 345 of February 25, 1862.

63 Raskin and Yermack, 'Digital Currencies, Decentralized Ledgers, and the Future of Central Banking', 7–8.

To consolidate this monopoly, the government had to restrain all private money, particularly banknotes. As we have seen, private banks operating under state charters issued thousands of banknotes of varying values during the early nineteenth century. To end this chaotic situation and establish a United States currency union, the National Banking System was created in 1863 under the direction of the Office of the Comptroller of the Currency (OCC). These new national banks would be able to issue their own notes, called National Bank Notes.[64]

In effect, the OCC re-established the private currency system on a government-controlled collection of national banks that met strict deposit (100 per cent reserves against issuance) and auditing criteria and issued government-approved banknotes. Congress completed the end of Free Banking by taxing private banknotes out of existence. Eventually, the banknotes of the national banks were replaced by those of the Fed.

1.4 Conclusion: The money monopoly and CBDC

So, by the twentieth century, the United States Government had secured a monopoly on what money meant in the country. However, this definition rested on a specific monetary technology, physical coins, and banknotes. Wire transfers and electronic records of money developed over the next 50 years or so. However, in the end, the money represented would still rest on and be finally settled using legal tender physical tokens. Hence, the shock and panic felt by central bankers in the late twentieth century with the rise of e-money. This new money technology representing a non-legal tender that could be widely used instead of the accepted legal tender technology was revolutionary and threatening. The money monopoly faced a serious threat for the first time in almost a century. And so began the journey to CBDCs. As we have seen, what drove the development of CBDC was the repeated challenge of new monetary technologies that threatened the legal tender monopoly of central banks. First, it was e-money and then it was cryptocurrency. These technologies could produce popular currencies that did not have legal tender status, unleashing decentralising forces that could undermine the monopoly of the central bank. Of course, these technological developments were not viewed

64 Ronnie Phillips and PAVB Swamy, 'Par Clearance in the Domestic Exchanges: The Impact of National Banknotes', *Economic History*, no. 18 (1998): 121–26. For an overview of the National Banking System see, for example, Bruce Champ, 'The National Banking System: A Brief History', *Working Papers*, no. WP 07-23R2 (1 May 2011), https://www.clevelandfed.org/newsroom-and-events/publications/working-papers/2011-working-papers/wp-0723r2-the-national-banking-system-a-brief-history; Phillip Cagan, 'The First Fifty Years of the National Banking System, an Historical Appraisal', in *Banking and Monetary Studies*, by Deane Carson (Homewood, Ill.: RD Irwin, 1963); and Franklin Noll, 'National Bank Notes and the Practical Limits of Nationalization', in *Banking Modern America*, ed. Jesse Stiller, 1st ed. (London: Routledge, 2016).

from this perspective at the time. Instead, they were considered a series of technical challenges to central bank functions. With the rise of e-money in the 1980s and 1990s, there were concerns about competing currencies that could impact monetary policy, seigniorage, and cash usage. In short, central banks were concerned about their business models and sought ways to fortify their positions in a changing monetary world. However, the challenge of e-money faded at the end of the decade. With the rise of cryptocurrencies in the late 2000s, after the launch of Bitcoin, central banks again became concerned about all these technical issues. Alternative cryptocurrencies grew in number and size, and by the early 2010s, they were increasingly viewed as threats to central banks and their operations. Consequently, more and more banks launched initiatives to study and create central bank digital currencies as a counter to the stablecoins and other cryptocurrencies exploding onto the scene. Furthermore, 2021 saw the launch of CBDCs by various countries with more in development. In short, CBDCs are the story of central banks responding to the threatened loss of their monetary power and monopolies by alternative currencies brought about by new monetary technologies.

2 The Technological Factor in the Conception of Central Bank Digital Currencies

Vincenzo Vespri and Andrea Bracciali

2.1 Introduction

Is cash disappearing? There was an acceleration in non-cash payments during the COVID-19 pandemic, but the use of non-cash payments was already on the rise. 'Plastic and contactless money,' such as debit and credit cards and mobile payment apps, are widespread. Cryptocurrencies, from Bitcoin onwards, have become mainstream over the last decade.[1] Such new forms of money and payments may lead to improvements and present difficulties, for example, efficiency, costs, compliance with AML and KYC, resistance to evasion, energy requirements, governance, on/offline availability, finality, customer protection, and systemic risks.

Noticeably, the development of a form of 'private' digital currencies, such as some stablecoins and proprietary digital tokens of Big Tech companies, must also be mentioned. The former includes cryptocurrencies run by private companies whose value is kept stable, for example, by pegging to fiat currencies or algorithmically controlling supply against demand. These have a predominant role in cryptocurrency and a consistent market cap but may sometimes run non-regulated and transparently, constituting a potential risk.[2] The latter includes experiments like Facebook's Libra/Diem, now suspended, a digital currency and payment system comprising a few billion users in a cross-nation cross-regulation monetary framework. It is reasonable to imagine that a push for state-controlled digital currencies is also motivated by the competition with such private frameworks. The actual impact of any digital currency and payment framework strongly depends on the supporting technology that strictly defines their properties. The fundamental technological aspect is generally underestimated. Not only is it often assumed that technology could overcome any issue, but even assuming the feasibility of an approach, the costs of one system over another, and the risks and opportunities that the new forms

1 Hitting a market cap of about 2,000 billion USD around 2021–22: CoinMarketCap, 'Global Cryptocurrency Market Charts', CoinMarketCap, accessed 11 June 2022, https://coinmarketcap.com/charts/.

2 CoinMarketCap.

DOI: 10.4324/9781003258261-3

of money have concerning each other and cash, have not been thoroughly evaluated.

CBDCs are electronic retail money issued by a central bank, twin to the existing fiat currency. The issuing of retail money, in principle directly usable by citizens, may lead to the definition of new business models and possibly the rethinking of the incumbent banking system. CDBCs should retain as much as possible the desirable properties of cash, for example, privacy, finality, and availability while adding efficiency, costs, regulation, and new business models. When compared with cash, several technological and structural issues arise. With CBDC being a claim on central banks, the CBDC *architecture* could consist of a single-tier framework, with the central bank in charge of an overall ledger and direct relationship with retail users. This solution would add demanding and spurious tasks to a central bank, for example, KYC, AML, and credit management, and potentially disintermediate incumbent banks, which might not be ideal. Indeed, the role of the private sector in this business must be considered and regulated. Otherwise, CDBCs would risk losing the characteristic of behaving like central bank currencies and becoming excessively like current cryptocurrencies. Two-tier frameworks are also considered, where the central bank liaises and delegates tasks like KYC to an intermediate layer of payment service providers, for example, banks and companies, which might or might not interact. In the former case, they could also execute retail payments among themselves.[3] Also, the proposal by Chaum et al.,[4] a pioneer in digital money, envisages a layered architecture with the central bank as an issuer and commercial banks in charge of KYC and payment supervision.

A significant issue in the design of CBDC is *privacy*. While cash transactions between custodian parties (who own the money) can generally be anonymous and privacy-preserving, CDBC transactions, based on the electronic recording of transactions, require careful design of the ledgers and their access to exhibit privacy-preserving properties. The ledger may be centralised or decentralised. If decentralised, based on blockchain technology, the distributed ledger requires a consensus mechanism to agree on valid transactions, for example, protecting from double spending. Many consensus mechanisms have been identified, most based on miners' work guaranteed by cryptocurrency rewards. In the case of CBDCs, what is the consensus mechanism that should be chosen, and who should possibly do the work of the miners?

Furthermore, how do we reward them for such work? Related aspects include identifying the custodians of the money since each custodian introduces

3 For further details, Raphael Auer et al., 'Central Bank Digital Currencies: Motives, Economic Implications and the Research Frontier', *SSRN Electronic Journal*, 2021, https://doi.org/10.2139/ssrn.3922836.

4 David Chaum, Christian Grothoff, and Thomas Moser, 'How to Issue a Central Bank Digital Currency', *SSRN Electronic Journal*, SNB Working Papers, no. 3 (2021), https://doi.org/10.2139/ssrn.3965032.

a further layer of aggregation of private information. Whether the ledger is transaction-based, i.e., like Bitcoin, it records pseudonymous transactions and their unspent outputs (UTXO), or account-based, i.e., it records balances of accounts of (identified) users. The former may better support privacy. The latter may better support compliance in terms of KYC and AML.

Another property of cash that is difficult to replicate is a form of *availability*, given that electronic transactions require a connection with a ledger to promptly record the payment of a coin and avoid it being double spent. Suppose CBDC is to be as good as cash. In that case, it must be usable even when offline, technologically impaired, or not accustomed to digital tools. This creates a complex trade-off between addressing double spending on the one hand and excessive centralisation and privacy guarantee on the other. What is the right compromise between the need to operate even in places without Wi-Fi, say, and the obligation to safeguard the protection of sensitive data as enshrined in the very stringent European regulatory framework?

It is reasonable to expect that in an initial attempt, CBDCs will be asked to replicate as many as possible valuable cash functions, not considering the structural and intrinsic differences between physical and digital money. It will also be the task of technology to manage the transition phase to make the adoption of CBDCs as frictionless as possible. It is important to mention other critical technological aspects, such as energy efficiency, performance and scalability, and the future impact of quantum computing.[5]

Finally, the great opportunities offered by CBDCs, if properly implemented, are worth considering. Digital technology allows unprecedented uses of digital money, which, unlike cash, can be spent anywhere and not just in physical proximity. It will enable micropayments, and fast finality reduces frictions and reconciliation efforts and drastically eases cross-border transactions. This implies a drastic change in trade. We are no longer forced to spend cash near us, i.e., the digital twin of usual banknotes, but we can spend it anywhere. It will also significantly impact globalisation: local currencies will suffer competition from stable currencies, resulting in the need for digital money to be accepted and regulated by common international laws. All parties would take the duty to protect weaker economies. On the other hand, if CBDCs are implemented correctly, they could boost the economies of developing countries.

CBDCs can be managed safely, responsibly, and efficiently through disintermediation. This means reducing costs and time if their structural properties are implemented correctly (both technologically and legally). Nevertheless, the opportunities for the monetary system are even more remarkable: digital currencies can also be linked to smart contracts, thus multiplying the uses and fields of application.[6] It means that everyone's wallet will have the same

5 These are currently fostering further research, for instance, in post-quantum cryptography.

6 As, for instance, for the climate change challenge: 'Programmability features of digital currencies (for example, smart contracts) could support precise policies such as incentivisation of

potential as a 'bank,' for instance, in DeFi applications, such as peer2peer automated lending. Moreover, we will soon have to deal more with online and digitalised activities. Consider, for example, the current interest in the *metaverse*, an extended transposition of our life online. Suppose the technological choices are the correct ones. In that case, CDBCs could be the right tools to manage the transactions that will take place across physical life and such a digital universe that is opening up to humanity. Another aspect to consider is that CBDCs will increasingly favour the development of DeFi, i.e., financial instruments without relying on intermediaries. Organising crowdfunding and launching microcredit initiatives and loan services between individuals will be easier without bank intermediation.

2.2 Technological choices

Starting from the arguments mentioned above in the BIS working paper,[7] we focus on the main technological challenges in adopting CDBCs.

2.2.1 CDBC architecture

The first aspect to consider is the private sector's role. This is one of the most overlooked aspects in academic papers, where it is generally assumed that central banks will fully manage CBDCs.[8] However, this solution is implausible. It would be impossible for central banks to handle the work associated with a digital currency. It would be deeply unfair because it would give them too much power over the private sector. It is necessary to leave the private operators the possibility of transferring funds from a bank account to a CBDC wallet by using various payment tools, such as prepaid devices, cards with offline capabilities, or smartphone wallets. If central banks reserved these assets for themselves, managing a unique, centralised ledger, not only would there be an excessive transfer of help from the private sector to the public sector, but also an unjustified distortion of the market and a reduction in efficiency. Think, for instance, about the lending sector. Would it also be managed by the central bank? One possibility would be to adopt a hybrid system: leave all retail activities to the private sector, including implementing regulatory tasks such as KYC and AML, and leave the central banks only to provide the backup infrastructure managing the issuing and regulation of the currency.

climate-friendly behaviours by users and environmental impact accounting'. See Itai Agur et al., 'Digital Currencies and Energy Consumption', FinTech Notes (International Monetary Fund), no. 6 (June 2022): 17, https://www.imf.org/en/Publications/fintech-notes/Issues/2022/06/07/Digital-Currencies-and-Energy-Consumption-517866.

7 Auer et al., 'Central Bank Digital Currencies'.

8 See namely Peterson K Ozili, 'Central Bank Digital Currency Research around the World: A Review of Literature', *Journal of Money Laundering Control*, 7 January 2022, https://doi.org/10.1108/JMLC-11-2021-0126.

Additionally, private payment service providers might be allowed to execute payments among themselves, i.e., manage and reconcile their local ledgers, similar to what banks currently do. The choices affect the ledger(s) architecture and citizens' privacy differently. A hybrid solution has the advantage that, as in the case of cash, the movements of money would not be traced directly by the central authorities but would leave the management of sensitive data, with all the associated risks, to the private sector. An intermediate solution would therefore be desirable in which central banks also have a (marginal but guarantee) role in retail activities. It should be noted that adopting one model or another would entail very different costs for central banks and taxpayers and have a considerable impact on consumer habits and the banking sector.

2.2.2 Privacy

A large number of recorded electronic transactions and their metadata pose a consistent problem of privacy for the users of CDBCs. A key aspect is the design and access to the transaction record. It could be implemented as a centralised ledger managed by central banks, allowing them a complete view of sensitive spending records. Implementing such records, for example, a distributed ledger over a public or private blockchain, or even without any ledger, is an open research question. The problem received institutional attention, such as the ECB study[9] on allowing privacy for lower-value transactions while still ensuring that higher-value transactions are subject to mandatory AML/CFT checks based on 'anonymity vouchers.' They enable users to anonymously transfer a limited amount of CBDC over a defined period, supported by a permissioned DLT.

Chaum's proposal[10] is based on a token-based system, which preserves transaction privacy, and meets regulatory requirements. The central bank provides money creation and the database, while all consumer and merchant interactions are with commercial banks. Informally speaking, the token is validated through a (blind) signature by the central bank. It does not require the central bank to know the user, who is authenticated by commercial banks when they withdraw CBDC or receive CBDC as payment, catering for KYC, AML, and taxes. Privacy is obtained by unlinking authenticated withdrawals from received amounts so that payers only need to authorise their transactions and do not need to identify themselves. Under such hypotheses, the framework does not require a blockchain-supported DLT. Other proposals[11] adopt unlinking between receiving and spending CDBC money, so obtaining

9 ECB, 'Exploring Anonymity in Central Bank Digital Currencies', *IN FOCUS* Issue no 4 (December 2019).

10 Chaum, Grothoff, and Moser, 'How to Issue a Central Bank Digital Currency'.

11 Geoff Goodell, D R Toliver, and Hazem Danny Nakib, 'A Scalable Architecture for Electronic Payments' (arXiv, 11 April 2022), http://arxiv.org/abs/2110.13840.

a winning trade-off between regulation and privacy, in a more elaborated construction, relying on a DLT and blind signatures to provide trust and validation to stateful assets. The framework Hamilton,[12] an ongoing MIT project, addresses scalability and real-life performances in the current phase, adopting an approach to privacy based on minimal data collection. In contrast, performance is based on the parallel processing of independent transactions.

Proposals based on DLTs present the problem of the consensus mechanism to choose. Currently, there are several mechanisms adopted by cryptocurrencies: there are permissioned ones and decentralised ones. Among the decentralised, we have tools based on PoW (as in the case of Bitcoin)[13] and PoS (as in the case of Cardano,[14] Algorand,[15] and Ethereum 2.0).[16] Almost all the consensus mechanisms reward the miners and require transition fees (with the noticeable temporary exception of Iota).[17] Now, let us try to analyse, from a technological point of view, what it means to choose one consensus mechanism over another. All blockchain technologies applied by banks are permissioned, as those who control financial information must be trusted and have credible structures. Even the Ripple[18] blockchain, explicitly designed for financial transactions, has a centralised consensus mechanism. It is obtained via a group of bank-owned servers, the validators, used to confirm transactions and account balances.

As far as traditional permissionless, open blockchains are concerned, the most tested and hacker-proof mechanism is Bitcoin's PoW. However, this approach is not quickly adopted for two reasons: the first requires considerable energy consumption[19] and the miners represent the second. Who should undertake the great work done by the miners? It would not be clear how to reward miners for their work. In the case of the Bitcoin blockchain, miners receive the reward through the bitcoins awarded when they manage to solve the PoW puzzle and publish a block. In the case of digital currency, it is impossible to adopt a system that charges a more or less fee to hide the circulation of money. The idea behind introducing CBDCs is to replicate the functionality

12 https://www.media.mit.edu/publications/a-high-performance-payment-processing-system-designed-for-central-bank-digital-currencies/.

13 For more details, Satoshi Nakamoto, 'Bitcoin: A Peer-to-Peer Electronic Cash System', October 2008, https://bitcoin.org/bitcoin.pdf.

14 Charles Hoskinson, 'Why We Are Building Cardano. A Subjective Approach' (IOHK, 28 June 2017), https://whitepaper.io/document/581/cardano-whitepaper.

15 Jing Chen and Silvio Micali, 'Algorand' (arXiv, 26 May 2017), http://arxiv.org/abs/1607.01341.

16 Vitalik Buterin, 'Ethereum Whitepaper', ethereum.org, accessed 12 June 2022, https://ethereum.org.

17 See Serguei Popov, 'The Tangle', 30 April 2018, http://www.descryptions.com/Iota.pdf.

18 For more details, Brad Chase and Ethan MacBrough, 'Analysis of the XRP Ledger Consensus Protocol' (arXiv, 20 February 2018), http://arxiv.org/abs/1802.07242.

19 Alex de Vries, 'Bitcoin Boom: What Rising Prices Mean for the Network's Energy Consumption', *Joule* 5, no. 3 (March 2021): 509–13, https://doi.org/10.1016/j.joule.2021.02.006.

of cash, not that of credit cards. The idea would be to use a consensus mechanism, such as PoS. PoS considerably reduces the computational work needed to secure the blockchain from hacker attacks. The owners offer their coins as collateral for the chance to validate blocks. Coin owners with staked coins become validators randomly selected to validate blocks. In other words, this system randomises who gets to mine rather than using a competition-based mechanism like PoW.

In this case, the problem is that the miners inevitably have the most money to put as collateral. A system of this kind has the characteristic that the reward for miners ends up rewarding the richest over the poorest. PoS proposals without rewards for miners and no penalties for bad behaviour may not be considered safe enough, making their adoption quite impossible by central banks. A similar argument holds for the consensus mechanism underlying Iota. Recall that Iota is not a blockchain based on the Tangle but a software protocol based on direct acyclic graphs. The innovation of the Tangle is that the transactions are processed in parallel. It allows Iota to scale directly in proportion to the growth of the network and not to charge any fees on transactions. This consensus mechanism is undoubtedly revolutionary and has enormous potential developments, but it is not yet entirely reliable.[20]

Another question concerns the technological choices to comply with stringent (mainly European) privacy laws. Choosing whether the CBDC is based on the user's account or a single transaction is necessary. In the first case, expenses made would be tracked and potentially known to the Central Bank, and as seen previously, the individual transactions could also be accounted for offline. In the second case, much more complicated, transactions could only be accounted for online. However, privacy would be more easily safeguarded, informally speaking, making it more difficult to reconstruct a personal history spread across the whole set of transactions. One also needs to consider what the user might want. Some transactions are best tracked, others do not matter if they are, and others that one would prefer were untraceable, as they reveal personal aspects that one would rather avoid. One can imagine that the choice of central banks is to adopt the most straightforward option from a technological point of view, that is, to implement a permissioned blockchain based not on the representation of single transactions but on users' accounts. This solution is undoubtedly the most feasible and is based on consolidated experiences such as those made by the R3 Consortium with the Corda financial platform.[21] We recall that R3 is an enterprise software company founded in

20 See, for instance, the paper by Pericle Perazzo, Antonio Arena, and Gianluca Dini, 'An Analysis of Routing Attacks Against IOTA Cryptocurrency', in *2020 IEEE International Conference on Blockchain (Blockchain)* (2020 IEEE International Conference on Blockchain (Blockchain), Rhodes Island, Greece: IEEE, 2020), 517–24, https://doi.org/10.1109/Blockchain50366.2020.00075.

21 For more details, see the white paper by Mike Hearn and Richard Gendal Brown, 'Corda: A Distributed Ledger', 20 August 2019, 73.

2015 that began as a consortium of nine major banks interested in exploring how blockchain could address inefficiencies in the ageing network of bank payments and settlements. This consortium has grown to include more than 100 financial institutions. Its blockchain platform Corda allows businesses to manage secure transactions directly between parties. Starting from this success story is easy to imagine a CBDC having the backbone of the central bank and the private sector managing retail services. Being an account-based blockchain, all the transactions would be registered. In this perspective, the CBDC digital wallet is more similar to a bank checking account than a wallet, as we understand it now for the early blockchains.

2.2.3 Availability

Another thing to consider when choosing between a permissioned or non-permissioned system is that cash must also work offline. There has yet to be complete internet coverage worldwide, even though we are moving towards this goal. If CBDCs want to replace cash, they must always be able to function, and in uncovered areas among unconnected users. According to the CAP theorem, also known as the Brewer theorem,[22] any distributed data store can only provide two of the following three guarantees:

i) *Consistency*: every read receives the most recent write or an error.
ii) *Availability*: every request receives a (non-error) response without the guarantee that it contains the most recent write.
iii) *Partition tolerance*: the system continues to operate despite an arbitrary number of messages being dropped (or delayed) by the network between nodes.

Non-permissioned technology overcomes the difficulties linked to partition tolerance (when the system is offline) by allowing the blockchain to temporarily fork and choose one forking branch once the system is back online. This approach cannot be adopted for structurally immediate cash payments as it would not prevent double spending or guarantee finality in acceptable times. So, it would seem that the only one could be a permissioned solution. Most likely, the choice will depend on a hybrid technology that enables a fair compromise between the need to prevent the phenomenon of double spending and also to work offline. Moreover, it will also depend on the need to protect individual freedoms by not having all financial transactions traced by the Big Brother of the central bank. The proposed initial solution has been discussed

22 As stated by Eric A Brewer, 'Towards Robust Distributed Systems (Abstract)', in *Proceedings of the Nineteenth Annual ACM Symposium on Principles of Distributed Computing - PODC '00* (the nineteenth annual ACM symposium, Portland, Oregon, United States: ACM Press, 2000), 7, https://doi.org/10.1145/343477.343502.

about *privacy*, for instance, based on the unlinking of possessing (withdrawing) and using CDBCs.

The need to simulate cash functionality would remain open. That is, to build a blockchain that is as decentralised as possible, not permissioned, based on individual transactions and not on the user account that protects privacy and anonymity. Based on that, the method of use is in the user's interest and not of the state (which would instead have the interest of having all transactions traced).

One might think that the best solution is a blockchain with PoS consensus and a fee to pay to incentivise the permissioned mode. In this case, the participation of the private banking sector would be much more limited precisely because there is sensitive information to protect. Another possibility is that the cash and CBDC will coexist for at least a while because it is not sensible and feasible to completely substitute cash with CBDC. And in our opinion, this is the most probable solution. Even if it means that, at least at the beginning, CBDCs will not enter the competition with the cryptocurrencies.

This description of the functionalities of the CBDC blockchain is a hypothesis as the major central banks have yet to decide in an incontrovertible way which IT architecture they will choose. Considering costs, technological limitations, required functionalities, privacy regulation, and the need to avoid invading the private banking sector too much, we believe it is difficult for central banks to adopt a radically different solution from what we have just described.

2.3 Cash versus CBDC

It is unlikely that CBDC can replace cash in a brief period. There are many reasons.

Parts of the population are not digital natives and would find it difficult to replace something physical like cash with a virtual currency. Digital wallets would be managed via mobile phones, which is a challenge to consider for the older population, who would have almost insurmountable difficulties in adapting to the pervasive use of the smartphone. Furthermore, there are still regions not fully covered by Wi-Fi, making it difficult for everyone, not just older people, to manage their digital wallets.

This problem can increase the differences between developed and developing countries.[23]

Another difference concerns the necessity of a digital identity and a password. If the CDBC is implemented with a permissioned blockchain, the

23 See for instance the technical paper by Katherine Foster et al., 'Digital Currencies and CBDC Impacts on Least Developed Countries (LDCs)', UN Dialogue on Global Digital Finance Governance, 10 May 2021, 24.

connection to the digital wallet will be made possible by the digital identity.[24] This is a significant difference from cash, which can be used without a valid identity document. That is very disruptive because one can only spend their own money if a digital record proves that this person is the wallet owner. It means that central banks should invest in cybersecurity to prevent the robbery of digital identities. In other words, in such a 'metaverse,' our identity will be linked, almost in an irreversible way, to our digital wallet, and our expenditures will be a sort of digital fingerprint of ours, revealing sensitive information. Paraphrasing Descartes, 'I spend the digital currency. Therefore I am.' Suppose the blockchain is not permissioned, and the digital wallet is not associated with a digital identity but with a pseudonym. In that case, it is not vital to protect digital identity, but access to digital money is only possible if one uses the correct password. If one forgets the password, digital money is no longer reachable.[25] If a thief gets the password, digital money is lost forever. This feature makes digital money seemingly similar to cash. Even in the case of cash, if a thief steals the wallet, the lost money is irrecoverable.

Furthermore, in a fully decentralised world, police might be unable to operate. However, losing or forgetting a password differs from a wallet's (physical) loss. In both cases, the introduction of CBDC will change our habits. In one case, a safe place to store the passwords will play the same role as a safe, and in this sense, the diffusion of cold storage, essentially hardware wallets, is telling. In the other case, a digital identity becomes essential to our life. Being robbed of one's digital identity means not being able to experience all aspects of one's existence, possibly including owning money.

Another apparent difference between cash and CBDC is that cash can only be spent in proximity, while CDBC does not have this constraint. Once one gets used to having a digital wallet, it will be apparent that the impact on our way of spending will be enormous. We currently use a credit card to purchase goods without proximity restrictions and cash to purchase goods only close to us. With CDBC, it will be the opposite: reasonably, the credit card will be reserved for purchases of particular importance, while CDBC will possibly be used much more than cash. Easier use of the money will impact the economy, perhaps boosting it.[26]

Nevertheless, perhaps the biggest change will be the marketing strategies that must radically change to account for this transformation. The shops will become virtual windows. The aim will be to interest the customer with unphysically present goods and push him to buy them. We will be subjected to

24 See, for instance, 'Why CBDCs Will Likely Be ID-Based', Financial Times, 5 May 2021.

25 See, for instance, Nathaniel Popper, 'Lost Passwords Lock Millionaires Out of Their Bitcoin Fortunes', *The New York Times*, 12 January 2021, sec. Technology, https://www.nytimes.com/2021/01/12/technology/bitcoin-passwords-wallets-fortunes.html.

26 See, for instance, Ajay S Mookerjee, 'What If Central Banks Issued Digital Currency?', *Harvard Business Review*, 15 October 2021, https://hbr.org/2021/10/what-if-central-banks-issued-digital-currency.

temptations close to us and the most distant ones. We will live in a metaverse where physical and digital realities will coexist, and CBDCs will be one of the tools that will connect real and virtual.

2.4 CBDC opportunities

CDBC is more than just a cash substitute. It has a lot more potential. In this section, we will talk about the new technological perspectives that could open up thanks to the widespread use of CBDC.[27]

The first aspect to consider is that much more than now, the currencies of neighbouring countries will be able to be compared with each other by their citizens. If changing currencies is no longer necessary, comparing a currency's purchasing power and strength will be much easier. The famous Big Mac index will no longer be a statistical curiosity but an experience that will be touched by hand. This situation will push the world economy more and more towards greater globalisation. It will depend on political choices and agreements between states, whether in this situation, the advantages deriving from an increase in transnational trade or the disadvantages that could derive from comparing strong currencies of strong states and weak currencies of weak states, such as hyperinflation and exploitation of the poorest countries. If digital currency were allowed to circulate freely, it would naturally create a free trade market area without the precautions to create these economic zones.[28] On the other hand, the CBDCs represent a unique opportunity for developing economically disadvantaged areas because CBDCs could provide the economic stability necessary to start an economic recovery. Already some cryptocurrencies have been used in place of the national currency. The main reason is that they are not subject to hyperinflation. A textbook case uses Bitcoin in El Salvador as legal tender money with all the consequences that this entails.[29] There have even been rumours that the Zimbabwean government was ready to accept cryptocurrencies as the state's currency. It was reasonable considering how the cryptocurrency Dash is essential for its economy. However, the news was subsequently denied but not wholly excluded.[30] Indeed, digital

27 See, for instance, BIS, 'Annual Economic Report' (Basel: BIS, 2021), pt. 3 III, https://www.bis.org/publ/arpdf/ar2021e.htm.

28 See 'Dash CEO Reveals How Crypto Is Changing Lives in Venezuela and Zimbabwe', Dash, 21 June 2018, https://www.dash.org/news/zim/.

29 See Cecilia Quirk, 'El Salvador's Bitcoin Law: Contemporary Implications of Forced Tender Legislation', Princeton Legal Journal, 29 November 2021, https://legaljournal.princeton.edu/el-salvadors-bitcoin-law-contemporary-implications-of-forced-tender-legislation/.

30 See 'Zimbabwe Says It Won't Adopt Bitcoin as Legal Payment', accessed 12 June 2022, https://finance.yahoo.com/news/zimbabwe-says-won-t-adopt-120748967.html?guccounter=1.

money issued by a central bank would have greater credibility and, therefore, would give excellent stability.[31]

Moreover, another positive impact will be greater inclusivity. CDBC transactions do not require any bank account. This is very important in developing countries, where typically a third of the population lacks access to traditional finance yet has mobile internet access.

Another potential CDBC effect being considered is the impact on the banking sector. CBDCs have the great advantage of eliminating intermediaries and, therefore, making financial transactions less expensive, but this feature, on the one hand, favours citizens who use digital money. On the other hand, it could reduce the financial returns of banks, causing substantial difficulties and systemic risks in a critical economic sector for today's society.[32] This means CBDCs must be technologically structured to reduce the systemic impact caused by their introduction. It is clear that when digital currencies are of everyday use, banks will have to adapt. The traditional branch business will no longer make sense, and the economic return given by the management of clients' assets will not be enough to support the elephantine structures that are currently the banks. However, the introduction of CBDCs opens up new business prospects. Digital wallets will need to be managed. Of course, this means that banks will have to become more and more like software (power-) houses. On the other hand, an agile bank with reduced costs seems to be the natural evolution for the future bank. The introduction of CBDCs, if well done, fits perfectly into this trend. Digital wallets will need to be user-friendly and feature-rich. The future bank's success will be measured more by the *fintech* services offered to its customers than by the deposit rate it will offer on the money in its custody. CBDCs come from cryptocurrencies; therefore, technologically, they will naturally have the same functionalities. Second-generation blockchains allow smart contracts and third-generation ones are designed for the IoT.

Smart contracts allowed digital wallets to be enriched with features that were unthinkable until recently. Many developments achieved in recent years can be transferred to digital wallets. We will be able to participate in crowdfunding, we will be able to invest in NFTs, and we will be able to automatically use oracles, i.e., sources of trusted information, to manage our portfolio. The bank that can offer the most innovative product will have won. It will be exactly like a smartphone app: more and more features and more and more services at very low or zero prices. Our digital wallet will (automatically) guarantee us many more features than a traditional bank. Creating smart contracts

31 This aspect is well considered in BIS, 'Annual Economic Report'.

32 The impact of CBDCs on private banks is studied, for instance, in David Andolfatto, 'Assessing the Impact of Central Bank Digital Currency on Private Banks', 2018, https://doi.org/10.20955/wp.2018.026.

on CBDCs is undoubtedly risky.[33] The central bank should not do it, but it would be very natural if financial institutions operating under the direct control of central banks did. Probably the CBDCs will also change the concept of banking surveillance. It will go from being financial, as it is now, to being more and more technological: smart contracts will be analysed to verify their semantic and IT, as well as legal, correctness.

The IoT paradigm associated with CBDCs will be even more disruptive. The metaverse is a dimension getting closer and closer—a foundational revolution of our way of life. No legislation, not even in embryos, still aims to regulate a new and unexpected world. It is reasonable to think that in the coming decades, we will all have to deal with our avatars operating in a world that is halfway between the physical and the digital and will be governed by artificial intelligence programs. CBDCs, combining aspects of the physical and digital worlds, not only respect the paradigm and philosophy of the metaverse but could represent the right tool to give order to the metaverse if adequately implemented.[34] Being digital currencies governed by central banks, CBDCs could be the natural tool governments will use to rationalise an entire universe that is opening up and cannot afford a total lack of regulation and surveillance. It will probably be impossible to avoid a dark or deep metaverse, but there must be a metaverse out in the open with rules governing it. If the currencies governing exchanges in this futuristic environment are currencies managed by central banks, the metaverse will be safer. At least, this is the wishful thinking of the toughest Bitcoin fundamentalist.

2.5 Conclusions

Reasoning only on the technological aspects, we have deduced that it is implausible that digital currency can be managed only by central banks for multiple reasons. The first reason is that running a digital currency requires significant resources far beyond those currently allocated to central banks. The second reason is that not involving private banks in managing digital money means taking away important spaces from the banking sector, which is vital for the economy. The third and final reason is that it is inappropriate for central banks to comply with very stringent legislation (think, for example, privacy legislation). It is much more practical for central banks to provide the basic architecture for money while private banks do retail.

We have discussed other technical aspects, including possible CDBC frameworks, privacy, availability, the need (or absence of) for blockchain-supported

33 See, for instance, Patrick McConnell, 'CBDC – How Dangerous Is Programmability?', The FinReg Blog, 21 September 2021, https://sites.law.duke.edu/thefinregblog/2021/09/21/cbdc-how-dangerous-is-programmability/.

34 See, for instance, the technical report of Benoît Cœuré, 'Central Bank Digital Currency: The Future Starts Today', 10 September 2021, https://www.bis.org/speeches/sp210910.htm.

DLTs, private and public blockchains, and the type of consensus to adopt proof of work or proof of stake. We argued that the easiest to adopt is technology linked to permissioned blockchains in the first instance. Such technology might also support some offline interaction and guarantee a form of user security based on an explicit representation of users' accounts. However, it has the drawback that, unlike cash, the central authority would easily trace the movement of money. Therefore, this approach might be less suitable for financial transactions that require a given level of privacy.

We then noticed that, in any case, as far as technology can prove, digital money is different from cash. It requires using smartphones and digital wallets, which could create problems for older people. Furthermore, having exceeded the physical proximity limit,[35] we will have new spaces and horizons opening up in marketing that will be profoundly modified to adapt to the new opportunities offered. Finally, to use digital wallets, we will have to increasingly deal with our digital identity, which will become more important in our lives.

CBDCs offer far more opportunities than cash. If they are implemented well, they will change the way of banking. Financial institutions will become more and more agile and increasingly like providers of software-based fintech services. Furthermore, digital currencies connected to smart contracts will concentrate the same functionalities of an entire bank in our digital wallets. They will also be the natural bridge that will take humanity from this physical universe to the metaverse. Allowing financial transactions to be carried out with only a smartphone, even without a bank account, will increase inclusion and favour the growth of developing economies. By making trade easier, CDBC can play a vital role in globalisation.

35 It is possible to pay for goods and services with digital currency even if not supplied in proximity.

Part II

Central Banking and Monetary Economics in the Digital Currency Era

3 Monetary Sovereignty in the Digital Currency Era

Christian Pfister

3.1 Introduction

References to 'monetary sovereignty' in the public debate have been pervasive since crypto-assets appeared, and mainly since the launch of projects for GSCs, also referred to as systemically essential stablecoins. For instance, following its meeting in Rambouillet in July 2019, the G7 declared, 'Regarding systemic concerns, Ministers and Governors agreed that projects such as Libra may affect *monetary sovereignty* and the functioning of the international monetary system.'[1] Some authors also deem it necessary that central banks issue CBDCs to preserve monetary sovereignty in the face of GSC projects or foreign CBDC initiatives. Both approaches can be found in the Common Statement of the Finance Ministries of Germany and France to the digital euro issued following their meeting in July 2021. The press communiqué states that the 'digital euro will be essential in preserving our *digital and monetary sovereignty*. It represents a relevant alternative to developing private crypto-assets as means of payment or developing foreign CBDCs.'[2]

However, the notion of monetary sovereignty is seldom defined in public statements. In my opinion, the definition concerns the capacity of an economy to set monetary policy—i.e., make a given level of interest rate prevail—and thus the value of its money based on its economic fundamentals.[3] In addition,

1 Group of Seven, 'Chair's Summary: G7 Finance Ministers and Central Bank Governors' Meeting', banque-france.fr, 17 July 2019, https://www.banque-france.fr/sites/default/files/media/2019/07/23/g7_chairs_summary_vff_en_0.pdf.

2 Ministère de l'Économie, des Finances et de la Relance, 'N° 1232-Common Statement of the Finance Ministries of Germany and France to the Digital Euro', minefi.hosting.augure.com, July 2021.

3 This definition is close to the one implicitly provided by Antonio Diez de los Rios and Yu Zhu, 'CBDC and Monetary Sovereignty', *Bank of Canada*, Staff Analytical Note, no. 5 (February 2020), https://doi.org/10.34989/san-2020-5. The authors write, 'Wide adoption of a digital currency denominated in a different unit of account threatens a country's monetary sovereignty. For example, most central banks conduct monetary policy by setting a target for short-term interest rates in the interbank market for reserves (…) If Libra were widely adopted, it could become the unit of account in the economy, replacing reserves as the settlement asset.

DOI: 10.4324/9781003258261-5

as shown in this chapter (see namely, § 3.4), the issuance of CBDCs by large economies, especially those already issuing reserve currencies, could question monetary sovereignty in foreign economies while not necessarily offering a meaningful alternative to private or foreign initiatives. Therefore, the issuance of CBDCs is ambiguous, as it does not necessarily preserve sovereignty but could also jeopardise it.

First, some notions are recalled, clarifying the issues (see § 3.2). As the idea of sovereignty is *de facto* intertwined with that of public intervention, reasons for the role of government in money (see § 3.3) are then highlighted; how and where digital assets acting as money can create risks to monetary sovereignty are examined (see § 3.4); policy recommendations to alleviate these risks (see § 3.5) are reviewed; and the conclusion summarises the findings (see § 3.6).

3.2 Notions

Understanding the difference between money and means of payment is crucial to assessing how digitalisation may affect money and sovereignty.

Money is a three-fold asset: a unit of account, a medium of exchange, and a store of value. In the past, different units of accounts were used in transactions and debt contracts, allowing governments to manipulate conversion rates to depreciate debts (§ 3.3). Wide acceptance (or general use) is also an essential feature of money: vouchers or even bonus points can be expressed in their unit of account and serve as a means of payment and store of value. However, they do not qualify as money as they are only used within a specific network. Here, I consider that assets that do not fulfil the three roles of money and are not widely accepted are not a currency. Money in the economy is measured using 'monetary aggregates' built along with a 'Matroska' principle: broader aggregates include narrower ones, starting with the most liquid forms of money (cash and sight deposits), to include other bank liabilities that can be easily transformed into them (for example, term deposits up to a given maturity). This measure shows that money is primarily a private-sector product in modern economies. For instance, in the Euro area, at the end of August 2023, cash represented around 15 per cent of the narrow aggregate M1, with overnight deposits representing the rest and less than 10 per cent of the broad aggregate M3.[4] This does not prevent monetary sovereignty. Hence, monetary sovereignty is not necessarily related to the provision of money by the public sector.

This would make monetary policy irrelevant' (page 1). However, my definition is more general. For instance, it considers the case of countries that participate in exchange rate arrangements, join monetary unions, or 'dollarise' their economy, thus surrendering partly or fully their monetary sovereignty (see § 3.4).

4 European Central Bank, 'Monetary Developments in the Euro Area: August 2023', 27 September 2023,https://www.ecb.europa.eu/press/pr/stats/md/html/ecb.md2308~af0185147b.en.html.

Means of payment are used to circulate money (i.e., to implement the medium of exchange function of money). To use an analogy, they are the 'pipes' that allow the 'liquid' (i.e., money) to flow during transactions. Cheques, debit, and credit cards are means of payment. The case of debit and credit cards exemplifies the difference between money and payment, and the absence of a direct relationship between means of payment and monetary sovereignty. Indeed, there has been a global oligopoly of American firms in cards in the past half-century. However, economies using these cards outside the United States did not adopt the U.S. dollar as their currency. Neither was it envisaged that this oligopoly could jeopardise monetary sovereignty. The frequent confusion in modern times between money and means of payment probably stems from the fact that fiduciary money (i.e., coins and notes), also known as cash, was long the most common form of money and is also a means of payment. However, fiduciary money is currently the only asset that possesses both features. The reason is that payment in fiduciary money (i.e., a cash settlement) is final: it does not have to be processed by intermediaries, such as banks or other payment service providers, such as card issuers. Definitions of money that implicitly or explicitly give prominence to its role as a medium of exchange often cause confusion between money and means of payment. This confusion is also common in the media.

Regarding notions apart from money and means of payment, the concepts of central bank money, legal currency, the 'auto-referential' feature of a currency, forced course and fiduciary money, and finally, money backing are introduced. As shown below, many of these notions relate foremost to public money, i.e., the money the central bank issues for the most part nowadays.

Central bank money—also called the 'monetary base'—is made of banknotes and reserves, the latter held only by banks in demand deposits.[5]

Legal currency (also called 'fiat currency')[6] is a system of money generally used in a particular country or area. Legal tender is a feature attached in most cases only to the cash component of money, making accepting payment mandatory. However, in some countries, this feature can extend to other liquid forms of money, such as bank deposits. Even where legal provisions regarding legal tender exist and are extensive, payments using an asset different from the legal currency (usually a foreign currency but possibly precious metals) are contractually allowed. Such transactions are then typically just considered as barter, which is nowhere illegal. In most countries, the legal currency is widely accepted. Parity is ensured between its different forms (central bank money and bank deposits), thus creating uniformity—or singleness—in the payment system under conditions discussed in § 3.3. In turn, this singleness eliminates frictions in the economy that could be very costly and, in the extreme, prevent

5 In most of countries, the central bank purchases coins, which the Treasury issues. This organisation can be seen as a legacy of the past.

6 To recall, a fiat is a royal decree.

transactions altogether if uncertainties surrounding the values of the different units issued by the private sector were too high. Singleness of the payment system also supports a predictable transmission to the economy of monetary policy impulses, and is thus currently essential for monetary sovereignty.

A distinct feature of legal currency in current monetary systems is that it is '*auto-referential*'—or autonomous—and thus, its value appears purely conventional (however, in abstract terms, this value can be equated with the inverse of the general level of prices (1/P)). For instance, the French Monetary and Financial Code stipulates, 'The currency of France is the euro' (Article 1), without defining either 'currency' or 'euro.' Yet, everyone understands that the sentence means the euro is the legal currency in France. No explanation is necessary to define legal currency results from the intention of the legislator to provide a single account unit in each circumscription and, in practice, from the *forced course*. In the past, 'fiduciary money'—originated from the Latin word 'fiducia' (trust)—expressed confidence that the issuer—if asked to—would have been able to exchange notes for precious metals at a pre-specified conversion rate. However, cash conversion into metal could be transitorily suspended, thereby implementing a forced course. Since World War II, the forced course of fiduciary money has become permanent. Consequently, banknotes issued by central banks in modern monetary systems are no longer claimed, since the issuer can only exchange them for some of the other central bank's liabilities (reserves or other banknotes). As a result, the phrase 'fiduciary money' now expresses confidence that the issuer will maintain the purchasing power of the legal currency.

Having to accept cash at face value, much above its intrinsic value (for example, the value of the paper in the case of banknotes), implies that an essential element of coercion is present in modern monetary systems, potentially allowing to despoil money holders. However, there are counterparts to the privilege of issuing currency that has forced course. One is that central bank money is backed, unlike what is frequently stated in the literature or the media (other counterparts are discussed in § 3.3). It is not backed by the government, even though the commitment of the government to recapitalise the central bank in certain circumstances can help support the central bank's reputation. It is not backed either by the mandatory use of legal currency to pay taxes.[7] A sovereign can only accept the currency it has made legal in paying taxes. Otherwise, no one would hold it.

Furthermore, in modern economies, the mandatory use of legal currency in tax collection is not powerful enough to support demand significantly. Instead, most payments are made in the private sector, specifically in financial markets. It is merely the assets the central bank holds that back central bank

7 Unlike in Georg Friedrich Knapp, *The State Theory of Money*, trans. Lucas, Mrs. H M and Bonar, James (London: Published on behalf of the Royal Economic Society by Macmillan and Co., 1924).

money. These assets, thus, must be of good quality for the public to have confidence that the value of the legal currency will be maintained, just like the loans backing bank deposits must be of good quality to avoid bank runs. Regarding central banks, their statutes often mandate that they refinance the banking sector against 'appropriate' (i.e., safe) collateral and that they invest the counterparty of the banknotes they issue in government bonds (as is the case, for example, for the BoE and the Fed).

Consequently, the best backing a government can offer the central bank is to run sustainable public finances, thus avoiding the value of the securities it has issued plummeting in the expectation of a default, triggering a 'flight from currency.' This is all the more the case nowadays because, as interest rates reached their lower bound following the GFC and the Covid-19 pandemic, central bank purchases of government securities have swollen central banks' balance sheets.[8] The difference between bank deposits and central bank money is that the public can only rid themselves of undesirable central bank money—doubting its value 'flying from currency'—by chasing assets, goods, and services, causing severe inflation pressures. It can occur through the exchange rate depreciation if the public flies into foreign currencies.

'Digitalisation' (or 'digitisation') is the process of changing data into a digital form that a computer can easily read and process. To examine how digitalisation could affect the notions mentioned above, I distinguish three possible forms of digital money: decentrally issued crypto-assets (or 'first-generation' crypto-assets), stablecoins, and CBDCs. I also examine how each category fares as a potential candidate for the role of money.[9] Besides CBDCs, which are legal currencies, only a stablecoin that would become auto-referential could be regarded as a self-standing currency (the latter case is discussed in § 3.4).

As of mid-October 2023, there were more than 18,000 *decentrally issued crypto-assets*, with a total capitalisation of around $1.06 trillion.[10] Although the total market capitalisation of stablecoins reportedly stood at about 12 per cent of total crypto-assets, which is well above the 2–3 per cent pre-pandemic levels, Bitcoin was still the first and largest cryptocurrency as it accounted for around 50% per cent of the whole industry.[11] For this reason, and because it aimed to play a monetary role from the outset, the focus here is on Bitcoin. Bitcoin and the other first-generation crypto-assets only partially fulfil the three functions of money. They are not units of account (they are rarely used solely to price goods and services). Nor are they payment instruments (very few purchases of goods and services are settled with them, partly because, in the case of Bitcoin,

8 For a survey of the literature on unconventional policies, see Christian Pfister and Jean-Guillaume Sahuc, 'Unconventional Monetary Policies: A Stock-Taking Exercise', *Revue d'économie politique* 130, no. 2 (2020): 137–69.

9 Christian Pfister, 'Digital Currencies: From Myth to Innovative Projects', *Bulletin de la Banque de France* 230, no. 1 (August 2020): 1–9.

10 Source: CoinMarketCap, https://coinmarketcap.com/, accessed 11 October 2023.

11 Source: CoinMarketCap, https://coinmarketcap.com/, accessed 11 October 2023.

the decentralised validation of transactions is time and energy-consuming). Finally, they are not stores of value (their prices, hence their value in goods and services, are too volatile).

Furthermore, Bitcoin is unbacked to the extent that it does not have an issuer or a corresponding balance sheet. It mainly derives its market value from its anonymous use, which helps protect privacy and facilitates the financing of illicit activities. Its limited supply makes it a speculative investment. However, this market value could collapse suddenly.[12]

Because of the apparent inability of decentrally issued crypto-assets to serve as money, at least at the current stage of technology, the focus in the following of this chapter is on stablecoins and CBDCs. However, it may be worth mentioning the initiative of El Salvador. This country has used the U.S. dollar as its official currency since 2001 and decided in July 2021 to give legal tender to Bitcoin. Given Bitcoin's poor monetary capacities, the public's chances to use it as money are slim. One apparent reason is that pricing will be made much more difficult if merchants must show prices in U.S. dollars and bitcoins since the crypto-asset's value is so volatile.

Furthermore, suppose prices are made stickier by imposing a fixed conversion rate between the two legal tenders during a given period, such as the day. In that case, the public will be able to game the system. Indeed, this could create a modern version of bimetallism. Under it, an official conversion rate is forced on the metals acting as legal tender. This leads to the so-called 'Gresham Law' (i.e., the public uses the metal whose official value is above the market in its transactions and stores the other).

Stablecoins first emerged in 2014. They are designed to maintain a stable price *vis-à-vis* a benchmark, most often the U.S. dollar. They do not bear interest in their current form, although they might have to remain attractive if interest rates reach significantly positive levels. Offering users the benefit of a stable environment while enabling them to stay in the 'crypto universe,' stablecoins seem to provide 'a brave new world.'[13]

Most stablecoins are backed by a reserve held 'off-chain' (i.e., invested in assets denominated in legal currencies). It implies an element of centralisation that differentiates them from 'first-generation' crypto-assets. Furthermore, even when invested in legal currencies, the governance of stablecoins is often opaque, with information on their investment policy remaining insufficiently detailed and timely. Stablecoins are also poorly capitalised, exposing users to losses if, for instance, the reserve managers take too much duration, currency, or credit risks. Finally, users' claims on the assets held in reserve are unclear.

12 Eric Budish, 'The Economic Limits of Bitcoin and the Blockchain', NBER Working Paper, no. w24717 (June 2018): 24.

13 Anastasia Melachrinos and Christian Pfister, 'Stablecoins: A Brave New World?', *Stanford Journal of Blockchain Law & Policy* 4, no. 2 (30 June 2021): 113–38.

There have thus been calls to regulate the sector, including from promoters of stablecoin projects.[14]

Stablecoins are mainly used as a 'safe asset' and a 'vehicle currency' within the crypto universe, avoiding costly transactions into and out of legal currencies. However, this relatively modest status of stablecoins could change with the arrival of GSCs, issued by considerable players, which are the only stablecoins envisaged in the rest of this chapter. Two main categories of GSC arrangements can be distinguished:[15]

- *Wholesale GSCs* are designed for large-value transactions and are aimed at financial institutions and large corporations. Two main projects stand out in this category: the USC project, promoted by a group of global banks and investors (Fnality)[16] and JPM Coin,[17] promoted by JPMorgan Bank. The USC would come in different denominations, each backed by reserves held with the corresponding central bank.[18] In contrast, JPM Coin would be available only in the U.S. dollar and backed with deposits with JPM Bank.
- *Retail GSCs* are designed for mass transactions. Among retail GSC projects, the most famous is Libra, made public in June 2019, and renamed Diem in December 2020.[19] Although different denominations were envisaged at the outset of the project, the ambitions of the promoters have then been scaled back. At least as a first step, Diem would seek parity with the US dollar, and its reserve would be invested in safe and liquid assets denominated in this legal currency.

Despite being backed, unlike Bitcoin, legal currencies, stablecoins differ radically from the latter since they are not auto-referential. Instead, in their most common form, they aim at maintaining a stable value vis-à-vis a legal currency.

14 See, for example, Christian Catalini and Alonso de Gortari, 'On the Economic Design of Stablecoins', SSRN Scholarly Paper (Rochester, NY: Social Science Research Network, 5 August 2021), https://doi.org/10.2139/ssrn.3899499.

15 Melachrinos and Pfister, 'Stablecoins'.

16 Fnality International, 'Fnality International', accessed 10 April 2022, https://www.fnality.org/home.

17 'JP Morgan Creates Digital Coin for Payments', accessed 10 April 2022, https://www.jpmorgan.com/solutions/cib/news/digital-coin-payments.

18 The Bank of England has taken a first step towards allowing the issuance of a sterling denomination of USC by opening the financial institutions participating in the Fnality project an 'omnibus account'.

19 'The Diem Association', accessed 10 April 2022, https://www.diem.com/en-us/. After the Diem shutdown, its assets and intellectual property have been acquired by Silvergate: 'Silvergate Purchases Blockchain Payment Network Assets from Diem', accessed 10 April 2022, https://ir.silvergate.com/news/news-details/2022/Silvergate-Purchases-Blockchain-Payment-Network-Assets-from-Diem/default.aspx. On March 8, 2023, Silvergate announced plans to wind down and liquidate, https://ir.silvergate.com/news/news-details/2023/Silvergate-Capital-Corporation-Announces-Intent-to-Wind-Down-Operations-and-Voluntarily-Liquidate-Silvergate-Bank/default.aspx, accessed 11 October 2023.

A GSC gaining wide acceptance by the public would thus leave a peripheral domain to crypto-assets, only to enter another environment that is an appendage to legal currency. It would not become a fully-fledged currency; it would not be new money. Instead, it would be a new form of already existing money, offering a new payment method and possibly a store of value. Thus, it would not put monetary sovereignty at risk in the economy whose currency it tries to mimic. Furthermore, as shown in § 3.4, it would be challenging for stablecoins to sever the link with legal currencies, thus transforming their issuers into *de facto* central banks.

CBDCs would be issued by the central banks and freely convertible at par with other forms of central bank money.[20] The separation between wholesale and retail uses could be even starker for CBDCs than for GSCs:

- Since reserves are already digital, *wholesale CBDCs* would be DLT-based. They would only be accessible to banks. However, access could also be allowed to other payment service providers, not necessarily large firms, that could use wholesale GSCs, or non-residents, be they banks or not. The primary purpose of issuing wholesale CBDC would be to support the digitisation trend in the economy, specifically the tokenisation of finance, by supplying a means of settlement available on the blockchain, allowing the conduct of end-to-end transactions in a DLT environment.
- *Retail (or all-purpose) CBDCs* are often the only form of CBDC envisaged in the literature. They would not necessarily be DLT-based and could simply be central bank electronic money. However, this could put them at a competitive disadvantage *vis-à-vis* GSCs and limit their potential uses by not enabling the introduction of 'smart contracts.'[21] They would be accessible to the public, including banks, whereas banknotes are currently the only form of central bank money the public can access. However, non-residents, except when travelling for business or tourism purposes, would not necessarily have access to retail CBDC (how non-residents might access CBDC and potential consequences are discussed in § 3.4 and § 3.5). The purposes for issuing retail CBDCs are diverse and often differ between developed economies on the one hand and developing and emerging economies on the other. In the former, this would allow keeping a link between the central bank and the public in the face of a possible—and even actual, in some countries such as Sweden—dwindling use of cash, supposing such a link

20 I use the conditional tense because there are currently very few examples of CBDCs, and none yet in developed economies, allowing wide-scale use. For an introduction to CBDCs, one can refer to Christian Pfister, 'Central Bank Digital Currency: One, Two or None?', *SSRN Electronic Journal*, 2019, https://doi.org/10.2139/ssrn.3470143; or to Christian Pfister, 'Central Bank Digital Currency', 4 February 2020, https://publications.banque-france.fr/en/central-bank-digital-currency.

21 Smart contracts are software programs on a blockchain that run when predetermined conditions are met.

is deemed useful (see § 3.3). In developing and emerging economies, the purposes are to promote financial inclusion and to lower the cost of distributing central bank money, especially in archipelago countries. However, the example of Kenya shows that issuing a retail CBDC is not indispensable to this end. One suggestion about retail CBDC is that it should be a legal tender. As this is the case for cash nowadays (see above), the answer seems straightforward.[22] However, from an economic point of view, the case is less clear-cut, and the legal tender of retail CBDC does not appear necessary (see § 3.3).

One feature CBDCs have in common with stablecoins is that both sorts of assets are not new monies: they are just new forms of money, the legal currency for CBDCs and intended copycats of the legal currency for stablecoins. At least so far, digitalisation has yet to lead to a change in the nature of money.

3.3 Government and money

There are two main approaches to account for government intervention in money.

The first approach is political: money would be part of sovereign functions, including police, justice, diplomacy, and war. It differs from the approach adopted here because this chapter is primarily an economic contribution to the issue of monetary sovereignty. In economic literature, in the so-called 'State Theory of Money' (STM), one can find that money is a creature of the government.[23] Modern Monetary Theory (MMT) has taken up this idea. However, this approach is circular (it defines money as issued by the state) and thus tautological. Mainstream economists have widely criticised it. It has remained marginal among academics, and has led to disastrous results when implemented.[24]

Furthermore, making money part of sovereign functions is hard to reconcile with the current institutional framework. Monetary policy is no more conducted by the executive branch of government (the 'sovereign') but rather by an independent central bank. The contrast with the current institutional framework is even starker in the case of constituencies participating voluntarily

22 Pfister, 'Central Bank Digital Currency', 4 February 2020.

23 Knapp, The State Theory of Money.

24 Françoise Drumetz and Christian Pfister, 'The Meaning of MMT', Banque de France, 27 September 2021, https://publications.banque-france.fr/en/meaning-mmt. One can also note that the so-called 'sovereign money' approach (one of the 100 per cent reserve streams) shares some features with the STM and MMT, notably a confusion between fiscal and monetary policies. Although it has never been implemented, it would likely lead to the same disastrous results as MMT (see Christian Pfister, 'The 100% Reserve Reform: Calamity or Opportunity?', *SSRN Electronic Journal*, 2020, https://doi.org/10.2139/ssrn.3749135.

in exchange rate agreements or a monetary union, the perimeters of which do not coincide with any of the constituting countries.

The second approach applies standard economic analysis to the case of money. This is the approach followed here. Within this approach, there are two streams of literature. The first stream is normative. The second stream—the 'political economy approach'—is positive. According to the *normative approach*, there is ground for public intervention if there is a market failure and if the benefits of a public intervention outweigh the costs. Public intervention does not imply public production, which is instead the extreme form of public intervention in market economies. This means that one should envisage public money supply only with great caution.

Market failures can result from monopolies, information asymmetries and externalities.

Network externalities in payment systems could lead to monopolies in the private money supply. However, this requires enforcement of competition policies in the payment services sector, not necessarily the provision of money by the public sector. However, introducing CBDCs could promote competition in an industry that is currently very concentrated. Furthermore, the conditions under which CBDCs would be supplied—mainly whether this seems 'free' or not—could limit competition and innovation in the payment services sector by preventing the entry of private players.

It is well known that information asymmetries are market imperfections[25] at the heart of banking activities, resulting *inter alia* in adverse selection.[26] However, in this case as well, it does not imply the provision of money by the public sector: public banks also thrive on information asymmetries. The most frequent sort of market failure results from externalities. Regarding money, externalities result from network effects (each agent's welfare increases when more potential counterparts join the network). Reaping the full benefits of network effects thus justifies the provision of a single unit of account within an economy. It is worth noting that, from an economic point of view, as illustrated by the theory of optimal currency areas,[27] such an economy does not necessarily coincide with a government constituency, hence with a 'sovereign.' As for the euro definition given above, one could imagine that the unit of account is defined abstractly. However, just as a measurement unit cannot only be defined abstractly, uniformity of the payment system can only

25 See, for example, Joseph E Stiglitz and Andrew Weiss, 'Credit Rationing in Markets with Imperfect Information', *American Economic Review*, Volume 71, Issue 3 (June 1981): 393-410.

26 George Akerlof, 'The Market for 'Lemons': Quality Uncertainty and the Market Mechanism', *Quarterly Journal of Economics,* Volume 84, Issue 3 (August 1970): 488-500.

27 Robert Mundell, 'A Theory of Optimal Currency Areas', *American Economic Review*, Volume 51, Issue 4 (September 1961): 657-665.

be achieved if 'outside money'[28] is provided and banks exchange it at par with their own liabilities. Whether this is a precious metal, paper, or code, 'outside money' is not a liability for anyone 'inside' the economy—i.e., anyone in the private sector—whereas 'inside money' is backed by private credit. Central bank liabilities provide 'outside money' in modern monetary systems.

More precisely, central bank money provides uniformity in the payment system, at least in principle, at two levels, the public and the central bank. The *public* is entitled to demand the total conversion of bank deposits into fiduciary money, as it is legal tender, which means that it is impossible to eschew their use when required to by the payee (see § 3.2). However, deposit insurance systems, in which banks' participation is mandatory in most countries, are in place. In addition, public institutions—in many cases, central banks—supervise banks, making it more difficult not to provide public assistance in case of difficulties in a specific bank or the banking system at large. Accordingly, and also because of banks' role in the economy, central banks intervene to bring liquidity to the banking sector when systemic crises occur as lenders of last resort. Furthermore, governments often bail out defaulting banks by acting as shareholders of last resort.[29] The policy recommendations outlined in the academic literature to avoid bank runs have been implemented by extending a safety net.[30] Depositors do not want to discipline banks anymore, since public intervention has withdrawn their incentives to do so and instead incentivises them to consider private money nearly as good as public money.

Although many payment systems handling smaller value payments operate in private money, systemic payment infrastructures settle in *central bank* money, which thus anchors the financial system. It is worth noting that banks using central bank money as outside money was mostly adopted spontaneously rather than under legal pressure. It is convenient for banks to use central bank money to avoid one of them (or a group of them, for instance, those managing a clearinghouse) providing the final means of settlement and thus acting both as a central bank and a competitor. Only recently has the joint suggestion of the CPSS, now CPMI, and the IOSCO[31] that systemic payment

28 John G Gurley, Edward S Shaw, and Alain C Enthoven, *Money in a Theory of Finance* (Washington, DC: Brookings Inst, 1979).

29 In the wake of the GFC, instruments and procedures, such as contingent capital and 'living wills' have been devised to limit bailouts and better protect taxpayers. However, whether these instruments and procedures will be used in systemic crisis situations remains an open issue.

30 See, for example, Douglas W Diamond and Philip H Dybvig, 'Bank Runs, Deposit Insurance, and Liquidity', *Journal of Political Economy* 91, no. 3 (1983): 401–19. It is worth noting that, just as in the case of central bank money, the guarantee provided by insurance deposit schemes can be credible only if the government preserves sustainable public finances.

31 Group of Ten et al., *Principles for Financial Market Infrastructures* (Basel, Switzerland]; [Madrid, Spain: Bank for International Settlements, Committee on Payment and Settlement Systems; International Organization of Securities Commissions, 2012), http://www.bis.org/publ/cpss101a.pdf, Principle 8. The Principles are commonly referred to as PFMIs.

infrastructures should settle in central bank money been passed into law in Europe under the EMIR and the United States through the Dodd-Franck Act.

It is thus when banks settle their net claims on each other in the interbank market, through the operation of their account with the central bank, rather than when the public demands the conversion of its deposits into cash, that the uniformity of the payment system is nowadays enforced. Accordingly, runs in current monetary systems occur mostly in the money market,[32] where participants have more incentives than the public to monitor their counterparties. And so, even though runs may occasionally extend to the retail deposit market, as was briefly the case for the Northern Rock bank in the United Kingdom in 2007. Overall, the uniformity of the payment system is currently implemented essentially through the provision of central bank reserves to the banking system. There are two consequences of this state of play. The first consequence is that, while cash provides valuable services, notably in preserving anonymity, its role in achieving uniformity in the payment system nowadays is optional. Retail CBDC would not materially alter this situation and might even make runs by the public easier in times of financial crises, thus possibly creating a new risk for financial stability and the singleness of the payment system.[33] However, this risk should be balanced since runs would still likely occur first in the wholesale market. In turn, possibly more frequent runs would call, in the first instance, for an already necessary clarification of the role of the central bank as a LoLR.[34] Yet, central banks rarely connect the possibility of issuing a retail CBDC with reforming their LoLR policies.[35] Instead, many of them have put themselves in an awkward position, where they both stress the safety of a possible retail CBDC compared to deposits and the risk that it might disintermediate banks, especially in financial crises. The second consequence is that if, in the longer run, the tokenisation of assets becomes standard practice, supplying the wholesale version of CBDC rather than the retail one could be

32 Gary Gorton and Andrew Metrick, 'Getting Up to Speed on the Financial Crisis: A One-Weekend-Reader's Guide', *Journal of Economic Literature* 50, no. 1 (March 2012): 128–50, https://doi.org/10.1257/jel.50.1.128.

33 See Pfister, 'Central Bank Digital Currency', 4 February 2020.

34 Christian Pfister and Natacha Valla, ''New Normal' or 'New Orthodoxy'?', Banque de France Working Paper, no. 680 (May 2018): 27.

35 One exception can be found in 'Central Bank Digital Currencies: Financial Stability Implications' (BIS, September 2021), https://www.bis.org/publ/othp42_fin_stab.pdf. This report envisages that central bank emergency liquidity frameworks could be reviewed to broaden collateral or access. However, this would represent a relatively marginal change to current practices. As far as collateral is concerned, this change has already been implemented several times by the ECB since the inception of the GFC in its primary refinancing operations, which have *de facto* played the role of lending-of-last-resort operations since then. Furthermore, the Fed also broadened access to its emergency liquidity operations at the inception of the GFC (see Pfister and Valla, ''New Normal' or 'New Orthodoxy'?' in which more substantive changes are envisaged). Finally, some central banks, including the Bank of England, broadened access during the Covid-19 pandemic episode of 'dash for cash.'

far more critical to preserving the role of the central bank in ensuring the singleness of the payment system. Banks themselves could require that a provider of DLT-based outside money steps in. The central bank could fill this role since it has historically played it.[36]

As Friedman and Schwartz put it:

> There is no economic reason why the determination of the unit of account linked with a medium of exchange cannot be left to the market. But history suggests that any privately issued unit of account will be linked to a commodity and that government will not long keep aloof.[37]

In other words, the authors resort to a *positive approach* to account for the public sector's involvement in money provision. Such an approach aims at elucidating the unofficial reasons for the government's role in money and at stressing ways and designing institutions to protect the private sector against the potentially destabilising effects of government intervention, which I refer to as 'safeguards.'

As regards the *government's role in money*, Selgin and White propose a *fiscal* [authors' emphasis] hypothesis:

> Governments have come to supply currency and to restrict the private supply of currency and deposits, not to remedy market failures, but to provide themselves with seigniorage and loans on favourable terms.

36 The point has been made that the issuance of a wholesale CBDC might not be a necessity since central bank money is already provided to banks under a digital—i.e., electronic—form (see, for example, Fabio Panetta, 'The ECB's Case for Central Bank Digital Currencies', *Financial Times*, 18 November 2021, https://www.ft.com/content/5e588cea-c218-4867-aeb7-e16e198ccd9a, and Ledger Insights, 'UK Has No Plans for a Wholesale CBDC, Envisages Banks Enabling Synthetic', Ledger Insights—enterprise blockchain, 26 November 2021, https://www.ledgerinsights.com/uk-has-no-plans-for-a-wholesale-cbdc-envisages-banks-enabling-synthetic/). Indeed, a 'bridge' could be built between financial market infrastructures using DLT and settlement systems operated by central banks, allowing smart contracts to trigger conventional RTGS transactions, thus settling DLT-based trade in central bank money ('Shaping the Future: Challenges in the European Payments Market', accessed 10 April 2022, https://www.bundesbank.de/en/press/speeches/shaping-the-future-challenges-in-the-european-payments-market-851850). However, if the tokenisation of assets became a standard practice, this approach would appear awkward. Indeed, settling the digital cash leg of transactions 'off-chain' would not allow benefiting from the blockchain architecture fully. Furthermore, a 'bridge' could create a single point of failure and a coordination problem could arise if issuers and investors view the central bank's initiative to create a 'bridge' too timid, since it could easily be reversed. Finally, it is worth noting that using stablecoins instead of CBDC to settle within the DLT infrastructure would create settlement risk.

37 Milton Friedman and Anna J Schwartz, 'Has Government Any Role in Money?', *Journal of Monetary Economics* 17, no. 1 (January 1986): 37–62, https://doi.org/10.1016/0304-3932(86)90005-X.

Government currency monopolies and bank regulations can thus be understood as part of the tax system.[38]

In particular, 'governments, and democratic ones especially, are more anxious to obtain seigniorage revenue, and to alter monetary arrangements to generate more seigniorage, during fiscal emergencies, especially wars.'[39] This hypothesis appears confirmed by Karaman et al.[40] The authors investigate the determinants of monetary stability in Europe from the late medieval era until World War I. During that time, the objective of monetary policy was monetary stability, as today, except that it was then defined as the silver or gold value of the monetary unit. They find that the primary determinant of monetary instability over the period was politics, executive constraints, warfare, and (lack of) fiscal capacity. This finding is particularly striking as commodity-based money was used during most of the period under review. Within a fiat-currency system, government interference gets easier and thus more tempting.

This fiscal hypothesis, particularly at the current high public deficits, implies that governments can be expected to support the issuance of CBDCs, especially in the retail form. Indeed, to the extent that banks usually only settle their net positions using central bank money, with netting taking place outside the central bank's books, that they already hold reserves they could convert into wholesale CBDC, and that the velocity of central bank money held by financial institutions is potentially infinite, the additional demand for it resulting from the issuance of wholesale CBDC can be expected to be minimal in normal circumstances, just as the demand for reserves for settlement purposes currently is. In contrast, the demand for retail CBDC, especially for significant economies, could be large, especially if it can circulate globally (§ 3.4). Then, central banks would spontaneously invest the counterpart of retail CBDC that substitutes for bank deposits in public securities. Supposing that, beyond possible short-term fluctuations, the demand for CBDC would increase in the long run, as has been the case for banknotes, this would mean that the governments of economies issuing CBDC would be granted what would amount to a perpetual loan by the central bank on that part of CBDC issuance that would substitute for bank deposits.[41]

38 George Selgin and Lawrence H White, 'A Fiscal Theory of Government's Role in Money', *Economic Inquiry* 37, no. 1 (January 1999): 155, https://doi.org/10.1111/j.1465-7295.1999.tb01422.x.

39 Selgin and White, 163.

40 K Kıvanç Karaman, Şevket Pamuk, and Seçil Yıldırım-Karaman, 'Money and Monetary Stability in Europe, 1300–1914', *Journal of Monetary Economics* 115 (November 2020): 279–300, https://doi.org/10.1016/j.jmoneco.2019.07.007.

41 A substitution of retail CBDC for cash, just as a substitution of wholesale CBDC for reserves, would leave the size of the central bank's balance sheet unchanged, see Christian Pfister, 'Monetary Policy and Digital Currencies: Much Ado About Nothing?', *SSRN Electronic Journal*, 2017, https://doi.org/10.2139/ssrn.3038906.

Furthermore, if the retail CBDC were remunerated at a zero-interest rate—as is the case for existing CBDCs and looks likely to remain so[42]—the interests paid on the corresponding assets could be entirely returned to the government in the form of increased seigniorage. It implies that the implicit perpetual loan would be free. Overall, the service of public debt would be significantly alleviated.

In contrast, interests would be kept by the GSC arrangements if they purchased the government debt or possibly passed it to the GSC users. In addition, GSC arrangements could be more active investors than central banks. Hence, from a political economy perspective, governments can be expected to support the launch of retail CBDCs rather than GSC arrangements, if not oppose the latter, especially in a period of high public debts. Indeed, issuing a retail CBDC would imply a transfer from the banking sector, which would lose deposits and have to collect other resources at higher costs, to the government that would re-appropriate seigniorage,[43] whereas issuing GSCs implies reallocating activities and profits within the private sector.

Political economy purposes could also give central banks reasons to supply retail CBDCs. For instance, in the face of dwindling demand for cash, central banks could see the preservation of a direct and obvious link with the public as helpful to rely more readily on it, thus keeping the government in check and ultimately maintaining their independence. Not remunerating retail CBDC or at a rate below the average return on its assets would also help preserve central bank's revenue if it does not fully return to the government the interests it receives on public debt. Thus, it would allow the central bank to decide its budget more autonomously, enabling it to keep its independence. Finally, the implicit perpetual loan granted by the central bank to the government (see above) would partly or totally replace the stock of public securities purchased at the occasion of large-scale asset purchases (so-called 'quantitative easing' operations) in the central bank balance sheet. This would lower the risk of a conflict between the central bank and the treasury when the latter would have to pay back the debt held by the central bank. It could even lower the risk of a selective default of the treasury on that debt.[44]

42 Christian Pfister, 'Retail CBDC Remuneration: The Sign Matters', SUERF Policy Note, no. 205 (November 2020): 8.

43 However, central banks may wish to temporarily compensate banks, paying them a fraction of the additional seigniorage generated by issuing CBDC, as envisaged by Ulrich Bindseil, Fabio Panetta, and Ignacio Terol, 'Central Bank Digital Currency: Functional Scope, Pricing and Controls', *SSRN Electronic Journal*, 2021, https://doi.org/10.2139/ssrn.3975939. As this would reduce seigniorage, it may need the approval of governments and could also be undertaken by them.

44 Christian Pfister and Natacha Valla, 'Whoever Pays off Their Debt Gets Rich', Fondation pour l'Innovation Politique, October 2020, https://www.fondapol.org/en/study/whoever-pays-off-their-debt-gets-rich/.

As regards *safeguards*, already mentioned in § 3.2, it means the preservation by the central bank of a sound balance sheet and the necessity of a sustainable fiscal policy. Central bank independence is another piece of a stable institutional environment indispensable to a stable currency. Central banks have been granted independence to avoid the government creating 'inflationary surprises,'[45] subject to pursuing price stability as their prime objective and supporting employment in the case of some central banks, such as the Fed, but there is no contradiction in the medium-term approach inherent to monetary policy.

Finally, as alluded to above, issuers of legal currency that have forced tender can be disciplined by the market through currency competition, i.e., the substitution of some other asset—usually foreign—for the legal currency, a process referred to in the literature as 'dollarisation,' or through the investment policy of GSCs.

This process differs from the one envisaged by Hayek,[46] which takes place at the domestic level and implies competition between other non-commodity-based monies supplied by the private sector, thus forfeiting the merits of a single unit of account in each economy.[47] It can also be official but, whether official or spontaneous, usually takes place after an episode of 'flight from currency,' thus sanctioning poor management of the domestic currency and enhancing social welfare.[48] In 2020, according to the International Monetary Fund, 13 of the economies surveyed were dollarised, and 11 operated currency boards, thus not enjoying any monetary sovereignty, in my view.[49] Furthermore, 105 countries managed pegs of different sorts, leaving 63 floating their currencies, with only 3—or 16 per cent of all economies surveyed—freely floating, thus fully exercising monetary sovereignty.

45 Robert J Barro and David B Gordon, 'Rules, Discretion and Reputation in a Model of Monetary Policy', *Journal of Monetary Economics* 12, no. 1 (January 1983): 101–21, https://doi.org/10.1016/0304-3932(83)90051-X.

46 Friedrich A von Hayek, Denationalisation of Money: The Argument Refined; An Analysis of the Theory and Practice of Concurrent Currencies, 1. ed, Hobart Paper 70 (London, 1976).

47 For a discussion and a comparison with other forms of market approaches to the supply of money, see George A Selgin and Lawrence H White, 'How Would the Invisible Hand Handle Money?', *Journal of Economic Literature* 32, no. 4 (1994): 1718–49.

48 One can refer to Alberto Alesina and Robert J Barro, 'Dollarization', *American Economic Review* 91, no. 2 (1 May 2001): 381–85, https://doi.org/10.1257/aer.91.2.381, for an introduction to the subject of dollarisation, and to Eduardo Levy-Yeyati, 'Financial Dollarization and De-Dollarization in the New Millennium', *Working Paper*, Fundo Latinoamericano de Reservas, January 2021, 69, for a recent and—perhaps excessively—critical assessment.

49 International Monetary Fund. Monetary and Capital Markets Department, *Annual Report on Exchange Arrangements and Exchange Restrictions 2020.*

3.4 Risks to monetary sovereignty

The digitalisation of money can create risks for monetary sovereignty by increasing currency competition. This is because of two reasons. The first reason is that CBDCs and GSCs could be easier to access globally than existing forms of money, primarily when issued on public blockchains. The second reason is that, despite current and foreseen improvements in the processing of international transactions, using digitalised assets in such transactions is likely to be more efficient and cheaper than using existing procedures relying on correspondent banking. Comparing the risks created by CBDCs and GSCs, respectively, is a problematic exercise.

On the one hand, CBDCs might create more risks because they are safer (they bear no credit or liquidity risk) and thus would potentially attract more demand. In addition, the not-for-profit organisations issuing them are less susceptible than GSC arrangements to sell data on user transactions and, therefore, likely to protect privacy better. On the other hand, GSC arrangements could more easily bundle the provision of a means of payment with other services, offering what Carstens has referred to as 'walled gardens.'[50] Remuneration should make a minor difference since both forms of digital money will likely not bear interest, at least in the short run (see above).

However, three sorts of qualifications are in order when assessing the risks the issuance of CBDCs or GSCs would create to monetary sovereignty. The first qualification is that, where capital movements are free, i.e., in all developed economies, except for China, considered a developed economy, currencies in the form of bank deposits are already available globally, with a few clicks from a smartphone or a personal computer Thus, digitised assets make a difference in degree rather than in nature.

The second qualification is that whether or not cross-border access to digitised assets would be easier than for pre-existing forms depends very much on their design. As shown in § 3.5, cross-border access to DLT-based records of digital assets acting as money could be limited by extending current restrictions or designing them—especially CBDCs—for that purpose.

The third qualification is that currency competition can enhance welfare, as indicated in § 3.3. First, it increases authorities' incentives to provide a sound currency, if only for fear of losing monetary sovereignty in part or total. Second, if a 'flight from currency' occurs, dollarisation offers a way out to the private sector. Similarly, competition of domestic currencies with foreign CBDCs and GSCs could also enhance welfare.

To assess the risks for monetary sovereignty, we must first consider attempts to quantify the potential reach of CBDC and GSC arrangements, then the

50 Agustín Carstens, 'Central Bank Digital Currencies: Putting a Big Idea into Practice' (Peterson Institute for International Economics (PIIE) discussion on Central Bank Digital Currencies, Basel, 31 March 2021), https://www.bis.org/speeches/sp210331.pdf.

two possible cross-border uses in international and domestic transactions. As shown below, both sorts of assets create similar but probably limited risks for monetary sovereignty.[51] Furthermore, the risks they create are similar. At the same time, CBDCs differ from GSCs since they bear no liquidity or credit risk, implying that both assets should be considered jointly when assessing digitalisation's risks for monetary sovereignty.

Estimates of the *potential reach of CBDCs and GSCs* are scarce and relate to retail use.

Regarding CBDCs, Ferrari and Mehl indicate that, according to model simulations, a CBDC (in the specific case, a digital euro) supports using a currency in cross-border payments. However, it 'is not a game-changer' since fundamental forces, such as the stability of economic fundamentals and size, remain the most important factors for international currency status' (see below).[52] It can also be helpful to consider central banks' vision of the possible cross-border use of CBDC. To this end, Auer et al. exploit the results of a survey of central banks' initial thinking on this issue, which drew 50 responses.[53] They distinguish between front-end (i.e., retail) and back-end (i.e., wholesale) uses. Overall, central banks have a cautious approach to allowing the use of a CBDC beyond their own jurisdiction.

Regarding the front end, there is a majority inclination for non-residents domestically (i.e., for tourism or business travels) and some more reluctance to use abroad, or more precisely, to use of a foreign CBDC by non-residents in their jurisdictions. Regarding the back end, central banks seem to be less well prepared. More than a quarter of them consider incorporating interoperability features to reduce frictions in the cross-border and cross-currency settlement in designing their CBDC (see § 3.5), and over one-half of those considering this option are undecided on the model.

Regarding GSCs, Adachi et al. have provided estimates of the potential size of a GSC arrangement.[54] They use the initial version of the Libra initiative—i.e., the basket version—as an example. They consider three scenarios. In the

51 The parallel between CBDCs and GSCs could extend further, since both sorts of assets could entail similar risks, in terms of bank disintermediation, for the domestic financial sector. This has been indicated above regarding the 're-appropriation' of seigniorage implied by a substitution of CBDC for bank deposits, but a GSC could also substitute for bank deposits and invest in securities issued by non-banks or abroad, thus leading to bank disintermediation.

52 Massimo Ferrari and Arnaud Mehl, 'Central Bank Digital Currency and Global Currencies', in *The International Role of the Euro*, ed. European Central Bank. (LU: ECB, 2021), https://data.europa.eu/doi/10.2866/070753.

53 Raphael Auer et al., 'CBDCs beyond Borders: Results from a Survey of Central Banks', BIS Papers, no. 116 (June 2021): 22.

54 Mitsutoshi Adachi et al., 'A Regulatory and Financial Stability Perspective on Global Stablecoins', Macroprudential Bulletin, no. 10 (5 May 2020), https://www.ecb.europa.eu/pub/financial-stability/macroprudential-bulletin/html/ecb.mpbu202005_1~3e9ac10eb1.en.html.

first scenario, in line with GSC promoters' declared intentions,[55] the GSC is used only as a means of payment, with average per-capita holdings of €64 and a global size of slightly more than €150bn.[56] The GSC is also used as a store of value in the second and third scenarios. In the second scenario, the average per capita holdings amount to €231 and total holdings to slightly more than €560bn. Although the second scenario could have adverse consequences for financial stability in case of a run on the GSC, neither the first nor the second scenarios would appear problematic for monetary sovereignty, except perhaps when the GSC would massively displace the legal currency in a tiny economy. In the third scenario, labelled 'extreme-case scenario' by the authors, the average per capita holdings reach €1,220, and the global size of the GSC stands slightly below €3tn. However, this scenario may not be realistic. As the authors point out, it has been designed on the pattern of Yu'E Bao,[57] which has since been sized down following regulators' intervention; hence, it may reflect a situation where a GSC arrangement remains largely unregulated.

Furthermore, in the third scenario, the authors use purchasing parity-adjusted exchange rates to consider the difference between the income levels in China and Europe. However, European savers have a broader range of possible investments than Chinese ones. While the purchasing power parity adjustment is warranted between China and Europe, it is likely to be lower between China and other parts of the world, where currency substitution can be higher than in Europe (see below). Finally, in all three scenarios, the considered basket version of the GSC limits the currency risk users are exposed to, making it appealing for its use as a store of value. However, the basket version of Diem has rapidly been abandoned.

Consequently, demand for a GSC could be lower in the three scenarios, especially the second and third ones. In the opposite direction, Adachi et al. consider the case of a single GSC, whereas there could be several of them, although most likely partly at the expense of every other. Furthermore, the demand for GSCs—just like for CBDCs—could spike during financial crises that would hit weaker economies, making both play the role of safe havens (see below).

Using a currency in *international transactions* has no direct impact on monetary policy and, thus, according to my definition, on monetary sovereignty. However, it can indirectly affect the conduct of monetary policy, notably as a source of shocks to the domestic economy resulting from exchange

55 See, for example, Christian Catalini, *From Cryptocurrencies, Stablecoins and Diem to CBDCs*, YouTube, OMFIF DMI Symposium Central Banks and Digital Currencies, 2021, https://www.omfif.org/from-cryptocurrencies-stablecoins-and-diem-to-cbdcs/, in the case of Diem.

56 Hence less than 7 per cent of the total market capitalisation of crypto-assets as of mid-December 2021.

57 The money market fund operated by Ant Group, itself part of the Chinese Alibaba Group: 'Tianhong Asset Management', accessed 10 April 2022, http://www.thfund.com.cn/en/yuebao.html.

rate fluctuations. Symmetrically, the internationalisation of a currency—i.e., its growing use in international transactions—can protect the issuing economy from exchange rate shocks (see § 3.5).

In the context of the digitalisation of money, three sorts of questions arise:

- How could the digitalisation of money affect the drivers of the international use of a currency and, in turn, monetary policy?
- Supposing that digitalisation does influence the international use of a currency, would the economy that would be the first to issue a CBDC benefit from a 'first-mover advantage,' allowing it to increase its currency's role in international trade finance?
- Could a multi-currency CBDC or GSC achieve international status?

Regarding *drivers*, empirical research has shown the roles of economic size, opening, development, and depth of financial markets, and credibility of the economic and financial system, in promoting the international use of a currency, with, as expected, the first factor at play in foreign trade and the following factors mainly influencing financial transactions.[58] Furthermore, there is substantial inertia in the role of a dominant currency, even though changes can occur brutally, and there can be periods without a dominant currency.[59] These factors favour the U.S. dollar, the dominant currency for over 60 years now. As indicated by Iancu:[60]

- The share of the U.S. dollar in global reserves was 61 per cent at the end of 2019, while the euro came second with 21 per cent, and other currencies played only a minor role.
- The dollar was also the most traded currency in the foreign exchange market (44 per cent of turnover), where it acts as the vehicle currency and is mainly used for trade invoicing (54 per cent of global trade). This is partly due to its role in the third country, commodity trade, and financial claim denomination (51 per cent of cross-border bank claims).

58 For recent reviews, one can refer to Georgios Georgiadis et al., 'Fundamentals vs. Policies: Can the US dollar's Dominance in Global Trade Be Dented?', *SSRN Electronic Journal*, 2021, https://doi.org/10.2139/ssrn.3894751, regarding the use of a currency in trade, and to Alina Iancu et al., 'Reserve Currencies in an Evolving International Monetary System', *IMF Departmental Papers* 2020, no. 002 (17 November 2020), regarding its use as a reserve currency (i.e., a currency that enters the foreign exchange reserves of central banks). In addition, Gita Gopinath and Jeremy C Stein, 'Banking, Trade, and the Making of a Dominant Currency', *The Quarterly Journal of Economics* 136, no. 2 (2021): 783–830, show the interaction between uses in trade and in banking.

59 Barry J Eichengreen, Arnaud Mehl, and Livia Chitu, *How Global Currencies Work: Past, Present, and Future* (Princeton: Princeton University Press, 2018).

60 Eichengreen, Mehl, and Chitu.

In contrast, whereas China is the world's largest exporter, its currency remains little used in foreign trade and financial transactions, even in its own ones. According to Poenish, the share of Chinese exports and imports settled in renminbi stood at 20 per cent in 2020, and the renminbi's share in global reserve holdings was 2.3 per cent.[61] However, both percentages have been growing fast in recent years, partly reflecting policies to encourage the international use of the currency, including establishing currency swaps between the People's Bank of China and foreign central banks that facilitate access to the renminbi.[62]

This example shows that although the infrastructure supporting a legal currency does not currently appear as a driver of its international use, more accessible access, to which CBDCs and GSCs could contribute, could, to a certain extent, play a supporting role. Consequently, cross-border capital flows and exchange rate volatility could increase, inflicting undesired shocks on the economy that would interfere with the smooth conduct of monetary policy in the issuing or receiving economies. For example, in periods of a financial crisis hitting developing or emerging economies, there could be an appreciation of the currency of the CBDC issuing economy acting as a haven (or the currency or currencies backing the GSC) and a depreciation in the currency hit by the economy in crisis, with stabilising consequences in the case of the economy in crisis and destabilising effects for the admittedly larger and more developed issuing economy.

Regarding a potential *prime-mover advantage*, the case of the U.S. should be singled out for two reasons. First, the U.S. dollar dominates the international monetary system, as seen above. Second, because of this dollar domination, projects of GSCs currently all include at least a U.S. dollar component, as seen in § 3.2. This probably accounts, at least partly, for the relatively relaxed attitude of some US policymakers in the face of foreign CBDC initiatives, such as the Chinese one.[63] In the case of the Chinese project of an e-yuan, the argument of the prime-mover advantage has been put forward since China is likely to become the first significant country to issue a CBDC. Suarez and Lanzolla show that first-mover status can confer benefits but does not so categorically, depending on circumstances.[64] More precisely, they argue that developing such an advantage is unlikely when 'technology leads' and very unlikely when 'the market gets rough'. Chorzempa notes that these two adverse conditions are

61 'Renminbi Internationalisation Getting Back on Track', *OMFIF* (blog), 13 August 2021, https://www.omfif.org/2021/08/renminbi-internationalisation-getting-back-on-track/.

62 Gopinath and Stein, 'Banking, Trade, and the Making of a Dominant Currency'.

63 See, for example, 'Randal K Quarles: Parachute Pants and Central Bank Money' (BIS, 28 June 2021), https://www.bis.org/review/r210705c.pdf, and Christopher Waller, 'CBDC: A Solution in Search of a Problem?', 5 August 2021, https://www.federalreserve.gov/newsevents/speech/files/waller20210805a.pdf.

64 Fernando F Suarez and Gianvito Lanzolla, 'The Half-Truth of First-Mover Advantage', *Harvard Business Review*, 1 April 2005, https://hbr.org/2005/04/the-half-truth-of-first-mover-advantage.

met in the digital currency space.[65] Andolfatto also stresses that a world currency supplier must be prepared to run potentially substantial current account deficits and that the Chinese economic model encourages the opposite.[66] On the Chinese side, the People's Bank of China has assured that the e-yuan was mainly designed for domestic use and should not disrupt other central banks' currency sovereignty.[67] Be it as it may, if not fear of losing monetary sovereignty, there could at least be a 'fear of missing out' on the part of central banks. In 2020, 86 per cent of the respondent central banks surveyed by the BIS indicated that they explored the benefits and drawbacks of CBDCs.[68] In addition, the ECB Report on a digital euro mentions the issuance of foreign CBDCs as one of the reasons.[69] Finally, being the first major economy to issue a CBDC could allow China to play a significant role in defining any international standards, as the US did at the inception of the Internet. This implies that the primary reserve currency issuers, starting with the US, cannot be absent from the definition of international standards.[70] Such standards could also be adopted by GSCs, possibly under the pressure of regulators, to promote interoperability between them (conversely, interoperability with other payment infrastructures could encourage the use of GSCs by allowing GSC holders to benefit from enhanced network effects).

Regarding the possibility of *a multi-currency CBDC or GSC achieving international status*, a proposal for the former was formulated by Carney under the label of a public 'Synthetic Hegemonic Currency' (SHC).[71] The SHC would

65 Martin Chorzempa, 'China, the United States, and Central Bank Digital Currencies: How Important Is It to Be First?', *China Economic Journal*, 5 January 2021, https://www.tandfonline.com/doi/full/10.1080/17538963.2020.1870278.

66 David Andolfatto, 'On the Necessity and Desirability of a Central Bank Digital Currency', in *Central Bank Digital Currency: Considerations, Projects, Outlook*, ed. Dirk Niepelt (London: Centre for Economic Policy Research, 2021), https://voxeu.org/content/central-bank-digital-currency-considerations-projects-outlook.

67 People's Bank of China, 'Progress of Research & Development of E-CNY in China' (Working Group on E-CNY Research and Development of the People's Bank of China, July 2021), http://www.pbc.gov.cn/en/3688110/3688172/4157443/4293696/2021071614584691871.pdf.

68 Boar Codruta and Andreas Wehrli, 'Ready, Steady, Go? Results of the Third BIS Survey on Central Bank Digital Currency', *BIS Monetary and Economic Department*, BIS Papers, no. 114 (January 2021), https://www.bis.org/publ/bppdf/bispap114.pdf.

69 Ferrari and Mehl, 'Central Bank Digital Currency and Global Currencies'.

70 Lael Brainard, 'Speech by Governor Brainard on Private Money and Central Bank Money as Payments Go Digital: An Update on CBDCs', Board of Governors of the Federal Reserve System, 24 May 2021, https://www.federalreserve.gov/newsevents/speech/brainard20210524a.htm.

71 Mark Carney, 'The Growing Challenges for Monetary Policy in the Current International Monetary and Financial System', Bank of England, 23 August 2019, https://www.bankofengland.co.uk/-/media/boe/files/speech/2019/the-growing-challenges-for-monetary-policy-speech-by-mark-carney.pdf?la=en&hash=01A18270247C456901D4043F59D4B79F09B6BFBC.

provide an alternative to multi-currency GSCs (at the time, Libra was mentioned by Carney), intending to replace the dollar in international payments. The benefits cited would be twofold. First, the SHC would help reduce the dollar's influence on international trade, exchange rates, and global financial conditions and thus reduce the volatility of capital flows to emerging economies. Second, the SHC would gradually make the currencies other than the dollar constituting the basket appear as reserve currencies. The SHC would spread, thereby increasing the supply of safe assets and reducing the downward pressure on the equilibrium interest rate.[72] However, the question arises about the reason why an already existing instrument, aimed to serve as an SHC and designed as a basket of currencies, as the Special Drawing Rights (SDRs), could not assert itself in international monetary relations beyond its—allegedly marginal—role as a unit of account.[73] Eichengreen underlines that the SDR has had no success with the private sector.[74] Also, as Melachrinos and Pfister note, who would determine the basket's composition and issue the SHC, the amounts to be issued, and according to what criteria remains to be seen.[75]

Furthermore, what would be the status of the SHC in the different economies? Would the SHC be used only in international transactions? How would its issuance be combined with the currencies of the various economies contributing to it? Finally, although it is not unthinkable that, in countries where a multi-currency GSC would have primarily displaced the domestic currency (see below), the central bank could include it in its foreign exchange reserves, the chances that issuers of reserve currencies do the same, putting a privately issued asset on the same footing as legal currencies, seem slim.

Whereas the issuance of GSCs and CBDCs could redistribute the roles among the various international currencies to some extent, their substitution for currency in ***domestic transactions*** could more severely disrupt monetary policy. I first envisage the issue in general terms and then discuss the case in which a GSC would become auto-referential.

In ***general terms***, one can distinguish the consequences for the economies issuing the CBDC or the legal currency the GSC arrangement is invested in—hereafter 'issuing economies'—and for the economies receiving

72 Ricardo J Caballero and Emmanuel Farhi, 'The Safety Trap', *Review of Economic Studies*, Volume 85, Issue 1 (January 2018): 233-274.

73 See especially the paragraph 'New opportunities and challenges of central bank issuance of digital assets for the governance of the international monetary system' in Filippo Zatti and Rosa Giovanna Barresi, 'La futura gobernanza del sistema monetario internacional: primeras consideraciones sobre el papel del euro digital', in *Dinero digital y gobernanza TIC en la UE*, ed. Carmen Pastor Sempere (Cizur Menor: Editorial Aranzadi, 2022), 397–424.

74 Barry Eichengreen, 'Libra: The Known Unknowns and Unknown Unknowns', *VoxEU.Org* (blog), 4 September 2019, https://voxeu.org/article/libra-known-unknowns-and-unknown-unknowns.

75 Melachrinos and Pfister, 'Stablecoins'.

them—henceforth 'receiving economies.'[76] The implicit assumption is that issuing economies would be developed economies with sound economic fundamentals and robust institutions, which already issue reserve currencies, while the receiving economies would be developing and emerging economies with weaker economic fundamentals and institutions. As Cunliffe puts it, answering a question on the risks for UK monetary sovereignty that the issuance of a digital euro might create: 'My own view is that (…), if we continue to provide credible, safe, reliable money in the UK, then I do not see "euroisation" or "dollarisation" as an issue.' [77]

Other important distinctions are between retail and wholesale applications and between normal circumstances, in which consequences can be limited, particularly for issuing economies, and crises, which can be more significant, especially for receiving economies.

Consequences for *issuing economies* could be limited to ancillary issues regarding the management of the monetary base and associated exchange rate volatility, as for international transactions (see above), in the case of CBDCs or wholesale GSCs. The issuance of wholesale GSCs could decrease demand for reserves if the wholesale GSC, as envisaged by JPM Coin, is backed by commercial bank deposits (§ 3.2). This is because the unwinding of transactions previously on the central bank's books could then be shifted to the GSC blockchain. More importantly, in a liquidity crisis, the central bank's less detailed knowledge of institutions' cash holdings could make its intervention in favour of the GSC arrangement as a LoLR more difficult. CBDCs and GSCs backed by base money, as in the USC project (§ 3.2) or possibly someday for retail GSCs,[78] could cause the demand for central bank money to increase significantly and become more volatile, especially during financial crises in receiving economies.

In *receiving economies*, the use of retail CBDCs or GSCs, if it were to be widespread, possibly leading to the crowding out of the legal currency, would raise serious difficulties for the transmission mechanism of monetary policy. The conversion of bank deposits into CBDC or GSC and the associated possible distribution of CBDC or GSC-denominated loans would weaken the transmission to the economy of changes in the legal tender interest rate. On the other hand, the credit channel would be ambiguously affected. The narrow credit channel could be weakened because the banking sector's liquidity would be partly in CBDC or GSC and could not be directly impacted by the central bank unless it intervenes in CBDC or GSC. Conversely, on the

76 In the case of a multi-currency GSC arrangement, there are several issuing economies, and all economies are potentially receiving economies. In this case, consequences for monetary policy, hence potentially monetary sovereignty, are more diffuse for issuing economies and for those receiving economies that are also issuing economies.

77 The Bank of England's Approach to Digital Currencies and Cross-Border Payments, 2021, https://www.youtube.com/watch?v=rsowfkOUHqM.

78 From Cryptocurrencies, Stablecoins and Diem to CBDCs.

one hand, the broad credit channel would be reinforced by increased financial frictions—if there were less substitutability—between the foreign CBDC or the GSC and legal tender financing than between different forms of funding in the legal currency (for example, between intermediated credit and securities issuance), on the other hand. Finally, suppose the legal currency remains the unit of account. In that case, the asset price channel could become more potent as interest rates on the exchange rate would influence a more significant proportion of assets. However, there would be few chances that the legal currency remains the unit of account if a GSC or a CBDC has displaced it as a medium of exchange and a store of value, except perhaps in public taxation and expenditure. Consequently, monetary policy would lose its potency, and monetary sovereignty would be foregone. Furthermore, as in the case of dollarisation, LoLR operations in favour of a domestic bank or a GSC arrangement could then be carried out only within the limits of the foreign exchange reserves held by the central bank.

The *specific case* of GSC becoming auto-referential has received some attention.[79] While inherently dramatic, this case is probably unrealistic. If a GSC became auto-referential, it would conduct its monetary policy. This case would differ from the one in which a multi-currency GSC substitutes for a legal currency. Indeed, a multi-currency GSC can be replicated, allowing arbitrage with the component currencies and preventing the GSC arrangement from deciding autonomously on the conditions—i.e., the interest rate—at which it supplies its units. As a first approximation, the consequences for a receiving economy of substituting an autonomous GSC for a domestic currency would not necessarily differ substantially from the general case envisaged above: the money issuer would just be private instead of public. However, the privatisation of monetary policy would be a dramatic development. In addition, as the issuer would be a profit-making institution, it would entail the risk of unbacked issuance. This risk is nevertheless present in public issuance schemes if there are reasons to think that the assets owned by the central are risky (§ 3.3).[80]

79 See, for example, International Monetary Fund, *Digital Money across Borders: Macro-Financial Implications*, 2020, and Markus Brunnermeier, Harold James, and Jean-Pierre Landau, 'The Digitalization of Money' (Cambridge, MA: National Bureau of Economic Research, September 2019), https://doi.org/10.3386/w26300.

80 In Maurice Obstfeld, 'Reprint: Two Challenges from Globalization', *Journal of International Money and Finance* 114 (June 2021), https://doi.org/10.1016/j.jimonfin.2021.102408, the author also points out that, as a GSC arrangement extends its liabilities, it must invest in ever-riskier assets, a fact that an individual user of the GSC may not internalise. However, a similar observation could also be attached to CBSCs: that the universe of safe assets is limited and is a feature that does not depend on the status of investors. Furthermore, as indicated below in the main text, there are reasons to expect that, at some point, users of a GSC will realise the risk they incur and then run on the GSC.

However, such a scenario would be unrealistic. It implies that the transition would be risky for users and issuers. Users of a GSC not referenced in the domestic legal currency expose themselves to currency risk. This is nearly nowhere the case currently for individuals, at least in developed economies. One exception is mortgaging in foreign currency, which does not involve everyday payments and mostly takes place in countries or regions with high financial frictions or where the borrower receives income in the foreign currency it borrows. For the public to accept exposure to an unpegged GSC, it would have to gain benefits, for instance, through bundling payment services with other services,[81] which would be extremely valuable to offset the exchange risk. This might draw a small part of the public, most probably not a share that would be high enough to incentivise the rest of the public to turn to the GSC to reap associated network effects. This scenario would have to build on a 'closed system.' Banks would have to accept the units the GSC arrangement issues as deposits. The securities the arrangement invests in would have to be denominated in its unit of account, and the GSC arrangement would have to be able to act as a credible LoLR—in its currency—for the banks that accept its money—i.e., potentially all the banks.

Moreover, the users would have to receive their income in the same unit of account. The latter would have to be accepted not only by the producers of the items sold on the platform on which the GSC circulates but, more generally, by all merchants, too (unless, of course, purchases are made on the issuer's platform). In other words, as in a scenario frequently mentioned at the inception of Bitcoin,[82] the preconditions that would allow the generalised use of a GSC are utopian. Furthermore, the public would understand that the profit-maximising objective of an unpegged GSC could be in conflict at any moment with the maintenance of price stability in this GSC. Its monetary policy would, therefore, not be credible. Overall, there are good reasons to think the GSC arrangement announcing its intention to unpeg would trigger a run on it. Finally, in order to precisely avoid a run on the GSC, regulators would quite sensibly oppose the decision by a GSC arrangement to issue an autonomous currency, whether it wishes to take that decision from the start—in which case, there would be no unpegging at all—or a later stage.

3.5 Policy recommendations

Here, I focus on retail uses since they could challenge monetary sovereignty much more than wholesale uses, as seen in § 3.4. Again, I distinguish between issuing and receiving economies, assuming that the former will likely be developed economies, and the latter ones will be developing or emerging economies.

81 Brunnermeier, James, and Landau, 'The Digitalization of Money'.

82 In which prices would fall as the use of Bitcoin would generalise due to the limited supply of the crypto-asset: Pfister, 'Monetary Policy and Digital Currencies'.

Regarding *issuing economies*, the design of CBDCs and the environment in which GSC arrangements would operate could significantly affect the risks they create. Due to different institutional settings and objectives, I distinguish between CBDCs and GSCs.

In designing *CBDCs*, central banks must choose their possible cross-border uses. Apart from legal constraints, such choices will likely depend on two factors: whether or not GSCs, which could play a similar role as CBDC, are available, and whether central banks wish to internationalise their currency. In that regard, central banks face a trade-off between hedging and creating spillovers.

On the one hand, the currency's internationalisation will help protect the economy against foreign exchange shocks. In the extreme, an economy that only uses its currency in trade and financial transactions with the rest of the world would perfectly insulate itself from exchange rate shocks. On the other hand, by internationalising its currency, an economy exposes its partners to more significant exchange rate risks, which can, in turn, adversely affect it. The internalisation of the currency may also limit the potency of monetary policy by reducing the role of the foreign exchange channel in the transmission of monetary policy. However, and possibly contrary to a stated desire to preserve monetary sovereignty, governments may not share such preoccupations. Indeed, fiscal objectives (see § 3.3) would make them prone to support the currency's internationalisation to increase *seigniorage*.

As explained in § 3.4, the central bank's approach to the cross-border use of CBDC is cautious. Concretely, the preliminary decision they must take relates to the possible access of non-residents. Other features are less important. For instance, wholesale CBDCs should bear the same remuneration as reserves,[83] whereas retail CBDCs will probably pay a zero-interest rate like retail GSCs (see above). Equally, whether the CBDC is account-based or token-based is of relatively minor importance. For instance, using tokens does not imply exemption from KYC and AML/CFT requirements or anonymity *vis-à-vis* the issuer.

The first possibility would be to refuse non-residents access to retail CBDC, except when travelling for business or tourism purposes, and within limits that could be as stringent as those possibly imposed on residents. It is, for instance, the option so far taken regarding the e-yuan.[84] However, adopting the same option would be more challenging to justify in the case of other developed economies with free capital flows. Indeed, for these economies, it would amount to turning over the principle that has prevailed in the past half-century, i.e., that free capital movements are the rule, and thus that capital movements should not be limited. Furthermore, by limiting the circulation of their CBDCs, developed economies might end up *de facto* supporting the use of GSCs pegged to their currencies.

83 Pfister, 'Central Bank Digital Currency', 4 February 2020.

84 Pfister, 'Retail CBDC Remuneration: The Sign Matters'.

The second possibility would be to allow access. It could be implemented either directly—i.e., by giving access to foreign payment service providers in the case of a two-tier distribution model[85]—or indirectly through multi-CBDC (m-CBDC) arrangements of three sorts, from the least integrated to the most integrated model:[86]

- Enhancing the compatibility of CBDCs by setting joint standards for domestic CBDC systems.
- Interlinking CBDC systems through a shared technical interface or a common clearing mechanism.
- Integrating multiple CBDCs in a single m-CBDC arrangement.

All three models, particularly the third one, would ideally have to be anticipated since profoundly re-designing a payment infrastructure is lengthy and costly. All could also incorporate holding and/or transaction limits, for example, the same limitations that could apply to residents to limit disintermediation, with the risk of supporting the corresponding GSCs. Furthermore, a fully integrated m-CBDC arrangement could a priori easily incorporate the possibility of activating capital control measures (see below).

Regarding *GSCs*, forbidding or limiting the holding or transaction amounts could be more difficult than when a CBDC is used, in the case of issuing economies with free capital flows. This *de facto* would constrain the central banks of these economies (see above) since a CBDC and the GSC referenced to the same legal currency are partly substitutable (see § 3.4). However, this does not imply that issuing economies could not influence the issuance of GSCs, and, thereby, the risks they create. Issuing economies inevitably place regulatory constraints on GSC arrangements for various widely accepted reasons, including by their promoters.[87] Requirements could *inter alia* be prudential, consumer protection, privacy, KYC, and AML/FT. Concerning more specifically risks that GSC arrangements could create, two sorts of actions would be crucial. First, prudential regulations should require demanding capital and liquidity requirements to avoid a run on a GSC triggering fire sales in the

85 Pfister, 'Central Bank Digital Currency', 2019.

86 Raphael Auer, Philipp Haene, and Henry Holden, 'Multi-CBDC Arrangements and the Future of Cross-Border Payments', *BIS Papers*, no. 115 (March 2021), https://www.bis.org/publ/bppdf/bispap115.pdf.

87 See, for example, Gopinath and Stein, 'Banking, Trade, and the Making of a Dominant Currency'; or David Marcus, 'Good Stablecoins, a Protocol for Money, and Digital Wallets: The Formula to Fix Our Broken Payment…', *Medium* (blog), 18 August 2021, https://medium.com/@davidmarcus/good-stablecoins-a-protocol-for-money-and-digital-wallets-the-formula-to-fix-our-broken-payment-f11f59fc92d7. For an official point of view, one can refer to the case of the President's Working Group on Financial Markets, the Federal Deposit Corporation, and the Office of the Comptroller of the Currency, 'Report on Stablecoins' (US Treasury, November 2021). *Inter alia*, the report urges Congress to limit the issuance of 'payment stablecoins' to banks and other insured depository institutions.

underlying securities markets, making it very difficult for the central bank not to intervene as a LoLR, as seen in § 3.3. Second, competition between GSC arrangements should be fostered, including by promoting and, if necessary, imposing interoperability. This would also be important for receiving economies and is accepted by the promoters of GSC arrangements.[88] In the same direction, compatibility with existing payment infrastructure should be sought. Nevertheless, just as they could favour the internationalisation of CBDCs, governments in the issuing economies may not oppose non-residents holding GSCs referenced on their legal currency, at least to the extent that the reserves of the GSC arrangements would be invested in public bonds they issue.

Apart from promoting competition between GSCs and compatibility with existing payment infrastructure, various policies could help receiving countries manage the risks potentially created by digitising money. These policies are the same as those recommended in the face of a risk of dollarisation and include monetary and foreign exchange policies.[89] While more exchange rate flexibility may be helpful in the first instance, to increase exchange rate uncertainty and thus the reluctance to hold foreign currency on the part of residents, authorities might be tempted to have recourse to more 'hands-on' policies if dollarisation gained ground despite sound economic fundamentals. Indeed, exchange rate fluctuations could have a destabilising effect on the domestic economy. More direct and forceful policies could include recourse to capital controls and exchange rate targeting, implying a reduction in monetary sovereignty. As mentioned above, it could be relatively easy to implement capital controls in a m-CBDC arrangement framework, as controls would then be centralised and applied to all transactions. However, rules on purchases of GSCs could probably only be put in place through recourse to 'gatekeepers,' i.e., primarily banks, which would be more cumbersome and probably less efficient. Also, if an exchange rate target puts a heavy constraint on monetary policy, the receiving economy could recoup at least part of its autonomy to smooth the economic cycle by increasing 'fiscal space.' Entering a recession with sustainable public finance would also increase the credibility of the economic framework, thus reducing risk premiums on the domestic currency and pressure on the foreign exchange markets, eventually increasing monetary sovereignty. Furthermore, prudential policies could apply at two levels. At the macroeconomic level, the central bank could build up foreign exchange reserves, negotiate credit lines, and enter foreign exchange swaps with foreign central banks. At the level of supervised entities, regulators could require higher capital and liquidity buffers and impose higher capital charges on loans denominated in foreign currency.

88 See, for instance, Marcus, 'Good Stablecoins, a Protocol for Money, and Digital Wallets'.

89 See Obstfeld, 'Reprint'; Board of Governors of the Federal Reserve System et al., 'Global Stablecoins: Monetary Policy Implementation Considerations from the US Perspective', *Finance and Economics Discussion Series* 2021, no. 020 (22 March 2021): 1–14, https://doi.org/10.17016/FEDS.2021.020.

Finally, launching a CBDC could diminish the attractiveness of GSCs, and, conversely, increase that of the domestic currency. However, it would not be a substitute for sound and credible fundamentals and institutions.

3.6 Conclusion

The following takeaways emerge, starting from the definition of monetary sovereignty as the capacity for an economic area to set monetary policy, and thus the value of its money, based on its economic fundamentals.

Money and means of payment are different things. Means of payment are used to make money circulate (i.e., to implement the medium of exchange function of money). In current monetary systems, only cash is money and a means of payment.

Monetary sovereignty does not imply that the public sector provides money: nowadays, *the private sector provides the bulk of money.*

Monetary sovereignty is not a universal rule, with many economies dollarised, participating in exchange rate arrangements, or pursuing an exchange rate objective.

The singleness of the payment system eliminates frictions in the economy that could be costly and supports a predictable transmission to the economy of monetary policy impulses. It is thus currently essential for monetary sovereignty.

A legal currency is auto-referential. It implies that stablecoins are not a substitute for legal currency. With possible government interference in managing legal currency, for fiscal purposes, legal tender means that safeguards, such as central bank independence, must be implemented to protect social welfare. Currency competition can also be valuable, even though it risks monetary sovereignty.

Public money is backed by the central bank's balance sheet, implying that the best government can do to support it is to run a sustainable fiscal policy. Unless a significant technological breakthrough takes place, allowing us to use decentrally issued crypto-assets in transactions and as stores of value while preserving the singleness of the payment system, they do not appear to have a future as money.

At least so far, digitalisation has not led to a change in the nature of money. CBDCs and stablecoins are not new monies: they are just new forms of money, the legal currency for CBDCs and intended copycats of the legal currency for stablecoins.

A GSC cannot put monetary sovereignty at risk in the economy that issues the currency it mimics.

The provision of central bank money ensures the singleness of the payment system. In contemporary economies, this does not necessarily call for providing central bank money to the public.

However, central banks may wish to issue retail CBDC for political economy reasons in developed economies and to support financial inclusion in developing and emerging economies.

In the future, if the tokenisation of assets were to become standard practice, supplying the wholesale version of CBDC, rather than the retail one, could be far more critical for preserving the role of the central bank in ensuring the singleness of the payment system.

From a political economy perspective, governments can be expected to support the launch of retail CBDCs rather than GSC arrangements, if not oppose the latter's creation, especially in a period of high public debts. Governments in issuing economies can also be expected to support holding retail CBDCs or GSCs referenced on their legal currency by non-residents.

The digitalisation of money implied by CBDCs and GSCs can create risks for monetary sovereignty by increasing currency competition in economies that neither issue them (for CBDCs) nor the invested currency (for GSCs). In countries where economic fundamentals and institutions are weaker, above all, in some developing and emerging economies, these risks are material. It could be the modern version of dollarisation.

Whether CBDCs or GSCs would spontaneously create more risks to monetary sovereignty is an open issue. Since they would be imperfect substitutes, both assets should be considered when assessing digitalisation's risks for monetary sovereignty. However, there is considerable uncertainty about the potential reach of CBDCs and GSCs. Thus, whether either digital asset can be a game-changer is an open issue.

It is not clear either whether there would be a prime-mover advantage in launching a CBDC, allowing China to transform the renminbi into a significant reserve currency without freeing its capital flows and significantly amending its economic policies.

However, the primary reserve currency issuers must be present in the definition of international standards, which would apply to CBDCs and could also be adopted by GSCs.

The prospects of a multi-currency CBDC or GSC achieving international status or a GSC becoming auto-referential are very slim.

There are ways through which issuing economies can limit risks to the monetary sovereignty of receiving economies. However, such measures would come at the cost of reversing the principle that capital movements into and out of developed economies—except China—are free and, when applied to CBDCs, might eventually *de facto* support the use of GSCs pegged to their currencies.

There are also ways in which receiving countries, where risks could be more material, can protect their monetary sovereignty.

In both sorts of economies, fostering competition between GSCs could play a valuable role.

Overall, even though the digitalisation of money will undoubtedly lead to profound changes in the provision of means of payment, the risks it could create for monetary sovereignty in developed economies seem overblown. In this respect, currency risks, legacy effects, and regulatory constraints make a *status quo* more likely than sweeping changes.

Furthermore, the main risk one can detect, dollarisation in developing or emerging economies, is familiar. Ways to manage it are also well known. Consequently, it would be a pity if the preservation of monetary sovereignty were taken as a motive to narrow the scope of choices offered to consumers, for example, by banning or unduly constraining GSC arrangements.

Other substantial issues are currently at stake in the global debate on digitalisation, including consumer protection, legal and governance frameworks, data privacy, competition, innovation, operational resilience and cybersecurity, illicit finance, and energy and the environment.[90]

90 See, for example, HM Treasury and Bank of England, 'G7 Finance Ministers and Central Bank Governors' Statement on Central Bank Digital Currencies (CBDCs) and Digital Payments', G7 UK 2021, 13 October 2021, https://assets.publishing.service.gov.uk/government/uploads/system/uploads/attachment_data/file/1025234/FINAL_G7_Statement_on_Digital_Payments_13.10.21.pdf; and the companion report: G7, 'Public Policy Principles for Retail Central Bank Digital Currencies (CBDCs)' (HM Treasury, 14 October 2021), https://assets.publishing.service.gov.uk/government/uploads/system/uploads/attachment_data/file/1025235/G7_Public_Policy_Principles_for_Retail_CBDC_FINAL.pdf.

4 Central Bank Digital Currencies

A New Nexus Between Central and Commercial Banks?

Arthur Rossi[1]

4.1 CBDCs, a game changer for the relationship between central and commercial banks?

From a competition perspective, what is the impact of a CBDC on commercial banks and central banking? In this chapter, we will go through it for then look at how the CBoB—the first to launch its own CBDC officially—arbitrated competing interests and what was the ensuing take-up by the population and financial sector. In a third sub-paragraph, we will identify which design choices for CBDCs could have a material impact on intermediation. In doing so, we will investigate the historical explanations for why central banks are granted monopolies for the issuance of paper currency; the reasons why commercial banks seek their own monopoly in the payment space; and, finally, we will look at the interaction between these competing forces in the context of a CBDC.

4.1.1 The legal monopoly of central banknotes

The allocation of the respective roles to different banks in the economy results from the long 'tried and tested'[2] evolution of central and commercial banking. Initially, some central banks were created because of the dire financial needs of their home governments, essentially to support rearmament efforts (for example, the BoE).[3] Those central banks were then granted the right to issue 'legal tender' banknotes as a privilege to compensate for their government funding. For example, after the short-term issuance of the banknote monopoly of John

1 The views expressed in this chapter are solely those of the Author and may not necessarily represent the position of the Saudi Central Bank.

2 See Thomas Jordan, 'How Money Is Created by the Central Bank and the Banking System' (Swiss National Bank, 16 January 2018).

3 In fact, the 'Bank of England Act', 20 § 5 & 6 Will. and Mar. (1694) directly refers to the war effort against France that followed, among others, the Royal Navy defeat of Beachy Head: 'An Act for granting to their Majesties several Rates and Duties upon Tunnage of Ships and Vessels, and upon Beer, Ale, and other Liquors, for securing certain Recompenses and Advantages in the said Act mentioned, to such Persons as shall voluntarily advance the Sum of Fifteen hundred thousand Pounds towards carrying on the *War against France*.'

DOI: 10.4324/9781003258261-6

Law's Banque Royale,[4] Banque de France was granted the monopoly to issue cash in 1803, three years after its founding. Another occurrence included the Swedish Riksbank, founded in 1668. Its notes became legal tender after the bank 'ran into difficulties in 1726 (…) after making unsecured government loans.'[5]

The second set of inducements for creating central banks, attributing them note issuance powers, can be found in the development of commerce. This effect was often fostered by entrusting the central bank to improve payment infrastructure. Early examples included the Amsterdam Wisselbank[6] or the Reichsbank for wholesale payments. Moreover, the development of commerce in the German Empire was also intended to thrive, with the Reichsbank organising retail payments *inter alia* parting from the seven 'different coinage systems' that existed heretofore.

Other circumstances that led to central banks being granted the monopoly of banknote issuance were linked to prudence. Commercial banks initially issued paper receipts or notes against gold deposits[7] and, after that, government bonds.[8] Those paper notes then circulated widely enough to become current and served as a payment method: they became currency. However, commercial banks routinely failed in their obligation to return gold against such notes[9] or had difficulty issuing enough banknotes to meet cash demand.[10] The need for the creation of central banks was felt. Central banks were thereafter typically entrusted with a financial stability mandate and could then step

4 See Liesse, André, United States. National Monetary Commission, and Sixty-First Congress, 'Evolution of Credit and Banks in France from the Founding of the Bank of France to the Present Time' (Government Printing Office, 1909).

5 See also, for instance, C A E Goodhart, *The Evolution of Central Banks* (Cambridge, Mass: MIT Press, 1988): 'as the unification of Italy proceeded, this bank became the government's bank, providing large loans to the government in return for which the government in 1866 freed it (…) from the obligation of redeeming notes in species by proclaiming the forced currency of the banknotes.'

6 The city of Amsterdam, in fact, had a requirement that all payments exceeding a certain amount were to be settled via accounts in the Wisselbank. See, Peter Douglas, 'The Amsterdamsche Wisselbank' (New Netherland Institute, 1974), https://www.newnetherlandinstitute.org/files/5313/5396/7824/Amsterdamsche_Wisselbank.pdf.

7 See Andrea Andréadès, *History of the Bank of England 1640 to 1903*, trans. Meredith Christabel (PS King & Son, 1909), 23: 'This policy succeeded beyond all expectations, and in the course of a few years the citizens had generally adopted the habit of depositing their savings with the goldsmiths. Receipts were given for these deposits, which, under the title of goldsmiths' notes, soon circulated better than the actual coins whose scarcity they often supplied.'

8 See for instance Vera C Smith, *The Rationale of Central Banking and the Free Banking Alternative* (Indianapolis: LibertyPress, 1990), 148, where the author reveals that American banks in the late 19th century 'could only issue notes to the extent of 90 per cent of the face value of the bonds it purchased.'

9 Michael Godfrey, *A Short Account of the Bank of England* (John Whitlock, 1695) noted that goldsmiths lost millions of pounds worth of gold because of bankruptcies or the 'disappearance' of their clerks.

10 See the crises in the US in 1873, 1884, 1890, 1893, and 1907.

in as 'lenders of last resort'. Such central banks were also given the monopoly to issue banknotes to facilitate the 'elastic supply' of currency to the economy regarding its structural and temporary needs. These early central banks inspired the design of most central banks, either on a one-off basis[11] or in the 20th century, due to the standardised formatting for creating central banks designed with the advice of multilateral organisations. As a result, most jurisdictions worldwide have granted their central bank the legal monopoly on issuing banknotes. Next to banknotes, coinage is either the responsibility of the Treasury for early central banks or a task vested to central banks for most institutions founded after 1945.

The confluence of these factors made clear one point. The seigniorage earned by the lords when they coined a local metallic currency and then by commercial banks—when they issued banknotes on deposits of precious metals—gradually shifted to central banks when they received the monopoly for issuing banknotes. This incentivised commercial banks to service the savings and payment needs of their clients by crediting and safekeeping bank deposits with scriptural money rather than banknotes.

4.1.2 The search for a private monopoly of commercial banks' scriptural money

Commercial banks have set up payment networks to encourage deposits rather than physical cash. Major payment networks include American Express—which was created by what would become Wells Fargo in 1850; Visa—which Bank of America launched in 1958; and MasterCard—which a group of commercial banks designed.[12] These payment networks made the disbursement of bank deposits ever more accessible with the increased use of debit and credit cards.[13]

Recent developments include contactless payments, which became mainstream in 2014. Growing in the UK from nearly zero in 2013 to about 700 million transactions per month in 2019, the global contactless payment market is expected to grow from $10.3 billion in 2020 to $18 billion by 2025 at a compound annual growth rate of 11.7 per cent.[14] Contactless payments allow customers to pay more seamlessly than before and increase health safety, which is particularly suited to modern times. The accelerating digitalisation of econo-

11 Essentially, during the 19th century: i.e., the Bank of Japan was primarily modelled after the Bank of Belgium, for instance.

12 United California Bank, Crocker National Bank, Wells Fargo, Bank of California, First National Bank, and Marine Midland Bank launched its predecessor Master Charge in 1966.

13 See, for instance, Fumiko Hayashi et al., *A Guide to the ATM and Debit Card Industry* (Kansas City, Mo.: Payments System Research Dept., Federal Reserve Bank of Kansas City, 2003), 13'ATM and Debit Card Timeline'.

14 See the MarketsandMarkets, 'Contactless Payment Market Size, Share and Global Market Forecast to 2025', Market Research Report, Contactless Payment Market, March 2020, https://www.marketsandmarkets.com/Market-Reports/contactless-payments-market-1313.html.

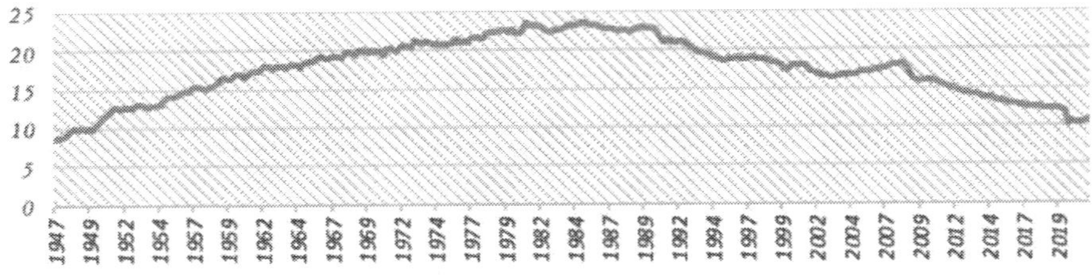

Figure 4.1 GDP/banknotes ratio in circulation in the US. (Analysis by the author based on the Federal Reserve data.)

mies from the 1980s put physical cash use under pressure. Scholars calculated that 40 countries in a sample of 129 had seen a percentage decline in their cash-to-GDP ratio between 2001 and 2018.[15] In developing economies, digitalising payments, skipping card payments altogether with alternative payment methods, essentially e-money providers, has led to significant revenue growth in recent years.[16]

In the US, the 2021 findings from the Diary of Consumer Payment Choice show an increasing number and value of cards and electronic payments and a shrinking share of cash (Figure 4.2). The dollar value of cash payments fell from $381 to $270 from 2005 to 2020 per customer surveyed, while digitalised payments (including both card and electronic payments) increased from $2,393 per customer to $2,745 during the same period. Net decrease in the average value of payments has not yet been transposed to the cash in circulation in the US: the cash-to-GDP ratio has gone back to its 1947 level. This impressive resilience of the circulation of US dollar banknotes may partially explain their heavy use outside the US, notably in dollarised economies (Figure 4.1). The same observation is valid for the euro area in general, as the currency-to-deposit ratio has increased from 2005 to 2016.[17]

On the other hand, a significant share of countries that do not have a currency used internationally has seen their cash in circulation shrink. Ironically, or maybe in a sign of things to come, one of the countries most impacted by this phenomenon has invented Sweden's modern standardised paper bank. It experienced a 43 per cent decrease in cash circulation between 2007 and 2019.

15 See Armelius Hanna, Claussen Andreas Carl, and Reslow André, 'Withering Cash: Is Sweden Ahead of the Curve or Just Special?', Sveriges Riksbank Working Papers, no. 393 (August 2020), https://ideas.repec.org/p/hhs/rbnkwp/0393.html. The full dataset from figure A1, 'Percentage change in currency-in-circulation between 2001 and 2018', was transmitted to the author on a bilateral basis.

16 See McKinsey & Company, 'The 2020 McKinsey Global Payments Report', October 2020. It shows the critical growth rate of e-money issuers in developing economies.

17 Jonathan Ashworth and Charles, A E Goodhart, 'The Surprising Recovery of Currency Usage', *International Journal of Central Banking* 16, no. 3 (2020): 250.

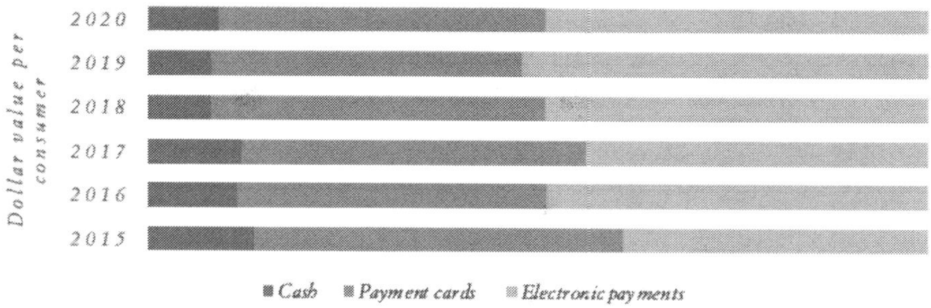

Figure 4.2 Average value payments by type of payment instruments in the US, October 2021. (Analysis by the author based on the Federal Reserve Diary of Consumer Payment Choice data.)

4.1.3 The interaction of the two monopolies in the context of CBDCs

The state of things between the competing interests of commercial and central banks when it comes to issuing money, whether in physical cash or bank deposits, can be significantly shaken by the introduction of a CBDC. Indeed, commercial banks operate in most jurisdictions in a competitive market to attract bank deposits. Therefore, they could see an important source of their funding threatened by the introduction of a default-free, highly efficient electronic payments that CBDCs have the potential to offer. Commercial banks' first response will likely be lobbying to ensure that introducing a CBDC does not jeopardise their interests. This will likely occur during the several formal and informal outreach rounds most central banks organise when designing their CBDC.[18] Valid arguments could include the Bank of International Settlements CBDC principles:[19]—Principle (ii) stating that the CBDC should 'coexist with cash and other types of money in a flexible and innovative payment ecosystem'[20]—as well as the G7 Public Policy Principles for retail CBDCs (principle five on competition).[21] Suppose lobbying does not prove fruitful enough. In that case, commercial banks may want to challenge the central banks' launch of the CBDC by, for instance, arguing that the central bank is abusing its monopolistic power to issue a digital version of money.

18 See, for instance, for the euro area, the two-year outreach being organised by the Eurosystem: ECB, 'Eurosystem Launches Digital Euro Project', 14 July 2021, https://www.ecb.europa.eu/press/pr/date/2021/html/ecb.pr210714~d99198ea23.en.html.

19 See Bank for International Settlements et al., 'Central Bank Digital Currencies: Foundational Principles and Core Features', 2020, https://www.bis.org/publ/othp33.pdf.

20 Bank for International Settlements et al., 10.

21 See G7, 'Public Policy Principles for Retail Central Bank Digital Currencies (CBDCs)' (HM Treasury, 14 October 2021), 9, https://assets.publishing.service.gov.uk/government/uploads/system/uploads/attachment_data/file/1025235/G7_Public_Policy_Principles_for_Retail_CBDC_FINAL.pdf.

One legal venue for contesting the validity of a CBDC would be to verify the CBDC's compliance with the corresponding central bank act and, sometimes, the monetary provision in their Constitution. Indeed, it was found that currently, many central banks need to have their central bank act amended to issue either a token or an account-based CBDC legally.[22] These numbers contrast with central banks advancing with their CBDC projects.[23]

Another venue for commercial banks contesting the validity of the CBDC would be to invoke competition law infringements against the central bank, at least in the EU. A provision that could inform such litigations could include Article 2 of the ESCB Statutes, reading that it 'shall act by the principle of an open market economy with free competition, favouring an efficient allocation of resources, and in compliance with the principles set out in Article 119 of the TFEU.' On the other hand, central banks may want to contest the abuse of the monopolistic behaviour stemming from commercial providers of payment solutions were they to misuse their dominant position of retail payment providers. A first means of contesting that dominant position is by introducing a CBDC themselves, as it was found that a significant—36 per cent of central banks—share of the key motivators for introducing a CBDC was precisely the 'monopoly distortions' stemming from the private sector.[24] A second means of contesting commercial providers' abusive practices could be through legal recourses. Anti-trust litigation has been ripe in the payments space. As per Metcalfe's law, payment networks (as with other networks) tend to increase in value by the square root of their number of users.[25] These tensions may surface regarding the interplay between physical cash and electronic payments. Some US states have passed laws to ensure that local businesses accepting payments via electronic payment networks should not refuse the tendering of coins and banknotes.

22 146 central banks need to amend their statutes. See Wouter Bossu et al., 'Legal Aspects of Central Bank Digital Currency: Central Bank and Monetary Law Considerations', *IMF*, IMF Working Paper, 20, no. 254 (November 2020), https://www.imf.org/en/Publications/WP/Issues/2020/11/20/Legal-Aspects-of-Central-Bank-Digital-Currency-Central-Bank-and-Monetary-Law-Considerations-49827.

23 For an updated picture of the number of CBDC projects currently being studied, see 'Central Bank Digital Currency (CBDC) Tracker', Central Bank Digital Currency (CBDC) Tracker, accessed 16 April 2022, https://cbdctracker.org/; 'Central Bank Digital Currency Tracker', Atlantic Council, accessed 16 April 2022, https://www.atlanticcouncil.org/cbdctracker/.

24 See Tommaso Mancini-Griffoli et al., 'Casting Light on Central Bank Digital Currencies', IMF Staff Discussion Note, 18, no. 8 (November 2018): 28, https://www.imf.org/-/media/Files/Publications/SDN/2018/SDN1808.ashx; Table 2.

25 See, for instance, Peter Rudegeair, AnnaMaria Andriotis, and Brent Kendall, 'Justice Department Probes Visa's Relationships With Fintech Firms', *Wall Street Journal*, 27 October 2021, sec. Markets, https://www.wsj.com/articles/justice-department-probes-visas-relationships-with-fintech-firms-11635358833.

4.2 The Bahamas sand dollar or the challenges of introducing a general, domestic, two-tier, permission-based CBDC

4.2.1 A timeline of the project

The Bahamas has many banking specificities, including a high share of international banks and a servicing of its local population complicated by its geography and relatively small demography. For instance, the Bahamas is composed of 30 islands of varying sizes; therefore, the banking system's servicing of the population is uneven. This is particularly acute for islands other than New Providence Island, where the capital and Nassau are located, especially following the 2008 financial crisis. Moreover, the rising costs of providing financial products through bank branches have further reduced access to financial services.

As a result, a National Payments Council was set up in May 2003 and entrusted with the Bahamian Payments Systems Modernization Initiative to ensure that payment services adapt to the needs of the local population. In 2012, with the adoption of the Payment Systems Act, the National Payments Council was replaced by the National Payments Committee to:

- Be an advisory body to the CBoB for its oversight function according to the national payment system.[26]
- Support the achievement of sound and efficient payment systems in the Bahamas and serve as a forum for cooperation to maintain orderly conditions in regional and international systems.[27]

Ensuing overhauls of the payments system included the introduction by the central bank of a real-time gross settlement system for large-value payments in May 2004, as well as the promotion by the CBoB of a local automated clearing house in 2010 for small-value retail payments of less than B$150,000. However, despite those advances, the declining number of commercial bank branches—30 per cent over the last seven years[28]—and ATMs[29] in the Bahamas has obliged the government to ship cash to smaller islands, a process

26 'Payment Systems Act', Pub. L. No. 7 (2012).

27 Art. 7 (3) of Payment Systems Act.

28 See 'Bank Branches Shrink 30% in Seven Years', accessed 16 April 2022, http://www.tribune242.com/news/2021/oct/15/bank-branches-shrink-30-seven-years/.

29 See the Central Bank of The Bahamas, '2020 Annual Report', 26 April 2021, 19, https://www.centralbankbahamas.com/viewPDF/documents/2021-05-05-14-14-43-2020-CBOB-Annual-Report.pdf: 'during 2020, the number of automated teller machines (ATMs) decreased by 1.0% to 381,' down from 393 in 2017. See also the 'Governor's Remarks at the Blockchain Seminar: "Digital Currency—Extending the Payments System Modernisation Initiative"—Central Bank of the Bahamas', 2 March 2018, https://www.centralbankbahamas.com/news/governor/governor-s-remarks-at-the-blockchain-seminar-digital-currency-extending-the-payments-system-modernisation-initiative.

that can be expensive[30] and hazardous and renders several Bahamian inhabitants unbanked. As a result of the drawbacks of physical cash circulation in the Bahamas, a recent Payments Systems Modernization Initiative project was the 'sand dollar' launch. In an early discussion paper issued in 2017 by the payment unit of the CBoB, the main objectives of the sand dollar were later identified:

- Increasing the efficiency of Bahamian payment systems through more secure transactions and faster settlement speed.
- Providing non-discriminatory access to payment systems without regard for age, immigration, or residency status.
- Achieving greater financial inclusion and cost-effectiveness and providing greater access to financial services across the Bahamas.
- Strengthening Bahamian national defences against money laundering, counterfeiting, and other illicit ends by reducing the ill effects of cash usage.[31]

The CBoB requested an Expression of Interest,[32] which received submissions from 30 bidders.[33] The bank selected and signed an agreement with NZIA Limited in March and May 2019. NZIA Limited offers a 'Decentralized Wireless Payment System' that uses distributed ledger technology dubbed the 'Cortex DLT.' The central bank launched a pilot in December 2019 where 48,000 sand dollars were distributed to selected island residents of Exuma and then to Abaco in February 2020. On 20 October 2020, the Bank of the Bahamas officially released the sand dollar to the public through six authorised financial institutions. Four were money transmission businesses and two (now three) payment service institutions, making it the first central bank in the world to officially go live with its CBDC.[34] By 2020, the bank had put B$130,000 sand dollars in circulation, which grew to B$300,000 in 2021.

30 For instance, cash shipment costs in 2019 and 2020 were respectively B$ 342k and B$ 109k, as per the Central Bank of The Bahamas, '2020 Annual Report', 91.

31 See the Central Bank of The Bahamas, 'Objectives Sand Dollar - Bahamas', accessed 16 April 2022, https://www.sanddollar.bs/objectives.

32 Central Bank of The Bahamas, 'Requests for Expressions of Interest (EOI) Design And Implementation of A Digital Fiat Currency System', accessed 16 April 2022, https://cdn.centralbankbahamas.com/download/036923300.pdf.

33 See Equity Bank Bahamas Limited, 'The Central Bank of The Bahamas Approved Digital Sand Dollar Is on Its Way', 2019, http://equitybankbahamas.com/en/central_bank_of_the_bahamas_approved_digital_sand_dollar.

34 Currently, the four Money Transmitting Businesses are Omni Financial Group Limited, SunCash, MoneyMaxx, and Cash N' Go, and the three PSPs are Kanoo, Mobile Assist, and Island Pay. In March 2021, the CBoB authorised three additional financial institutions to distribute the sand dollar, thereby approving the first bank and credit union. See, The Central Bank of The Bahamas, 'Central Bank Announces Additional Sand Dollar Authorised Financial Institutions- Central Bank of the Bahamas', Central Bank of The Bahamas, 2 March 2021, https://

After the October 2020 launch, significant steps included releasing a consultation paper setting out the CBoB's proposals for legislation to regulate the provision and using central bank-issued electronic Bahamian dollars.[35] Among these proposals, the Bahamian Dollar Digital Currency Regulations confirmed that the digital sand dollar would not pay any interest and be legal tender. Regarding financial stability in particular, it was enacted that when 'the Central Bank is of the view that continued cash withdrawals of deposits settled or transferred in BDDC, poses risks to the stability of the financial system of the Bahamas',[36] the Central Bank may—(a) suspend the withdrawl of such deposits; or (b) limit the maximum amount of withdrawals.[37]

4.2.2 *The sand dollar structure*

The sand dollar has a two-tier distribution model, where transactions are booked on a permissioned[38] DLT on CBDC wallets, and it is only available for payments in the Bahamas. It is unclear whether the sand dollar is an

www.centralbankbahamas.com/news/press-releases/central-bank-announces-additional-sand-dollar-authorised-financial-institutions.

35 The Central Bank of The Bahamas, 'Consultation Paper: Proposed Legislation for the Regulation of the Provision and Use of Central Bank Issued Electronic Bahamian Dollars', 15 February 2021, https://www.centralbankbahamas.com/viewPDF/documents/2021-02-15-11-24-12-Central-Bank-Electronic-Bahamian-Dollars-Regulations-2021.pdf.

36 The Central Bank of The Bahamas, 'Bahamian Dollar Digital Currency Regulations', 88 § (2021), art. 18, https://www.centralbankbahamas.com/viewPDF/documents/2022-02-11-11-53-25-Bahamian-Dollar-Digital-Currency-Regulations-2021-Final-Gazetted.pdf. See also The Central Bank of The Bahamas, 'Bahamian Digital Dollar Currency (Holding and Transactional Limits) Notice', 49 § (2022), https://www.centralbankbahamas.com/viewPDF/documents/2022-08-02-16-38-17-Bahamian-Dollar-Digital-Currency-Holding-and-Transactional-Limits-Notice-2022.pdf.

37 Chester Robards, 'Central Bank Completes Sand Dollar's Link to Automated Clearing House', The Nassau Guardian, 3 March 2022, https://thenassauguardian.com/central-bank-completes-sand-dollars-link-to-automated-clearing-house/.

38 See Central Bank of The Bahamas, 'Project Sand Dollar: A Bahamian Payments System Modernization Initiative- Central Bank of the Bahamas', 24 December 2019, 12, https://www.centralbankbahamas.com/publications/main-publications/project-sanddollar-a-bahamian-payments-system-modernization-initiative: 'In particular, although the Bank will not provide front-end customer service, nor directly sponsor digital wallets, it will ultimately maintain the ledger of all individual holdings of the digital currency. On a near-to medium-term timeline, the Bank will also promote a centralised KYC register to maintain identification and profile data that would either mandate or allow individuals who do not maintain such information within banks or licensed intermediaries, to supply the data for the register.'

account- or token-based CBDC.[39] However, the CBDC is general purpose[40] and open to wholesale payment participants and the wider public.

According to the 2021 annual report, the costs associated with developing the sand dollar CBDC amounted to B$7,499,753 and further outstanding contractual commitments to the developer of B$312,801 (2020: 1,417,121).[41] It will be amortised over five years as an intangible asset of the central bank. Why has take-up been slow? Despite the successful pilot projects in 2019 and early 2020, the CBDC has grown slowly since its official launch. As of 2021, it was estimated by the central bank governor that 20,000 individuals have their own wallets to source the CBDC and that seven entities are authorised to distribute the CBDC through 231 agents.[42] However, sand dollars are mainly used to settle amounts between wallet platforms rather than actual spending towards merchants.[43] Therefore, the government seeks to promote the broader use of the sand dollar for trade on the island and increase Bahamians' access to the sand dollar to pay taxes.[44] Reportedly, factors that slowed the adoption of the CBDC included conjunctural factors such as the Covid-19 pandemic and structural elements tied to the design choices of the CBDC itself. Indeed, while the design choices of the Bahamian CBDC show regard for limiting its impact on financial intermediation by avoiding competing against existing e-money providers or banks, the slow take-up of the CBDC by both wholesale and retail users also demonstrates the inherent limits of relying on third

39 See Central Bank of The Bahamas, 10: 'Each holder would maintain direct claims on the Central Bank and legally have the equivalent of accounts with the Central Bank', which conflicts with a more recent Central Bank of Bahamas presentation titled 'Project Sand Dollar Central Bank of the Bahamas Digital Currency Project' stating that it is a 'Token-Based Model' and that the 'Digital B$ would be available for use across all payment platforms and existing or proposed e-wallets.'

40 See Central Bank of The Bahamas, 10: 'The digital version of the Bahamian dollar would be available for both wholesale and retail applications.'

41 The Central Bank of The Bahamas, '2021 Annual Report' (Nassau, NP, Bahamas, 25 April 2022), 73, https://www.centralbankbahamas.com/viewPDF/documents/2022-05-05-11-51-31-CBOB-2021-Annual-Report-and-Financial-Statements.pdf.

42 See Paige McCartney, 'Central Bank on Target to Integrate Sand Dollar Platform with RTGS, ACH Systems', *The Nassau Guardian*, 29 December 2021, https://thenassauguardian.com/central-bank-on-target-to-integrate-sand-dollar-platform-with-rtgs-ach-systems/ where the Governor also reports that 'Person-to-person transactions averaged 2,951 monthly, for an average value of B$ 0.9 million; and person-to-business transactions averaged 14,792 monthly, with a corresponding value of B$ 3.4 million. Conversely, withdrawal transactions averaged 19,549 monthly, valued at B$ 7.2 million.'

43 See the interview with Jhon Rolle, Sand Dollar circulation grows but spend still low, The Nassau Guardian, 2 November 2021, https://thenassauguardian.com/sand-dollar-circulation-grows-but-spend-still-low/ where the Governor says: 'What we're seeing now are funds that are being exchanged between platforms [...] in many cases, these are net settlements going on across platforms.'

44 Government of the Bahamas—Office of the Prime Minister, 'The Future of Digital Assets in The Bahamas—Policy White Paper', 20 April 2022, 7, https://opm.gov.bs/the-future-of-digital-assets/.

parties for the distribution model of a CBDC. It was reported by a key CBoB decision-maker working on the project that one of the first challenges was to convince banks, credit unions, payment service providers, and money transmission businesses to become authorised financial institutions. That is because 'not every institution initially joined and wanted to be an early adopter of Sand Dollar,'[45] as they perceived the 'Sand Dollar as a threat to traditional banking services—a deposit alternative that might draw resources out of banks and other financial institutions.'[46]

To help convince commercial banks, for instance, of the benefits of distributing the CBDC, the CBoB developed a centralised KYC system designed to alleviate some of the back-end costs stemming from running AML/CFT checks on new wallet users. The first phase of the national rollout focused on the immediate readiness within the private sector for the different tiers of authorised accounts that were ranked depending on risk-based customer due diligence or 'KYC' requirements:

- The low-value personal wallets have minor account opening requirements but restricted transaction limits.
- Regular personal accounts align with established, flexible customer due diligence for existing banking and financial services.
- Business or enterprise accounts are subject to other KYC rigour with higher limits for transactions and holdings of the digital currency.

However, even the first phase was complex to implement as the CBoB chose a new infrastructure for transacting electronically via a permissioned distributed ledger technology. It necessitated private sector entities overhauling their payment systems. Indeed, one of the critical design choices was for the CBDC to be distributed by e-money providers and banks. Those payment service providers needed to upgrade their systems to be interoperable with the blockchain-powered CBDC. A year after the launch of the CBDC, the automated clearing houses (ACH) were reportedly being overhauled for the CBDC to be transacted in deposit accounts and vice versa. As for the non-bank authorised financial institutions, although the CBoB planned to launch the currency with six AFIs, only two were ready to market on time.

The second phase of national engagement was targeted at government services and public utilities, allowing, for instance, courts to take payments via the CBDC while only accepting cash payments before. This phase was crucial as

45 See the interview of Kimwood Mott, the project manager who led the implementation of the sand dollar at the Central Bank of the Bahamas: Island Pay, 'Sand Dollar CBDC—#1 Most Influential Project of 2021 in Finance', *Island Pay* (blog), 22 October 2021, https://islandpay.com/sand-dollar-cbdc-1-most-influential-project-of-2021-in-finance/.

46 Island Pay.

it was estimated that the Bahamian government is the biggest cash distributor and one of the most prominent cash collectors in the economy.

4.3 The design choices of CBDCs are a crucial determinant of the potential impact on the banking architecture

Five main features of a CBDC have been identified to date: (1) wholesale vs. retail vs. general purpose; (2) direct/one-tier vs. indirect/two-tier; (3) centralised vs. decentralised; (4) account-based vs. token-based; and (5) international vs. domestic. Each of those has the potential to impact the commercial banking sector.[47]

4.3.1 What is the user base? Wholesale-retail-general purpose CBDC

The first question a central bank must answer when embarking on a CBDC initiative is: What would the intended user base for the CBDC be? To date, there are three main categories of CBDCs in that regard. The wholesale CBDCs are the instruments that would be available to the current central bank reserve holders and participants in RTGS systems.[48] Retail CBDCs, however, are designed to be accessed by users (businesses or individuals) other than the institutions currently dealing with central bank reserves and RTGS. Finally, the general-purpose CBDCs are designed to be accessed by wholesale and retail users.

Of the 25 wholesale CBDC projects currently compiled by the BIS,[49] project Aber conducted by the central bank of the United Arab Emirates and the Saudi Central Bank, for instance, has selected a 'CBDC that would be used as an instrument of settlement by participating commercial banks and would not be made available to the general public: hence, is considered a wholesale CBDC.'[50] As already discussed by others,[51] a wholesale CBDC would not dra-

47 Other vital features that are being debated that have the potential to modify banking intermediation substantially include CBDS' remuneration with, for instance, the possibility to implement deep negative interest rates, thereby potentially breaking the zero lower bound, as well as eventual limits in wallets/accounts holdings of the CBDC. See developments on these aspects, for instance, in Jean-Pierre Landau and Markus K Brunnermeier, 'The Digital Euro: Policy Implications and Perspectives', 2022, 53.

48 See Bossu et al., 'Legal Aspects of Central Bank Digital Currency', 9.

49 See the different CBDC projects as compiled by the BIS: Raphael Auer, Giulio Cornelli, and Jon Frost, 'Rise of the Central Bank Digital Currencies: Drivers, Approaches and Technologies', *BIS Working Papers* No 880 (August 2020).

50 See the white paper of project Aber: Saudi Central Bank, 'Project Aber. Saudi Central Bank and Central Bank of the UAE Joint Digital Currency and Distributed Ledger Project', Final Report, 2020, sama.gov.sa/en-US/News/Documents/Project_Aber_report-EN.pdf.

51 See, for instance, Ulrich Bindseil, 'Tiered CBDC and the Financial System', *ECB Working Paper Series* No 2351 (January 2020): 4, 'This paper discusses general purpose CBDC since wholesale CBDC is of more limited scope and does not really question the established structure of the monetary base.'

matically alter the banking structure given that their targeted user base already has access to a digital form of central bank money: The central bank reserves. However, central banks offering a digital means of payment directly to retail users could have severe implications for the structure of the banking system. Indeed, currently, central banks are only offering wholesale users electronic payments and settlement means. Only cash is directly available to retail users and is now distributed to the public, primarily through commercial banks.

4.3.2 *How to distribute a CBDC? A direct/one-tier or indirect/two-tier CBDC*

A central bank should decide whether it aims to issue and manage the CBDC directly (one-tier CBDC); or, instead, to credit the CBDC to commercial banks. In the latter, they would then process the payments from one user to the next (two-tier CBDC) and ensure the commercial relationship with the user. As per the latest BIS statistics on the topic, 35 central banks working on a retail CBDC project have yet to decide whether they aim to issue a one-tier or two-tier CBDC. Two central banks are experimenting with a direct CBDC, and 23 are looking into indirect CBDCs. There are two sub-categories of two-tier CBDCs: The ones that are a central bank liability (22 central banks so far) and those to be issued by commercial banks and backed by central bank liabilities called synthetic CBDC[52] (one so far).[53]

The functioning of an indirect CBDC is comparable to how physical cash currently flows in the economy. Commercial banks allocate a certain amount of cash to their customers via ATMs.[54] However, the CBDC would differ since it would essentially be an electronic version of cash. Therefore, one customer could not simply pass it along to the other by physically tendering the banknotes but by initiating payment requests in a payment system. From a financial architecture perspective, the most disruptive CBDC would be directly issuing digital cash to retail users. Indeed, currently, central banks only interact with commercial banks when issuing banknotes. Therefore, a direct model of CBDC issuance would imply that central banks onboard customers and process retail users' payments, much like e-money service providers such as M-Pesa.[55]

52 On synthetic CBDCs, see Tobias Adrian and Tommaso Mancini-Griffoli, *The Rise of Digital Money*, FinTech Notes 19/01 (International Monetary Fund, 2019).

53 Anneke Kosse and Ilaria Mattei, *Gaining Momentum: Results of the 2021 BIS Survey on Central Bank Digital Currencies* (Basel: Bank for International Settlements, Monetary and Economic Department, 2022).

54 Note that in certain countries. including the US, retailers also distribute cash to their customers.

55 See, regarding critical risks that arise from e-money issuance, Marc Dobler et al., 'E-Money: Prudential Supervision, Oversight, and User Protection', *IMF*, Departmental Paper, no. 027 (December 2021).

4.3.3 How many stakeholders would be maintaining the ledger? Centralised v. decentralised CBDC

The discussion around making digital payments from central banks more widely accessible to the public was (re-)launched[56] in the context of private digital currencies, especially so-called global stablecoins, in 2019.[57] Hence, it is natural for central banks to adopt private digital currencies' desirable, innovative features. In that regard, the most innovative aspect of several digital currencies is that their issuance and transactions are decentralised and processed via distributed algorithms. The term 'decentralised' refers to the fact that, unlike the current system,[58] digital assets, such as bitcoins, are issued and transacted on a ledger maintained by several computers that contribute to the system simply by downloading and running the source code. There are two types of decentralisation, permissioned and permissionless ones. The permissionless ledgers are the ones where any individual can participate in running the source code on his computer, thereby processing transactions on the distributed ledger. Permissioned ledgers, on the other hand, only allow the nodes selected by a central entity to participate in that process, much like how CCPs currently choose their clearing members.[59]

A permissionless, decentralised CBDC would be a significant architectural shift for any central bank. It would allow any person to take part in running the ledger of transactions. However, most central banks are looking at permissioned systems whereby, depending on the entities chosen to run the nodes on the distributed ledger, mainly if commercial banks operate such nodes, the system could involve the same stakeholders as with the distribution of banknotes today.

4.3.4 How is the CBDC held? Account-based vs token-based CBDC

One of the main design elements that central banks will have to decide on is whether the CBDC should be held in traditional bank accounts (account-based CBDC) or whether it could be transacted by wallets (token-based CBDC).

56 In the 1990s, in the context of electronic money, scholars had already debated the interest of issuing money from the central bank directly to retail users. See, for instance, Bank for International Settlements, ed., *Implications for Central Banks of the Development of Electronic Money* (Basle, 1996).

57 In particular, the announcement of the Libra (now Diem by Facebook) in June 2019 is tied to a continuous increase in positive speeches from central banks. See Auer, Cornelli, and Frost, 'Rise of the Central Bank Digital Currencies: Drivers, Approaches and Technologies'.

58 Where the Central Securities Depository, for instance, has a single ledger of the stocks and bonds being held and settled; or, in the central banking context, the amounts of M-0 are recorded in the books of one central bank.

59 As per the BIS, as of January 2022, seven retail CBDC projects are decentralised, while seven others are looking at centralised CBDCs, and 12 are exploring a centralised and a decentralised model. Forty central bank retail CBDC projects are still undecided in that regard.

Per the BIS updated database, ten central banks are currently exploring an account-based infrastructure, while four have chosen a token-based one, and nine are looking both into an account-based and a token-based CBDC.[60]

Deciding for an account-based CBDC transaction model would be the least disruptive option, as bank deposits are mostly held on such accounts. This would make the account-based CBDC compatible with current payment infrastructures such as RTGS and ACH. However, for the central bank to issue an account-based CBDC, several legal hurdles must be checked, including whether the central bank is legally allowed to open bank accounts to the public.[61]

On the other hand, choosing a token-based CBDC would be disruptive as the most widely used token-based electronic payment instrument currently is none other than Bitcoin. Indeed, Bitcoin and other altcoins typically allow their users to pay anyone on the distributed ledger only by having a public key on the relevant network. Therefore, a token-based CBDC would allow designing a CBDC that closely resembles the characteristics of physical cash as a payment instrument, with its benefits (universal accessibility of the payment instrument, anonymity) and risks (AML/CFT risks, risk of loss of tokens)[62]. A token-based or account-based CBDC in the banking system will vary depending on the design choices taken to reap the benefits of those two techniques while clearing their inherent risks. For example, suppose the central bank chose a token-based CBDC that would be granted high privacy. Retail users might be tempted to use the CBDC instead of their bank's deposits. They have less confidence in protecting their privacy due to new business models, such as open banking initiatives that aim to monetise bank transfer data.

4.3.5 *Can the CBDC be used across borders? International or domestic central bank digital currencies*

Another essential criterion when designing CBDCs is whether the CBDC will be deployed only in its home market or is intended to be used internationally. These choices will depend on the exchange control regimes countries/currency zones put in place, as economies with stringent capital controls could hardly allow a CBDC to be used or converted cross-border. On the other hand, for open economies with free capital accounts, allowing a CBDC to be

60 Kosse and Mattei, Gaining Momentum: Results of the 2021 BIS Survey on Central Bank Digital Currencies.

61 On assessing the public law legal requirements for central banks to issue a CBDC, see Bossu et al., 'Legal Aspects of Central Bank Digital Currency'.

62 See, the prescient quote from National Taxpayers Union, *Milton Friedman Full Interview on Anti-Trust and Tech*, 1999, https://www.youtube.com/watch?v=mlwxdyLnMXM: 'of course it [referring to token-based money] has a negative side. It means that the gangsters, the people who are engaged in illegal transactions will also have an easier way to carry on their business.'

used cross-border could have international implications for commercial and central banks if it were to lead to a rapid rate of currency substitution in some countries.[63]

4.4 Conclusion

Central and commercial banks have long and complex relationships where both could compete directly to collect deposits and provide access to M-0 monetary aggregate to non-financial users. Over time, this relationship has been settled, with commercial banks primarily responsible for providing electronic payments to non-financial users. Central banks issue banknotes—often coins—to the public and provide electronic payment systems only to institutions with access to central bank reserves and RTGS. As central banks embark on CBDC projects whereby they could offer electronic payments to retail users, this state of things could change with central banks competing directly with commercial banks and e-money payment service providers. Depending on the selected CBDC design, competition from central banks to commercial banks will be more or less crucial. The CBoB precedent shows that choosing the least disruptive option for commercial banks and e-money issuers can also be challenging for the CBDC project's success. Such an option typically relies on private sector entities for distributing the CBDC. Indeed, the conundrum is to design a CBDC that 'should be successful but not too successful.' Private sector actors can ensure that a CBDC is not successful if they are to be entirely relied upon to make it available to the public.

63 In fact, one of the motivators for accelerating the digital yen project was the fear of the cross-border distribution of the digital yuan. See Leika Kihara, 'Analysis: Japan Keen to Speed up Digital Yen Launch as China Adds Geopolitical Twist', *Reuters*, 1 December 2021, sec. Currencies, https://www.reuters.com/markets/currencies/japan-keen-speed-up-digital-yen-launch-china-adds-geopolitical-twist-2021-12-01/.

5 Unlocking the Potential of Central Bank Digital Currencies in Developing Countries

Sangita Gazi

5.1 Introduction

Modern discussion of 'digital money' began with the introduction of mobile money, which showed its groundbreaking impact on Africa and South Asia's unbanked and underbanked populations. Starting with Kenya's M-Pesa in 2007, mobile money revolutionised the concept of financial inclusion by giving people in developing and least-developed countries access to standard and alternative financial services without the involvement of any formal banking systems. With simple access to mobile phones, mobile money helps millions of people transfer money from one to another and store money in digital wallets just by linking a user's mobile number. Since its emergence, a mobile-money-led digital financial ecosystem has demonstrated the potential to enable unbanked women and other disadvantaged populations in developing and least-developed countries to bypass traditional physical banking networks. It showed a path to financially include a large group of the population who would otherwise be excluded, decreasing the gender gap in the financial system.[1]

Although mobile money was one of the very first instances that showed that money could be virtual and transferred seamlessly without a bank account, Bitcoin's launch in 2009 further modernised the idea of digital money. This novel digital currency successfully conceptualised the use of DLT to form a distinctive type of cryptographically encrypted currency. Bitcoin's potential to be issued on a DLT and its ability to complete a transaction without involving an intermediary have shown the promise of adopting a new form of digital money and establishing a decentralised peer-to-peer payment system that is more transparent, efficient, and interoperable. Keeping these potentials at the centre of the discourse, market participants, such as fintech start-ups, Big Tech, and incumbent financial institutions, have been exploring the use cases of DLT for a while. These use cases primarily include privately issued cryptocurrencies

1 Douglas W Arner, Ross P Buckley, and Dirk A Zetzsche, 'Fintech for Financial Inclusion: A Framework for Digital Financial Transformation', *SSRN Electronic Journal*, 2018, https://doi.org/10.2139/ssrn.3245287.

DOI: 10.4324/9781003258261-7

and stablecoins, disintermediated lending-borrowing platforms, non-fungible tokens, and tokenisation of assets. However, the novel technology and oftentimes lack of centralised authority in issuing and operating DLT-based platforms raised numerous regulatory tensions and consumer protection issues, prompting a cautious approach by regulators across the globe.

The recent public health emergency has shifted the regulators' concern from a 'wait and see' approach to innovation to creating a contactless and faster digital payments system. Such a push encourages central banks worldwide to examine and evaluate the idea of using emerging technologies to adopt CBDC, which can eliminate the risks and inefficiencies of the existing private digital currencies. Emerging economies and small island countries are particularly interested in adopting CBDC. Nonetheless, the advanced economies are also speeding up their efforts to understand and assess the potential legal and macroeconomic implications of CBDC. Like developed countries, many emerging economies evaluate the risks and benefits of issuing a CBDC, suggesting that the global financial and monetary systems will soon shift significantly and become cashless.

The current momentum of sovereign banks to digitalise central bank money as an alternative or complementary to physical cash is multipronged.[2]

First, many economies are on the verge of becoming cashless. The Swedish CBDC project 'e-krona' spearheaded by the Riksbank highlighted the declining use of cash in Sweden as the driving factor for issuing a CBDC.[3] Over the past decades, Sweden saw an almost 50% decrease in cash circulation due to the widespread adoption of electronic payment cards since the 1950s, digitalisation and modernisation of banking sectors through the internet post-1990s, and outsourcing of printing and cash distribution.[4] Similarly, triggered by the rise of Big Tech and the proliferation of private digital currencies, the use of

2 For a general discussion on central banks' motives regarding issuing CBDC, see Raphael Auer et al., 'Central Bank Digital Currencies: Motives, Economic Implications and the Research Frontier', *Monetary and Economic Department*, BIS Working Papers, no. 976 (November 2021): 30. Soderberg et al. analysed several CBDC projects, such as the Sand Dollar (the Bahamas), e-CNY (China), DCash (ECCB), e-krona (Sweden), and e-peso (Uruguay). They highlighted eight central banks' motives for issuing CBDC. They are financial inclusion, efficiency and resiliency of payment systems, access to payments, curbing illicit use of money, monetary sovereignty, and competition. See Gabriel Soderberg et al., *Behind the Scenes of Central Bank Digital Currency: Emerging Trends, Insights, and Policy Lessons*, FinTech Notes 4 (Washington, DC: IMF, 2022), https://www.imf.org/en/Publications/fintech-notes/Issues/2022/02/07/Behind-the-Scenes-of-Central-Bank-Digital-Currency-512174.

3 Sveriges Riksbank, 'E-Krona Pilot Phase 2', E-Krona Report (Sveriges Riksbank, April 2022), https://www.riksbank.se/globalassets/media/rapporter/e-krona/2022/e-krona-pilot-phase-2.pdf.

4 Jonas Hedman, 'Going Cashless: What Can We Learn from Sweden's Experience?', Knowledge at Wharton, 31 August 2018, https://knowledge.wharton.upenn.edu/article/going-cashless-can-learn-swedens-experience/.

cash was declining in China, which pushed the PBoC to expedite adopting a digital yuan.

Second, there is a growing demand that cross-border payment systems be efficient and effective to achieve faster and more secure payment mechanisms.[5] Due to globalisation, national payment systems are integrated, and financial institutions are interconnected, with increased capital flow transcending national boundaries. That also created a 'complex patchwork of national and cross-border systems that is not seamless and uniform, yet closely connected.'[6] The complex cross-border payment infrastructure also demonstrated specific challenges as it is slow, inefficient, and highly costly. Early research suggests that CBDC can integrate interoperability features within its design, fundamentally increasing the connectivity of multiple payment systems across various jurisdictions.[7]

Third, since the advent of fintech-led financial services, there is also a growing expectation of end-users demanding a more user-friendly, efficient, and trustworthy payment that accommodates an inclusive financial system.

Finally, emerging economies focus on CBDC's potential to enhance financial inclusion among the unbanked and underbanked communities—one of the top policy goals for central banks that have already rolled out or are looking to roll out CBDCs.

The existing international efforts regarding CBDC projects in developed and emerging economies revolve around exploring CBDC's designs and underlying technologies and assessing their risks and benefits in each economic context. CBDC's synergies with private payment solutions can encourage payment service providers to achieve greater digitalisation in emerging markets. This will significantly foster an 'innovative, competitive, and resilient' payment

5 Park (2006) described three reasons for such slow, inefficient, and costly cross-border payment systems: (1) the payment systems are subject to national laws and practices. (2) There is a lack of 'common global standard and variations' between domestic and international payment systems that prevent the banks from passing data between each other seamlessly. (3) Government regulations affect cross-border payments as they may vary between an originating and receiving country. See, Yoon S Park, 'The Inefficiencies of Cross-Border Payments: How Current Forces Are Shaping the Future' (Visa Commercial, 2006), http://euro.ecom.cmu.edu/resources/elibrary/epay/crossborder.pdf.

6 Timothy F Geithner, 'Challenges Facing the Global Payments System,' the SIBOS 2004 Atlanta Conference, Atlanta, 14 October 2004, https://www.bis.org/review/r041020a.pdf.

7 For example, the mCBDC project aims to develop a prototype of multiple central bank digital currencies. Built by the Bank for International Settlements (hereinafter, BIS) Innovation Hub, in collaboration with the Hong Kong Monetary Authority, the Bank of Thailand, the Central Bank of the United Arab Emirates, and the Digital Currency Institute of the People's Bank of China, the project demonstrates the potential of capitalising on CBDC's interoperable feature to complete international transactions in seconds. See BIS Innovation Hub Hong Kong SAR Centre, 'Inthanon-LionRock to MBridge: Building a Multi CBDC Platform for International Payments' (BIS, 28 September 2021), https://www.bis.org/publ/othp40.htm.

system within a country.[8] With central banks' control over money transmission and monetary policies, large-scale adoption of digital currencies by emerging market economies is likely to increase financial inclusion and enhance access to financial services, thereby bringing the unbanked and underbanked population within the traditional financial system.[9]

As more banks are invested in exploring the possibility of adopting CBDCs as a tool to promote financial inclusion, the intersection of CBDC and its potential impacts in a given economic condition[10] requires further consideration.

Despite CBDCs' benefits of achieving greater financial inclusion, there is a lack of discussion on how it can be achieved while keeping the developing countries' context at the centre of the discourse. CBDC's promise to improve financial inclusion could be thwarted by a country's weak financial infrastructure, lack of technological know-how and digital identification, and low-level mobile and Internet coverage. The existing policy discussion fails to adequately address CBDC's possible risk factors, especially the macroeconomic shocks that can arise in developing countries from CBDC's operation across borders. Absent capital control regulation and regulatory and institutional changes, the introduction of CBDC in emerging economies or its adoption in significant economies could limit central banks' control of monetary supply and implement macroeconomic policies independently. Against this backdrop, this chapter will assess the conditionality that developing countries should establish before launching a successful CBDC project, amplifying their efforts to promote financial inclusion and trust across borders while curbing adverse macroeconomic instabilities. The chapter will investigate the possibility of leveraging the existing digital infrastructure to unlock CBDC's positive effects on financial inclusion. In particular, it will analyse the efficacy of exploiting developing countries' mobile money ecosystem, agent-banking model, and collaboration with fintech actors to pursue CBDC's goal of furthering financial inclusion among unbanked communities. Finally, the chapter will highlight the importance of building an inclusive digital currency ecosystem that lays the foundation of financial inclusiveness in a digital economy. The chapter argues that the inclusiveness of a digital currency ecosystem needs some prerequisites that cannot be renounced, using India Stack as an example.[11] They must be underpinned by an interconnected digital payment platform, combined with a digital identification system, simplified KYC requirements, and access to digital devices and Internet coverage.

8 ECB. *Report on a Digital Euro*. European Central Bank. Frankfurt, Germany. October 2020.

9 See Tommaso Mancini-Griffoli et al., *Casting Light on Central Bank Digital Currencies*, IMF Staff Discussion Notes 08 (Washington, DC: IMF, 2018); Itai Agur, Anil Ari, and Giovanni Dell'Ariccia, *Designing Central Bank Digital Currencies*, IMF Working Paper 252 (Washington, DC: IMF, 2019), https://www.imf.org/en/Publications/WP/Issues/2019/11/18/Designing-Central-Bank-Digital-Currencies-48739.

10 Especially in developing and least-developed countries with fragile financial infrastructure and low rates of digital skills and financial literacy.

11 'India Stack', accessed 14 September 2022, https://indiastack.org/.

The chapter is organised as follows:

- § 5.2 provides a thematic discussion on what constitutes financial exclusion and the underlying reasons thereof. It also draws references from developing countries to analyse the current landscape of financial inclusion strategies and the role of digitalisation in creating low-cost and easy access to payment channels.
- § 5.3 analyses technology's evolving role in financial systems. From mobile money to CBDC, technology has been instrumental in creating novel forms of digital money. This has also been crucial in bringing the unbanked population into the traditional banking system, who would otherwise be excluded. This section further highlights a conventional bank's vantage point in intertwining new business models and technology-led financial innovation to facilitate access to financial services by the unbanked population.
- § 5.4 presents a nuanced approach to CBDC's impact on financial inclusion in developing countries. It explores the potential avenues of adopting, distributing, and scaling CBDC in developing and least-developed countries. Central banks can potentially capitalise on the existing digital infrastructure, such as mobile money, agent-banking model, and fintech service providers, to make a successful CBDC case in those countries.
- § 5.5 discusses the prerequisites for establishing a digital currency ecosystem, particularly in a country with a high financial exclusion rate. Drawing on the 'India Stack' example, an interoperable payments platform accessible via digital identification, simplified KYC, and a secure data management system is critical in designing a digital currency ecosystem. The section also briefly highlights the potential technological risks arising from a CBDC digital infrastructure.
- § 5.6 highlights CBDC's macroeconomic challenges in the context of a developing country. Despite its significant potential to increase financial inclusion among unbanked communities, central banks must consider CBDC's design choices, underlying technology, and operating model carefully to curb adverse macroeconomic shocks.

5.2 Financial exclusion vs financial inclusion: Existing trends of innovative financial services in developing countries

The 'financial exclusion' concept focuses on the unbanked or underbanked population. In a broader societal context, it is considered a form of 'social exclusion' that prevents certain social groups or individuals from accessing the traditional financial system.[12] The lack of access to financial services was explained in economics from neoclassical, new-Keynesian, and behavioural economics perspectives. In the neoclassical economic model, agents are assumed to be

12 Andrew Leyshon and Nigel Thrift, 'Geographies of Financial Exclusion: Financial Abandonment in Britain and the United States', *Transactions of the Institute of British Geographers* 20, no. 3 (1995): 312, https://doi.org/10.2307/622654.

rational, self-interested, well-informed, and competitive.[13] Therefore, financial exclusion is the result of consumers' choices. The neoclassical model further argues that an individual may choose not to use a formal bank account due to economic costs associated with or perceived difficulties physically accessing a bank.

In contrast, the new-Keynesian analysis emphasises market distortions, such as information asymmetries, to explain credit exclusion. Stiglitz and Weiss (1981) show the impact of information asymmetries on credit exclusion, whereby credit institutions tend to charge higher interest rates or other metrics to avoid risky borrowers.[14] Behavioural economists attribute financial exclusion to consumers' distrust of financial institutions, often accentuated by negative experiences or perceptions.[15]

Regardless of the various thematic discussions and underlying reasons, financial exclusion has been challenging in many economies for several decades. The problem is particularly acute in developing countries. In 2021, the World Bank's Global Findex reported that almost 1.4 billion adults were unbanked, and 54 per cent were from seven developing economies: Bangladesh, China, India, Indonesia, Mexico, Nigeria, and Pakistan.[16] From a developing country's perspective, the root causes of the uneven financial coverage are underpinned primarily by the poor banking infrastructure, insufficient banking coverage in rural areas, lack of access to payment channels, costly financial services, and the lack of legal framework conducive to the growth of financial institutions beyond urban areas. The other reasons include the unavailability of affordable financial products catering to the financial needs of the poor and uneducated, lack of financial literacy among the disadvantaged population, and socio-cultural barriers. On the supply side, banks' requirements to open accounts and maintain a minimum balance are often cumbersome for low-income groups in a developing country, excluding them from participating in the financial system. Besides, a country's legal and policy framework can significantly impact the unbanked population's economic empowerment and ability to access financial services. Discriminatory laws can restrict women and

13 Veblen (1900) first used the term 'neoclassical.' For Veblen's original work, see Thorstein Veblen, 'The Preconceptions of Economic Science', *The Quarterly Journal of Economics* 14, no. 2 (February 1900): 240, https://doi.org/10.2307/1883770; also, Tony Aspromourgos, 'On the Origins of the Term "Neoclassical"', *Cambridge Journal of Economics* 10, no. 3 (1986): 265–70.

14 Joseph E Stiglitz and Andrew Weiss, 'Credit Rationing in Markets with Imperfect Information', *The American Economic Review* 71, no. 3 (1981): 393–410.

15 Savita Shankar, 'Financial Inclusion in India: Do Microfinance Institutions Address Access Barriers?', *ACRN Journal of Entrepreneurship Perspectives* 2, no. 1 (2013): 60–74. A major demonstration of the distrust of formal institutions was seen in the post-global financial crisis era when banks were exposed and condemned for their reckless and risky behaviour with depositors' funds.

16 Asli Demirgüç-Kunt et al., The Global Findex Database 2021: Financial Inclusion, Digital Payments, and Resilience in the Age of COVID-19 (The World Bank, 2022), 33, https://doi.org/10.1596/978-1-4648-1897-4.

other disadvantaged people from making economic decisions independently, thus creating a barrier to being a part of the formal financial system.[17] Also, some laws and regulations make it tricky for women to access an identification card or passport without their husband's permission, making their financial options very limited, if not inaccessible.[18] Financial exclusionary processes are also embedded in a country's legal, economic, and financial structures.

In contrast, financial inclusion means that 'adults have access to and can effectively use a range of appropriate financial services.'[19] It is the process that ensures low-income and vulnerable populations can participate in obtaining mainstream financial products and services at low costs fairly and transparently.[20] According to the RBI, financial inclusion accommodates 'convenient access' to essential financial products and services, such as savings, credit, remittance, insurance and pension for the marginalised population, low-income households, and SMEs at a reasonable cost with adequate protection. Therefore, financial inclusion discourse entails affordability, accessibility, and security for everyone who wants to use financial services.[21]

Countries' approach to providing basic financial services to vulnerable and low-income populations is not old. For instance, in 1977, Congress enacted the Community Reinvestment Act (CRA) to encourage banks and thrift institutions to provide credit facilities and financial services to low-income neighbourhoods where they were chartered.[22] At the same time, developing countries introduced numerous innovative approaches and credit mod-

17 For a general analysis of the impact of gender-discriminatory legislation on women's asset ownership and access to finance, see Mala Htun, Francesca R Jensenius, and Jami Nelson-Nuñez, 'Gender – Discriminatory Laws and Women's Economic Agency', Social Political International Studies in Gender, State & Society, 26, no. 2 (2019), 193–222, https://doi.org/10.1093/sp/jxy042.

18 The World Bank's Women, Business and the Law data show highlight at least 48 legal differences for women compared with men when applying for ID or passport. See World Bank, *Women, Business and the Law 2018* (The World Bank, 2018), https://doi.org/10.1596/978-1-4648-1252-1.

19 Asli Demirguc-Kunt, Leora Klapper, and Dorothe Singer, *Financial Inclusion and Inclusive Growth: A Review of Recent Empirical Evidence* (World Bank, Washington, DC, 2017), https://doi.org/10.1596/1813-9450-8040.

20 RBI, 'National Strategy for Financial Inclusion 2019-2024', 10 January 2020, https://www.rbi.org.in/scripts/PublicationReportDetails.aspx?ID=1154.

21 Anita Gardeva and Elisabeth Rhyne, 'Opportunities and Obstacles to Financial Inclusion' (Center for Financial Inclusion at Accion International, July 2011), https://www.gsma.com/mobilefordevelopment/wp-content/uploads/2012/06/opportunitiesandobstaclestofinancialinclusion_110708_final.pdf. For a literature review on financial inclusion, see Tatjana Boshkov, 'Virtual Banking and Financial Inclusion,' *Research Journal of Finance and Accounting* 10, no. 13 (November 30, 2019), https://core.ac.uk/download/pdf/224837027.pdf.

22 Before the enactment of the CRA, many banks and financial institutions did not include low-income areas (known as 'redlined areas'—the colour-coded maps developed by the New Deal-era Homeowners' Loan Corporation) because they were deemed highly risky and hazardous. Inhabited by low-income poor households, racial, ethnic, and other minority groups, these government-sponsored policies prevented them from accessing credit markets. See 'Com-

els to reach out to the population who would otherwise be unbanked and underbanked. One of the earliest evolutions in this regard is the Grameen Bank's microcredit model—a 'poverty lending' approach instead of the traditional 'financial systems' approach.[23] Pioneered by Muhammad Yunus in 1976, under this model, potential borrowers are grouped into categories and deposit a small amount of savings to build their own resources. A participating member is entitled to a small loan that the borrower repays in equal instalments. Although collective and community finance long existed in various forms,[24] the Grameen Bank microcredit model was the first institutionalised intervention that became a global phenomenon.[25] Following the success of the Grameen Bank in Bangladesh and other developing countries, in 2003, the United Nations announced that 2005 would be the 'Year of Microcredit.'[26] This announcement reflected a growing recognition of the large numbers of people unable to avail themselves of the benefits of formal financial institutions. Subsequently, the microcredit model was expanded to include small savings deposits and micro-insurance. Currently, microcredit and microfinance institutions are institutionalised mainly in developing countries. They have scaled up to provide other financial services to an underserved population, such as money transfers, remittances, housing loans, education loans, and SME financing.[27]

5.3 The transformative potential of technology in promoting financial inclusion: From mobile money to CBDC

The beginning of the 21st century is marked by the rapid growth of mobile technology and innovation, leading to a paradigm shift in financial inclusion—from microcredit to microfinance, encouraging savings to modernise payment services. While microcredit institutions were able to facilitate the credit and

munity Reinvestment Act of 1977 | Federal Reserve History', accessed 14 September 2022, https://www.federalreservehistory.org/essays/community-reinvestment-act.

23 Cf Marguerite S Robinson, *The Microfinance Revolution* (Washington, DC: New York: World Bank, Open Society Institute, 2001), 2–7, 22–23.

24 The earliest example of a collective financing platform could be found in the 1700s when Jonathan Swift—an Irish author and nationalist, established the 'Irish Loan Fund'—a fund made of wealthy people's charity contributions. The Fund was used to lend money to creditworthy poor people. In 1852, credit unions were developed in Germany in response to crop failure and famine. Under the credit union model, the members deposited their money and were able to secure a loan with an interest rate lower than traditional banks.

25 David Hulme, 'The Story of the Grameen Bank: From Subsidised Microcredit to Market-Based Microfinance', *SSRN Electronic Journal*, 2008, https://doi.org/10.2139/ssrn.1300930.

26 Kathryn Imboden, 'Building Inclusive Financial Sectors: The Road to Growth and Poverty Reduction', *Journal of International Affairs* 58, no. 2 (2005): 65–86.

27 Ira W Lieberman, 'The Growth and Commercial Evolution of Microfinance', in *The Future of Microfinance*, ed. Ira W Lieberman et al. (Washington: Brookings Institution Press, 2020), 27.

saving needs of marginalised groups, the lack of access to the payment channels and costly transactions caused a hindrance for activities for the unbanked population to transfer money and conduct payment activities. Further, the changing dynamics of economic activities and labour movement within and across the country created a market demand for user-friendly, peer-to-peer, and efficient payment channels. In response to consumers' needs and demands, during the 2000s, mobile phone companies played a critical role in shaping an 'inclusion' centric financial service by introducing mobile money and leveraging mobile devices.[28]

The advancement of modern technologies in the communication sector has played a pivotal role in shaping the financial landscape in recent decades. The invention of revolutionary devices like smartphones, payment wallets, and social media applications has created an integrated digital ecosystem, streamlining easy access to payments and digital money. Furthermore, the use of cutting-edge technologies like artificial intelligence and big data in the banking and finance industries has been a game-changer. They have not only enhanced the efficiency and convenience of financial services but have also expanded access to financial services, particularly for unbanked and underserved populations.

From a consumer's perspective, the transformative role of technology has reshaped people's expectations and perception of money itself. Money is now virtual and cashless, allowing seamless storage, deposits, and transfers between users without the need for traditional bank accounts. The following section discusses the instrumental role of technology in modernising the concept of money and its impacts on financial inclusion.

5.3.1 Mobile money

The mobile money regime primarily started in 2007 with the adoption of M-Pesa in Kenya—a mobile financial service model pioneered by Kenya's largest telecom company, Safaricom. The earlier financial inclusion models utilised either 'credit-led' or 'savings-led' approaches.[29] However, the M-Pesa experience suggested that 'focusing on building the payment "rails"' could potentially increase access to financial services as it can serve as a meeting point for

28 Slade, Williams, and Dwivedi (2013) define mobile money as 'a culmination of innovations' that 'combines payment systems with mobile device' and enables users 'to initiate, authorize, and/or complete a financial transaction in which money or funds are transferred over the mobile network or wireless communication technologies to the receiver through the use of a mobile device.' Emma L Slade, Michael D Williams, and Yogesh K Dwivedi, 'Mobile Payment Adoption: Classification and Review of the Extant Literature', *The Marketing Review* 13, no. 2 (30 August 2013): 167, https://doi.org/10.1362/146934713X13699019904687.

29 For a general discussion, see Ignacio Mas and Daniel Radcliffe, 'Scaling Mobile Money', *SSRN Electronic Journal*, 2011 https://papers.ssrn.com/abstract=1681245.

a broad range of financial services.[30] In Sub-Saharan African countries, mobile money demonstrated the benefits of establishing an improved infrastructural payment rail for additional innovations, such as payments of utility bills without going to a bank or standing in a long queue and being a means for efficient conditional cash transfers for drought relief or government compensation.[31] In places with no financial infrastructure, mobile money revolutionised the concept of financial inclusion by bringing people living in remote locations into formal financial systems.

Mobile money, therefore, unlocked technology's transformative potential of alleviating poverty and reducing economic inequality in developing and low-income countries.[32] Mobile money has also provided a channel for cross-border remittances and payments for commercial transactions, allowing households and SMEs easy and cheap access to such payments.[33] Mobile money is now available in 96 countries with 1.2 billion registered mobile accounts with over two billion US dollars in daily transactions.[34]

The digitalisation of financial services through seamless devices is further accelerated through innovative business models adopted by mainstream financial and telecommunication entities. One such example is the 'agency banking model.'[35] The success of mobile money has been significantly amplified by introducing an 'agency banking model' in Africa and Asia. Agency banking is a hub-and-spoke model whereby an agent, rather than a teller/cashier, conducts banking transactions on behalf of a bank (Figure 5.1). An agency

30 Mas and Radcliffe, 'Scaling Mobile Money.'

31 Kevin Donovan, 'Mobile Money for Financial Inclusion', in *Information and Communications for Development 2012*, by World Bank (The World Bank, 2012), 61–73, https://doi.org/10.1596/9780821389911_ch04.

32 Stephen C Rea and Taylor C Nelms, 'Mobile Money: The First Decade', *IMTFI Working Paper*, no. 1 (2017): 3.

33 With the rise of blockchain technology, mobile financial service (MFS) providers are partnering with traditional banks to develop a peer-to-peer transfer of remittances across the border. Recently, bKash, an MFS provider, developed a blockchain-enabled mobile wallet in collaboration with Standard Chartered Bank, which would allow remittance to be transferred from Malaysia to a bKash wallet-holder instantly.

34 Rishi Raithatha, 'GSMA Mobile Money Programme Mobile Money Policy and Regulatory Handbook' (GSMA, October 2021), 8, https://www.gsma.com/mobilefordevelopment/wp-content/uploads/2021/10/Mobile-Money-Policy-Handbook.pdf.

35 The agency banking model refers to the arrangement in which licensed, or registered entities, allow third parties to provide certain banking services on their behalf. See, Tariro Mavaza, Dauglas Halimani, and Farai Dzapasi, 'Agent Banking Model', *PM World Journal* IX, no. I (January 2020): 1, https://pmworldjournal.com/article/agent-banking-model. For a general analysis, see Aduda Josiah, Kiragu Patrick, and Jackline Murugi Ndwiga, 'The Relationship between Agency Banking and Financial Performance of Commercial Banks in Kenya', *Journal of Finance and Investment Analysis* 2, no. 4 (2013), https://www.proquest.com/openview/9f2a89d0763186c146512ee19ff54547/1?pq-origsite=gscholar&cbl=5222963. Also, Dr Josephat Lotto, 'The Role of Agency Banking in Promoting Financial Inclusion: Descriptive Analytical Evidence from Tanzania', *European Journal of Business and Management*, 2016, 10.

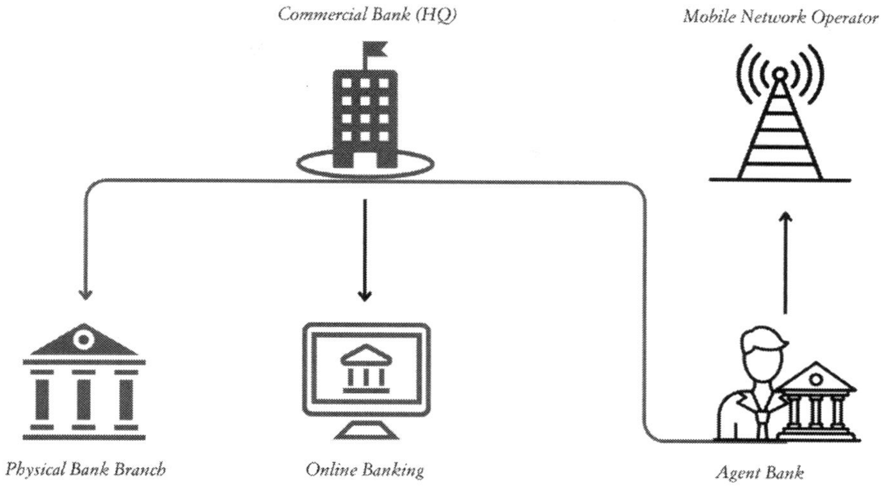

Figure 5.1 Agency banking model. (Elaboration by the author.)

bank—an alternative delivery channel—offers some services on behalf of its principal banks, such as depositing, card-based withdrawals, internal transfers, bill payments, balance inquiring, and the provision of mini statements.[36] From a mobile network operator's perspective, an agent is a point of sale facilitating transactions, cashing out, customer onboarding processes, and ensuring the compliance norms of KYC with biometrics.

In areas with limited mobile services or no brick-and-mortar bank branches, agency banking helps close rural-urban areas by making financial services more accessible to excluded population groups. A report published by the Bank of Tanzania stated that since the introduction of agency banking, deposits and withdrawals in Tanzania have increased by 200% and 400%, demonstrating an increased rate of financial inclusion.[37] Agency banking also increased financial inclusion in Nigeria. Such banking model employed by Nigerian microfinance banks help small businesses and micro-entrepreneurs deposit their earnings and savings.[38]

While mobile money is significantly successful in this part of the world, the lack of an enabling regulatory environment for agents and prudential

36 Mavaza, Halimani, and Dzpasi, 'Agent Banking Model in Zimbabwe,' 1.

37 Bank of Tanzania, '2015 Banking Supervision Annual Report' (Bank of Tanzania, October 2016).

38 Maarten Froeling, Angela G Vargas and Beniamino Savonitto, 'LAPO Agent Banking: Increased Reach and Client Diversity' (International Finance Corporation, 2021): 2–8, https://www.ifc.org/wps/wcm/connect/5eae1f1d-ad47-41db-93c9-eebd858b07e7/LAPO+Agent+Banking-+Increased+reached+and+client+diversity.pdf?MOD=AJPERES&CVID=nyyOk5M.

oversight over mobile financial services provides burdensome customer due diligence, regulatory uncertainty (division between financial services regulators and communication regulators), and often hinders mobile money's scalability and impact in rural areas. Further, the lack of interoperability among various mobile network operators increases the processing costs, which are passed on to consumers.

5.3.2 DLT-based digital currencies (cryptocurrency and stablecoins)

In the post-global financial crisis in 2007, the use of DLT showed the enormous potential of creating a fast, efficient, and secure payment system with minimal involvement of third-party financial intermediaries.[39] The essential features of DLT applications are that the transaction is direct, does not need intermediaries, reduces the third-party costs substantially,[40] and establishes a direct relationship between counterparties.[41] Therefore, DLT can potentially achieve tremendous success in the cross-border payment system. A DLT-based payment infrastructure can cure the existing problem of the 'fractional-reserve banking model'[42] and could be instrumental in accelerating financial inclusion.

The first instance of a DLT-based payment instrument is cryptocurrency. Although cryptocurrencies represented both innovations in payment systems and an alternative means of financial inclusion, they also gave rise to unique problems. For instance, cryptocurrencies are volatile and not a reliable means of payment. They require a piece of advanced knowledge on the underlying technology, and therefore, are not for widespread use. In addition, since inception, cryptocurrency exchanges have been susceptible to market manipulation, security breach, fraud, and scams, causing consumers monetary losses.

Further, when cryptocurrencies are traded on decentralised exchanges, fall outside regulatory oversight. Due to regulatory challenges and opacity in the market, until now, cryptocurrencies failed to achieve the role of 'money' in society. Nonetheless, they challenge the current state of monetary stability, financial regulation, consumer protection, and taxation frameworks. Given

39 For a review of DLT's impact on the payments system, see David Mills et al., 'Distributed Ledger Technology in Payments, Clearing, and Settlement,' Finance and Economics Discussion Series, no. 095 (Washington: Board of Governors of the Federal Reserve System, 2016), https://doi.org/10.17016/FEDS.2016.095; Paul Wong and Jesse Leigh Maniff, 'Comparing Means of Payment: What Role for a Central Bank Digital Currency?', FEDS Notes, 13 August 2020, https://doi.org/10.17016/2380-7172.2739.

40 It could reduce transaction costs to below 1 per cent.

41 Roger Maull et al., 'Distributed Ledger Technology: Applications and Implications,' *Special Issue: The Future of Money and Further Applications of the Blockchain*, 26, no. 5 (September 2017): 481–489.

42 Alexander Lipton, 'Toward a Stable Tokenized Medium of Exchange,' in *Cryptoassets: Legal Regulatory, and Monetary Perspectives*, ed. Chris Brummer (The United States: The Oxford University Press, 2019): 89–115.

cryptocurrencies' risks, many countries (developing and least developed) banned the trading of cryptocurrencies, while other countries investigated the possibility of bringing cryptocurrency under a robust regulatory framework.

Another form of innovative DLT-enabled digital money is stablecoins. Unlike cryptocurrencies, stablecoins are non-volatile as they derive their 'stable' value from underlying fiat money or a pool of assets/currencies, and their supply is not predetermined (for example, tether). Domestically, stablecoins are accessed through digital wallets or mobile apps and thus can be a convenient tool to support financial inclusion by enabling people to transact and save digitally without the need for a formal bank account. Used as a means of cross-border payment or settlement, stablecoins can reduce the frictions and shortcomings of the existing transnational payment systems by allowing people to transact seamlessly and bypassing the cost of interbank settlements. Stablecoins comes with a redemption option, allowing users to convert these currencies into either fiat money or assets linked to it. These features enhances their trustworthiness as a method of payment and store of value in countries with hyperinflation and economic instability.

Despite stablecoins' efforts to achieve trust and be a reliable alternative payment instrument, like cryptocurrencies, they also pose a risk to monetary sovereignty and limit a country's efforts to counter money laundering, illicit activities, and tax avoidance. In addition, Big Tech-backed global stablecoin, such as Facebook's Diem and PayPal's PYUSD, can widely substitute cash and deposits in developing economies and jeopardise their monetary and financial systems' safety, efficiency, and integrity, thereby undermining global financial stability.

5.3.3 Sovereign-backed digital currencies

Considering the risks associated with cryptocurrencies and stablecoins, these DLT-based digital monetary instruments have not evolved into a stable and reliable means of payment. Nonetheless, these new forms of digital money and the underlying technology have sparked interest among central banks, financial regulators, legislators, policymakers, and academics to explore DLT's potential in payment systems. With a wide range of applications and use cases, DLT promises a drastic change in the existing payments and financial systems landscape by increasing inclusivity, efficiency, and safety. Therefore, central banks worldwide are actively exploring DLT's potential in developing digital central bank money, i.e., CBDC, as a safe, trustworthy, and convenient payment instrument.

A CBDC is the digital version of a fiat currency backed and regulated by a sovereign central bank.[43] Deployed on either DLT or non-DLT, a CBDC

43 Despite growing literature, the CBDC discourse lacks a standard and uniform definition. Barrdear and Kumhof (2016) define a CBDC as a 'central bank granting universal, electronic,

is a legal tender that can exist in a digital or algorithmic format (such as programmable money executed in a smart contract).[44] It serves the traditional functions of money (a means of payment, a stable unit of account, and a store of value), which is 'different from balances in traditional reserve or settlement accounts.'[45] It represents a legally mandated payment means as a universally accepted legal tender.[46] CBDC restores the 'trust' element within the discourse of DLT-based digital currencies—a pivotal aspect in ensuring wider usage and access to this new form of digital money. Issued by a sovereign bank, CBDC eliminates the volatility and regulatory risks of privately issued cryptocurrencies and stablecoins and thus could serve as better complements or substitutes to physical cash than other forms of cryptocurrencies.[47]

More than 100 central banks are exploring the possibility of introducing CBDC, while China, Nigeria, Cambodia, and the Bahamas introduced their versions of sovereign-backed digital currencies. Within the CBDC discourse, one of the central banks' key considerations is assessing how a CBDC can foster its policy objectives, mainly to increase financial inclusion among unbanked communities in developing countries.[48]

24×7, national-currency-denominated and interest-bearing access to its balance sheet.' See John Barrdear and Michael Kumhof, 'The Macroeconomics of Central Bank Issued Digital Currencies', *SSRN Electronic Journal*, 2016, 7, https://doi.org/10.2139/ssrn.2811208. The European Central Bank considers a digital euro as the digital version of euro banknotes issued by the Eurosystem and which is a central bank liability. See ECB, 'Report on a Digital Euro', October 2020, 6, https://www.ecb.europa.eu/pub/pdf/other/Report_on_a_digital_euro~4d7268b458.en.pdf. The US Federal Reserve Bank considers both general-purpose and narrower-purpose CBDC. A general-purpose CBDC is widely available to the public, while a narrower-purpose CBDC can be designed to facilitate large-value institutional payments. See Board of Governors of the Federal Reserve System, 'Money and Payments: The U.S. Dollar in the Age of Digital Transformation', January 2022, 13, https://www.federalreserve.gov/publications/files/money-and-payments-20220120.pdf.

44 Although ill-defined, programmable money is different from a CBDC and programmable payments. According to Lee (2021), programmable money consists of digital money and a computer-programmed automated behaviour of money. However, in a CBDC context, programmability could be integrated into the CBDC core infrastructure. For a general discussion on programmable money, see Alexander Lee, 'The Fed: What Is Programmable Money?', FEDS Notes, 23 June 2021, https://www.federalreserve.gov/econres/notes/feds-notes/what-is-programmable-money-20210623.html.

45 Benoît Cœuré and Jacqueline Loh, 'Central Bank Digital Currencies', ed. Committee on Payments and Market Infrastructures (BIS, March 2018), 4, https://www.bis.org/cpmi/publ/d174.pdf.

46 Michael Bordo and Andrew Levin, 'Central Bank Digital Currency and the Future of Monetary Policy' (Cambridge, MA: National Bureau of Economic Research, August 2017), 5, 20, https://doi.org/10.3386/w23711.

47 Max Raskin and David Yermack, 'Digital Currencies, Decentralized Ledgers, and the Future of Central Banking' (Cambridge, MA: National Bureau of Economic Research, May 2016), 7, https://doi.org/10.3386/w22238.

48 Bordo and Levin, 'Central Bank Digital Currency and the Future of Monetary Policy', 2; Walter Engert and Ben . Fung, 'Central Bank Digital Currency: Motivations and Implications', 2017, 2–8, https://doi.org/10.34989/SDP-2017-16.

5.4 CBDC's promise of accelerating financial inclusion: Capitalising on existing infrastructure to adopt, distribute, and scale CBDC

Despite the transformative integration of emerging technologies in the financial system, the truth is that more than one billion people are still financially excluded, mostly found in developing and least-developed countries.[49] Hence, CBDC could be pivotal in bringing financially excluded populations into the realm of the traditional financial system. It can be a convenient mode of carrying central bank money instead of physical cash during any uncertain situation like the Covid-19 pandemic.[50] For instance, Andolfatto studied the positive impact of an interest-bearing CBDC to increase financial inclusion.[51] Bordo and Levin argue that CBDC usage can stimulate greater credit intermediation by encouraging increased liquidity flows within the formal financial system.[52] Depending on the design and features, CBDC can function offline and, thus, can be accessed in regions with poor or no internet connectivity.

CBDC's universal acceptance as a legal tender will ensure that it enjoys the same regulation and prudential supervision as a legal tender. Therefore, any financial products or alternative monetary instruments associated with CBDC can achieve 'true system-wide interoperability' across the payments and financial systems, reducing the cost and complexity of the existing system.[53] CBDC's ability to remove third-party financial intermediaries, such as ACH in the clearing and settlement system, is likely to reduce counterparty risks and eliminate reconciliation steps, thereby harmonising different payment service providers, including e-money entities, mobile-money schemes, and interbank settlements.[54] From a consumer's standpoint, this also ensures timely payment cost-effectively. Further, it may incentivise the digitalisation of merchant and agricultural value chains through more efficient person-to-business and business-to-business

49 Demirgüç-Kunt et al., The Global Findex Database 2021.

50 FinTech Department, 'Concept Note on Central Bank Digital Currency' (RBI, October 2022), https://rbidocs.rbi.org.in/rdocs/PublicationReport/Pdfs/CONCEPTNOTEACB531172E0B4DFC9A6E506C2C24FFB6.PDF.

51 David Andolfatto, 'Assessing the Impact of Central Bank Digital Currency on Private Banks', *The Economic Journal* 131, no. 634 (3 March 2021): 525–40, https://doi.org/10.1093/ej/ueaa073; David Andolfatto, 'Some Thoughts on Central Bank Digital Currency', *Cato Journal* 41, no. 2 (Spring/Summer 2021), https://doi.org/10.36009/CJ.41.2.12.

52 Bordo and Levin, 'Central Bank Digital Currency and the Future of Monetary Policy'.

53 Barry Cooper, Antonia Esser, and Michaella Allen, 'The Use Cases of Central Bank Digital Currency for Financial Inclusion: A Case for Mobile Money' (cenfri, June 2019), 14, https://cenfri.org/wp-content/uploads/2019/06/CBDC-and-financial-inclusion_A-case-for-mobile-money.pdf.

54 Barry Cooper, Antonia Esser, and Michaella Allen, 'The Use Cases of Central Bank Digital Currency for Financial Inclusion: A Case for Mobile Money' (cenfri, June 2019), 15, https://cenfri.org/wp-content/uploads/2019/06/CBDC-and-financial-inclusion_A-case-for-mobile-money.pdf.

transactions.[55] Central banks' ability to trace CBDC transactions can support regulatory efforts to identify and mitigate illicit financial flows and track potential money laundering and terrorist financing for improved financial integrity and AML and CFT compliance.[56] Yet, there are trade-offs. The primary concerns around any digital platform include data privacy, anonymity, and a KYC verification process that could discourage many consumers from using CBDC. Using a digital currency creates digital footprints—an antithesis to the anonymity offered by cash. Moreover, central banks are interested in CBDC due to its potential benefits to provide a robust and effective AML/CFT enforcement mechanism that connotes a certain degree of government surveillance.

Several active projects have provided a tiered CBDC wallet with different levels of thresholds for deposits to minimise the friction between two opposing policy objectives. For instance, a CBDC wallet holding a minimum amount of CBDC will have greater anonymity and fewer regulatory requirements in complying with reporting requirements. Therefore, CBDC can be easily rolled out into rural or disadvantaged areas.[57] An example of CBDC's successful impact on financial inclusion can be drawn from Cambodia's Bakong—the first-ever sovereign-backed digital currency adopted by the National Bank of Cambodia (NBC). Since Bakong's rollout in 2020, Cambodia recorded more than 1.4 million Bakong transactions among its 5.9 million users,[58] demonstrating a remarkable prospect for increasing financial inclusion in Cambodia. Nonetheless, a CBDC does not guarantee automatic success. For instance, only 0.5% of Nigeria's 217 million population uses eNaira, although it is one of the most crypto-savvy nations in the world.[59]

Like any other form of money, CBDC needs users' trust and confidence for its successful adoption. Public confidence in a new form of money is likely to generate frequent usage of CBDC as a mode of payment and settlement and its circulation in the economy. Therefore, in order to generate trust and public confidence, central banks must consider four key areas. These encompass legal, regulatory, technological, and structural considerations (see Table 5.1).

55 Barry Cooper, Antonia Esser, and Michaella Allen, 'The Use Cases of Central Bank Digital Currency for Financial Inclusion: A Case for Mobile Money' (cenfri, June 2019), https://cenfri.org/wp-content/uploads/2019/06/CBDC-and-financial-inclusion_A-case-for-mobile-money.pdf.

56 Barry Cooper, Antonia Esser, and Michaella Allen, 'The Use Cases of Central Bank Digital Currency for Financial Inclusion: A Case for Mobile Money' (cenfri, June 2019), https://cenfri.org/wp-content/uploads/2019/06/CBDC-and-financial-inclusion_A-case-for-mobile-money.pdf.

57 Gabriel Soderberg, 'Behind the Scenes of Central Bank Digital Currency', 13.

58 Makoto Takemiya, 'Is Cambodia's Bakong the Future of Digital Currencies?', World Economic Forum, 30 August 2021, https://www.weforum.org/agenda/2021/08/cambodias-digital-currency-ishowing-other-central-banks-the-way/.

59 Jordan Finneseth, 'Nigerians Reject the Country's CBDC in Favor of Decentralized Cryptocurrencies', Kitco News (03 November 2022), https://www.kitco.com/news/2022-11-03/Nigerians-reject-the-country-s-CBDC-in-favor-of-decentralized-cryptos.html.

Table 5.1 Legal, regulatory, technological, and structural considerations for a trustworthy CBDC.[a, b] (Author's elaboration.)

Contexts	*Areas of consideration*
Legal	• Determining CBDC's status as legal tender. • In case the existing law is unclear about any such mandate, providing legal clarity, i.e., a clear legal framework mandating the central bank to issue a CBDC. • Analysing CBDC's legal implications and challenges in the context of public and private law.
Regulatory	• Enforcing AML/CFT framework for retail and wholesale CBDC transactions. • Determining prudential regulatory framework, stress-testing, and capital adequacy requirements for financial institutions in a CBDC economy. • Providing a regulatory framework for data governance, usage, and privacy.
Technological	• Adopting privacy-enhancing techniques and strong cybersecurity measures. • Preserving technical stability and resilience of a CBDC infrastructure. • Establishing sound IT governance mechanisms.
Structural and policy	• Implementing a robust and efficient digital identity system. • Introducing a simplified e-KYC compliance requirement. • Enhancing digital skills and financial literacy. • Ensuring access to the internet and smartphones.

[a] Commercial banks generally operate in physical branches and online banking. In developing countries, traditional banks partner with agent banks to reach customers who would otherwise not have access to banking. Similarly, under the mobile money framework, telecommunication mobile operators utilise third-party agents to extend mobile financial services to unbanked communities in rural areas.
[b] The list is not exhaustive.

Legal considerations. CBDC must be issued in a clear and certain legal environment. This may require a country to enact specific legislation setting out CBDC's status as legal tender as well as its relationship with a country's existing legal settings.[60] Additionally, a data governance law can set forth how data generated through CBDC accounts should be used and repurposed.

Regulatory considerations. A safe and sound CBDC resolves regulatory concerns surrounding it. Regulators must come up with a specific framework to enforce AML/CFT regulation for domestic and transnational transactions involving CBDC. Financial institutions must also have clarity regarding CBDC's prudential regulatory treatments, particularly with respect to holding CBDC as assets or liabilities on their balance sheet.

60 For instance, the Bahamas was required to reform its laws prior to adopting the Sand Dollar. Sweden, China, and the Eastern Caribbean countries are on the verge of reforming their laws to provide a certain legal environment for their respective CBDCs.

Technological considerations. CBDC's trust is also hinged upon its ability to preserve users' privacy and security.[61] Authorities must consider deploying privacy-preserving techniques to ensure CBDC offers cash-like anonymity and mitigates technological risks.[62] Adopting strong cybersecurity measures and a sound IT governance mechanism safeguards the resilience and robustness of the infrastructure on which CBDC is deployed.

Structural and policy considerations. The success of CBDC depends on an efficient digital identification system and a simplified electronic KYC compliance requirement, facilitating convenient customer onboarding. The novel digital structure of CBDC needs enhanced digital skills and financial literacy, as well as wide coverage of Internet and smartphone access.

An essential aspect of any currency is trust. Without trust and confidence, a currency, physical or digital, loses value, disrupting a country's economic and political stability.[63] Therefore, it is safe to say that CBDC's success in bringing unbanked communities into the financial system largely depends on its trustworthiness.[64] Moreover, a CBDC needs to be operated in a safe environment. Its design, features, and operating models should be curated to unlock its maximum potential and benefits for the financially excluded population. To build a safe end-to-end environment, careful consideration must be given to CBDC's wide range of implications in each economy.

Finally, achieving financial inclusion through CBDC will depend on a country's infrastructure and intermediation design to issue, distribute, and scale CBDC among its citizens. While no 'one size fits all' CBDC solution exists, central banks can use their existing digital infrastructures to design an intermediated CBDC model. The following sub-section offers a curated analysis exploring possible infrastructure options that developing countries can utilise to accelerate the growth and promotion of CBDC among the financially excluded population.

61 Lerong Lu and Alice Lingsheng Zheng, 'Could the Dragon Now Fly Beyond Borders? Contextualising Regulatory Aspects and Risks for China's CBDC Cross-Border Use', *SSRN Electronic Journal*, 2021, https://ssrn.com/abstract=3935854.

62 For a study on what is technologically feasible for a privacy-preserving CBDC, see Siram Darbha and Rakesh Arora, 'Privacy in CBDC Technology' (Bank of Canada, June 2020), https://www.bankofcanada.ca/2020/06/staff-analytical-note-2020-9/.

63 Tarik Hansen and Katya Delak, 'Security Considerations for a Central Bank Digital Currency,' FEDS Notes (03 February 2022), https://www.federalreserve.gov/econres/notes/feds-notes/security-considerations-for-a-central-bank-digital-currency-20220203.html.

64 Neha Narula, Lana Swartz, and Julie Frizzo-Barker, 'Expanding Financial Inclusion or Deepening the Divide? Exploring Design Choices that Could Make a Difference', MIT DCI (January 2023), https://static1.squarespace.com/static/59aae5e9a803bb10bedeb03e/t/63c01f1bcf425f01973b4889/1673535260873/MIT+DCI+%26+Maiden+Labs+-+CBDC+%26+Financial+Inclusion+%28Jan.+2023%29.pdf.

5.4.1 Using the existing mobile-money infrastructure to ensure CBDC penetration

In many countries, smartphone access is cheaper and more available than bank accounts. Further, during the Covid-19 pandemic, mobile phones and fintech played a critical role in accelerating the penetration of digital finance.

The drastic measures of social distancing and lockdowns warranted the easy availability of digital payments and contactless financial services, which helped SMEs continue business (for example, food and essentials delivery).[65] Due to the banks' limited operating hours amidst the pandemic, individuals could quickly and cheaply transfer money to their loved ones using digital financial services. This also allowed business entities to develop innovative solutions to manage faster money transfer services.

In a country where mobile money has proven successful, CBDC can achieve legal and regulatory harmonisation across payment systems by facilitating an interoperable framework. Central banks can use these existing digital infrastructures to supply money to the digital economy and satisfy public policy goals. CBDC can be linked to mobile money and thus can integrate the consumer base to scale domestic and cross-border payments.[66] The fungibility of CBDC can facilitate interoperability among various mobile money providers to ease the process of sending and receiving CBDC from one account to another using different services. The interoperability feature can also integrate the transfer of CBDC from mobile wallets to traditional bank accounts or a point-of-sale facility, boosting the drive and user adoption at a large scale.[67]

5.4.2 Utilising the agent-banking model in CBDC distribution

In developing countries, the 'agent banking' model has transformed the financial sector and expanded the financial inclusion rate from 23% in 2011 to 43% in 2017.[68] Agency allows an agent, rather than a teller/cashier, to conduct banking transactions on behalf of a bank. Mobile financial services providers use the agent banking model to access customers without a digital device or skills to conduct banking activities. The success of this model is primarily attributed to

65 It is reported that the government utilised fintech solutions to transfer cash and other forms of financial services to the poor and vulnerable, provide emergency liquidity to business entities, and facilitate cross-border remittances. See Ceyla Pazarbasioglu et al., 'Digital Financial Services' (World Bank Group, April 2020), 9–17, https://pubdocs.worldbank.org/en/230281588169110691/Digital-Financial-Services.pdf.

66 Cooper, Esser, and Allen, 'The Use Cases of Central Bank Digital Currency for Financial Inclusion: A Case for Mobile Money'.

67 Cooper, Esser, and Allen, 14.

68 Christian Rodriguez et al., 'A New Banking Model for Africa' (International Finance Corporation | World Bank Group, April 2019), 11, https://www.ifc.org/wps/wcm/connect/ccfc72e8-1434-4fcb-9262-990fb864e22c/Longitudinal–study_New+Banking+Model+for+Africa_final.pdf?MOD=AJPERES.

agents' strategic and convenient location, their ability to facilitate transactions immediately, and customers' confidence in the system.[69] Subsequent to the success of mobile money, several jurisdictions, such as Kenya and Bangladesh, have streamlined the use of the agent banking model in their traditional financial systems and adopted the necessary regulatory frameworks to ensure compliance with AML/CFT standards.[70] Regulators have also issued technical guidelines for agent banks to make sure agents are equipped with technological solutions and IT devices, such as mobile phones, point of sale with biometric features, card readers, personal identification numbers (PINs), data connection, and connectivity with their bank's server. A regulated agent banking model can be instrumental for a developing country, especially during the CBDC's initial adoption stage. It can be utilised to gradually distribute retail CBDCs among the rural population who may not have access to smartphones or mobile wallets required for accessing CBDCs. From a regulatory point of view, central banks can potentially use the existing regulatory framework and infrastructure to distribute CBDC via agent banks and thus provide consumers with various financial services to people who live in geographically dispersed locations or lack digital skills.[71] On the consumer side, if issued as a complementary to cash, people who previously relied on mobile money services will have an easier transition from a cash-based economy to a CBDC-based economy. For elderly population who may not have a CBDC account, an agent can facilitate the digital transaction on their behalf over the counter. Although the effectiveness and usefulness of CBDC distribution via an agent banking model will primarily depend on CBDC's design, associated features, and underlying technologies, central banks can analyse its viability and impact on financial inclusion before its large-scale adoption.

5.4.3 Collaboration with fintech service providers to design a CBDC's core infrastructure

Another potential (and the most common) way to materialise CBDC's benefits in developing countries is to engage fintech companies and use their innovative technological solutions to craft a novel CBDC solution that supports countries' specific needs and policy goals. A curated technological infrastructure can prioritise consumers' needs and engage financial intermediaries

69 Neil Davidson and Paul Leishman, 'Building, Incentivising and Managing a Network of Mobile Money Agents: A Handbook for Mobile Network Operators' (London: GSMA, November 2010), https://www.gsma.com/mobilefordevelopment/wp-content/uploads/2011/02/Agent-Networks-full.pdf.

70 See Bangladesh Bank, 'Guidelines on Agent Banking for the Banks', n.d., https://www.bb.org.bd/aboutus/regulationguideline/psd/agentbanking_banks_v13.pdf.

71 An effective regulatory framework of the agent banking model enables banks and other financial services providers to reach the underserved population. It ensures agent banks' regulatory compliance with AML/CFT standards set by regulators. Regulators also issue technical guidelines for agent banks to make sure agents are equipped with technological solutions and IT devices, such as mobile phones, point of sale with biometric features, card readers, PINs, data connection, and connectivity with their bank's server.

meaningfully. For instance, the Sand Dollar, built on NZIA Cortex DLT, supports 'offline functionality' even if communication is disrupted in the region. This novel solution is an important feature for the Sand Dollar, given that the Bahamas is prone to hurricanes, and any loss of power connectivity could disrupt the operation of a CBDC payment platform if an offline functionality is not incorporated into its design. The Sand Dollar arrangement further integrates the financial intermediaries as 'authorised financial institutions' and thus modernises the Bahamas' payment systems while retaining the financial institutions' existing consumer base. NBC co-developed 'Bakong' with Soramitsu, a blockchain-based fintech company in Cambodia. Developed on the open-source Hyperledger Iroha, Bakong's core digital infrastructure run by NBC supports the financial intermediaries' role as 'payment gateways' wherein end-users connect to these payment gateways using a mobile app. The design of Bakong allows retail consumers to transact without having a traditional bank account, which is crucial considering the high rate of financial exclusion in Cambodia before the adoption of Bakong.

5.5 Promoting financial inclusion in a CBDC economy: A digital currency ecosystem as the primer

For CBDC to enhance financial inclusion, it must address the causes of exclusion, which may vary by country. A CBDC's success will largely hinge upon a country's technology readiness, specifically in the form of the availability of an accessible digital ID and simplified electronic KYC (e-KYC) systems, high-level of internet and mobile coverage, digital skills, and financial literacy laying out the foundation for CBDC's operation. Also, given the complexity of this issue and possible underlying obstacles to digital financial inclusion, any CBDC initiative would likely need to be embedded in the broader set of reforms.[72] In this respect, before a country takes the leap, a consumer-centric digital currency ecosystem leverages a country's digital infrastructure that gradually builds consumers' behaviour and develops trust in the use and convenience of digital currencies.

'India Stack'[73] provides valuable insights into how a digital platform integrates interoperability to provide consumers with accessible, convenient, and trust-based digital financial services. Architecturally, India Stack has four principal layers comprising a unique citizen identifier system, a paperless verification process, a uniform payment network connecting banks, fintech firms, various digital wallets, and consent-based data management.[74]

72 Committee on Payments and Market Infrastructure and World Bank Group, 'Payment Aspects of Financial Inclusion in the FinTech Era,' Working Paper (BIS, April 2020): 43, https://www.bis.org/cpmi/publ/d191.pdf.

73 India Stack refers to the digital infrastructure comprising a set of open APIs and digital public goods.

74 Yan Carrière-Swallow, Vikram Haksar, and Manasa Patnam, 'The India Stack Is Revolutionizing Access to Finance—IMF F&D', July 2021, https://www.imf.org/external/pubs/ft/fandd/2021/07/india-stack-financial-access-and-digital-inclusion.htm. For a full discussion

The development of India Stack started in 2010 with the launch of a digital identification system (called 'Aadhar'). Aadhar provides each person with a unique 12-digit identification number that can be used to open bank accounts and obtain a wide range of services, including government benefits. Aadhar incorporates a simplified online KYC process that helps commercial banks verify a new customer's identity quickly and efficiently. Currently, 90 per cent of India's 1.2 billion population have a digital identity, and almost half of them have linked their Aadhar card to their bank accounts. India Stack further built a harmonised payment platform (known as 'Unified Payments Interface' or UPI) that interacts with different forms of mobile money and digital wallets, allowing customers to transact with all kinds of financial entities—bank, non-bank, and fintech. Under this framework, the central bank regulates all payment service providers. The final layer of India Stack comprises data aggregators—a third party facilitating a consent-based financial data flow, storage, and use among financial service providers. The existing digital ecosystem could effectively help the 'Digital Rupee' to be a part of the Indian payment landscape,[75] especially by instilling 'trust' among its citizens. The interoperable payment platform can essentially contribute to the large-scale adoption and use of CBDC among Indian consumers.

Figure 5.2 demonstrates an example of what a digital currency ecosystem may look like. In this design, central banks maintain a uniform digital infrastructure and centralised AML/KYC compliance mechanisms that can be utilised by financial intermediaries for customer onboarding. Consumers use

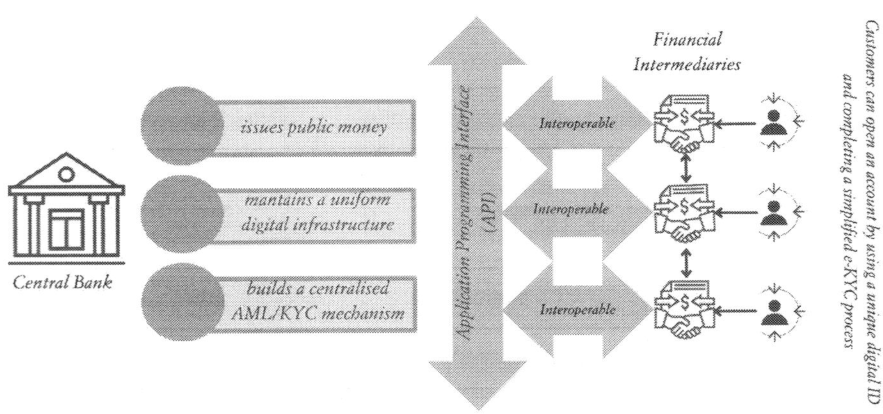

Figure 5.2 A digital currency ecosystem. (Elaboration by the author.)

see Yan Carriere-Swallow, V Haksar, and Manasa Patnam, 'India's Approach to Open Banking: Some Implications for Financial Inclusion' (IMF, 26 February 2021), https://www.imf.org/en/Publications/WP/Issues/2021/02/26/Indias-Approach-to-Open-Banking-Some-Implications-for-Financial-Inclusion-50049.

75 FinTech Department, 'Concept Note on Central Bank Digital Currency'.

digital devices to open accounts with financial institutions using digital identification and simplified KYC processes. In such an ecosystem, public money and private money are interoperable. Central banks can use an application programming interface (API) or similar technologies to ensure interoperability between financial intermediaries and central banks, and also between financial intermediaries.

A similar integrated digital infrastructure can potentially boost the success of a CBDC, particularly in developing countries. The foundation of a consumer-centric digital currency ecosystem is underpinned in its interoperability,[76] secure digital infrastructure, and harmonised customer onboarding requirements, including a digital identification system and simplified e-KYC requirements. An interoperable platform that supports digital payments between public and private monies can foster competition and innovation, bringing efficiency to the payments and financial systems.

However, there are additional challenges and risks. A digital CBDC infrastructure, by its very nature, raises technological risks. These risks are potentially amplified in the context of the mass use of a centralised ledger. For instance, Nigeria's eNaira and Eastern Caribbean Central Bank's DCash pilot both used Bitt—a blockchain-based fintech company's digital currency management system (DCMS)—a market solution for digital currency infrastructure. Several countries are actively looking into the potential of using Bitt's DCMS across Africa and Central America. While deploying a fintech solution does not bring negative effects on its own, using the same infrastructure from a single vendor for issuing CBDCs across multiple jurisdictions concentrates on technological risks. In the event of technological failures, the spill-over effects will significantly impact the entire financial services ecosystem.

5.6 Looking ahead: Additional macroeconomic challenges for developing countries hindering CBDC's success

It is generally agreed that with a suitable design choice, features, and characteristics, CBDCs can achieve financial inclusion in developing countries while maintaining their monetary and financial stability.[77] Yet, there are challenges. For a developing country, the developmental challenges of a CBDC are underpinned by the absence of efficient digital infrastructure, structural barriers, and a weaker capacity to counter money laundering and terrorist financing risks. While the earlier section stresses optimising the use of a country's existing digital infrastructure, in fact, the success of a CBDC will largely depend on a country's technology readiness, specifically in the form of the availability of

76 Interoperability among various private monetary instruments, as well as interoperability between public and private money.

77 BIS et al., 'Central Bank Digital Currencies: Foundational Principles and Core Features', 2020, https://www.bis.org/publ/othp33.pdf.

an accessible digital ID and simplified electronic KYC systems, high-level of Internet and mobile coverage, and digital skills. For instance, the adoption and diffusion of Bakong and the Sand Dollar are attributed to the tech-savviness of the population in Cambodia and the Bahamas, respectively. In Cambodia, around 70% of the total population is under the age of 30 and has access to high speeds and smartphones.

Similarly, even before the adoption of the Sand Dollar, the Bahamas transformed the archipelago into a smart island by integrating smart technologies into its tourism and financial industries. Therefore, the inclination of the general population to embrace new technology, coupled with a tech-savvy demographic and a greater degree of technological adoption, can play a crucial role in facilitating a seamless shift from a traditional economy to a fully digital one. Further, launching a CBDC requires central banks to undertake multidimensional responsibilities ranging from exceptional information technology skills to competence within its management framework.

CBDC arrangements raise several macroeconomic concerns, particularly for developing countries. A CBDC issued on DLT may lead to the gradual disintermediation of traditional financial institutions and their lending activities.[78] Moreover, a central bank-operated digital wallet may enable consumers to withdraw deposits from banks swiftly, triggering bank runs during financial turmoil. A large movement of capital floating outside the commercial banking system could give rise to a liquidity crunch, impacting banks' ability to offer credit and thus limiting access to financial services. CBDC's interoperable feature can connect multiple payment systems across various jurisdictions. Hence, absent capital control regulation, a CBDC could trigger a potential capital flight from developing economies, especially countries with less stable economies, to other advanced open market economies. Amidst a large-scale capital flight, the government may lose its ability to collect taxes and maintain its fiscal and monetary policy control. This can also increase significant concerns regarding money laundering and illicit activities. If central banks from developing countries fail to adopt effective safeguard measures, adopting CBDC could backfire and significantly hurt countries' economic growth and development. CBDC's benefits can hardly be achieved if a domestic CBDC is pegged to a foreign CBDC or foreign CBDCs are easily accessible. Unlike the current international monetary system where domestic currencies, such as the Cambodian riel and the Hong Kong dollar, are pegged to the US dollar, the macroeconomic impact of a CBDC tied to a foreign CBDC could be multidimensional and bring unexpected spill-over implications on global financial stability. There is a concern that it will impede a central bank's autonomy over monetary policy, thereby hurting its policy objectives, including its goal

78 David Andolfatto, 'Assessing the Impact of Central Bank Digital Currency on Private Banks', Economic Research Working Paper Series, no. 026 (Missouri: Federal Reserve Bank of St. Louis, 2018), https://doi.org/10.20955/wp.2018.026.

to pursue financial inclusion through CBDC adoption. Despite these risks, central banks' decision to adopt CBDCs should consider how they would encounter these risks, generally in combination with adopting safeguard measures integrated into the CBDC ecosystem and effective financial and monetary policies.[79] The implementation of a secure and trustworthy CBDC is likely to create an inclusive digital economy in developing countries, integrating the marginalised and disadvantageous population into the traditional financial system.

79 BIS, 'Central Bank Digital Currencies'.

6 A Universal Stablecoin to Rule Them All?

David Tercero-Lucas[1]

6.1 Foreword

The development of money and payment is closely linked to technological developments. Money is meant as an asset that performs the three functions described by Keynes—a medium of exchange, a unit of account, and a store of value—while a means of payment can only fulfil the first two functions. Since humankind began exchanging goods due to excess production, different highly valued goods, for example, agricultural commodities, cattle, and metals, were considered valid means of payment. This primitive monetary system is known as barter, and it was widely introduced by the tribes of Mesopotamia (6000 BC). However, barter relies on the double coincidence of wants. Both exchange parties must agree to sell and buy a commodity. As this has proved unfeasible, metals were market-borne as the most effective asset to fulfil the functions of the medium of exchange and unit of account.

Technological developments in metallurgy in the 7th century BC led to the invention of minting. In a short time, metals in the form of coins became a widely accepted means of payment.[2] With the increasing cash demand, this payment also fulfilled the stored-value function. After that, paper money surged. This was the first unvalued cash claim on bank metal assets that was widely used for payment. Although it was introduced in Europe in the colonialism era, Kublai Khan, grandson of Genghis Khan and the first emperor of the Yuan dynasty, implemented paper money in China in 1260.[3] After passing the 1844 Peel's Bank Act, in which the UK banned loan-driven cash creation by commercial banks, bank deposits settled through bills of exchange became the most demanded form of money. These bank deposits were both

1 I want to express my gratitude to Carlos Viñuela Valcarce from UCAM for his insightful feedback and recommendations. This chapter has been revised from a previous working paper. The research that led to these findings was aided by a fellowship grant from the 'la Caixa' Foundation.

2 Ian Carradice and Martin Price, *Coinage in the Greek World* (London: Braintree, Essex: Seaby; Distributed by BT Batsford, 1988).

3 John Pickering, 'The History of Paper Money in China', *Journal of the American Oriental Society* 1, no. 2 (1844): 136–42, https://doi.org/10.2307/3217743.

DOI: 10.4324/9781003258261-8

account-based and a means of payment since the bank redeemed the cash or coins upon demand and at face value. The widespread use of bank deposits as money and a means of payment occurred alongside the advent of digital methods of registering and settlement in the mid-1960s.[4] This marked the beginning of digital account-based means of payment.

In the twenty-first century, digital technologies are much more refined than those of the past, changing societies and the global economy.[5] The digital currencies era has allowed non-bank private institutions to enter the payments landscape. E-money issuance first took place in the 1990s, and PayPal,[6] TransferWise (now Wise), Alibaba, and WeChat are now commonly used. They aimed to offer faster, more cost-effective, and user-friendly payment systems than the bank-based ecosystems could. E-money issuance is an account-based means of payment. They represent a claim for the user since the issuer must exchange, upon demand and at face value, the e-money issuance for bank deposits. In 2008, a blockchain-based technology and pseudo-anonymous[7] means of payment was established: Bitcoin.[8] Since then, tens of thousands of virtual currencies have been launched.[9]

It was the American computer scientist, David Chaum, who introduced the idea of digital cash three decades ago. He proposed a new kind of cryptography that would allow an automated payment system and the execution of untraceable payments.[10] One of the latest financial innovations was Facebook's (now Meta) digital currency: Diem (previously Libra). In 2019, the Libra Association—later called Diem Association—launched a digital currency issuance with the same design features as stablecoins. Unlike non-stable virtual currencies, the Diem would be backed with a pool of assets and could be a claim for the user. After some years of development, the project was cancelled. However, what is relevant is that this kind of global stablecoins could

4 Pablo Hernandez de Cos, 'Central Banks, Financial Inclusion and Digitalization: Harnessing Technology for Inclusive Growth' (Financial integration and inclusive development: A view from the Mediterranean Countries, Banco de España, 2019), https://www.bis.org/review/r191213f.pdf.

5 Klaus Schwab, *The Fourth Industrial Revolution*, First U.S. edition (New York: Crown Business, 2016).

6 PayPal started as an e-money issuer but received a banking license in Europe in 2007. See, moreover, 'PayPal Stablecoin | US Dollar Cryptocurrency', accessed 9 August 2023, https://www.paypal.com/us/webapps/mpp/digital-wallet/manage-money/crypto/pyusd.

7 Bitcoin addresses are public. Nevertheless, the identity of the user behind the address is private.

8 Morten Bech and Rodney Garratt, 'Central Bank Cryptocurrencies', BIS Quarterly Review, September 2017, 16.

9 Some of them have cash-anonymity as their main design feature but the majority are not anonymous.

10 David Chaum, 'Blind Signatures for Untraceable Payments', in *Advances in Cryptology*, ed. David Chaum, Ronald L Rivest, and Alan T Sherman (Boston, MA: Springer US, 1983), 199–203, https://doi.org/10.1007/978-1-4757-0602-4_18.

potentially become a widely accepted means of payment due to the large customer base of Facebook or similar Big Techs.

As a result of monetary evolution in modern economies, people may demand five different means of payment, including central bank money, bank deposits, e-money, virtual currencies, and stablecoins. Central bank money can be classified as cash or, maybe in the future, CBDC.[11] Bank deposits, named 'b-money,'[12] feature a redemption guarantee backstopped by the Estate. On the other hand, e-money is a claim that can be exchanged for currency at face value.[13]

The EU's regulatory framework summarises these means of payment into three main categories.[14] The first category is 'funds,' which comprises cash, bank deposits, and e-money. These means of payment are either issued or guaranteed by a public authority and, therefore, have a sovereign fiat value, i.e., they are denominated in sovereign units of account. The second category is 'virtual currencies,' which are neither issued nor guaranteed by public authorities and, therefore, have their own fiat value, i.e., denominated in their own private unit of account. They are not attached to a legally established currency. Finally, the last means of payment is stablecoins.[15] They are neither issued nor guaranteed by public authorities and, therefore, have their own fiat value, i.e., denominated in their own private unit of account. Still, they are attached to a legally established currency.

Means of payment denominated in sovereign units of account—cash, bank deposits and e-money—generally have a more robust demand and could be considered money. Non-stable virtual currencies and stablecoins, however, due to their currently weaker money demand, fail to fulfil, so far, all the money functions.

Cash usage for payments has decreased over the last decade in many countries. Adopting retail payment innovations and digital currencies suggests

11 For a summary of the possible features of a CBDC, see Raphael Auer, Giulio Cornelli, and Jon Frost, 'Rise of the Central Bank Digital Currencies: Drivers, Approaches and Technologies', *SSRN Electronic Journal*, 2020, https://doi.org/10.2139/ssrn.3724070; David Tercero-Lucas, 'Central Bank Digital Currencies and Financial Stability in a Modern Monetary System', Working papers GEAR, no. 2022–01 (2022): 37, https://ddd.uab.cat/record/258890.

12 Tobias Adrian and Tommaso Mancini-Griffoli, 'The Rise of Digital Money', *Annual Review of Financial Economics* 13, no. 1 (1 November 2021): 60, 61, 62, 63, 64, 66, 67, 69, 73, 75, https://doi.org/10.1146/annurev-financial-101620-063859.

13 Adrian and Mancini-Griffoli, 61–62.

14 See, namely, art. 2 in the Directive 2009/110/EC of the European Parliament and of the Council of 16 September 2009 on the taking up, pursuit and prudential supervision of the business of electronic money institutions amending Directives 2005/60/EC and 2006/48/EC and repealing Directive 2000/46/EC.

15 Dirk Bullmann, Jonas Klemm, and Andrea Pinna, 'In Search for Stability in Crypto-Assets: Are Stablecoins the Solution?', Occasional Paper Series (European Central Bank, August 2019), https://ideas.repec.org/p/ecb/ecbops/2019230.html.

an evolution towards a cashless society.[16] The emergence of new digital currencies—non-stable virtual currencies and stablecoins—as a substitution for cash and bank deposits may alter the bank-based ecosystem and disrupt the monetary policy mechanism and financial stability. As Carstens argues, 'technological innovations have continually reshaped the monetary system, either by changing the nature of money or the workings of the payment system.'[17] Cryptocurrencies such as Bitcoin do not fulfil money functions successfully since their value is unstable (relatively high volatility). Their user network is not sufficiently large. They are often treated as speculative assets rather than money because of distrust in fiat currencies and the financial system.[18]

In contrast, if it had been, the creation of the Diem digital currency could have fulfilled all the previous features and significantly disrupted the bank-based ecosystem. Meta saw an opportunity to launch its digital currency in the context of cash disappearing and non-bank universal services. Governments, regulators, and central banks were worried about how to monitor a digital currency that could be available to more than 2.5 billion users.[19] Diem reserves total assets under management could range from €152.7 billion in the 'means of payment' scenario to around €3 trillion if the currency became a widely adopted store of value.[20]

The monetary-financial implications of fully backed stablecoins, starting from the Diem experience, are the focus of this chapter.[21] In § 6.2, some risks stemming from the current monetary-financial system are identified. The third and fourth §§ analyse how a wide-acceptability scenario of a multi-cur-

16 In countries like Norway and Sweden, the demand for cash as a means of payment is rapidly declining. Partly because of this, some central banks are assessing the possibility of launching their own public digital currencies. For instance, the Riksbank launched the e-Krona project in order to determine whether it should supply CBDC to the general public: see 'E-Krona Reports', accessed 20 April 2022, https://www.riksbank.se/en-gb/payments--cash/e-krona/e-krona-reports/. For an analysis of the economics of CBDCs, see, among others, Raphael Auer and Rainer Boehme, 'The Technology of Retail Central Bank Digital Currency', *BIS Quarterly Review*, March 2020; Raphael Auer, Giulio Cornelli, and Jon Frost, 'Rise of the Central Bank Digital Currencies: Drivers, Approaches and Technologies', *BIS Working Papers* No 880 (August 2020); and David Tercero-Lucas, 'Moneda digital: ¿disrupción o evolución?', *Política Exterior*, no. 204 (1 November 2021), https://www.politicaexterior.com/articulo/moneda-digital-disrupcion-o-evolucion/.

17 Agustín Carstens, 'The Future of Money and Payments - Speech at the Central Bank of Ireland, 2019 Whitaker Lecture, Dublin' (BIS, 22 March 2019), 2, https://www.bis.org/speeches/sp190322.htm.

18 Raphael Auer and David Tercero-Lucas, "Distrust or speculation"? The Socioeconomic Drivers of US Cryptocurrency Investments", *Journal of Financial Stability*, 62, 2022.

19 It is the total number of monthly active users in 2019.

20 Mitsutoshi Adachi et al., 'A Regulatory and Financial Stability Perspective on Global Stablecoins', Macroprudential Bulletin, no. 10 (5 May 2020), https://www.ecb.europa.eu/pub/financial-stability/macroprudential-bulletin/html/ecb.mpbu202005_1~3e9ac10eb1.en.html.

21 Algorithmic stablecoins will not be analysed in the current chapter.

rency stablecoin and a single-currency e-money could challenge the current bank-based ecosystem and, therefore, the associated risks; § 6.5 focuses on a regulatory response to fully backed stablecoins and § 6.6 concludes.

6.2 The risks posed by the euro area monetary system and its regulatory framework

Since the advent of the digital-account-based means of payment—i.e., digital currencies—monetary systems have included two main elements: (i) the infrastructures through which funds are transferred between users' accounts, i.e., the payment systems, and (ii) the means of payment. Adequate functioning of the monetary system is a critical issue in the current market-based economies. To ensure this, public authorities must identify and control the risks posed to the users and the economy.

Any means of payment inherently has two risks: losing value[22] and operational failure. The fiat-value risk is defined as a reduction in the value of the unit of account held by the user arising from the following two causes: (i) materialisation of the currency substitution risk stemming from a reduction in money demand both domestically and from abroad, which may trigger long-term periods of currency depreciation and high inflation; and (ii) an over-issuance of money, which may generate an excess-aggregate-demand scenario and, therefore, high inflation. Operational risk is defined as suffering losses resulting from inadequate designs and information and communications technology (ICT) failures in the payment system. Any digital-account-based means of payment has one or multiple ledgers that digitally record the users' accounts and one or several infrastructures to move funds between users. These infrastructures may be conventional-based, such as the market-based deferred-net-settlement networks, for example, Visa Europe; the public real-time gross-settlement networks, for example, TARGET2; and the parallel e-money networks, for example, PayPal and Alibaba. The infrastructures can also be DLT-based, in which participants jointly update the central ledger—as with Bitcoin and some stablecoins and CBDC proposals.[23]

Additionally, debt-like means of payment such as bank deposits, e-money, and stablecoins also have credit risk, defined as the possibility of suffering losses from the issuer's failure to redeem its sight obligations. Debt-like or claim-like issuance could be either fractional backed, with commercial banks' assets mainly consisting of long-term debt and loans, or semi-fractional backed, with e-money institutions' assets consisting of short-term debt and cash equivalents.

22 Fiat money, also known as fiduciary money, is a means of payment that does not have an intrinsic value. All account-based means of payments lack an intrinsic value because they are an intangible accounting entry in a ledger convertible into another fiat-value asset, cash.

23 Auer and Boehme, 'The Technology of Retail Central Bank Digital Currency'.

The euro area's monetary-regulatory framework aims to ensure that households and companies can access a low-risk, efficient, cost-effective means of payment in the current bank-based ecosystem. This regulatory approach is based on four key elements: (i) a monetary policy to mitigate the fiat-value risk; (ii) a payment system oversight to control the operational risk; (iii) a microprudential and deposit-insurance framework to limit the credit risk on a microeconomic basis; and (iv) a macroprudential, deposit insurance, and lender of last resort (LOLR) framework to mitigate the risks—risks of systemic bank runs and risk of economic and financial bubbles—for the economy on a macroeconomic basis.

The ECB takes a two-pillar approach—and economic and monetary analysis—to implement its instruments (open market operations, standing facilities, minimum-reserve requirements, and asset purchase programs) to fulfil price stability. One of the ECB's tasks is to promote the smooth operation of payment systems, as established by the TFEU. In performing this task, the Eurosystem operates the RTGS system for the Euro—TARGET2—and oversees the market-based deferred-net-settlement networks—also known as wholesale interbank clearinghouses—such as MasterCard or Visa Europe. The ECB also tries to ensure the financial system's stability, as assumed by the TFUE.

Nowadays, bank deposits are the most demanded form of money. This means of payment—which *a priori* should have credit risk due to its fractional-backed reserve—is guaranteed by public authorities up to €100,000 and is generally considered a credit-risk-free means of payment. The present configuration of the monetary-financial system, known as fractional reserve banking, poses some risks to the economy: (i) risk of systemic bank runs and (ii) risk of economic and financial bubbles because of the ability of commercial banks to overshoot the economy by creating new money in the process of bank lending.[24]

On a microeconomic basis, the credit risk of bank deposits is controlled by the EU prudential regulatory framework—the so-called Basel III—and deposit insurance schemes. The Basel III framework is based on a microprudential three-pillar approach, which aims at minimising the commercial banks' probability of default. Pillar 1 aims at (i) converging minimum risks stemming from the assets side of the commercial banks' balance sheets through a capital ratio, a liquidity ratio, and large-exposures limits; and (ii) containing system-wide build-ups of leverage through a leverage ratio. Within Pillar 2, a commercial bank (i) performs an internal capital and liquidity auto-evaluation process, and public authorities (ii) supervise these banks and require additional capital requirements based on different risks. In Pillar 3, the financial market disciplines commercial banks by publishing recurrent reports. Finally,

24 Adair Turner, 'The Case for Monetary Finance - An Essentially Political Issue' (16th Jacques Polak Annual Research Conference, Washington, DC: IMF, 2015).

the resolution framework avoids bankruptcy once the ECB determines that a commercial bank fails or is likely to fail.

As mentioned above, deposit insurance schemes are state-owned reserves that guarantee commercial bank deposits up to €100,000 per person and bank account. However, these reserves only cover a small fraction of total deposits. Suppose a systemic bank run becomes a reality due to complete migration from bank deposits to cash to comply with the guarantee of bank deposits. In that case, public authorities should either (i) recapitalise the banking system or (ii) act as a LoLR through the central bank, which may disintermediate the commercial banking system. On a macroeconomic basis, apart from the instruments mentioned above to control systemic bank-run risks, public authorities also have macroprudential tools, such as the countercyclical buffer and loan-to-value caps, to limit over-indebtedness processes that can trigger economic and financial bubbles.

Electronic money institutions' issuance poses a credit risk since e-money is a debt-like and semi-fractional-backed means of payment. Hence, its reserve is composed of short-term high-liquid securities and interbank loans. For this reason, the EU prudential regulatory framework of the e-money institutions is primarily based on two pillars: (i) a minimum requirement of safeguarding the funds that have been received in exchange for electronic money issued and a capital ratio, and (ii) prudential supervision of these two requirements. This considerably limits the credit risk of e-money.

6.3 A multi-currency stablecoin issuance

In June 2019, (then-)Facebook—in partnership with some crucial companies in payments, technology, and venture capital, such as Visa and Uber Technologies[25]—announced that they were planning to create their own digital currency, called 'Libra.'[26] In the first white paper, Libra was designed as a stablecoin with the following arrangements: (i) its fiat value was planned to be denominated in its own unit of account; (ii) its issuance would have been semi-fractional backed by a reserve mainly denominated in USD; and (iii) it wouldn't have been guaranteed redeemable upon demand at face value. In their words, the reserve was established 'to help instil trust in this new

25 Along with Facebook, the following companies have been involved in version 1.0 of the project: Mastercard, PayPal, PayU, Stripe, Visa, Booking Holdings, eBay, Farfetch, Lyft, Mercado Pago, Spotify AB, Uber Technologies, Inc., Iliad, Vodafone Group, Anchorage, Bison Trails, Coinbase, Inc., Xapo Holdings Limited, Andreessen Horowitz, Breakthrough Initiatives, Ribbit Capital, Thrive Capital, Union Square Ventures, Creative Destruction Lab, Kiva, Mercy Corps, and Women's World Banking.

26 Diem Association, 'Introducing Libra', 18 June 2019, https://www.diem.com/en-us/updates/introducing-libra/.

currency and gain widespread adoption during its infancy.'[27] Fatás and Weder di Mauro said this feature made it like a currency board.[28] Apart from the economic characteristics, it was designed as a DTL-based payment system to allow movement between users' accounts.

This stablecoin issuance could challenge the monetary sovereignty of countries with weak currencies and that of reserve currency countries.[29] Moreover, whether regulators could ensure privacy standards, consumer protection, and legal payments was unclear.[30] Williamson argued that Libra evaded regulation because it did not have a difference from coin offerings.[31] Even though Libra would have provided significant network externalities, it raised privacy and crime issues and concerns regarding the possible inappropriate use of data. The Diem (Libra) Association would have monopolised the whole transaction data.[32] Nearly one year after the first Libra announcement, and in response to regulatory authorities' concerns stemming from this digital currency design, Meta published a second paper with a new design for Libra.[33] In this second white paper, Facebook introduced two versions of Libra: a multi-currency approach (Libra 1.0) and a single-currency system (Libra 2.0). Libra 2.0 offered the same path as in the first white paper but was guaranteed redeemable upon demand at face value and provided a commitment to perpetually maintaining a reserve composed of short-term public debt and cash equivalents denominated in reserve currencies of account. These design features made Libra 1.0 a stablecoin and ensured it fell outside the current (pre-MiCA)[34] EU regulatory framework. Whether a stablecoin like Diem would have become a global digital currency or not could matter from a policymaking perspective. Suppose European authorities would grant Meta, or a similar company, a license to

27 Colby Smith and Izabella Kaminska, 'What Exactly Is Facebook's Libra Reserve?', *Financial Times*, 18 June 2019, https://www.ft.com/content/7884a51a-c3bf-3740-9739-9e933e2e8471.

28 Antonio Fatás and Beatrice Weder di Mauro, 'The Benefits of a Global Digital Currency', *VoxEU.Org* (blog), 30 August 2019, https://voxeu.org/article/benefits-global-digital-currency.

29 G7 Working Group on Stablecoins, 'Investigating the Impact of Global Stablecoins', October 2019, https://www.bis.org/cpmi/publ/d187.htm.

30 Dirk Niepelt, 'Reserves for All? Central Bank Digital Currency, Deposits, and Their (Non)-Equivalence', *International Journal of Central Banking*, 16, no. 3 (June 2020), https://www.ijcb.org/journal/ijcb20q2a6.htm.

31 Stephen Williamson, 'New Monetarist Economics: Libra: Financial Inclusion for the World's Poor, or Scam?', *Stephen Williamson* (blog), 21 June 2019, http://newmonetarism.blogspot.com/2019/06/libra-financial-inclusion-for-worlds.html.

32 Fatás and Mauro, 'The Benefits of a Global Digital Currency'.

33 'Libra Reinvents Itself', *OMFIF* (blog), 22 April 2020, https://www.omfif.org/2020/04/libra-reinvents-itself/.

34 'Proposal for a Regulation of The European Parliament and of The Council on Markets in Crypto-Assets, and Amending Directive (EU) 2019/1937' (2020), https://eur-lex.europa.eu/legal-content/EN/TXT/?uri=CELEX%3A52020PC0593.

issue Libra 1.0 without properly regulating these crypto-assets.[35] In that case, a risk of currency substitution could materialise, and the euro area's monetary sovereignty could be jeopardised. Given the composition of its reserve, by acquiring that kind of stablecoin, people indirectly would have demanded a basket of short-term debt and cash equivalents denominated in 50 per cent USD, 18 per cent EUR, 11 per cent GBP, and so on. For the eurozone, a shift from EUR-denominated bank deposits to Libra 1.0 would have indirectly been a demand for USD-denominated assets. With households and companies holding ≈LBR-denominated means of payment domestically and abroad, commercial banks will increase their assets and liabilities in foreign currency and not need to borrow liquidity from their central bank. This may imply that there will be no monetary policy transmission via reserves (see Table 6.1).

The weakened currency could lead to (i) a reduction in the country's ability to import in its currency, which could result in public debt problems stemming from the issuance of foreign-denominated public debt and (ii) long-term periods of high inflation and currency depreciation.[36]

This shift in money demand may be driven in the EU by technological features, such as a user-friendly interface and fast and cost-effective transactions. However, in emerging market economies, this shift would also be driven by economic characteristics such as a more reliable fiat value, which could fully materialise a risk of currency substitution.

As a global currency outside the control of monetary authorities, Libra also posed financial stability concerns. Cecchetti and Schoenholtz emphasised that Libra could be subject to essential runs on less liquid or illiquid assets.[37] Depending on the use of Libra worldwide, it could trigger a global bank run in times of distress, resulting in unknown consequences.

From the user's perspective, the fiat value of Libra 1.0 would have depended on: (i) the sovereign denomination of the assets in reserve and (ii) Libra's commitment to fulfilling the convertibility at par. The main drawback was that users would have been subject to a disproportionate exchange rate risk.[38] As it would not have provided completely stable purchasing power, people would not have been able to smooth their consumption perfectly. This was especially relevant as ordinary people and companies made most of their purchases in domestic currency. In countries with weaker currencies, it could be beneficial.

35 In MiCA, these assets belong to the category of 'asset-referenced tokens.'

36 Guillermo Calvo, *Currency Substitution in Developing Countries: An Introduction* (International Monetary Fund, 1992), http://elibrary.imf.org/view/IMF001/01487-9781451845884/01487-9781451845884/01487-9781451845884.xml.

37 Stephen Cecchetti and Kim Schoenholtz, 'Libra: A Dramatic Call to Regulatory Action', *VoxEU.Org* (blog), 28 August 2019, https://voxeu.org/article/libra-dramatic-call-regulatory-action.

38 Niepelt, 'Reserves for All?'

Table 6.1 Transmission of monetary policy via reserves. (Elaboration by the author.)

Assets		*Liabilities*		*Assets*			*Liabilities*		
EA commercial banks (EACB)				EA commercial banks (EACB)					
Reserves	30	*Retail deposits*	390	*Reserves*		30	*Retail deposits*	(–40)	**350**
Loans	280	*Wholesale funding*	30	*Loans*		280	*Wholesale funding*		30
Deposit to USCB	30	*Deposit from USCB*	40	*Deposit to USCB*		30	*Deposit from USCB*	(+30)	**70**
EUR-Public debt	120			*EUR-Public debt*	(–10)	**110**			
US commercial banks (USCB)				US commercial banks (USCB)					
Reserves	50	*Retail deposits*	300	*Reserves*		50	*Retail deposits*		300
Loans	200	*Wholesale funding*	60	*Loans*		200	*Wholesale funding*	(+10)	**70**
Deposit to EACB	40	*Deposit from EACB*	30	*Deposit to EACB*	(+30)	**70**	*Deposit from EACB*		30
USD-public debt	100			*USD-Public debt*	(–20)	**80**			
Libra reserve				Libra reserve					
USD-Public debt	0	*Stablecoins*	0	*USD-Public debt*	(+20)	**20**	*Stablecoins*	(+40)	**40**
EUR-Public debt	0			*EUR-Public debt*	(+10)	**10**			
USD-Wholesale funding	0			*USD-Wholesale funding*	(+20)	**10**			

6.4 A single-currency, e-money issuance

As mentioned above, Meta put forward a single-currency stablecoin arrangement in the second white paper. Libra 2.0 would have maintained the same DLT-based payment system and had the following economic features: (i) its fiat value was designed to be denominated in sovereign units of account—in the case of the euro area, the EUR; (ii) its reserve would have been semi-fractional backed by EUR-denominated short-term public debt and cash equivalents; and (iii) the Libra 2.0 issuances would have been redeemable upon demand at face value so that end users would have had a claim on Facebook. These design features make Libra 2.0 a stablecoin whose value is backed by one single currency that is legal tender. Libra 2.0, therefore, would be close to the definition of e-money under the Electronic Money Directive. Because of Facebook's large customer base in the EU, a EUR-denominated Libra 2.0 could have been a widely and rapidly adopted means of payment. Allowing Facebook or other Big Tech to issue a stablecoin like Libra 2.0 would pose significant risks. As with any further e-money issuance, an EU stablecoin like Libra 2.0 would have a fiat-value risk, operational risk, and credit risk from the users' perspective. The fiat-value risk would be the same as cash and bank deposits since it stems from the sovereign unit of account (EUR).

Regarding operational risk, Libra 2.0 would develop a new type of payment system, DLT-based infrastructures with unknown ITC risks, which the ECB and the NCBs would supervise. The credit risk for users would depend on the asset side. In the case of Libra 2.0, Facebook's idea was putting forward a reserve comprised of A+ short-term public debt (80 per cent) and cash equivalents (20 per cent) denominated in EUR. If a bank run on Libra 2.0 had taken place, the high liquidity composition of the reserve would have allowed Facebook to redeem its sight obligations effectively. From a macroeconomic perspective, the risks would also have depended on reserves. A migration from bank deposits to Libra 2.0 would have triggered three main threats to the euro area's monetary-financial infrastructure: structural bank disintermediation, systemic bank runs, and sovereign-debt-market fragmentation. Structural bank disintermediation risks shrinking commercial banks' balance sheets would have been due to non-bank financial institutions investing client funds in money markets, including the interbank market.

As is shown in Table 6.2, migration from bank deposits to a stablecoin such as Libra 2.0 would have implied that Meta should have invested the new funds collected in short-term A+ public debt (more than 80 per cent), purchasing it from the commercial banks and in wholesale deposits (less than 20 per cent) in commercial banks. This reduced the commercial banks' balance sheet by the amount sold, and banks also replaced retail deposits with wholesale deposits, which are less stable and more expensive. This would also widen the structural liquidity deficit of the banking system, which could materialise a risk of systemic bank runs.

Table 6.2 The impact on the commercial bank's balance sheet of migration from bank deposits to e-money. (Elaboration by the author.)

Assets		*Liabilities*		*Assets*			*Liabilities*		
Commercial banks				Commercial banks					
Public debt	100	*Retail deposits*	280	*Public debt*	(−16)	**84**	*Retail deposits*	(−20)	**260**
Loans	200	*Wholesale funding*	20	*Loans*		200	*Wholesale funding*	(+4)	**24**
E-money providers				E-money providers					
Wholesale funding	20	*E-money*	40	*Wholesale funding*	(+4)	**24**	*E-money*	(+20)	**60**
Public debt	20			*Public debt*	(+16)	**36**			
Real sector				Real sector					
Retail deposits	280	*Loans*	200	*Retail deposits*	(−20)	**260**	*Loans*		200
E-money	40	*Public debt*	120	*E-money*	(+20)	60	*Public debt*		120

Hernández de Cos[39] and Adrian and Mancini-Griffoli[40] considered different scenarios in which e-money could replace bank deposits and trigger different levels of structural bank disintermediation. The worst-case scenario for commercial banks would be a full-disintermediated commercial banking system, where fractional banking and money creation would be significantly limited. The Chinese commercial banking system has experienced significant bank disintermediation for several years due to its leading e-money issuers, for example, Alibaba and Tencent. These Big Techs have played an essential role in the interbank market operating as money market funds (MMFs) since their liabilities are substitutes for bank deposits. These deposits were invested in the interbank market on a collateral uncollateralised basis. The last risk for the economy is the risk of sovereign-debt-market fragmentation. As 80 per cent of the Meta reserve would have been composed of A+ public debt issuances, some euro area-country allocations under that rate[41] would have become less in demand, which could increase the risk premium of those countries.

6.5 What comes next? Improving the regulatory framework

This paragraph outlines a monetary-financial regulatory response to Meta's two digital currency proposals. Regarding Libra 1.0 or, in terms of MiCA, significant asset-referenced tokens, they would have been authorised to be issued within the euro area's jurisdiction if they had complied with strict regulatory standards of transparency, operation, and governance. However, some of the risks would have remained. As was mentioned in § 6.3, a massive migration from EUR-denominated bank deposits to Libra 1.0 would have implied an indirect USD demand and, hence, a depreciation of the EUR. Following the EU free movement of capital, any person could replace their EUR-denominated assets with USD-denominated assets. The EUR could have partially lost its power as an international reserve and could experience higher volatility. This currency substitution would only have been justified due to a loss of trust in the euro area's monetary-financial system, not because of technological features—as would have been the case with Libra 1.0. As for Libra 2.0 or, in terms of MiCA, an e-money token should have been authorised to be issued in the euro area jurisdiction, subject to some changes to the European regulatory framework. First, European public authorities should have reinforced and adapted the oversight framework to a new DLT-based payment system to limit operational risk. MiCA goes in this direction. Second, concurring with issuing the second Libra white paper, the FSB issued new comprehensive guidelines on the regulatory approach for global stablecoins,

39 de Cos, 'Central Banks, Financial Inclusion and Digitalization: Harnessing Technology for Inclusive Growth'.

40 Adrian and Mancini-Griffoli, 'The Rise of Digital Money'.

41 For example, Spain, Italy, Portugal, and Greece.

Table 6.3 E-money institutions setting up a 100 per cent CBDC reserve. (Elaboration by the author.)

Assets		*Liabilities*		*Assets*			*Liabilities*		
Central banks				Central banks					
Assets	50	*Reserves*	50	*Assets*		50	*Reserves*	(–40)	**10**
		CBDC	0				*CBDC*	(+40)	**40**
Commercial banks				Commercial banks					
Reserves	50	*Equity*	50	*Reserves*	(–40)	**10**	*Equity*		50
Public debt	100	*Retail deposits*	280	*Public debt*		100	*Retail deposits*	(–40)	**240**
Loans	200	*Wholesale funding*	20	*Loans*		200	*Wholesale funding*		20
E-money providers				E-money providers					
CBDC	0	*E-money*	0	*CBDC*	(+40)	**40**	*E-money*	(+40)	**40**

which we assimilated into a reinforcement of the e-money regulatory framework.[42] The policies cover prudential, competitive, resolution, AML, and market discipline regulation, which were fields that should have been reinforced because of Libra's systemic asset reserve. Finally, the ECB has different possibilities to limit credit risk to the user and the risk of structural bank disintermediation, systemic bank runs, and sovereign-debt-market fragmentation to the economy. If the digital Euro is not issued in the short/medium term, one of them may be granting Meta access to its balance sheet to establish a 100 per cent CBDC-backed reserve. This would imply a synthetic CBDC[43] issuance and the configuration of Facebook as a narrow bank.

In Table 6.3, we show how a migration from bank deposits to CBDC.

Even though there is a risk of structural bank disintermediation, it also lowers the risk of systemic bank runs. It eliminates the interlinkages between the bank and non-bank financial institutions. At the same time, it mitigates the risk of sovereign-debt-market fragmentation. This 100 per cent CBDC reform relating to e-money issuers was implemented by the PBoC for two years, from 2017 to 2019. This reform required e-money Big Techs in China, for example, Alibaba and WeChat, to gradually establish a 100 per cent CBDC reserve. The main aim of this reform was to limit the risk of structural bank disintermediation. So, interlinkages between banks and these e-money providers stemmed.[44] Moreover, in its second white paper, Meta introduced a Libra 2.0 100 per cent backed by CBDC to save the reserve's costs.

6.6 Conclusion

With the announcement of Libra in the first white paper, it was thought that the Libra Association's stablecoin would have become a global digital currency that would have ruled all private cryptocurrencies. After the announcement, Meta changed its plan and designed Libra 2.0 to please public authorities. Later, the project was cancelled. Nevertheless, Diem would have posed several risks to the euro area monetary-financial structure. Due to Facebook's large customer base in the EU, EUR-denominated Libra 2.0 could have been a widely adopted means of payment. It would have derived risks of structural bank disintermediation, systemic bank runs, and risks of sovereign-debt-market fragmentation. At the same time, e-money issuance presents three risks from the users' perspective: fiat-value, operational, and credit risk. These

42 Financial Stability Board, 'Addressing the Regulatory, Supervisory and Oversight Challenges Raised by "Global Stablecoin" Arrangements: Consultative Document', 14 April 2020, https://www.fsb.org/2020/04/addressing-the-regulatory-supervisory-and-oversight-challenges-raised-by-global-stablecoin-arrangements-consultative-document/; BIS, 'III. Big Tech in Finance: Opportunities and Risks', BIS Annual Economic Report (BIS, 23 June 2019), https://www.bis.org/publ/arpdf/ar2019e3.htm.

43 In a synthetic CBDC, the access to the currency is provided by private financial institutions.

44 BIS, 'III. Big Tech in Finance'.

drawbacks of Diem or possible similar stablecoins, being a digital euro not issued before Big Tech's stablecoins, would have been minimised by configuring the Diem Association (or the association of cther Big Techs) as a narrow bank and allowing it to create a synthetic CBDC. To do that, the ECB would have granted the Diem Association access to its balance sheet to establish a 100 per cent CBDC-backed reserve. In the meantime, the regulatory framework of the EU had to be strengthened. Uncertainty about the rule of law should have been avoided, and all legal *vacuums* regarding stablecoins and private digital currencies removed. Something that MiCA aims to do.

Part III

The Central Bank Digital Currencies in the Mirror

7 Implications of the Digital Euro for Monetary Policy Transmission Outside the Euro Area

Deyan Radev

7.1 Motivation

The international implications of introducing the digital euro cannot be overstated. Aside from the apparent effect on cross-border payments, the digital euro will significantly affect monetary policy transmission, financial stability, and cross-border funding. Figure 7.1 presents the seniority of consumer needs against CBDC design choices that satisfy them. The lower-level needs correspond to lower-level design choices. We notice that the cross-border dimension is at the top of the pyramid, indicating the highest level of coordination in the international monetary system.

The international view must be integrated into the design of the digital euro from the start to reap the benefits of faster, cheaper, and safer payments and economic transactions. And yet, the cross-border dimension of CBDCs has had a relatively low priority in the current CBDC projects of central banks. Boar and Wehrli document that the focus for retail CBDCs is primarily on financial inclusion, domestic payment efficiency, and the effects on domestic monetary policy.[1] This chapter aims to provide an overview of the main effects of the digital euro across borders. We start with the digital euro's primary features in policy and technical group discussions: objectives, principles, architecture, design, and back-end infrastructure. Based on the most likely final design, we discuss the monetary policy implications domestically and abroad. Then, we discuss the effects on cross-border payments based on the most likely setup: an interconnected multi-CBDC system. We conclude with the contentious issue of *euroisation*—the substitution of domestic currencies with the digital euro in countries with weak institutions and monetary systems. We make the case that allowing access to the digital euro to non-residents from the EU and other European countries would provide new impetus to European integration and put the euro in a position to become a global currency. In the final section, we conclude and give a policy discussion.

1 Codruta Boar and Andreas Wehrli, 'Ready, Steady, Go? Results of the Third BIS Survey on Central Bank Digital Currency', *BIS Papers*, no. 114 (January 2021): 10, Graph 5.

DOI: 10.4324/9781003258261-10

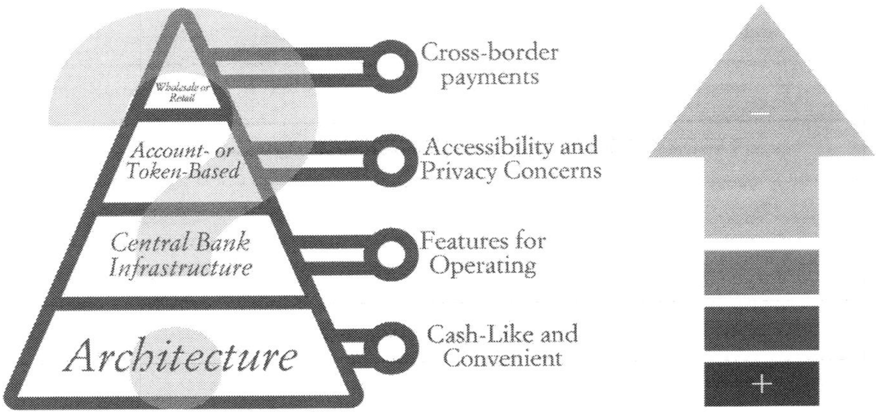

Figure 7.1 CBDC pyramid and consumer needs. (Elaboration by the author. Based on Raphael Auer and Rainer Boehme, 'The Technology of Retail Central Bank Digital Currency', BIS Quarterly Review, March 2020, fig. 1, https://www.bis.org/publ/qtrpdf/r_qt2003j.htm.)

7.2 Overview of digital euro designs

This section summarises the main goals, purposes, architectures, and designs that are being considered regarding the digital euro. We aim to distinguish the most likely line of action and design, which we will then elaborate upon and critically analyse in the context of the international monetary system.

7.2.1 Goals and principles

A report on a digital euro, issued by the ECB in October 2020,[2] outlines the main objectives and principles the new currency should follow.

Among the former are:

i) *An electronic alternative to cash.* Observing the trends and changes in consumer behaviour, the ECB has identified a lower demand for physical money and more considerable use of electronic payments. A digital euro will therefore address the changes in the consumer behaviour of European citizens.
ii) *Emblem of European integration.* The digital euro will be a tool to position the euro as the primary global currency. Whatever the final design, the digital euro should have solid European branding.

2 ECB, 'Report on a Digital Euro' (European Central Bank, October 2020).

iii) *Alternative to solutions by foreign payment providers.* If society completely abandons using cash,[3] the Eurosystem should be equipped to provide solutions that compete with existing and future services by private, domestic, and foreign entities.
iv) *Innovation in the payments system.* To ensure continued economic growth and prosperity for European citizens, the Eurosystem must always be ready to innovate and maintain a high level of financial development.
v) *Financial inclusion.* In case of the abandonment mentioned above of cash, the digital euro should be easy to use by vulnerable groups of citizens, such as the 'unbanked people.'

Instead, among the latter are:

i) *Accessibility.* The digital euro should be accessible throughout the euro area and supported by the existing private payment solutions. It should also be possible to be used by citizens who do not have a bank account.
ii) *Safety.* The infrastructure should be robust to cyber-attacks and ensure the digital euro's effectiveness.
iii) *Efficiency.* The features of the digital euro will be selected after an extensive cost-benefit analysis.
iv) *Privacy.* Users' privacy should be protected to not interfere with the public interest. The latter may include conditionalities to limit the use by non-euro area residents, prevent excessive cash outflows, and others. Also, privacy may be limited by the legal requirement that electronic payments need identification to comply with existing laws.
v) *Compliance.* The digital Euro must comply with the existing legal frameworks, including the legislation on money laundering and the payments industry standards.

The BIS adds a guiding principle, which is indispensable for the smooth functioning of the financial system.[4]

3 Sweden has seen a strong decline in the use of cash, with many shops declining to accept it already. This has prompted the strong investigation into digital currencies by the Sveriges Riksbank: Sveriges Riksbank, 'Why Are We No Longer Using Cash? | Sveriges Riksbank', 7 November 2019, https://www.riksbank.se/en-gb/payments--cash/payments-in-sweden/payments-in-sweden-2019/the-payment-market-is-being-digitalised/cash-use-in-constant-decline/why-are-we-no-longer-using-cash/.

4 Minimally invasive technology: see Raphael Auer and Rainer Böhme, 'Central Bank Digital Currency: The Quest for Minimally Invasive Technology', BIS Working Papers (BIS | Monetary and Economic Department, June 2021). CBDC architectures should maintain the private sector's primary role in retail payments and financial intermediation within a two-tier system.

7.2.2 Purposes

In terms of purposes and user scope, CBDCs are commonly divided into wholesale and retail CBDCs:[5]

i) *Wholesale CBDCs.* These digital currencies are used to settle interbank transfers and other wholesale transactions. They serve similar purposes as reserves at the central bank but may include additional functionalities, such as conditional settlements.
ii) *Retail CBDCs.* Retail CBDCs serve for transactions in the economy at large. They modify the traditional two-tier financial intermediation system and allow the public to hold claims at the central bank.

The digital euro will possess the features of both types of digital currencies, as the Eurosystem already operates an efficient digital wholesale infrastructure through its TARGET services. For this exposition, we put more emphasis on applying the digital euro as a *retail CBDC*. The BIS suggests two architectures for this setup: single-tier and two-tier retail CBDCs.[6]

In all cases, the ECB issues the digital euro. In the case of a direct CBDC (top panel), all transactions are handled by the ECB, which also keeps records of all retail holdings. The middle panel presents a hybrid CBDC with a two-tier structure: direct claims on the ECB but intermediated real-time payments. In that case, the ECB periodically should update its copy of all retail digital euro holdings. The bottom panel presents an intermediated CBDC, which includes the features of the hybrid CBDC, but the ECB will process only wholesale transactions. In that case, the ECB should supervise closely to ensure that the wholesale records correspond to the retail records. All three architectures will allow for account- or token-based transactions.

The single-tier architecture will shift operational risks to the ECB. It may completely substitute private financial intermediaries, which is at odds with the intent of the bank to avoid disruptions in financial intermediation. ECB's report on a digital euro provides arguments in favour of the two-tier model, with a preference for a fully intermediated retail digital euro. This approach will ensure the minimum invasiveness of the new currency. Nevertheless, the bank points to specific operational and reputational risks that discrepancies in wholesale and retail records can lead to. The solutions that the bank discusses internally are real-time auditing like the hybrid model or allowing the users to check whether their balances at the intermediary correspond with the balances at the ECB before they request the bank to initiate a transaction.

5 BIS, 'Annual Economic Report' (Basel: BIS, 2021), chap. III. CBDCs: an opportunity for the monetary system., https://www.bis.org/publ/arpdf/ar2021e.htm.

6 See Auer and Böhme, 'Central Bank Digital Currency: The Quest for Minimally Invasive Technology', fig. 4.

7.2.3 Architecture

Regarding access to the payments system, two types of architectures provide different functionalities and serve other goals.

i) *Account-based access.* This form of the digital euro would allow the opening of an account with the Eurosystem directly. In case of a transaction, a third party will record the users' holdings and will update the accounts of payees and payers. This form of the digital euro provides the broadest functionality for users, including possible remuneration, but cannot be used offline and is not anonymous.
ii) *Token-based access.*[7] This form resembles cash because the payer and payee will verify the transaction. This method will theoretically allow fully anonymous use of the digital euro, which conflicts with the existing legislative framework for electronic payments. It will require additional arrangements at the payment divide levels that may restrict the amount of the holdings, the value of international transactions, and the access of user groups, such as, for example, non-residents of the euro area.

Auer and Böhme present the different setups behind both types of access.[8] On the left-hand side, within an account-based design, the ownership of the digital euro is linked to the user's identity, and any transaction between users needs authorisation through identification. In a token-based digital euro, represented on the right-hand side, any user verifying the transfer via the digital signature can operate with the funds. Some analysts point out that the differentiation between account-based and token-based CBDCs is artificial, and both types are not mutually exclusive.[9]

Three additional distinctions are relevant to the current analysis.

i) *Non-remunerated vs remunerated digital euro.* To encourage the adoption of the digital euro, the ECB may offer remuneration to holders of accounts with the Eurosystem. Since the token-based access is anonymous and mainly out of the control of the bank, the token-based digital euro will not be remunerated. Hence, remuneration will be a functionality only available to account-based forms of the digital euro and is one of the

7 The ECB Report on a digital euro uses the term 'bearer digital euro' to avoid confusion with assets based on distributed ledger technologies such as blockchain, to which the term 'token-based' has been mostly related.

8 Raphael Auer and Rainer Boehme, 'The Technology of Retail Central Bank Digital Currency', 2020, 94, Graph 4.

9 Rod Garratt et al., 'Token- or Account-Based? A Digital Currency Can Be Both - Liberty Street Economics', Federal Reserve Bank of New York, 12 August 2020, https://libertystreeteconomics.newyorkfed.org/2020/08/token-or-account-based-a-digital-currency-can-be-both/.

potential new monetary policy tools at the ECB's disposal. Remuneration should be assessed carefully due to the risk of substituting deposits at private financial intermediaries, disturbing the functioning of the two-tier financial system.

ii) *Standalone CBDC vs multilateral CBDC agreements.* The issue of cross-currency transactions is of utmost importance for cross-border payments. There are many suggestions on how the interoperability of CBDCs could be achieved. Auer et al. (2021) summarise their features in three models.[10] Model 1 suggests improvements in compatibility through the synchronisation of legislation, market practices, formats for messaging, and requirements for data. This is the weakest form of interaction of CBDCs and provides limited benefits in terms of efficiency. Model 2 suggests interlinked CBDCs that share an interface and use a common clearing mechanism, centralised or decentralised. This system improves on Model 1 regarding efficiency and safety. Model 3 involves multiple CBDCs hosted on a single, integrated platform. This model provides the highest operating efficiency and safety by reducing the international monetary system's complexity, fragmentation, and concentration. The integrated approach is advocated by Auer et al. (2021) and suggested in the ECB's report as the optimal solution for the interoperability of currencies. It makes full use of the advantages of CBDCs and, if implemented fully and correctly, will provide a significant overhaul of the international monetary system. However, it will require the highest level of international coordination and compromises on a large scale. It also resembles a process towards a monetary union, which may spark fears for the sovereignty of the national currency, as discussed in the following sections. Given these conjectures, we believe the most likely application will be an advanced form of Model 2.

iii) *Conditional vs unconditional use of the digital euro by non-residents.* ECB's report does not provide clear-cut guidance on whether non-residents will have unlimited access to the digital euro. First, this will depend on the conditionalities regarding residents' access: remuneration, limits to holdings, account-based or token-based versions of the euro, and so on. Second, the account-based design will be necessary to enforce these conditions and assign additional constraints if foreign residents have even more limited rights. Third, the availability of non-residents will depend on the level of integration of the different CBDCs. ECB argues that in a well-integrated multilateral CBDC system, there may not be a need to grant rights to foreigners to hold digital euros.

10 Raphael Auer, Philipp Haene, and Henry Holden, 'Multi-CBDC Arrangements and the Future of Cross-Border Payments', BIS Papers, no. 115 (March 2021): 4.

7.2.4 Back-end infrastructure

Centralised vs decentralised. Under a centralised approach towards the back-end infrastructure, all transactions will be recorded in the Eurosystem's ledger. Under a decentralised approach, the ECB issues a rule for settling transactions, which users or financial intermediaries will then record. The ECB argues that decentralisation is vital for providing a token-based digital euro. As the current distributed ledger technology and consensus mechanisms are not suited for the number of operations occurring within the euro area and do not comply with AML rules, a hybrid account-based and token-based approach is suggested, where the wholesale operations may be handled in a decentralised manner. In contrast, the retail operations are verified by supervised intermediaries on behalf of end users. Regardless of the choice of infrastructure, it will be under the control of the ECB.

7.2.5 The most likely final design of the digital euro

Taking stock of the features listed above and given the ongoing discussions since the publication of the report in October 2020 and the research done at the BIS and major central banks, the digital euro is most likely to be a two-tier retail CBDC, with an account-based architecture and a hybrid centralised back-end infrastructure with some degree of decentralisation.[11] Cross-currency payments will most likely be handled in an interlinked multi-CBDC arrangement.

This model of the digital euro will be used for the remainder of the exposition, with alternative options also being analysed when applicable.

7.3 Monetary policy implications

The issuing of a digital euro is an act of monetary policy of significant proportions. Although the functions of the digital euro as a monetary policy tool are not explicitly addressed in the ECB report, it will have important domestic and international implications. The monetary policy implications of CBDCs are still under-researched, and this section aims to shed more light on the first line of effects.

11 Another design option that is currently discussed is to limit the number of holdings in the digital euro or penalise large holdings with prohibitive interest rates. In this chapter, we decided not to take a stance on the introduction of *ex ante* limits for digital euro holdings as that may lead to a suboptimal choice that does not reflect an equilibrium market outcome. It is also against the objective of the digital euro to become a global currency. However, in times of crises, the programmability of the digital euro could be used to monitor, control, and steer transfers to prevent contagion within economies and cross-border transmission of crises.

7.3.1 Domestic implications

i) *Digital cash.* The ECB report on the digital euro states that the new currency will supplement rather than substitute cash. At the same time, the digital euro can provide much broader functionality to users than physical cash. It will also extend the role and powers of the ECB to determine what constitutes money and cash in the digital age. For instance, the bank will have the discretion to switch on and off features and provide access to services to make it more akin to cash or to augment it with broader functionality, allowing, for instance, smart contracts.

ii) *Direct monetary policy tool.* The report states on several occasions that using the digital euro as a monetary policy tool is not in the internal policy discussions yet but provides guidance as to what specific designs affect essential ingredients of the monetary system. For instance, whether to remunerate deposits with the euro system and how much or not has the potential to open a new monetary policy channel to affect interest rates on deposits directly. The report points out several ways to sterilise the effect of these direct deposit rates, for instance, by reimbursing commercial banks for the loss of deposits or by directing end users to interact with the ECB only via supervised intermediaries.

iii) *The danger of substitution effects.* The main direct threat to financial intermediation and the financial system's stability from having accounts directly with the Euro system is the highly likely substitution effect it will bring. Other things being equal, users will prefer to hold riskless deposits with the Eurosystem instead of risky deposits with commercial banks. This will increase the cost of funding for banks, which may increase their default risk. The famous Modigliani and Miller theorem[12] postulates that there is no particular need for financial intermediation without friction in financial markets. *CBDCs will be able to reduce some friction in the financial system.* Still, not all, and the ECB does not have the physical and technical capacity to maintain and operate accounts of over 300 million users in the euro area. For instance, one of the most critical roles of financial intermediation is to reduce information asymmetry among economic agents. CBDCs must sufficiently address information asymmetries to provide a viable substitute for financial intermediaries. Therefore, the ECB needs to take the required precautions to avoid disruptions in financial intermediation and the two-tier structure of the financial system. The suggestions in the report are along several dimensions that address different negative externalities of issuing a digital euro.

iv) *Financial stability implications.* Another dimension related to the issuing of a digital euro concerns financial stability. The impact on financial

12 Franco Modigliani and Merton H Miller, 'The Cost of Capital, Corporation Finance and the Theory of Investment', *The American Economic Review* 48, no. 3 (1958): 261–97, http://www.jstor.org/stable/1809766.

stability is not necessarily the same or related to the substitution effects above—if financial intermediaries are not needed or add frictions to the system, their demise will not negatively affect the financial system or financial development. It is important not to disturb the functioning of the financial system because it will send shockwaves to the real economy and have negative repercussions abroad (see below). Examples of adverse effects on financial stability from a potential increase in funding costs and loss of business are the deleveraging reduction of credit supply and the reduction in risk assessment capacity due to fewer bank customers.

7.3.2 International implications

i) *Global financial stability.* A significant threat to global financial stability is the tendency of investors and households in developed and emerging economies to shift to safer and more liquid assets, especially during financial and economic crises.[13] In the case of the digital euro, these 'digital runs' may involve a shift to Eurosystem deposits at unprecedented speed and magnitude, which may exacerbate exchange rate volatility. The increased integration of payment systems may also facilitate the contagion and transfer of crises and systemic risk across borders.[14] These issues should be considered when choosing the digital euro's design features, for example, through account-based access or channelling funding from an increase in deposits with the Eurosystem back into financial markets.

ii) *Interest rates and inflation.* The increased integration may lead to the transfer of the ECB's monetary policy across borders and endanger the independent monetary policy of foreign countries.

iii) *International bank lending.* Providing a liquid, safe asset affects global liquidity through the operations of global banks.[15] The effect of issuing the digital euro is ambiguous, since increased efficiency may be conducive to cheaper access to cross-border funding. Still, the threat of disintermediation may reduce bank lending both domestically and abroad.

iv) *Capital flows.* The ECB states that the digital euro should be administered to avoid attracting substantial investment flows into the Eurosystem. Still, such policies may not align with the goal of the euro to become a global

13 CPMI, 'Central Bank Digital Currencies' (BIS, March 2018), www.bis.org.

14 Deyan Radev, *Measuring Systemic Risk: A Probabilistic Perspective*, vol. 409, Studies in Systems, Decision and Control (Cham: Springer International Publishing, 2022), https://doi.org/10.1007/978-3-030-94281-6.

15 Elod Takats and Abraham Vela, 'International Monetary Policy Transmission', in *The Transmission of Unconventional Monetary Policy to the Emerging Markets*, ed. Bank for International Settlements, vol. 78 (Bank for International Settlements, 2014), 25–44, https://EconPapers.repec.org/RePEc:bis:bisbpc:78-02; Deyan Radev, 'Liquidity Regulation and the Transmission of Lending Shocks Across Borders', *Economic Alternatives*, no. 4 (2022): 711–37, https://EconPapers.repec.org/RePEc:nwe:eajour:y:2022:i:4:p:711-737.

currency or possibly altogether. Due to increased volumes and fluctuations of cross-border capital flows, capital controls lose effectiveness.[16]

v) *Cross-border payments.* Issuing a digital euro within an integrated multi-CBDC system may reduce costs and improve the speed and security of cross-border transactions; § 7.4 provides a more in-depth discussion of the benefits of interoperable CBDCs, and the digital euro based on research by the BIS.

vi) *Global currency and euroisation.* Introducing a programmable digital euro will put the Eurosystem at the forefront of financial innovation and make it a chief candidate for a global digital currency. The increase in reputation and the design-dependent benefits of the digital euro will increase its adoption rate abroad. In some cases, countries with unstable monetary systems may wish to adopt it as their primary currency, leading to so-called euroisation. While this issue is politically contentious and challenges diplomacy and economic policy, it may benefit the countries in question; § 7.5 presents several cases in which the fixation of the local currency to the euro within a currency board (Bulgaria) and the absolute unilateral adoption as a domestic exchange unit (Montenegro) have benefitted the respective economies.

7.4 Cross-border payments

Cross-border payments play an ever-growing role in the interconnected global economy. Boar et al. and Auer et al. document that international tourism expenditures have tripled, while migrant remittances have increased by as much as six times between 2000 and 2019.[17] The number of internationally dispatched parcels has increased five times throughout the period, reflecting the globalisation of trade.

At the same time, the efficiency of the international payments system is currently compromised: Despite significant efforts throughout the years, cross-border payments remain costly, non-transparent, and take a substantial amount of time to settle.[18] While Boar et al. and Auer et al. find that central banks do not put cross-border retail payments high on their agenda, CBDCs, in general, and the digital euro could play a leading role in reducing these frictions. The three models developed by Auer et al. (2021), mentioned above, present a good starting point for ensuring the interoperability of CBDCs. The authors outline some frictions that these models can reduce or eliminate:

16 Sarah Allen et al., 'Design Choices for Central Bank Digital Currency: Policy and Technical Considerations' (Cambridge, MA: National Bureau of Economic Research, August 2020), https://doi.org/10.3386/w27634.

17 C Boar, H Holden, and A Wadsworth (2020) and R Auer, P Haene, and H Holden (2021).

18 Auer, R, P Haene, and H Holden (2021), Multi-CBDC arrangements and the future of cross-border payments, BIS Papers, no 115, p. 1.

i) Operational costs to sustain cross-border banking relations and pre-funding. Model 1 provides efficiency gains by improving existing relations between banks, while the clearing mechanism within Model 2 will decrease the number of connections and introduce economies of scale. Model 3, with a single mCBDC multicurrency system, does not require such relations to exist but may add operational costs for its maintenance.
ii) *Mismatch of opening times across time zones.* Within all three models, mCBDCs allow operations to be settled 24/7, thus wholly removing frictions from different closing and opening times worldwide.
iii) *Mismatch of communication standards.* mCBDCs will incorporate consistent messaging standards or use a single messaging standard altogether.
iv) *Unclear FX rates and incoming fees.* Although the models do not establish an exchange rate mechanism, they will reduce operational and settlement risk and reduce segmentation, reducing transaction fees.
v) *Limited transparency on the status of payment.* Integrated mCBDCs will allow instantaneous settlements, eliminating settlement risk.
vi) *High costs of compliance across borders.* A well-designed joint mCBDC system will have a single set of rules, eliminating compliance costs.

The Eurosystem has decades of experience in integrating many different currencies, and the digital euro has the potential to be a central element in a joint mCBDC system. However, as the history of the eurozone shows, coordinating and maintaining an optimal currency area involving many sovereign interests is challenging. To this end, we believe that Model 2 is the most viable compromise in international affairs.

Including the objective of interoperability from the start is necessary to reap the benefits of CBDCs. Although surveys across central banks show that this task is not high on their agenda[19], there is a significant push from G20.[20]

7.5 Euroisation: Point of concern or an opportunity?

Providing access to a safe, liquid, and convenient digital euro may lead to its adoption as a main monetary unit in non-euro area countries. Most sources argue that this process has excessively adverse effects on the sovereignty of the adopting monetary system. These arguments serve as a motive for introducing account-based access instead of token-based access to the digital euro. In this section, we provide two case studies that show that euroisation may have

19 Boar and Wehrli, 'Ready, Steady, Go? Results of the Third BIS Survey on Central Bank Digital Currency'.

20 G20 Finance Ministers and Central Bank Governors Meeting, '2020 G20 Finance Communiqué: Realizing Opportunities of the 21st Century for All', *G20 Research Group* (blog), 23 February 2020, http://www.g20.utoronto.ca/2020/2020-g20-finance-0223.html.

positive implications for the financial and economic stability of the adopting country, which can lead to an increase in the welfare of its citizens.

7.5.1 The case of Bulgaria

Due to failed economic, fiscal, and monetary policies in its transition from a planned to a market economy, Bulgaria experienced a banking and economic crisis in 1996 and 1997. Failures in banking supervision led to bank defaults and loss of savings, while lax monetary policy to window-dress bad economic policy decisions led to hyperinflation and social unrest in the winter of 1996. Bulgarian citizens lost trust in the Bulgarian currency, the lev, and private transactions were made exclusively in US dollars and Deutsche Marks. These events led to instituting a currency board on July 1, 1997, with a peg to the then-existing Deutsche Mark and later to the Euro. The Board included a traditional rule-based exchange rate arrangement with specific innovations. As part of the rules for the Currency Board, the Bulgarian National Bank (BNB) received a mandate to guard banking and financial stability—at the time, one of the few central banks in the world with such a mandate.[21] The design of the Board and the incorporated safeguards to financial stability were aimed at making it credible, which ultimately reflected the credibility of the national currency. Strict fiscal and monetary discipline and the financial stability guarded by the Board led to economic stability that allowed the Bulgarian economy to experience its highest economic growth in the post-Communist era and to become a candidate and then a member of the European Union. Due to the peg to the euro, the restrictions to the monetary policy toolkit of the BNB, and the close integration with euro area economies, the EC monetary policy transmitted almost without friction to the Bulgarian economy. At the same time, being outside the Eurosystem, Bulgaria was left out of the monetary policy decision-making process. An attempt to apply to the Exchange Rate Mechanism II was precluded due to the global financial crisis of 2008–2009 and the following sovereign debt crisis in the euro area. Because of meeting most macroeconomic and institutional conditions, Bulgaria entered the ERM II and the European Banking Union in late 2020, adopting the euro on January 1, 2024. The entry to the euro area is not without opponents in Bulgaria. The euro is already in circulation in Bulgaria, and most of the significant household transactions, such as property purchases, are negotiated in euros and settled in lev with a minor but positive commission. The decision on issuing a digital euro will not be made before 2024. Still, closer integration with the euro area via access to a digital euro before the official adoption rate would improve the integration of Bulgaria with the Eurosystem and

21 The main mandate of the ECB is to maintain price stability, while Deutsche Bundesbank received the task to identify and assess financial stability risks as part of its macroprudential mandate only in 2013.

enhance the acceptance of the euro and the efficiency of the financial system and economy.

7.5.2 The case of Montenegro

The following example presents an outright euroisation of a country outside the European Union. Following World War II, Montenegro adopted the Yugoslav dinar as a member country of the Socialist Federal Republic of Yugoslavia (SFRY). After the dissolution of SFRY in 1992, Montenegro joined Serbia in the new Federal Republic of Yugoslavia. The National Bank of Montenegro lost its autonomy in favour of Belgrade's National Bank of Yugoslavia. The new country's lack of financial discipline and lax monetary policy led to a prolonged period of hyperinflation between 1992 and 1994. Like Bulgaria, Yugoslav citizens switched to the Deutsche Mark as their main exchange unit. After several attempts to stabilise the dinar, on January 24, 1994, it was pegged to the Deutsche Mark.

In November 1999, Montenegro introduced a dual currency system, where the Deutsche Mark was accepted as a second official currency alongside the dinar. In January 2002, Montenegro officially and unilaterally adopted the euro as the sole legal tender in the country. Except for the periods around the global financial crisis and the Covid-19 pandemic, Montenegro has experienced annual economic growth between 3 and 7 per cent. The ongoing economic stabilisation policies led to the country officially becoming an EU candidate in 2010. As in the case of Bulgaria, the ECB's monetary policy is transmitted with no obstructions to the economy of Montenegro. Any difference between the ECB policy rate and local interest rates is attributed to domestic banking and economic conditions.[22] However, while the Currency Board in Bulgaria allows the national bank to serve as a lender of last resort in particular cases, the Central Bank of Montenegro cannot perform such duties. It must rely on international institutions in case of banking crises. The issue of unilateral euroisation has been contentious since its introduction, primarily after Montenegro was assigned an EU candidate status in 2010. The EC has stated on numerous occasions that even though all EU members are bound to adopt the euro, they should satisfy the convergence criteria in the TFEU, which include the exchange rate of their national currency with the euro within a specific band. The Commission believes a unilateral adoption does not comply with the Treaty. One possible solution is for the country to adopt a currency board with conditions like the Bulgarian one for at least two years before the eventual admission to the euro area. However, given the high

22 Alexandre Sokic, 'Euroisation and Cyclical Stabilisation in Montenegro', *Revue d'études Comparatives Est-Ouest* 47, no. 3 (September 2016): 83–100, https://doi.org/10.4074/S033805991600303X.

adoption rate and trust in the euro, introducing a new currency in the country may be economically costly and risky.

The cases of Bulgaria and Montenegro provide positive examples of countries with a limited monetary policy toolkit that benefitted from tying their economies to the euro. The peg to the euro in Bulgaria and the outright adoption in Montenegro were coupled with structural reforms in the financial sector and the real economy in joining the EU. These have led to improved financial and economic stability, better integration with developed countries and an increase in the welfare of the citizens in the adopting country.

7.6 Conclusion and policy discussion

The introduction of a digital euro is the next major milestone in the evolution of the Eurosystem. Providing a liquid, safe, and convenient digital medium of exchange will improve the welfare of European citizens in an environment of ever-decreasing use of physical cash and the advent of private challengers. While there are many ongoing CBDC projects around the globe, the focus is usually on the domestic economy, leaving cross-border effects as a secondary objective. We argue that the international dimension should be considered and integrated into its design to reap the benefits of introducing the digital euro. The euro will require careful analysis of the implications on global financial stability, international lending, and capital flows, as well as a significant coordination effort between authorities regarding cross-border payments.

Providing foreign residents access to the digital euro is a delicate political issue. However, the risks for the Eurosystem and the adopting country tend to be overestimated. We argue that such access will improve the euro's role internationally, and the possible risks could be quickly addressed with the instruments mentioned throughout this chapter. Even more, this could be done without taking an explicit stance on the monetary system of these countries, avoiding political tensions. Moreover, the ECB may need to consider foreign economy implications when deciding to switch on or off some features for non-residents, which is an exciting venue for future policy research and deliberation.

8 Digital Euro

Issued by Commercial Banks, Digitally Transforming the Industry

Philipp Sandner, Jonas Gross, and Roman Avdeev

8.1 Motivation

Recent developments have shown that cash is becoming gradually less important as a means of payment.[1] Increasingly, people are turning towards digital payments, such as mobile payments, cryptocurrencies, or stablecoins. During these paradigm shifts, El Salvador was the first country to introduce Bitcoin as an official legal tender, and China is establishing its digital version of the yuan, the eCNY. Driven by technological advancements, increasing competition, and the growing need for innovative payment solutions, European institutions, including central and commercial banks, aim to satisfy this demand by establishing a new technological basis for money. With the ever-increasing complexity of business processes, legacy payment infrastructures cannot provide the capabilities required to achieve high automation and efficiency. Accordingly, a programmable euro, a blockchain-based form of the euro that enables programmable payments, could address these issues by allowing digital delivery-versus-payment (DvP) transactions, micro, streaming, and machine-to-machine (M2M) payments. The DLT-based infrastructure would be the foundation for an advanced monetary system facilitating the digital euro.[2] In this sense, the established reputation of banks as trusted and regulated entities can be leveraged to introduce the digital euro and enable new business models for various industries. Alongside industry applications and the increased efficiency in payment processes, the numerous possibilities offered by DLT would likewise result in advantages for banks. For instance, internal bank processes such as compliance, risk management, or the provision of banking services could be fully automated, thus further improving banks' operational efficiency. The advantages mentioned above will attain a unique role following constant digitalisation within the scope of Industry 4.0 and the IoT economy.

1 ECB, 'Study on the Payment Attitudes of Consumers in the Euro Area (SPACE)', 16 December 2022, https://www.ecb.europa.eu/stats/ecb_surveys/space/html/index.en.html.

2 Philipp Sandner et al., 'The Digital Programmable Euro, Libra and CBDC: Implications for European Banks', *SSRN Electronic Journal*, 2020, https://doi.org/10.2139/ssrn.3663142.

DOI: 10.4324/9781003258261-11

Hence, it is crucial to demonstrate the various opportunities of a digital euro through illustrative examples.

Considering this, we will give a broad overview of the various digital euro solutions the public and private sectors offer. These include but are not limited to CBDCs, tokenised commercial bank money, tokenised e-money, and stablecoins. Moreover, we will elaborate on the features of the digital euro and the resulting benefits for the banking industry. Lastly, specific applications within the industry will be presented to further stress the composability benefits between the digital euro, emerging technologies, and business models.

8.2 Forms of the digital euro

Today, the euro has three forms: central bank reserves, bank money (deposits), and physical cash. The emergence of the digital euro would constitute a fundamental change to these existing forms. In this sense, the concept of the digital euro encompasses a taxonomy of alternatives that can be regarded as a technological extension of prevailing money conditions.

Figure 8.1 shows how private and public institutions can issue the euro in digital form. In addition to purely public initiatives such as CBDCs, private institutions could be equally engaged by issuing stablecoins, tokenised e-money, tokenised commercial bank money, or deploying a trigger solution. Alternatively, a public-private initiative (synthetic CBDC, sCBDC) could

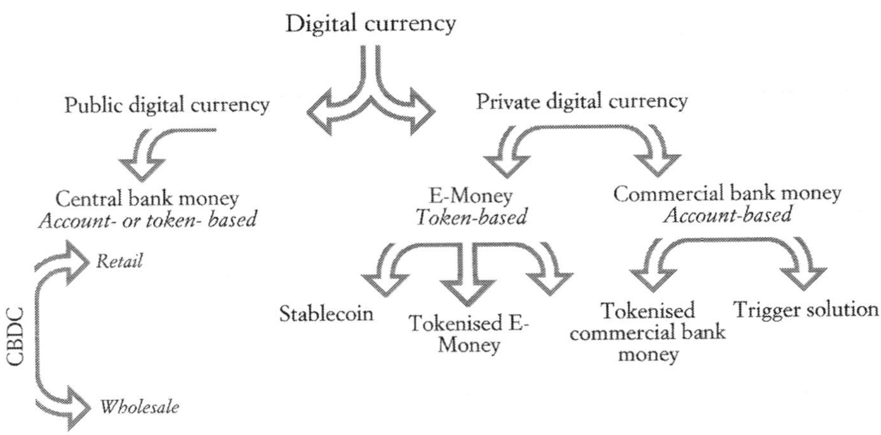

Figure 8.1 Taxonomy of a digital currency. (Adaptation by the authors. Based on Maximilian Forster et al., 'The Future of Payments: Programmable Payments in the IoT Sector – CashOnLedger', *CashOnLedger* (blog), 5 April 2022, https://cash-on-ledger.com/insights/the-future-of-payments-programmable-payments-in-the-iot-sector/.)

involve both parties in which a private institution would issue the digital euro, which would be backed 100 per cent by central bank reserves.[3]

Generally, a distinction can be made between account- and token-based systems. In account-based systems, transactions occur by message exchange, after which intermediaries (banks) update the account balances. In contrast, token-based forms of money do not rely on intermediaries, as they represent a bearer instrument that can be exchanged directly between two parties.

8.2.1 Public sector initiatives

Most central banks are currently exploring the issuance of CBDCs. This form of money represents a digital currency issued directly by the central bank and is thus central bank money. In the current monetary system, only financial institutions can hold central bank money/reserves (excl. cash), primarily designed for credit institutions for purposes such as settlements and not publicly available. However, with a retail CBDC, entities other than financial institutions would be granted the ability to hold central bank money on electronic devices. As a result, the critical benefit would lie in having risk-free central bank money through digital legal tender. In contrast, bank money does not represent an official legal tender but rather a claim on the bank that can be exchanged at par value for cash or be transferred to other financial institutions, hence incorporating credit default risk.

As outlined in Figure 8.1, another variant of the public sector digital euro is a wholesale CBDC, which could be employed for efficiency enhancement purposes in interbank transfers.[4] It should be noted that all forms are not mutually exclusive and will very likely coexist. The ECB is pursuing a digital alternative to cash in the long term.[5] Further, it should be noted that digital euro solutions provided by the ECB do not necessarily have to be DLT-based. An account-based CBDC would be likewise conceivable. Like standard bank accounts of financial institutions, the users would have access to a digital account provided by the central bank.

3 Manuel Klein, Jonas Gross, and Philipp Sandner, 'The Digital Euro and the Role of DLT for Central Bank Digital Currencies', *FSBC Working Paper*, May 2020, http://explore-ip.com/2020_The-Digital-Euro-and-the-Role-of-DLT-for-Central-Bank-Digital-Currencies.pdf.

4 'Digital Euro Could Be Reality by 2026 – ECB's Panetta', Central Banking, 16 May 2022, https://www.centralbanking.com/node/7947766; Benoît Cœuré and Jacqueline Loh, 'Central Bank Digital Currencies', Committee on Payments and Market Infrastructures-Markets Committee, March 2018, https://www.bis.org/cpmi/publ/d174.pdf.

5 Alexander Bechtel et al., 'The Future of Payments in a DLT-Based European Economy: A Roadmap', *SSRN Electronic Journal*, 2020, https://doi.org/10.2139/ssrn.3751204; European Central Bank, 'Publications on Digital Euro', 3 January 2023, https://www.ecb.europa.eu/home/search/html/digital_euro.en.html.

8.2.2 Private sector initiatives

Private institutions are equally engaged in developing their digital euro solutions. The private digital euro issued by financial or e-money institutions would be based on DLT to meet industry demand for a more efficient means of payment, enabling a wide range of novel use cases. As such, the multiple solutions for providing a private digital euro will be elaborated in the following sections.

8.2.3 Payment rails and trigger solutions

In principle, the DLT can be used to either facilitate a token-based payment infrastructure or as a platform for programmable payments settled on legacy bank accounts. A conceptual distinction can be made, differentiating between the contract execution system, the digital payment infrastructure, and the monetary unit.

- *Contract execution system*. The first pillar of the process flow represents a system with a programmable sequence for which payment can be triggered.[6] Within a DLT-based environment, this system would be realised through a smart contract following pre-programmed business logic. In particular, the smart contract could, for example, query the position of a shipped container and trigger a payment if the geographical coordinates lie within a predetermined range.
- *Digital payment infrastructure*. The possible precursor to a (native) DLT-based payment infrastructure could be the so-called trigger (or bridge) solution that would provide a bridge between DLT and conventional payment systems. Such a solution would likewise allow for the use of complex business logic implemented via smart contracts. However, the ultimate value transfer would occur outside the DLT and be settled on conventional central or commercial bank accounts. As the name suggests, payment would be triggered by message exchange and through interfaces established between DLT and conventional payment systems.[7]
- *Monetary unit*. Depending on the choice of the digital payment infrastructure, different monetary units are used for the ultimate exchange of monetary value. The monetary unit can only be fiat-denominated in the upper rail and settled between bank accounts. Conversely, a (native) DLT-based digital payment infrastructure would allow for the transfer of token-based fiat money or cryptocurrencies, which would be settled on the blockchain directly between two parties.

6 See Alexander Bechtel et al., 'The Future of Payments in a DLT-Based European Economy: A Roadmap', *SSRN Electronic Journal*, 2020, 18, https://doi.org/10.2139/ssrn.3751204, Figure 2.

7 Bechtel et al., 'The Future of Payments in a DLT-Based European Economy', 2020.

8.2.3.1 Trigger solutions vs native DLT-based systems

In the literature, the trigger solution has not received substantial attention yet. A further distinction of various implementation forms of the trigger solution is required to draw a clear line between trigger solutions and native token-based systems.

As depicted in Figure 8.2, there are three types of possible implementations of a trigger solution. A smart contract communicates through interfaces with banks' current legacy settlement systems in all three variants. Thereby, the final settlement takes place outside the blockchain. The smart contract triggers the payment in the first variant, and no blockchain token transfers monetary value. Because the sole use of the smart contract is to trigger payments, this variant can be identified as a *pure trigger* solution. The second variant, *sync trigger*, synchronises the token transfers by forwarding the state change of the blockchain, thus triggering a payment between bank accounts. Here it is important to note that the tokenised claims can only be accessed via the DLT. This can be considered a sub-account to which the user has no access via legacy systems but instead uses DLT-based tokens. In this case, the user passively triggers the payments on legacy systems. The third and last variant, the *full sync trigger*, works similarly to the previous one, except that the token balance is not separated but fully synchronised with the account balance on the legacy infrastructure. This would allow the user to transfer his funds by traditional means of access, such as online banking or via DLT. The advantage of a token-based trigger solution is that the user is not limited to the payment trigger function but can virtually tap into the same capabilities of a DLT native infrastructure.

Thus, the monetary unit would be a quasi-bearer instrument that could, for example, be locked into smart contracts for settlement purposes. Solutions built around the sync trigger variants would also be inherently upward compatible and interoperable concerning future token-based variants of the digital euro.

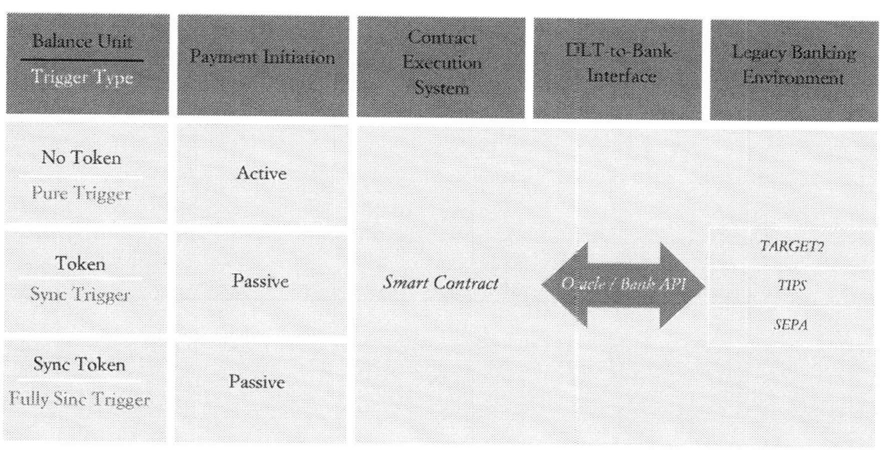

Figure 8.2 Different variations of the trigger solution. (Elaboration by the authors.)

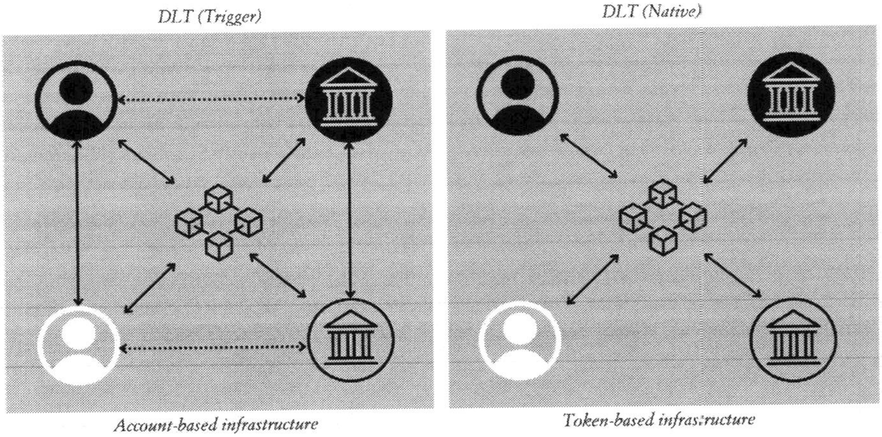

Figure 8.3 Trigger solutions—DLT trigger vs. DLT native. (Depiction by the authors.)

Generally, for all three solutions to work, both sender and recipient must be identifiable to trigger payments between the parties. This, and the settlement taking place on legacy systems, separates the trigger solution from a DLT-based digital payment infrastructure. Figure 8.3 depicts the difference between the two setups.

In contrast to the trigger solution, a DLT-based payment infrastructure does not require a bridge between the blockchain and legacy settlement systems. Individual parties can freely transact with each other and use the token as a bearer instrument.

8.2.3.2 Stablecoins and tokenised e-money

With the advent of cryptocurrencies and their ever-growing market capitalisation, fiat-backed stablecoins became increasingly popular by providing investors with an asset that could be used as a store of value and would reduce volatility. The latter also plays a significant role in DeFi applications such as decentralised exchanges, lending protocols, and derivatives platforms, in which stablecoins are used as a medium of exchange and for collateralisation purposes.[8] Depending on the collateralisation and stability mechanisms, stablecoins can be classified into three categories.[9] The first category describes off-chain collateralised stablecoins. They require a custodian to safeguard the

8 Alexander Lipton et al., '11. Stablecoins, Digital Currency, and the Future of Money', *Works in Progress*, Building the New Economy, 30 April 2020, https://doi.org/10.21428/ba67f642.0499afe0.

9 Aleksander Berentsen and Fabian Schär, 'Stablecoins: The Quest for a Low- Volatility Cryptocurrency', in *The Economics of Fintech and Digital Currencies*, ed. Fatas Antonio (London: CEPR Press, 2019), 65–71.

tokenised (off-chain) assets. The stablecoin value could be pegged to a currency, an asset such as gold, for example, or a basket of different kinds of assets. Usually, such stablecoins are issued by private institutions that form custody partnerships with financial institutions.

The stablecoins can be redeemed or purchased on the secondary market or directly from the issuer.[10] In contrast, the second category of on-chain collateralised stablecoins relates to a concept for which neither an issuer nor a custodian (in the form of a legal entity) is required. The operationalisation of such a stablecoin is realised solely with smart contracts, which issue and destroy (upon redemption) stablecoins in exchange for on-chain assets that are being used as collateral. The third category is another example of decentralised smart contract-based protocols, the so-called algorithmic stablecoins. As opposed to the previously mentioned variants, algorithmic stablecoins do not necessarily need to be collateralised. Instead, they attempt to maintain their peg by employing a stability mechanism that expands or contracts the supply in reaction to price fluctuations. While some projects like Ampleforth, for example, turn to a purely algorithmic approach by adjusting the supply of all token holders, others attempt to stabilise the peg by selling accumulated fees or future revenues (comprised of fees) against the stablecoin.[11] Some classes of stablecoins will be regulated under the MiCA Regulation as e-money tokens or asset-referenced tokens. The MiCA defines e-money tokens as 'crypto-assets that are intended primarily as a means of payment aimed at stabilising their value by referencing only one fiat currency.'[12] In this context, the 'e-money' prefix was derived from the similarities of stablecoins to electronic money that the ECB defines 'as an electronic store of monetary value [...] that may be widely used for making payments to entities other than the e-money issuer.' Asset-referenced tokens, on the other hand, describe those tokens that attempt to hold a stable value by reference to the value of several different currencies, single or multiple commodities, or other crypto-assets.[13] Accordingly, the critical difference between a broad definition of stablecoins and tokenised e-money is that the latter is issued and can be claimed at par value.

10 Dirk Bullmann, Jonas Klemm, and Andrea Pinna, 'In Search for Stability in Crypto-Assets: Are Stablecoins the Solution?', *SSRN Electronic Journal*, 2019, https://doi.org/10.2139/ssrn.3444847.

11 Berentsen and Schär, 'Stablecoins: The Quest for a Low- Volatility Cryptocurrency'; Bullmann, Klemm, and Pinna, 'In Search for Stability in Crypto-Assets'; Ayten Kahya, Bhaskar Krishnamachari, and Seokgu Yun, 'Reducing the Volatility of Cryptocurrencies – A Survey of Stablecoins' (arXiv, 1 March 2021), http://arxiv.org/abs/2103.01340.

12 'Proposal for a Regulation of the European Parliament and of the Council on Markets in Crypto-Assets, and Amending Directive (EU) 2019/1937' (2020), art. 3 (1) (4), https://eur-lex.europa.eu/legal-content/EN/TXT/HTML/?uri=CELEX:52020PC0593&from=EN.

13 European Central Bank, 'Report on a Digital Euro', European Central Bank, 14 January 2021, https://www.ecb.europa.eu/euro/html/digitaleuro-report.en.html.

8.2.4 Tokenised commercial bank money

The German Banking Industry Committee (GBIC) published a paper that is among the latest efforts around tokenised commercial bank money.[14] They proposed a concept that aims to tokenise existing bank deposits. Hence, the resulting monetary unit would be called the commercial bank money token (CBMT). This approach would offer the benefits of DLT and enhance the liquidity provision possibilities of commercial banks due to an additional distribution channel. The fundamental difference compared with stablecoins lies in banks' case of credit creation. While stablecoins or e-money tokens imply full collateralisation, banks, in theory, are free to leverage following fractional reserve banking. Financial institutions must establish a common technological standard for tokenised commercial bank money issuance to ensure interoperability between the various financial institutions. Likewise, fungibility must be guaranteed as the various institutions' tokens inherently imply different credit risks and hence cannot be considered equivalent at any given time.[15] To prevent exchange rates between tokens from other issuers and ensure fungibility, the GBIC proposed the following three possible governance models for CBMTs:

- *Fully collateralised stablecoin*. In this model, the CBMT would be 100 per cent backed by central bank reserves regardless of the issuing bank. Because the collateral is central bank money, the counterparty credit risk of the issuing institutions can be disregarded; hence fungibility is ensured.
- *Special purpose vehicle (SPV)*. Another potential solution could be an SPV created and maintained by banks participating in the CBMT scheme. In this model, the banks would move credit claims onto the balance sheet of the SPV, for which the SPV would issue CBMT in exchange. Because the CBMT would be a liability of the SPV at any time, only one counterparty is involved, which makes all issued tokens equivalent as they have the same credit risk.
- *The CBMT*. Like the first solution, the CBMT would be the liability of the issuing banks. To address the issue of exchange rates and provide fungibility, the banks could grant each other credit lines when the CBMT is transferred between two customers (with different banks). In doing so, the receiving bank would assume the credit risk of the paying bank until the final settlement on legacy clearing accounts.

14 German Banking Industry Committee, 'Europe Needs New Money – an Ecosystem of CBDC, Tokenized Commercial Bank Money and Trigger Solutions', 5 July 2021, https://perma.cc/4SJS-F9VE.

15 German Banking Industry Committee.

8.3 Digital euro issued by commercial banks

The introduction of a digital euro by the private sector and the resulting use of DLT would constitute a technological entry point for various industries, including banks, that seek to introduce new services and improve existing business processes. This chapter focuses on the complementary capabilities arising from commercial banks' introduction of the digital euro. They are primarily divided into the programmability of money and payments, data-driven process automation, and new services and business models that could emerge from the appliance of DLT.

8.3.1 Benefits of banking services and novel business models

8.3.1.1 Programmable money and programmable payments

Today, the banking industry can already provide digital access to payment and account information functionality, including web, mobile apps, or application programming interfaces (API). The banking system offers essential programming functions such as scheduled payments, standing orders, or direct debit mandates. Although countless other functions could be programmed externally and executed via APIs, the involved payments are still constrained by the underlying payment infrastructure of banks and their limitations. For example, conventional SEPA credit transfers usually require one business day to reach the recipient. This is a significant obstacle, especially in DvP transactions. Due to the delay, the parties involved in the value exchange are exposed to counterparty risk until the final settlement. While real-time credit transfers may address this issue, not all financial institutions can accept or provide real-time payments. Furthermore, for regulatory reasons, payments can only be initiated through human interaction that involves two-factor authentication, rendering the technology unsuitable for automated M2M payments.[16]

Banks could address these issues by providing an environment that allows unconstrained programmability of money and payments. Because the cash leg is also embedded in a programmable, Turing-complete environment, virtually any complex payment process could be implemented securely and trusted. Thereby, for example, self-executing smart contracts could automatically check predetermined conditions that are part of a trade procedure and trigger payments to one or several stakeholders. Likewise, this technology enables the programmability of money, whereby the monetary unit could be equipped with inherent properties. Examples of such properties include interest-bearing capabilities (proportionally in- or decreasing the supply), permission or blocklisting recipients for usability boundaries (for example, food stamps), or expiration dates.

16 Forster et al., 'The Future of Payments'.

8.3.1.2 Data-driven process automation

Apart from the programmability of payments and money, the DLT could likewise be utilised to automate processes within banks. These do not necessarily have to represent payments but rather business processes where human interaction is required to collect, process, and evaluate data. By programming the respective procedures, smart contracts could take over time-consuming and repetitive tasks. For example, bank customers could acquire a loan by depositing digital assets into the smart contract. Thereby an embedded logic would perform a valuation of the collateral and grant a loan according to predefined risk parameters. Subsequently, the loan could be used as a down payment to purchase a property via decentralised housing markets. In this case, the bank could again act as an intermediary for financing purposes.

Similarly, a smart contract would perform an enhanced credit rating of the bank customer, value the property, grant a mortgage, and lock in the tokenised property as collateral. In addition to the programming capabilities, the DLT-based environment would also provide vast amounts of on-chain data that could be repurposed for concepts like embedded supervision. By leveraging the integrity and availability of data, compliance and oversight processes can be improved. Banks can use this technology to conduct real-time sensitivity and risk analyses of their balance sheet exposure to market volatility. If certain risk parameters are exceeded, the bank can initiate a securitisation process, where ongoing loans are bundled into mortgage-backed securities, tokenised, and sold to investors. That could, in turn, transfer risk off the balance sheet and further contribute to the stability and resilience of financial institutions in an automated manner.[17]

8.3.1.3 Enabling new services and business models

With a growing and interconnected Industry 4.0 ecosystem, the data collected by IoT devices could be used in conjunction with DLT to construct new business models and services.[18] One such solution actively explored in the industry is the Assets-as-a-Service (AaaS) model. In this model, the bank aims to refinance physical assets (for example, laundry machines and tractors) and is responsible for the rental process. The core innovation in AaaS lies in the fully automated payment procedure in which the user is billed directly after a machine or device has been used. This process is supported by IoT devices that forward the state change of a machine to a smart contract which then debits the client for the usage period. Another complementary service that might inherently arise from such offerings could be (dynamic-) Pricing-as-a-Service (PaaS). One specific example could be a dynamic price adjustment at electric

17 The Joint Forum, 'Report on Asset Securitisation Incentives' (Basel: BIS, July 2011), https://www.bis.org/publ/joint26.pdf.

18 Forster et al., 'The Future of Payments'.

charging stations. Different data endpoints such as traffic volume, electricity prices, distance to the nearest city, and others could be sourced to calculate the kW/h price at the electric charging station. Especially in IoT-driven economies, the DLT would serve as a technological underpinning allowing for the seamless construction of new services in a secure and decentralised environment. Furthermore, service providers, including banks, could take advantage of network effects in terms of established access standards that have evolved around the vision of Web 3.0. In practice, this would enable end consumers to access services through the same application and technology stack already being used broadly in the decentralised economy of cryptocurrencies.

8.3.2 Addressing inefficiencies

One benefit of DLT is realising efficiency gains when using this technology to improve existing processes. Well-known examples include transactions, clearing processes, and securities settlements. As outlined in the previous section, many use cases can be implemented due to the blockchain's programmability and availability of all transaction data. The following section will explain how a DLT can eliminate inefficiencies that are indirectly related to payments or settlements.

8.3.2.1 Settlements

As previously discussed, transactions in today's payment and settlement systems are subject to settlement risks. These risks are characterised by the probability that the counterparty will not deliver after paying (also known as counterparty risk). In this sense, using DLT for digital money transfers can alleviate risks due to the provision of a perfect DvP settlement. Thereby, the monetary value or securities are exchanged simultaneously; hence counterparty risks are eliminated for both parties.[19]

8.3.2.2 Cross-border and FX transactions

Another risk in the context of settlement processes is foreign exchange (FX) risks in cross-border transactions. The risk is a substantial exchange rate fluctuation between the currencies involved, which can happen between the payment initiation and the final settlement between two parties.[20] When a bank

19 Forster et al.; Board of Governors of the Federal Reserve System (U.S.) et al., 'Distributed Ledger Technology in Payments, Clearing, and Settlement', *Finance and Economics Discussion Series* 2016, no. 095 (December 2016), https://doi.org/10.17016/FEDS.2016.095.

20 Bank for international settlements and Comité sur les systèmes de paiement et de règlement des banques centrales du Groupe des dix, eds., *Settlement Risk in Foreign Exchange Transactions* (Basle [Paris]: Bank for international settlements [diff. Banque de France], 1996), https://www.bis.org/cpmi/publ/d17.pdf.

client intends to conduct a cross-border transfer in foreign currency, the bank obliges the client to pay a fee to compensate for the FX risk.[21] With a DLT-based digital euro, FX transactions can promptly be atomic and settled between two parties. Because the payment is processed immediately, the involved FX risks are effectively eliminated, reducing transaction costs.[22] For this to work in practice, DLT-based forms of money backed by the euro and other currencies are required.

8.3.2.3 Compliance costs

As explained in § 8.3.1, it would be conceivable to integrate compliance guidelines and related processes directly into a DLT as part of the 'embedded supervision' concept. Apart from international regulatory frameworks (Basel III), KYC and AML measures could be integrated into the DLT. For this to happen, a global identity network would be necessary. Once in place, this could not only allow the use of financial services on a DLT but would also significantly improve the efficiency of compliance processes within banks.

8.4 Digital transformation driven by the digital euro

8.4.1 The role of commercial banks

In the wake of digital transformation, the role of commercial banks should be particularly highlighted. Already today, it can be observed that consumers and companies are slowly turning towards usage-based business offerings.[23] Due to the lack of long-term commitment to an asset or service, such models offer considerable financial flexibility. The lack of commitment also contributes to a highly competitive atmosphere, as suppliers must constantly innovate and add value to attract new customers. Apart from changing consumer and corporate trends, ecological incentives might as well play a role alongside purely economic ones. Usage-based business models could incentivise manufacturing companies to design long-lasting products and extend their production cycles.[24] At the same time, customers will become more aware of their consumption patterns and will seek ways to reduce costs by avoiding

21 Board of Governors of the Federal Reserve System (U.S.) et al., 'Distributed Ledger Technology in Payments, Clearing, and Settlement'.

22 Forster et al., 'The Future of Payments'.

23 Laurent Probst et al., 'Servitization: Pay-per-Use (Business Innovation Observatory Contract No 190/PP/ENT/CIP/12/C/N03C01)' (EC, April 2016), https://ec.europa.eu/docsroom/documents/16595/attachments/1/translations/en/renditions/native.

24 Gianmarco Bressanelli, Marco Perona, and Nicola Saccani, 'Reshaping the Washing Machine Industry through Circular Economy and Product-Service System Business Models', *Procedia CIRP* 64 (2017): 43–48, https://doi.org/10.1016/j.procir.2017.03.065.

excessive usage of resources.[25] Undoubtedly, both of these phenomena contribute towards sustainability. Banks are in a pivotal position to trigger these far-reaching changes and hence have a responsibility to identify emerging trends and provide their clients with the necessary tools required to harness these new opportunities.

8.4.2 Potential use cases

8.4.2.1 AaaS and pay-per-use business models

Following the previous example of usage-based offerings, such business models can be combined with a pay-per-use billing modality and an AaaS solution provided by banks. AaaS employs a model where the customer is only charged for the actual utilisation of an asset or service. Compared with financing or fixed-term leasing models, AaaS offers more financial flexibility for customers, as their capital is not tied to the asset or the agreed lease term. However, challenges remain because the asset providers (for example, manufacturers) bear the risk of low utilisation and hence reduced profitability. To address this issue, manufacturers could outsource their assets to banks within the scope of an AaaS partnership. In turn, banks would provide renting services and be responsible for pricing and selling the assets on secondary markets. By transferring the risks and releasing capital, manufacturers would benefit from being able to focus more on their core business.[26] Conversely, given the current low-interest-rate environment, banks or asset managers would be offered a more attractive investment opportunity.

Combining IoT interfaces with financial services makes achieving higher efficiency within the context of the said example possible. Instead of charging a fixed amount, the machine would determine the incurred costs by analysing the utilisation rate of single-use. Thus, the over- and under-utilisation risk would be effectively alleviated, and at the same time, this would allow the calculation of the residual value after individual uses.

One example could be a laundry machine, where a variable price is determined by the selected cycle profile (revolutions per minute, duration, temperature).

Figure 8.4 shows that the IoT interfaces transmit usage-based telemetry data to a cloud, which calculates the incurred costs. Subsequently, the laundry machine would initiate a payment on behalf of the user. Especially in such complex implementations, it is necessary to enable the programmability of payments and provide a technology-agnostic infrastructure that allows

25 Georgios Zervas, Davide Proserpio, and John W Byers, 'The Rise of the Sharing Economy: Estimating the Impact of Airbnb on the Hotel Industry', *Journal of Marketing Research* 54, no. 5 (October 2017): 687–705, https://doi.org/10.1509/jmr.15.0204.

26 Deutsche Bank, 'Asset-as-a-Service – Corporates and Institutions', April 2021, https://corporates.db.com/publications/White-papers-guides/asset-as-a-service?language_id=1.

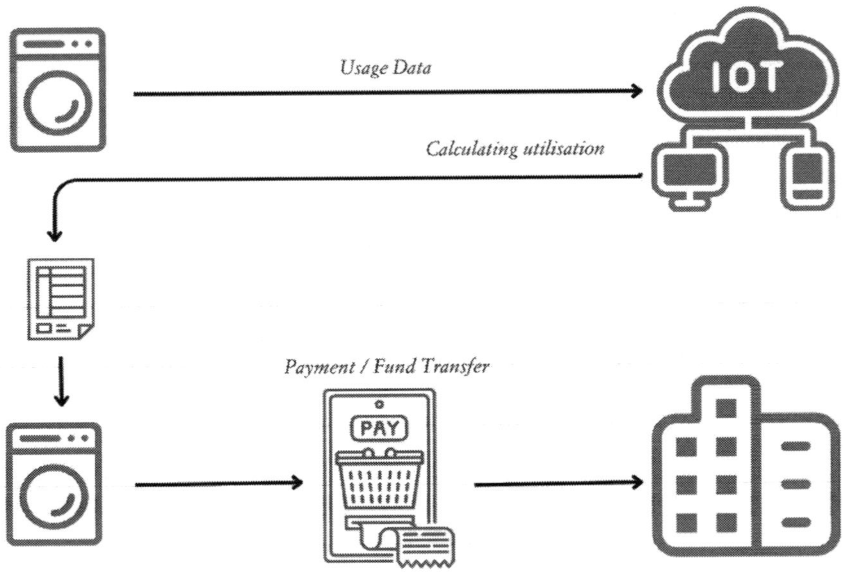

Figure 8.4 Asset-as-a-service model based on IoT data. (Adapted by the authors. Based on Bechtel et al., 'The Future of Payments in a DLT-Based European Economy', 2020.)

interactions with different systems and stakeholders of the industry. A DLT-supported digital euro can meet both requirements.

8.4.2.2 Streaming payments: Pay-as-you-use

With the applicability of DLT, specifically the ability of a continuous stream of nano payments, it would likewise be possible to operate a pay-as-you-use billing modality. Instead of being charged after using an asset or machine, the user is charged in real time through streaming payments. This would allow for perfect DvP as the involved settlement risks are virtually eliminated. Practical applications of such a billing modality include industries where the utilisation period and its costs are difficult to predict, posing an undefined settlement risk for the asset or service provider. While the costs of predetermined activities (for example, laundry cycles) are more or less predictable and constrained, others, such as computational tasks, might not be. In the case of cloud computing, the provider may not be able to estimate how long the processing power will be needed to solve complex computational tasks. These could, for example, involve nondeterministic algorithms like machine learning models, where the total resource consumption can only be determined after the execution of the algorithm. Another practical application of streaming payments could be in industries where commodities are delivered via pipelines. Especially in cases where the sum of regular payments is high and operationally critical, suppliers might want to consider using streaming payments to alleviate counterparty risks. From a technical viewpoint, current payment systems cannot provide streaming payments for two main reasons. First, such a solution would require multiple stakeholders within the financial services industry to upgrade their legacy payment infrastructure to support streaming functionality and ensure interoperability. However, due to the narrow applicability of streaming payments, the cost-benefit outcome will likely be negative. Second, a centralised solution would still involve parties between the payer and payee, which defeats the purpose of achieving zero settlement risk at the fundamental level. With the digital euro and DLT, both issues can be addressed by enabling the programmability of payments in a decentralised and trustless environment.

8.4.2.3 Machine-to-machine payments

When automation is being introduced into many industry domains, the changes go hand in hand with the application of IoT interfaces. These interfaces allow machines to exchange information with each other, hence also enabling M2M payments. One notable example that could soon become a reality is autonomous vehicles. In addition to autonomous driving capabilities, the entire handling and maintenance of cars could be further automated with M2M payments. A real-world example could be a concierge functionality responsible for autonomously managing the parking procedure. For this to work in crowded cities, where most parking spaces are not free of charge, M2M payments are required. Other possible applications could involve maintenance cases in which a vehicle performs cleaning, repair, or recharging procedures. The latter would particularly interest car rental agencies or companies operating a vehicle fleet. Combining process automation with M2M payments would almost eliminate the manual administrative effort around fleet management. At present, neither complex transactions nor fully automated payments are possible.

Additionally, current regulatory frameworks only allow for human-initiated transactions, and thus the full potential of process automation is limited.[27] In this sense, the benefit of a DLT-based digital euro would be the ability to automate tasks and initiate complex transactions such as streaming or conditional payments. A smart contract could, for example, distribute a split payment between the charging station operator and electricity supplier.[28]

27 Forster et al., 'The Future of Payments'.
28 Bechtel et al., 'The Future of Payments in a DLT-Based European Economy', 2020.

8.5 Outlook and conclusion

Based on the strong industrial demand for an innovative means of payment and its relatively slow development by the public sector, there is a clear need for a private-sector solution regarding a digital euro in the short term. While many different forms of a privately issued digital euro exist, the common denominator is the underlying DLT and its potential. Launching a commercial bank-issued digital euro would introduce programmability capabilities that, alongside industrial applications, could likewise be used to automate many processes within banks. Thus, the digital euro could lead to new business models and services and increase banks' operational efficiency and resilience. To deploy a DLT infrastructure, banks could leverage the developed and publicly maintained open-source blockchain systems and established standards. Because the application layer is separated from the infrastructure, the business logic (embedded in smart contracts) can be developed and maintained in a less complex programming environment. These composability benefits are significant for the fast adoption and deployment of the digital euro as they would allow the industry to freely develop its own applications independently of the payment infrastructure. The most compelling opportunities for the industry abide in the programmability that a digital euro would offer. This can enable concepts such as M2M payments that could be applied for various use cases, such as trade finance and pay-per-use business models, within the context of Industry 4.0 and the IoT. In particular, inefficiencies related to counterparty risk could be addressed while providing innovative payment functionality such as streaming payments or micropayments. It can be said that alongside industrial applications, the changes will also likely impact the environment and consumer behaviour, thus further stressing the crucial role and reason for banks to establish innovative payment solutions, that is to say, the digital euro.

Finally, yet important, is the collaborative work between the public and private sectors surrounding emerging innovation in the payments industry. For a sustainable deployment of new payment solutions, international standards regarding interoperability and access to the digital euro must be set to avoid exponential technological complexity. Moreover, given the different ways private digital money is, or can be, developed, a technology-neutral legal framework is required for said innovations to launch without impediments.

9 How To Design a Private and Compliant Central Bank Digital Currency?

Jonas Gross

9.1 The CBDC landscape

Digital currencies are on the rise. While private-sector cryptocurrencies and stablecoins steadily gain market shares, public-sector central banks are considering issuing their own digital currencies, so-called CBDCs. According to a study by the BIS, almost 90 per cent of surveyed central banks worldwide study the potential of CBDCs.[1] The Bahamas was the first country to fully launch a CBDC in October 2020. Other jurisdictions like the Eastern Caribbean Currency Union, Nigeria, and Jamaica have completed pilot programmes to test the implemented CBDC payment infrastructure.[2] Also, China is currently in the process of experimenting with its eCNY CBDC system. Besides these frontrunners, most central banks worldwide conduct research and investigate how a CBDC should be designed. One example is the ECB which started an investigation phase for its CBDC project, the digital euro, in October 2021.[3] The investigation phase would explore the potential CBDC design, use cases, and desired features that will be derived. So far, the ECB has not yet decided whether to issue a CBDC.[4]

9.2 Why privacy matters for CBDC

One crucial design dimension is the degree of privacy of CBDC transactions. From a technical perspective, a CBDC system can enable any desired degree of privacy. It allows transactions to be transparent, pseudonymous, or private/

1 Codruta Boar and Andreas Wehrli, 'Ready, Steady, Go? Results of the Third BIS Survey on Central Bank Digital Currency', *BIS Papers*, no. 114 (January 2021): 10.

2 This information was last updated in February 2023.

3 ECB, 'Eurosystem Launches Digital Euro Project', 14 July 2021, https://www.ecb.europa.eu/press/pr/date/2021/html/ecb.pr210714~d99198ea23.en.html.

4 ECB, 'Progress on the Investigation Phase of a Digital Euro—Second Report', 21 December 2022, https://www.ecb.europa.eu/paym/intro/news/html/ecb.mipnews221221.en.html. To stay updated, please refer to the European Central Bank's website for information on the Digital Euro: see European Central Bank, 'Digital Euro', 8 November 2022, https://www.ecb.europa.eu/paym/digital_euro/html/index.en.html.

DOI: 10.4324/9781003258261-12

anonymous. In the case of fully *transparent* payments, transaction data can be assigned to the respective sender and receiver by at least one payment service provider (for example, bank transfers). For *pseudonymous* transactions, transaction data cannot be assigned to a specific person but to a pseudonym (for example, Bitcoin). In the case of fully *private/anonymous* transactions, transaction data cannot be assigned to the transaction parties or pseudonyms and are only accessible to the parties involved. As a sequence, such payments provide the highest degree of privacy.

Total privacy of transactions is desirable for a multitude of reasons. First, a high degree of privacy constitutes a fundamental civil right, as the United Nations Declaration of Human Rights, the Convention for the Protection of Human Rights and Fundamental Freedoms, and the Charter of Fundamental Rights of the EU declared. Thus, privacy is protected by law. Second, privacy prevents surveillance abuses and the restriction of transactions of specific individuals. As third parties, such as banks or central banks, cannot infer who has sent or received money, public sector surveillance abuses and censorship of specific citizens can be enforced. Third, privacy protects users from data exploitation by a payment service provider and by data leaks. Previous incidents have shown considerable risks of cyber-attacks with devastating consequences for users. Even financial losses or identity thefts can occur in the most extreme cases. Storing only non-personal and non-interpretable data that do not reveal the transaction parties or the transaction amount would limit the negative consequences of such hacks (or data leaks) because the hacker cannot monetise or misuse the stolen data.

As financial transaction data is particularly sensitive, privacy plays an essential role in the context of payments. For these reasons, a payment solution should allow for fully private payments. Today, cash provides such a payment solution. Cash transactions are not recorded anywhere, and transaction details are inaccessible to third parties. Only the transaction parties involved know the amount of the trade and the respective transaction partner. While cash has the advantage of preserving privacy, it also has disadvantages. It is costly and risky to store and, due to its non-digital nature, inconvenient to transact as it cannot be used for transactions over distances, i.e., it cannot be used for online transactions.

Consequently, cash is already marginalised in some countries, with market shares in the single digits, such as China and Sweden.[5] In these countries, not all merchants accept cash payments anymore, lowering the demand for cash

5 Sveriges Riksbank, 'Cash Is Losing Ground', accessed 9 January 2023, https://www.riksbank.se/en-gb/payments--cash/payments-in-sweden/payments-in-sweden-2020/1.-the-payment-market-is-being-digitalised/cash-is-losing-ground/; 'China: Penetration Rate of Online Payment 2022', Statista, accessed 9 January 2023, https://www.statista.com/statistics/248962/penetration-rate-of-online-payment-in-china/.

payments. Due to the lower demand from users, even fewer shops accept cash payments. This vicious cycle leads to a further decline in the usage of cash.

In the euro area, cash is still the predominant means of payment, even if its usage has declined steadily over the last decade.[6] It does not seem unlikely that—even if central banks do not have any plans to abolish cash—the market could drive out cash in the euro area in the following decades, like what happened in Sweden and China. In an extreme scenario of a cashless economy, anonymous payments would not be possible anymore. Today, there are no private-sector digital payment methods that support anonymous payments.[7] The private sector seemingly lacks incentives to provide such privacy-preserving forms of money as business models often rely on analysing and monetising personal data. This business model would not be possible with anonymous payments. Due to such market failure, the public sector could and should provide such a digital, private form of money as a privacy-preserving CBDC.

In a consultation in April 2021, the ECB asked the public which features are most important for the digital euro. Citizens' responses indicated that privacy was the most demanded feature for a CBDC—43 per cent of all consultation participants stated that privacy is essential for the digital euro.[8]

9.3 Privacy and compliance

From a regulatory perspective, allowing fully private payments is controversial because third parties can't identify the individuals behind specific transactions. On the one hand, such privacy is beneficial for the above reasons. On the other hand, third parties and regulatory authorities cannot do proper AML checks because the sender and receiver of the money are kept secret in the case of fully private transactions. Therefore, the origin of the money is unknown. A disadvantage of fully private forms of money is that they can also be used to finance illegal activities.

For this reason, regulators worldwide restricted the use of anonymous cash payments.[9] The buyer can stay anonymous if the payment amount lies below

6 ECB, 'Study on the Payment Attitudes of Consumers in the Euro Area (SPACE)'.

7 One exception is e-money. However, its practical importance is limited by the fact that, in the euro area, anonymous payments are limited to €150 per month. See Art. 12 'Directive (EU) 2015/849 of the European Parliament and of the Council of 20 May 2015 on the Prevention of the Use of the Financial System for the Purposes of Money Laundering or Terrorist Financing, Amending Regulation (EU) No 648/2012 of the European Parliament and of the Council, and Repealing Directive 2005/60/EC of the European Parliament and of the Council and Commission Directive 2006/70/EC as amended by the Directive (EU) 2019/2177 of the European Parliament and of the Council of 18 December 2019', Pub. L. No. L 334 (2019).

8 ECB, 'Eurosystem Report on the Public Consultation on a Digital Euro', April 2021, https://www.ecb.europa.eu/pub/pdf/other/Eurosystem_report_on_the_public_consultation_on_a_digital_euro~539fa8cd8d.en.pdf.

9 Nadia Pocher and Andreas Veneris, 'Privacy and Transparency in CBDCs: A Regulation-by-Design AML/CFT Scheme', in *2021 IEEE International Conference on Blockchain and Cryp-*

the regulator's specific threshold. If the threshold is exceeded, the buyers must share their personal information and cannot remain anonymous.

As part of a research project on privacy and compliance with CBDC, my research team has proposed a CBDC system that allows for fully private CBDC payments while complying with AML regulations. From a technical perspective, it is already possible to fully implement private payments in the digital realm using privacy-preserving technologies.[10] Also, a CBDC system could utilise such privacy-preserving technologies.[11] AML compliance can be reached using a threshold approach, like anonymous cash payments today. Anonymous payments are then allowed until a specific threshold can, for instance, limit the volume of anonymous transactions per time (turnover limit) or maximum balances on anonymous accounts (account limit). By conducting expert interviews with central bankers, regulators, academics, and other entities, we found support for our hypothesis that there is no substantial interest in conducting AML checks for small payments because they are burdensome and expensive to carry out.[12] This finding supports using such a threshold approach for anonymous payments with CBDC.

In practice, using a threshold approach, hardware- and software-based solutions can allow fully private and AML-compliant CBDC transactions. In the case of a hardware-based solution, special hardware, for example, a secure element in the chip of a smartphone, guarantees the correctness of specific calculations and, thus, checks whether the client complies with the limits on anonymous payments and conducts a correct accounting following the logic of the monetary system. In the case of software-based solutions, software, mainly cryptographic techniques, guarantees the correctness of such calculations and thus checks the authorisation for anonymous transactions. While history has revealed security breaches with hardware-based solutions, software-based solutions have proven difficult to hack and compromise.[13]

We showed how a software-based CBDC system can be designed that allows for fully private transactions until a specific threshold but also addresses

tocurrency (ICBC) (2021 IEEE International Conference on Blockchain and Cryptocurrency (ICBC), Sydney, Australia: IEEE, 2021), 1–9, https://doi.org/10.1109/ICBC51069.2021.9461090.

10 Examples are David Chaum, 'Blind Signatures for Untraceable Payments', in *Advances in Cryptology*, ed. David Chaum, Ronald L Rivest, and Alan T Sherman (Boston, MA: Springer US, 1983), 199–203, https://doi.org/10.1007/978-1-4757-0602-4_18; Eli Ben-Sasson et al., 'Zerocash: Decentralized Anonymous Payments from Bitcoin', 2014, https://eprint.iacr.org/2014/349.

11 An example of utilising Chaum's approach for CBDC is David Chaum, Christian Grothoff, and Thomas Moser, 'How to Issue a Central Bank Digital Currency', 2021, https://doi.org/10.48550/ARXIV.2103.00254. An example of using a ZCash-oriented model is in Jonas Gross et al., 'Designing a Central Bank Digital Currency with Support for Cash-Like Privacy', *SSRN Electronic Journal*, 2021, https://doi.org/10.2139/ssrn.3891121.

12 Gross et al., 'Designing a Central Bank Digital Currency with Support for Cash-Like Privacy'.

13 Chaum, Grothoff, and Moser, 'How to Issue a Central Bank Digital Currency'.

regulatory constraints related to AML.[14] Our system uses many concepts of the protocol of ZCash. This cryptocurrency uses ZKPs to preserve the privacy of transaction data, thus allowing for anonymous payments. ZKPs are cryptographic protocols in which a user can convince another party that a computation was performed correctly without revealing the computation's inputs, computational traces, and outputs. While ZCash is based on *tokens* in the form of unspent transaction outputs (UTXOs), we use an account-based system in which money is linked to user accounts. This modification allows us to implement account limits for anonymous payments.

Moreover, this approach would not be feasible in a token-based system because transactions are not assigned to user accounts. We assume a digital ID is available to all citizens for onboarding. The digital ID allows for deriving a unique identifier for every citizen employing a user's account number. This setup is necessary to prevent users from opening more than one account, which would undermine the efficiency of the limit on anonymous payments.

9.4 A detailed proposal

This chapter proposes adopting a CBDC payment infrastructure with two payment rails within the CBDC system, as illustrated in Figure 9.1: private accounts in the so-called privacy pool and transparent accounts.[15]

Transactions in the privacy pool are anonymous, i.e., transaction details are not revealed to third parties. For transactions via the transparent account, like today's bank accounts, users must identify themselves, and transaction details

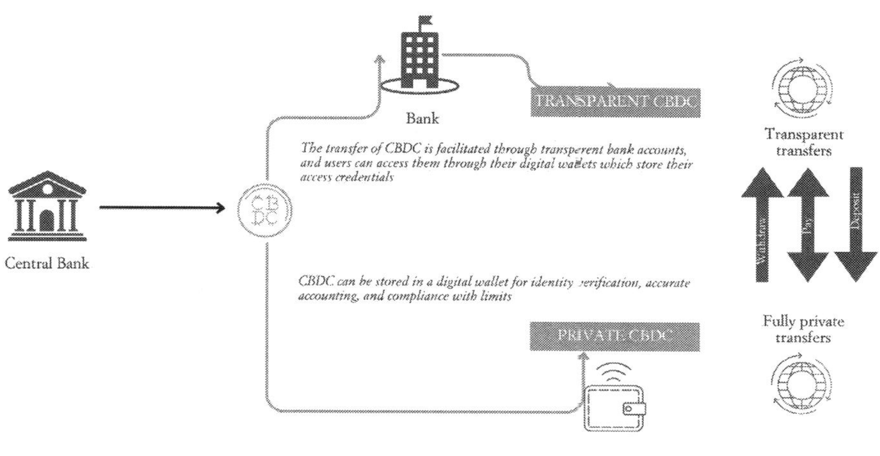

Figure 9.1 CBDC payment infrastructure. (Depiction by the authors.)

14 Gross et al., 'Designing a Central Bank Digital Currency with Support for Cash-Like Privacy'.
15 Gross et al., fig. 1.

are available for the payment service provider. Due to these two payment rails, our infrastructure enables anonymous transactions for both sender and receiver (fully private payments) and anonymous transactions for one party. In contrast, the other party remains transparent, thereby both accounting for semi-private payments and the depositing and withdrawal of funds, or transparent transactions for both sender and receiver.

The central bank issues CBDC as a novel form of central bank money available to the public. For transparent accounts, a third-party bank interacts with customers by conducting administrative tasks, for example, setting up accounts/wallets, onboarding users, or conducting AML checks. Further, the bank distributes the CBDC on behalf of the central bank. The role of banks for transparent accounts is very similar to banks' role today in the distribution of cash. The central bank issues cash and banks demand cash from the central bank based on clients' demand and distribute it to end-users via automated teller machines (ATMs).

There are no banks involved in fully private transactions inside the privacy pool. The central bank directly interacts with the end-users by checking the transaction proposals by the users (details see below). Note that this task is not burdensome to carry out as it is highly automated and not computationally intensive.

9.4.1 Onboarding users

Users would have to consult their banks to open a transparent CBDC account by going to the bank branch in person or telling the bank digitally via an app. Banks then create such an account for the clients on behalf of the central bank. Note that banks only move CBDC on behalf of the central bank, i.e., central bank money. Such CBDC accounts can be compared to today's existing bank accounts with the key difference that, in the end, central bank money, and not commercial bank money, is moved.

The procedure to open an account in the privacy pool differs. Suppose users seek to open a private CBDC account. In that case, they must prove via a ZKP that they own a valid digital ID, which an authorised entity has issued (signed with their private key, for instance, a national ID card authority). Based on the digital ID, a unique identifier is determined that does not change for individuals over time, for example, capturing attributes such as name, date of birth, and nationality. The user submits the proof and the unique identifier to the central bank. The central bank checks the validity of the evidence and that the unique identifier does not have an account in the privacy pool yet. As this identifier is deterministically derived from a person's digital ID, users trying to open two accounts are rejected. This procedure ensures that users cannot open multiple accounts in the privacy pool, which is essential to ensure the efficiency of limits on fully private payments. If the user does not have an account yet, the central bank will create such a user account in the next step.

9.4.2 Depositing and withdrawing CBDC

To deposit money in transparent CBDC accounts, users interact with an app. In this app, they tell the bank that they would like to convert commercial bank money into CBDC. Afterwards, the bank deducts funds from the individual bank account balance and adds these funds to the users' transparent CBDC account. Users can then use these funds in the transparent CBDC account to deposit money in their private CBDC accounts, with which they can pay anonymously. In this case, the bank sends proof of deducting funds (i.e., a digital receipt) to the central bank, and the user proves that they added the same amount of money to their balance in the privacy pool. After checking the proof, the central bank adds the user's new account state to the ledger.

The second way to deposit money in the privacy pool is via specific ATMs. These CBDC-specific ATMs can convert physical cash directly into CBDC. In the case of adding funds to the privacy pool balance, the ATM sends proof that the user has deposited a specific amount of cash. The user proves that they added the respective amount to their privacy pool balance. Again, the central bank checks the proofs and maintains a ledger that detects double-spending attempts without storing sensitive information. The advantage of depositing money in the privacy pool via ATMs instead of using the transparent CBDC account is that users remain anonymous. If money is deposited from the transparent CBDC account, the bank knows the owner of the transparent CBDC account and the deposit's size. In the case of ATMs, the owner is hidden.

9.4.3 Conducting fully private payments

If users seek to conduct a fully private payment, they need to indicate the desire to transact privately in the app so that the privacy pool is selected as the payment rail. The sender proposes a transaction by showing the new account balance, the recipient's address, and a unique transaction ID locally in their wallet. Further, the sender generates proof that they comply with the account and turnover limits for private payments. The recipient proposes a counter transaction and indicates the new account balance, the sender's address, and the transaction ID in their wallet, proving that compliance with account and turnover limits is ensured. Based on this information, both parties send proof to the central bank. Again, no confidential transaction data is shared with the central bank. The central bank checks that the transaction ID is correct and that the amount of money added to the receiver's balance is the same as the amount of money being deducted from the sender's balance (to make sure no money is being created). Eventually, it verifies that the sender's/receiver's addresses match. If the proof is valid, the central bank adds the new account states to the ledger and puts the old account states on a list of spend account states.

9.4.4 How to ensure privacy

Preserving privacy is at the core of our CBDC proposal. In the onboarding process, the users only need to prove that they own a valid digital ID without sharing confidential information about their ID, for example, name, address, or date of birth. In depositing through transparent CBDC accounts, the sender and recipient must prove that the same amount of funds has been deducted from one account and added to the other. Here, it is necessary to reveal the deduction/withdrawal amount to the bank, and the bank knows the holder of the transparent CBDC account. The transaction amount must be displayed in the depositing process via CBDC-specific ATMs, but third parties do not see the transaction party that deposits cash via the ATM. Thus, the degree of data privacy is higher. In the fully private transaction process, no confidential transaction data are shared with the central bank or banks. The only proof shared is that the integrity of the monetary system and compliance with limits for anonymous payments are ensured. The payment amount is not revealed, ensuring maximum privacy.

9.4.5 A centralised ledger as the technical basis

As explained previously, our approach to using ZKPs for CBDC in the privacy pool is based on the concepts used in the privacy coin ZCash. Even if inspired by a blockchain-based cryptocurrency, our CBDC system is based on a centralised instead of a distributed ledger because we believe that is a more secure way to manage the currency. We used a centralised setup where the central bank is solely responsible for validating transactions. It seems a reasonable choice for a payment infrastructure hosted and governed by the central bank and where central bank money is transacted. The advantages of such a centralised setting are higher scalability and privacy in the transparent domain. As only one party validates transactions in the form of proofs, transaction throughput can be higher than in the scenario where many entities validate transactions in a decentralised setup. Privacy is higher because, for transparent CBDC accounts, banks communicate directly with a central entity, the central bank, so only the central bank receives bank-related information. In the case of using a distributed ledger, balances of banks would not just be shared with the central bank but also with other (competing) banks, thereby reducing privacy. Even if ensuring privacy is feasible in such a setup, it would complicate the payment infrastructure and lower scalability. However, if a central bank decides to use a distributed ledger as the underlying technology for its CBDC, it would be, in principle, feasible to use our approach in such a scenario because the privacy pool does not include any sensitive data. Thus, replicated data storage is not an issue for privacy. Reasons to use a DLT could be the desire for higher resilience due to eliminating a single point of failure or benefits regarding programmability. First central banks worldwide, for example, in the Bahamas, the Eastern Caribbean, and Nigeria, have decided to use a DLT for a CBDC. In contrast, other jurisdictions such as China, Jamaica, and Ghana use a centralised variant.[16] In the context of advanced economies besides China, it has not been decided yet whether a distributed or a centralised ledger will be used as the underlying technology.

9.5 Conclusion

Revolutionary technical improvements around privacy allow us today to transfer the privacy-preserving attributes of cash to the digital world. From a technology perspective, as shown in this chapter, it is possible to conduct fully private payments in the digital realm. The degree of privacy for a CBDC is thus not a technical question. Instead, it is a political and regulatory question. Our concept shows that it is even possible for users to remain completely private while complying with AML regulations by using a threshold approach. To date, regulation for CBDC does not exist as CBDC constitutes a novel form of money. Thus, regulatory thresholds for conducting anonymous CBDC payments do not exist, as they do for anonymous cash and e-money payments in many European jurisdictions. Regulators and politicians should carefully assess the desirable degree of privacy of a CBDC, as privacy, in general, must be preserved. While opponents of a partly anonymous CBDC may argue that there is no need for a CBDC to allow anonymous payments as such payments are already possible with cash today, this argumentation is problematic. The use of cash as a means of payment is in decline. Even if central banks do not intend to abolish cash, there is a reasonable likelihood that cash might indeed be driven out of the market someday. If such a scenario materialises and cash is not universally accepted as a payment at points of sale anymore, another fully private means of payment must exist. Otherwise, the opportunity for fully private payments would be completely gone. As the private sector so far has failed to provide such a form of money, the public sector should take precautions and issue a CBDC that supports transactions with a high degree of privacy. Then, the CBDC would indeed be a digital form of cash in a strict sense. Furthermore, as central banks worldwide state that they seek to issue digital cash, they also must value the privacy-preserving properties of cash. Otherwise, central banks fail in their mission around CBDCs.

16 Igor Mikhalev, Kaj Burchardi, Bihao Song, Igor Struchkov, Jonas Gross, Gourav Roy, and John Kiff, 'CBDC Tracker' (October 26, 2021).

10 Beyond Central Bank Digital Currencies

Lessons from Japan's experience

Shuji Kobayakawa

10.1 Introduction

Central banks worldwide have started accelerating their efforts to advance the work of CBDCs. Two-track developments depend on the speed of CBDC implementation.

On the one hand, some emerging economies have adopted a fast-track approach and introduced general-purpose (or retail) CBDCs for the public to use daily. Cambodia introduced a CBDC-equivalent smart wallet service called *Bakong* in October 2020.[1] Around the same time, the Bahamas officially launched its CBDC, called the sand dollar.[2] It was reported that CBoB would eliminate cheque payments to accelerate cashless payment centring on the sand dollar. In Africa, Nigeria issued the eNaira in September 2021. Such development in emerging economies has a ripple effect on neighbouring countries. In Asia, Thailand, in cooperation with several other countries, has published the outcome of several projects which examine the feasibility of CBDCs. Other countries, like Singapore, Malaysia, and India, are also working on CBDC-related projects, mainly from the perspective of improving cross-border transactions. In Latin America, the Eastern Caribbean Central Bank (ECCB), which presides over the Eastern Caribbean Currency Union, launched a pilot of its CBDC, called *DXCDCaribe pilot*, in March 2019. The pilot involves issuing a digital version of the EC dollar, *DCash*. While the DCash system experienced some interruption at the start of 2022, the ECCB has made the DCash platform available to the public since March 2022. For these economies, the motivation behind CBDC implementation is clear: to accelerate financial inclusion by introducing CBDCs.

Major economies have mostly taken a cautious approach to studying how general-purpose CBDCs affect financial intermediation and the monetary system. China is undoubtedly an exception; it has launched large-scale pilot programmes in major cities such as Beijing, Shanghai, and Shenzhen to introduce

1 'បាគង | Bakong – The Next-Generation Mobile Payments', accessed 13 January 2023, https://bakong.nbc.org.kh/en/.

2 'Digital Bahamian Dollar Sand Dollar', accessed 13 January 2023, https://www.sanddollar.bs.

DOI: 10.4324/9781003258261-13

eCNY in the future. Japan has been examining the CBDC's function in a test environment, although a decision has yet to be made on its introduction. Likewise, the ECB officially launched its digital euro project preparation phase in October 2023. In the US, the Fed has undertaken public consultation concerning whether they need a digital dollar. Several senior officials at the Fed publicly expressed scepticism towards the possible benefit a digital dollar might provide.[3] At this stage, it is still being determined whether the United States will eventually introduce its own version of CBDC.[4]

Among many advanced economies, one of the major concerns is that CBDCs have significant ramifications for financial intermediation, which go well beyond the role of commercial banks and private money (i.e., deposits) created by those banks. If not correctly designed, CBDC could generate large outflow from deposits, particularly during stress periods, leading to credit disintermediation. Banks need to rely heavily on market funding, which tends to be more volatile and costly than retail deposits, to continue to perform their role as credit intermediaries.

Partly driven by such concerns, banks and other financial entities in the private sector have started taking their own initiatives to upgrade their financial market infrastructures (FMIs). Their efforts aim to build next-generation FMIs and ensure their deposit money. CBDC will create a symbiosis in which each money will provide services indispensable for the other to continue its operation. Ultimately, these currencies will be expected to provide services that meet the various end-users' needs in the digital economy. Such developments in major economies suggest that CBDCs will not be enough to sustain digital transactions in the future. Every country will need financial intermediaries to distribute, transfer, and collect CBDC on behalf of a central bank to meet payment-service users' needs. However, those intermediaries must also collect deposits and effectively allocate credit to the real economy. How can we articulate a vision for the next-generation FMIs where deposit money and CBDC coexist in symbiosis? The challenge of building such a symbiosis

3 See, for example, Randal K Quarles, 'Parachute Pants and Central Bank Money' (remarks by the Vice Chair for Supervision Board of Governors of the Federal Reserve System at the 113th Annual Utah Bankers Association Convention Sun Valley, Idaho, 28 June 2021), https://www.federalreserve.gov/newsevents/speech/files/quarles20210628a.pdf; Christopher J Waller, 'CBDC: A Solution in Search of a Problem?' (Remarks by Member Board of Governors of the Federal Reserve System at the American Enterprise Institute Washington, DC, 5 August 2021), https://www.federalreserve.gov/newsevents/speech/files/waller20210805a.pdf; Christopher J Waller, 'Reflections on Stablecoins and Payments Innovations' (Remarks by Member Board of Governors of the Federal Reserve System at "Planning for Surprises, Learning from Crises" 2021 Financial Stability Conference, co-hosted by the Federal Reserve Bank of Cleveland and the Office of Financial Research Cleveland, Ohio, 17 November 2021), https://www.federalreserve.gov/newsevents/speech/files/waller20211117a.pdf.

4 Office of Science and Technology Policy, 'Technical Evaluation for a U.S. Central Bank Digital Currency System' (The White House, September 2022), 52, https://www.whitehouse.gov/wp-content/uploads/2022/09/09-2022-Technical-Evaluation-US-CBDC-System.pdf.

is shared by the international community.[5] It is difficult to determine what details would be required, and it is also unclear if the possible measures and actions would be something the private sector would need to take care of.

This chapter is an attempt to draw some lessons from developments in Japan. It is organised as follows: § 10.2 outlines the overview of payment, clearing, and settlement in Japan; § 10.3 details recent initiatives by the Bank of Japan and the Japanese banking sector, emphasising the importance of creating a symbiosis in which CBDC and private money coexist in the financial system; § 10.4 describes medium- to long-term strategies against the rapidly changing payment landscape, arguing that the arrival of stablecoins presents further challenges for the central bank and the banking sector; finally, § 10.5 summarises some lessons for emerging economies. It emphasises that those economies that have been making efforts to implement CBDC will also need to lay out foundations for banks to generate sustainable business models.

10.2 Overview of Japan's payment, clearing, and settlement

Fund settlement in Japan relies on two FMIs: the Bank of Japan Financial Network System (BOJ-NET) and the Zengin Data Telecommunication System (Zengin System). These FMIs are at the heart of Japan's financial system, underpinning economic activity. More specifically, the BOJ-NET is operated by the Bank of Japan (BoJ) and immediately executes funds transfers per instruction in RTGS using central bank money. The Zengin System, run by Japanese Banks' Payment Clearing Network (Zengin-Net), a funds clearing agency (i.e., a central counterparty, CCP) under the Payment Services Act, handles funds transfers between financial institutions, primarily providing a clearing function. It is an online network linking almost all financial institutions in Japan through computers and telecommunication lines. It processes messages from remittances and other financial transactions, handling the daily settlement of interbank credit/debit positions resulting from those transactions.

These FMIs work closely with each other. Depending on the value of funds transfers, they process those transfers in two ways while ensuring efficiency gains from conducting clearing operations. First, funds transfers exceeding 100 mln ¥ per transaction are automatically transmitted to the BOJ-NET. They are processed through the BOJ-NET on an RTGS basis via the BoJ settlement accounts. Second, for those transfers less than 100 mln ¥ per transaction, the Zengin System pools payment instructions and calculates net credit/debit positions for each participating financial institution. These net positions are settled on a deferred net settlement basis using BoJ settlement accounts.

To better understand FMIs' roles in the financial system, Figure 10.1 outlines payment processes from initiation to settlement. It also includes several

5 See Tobias Adrian and Tommaso Mancini-Griffoli (2021).

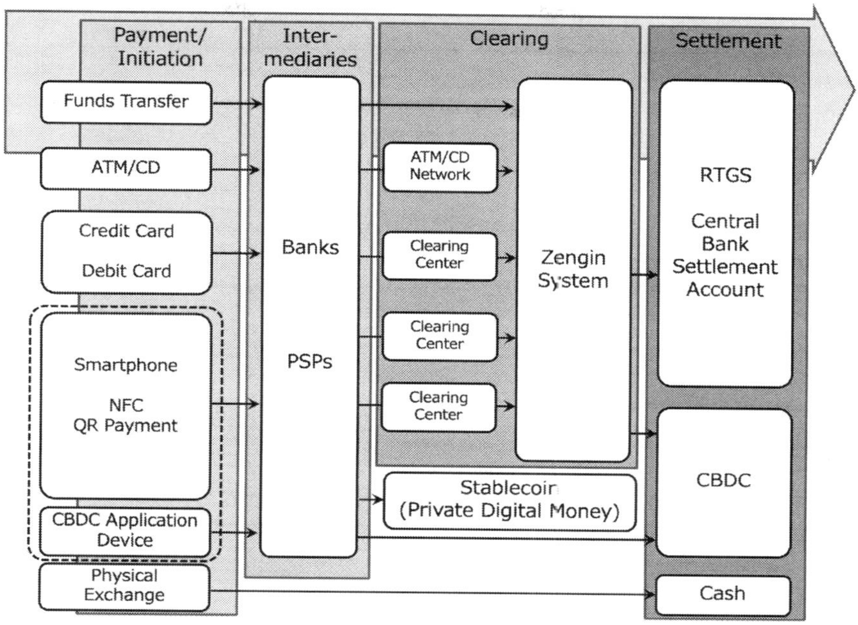

Figure 10.1 Overview of payment, clearing, and settlement in Japan. (Elaboration by the author.)

new initiatives, including the BoJ work on CBDC, the emergence of PSPs as an intermediary, and the arrival of Stablecoins, including the issuance of digital money in the private sector. Figure 10.1 captures the process in which 1) end-users initiate their payments, which go through financial intermediaries, 2) payment instructions are being cleared, and 3) net debit/credit positions of participating intermediaries are settled in the RTGS system providing finality and irrevocability by making use of central bank money. Such processes are universal across major economies.

At first glance, the whole process looks somewhat complex. However, it provides crucial benefits to end-users. First, the tiered structure in which the private sector and the central bank play their respective roles enables those users to enjoy diversity and integrity simultaneously. To be specific, at their discretion, they are free to choose a payment method among many (i.e., credit card, debit card, QR-code payment, to name a few). While such diversity is ensured, all the payments will eventually be cleared and settled on the same infrastructure (i.e., Zengin System and BOJ-NET). Such a centralised structure in clearing and settlement provides end-users with flexibility. As long as they have money in their bank accounts, they can choose the type of payment that fits best with their lifestyle.

Another benefit derived from the tiered structure is ensuring the settlement's safety. Because most payment methods are eventually linked to settlement using the central bank money, end-users can rely on these methods without fear of settlement failure. That starkly contrasts with a stablecoin that is not generally designed to settle using the central bank money. Thus, finality and irrevocability of settlement are not guaranteed, exposing users to risk.

The tiered structure also provides benefits to intermediaries. It notably incorporates the Zengin System's netting capability, enhancing the participants' liquidity efficiency. In other words, the System calculates the net balances between the participants. The Zengin-Net will be a central counterparty, meaning that a balance between the respective participant and the Zengin-Net will replace any balance between a sender and a receiver. By replacing the bilateral debit/credit relationship between participants with a debtor/creditor relationship between a respective participant and the Zengin-Net as a CCP, the system provides safety by preventing possible settlement failure by one participant from spreading to the others.

While settlement by the central bank usually takes the form of real-time gross settlement, clearing is one of the most important functions the private sector can contribute to the whole payment process.

10.3 Recent initiatives for next-generation FMIs

Over the years, such coordination between the two FMIs has been kept intact. More recently, there have been several efforts for the BoJ and the Zengin-Net to meet the potential demand of end-users in the digital economy. The BoJ has officially launched the project regarding CBDC. At the same time, the Zengin-Net is widening access to the Zengin System while helping major banks launch an infrastructure designed for small-value, high-frequency transactions. In a nutshell, these efforts aim to create a symbiosis between CBDC and private money.

10.3.1 Bank of Japan initiatives

The BoJ has started exploring the proof-of-concept study of general-purpose (or retail) CBDC in parallel with the private sector's efforts to modernise its market infrastructure. For some years, the BoJ has joined efforts with the ECB to study the possible application of DLT for FMIs, including the potential benefit of issuing wholesale CBDCs. The joint effort, 'Project Stella,' published its outcome in September 2017. It concluded that DLT-based solutions using liquidity-saving mechanisms could meet the current performance needs of the RTGS systems. In the second phase, the project published another report in March 2018, investigating the DLT application for delivery versus payment transactions, followed by the synchronisation of cross-border transactions in the third phase (June 2019) and the balancing between confidentiality and auditability in the DLT environment in the fourth phase (February 2020).

On top of these joint research efforts with the ECB, the BoJ explored a general-purpose CBDC and published its thinking in October 2020. While the BoJ has yet to plan to issue such a CBDC at this stage, the BoJ finds it essential to prepare for changes in circumstances in which the public will likely use a CBDC in the future. Based on such thinking, the BoJ explored a general-purpose CBDC in three stages. In the first stage, called 'proof of concept phase 1' (Phase 1), starting in April 2021, it developed a test environment for the CBDC system. It conducted experiments to examine basic functioning in that environment, such as issuance, distribution, and redemption of CBDC. In the second stage started in April 2022, proof of concept phase 2 (Phase 2) examines the additional CBDC functioning in the test environment developed in Phase 1. Those functions could include offline capability, programmability, and the balance between privacy and transparency. In the final phase, based on the results from the PoC, it launched a pilot programme involving intermediaries and end-users in April 2023.

The BoJ has yet to make an official decision on whether to release a general-purpose CBDC. However, the work programme set out in three stages should give them the necessary knowledge and understanding of technology requirements that would be essential for issuing a CBDC in the future. This work programme is crucial in making an informed decision on releasing a general-purpose CBDC. Such an approach also proceeds in other jurisdictions, such as the euro area, where the ECB initiated the work related to a digital euro. An official decision on issuing the digital euro has yet to be reached at the time of writing. Other advanced economies like the UK and Canada also engage in an in-depth study of a general-purpose CBDC in their jurisdictions without any commitment to issue one.

10.3.2 Private sector initiatives

As for the private sector initiatives, the Zengin-Net has decided to implement two significant changes in fiscal 2022 (April 2022–March 2023).

First, the Zengin System broadened the participation of non-banks and PSPs. PSPs have only been able to participate in the System as indirect participants without having a direct relationship with the AISP or PISP. This means they can send their payment instructions only via their sponsored financial institutions, which have direct access to the System. A new access policy will allow PSPs to join the System as 'agency participants' or 'clearing participants.' The former, often termed 'directly connected non-settling participants,' implies that they will directly connect to Zengin's infrastructure, allowing them to submit and receive messages. However, because they do not have settlement accounts at the BoJ, they need to use sponsors' settlement accounts to settle their positions. By contrast, the option to join the System as clearing participants, sometimes called 'directly connected settling participants,' puts PSPs in the same position as financial institutions. They will have direct access to the System and use their own settlement accounts at the BoJ to settle their positions. While the discussion is still underway as to which PSPs will be qualified to join the Zengin System, broadening the System's access policy will put them on an equal footing with depository institutions, thereby promoting competition and innovation in payment services.

Second, the consortium of leading Japanese banks built a new infrastructure called 'Cotra,' specifically designed to handle small-value/high-frequency payment transactions for retail customers free of charge. One of the striking features of the Zengin System compared with FMIs in the US and the euro area is that it handles payment transactions of all values. As shown in Figure 10.2, the daily average volume of transactions via the Zengin System is remarkably higher than other systems because it processes small-value/high-frequency and large-value transactions. The daily average value of transactions via the Zengin System remains at ¥12 trn, which is less than half the value of those processed in EURO1 (i.e., €194.4 bln), and much less than that in CHIPS (i.e., $1.6 trn).

Against such a background, Japanese banks' Cotra initiative aims to enhance the convenience of end-users who have often resorted to banknotes and coins when making small-value payments at retail stores. By closely cooperating with the Zengin-Net, Cotra launched its operation in October 2022. The main objective of these initiatives is to ensure that the services provided by commercial banks and PSPs will be interoperable so that the convenience of private money will be further enhanced.

	CHIPS (US)	EURO1 (Euro Area)	Zengin System (Japan)
Operator	The Clearing House (TCH)	EBA Clearing	Zengin-Net
Participant	Depository Institutions	Depository Institutions	Depository Institutions PSPs (FY2022-)
Number of participants	43 (December 2021)	92 (December 2021)	138 (December 2021)
Volume of transaction	450,000	170,000	7,130,000
Value of transaction	1.6 trillion US dollar	194.4 billion euro	12 trillion yen
Settlement mode	Continuous Net Settlement	RTGS-equivalent through Single Obligation Structure (SOS)	Designated Net Settlement
Risk management	- Prefunding the omnibus account of the CHIPS at the NY Fed (Abolishing collateral posting and sender net debit cap)	- Prefunding the omnibus account of the EBA Clearing at ECB - Sender net debit cap, Receiver net credit cap	- Covering credit risk by posting collateral (e.g., JGB) - Establishing "liquidity providing banks" - Sender net debit cap

Figure 10.2 Large-value payment systems in three economies. (Note that the number of participants is that of 'direct participants' in respective systems. Volume and value of transactions are those of daily average in 2020.) (Elaboration by the author.)

10.3.3 Some background behind recent initiatives

The most important reason for the BoJ and the private sector to accelerate their projects is to meet end-user needs in the digital era. With the arrival of smartphones as a payment device and the proliferation of QR-code payment in Japan, it has become evident, particularly after the outbreak of Covid-19, that the current structure of payment, clearing, and settlement does not satisfy the diversifying needs for payment services of end-users.

Indeed, smartphones enable people to be connected to the Internet regardless of where they live and when they want to use it. The dramatic change in people's daily lives with the introduction of the Internet has triggered new players—such as PSPs—to provide cutting-edge payment services. As a result, many service providers have entered the market to gain access to users' data. It did not take long before the market for payment services became the red ocean in which companies fiercely competed for users' demands. However, the lack of interoperability between services provided by those entrants and incumbents (i.e., banks) has become increasingly apparent. For example, there are currently several dominant smart wallet service providers in Japan, such as PayPay and Rakuten Pay. Even though it is more convenient not to use cash, people who use PayPay cannot send money to others who use different types of 'Pays,' like Rakuten Pay. These services are incompatible; neither are they compatible with bank services.

While smart wallets provided by PSPs can be charged from users' bank accounts, sending money to other users' bank accounts is either a) infeasible or b) possible but requires transaction fees and time. Such fragmentation in payment services does not meet users' expectations. Under those circumstances, major Japanese banks have decided to launch Cotra to ensure interoperability between different service providers by encouraging PSPs to join the same platform with banks when handling small-value/high-frequency payments for their customers. Cotra handles retail payments up to ¥100,000 and provides services as a clearing centre before payment instructions flow into the Zengin System. Such a sub-clearing function overarching banks and PSPs is a novel approach to ensure interoperability between the two, thereby enhancing end-user convenience.

In parallel with Cotra, those PSPs gaining access to the Zengin System can provide interoperable payment services beyond ¥100,000 to their customers, who will gain further flexibility to transfer money between PSP wallets and bank accounts. It is also important to note that these measures will benefit customers, retail stores, and shops. For years, these retailers have had to pay a higher commission fee to their PSPs when the total amount from the sale is credited to their bank accounts. PSPs joining the same platform with banks will eliminate the fee paid to their sponsor banks for clearing and settlement. They can offer pay-in/pay-out services to retailers at competitive prices. Because the Zengin System runs on a 24/7/365 basis, they can also provide services throughout the day for those wishing to receive proceeds from sales in real time.

10.4 Medium- to long-term strategy for next-generation FMIs

10.4.1 Rapidly changing payment landscape

Looking further ahead, end-users will likely expect seamless UI/UX (user interface/user experience) from payment activity. In the future, taking advantage of IoT technology, people will likely be accustomed to 'smart payment,' such as automated delivery and payment of daily commodities at smart homes, automated battery charging of electric vehicles at a smart charge station, and automated delivery versus payment between retail shops and wholesale distributors, to name a few. Furthermore, micropayments for downloading a favourite piece of music or an article from journals/magazines may eventually require payments whose denomination will likely be less than a unit of yen. For these activities to proliferate, the ongoing initiatives may not be sufficient to meet the users' future expectations. The arrival of stablecoins is expected to change how payment, clearing, and settlement are conducted in the financial system. Stablecoins are the second generation of crypto-assets, designed to address volatility in value, a drawback of the first generation, by linking their value to safe assets such as legal tender and sovereign bonds. By stabilising their value, they aim to function as a store of value and a means of payment. Some stablecoins, such as Tether, are heavily traded in the crypto-asset market and have allegedly become a 'key currency' in the metaverse. While the emergence of stablecoins attracts much attention from policymakers and central bankers, the legal framework in many jurisdictions is immature.[6] It is unclear whether their safety and soundness are embedded in society. Above all, the striking difference between current payment instruments and stablecoins is that the latter is by no means settled by central bank money, raising an essential question concerning its safety. As Figure 10.1 shows, stablecoins could contribute to further diversity in the payment means, though they will not help integrate those users' money with bank accounts.[7] [8]

6 Authorities in the United States and Japan are stepping up their efforts to set up the legal framework for stablecoins. For details, see President's Working Group on Financial Markets, the Federal Deposit Insurance Corporation, and the Office of the Comptroller of the Currency, 'Report on Stablecoins', November 2021, https://home.treasury.gov/system/files/136/StableCoinReport_Nov1_508.pdf; Financial Services Agency, 'Study Group on Digital and Decentralized Finance Interim Report' (FSA, 17 November 2021), https://www.fsa.go.jp/en/refer/councils/digital/20220518/01.pdf.

7 Japan passed a new legislation in June 2022 under which commercial banks, PSPs, and trust companies can issue stablecoins backed by commercial bank deposits. This creates a 'bridge' between stablecoins and private money in the form of bank deposits; however, the finality of stablecoins settlement is not guaranteed.

8 Another aspect of the new legislation is related to the fact that checking accounts are fully covered by deposit insurance in Japan. It means that stablecoins backed by checking accounts will likely be fully covered by the government safety net.

10.4.2 Building a common platform for overlay services

With the emergence of stablecoins, discussion for the future payment system has intensified in the Japanese financial sector. The question is whether CBDC and private money could be integrated to form a symbiosis and how such a structure could be further enhanced. Several ideas are currently being discussed. Among them is an idea to build a common platform to provide value-added services to customers using existing money and CBDC. These could include the following overlay services, among others:

- *Account verification service.* Internet and mobile banking usually offer a service in which the sender, who enters detailed information about the receiver's bank account, is notified in advance whether such an account under the receiver's name exists in the registry before a payment instruction is finalised. It prevents the sender from transferring money to the wrong receiver. With the arrival of Cotra, this service accepts *alias* information of the receiver so that the sender only needs to enter such information (receiver's e-mail address, mobile phone number, etc.) instead of typing in all the account information. This service is likely to provide value added to CBDC.
- *AML/CFT service.* Financial institutions have complied with AML and CFT requirements. While the risk of terrorist financing is somewhat low in Japan, the evaluation report published by the Financial Action Task Force in August 2021 stated that Japan needs to prioritise efforts to improve the AML/CFT framework.[9] To raise the framework's effectiveness, banks are considering a common platform in which users' identities undertaking large-value transactions can be checked based on the data from participating banks and authorities. Building an industry-wide platform for such purposes will prevent the duplication of similar functions by separate entities.

  In addition, the extent of AML/CFT monitoring will become more effective as more banks join the platform. There is scale merit in performing such a function. The platform is also expected to provide an essential underpinning for CBDC in the future. Without objection, CBDC must comply with the highest AML/CFT requirements, but a central bank is not generally geared towards carrying out such tasks. In its early research report, the ECB proposed a digitalisation solution for AML/CFT compliance procedures,[10] which could be undertaken by a separate entity called 'AML Authority,' without the interference of central banks. While the ECB's motivation was primarily driven by how to segregate users' data from a central bank to preserve anonymity in payment transactions, the

9 See FATF, 'Japan's Measures to Combat Money Laundering and Terrorist Financing', Fourth Round Mutual Valuation Report (Paris, August 2021), https://www.fatf-gafi.org/publications/mutualevaluations/documents/mer-Japan-2021.html.

10 See ECB, 'Exploring Anonymity in Central Bank Digital Currencies', In Focus Issue no 4 (December 2019).

idea is somewhat complementary to the platform approach proposed by the banking sector in Japan. Segregating AML/CFT functions from central banks can preserve anonymity and allow the private sector to earn revenue from CBDC-related operations.

- *EDI service.* Another area in which value-added service could be provided is the extensive use of electronic data interchange (EDI). EDI includes information related to payment notifications and invoice numbers. Over the years, the industry has suffered from the cost and inefficiency of manual operation and disconnect among sales orders, invoice issuance, and payment. Collecting accounts receivables and recording on the ledger (i.e., accounts receivable ledger) have yet to be synchronised. That often required manual operation (for example, deleting accounts receivables on the Excel sheet manually), which could be erroneous and time-consuming, particularly for small and medium-sized enterprises. The platform could be shared with the industry, which can upload data to automate the whole process, from sales orders to payment. These data could be an essential source of information for sponsor banks, which can access the microdata of their customers so that they can control risk effectively and propose new businesses by monitoring their pay-ins and pay-outs.
- *Programmability service.* Finally, programmability is one of digital money's most heavily discussed value-added functions. Programmable payments enable automatic money transfers when pre-determined conditions are met. It is important to note that a programmable feature has already been implemented using the current infrastructure. For example, under a delivery-versus-payment (DvP) transaction involving two linked obligations, the final settlement of one obligation can only occur if and only if the final settlement of another obligation occurs. In most jurisdictions, DvP transactions are widely implemented for those involving sovereign bonds. However, introducing smart contracts using DLT makes such implementation more flexible and easier. In the future, one could add more complexity and conditionality to any transactions without building an infrastructure to enable DvP transactions. This is another area that can provide the crucial underpinning for CBDC. It may not be in the central banks' domain to develop a business application for programmability, which should be left to the private sector's innovation. While central banks may want to oversee specific applications for programmable payments using CBDCs, having a platform may facilitate the private sector to provide such services.

10.4.3 Adapting to the arrival of new technology

Another consideration is how to make the Zengin System conducive to new technology. Over the years, the System has accommodated a wide range of payment instructions. These include credit transfers (on the same day or post-dated), payroll and bonus transfers that are likely processed in bulk on specific dates, benefit transfers from pension/insurance funds, and other miscellaneous transfers. However, the technology standard required for these transfers could be diverse, making it somewhat tricky for the System to flexibly adapt its infrastructure to the arrival of new technologies. Given this context, there is a proposal to split the infrastructure into two separate systems: one designed to handle mission-critical services such as credit transfers that need real-time processing 24/7/365 and transfers that can be processed in bulk; the other concentrating on value-added services whose development can be handled in an agile manner. Doing so will ameliorate flexibility in the future; for example, the system for value-added services could consider adopting cloud infrastructure in which DLT nodes can be set up without interfering with the mission-critical services. In sum, the arrival of stablecoins raised the awareness, for the banking sector and the central bank, that they need further efforts to ensure their currencies and services will continue to provide a crucial underpinning for the financial system and the real economy. Initiatives described in this section give some examples to meet that goal, bearing in mind that the extent of development in financial systems may vary across countries.

10.5 Conclusion

Considering such developments in Japan, emerging economies adopting the fast-track approach may need to consider the role of commercial banking in the future. While duplicating what the Japanese banking sector is undertaking is not realistic, some thinking behind building a system where CBDCs and deposits coexist and play their respective roles may provide some clues on how to proceed.

Ultimately, those emerging countries need to draw a picture in which commercial banks will distribute and redeem CBDCs to the public and conduct credit allocation to the real economy. Those banks are the only entities that can perform the latter function, not a central bank. In a tiered financial structure, it is essential to articulate the vision for the future of the monetary system from medium- to long-term perspectives and ensure that private money will continue to provide vital services for the public, along with the new role played by CBDCs.

Part IV

Digital Currencies, Cryptocurrencies, and Stablecoins: Fiat Money and Legal Tender

11 The Applicable Laws to Cross-Border Payments in Central Bank Digital Currencies

The Late *Lex Monetae* or Long Live the *Lex Monetae*?

Caroline Kleiner

11.1 Premise

One of the numerous benefits of discussing the legal nature and legal impact of CBDCs is giving fresh air to discussing what money is.

Many speeches come back to the nature of money when assessing whether introducing CBDCs would be valuable.

It is remarkable that in a very recent speech, the executive director of the BIS, Augustin Carstens, insisted on the function of trust in the mechanism of money.[1]

Like blood in the human body, trust is essential to the functioning of a currency.[2] The origins of trust in a currency have been very convincingly divided into three categories by French economists Michel Aglietta and André Orléan.[3] They have identified three different kinds of trust which allow 'fiat currencies' to play their function. In short, hierarchical trust expresses the individual's confidence in an institution. It is described as an institution that sets out the rules for using money and issues the ultimate settlement. This institution is an authority that guarantees the quality of monetary relations, i.e., their conformity to the enacted norm. According to the authors, 'hierarchical trust is based on the hierarchical structure of the banking system.'[4] In other words, the basis

1 During a conference organised by the Institute for Law and Finance on 18 January 2022 on the Future of the Financial Sector (Data, Digitalization, Decentralized Finance and Central Bank Digital Currencies: The Future of Banking and Money), available at Agustín Carstens, 'Digital Currencies and the Soul of Money,' BIS management speeches, January 18, 2022, https://www.bis.org/speeches/sp220118.htm.

2 See Rémy Libchaber, *Recherches Sur La Monnaie En Droit Privé*, Bibliothèque de Droit Privé, t. 225 (Paris: Libr. générale de droit et de jurisprudence, 1992), 49; Caroline Kleiner, *La Monnaie Dans Les Relations Privées Internationales*, Bibliothèque de Droit Privé, t. 516 (Paris: LGDJ, 2010), 22 ff.

3 Michel Aglietta and André Orléan, *La Monnaie Entre Violence et Confiance* (Paris: O Jacob, 2002) (translation by the author).

4 Aglietta and Orléan, 27.

DOI: 10.4324/9781003258261-15

for people's trust in money is the 'central bank' and the fact that it lies at the top of the pyramid of the banking system.

A second type of trust is called methodical trust, which comes into play in relations between individuals and 'proceeds from the repetition of acts of the same nature that bring exchanges to a successful conclusion. Routine is, therefore, the source of this form of trust.'[5]

The third and final type of trust, *ethical trust*, is, according to these authors, the highest form of trust. This is the trust citizens place in the state as the supreme institution that is legitimate to organise legal relationships within a society. In other words, trust in the public authority allows confidence in the institution. Ultimately, trust lies in the state that created the issuing institution. All this shows that the monetary value relies on relationships rather than substance.

In a way, the project of many central banks to issue CBDCs reveals the need to renew the desire to be more trusted by currency users, i.e., by citizens. In other words, to restore the social contract between, on one side, the authorities to which states have delegated their sovereign power to issue and manage a currency; and, on the other side, the population of those states. The fear that private cryptocurrencies, even stablecoins pegged to a national currency or a basket of national currencies, attract more and more users and deviate them from the use of national currencies, which in turn might lead to a disorganisation of the international monetary system with significant risks for global financial stability, is probably the most salient incentive to the considerable efforts undertaken today to create CBDCs.[6] According to the 2021 BIS annual report, 'CBDC design can protect monetary sovereignty by making legitimate cross-border and cross-currency payments easier, thereby obviating the need to hold other currencies and helping a central bank to monitor transactions.'[7] In that regard, issuance by central banks of CBDCs is a striking reaffirmation of monetary sovereignty, the core principle in international law that justifies applying the *lex monetae*.

It is noteworthy that although different central banks jointly lead some current experiences,[8] those cooperations do not aim to create an 'international'

5 Aglietta and Orléan, 27.

6 This fear is formulated by the G7 Working Group on Stablecoins, 'Investigating the Impact of Global Stablecoins,' October 2019, https://www.bis.org/cpmi/publ/d187.htm., and also in the explanatory memorandum of the 'Proposal for a Regulation of the European Parliament and of the Council on Markets in Crypto-Assets, and Amending Directive (EU) 2019/1937' (2020), 2, https://eur-lex.europa.eu/legal-content/EN/TXT/HTML/?uri=CELEX:52020PC0593&from=EN. See also Hossein Nabilou, 'Testing the Waters of the Rubicon: The European Central Bank and Central Bank Digital Currencies,' *Journal of Banking Regulation* 21, no. 4 (December 2020): 299–314, https://doi.org/10.1057/s41261-019-00112-1.

7 BIS, 'Annual Economic Report' (Basel: BIS, 2021), 10, https://www.bis.org/publ/arpdf/ar2021e.htm.

8 For instance, the ECB, the Bank of England, the Federal Reserve, the Bank of Canada, the Bank of Japan, the Sveriges Riksbank, and the Swiss National Bank, together with the Bank for

digital currency created by the states.[9] This means that despite the new doors offered by the latest technology in terms of future monetary architecture, we are still driven by the same old scheme of monetary sovereignty, expressing every state's right to issue its own currency.[10] No project of an international digital currency jointly issued by several central banks can be seen today. CBDC projects are national or supranational (in the euro case).

CBDCs, like other forms of money, will then be confronted with the variety of legal regimes potentially applicable to a transaction made in CBDCs, for the simple reason that CBDCs will likely be used abroad, i.e., outside the territory of the state of the issuing central bank.[11]

This contribution will focus on the cross-border use of CBDCs, i.e., on the situations involving conflict-of-laws issues, by investigating whether the *lex monetae* will stop playing a role in the regime of international payments made with CBDCs; or, to the contrary, whether increasing importance of the relevance of the *lex monetae* should be expected with the issuance of CBDCs. Cross-border use of CBDCs is defined as a cross-border payment, or a payment where the payer/debtor and payee/beneficiary are located in different countries, using a currency that is not common to both parties (one party pays or receives payment in a currency which is not the one in force in the state where they are domiciled—*cross-currency payment*). Even though international payments do not necessarily imply a cross-currency operation,[12] as is the case for payments made within a monetary union composed of different states, the focus of this contribution should be the 'extraterritorial use' of CBDCs.

Of course, technological design may restrict cross-border use, for instance, by conditioning the holding and spending of CBDCs to a residence in the issuing state, which is indeed a particular feature of CBDC as we understand

International Settlements (BIS), have created a group to share experiences as they assess the potential cases for CBDC in their home jurisdictions. The group will closely coordinate with the relevant institutions and forums, particularly the Financial Stability Board and the Committee on Payments and Market Infrastructures (CPMI). But other cooperations between central banks exist.

9 Except for one of the models of the joint experiment of the Bank of Canada and the Monetary Authority of Singapore as explained in the research paper of the World Bank Group, which is based on a 'universal wholesale CBDC': The World Bank Group, *Central Bank Digital Currencies for Cross-Border Payments: A Review of Current Experiments and Ideas* (Washington DC: World Bank, 2021), 7, https://doi.org/10.1596/36764.

10 See, Ch. 3.

11 This observation does not mean that current projects ignore the necessary coordination with other national projects. As noted by the World Bank Group, *Central Bank Digital Currencies for Cross-Border Payments*, 2: 'While no CBDC project has an explicit focus on payments beyond the jurisdiction of the issuing central bank, a number of central banks are working on cross-border payment models in parallel to their CBDC efforts, and international cooperation among central banks on CBDC, including for cross-border payments, is intensifying.'

12 See Report of the Bank for International Settlements et al., *Central Bank Digital Currencies for Cross-Border Payments: Report to the G20* (Basel: Bank for International Settlements, 2021), 3.

it. Such was the case of the Chinese CBDC, the eCNY, when it was initially launched.[13] The PBoC restricted the use of payments within China. However, 'there is scope to change.'[14] The level of interconnection between companies and banks across borders is such that it is probably naïve to think that the circulation of CBDCs may be limited to one specific territory. Moreover, most projects include a provision for cross-border use and interoperability between CBDCs, which shows that central banks are willing to be prepared for this step.[15] Hence, even though this issue has been kept silent in the numerous reports and studies published on CBDCs, it becomes necessary to study the interplay between legal systems that could apply to the cross-border use of CBDCs.

Answering the question of whether the traditional concept, maybe old fashioned, of *lex monetae* will be persistent in the CBDCs area requires:

i) Starting with a definition of the concept.
ii) Outlining these different interactions of the *lex monaetae* with other possible laws that could apply to a cross-border payment.
iii) Verifying if the emergence of CBDCs offers a resurgence of the *lex monetae* as a new digital law of money.

11.2 The concept and scope of the *lex monetae*

One core principle in international monetary law is the so-called principle of the *lex monetae*,[16] recognised in two famous decisions of the Permanent Court of International Justice (PCIJ) in the Serbian and Brazilian loan cases of 1929.[17] Previous findings of national courts had already affirmed the principle that the state is empowered to issue its own currency and use a more modern

13 China's CBDC is already in trial with some 24 million users.

14 According to the House of Lords Economic Affairs Committee, 'Central Bank Digital Currencies: A Solution in Search of a Problem?,' Session 2021-22 (Authority of the House of Lords, January 13, 2022), para. 101, https://committees.parliament.uk/publications/8443/documents/85604/default/.

15 The experiment conducted by various central banks already tackled the issue of their international use and thus tried how their schemes should be coordinated: Project mCBDC Bridge is testing interoperability between CBDC systems of four different jurisdictions (the Hong Kong Monetary Authority, the Bank of Thailand, the Digital Currency Institute of the People's Bank of China, and the Central Bank of the United Arab Emirates) on the same DLT platform while Project Dunbar is exploring the interoperability between multiple CBDCs on a shared platform (the Reserve Bank of Australia, Bank Negara Malaysia, the Monetary Authority of Singapore, and the South African Reserve Bank).

16 Charles Proctor et al., *Mann on the Legal Aspect of Money*, Seventh edition (Oxford, United Kingdom: Oxford University Press, 2012), 367.

17 Case concerning the payment of various Serbian loans issued in France, Series A No. 20, 44; Case concerning the payment in gold of the Brazilian Federal loans issued in France, Series A No. 21, 122 (July 12, 1929).

expression to 'design it.'[18] The US Supreme Court, in the Legal Tender Cases, went further than that when it explained that 'every contract for the payment of money, simply, is necessarily subject to the constitutional power of the government over the currency, whatever that power may be, and the obligation of the parties is, therefore, assumed concerning that power.'[19] More than a century old, this decision explains how currency is a *conveyor* of legal rules.[20]

The *lex monetae* principle, as stated by the PCIJ, has been understood as expressing the idea that only states can issue a currency, an interpretation backed by Knapp's State Theory of Money, first published in 1905.[21] The first sentence of this seminal book is crystal clear: 'Money is a creature of law.'[22] Further, Knapp writes: 'The soul of currency is not in the material of the pieces, but in the legal ordinances which regulate their use.'[23] The concept is still fundamentally enshrined in the legal theory of money today, as recognised by the Advocate General in the *Hessischer Rundfunk* case of the ECJ, who wrote:

> In economic theory, a functional definition of money—understood in the more general sense of 'money' or 'Geld'—tends to be used, which, according to a concept dating back to Aristotle, reveals the three functions it serves, namely: (i) a unit of account; (ii) a means of payment (or exchange); and (iii) a store of value. From a legal point of view, it seems that this economic definition must be supplemented by elements arising from the state theory of money, in the sense that money is a creation of the State or, in the case of the euro, of the Economic and Monetary Union, and that its existence can only be understood within a given legal system.[24]

18 See *Emperor of Austria v. Day and Kossuth* (1861), 2, Giffard 628, 678: 'The regulation of the coin and currency of every State is a great prerogative right of the sovereign power… Money is the medium of commerce between all civilized nations; therefore, the prerogative of each sovereign State as to money is but a great public right recognized and protected by the law of nations.'

19 Legal Tender Cases (*Knox v. Lee* and *Parker v. Davis*), 79 U.S. 457 (1870), 549.

20 What we named the bagages législatifs in Kleiner, La Monnaie Dans Les Relations Privées Internationales, 188.

21 Georg Friedrich Knapp, *The State Theory of Money*, trans. Lucas, Mrs. H M and Bonar, James (London: Published on behalf of the Royal Economic Society by Macmillan and Co., 1924). The core of the theory, as explained by the author himself in this preface: 'The money of a State is not what is of compulsory general acceptance, but what is accepted at the public pay offices; and that the standard is not chosen for any properties of the metals, but for the deliberate purpose of influencing exchanges with the commercially important neighbouring States.'

22 This theory has been diffused among economists as the 'chartalist theory of money.'

23 Knapp, The State Theory of Money, 2.

24 See the Opinion of AG Pitruzzella delivered on 29 September 2020 in Joined Cases C-422 & 423/19, *Johannes Dietrich and Norbert Häring* v. *Hessischer Rundfunk*, EU:C:2020:756, para. 77 and 78 (footnotes omitted).

This assertion made in 2020, when so-called cryptocurrencies were flourishing, shows the strength of the state theory of money, which some authors had already buried.[25]

From a methodological point of view, the principle of *lex monetae* is either seen as a conflict of laws rule or a principle of international law related to the allocation of competencies of the states.[26] Whatever the retained analysis, the issuing State of a currency has the sole and exclusive competence to rule on that currency, defined as a mere monetary unit.

What does the issuance of a currency mean? It means to install and usually impose a specific unit of account as the unit of value within a particular area or territory. The use of the unit of value relates to the abstract aspect. This concept suggests that the scope of the *lex monetae* was, at least initially, entirely restricted. It consisted merely of issues of the currency's name chosen by the states and the determination of its value, originally in terms of gold or silver. For a long time, the concept did not evolve. A 1998 Resolution of the Monetary Committee of the International Law Association recognised that:

> The State of issue of a currency, or a group of States adopting a common currency, has the exclusive competence to define its currency, to change the definition of such currency and to define the right of exchange between any new monetary unit and the former monetary unit or units it is intended to replace.[27]

This concurs with other opinions that:

> The law of the currency determines which chattels are legal tender of the currency referred to; to what extent they are legal tender, and how, in

25 See Dominique Carreau, 'La souveraineté monétaire de l'Etat à la fin du XXe siècle : mythe ou réalité ?' in Souveraineté étatique et marchés internationaux à la fin du 20ème siècle: à propos de 30 ans de recherche du CREDIMI mélanges en l'honneur de Philippe Kahn, ed. Centre de recherche sur le droit des marchés et des investissements internationaux, Travaux du Centre de recherche sur le droit des marchés et des investissements internationaux 20 (Paris Dijon : Litec CREDIMI, 2000), 491.

26 Art. 147 (1) of the Swiss Private International Law Act and art. 2.646 (1) of the Romanian Civil Code frame this rule as a conflict-of-law rule. For further analysis, see Caroline Kleiner, 'Money in Private International Law: What Are the Problems? What Are the Solutions?' in *Yearbook of Private International Law*, ed. Andrea Bonomi and Paul Volken (Sellier—De Gruyter, 2010), 578, https://doi.org/10.1515/9783866539174.565.

27 Committee on International Monetary Law, 'Taipei Conference,' *International Law Association*, February 10, 1998, 17, https://www.mocomila.org/publication/1998-mocomila-taipei-report.htm. Also see François Gianviti, 'Current Legal Aspects of Monetary Sovereignty,' in *Current Developments in Monetary and Financial Law*, ed. International Monetary Fund and IMF Institute, vol. 4, Seminar Volumes (Washington, DC: International Monetary Fund, 2008), 3–16, https://www.elibrary.imf.org/view/books/072/01500-9781589065079-en/01500-9781589065079-en-book.xml.

the case of a currency alteration, sums expressed in the former currency are to be converted into the new one.[28]

While firm on applying the norms of the state of issue of the currency, public international law adopted a restrictive view on the scope of the *lex monetae*. The traditional interpretation of the *lex monetae*—retrospectively seen as the narrow interpretation—reduces the scope of the *lex monetae* to the name of the currency and its value, more precisely, the method according to which the value is calculated.[29] That conception of the *lex monetae* is that of the 1929 PCIJ decisions. However, since 1929, the state's role over its currency has changed in practice. Indeed, states had tied their monetary competence over their currencies to respect their obligations undertaken when they became a party to the IMF, even after the demise of the fixed exchange rate policy. Determination of the value of a currency is today left to the market and the supply and demand rule. This phenomenon is corroborated with the development of book money and makes it necessary to adopt a newer and wider conception of the *lex monetae*.

A more extensive interpretation of the scope of the *lex monetae* that prevails today—although not always clearly—also refers to the security of the payment system. *Lato sensu*, monetary policy concerns issues related to the payment system,[30] which is one of the bases of guaranteeing financial stability, a common objective of many central banks. Furthermore, the Covid-19 crisis has enlightened this and the decisions adopted by major central banks globally. A currency is a vehicle for a specific monetary policy.[31]

No matter how narrow or broad the scope of application of the *lex monetae* is to be understood until CBDCs are created, it should be determined according to the function of the abstract aspect of the currency. One seminal distinction for legal money analysis is between money's abstract and concrete elements. The conceptual aspect deals with what a currency is (in terms of name and value). In contrast, the substantial aspects concern the currency as a way to perform and extinguish monetary obligations. In other words, the abstract aspect of money answers the question of *what* is owed in a monetary

28 Proctor et al., Mann on the Legal Aspect of Money, 332.

29 See, among others, Bertold Wahlig, 'European Monetary Law: The Transition to the Euro and the Scope of the Lex Monetae,' in *International Monetary Law: Issues for the New Millennium*, ed. Mario Giovanoli (Oxford [England]; New York: Oxford University Press, 2000), para. 6.06.

30 Francesco Martucci, *L'ordre économique et monétaire de l'Union européenne*, Collection Droit de l'Union européenne 45 (Bruxelles: Bruylant, 2016), 105.

31 Lael Brainard, 'Speech by Governor Brainard on Private Money and Central Bank Money as Payments Go Digital: An Update on CBDCs,' Board of Governors of the Federal Reserve System, May 24, 2021, https://www.federalreserve.gov/newsevents/speech/brainard20210524a.htm.

obligation. The concrete element addresses *how* the monetary obligation may be discharged.

And the *lex monetae* does not answer the last question. Indeed, the discharge of a monetary obligation in an international context, i.e., the cross-border payment, potentially implies the application of different legal systems. This is the subject of the following paragraph.

11.3 The interaction between the *lex monetae* and other laws applicable to a cross-border payment

Payment, being the performance of an obligation, is usually governed by the law applicable to the debt itself, the *lex causae*.[32] This solution is widely recognised in EU conflict of laws and elsewhere. However, a closer legal analysis of what a payment shows that two other legal systems may come into play: the law where the payment takes place and the law governing the specific means of payment used for the performance of the cross-border payment.

There is a general principle, known both in common law and civil law, that a contract, whether lawful under its governing law or not, is in general invalid insofar as its performance is unlawful by the law of the country where the contract is to be performed (*lex loci solutionis*).[33] This principle is firmly considered in EU private international law.

First, Article 9 of the Rome I Regulation[34] permits an EU member state jurisdiction to give effect to the overriding mandatory rules of the law of the state where the obligations arising out of the contract have to be or have been performed, notwithstanding another choice of law made by the parties, in so far as those overriding mandatory provisions render the performance of the contract unlawful.

Second, even if article 12 (1) of the same Regulation provides that the law applicable to a contract governs its implementation, the second paragraph of the provision states that:

> [i]n relation to the manner of performance and the steps to be taken in the event of defective performance, regard shall be had to the law of the country in which performance takes place.[35]

32 Luca G Radicati di Brozolo, 'International Payments and Conflicts of Laws,' *The American Journal of Comparative Law* 48, no. 2 (2000): 318, https://doi.org/10.2307/840973; Proctor et al., *Mann on the Legal Aspect of Money*, 113.

33 Andrew Haynes, *The Law Relating to International Banking* (London: Bloomsbury Professional, 2018), 313.

34 Regulation (EC) No 593/2008 of the European Parliament and of the Council of 17 June 2008 on the law applicable to contractual obligations (from now on *Rome I Regulation*).

35 A more detailed analysis of the lex loci solutionis may be found in Kleiner, La Monnaie Dans Les Relations Privées Internationales, 294.

Therefore, this provision leaves room for the possible considering of the state's law where the payment is made, i.e., the *lex loci solutionis.*

Indeed, many countries either prohibit using a specific means of payment for certain monetary transactions[36] or compel the use of one particular means of payment for other transactions *when those transactions are made in their territories.*[37] Various norms regulate the payment itself, all the more so since a genuine market for payment services has been created in the EU.[38] Hence, the *lex loci solutionis* is necessarily one element of the legal regime of cross-border payments.

Besides considering the *lex loci* solutions, a third legal system should be considered. The characteristic of payment as the performance of a monetary obligation originates in legal relationships with and by itself. Indeed, in any payment transaction, the implication of a third party is always needed, be it the monetary authority which issued the banknote or the coin or the banking or payment institution that allows a 'book-money' payment to be achieved. In other words, depending on the method of payment chosen, the third legal system involved in a cross-border payment will be different.

Payment made in cash (called 'Payment 1.0') supposes using monetary chattels created by monetary institutions, which nowadays are public. The creation of 'physical money,' as it is sometimes called, is a source of revenue for the states, the *Seigniorage*. Created by a public institution, coins and notes may be considered public chattels and raise the question of the right of property.[39] In any case, their use is submitted to the state's law which issued them. So, for instance, a payment made with a sterling banknote or dollar banknote implies the respect of the law related to the legal tender of the UK or the US.

The legal complexity of international payment involving book money (which in turn can be named 'Payment 2.0') is very well described in the

36 See, for instance, art. L. 112-6 of the French monetary and financial code that limits payment in cash above a certain threshold.

37 As decided, for instance, by the Conseil d'Etat, in the case *Ministre du budget v. Eurospeed Technic France* (May 10, 2012), the French Supreme Court (for public law cases) decided that art. L. 112-6 of the French Monetary and Financial Code (mentioned above) was applicable only if the payment takes place in France. See Caroline Kleiner, 'La prohibition de payer en espèces : une loi de police applicable aux seuls paiements faits en France,' *Recueil Dalloz* 34 (2012): 2289.

38 The EU set up standard rules for payments (via book money) with the adoption of the first Payment Services Directive (Directive 2007/64/EC of the European Parliament and of the Council of 13 November 2007 on payment services in the internal market amending Directives 97/7/EC, 2002/65/EC, 2005/60/EC and 2006/48/EC and repealing Directive 97/5/EC), which the second payment services have reformed (Directive (EU) 2015/2366 of 25 November 2015 on payment services in the internal market, amending Directives 2002/65/EC, 2009/110/EC and 2013/36/EU and Regulation (EU) No 1093/2010, and repealing Directive 2007/64/EC).

39 See Proctor et al., Mann on the Legal Aspect of Money, 30 ff.

already mentioned World Bank Group Research Paper, being this type of cross-border payment:

> to be largely based on the old correspondent banking model, which has not quite benefited from the sale flow of innovations as domestic payments have over the recent decade. This is mainly because managing change in the cross-border payment and settlement space is considerably more challenging than doing so in domestic payments and settlements due to the inevitable presence and complex interactions of multiple jurisdictions that feature different policy and regulatory requirements, use dissimilar standards and operating procedures, and difficulties in the organisation of the necessary collective action.[40]

What are those multiple jurisdictions? Two elements give rise to the potential application of different national laws. The first element comes from the fragmentation of the operation of payment itself, which can be divided into:

i) The segment between the payor and its banking institutions.
ii) The segment between the payee or beneficiary and its banking institution.
iii) And the legal relationships between the banking institutions.[41]

Different legal systems may govern those relationships. The law governing the contractual relationship between the bank and its client is, as a matter of principle, in EU private international law and other countries, the law chosen by the parties,[42] with all the *caveats* provided by consumer law. Absent a choice of law, the state law where the payor's bank is located can also be applied as it is where the service provider has its habitual residence[43] or where the payment operations are being performed (or technically supervised). It is not relevant whether the bank is a branch of a bank established abroad or has its registered office in the same state: The law of the place where the payor's bank manages the account is applicable.[44] This solution favours legal certainty, as many rules relating to bank accounts are mandatory (*lois de police*).

40 The World Bank Group, Central Bank Digital Currencies for Cross-Border Payments, 1.

41 Philip Wood, *Conflict of Laws and International Finance*, Second edition, Law and Practice of International Finance Series, volume 8 (London: Sweet & Maxwell, 2019), 429. See also di Brozolo, 'International Payments and Conflicts of Laws,' 314, who notes that 'whether an international payment is to be considered as a single transaction or as a series of juxtaposed segments is, in any event, an issue of characterization.'

42 Under Article 3 of the Rome I Regulation; Article 116 of the Swiss Private International Law Act; and the general principle of party autonomy.

43 Article 4 (1) b) of the Rome I Regulation; Article 117 of the Swiss Private International Law Act.

44 Kleiner, La Monnaie Dans Les Relations Privées Internationales, 145.

Which of these laws should prevail to apply to the transaction? One possible solution is to use the law applicable to the specific legal relationship to the segment of the payment transaction concerned.[45] Another approach is to select the most relevant one among all those possible rules. This is the position of the UNCITRAL Model Law on International Credit Transfers,[46] which, although it concerns only definite rules relating to international payments, proposes, in a footnote, a conflict-of-laws rule, which provides that 'the rights and obligations arising out of a payment order shall be governed by the law chosen by the parties. In the absence of agreement, the law of the state of the receiving bank shall apply.'[47] This conflict-of-laws rule, however, has not met great success. No specific conflict-of-law rule exists in EU private international law.

Furthermore, even though the rules governing the payment (made with 'book money') have been harmonised in the EU member states,[48] the question of the law applicable to the payment (to determine the extent of the liability in case of late payment, for instance) is not harmonised. Concerning its scope, the law governing the contractual relationships between the holder of a bank account and the bank will decide various issues, such as the date and the place of the payment, which can be either in the state of the payor or the state of the beneficiary. As explained above, the law which applies to the 'book-money' payment needs to be coordinated with the law of the place of performance.

The problem is that the 'place of the payment' concept becomes more artificial when payment is made through a transfer. Indeed, the legal localisation of payment depends on its legal conception, which in turn can be influenced by civil law rules on the determination of the place of payment[49] and by the analysis of commercial (or banking) law rules, which determine precisely when the final payment is made, depending on the instrument used.[50] The difficulty

45 This is the prominent view in the United States: See di Brozolo, 'International Payments and Conflicts of Laws,' 314; and Eric E Bergsten, 'Legal Aspects of International Electronic Funds Transfers,' *International Business Law Journal* 1987, no. 7 (1987): 661. It is also the only one foreseen in The World Bank Group, *Central Bank Digital Currencies for Cross-Border Payments*, 25.

46 Adopted by UNCITRAL on 15 May 1992: UN, ed., *UNCITRAL Model Law International Credit Transfers*, United Nations Publication (New York United Nations, 1999), https://uncitral.un.org/sites/uncitral.un.org/files/media-documents/uncitral/en/ml-credittrans.pdf.

47 di Brozolo, 'International Payments and Conflicts of Laws,' 317.

48 With the adoption of the Payment Services Directive. See footnote 38.

49 For instance: Article 1343-4 of the French Civil Code; §270 of the German Civil Code (BGB); Article 74 of the Swiss Code of Obligations.

50 In French law, according to Article L. 133-6 of the monetary and financial code—which transposed Art. 80 of Directive (EU) 2015/2366 of the European Parliament and of the Council of 25 November 2015 on payment services in the internal market (OJ L 337, 23.12.2015, 35–127)—the date of the payment is deemed to be the date of reception of the funds by the beneficiary or by the payment services provider of the beneficiary. By contrast, the date of the payment made by cheque is when the bank of the drawer transfers the funds to the bank of the beneficiary.

of determining the place of payment is increased with the use of a currency that is not the currency of the state where the payment service provider is located and requires the participation of a corresponding bank established in the state of the currency used for the payment.[51] Given the delocalisation of payments, the importance of the *lex loci solutionis* is declining.

The following and last paragraph will analyse whether the intertwinement already observed between the *lex monetae* on one side, which determines *what is due* in a monetary obligation, and the *lex loci solutionis* and the law applicable to the specific means of payment which indicates *how* the payment can be performed, on the other side, is still operable when cross-border payments will be realised through CBDCs.

11.4 The resurgence of the *lex monetae* within CBDCs: A new digital *lex monetae*?

Conflict-of-laws issues are scarcely addressed in the research papers concerning CBDCs[52] as if the technology is without border, so are the legal monetary relationships that use that technology. This absence could also be justified by the idea that 'Code is law'[53] because the code enshrines itself in the rules of law.[54] However, using CBDC will necessarily trigger a conflict of laws situation.[55] Their solutions will, of course, depend on the architecture the states chose for issuing their CBDCs.

In one of the numerous BIS research papers on CBDCs, the authors envisage two arrangements for their international use.[56] The authors suggest three models in another research paper published by the World Bank Group.[57] In

51 Argument used by some states to justify the competence of their public authorities, hence their national legislation. See Kleiner, *La Monnaie Dans Les Relations Privées Internationales*, 306; Samuel Hatcher, 'Circuit Board Jurisdiction: Electronic Payments and the Presumption Against Extraterritoriality,' *Georgia Journal of International & Comparative Law* 48, no. 2 (April 22, 2020): 602.

52 One of the very few papers dealing with this issue is Wouter Bossu et al., 'Legal Aspects of Central Bank Digital Currency: Central Bank and Monetary Law Considerations,' *IMF*, IMF Working Paper, 20, no. 254 (November 2020), https://www.imf.org/en/Publications/WP/Issues/2020/11/20/Legal-Aspects-of-Central-Bank-Digital-Currency-Central-Bank-and-Monetary-Law-Considerations-49827. The authors acknowledge the fact that CBDC raises new private international law issues but their research paper focus on monetary law. See also The World Bank Group, *Central Bank Digital Currencies for Cross-Border Payments*, 23–26.

53 Title of the famous article by Lawrence Lessig, 'Code Is Law,' Harvard Magazine, January 1, 2000, https://www.harvardmagazine.com/2000/01/code-is-law-html.

54 Dominique Legeais, *Blockchain et actifs numériques*, 2e éd. [refondue], Actualité (Paris: Lexis-Nexis, 2021), 51.

55 Mathias Audit, 'Le droit international privé confronté à la blockchain,' *Revue critique de droit international privé* 4, no. 4 (2020): 669, https://doi.org/10.3917/rcdip.204.0669.

56 Raphael Auer, Philipp Haene, and Henry Holden, 'Multi-CBDC Arrangements and the Future of Cross-Border Payments,' BIS Papers, no. 115 (March 2021): 4.

57 The World Bank Group, Central Bank Digital Currencies for Cross-Border Payments, 4–20.

the arrangements studied by the BIS Report, the matrix of the first architecture would be interoperability between CBDC systems. This would require (if we understand the different scenarios of 'multi-CBDC arrangements' correctly) the conclusion of either bilateral agreements between central banks to make their CBDC system compatible or multilateral agreements that would create a standard clearing system (centralised or decentralised). Experiments conducted by various central banks currently test both types of arrangements.[58] Under this architecture, each CBDC would be governed by its own rule book (the rules of the *lex monetae*). In our understanding, in this architecture, any cross-border payment with CBDC of country A made by a payer in country A to a beneficiary in country B would then require a conversion of CBDC A to CBDC B or currency B (if country B did not issue CBDC or if so wishes the beneficiary of the payment), made at an exchange rate that could be already 'embedded' in the programme.

The second scheme envisages the direct international use of CBDC. Still, such use can occur only if central banks authorise non-residents to hold CBDCs of their jurisdiction or allow their use outside its territory. Again, those choices (and their feasibility) will depend on the CBDCs type: 'account-based' or 'token-based.' The method of circulation of CBDCs and the legal relationships deriving from a transaction made with CBDCs will differ depending on those choices.

Allowing cross-border payments with CBDCs will also accrue risk in the transaction. Whereas a payment with cash (Payment 1.0) is performed by delivering the banknotes or coins, the payment with digital currencies, as it does already with the electronic transfer of book money, implies electronic fingerprints. This raises the risk of different levels of protection of personal data. The requirement level in applying KYC and AML/FT might also differ among the CBDC jurisdictions.

The issuance of CBDCs will allow central banks to shape, in the software programme designing CBDCs, characteristics that so far escaped their capacity to control.[59] Indeed, they will be able to decide:

i) Who owns CBDCs.
ii) Where they can be used.
iii) Moreover, possibly at which rate they can be exchanged.

58 Project mCBDC Bridge is testing interoperability between CBDC systems of four different jurisdictions (The Hong Kong Monetary Authority, the Bank of Thailand, the Digital Currency Institute of the People's Bank of China, and the Central Bank of the United Arab Emirates) on the same DLT platform while Project Dunbar is exploring the interoperability between multiple CBDCs on a shared platform (the Reserve Bank of Australia, Bank Negara Malaysia, the Monetary Authority of Singapore, and the South African Reserve Bank).

59 Legeais, Blockchain et actifs numériques, 9.

Nevertheless, the two first choices seem possible only if CBDCs are distributed by an account-based architecture.[60]

First, contrary to monetary tokens issued until now by monetary authorities—coins and banknotes—central banks will have the power to control the circulation of the CBDCs they will issue in terms of quality and quantity. Central banks may restrict *their* CBDCs only to the residents in their jurisdiction or, on the contrary, may extend the use to non-residents.

Second, central banks could also define the territory where their CBDCs circulate,[61] i.e., whether an 'extraterritorial' use would be permitted. Third, we can also imagine that the program enshrines rules (already programmed) to determine the exchange rate, should the CBDCs be convertible into other CBDCs or national non-digital currencies.

What are the implications of those new powers for the law applicable to a monetary obligation whose payment is made by CBDCs? What has just been explained suggests that the role of the *lex monetae* could increase.

The first expansion of the *lex monetae* will undoubtedly occur in parallel with the evolution of the role played by the CDBCs as conveyors of the monetary policy decided by the state issuing the CBDC.[62] In the future, CBDCs will likely be exposed to a rate of interest (positive or negative) or even to an 'expiration date' enshrined in the programme, thus transforming CBDCs into a *direct* (and not merely indirect) monetary policy tool. If this parameter is set for CBDCs, this will mean that questions of time limitation of use of CBDCs will be subjected to the *lex monetae*, although this issue had never so far been contemplated by the *lex monetae*.

However, the expansion of the *lex monetae* is not limited to those issues about monetary policy but goes beyond that sphere. Indeed, the software program will also enable central banks to determine the right final users for CBDCs. Those rights can range from the right of claims to ownership rights over CBDCs. Whether or not those categorisations will still be relevant for CBDCs is also an issue. For instance, MiCA excludes crypto-assets issued by a central bank from its scope of application.[63] So, it is still unclear what kind of rights CBDCs users will have. In this context, it is worth asking whether the law applies to the holding of CBDC or, as formulated by the World Bank

60 Indeed, the anonymity deriving from the very nature of a bearer instrument, on the contrary, should not permit central banks to select the criteria that a potential holder of CBDCs should meet. The control of the extraterritorial circulation of the currency would then be—as far as we understand the technology—impossible, or at least more difficult.

61 If we accept the idea that a currency has a specific 'territory' linked to one of the states which enacted the currency as its legal currency.

62 Brainard, 'Speech by Governor Brainard on Private Money and Central Bank Money as Payments Go Digital.'

63 See recital 7 of the Proposal for a Regulation of the European Parliament and of the Council on Markets in Crypto-assets and amending Directive (EU) 2019:1937, COM (2020) 593 final.

Group,[64] to the mere existence of CBDC. This question cannot be answered with certainty, as the conflict-of-law rule depends on the legal nature of the relationship between the user and CBDCs or the account holder of CBDCs. Without giving a straight answer, we can nevertheless suggest basing the future analysis on tried and tested principles.

The right of ownership is traditionally subjected to the *lex rei sitae*, i.e., the law where the chattel is located.[65] It might well be considered that a CBDC is presumed—by the law issuing it—to be found in the issuing country, thus giving an even more critical position to the *lex monetae*. If the account-based model is preferred, then it is likely that the conflict-of-laws rule that would apply to determine the law applicable to the relationship between the account beneficiary and its holder would be the same as the one used today regarding 'book money,' whichever solution is adopted (i.e., a 'direct' account with the central bank or an 'indirect approach,' opting for the use of intermediaries which would hold accounts with the central banks for retailed CBDC users). In the EU, this contractual relationship is governed by the law chosen by the parties, without prejudice to applying the law of the consumer's habitual residence. Even if the account beneficiary is not a consumer, the law chosen by the parties cannot derogate from the EU mandatory provisions and national mandatory provisions of the *lex fori*. In the case of the digital euro, the regulation that will embrace its creation and governance is likely considered compulsory. Again, this shows an extension of the role of the *lex monetae*.

However, that is not all. Payment made with CBDC also involves issues of protection of personal data. The quantity of information that passes in the payment process will also be determined *electronically* upon the choices made by central banks, i.e., how they are programmed. Even in its broadest sense, all those new characteristics that exceed the traditional domain of monetary law will yet be governed by the law of the issuing central bank, i.e., the *lex monetae*.

The account-based architecture, which requires access to the person's identity holding the account, poses the additional risk of differing legal protection concerning personal data.

The right to have one's own personal data protected and not transferred is an individual right. Hence, it is conceivable that the account holder's national law—or the law of the habitual residence—interferes with the payment operation. For instance, if a payor in country E pays in CBDC E to a beneficiary in country F and by receiving the payment, this beneficiary receives personal data that the debtor did not consent to give because the law of protection of in-country personal data F is less stringent than the law of country E, may the debtor claim the application of law E? An easy answer relies on technology. If payment can be made in CBDC E in country F, country E and country F

64 The World Bank Group, Central Bank Digital Currencies for Cross-Border Payments.
65 Proctor et al., *Mann on the Legal Aspect of Money*, para. 1.56.

will have concluded an arrangement for the cross-border use of their CBDCs, which means that both central banks should have validated the level of data protection in the transfers.[66] So, technology should nip the risk in the bud.

Nevertheless, what happens if there is a 'glitch'? Which law should apply? A clear conflict-of-laws rule solving this issue should be part of the legal toolkit accompanying the issuance of CBDCs.

In conclusion, it should be outlined that the law applicable to the characteristics of a CBDC should be the one of the central bank itself, not the one of the issuing *state*.

This remark is essential, especially in a 'supranational' currency shared by a group of states, as with the eurozone.

If we apply this position to the digital euro—whose investigation phase is still ongoing at the time of this writing[67]—the decision of who may own a digital euro and where it can be used lies in the competence of the ECB and the SECB, not in the member states' competence.[68] In concrete terms, this means that this is not a decision adopted by the legislative power but by the monetary authority, which usually is not an elected body within the states. This tendency shows the growing importance of the role of central banks in the conduct of monetary policy, *largo sensu*, and even beyond.

The *lex monetae* should be reformulated as the law *of the issuing central bank* (or *of the monetary authority)* and not the law of the issuing *country*. Given the power vested in the central banks with the creation of CBDCs, further reflections should be carried out on the democratic process leading to central bank governors' nominations.

66 Authorities in charge of data protection are increasingly attentive to the development of data transfer that occurs in a payment. See, for instance, the white paper of the French Commission of data protection : Commission nationale de l'informatique et des libertés, 'Quand la confiance paie: Les moyens de paiement d'aujourd'hui et de demain au défi de la protection des données' (Collection Livre Blanc de la CNIL, September 2021), https://www.cnil.fr/sites/default/files/atoms/files/cnil_livre_blanc_2-paiement.pdf.

67 European Central Bank, 'Investigation Phase,' September 27, 2021, https://www.ecb.europa.eu/paym/digital_euro/investigation/html/index.en.html.

68 This chapter does not tackle the issue of whether creating a digital euro is feasible, from a legal point of view, without modifying the existing legal framework. For that question, see Corinne Zellweger-Gutknecht, Benjamin Geva, and Seraina Neva Grünewald, 'Digital Euro, Monetary Objects, and Price Stability: A Legal Analysis,' *Journal of Financial Regulation* 7, no. 2 (September 1, 2021): 284s–2318, https://doi.org/10.1093/jfr/fjab009; Annelieke Mooij, 'The European Central Bank's Monetary Policy and Central Bank Digital Currency: Can the ECB Lawfully Introduce a Digital Euro under Its Monetary Mandate?,' *Irish Journal of European Law* 23 (September 24, 2021): 163–88; A M Mooij, 'A Digital Euro for Everyone: Can the European System of Central Banks Introduce General Purpose CBDC as Part of Its Economic Mandate?' *Journal of Banking Regulation*, January 21, 2022, https://doi.org/10.1057/s41261-021-00186-w.

12 'Legal tender' and Central Bank Digital Currency

Filippo Zatti

12.1 Changes in legal tender

Scholars who study money should focus more on the history and significance of legal tender. The rise of digital central bank money has brought it back into focus. For monetary stability and sovereignty aims, the digital currency issued by a central bank must be recognised as legal tender status like physical currency.[1] See, for example, the digital euro: the regulatory proposal aims to address its main features to make it easily accessible to the general public.[2] Due to their possible programmable nature, the EU is concerned about stablecoins potentially replacing euro payments in e-commerce, capital markets, and Industry 4.0.

As we examine the shift towards digital currency, will the definition of legal tender be altered?[3] Can physical and digital systems coexist with the same legal status, or are *ad hoc* rules necessary? These questions prompt us to re-evaluate money's characteristics, regulation, and the potential effects of divided monetary control on liquidity management.

Economists and legal scholars commonly accept[4] that (fiat) money is a (global) public good, even if peculiar. This statement has sparked a complex debate.[5] The definitions of 'public good' and 'money' are unclear from an

1 For instance, in the EU, a draft bill for introducing digital legal tender was first released in June 2023 as a Proposal for a Regulation of the European Parliament and of the Council on the establishment of the digital euro, COM/2023/369 final.

2 In order to enable all payment service providers in the EU to distribute the digital euro throughout the euro area, it is accompanied by a Proposal for a Regulation of the European Parliament and of the Council on the provision of digital euro services by payment services providers incorporated in Member States whose currency is not the euro and amending Regulation (EU) 2021/1230 of the European Parliament and the Council, COM/2023/368 final.

3 See, among others, Damian Lloyd, 'Bitcoin: Property, Money, Currency or Legal Tender?', SSRN Scholarly Paper (Rochester, NY, 9 March 2022), 52 ff., https://doi.org/10.2139/ssrn.4051062.

4 See Sarah Green, 'It's Virtually Money', in *Cryptocurrencies in Public and Private Law*, ed. David Fox and Sarah Green, First Edition (Oxford: Oxford University Press, 2019), 13 ff.

5 The information and analysis in this article is largely based on my previous article 'The Economic Law of (Central Bank) Digital Currency'. *Law and Financial Markets Review*, 2023, 1–13. https://doi.org/10.1080/17521440.2023.2261668

DOI: 10.4324/9781003258261-16

economic and legal point of view. It is crucial to solve this *puzzle* because if a currency is not just a public good and there is no reason for the government to make it the only legal tender, then the argument for only the government-issuing currency can be challenged.[6] This point must be clarified, regardless of any potential difficulties it may cause.

One challenge in establishing economic law standards is incorporating political principles to design regulatory models.[7] It is worth noting that the arguments supporting a widely accepted statement are founded on various assumptions. Although legal arguments may appear more straightforward, discussing the public good concerning money requires careful consideration of economic concepts. This involves assessing the nature of money as a commodity and the role of those who produce it.[8] A more relevant question is what qualities a currency needs to have in order to be acknowledged and commonly used.[9] When it comes to the law, fiat or legal tender is the preferred option, while economists recommend the trust design approach to currency.[10]

Understanding the role of money in payment systems may seem like an insignificant debate to some, but it is a crucial step in comprehending the unique characteristics of different currencies. Exploring the difference between money production and issuance can open up a whole new level of understanding regarding the intricacies of our financial system. The suggested technology to create a payment system that works without a middleman, like Bitcoin, confirms that money production can happen independently of politics and law. This

6 Nicolas Cachanosky, 'Is Money a Public Good? | AIER', 17 February 2011, https://www.aier.org/article/is-money-a-public-good/; Lawrence H White, *The Theory of Monetary Institutions* (Malden, Mass: Blackwell, 1999), 89 ff.; Corinne Zellweger-Gutknecht and Rolf H Weber, 'Digital Money – Taxonomy and Regulatory Approaches – EIZ Publishing', *Zeitschrift Für Europarecht*, no. 6 (2022): G27-8, https://eizpublishing.ch/artikel/euz/06-2022/digital-money-taxonomy-and-regulatory-approaches/.

7 See Box 1: Public versus private money, or a mix of both? In Jean-Pierre Landau and Markus K Brunnermeier, 'The Digital Euro: Policy Implications and Perspectives', *Policy Department for Economic, Scientific and Quality of Life Policies Directorate-General for Internal Policies*, Study requested by the ECON committee of the European Parliament, January 2022, 12.

8 For the concept see at length Ann Pettifor, *The Production of Money: How to Break the Power of Bankers* (London: Verso, 2017).

9 On this point see, for instance, the considerations proposed by White, *The Theory of Monetary Institutions*, 134–37.

10 'The use of money is limited as in the case of the park bench, and therefore, money is, according to the currently common scientific definition, an "*impure public good.*" However, an important aspect of money constitutes a "*pure public good*": money creates trust between people who do not know each other. The state establishes and supports the trust in *legal tender* and the official currency, making this trust a "*pure public good*"—non-excludable and non-rivalrous. The state puts various measures to create and maintain this trust: it issues money via the central bank; prescribes compulsory acceptance for legal tender; secures a portion of bank deposits; protects private property, and bails out banks': see Christian Felber, *Money - The New Rules of the Game* (Cham: Springer International Publishing, 2017), 30, https://doi.org/10.1007/978-3-319-67352-3. For a different conclusion about non-excludability and non-rivalry in money, see White, *The Theory of Monetary Institutions*, 89 ff.

means that an exchange can potentially occur without requiring the presence of a trusted third party.[11] The potential of Bitcoin and other digital coins has often been overlooked and even dismissed by those in power as if they were a threat to the status quo and heresy for their similarity to the Ponzi scheme,[12] and even worse,[13] the coin's value meant a security or a commodity.[14] Bitcoin and digital currencies based on DLT remind us that currency is, above all, a social agreement aimed, in a market economic system, at enabling the development of societies in economic and social terms.[15] This refers to something provided for the general public benefit. As a result, not only are the stability of the financial system and the protection of savings considered public goods but the very concept of credit and savings are also transformed into public goods.[16] The current question is whether the government should permit the development of private currency like Bitcoin or restrict it. Each governing body can assess this shift based on its own principles, values, and monetary goals. The concept of legal tender currency results from combining these three factors. Closed systems highlight monetary differences, while increased exchange reduces design model

11 See Satoshi Nakamoto, 'Bitcoin: A Peer-to-Peer Electronic Cash System', October 2008, 2, https://bitcoin.org/bitcoin.pdf.: 'In the mint-based model, the mint was aware of all transactions and decided which arrived first. To accomplish this without a *trusted party*, transactions must be publicly announced. We need a system for participants to agree on a single history of the order in which they were received.'

12 See SEC – The Office of Investor Education and Advocacy, 'Ponzi Schemes Using Virtual Currencies' (SEC, n.d.), https://www.sec.gov/files/ia_virtualcurrencies.pdf.

13 As stated by the Deputy Governor of the Reserve Bank of India: Shri T Rabi Sankar, 'Cryptocurrencies – An Assessment, *Reserve Bank of India - RBI Bulletin*, March 2022, 11, https://rbi.org.in/scripts/BS_ViewBulletin.aspx?Id=20870 quoting Robert McCauley, 'Why Bitcoin Is Worse than a Madoff-Style Ponzi Scheme', *Financial Times*, December 22, 2021, https://www.ft.com/content/83a14261-598d-4601-87fc-5dde528b33d0.

14 Jason G Allen, Henry Wells, and Marco Mauer, 'Cryptoassets in Private Law: Emerging Trends and Open Questions from the First 10 Years', *SSRN Electronic Journal*, 2022, https://doi.org/10.2139/ssrn.4206250; Chiara Zilioli, 'Crypto-Assets: Legal Characterisation and Challenges under Private Law', *SSRN Electronic Journal*, 2020, https://doi.org/10.2139/ssrn.3532316; JG Allen, 'Property in Digital Coins', *European Property Law Journal* 8, no. 1 (13 May 2019): 69, https://doi.org/10.1515/eplj-2019-0005.

15 For more on this concept see the valuable contribution by Emilios Avgouleas and Sir William Blair, 'The Concept of Money in the 4th Industrial Revolution – A Legal and Economic Analysis', *SSRN Electronic Journal*, 2020, https://doi.org/10.2139/ssrn.3534701.

16 'When non-residents use national money, as is extensively the case for the world's major national monies, national monetary policies acquire aspects of *global public goods*. Exchange rates always, to some extent, involve issues of international public goods because an exchange rate is the relative price of two national monies and is affected by the corresponding national monetary policies. This international public goods aspect rises to global significance for exchange rates among the world's major currencies because their use is global and movements in their exchange rates have widespread effects': see Michel Camdessus, 'International Financial and Monetary Stability: A Global Public Good', in *Reforming the International Monetary and Financial System*, ed. Peter B Kenen and Alexander K Swoboda (Washington, DC, USA: International Monetary Fund, 2000), 10, https://doi.org/10.5089/9781557758354.071.ch002.

discrepancies. However, the shift from perceiving money as a societal advantage to acknowledging it as a legitimate form of payment only captures a part of the legal and economic complexities. The idea of legal tender for money comes from the authority of a governing body. The concept of sovereignty has varying implications and outcomes depending on the jurisdiction, both in the past and currently. Upon constitutional investigation, it is evident that legal tender is closely associated with creating and regulating currency and ensuring the safety of savings in the face of credit changes.[17] The Italian legal system specifies the currency that must be used to fulfil a contract in its civil code, making it legal tender.[18] Legal scholars have overlooked certain aspects, like questioning the effects of the shift in monetary sovereignty that came with joining the euro, particularly in civil law.

Meanwhile, economists have muddled these concerns. The rise of alternative payment methods, such as cryptocurrencies, and the potential for worldwide payment systems utilising stablecoins and digital currencies issued by central banks, are leading to new economic and legal inquiries. Considering how these changes will affect the perception of money as a public good and legal tender is essential.

Exploring the concept of legal tender concerning both cryptocurrencies and central bank digital currencies can be beneficial. El Salvador's decision to make Bitcoin legal has made parallelism a viable option in today's world.

12.1.1 The case for a 'forced legal tender'

The recent situation in El Salvador is significant. On 7 September 2021, a bill that made Bitcoin a legal tender in the country was passed.[19] There are several factors to consider in this regard. We can refer to the information provided by various media and scientific sources. We would face economic, legal, and political concerns for or against them,[20] pointing out the risks[21] or opportunities that adopting Bitcoin as a 'forced' legal tender brings. However, two aspects require further investigation.

17 As in the case of the Art. 47, Constitution of the Italian Republic.

18 The Italian civil code at art. 1277, in its book of obligations, provides that 'pecuniary debts are extinguished in the currency which is *legal tender* in the State at the time of payment and for its nominal value.'

19 'Ley Bitcoin', Decree No. 57, published in the Official Gazette No. 110, volume No. 430, 13 (June 9, 2021).

20 As Steve Hanke, professor of applied economics at Johns Hopkins University, pointed out: see Shawn Tully, 'El Salvador's Plan to Create the First Bitcoin-Powered Nation Is Tanking the Economy—and Is a Mess by Every Measure', Fortune, 20 January 2022, https://fortune.com/2022/01/19/el-salvador-bitcoin-economy-distressed-debt/.

21 And how they can be addressed: see the El Salvador country team and IMF Western Hemisphere Department, 'El Salvador's Comeback Constrained by Increased Risks', IMF, 16 February 2022, https://www.imf.org/en/News/Articles/2022/02/15/cf-el-salvadors-comeback-constrained-by-increased-risks.

It should be noted that El Salvador adopted the US dollar as its official currency in 2000.[22] It faces a rise in debt within a political climate that can be categorised as undemocratic. The primary issue pertains to El Salvador's dealings with the International Monetary Fund. The second is the relationship between the Salvadoran government and its citizens, as expressed by the welcome to the new fiat money.

The country has shown its efforts to break away from relying on the International Monetary Fund regarding financial independence. This has been demonstrated by its decision to issue a bond denominated in Bitcoin, which is worth the same amount as a maturing bond denominated in US dollars with a high interest rate.[23]

The second concerns the use of Bitcoin made so far by Salvadoran citizens, considering that one of the reasons given by the government for adopting Bitcoin as legal tender is the problem of financial inclusion[24] and the significant weight of immigrants' remittances to the United States.[25] The adoption of Bitcoin has been met with protests among citizens.[26] Despite the setting up of a government wallet, the Chivo,[27] with an amount loaded with Bitcoin for a counter-value of $30, the data concerning its use is still unclear.[28] In simple terms, the external and internal factors come together through the design model chosen by the Salvadoran government for implementing Bitcoin as an

22 The 'Monetary Integration Act (El Salvador)', Pub. L. No. 201 (2020), https://www.global-regulation.com/translation/el-salvador/3370061/monetary-integration-act.html., which came into force on 1 January 2001, states art. 3 that 'The dollar will have an unrestricted legal tender with the unlimited release for payment of obligations in money in the national territory.' Colón is still legal tender but not in circulation anymore. The fixed exchange rate was determined as follows: $1 for ₡8,75.

23 Joshua Oliver and Tommy Stubbington, 'El Salvador Courts Crypto "Whales" as Traditional Investors Shun Bitcoin Bond', *Financial Times*, 30 March 2022, https://www.ft.com/content/4fa63c8c-51f5-4512-b522-76dd75e62916.

24 Banco Central de Reserva de El Salvador, 'Inclusión y educación financiera', Inclusión Financiera, n.d., http://inclusionfinanciera.gob.sv/.

25 Statista, 'Topic: Bitcoin in El Salvador', Statista, 7 September 2021, https://www.statista.com/topics/8401/bitcoin-in-el-salvador/; 'El Salvador Is Betting on Bitcoin to Rebrand the Country — and Strengthen the President's Grip', Time, accessed 26 April 2022, https://time.com/6103299/bitcoin-el-salvador-nayib-bukele/.

26 Statista, 'Topic'.

27 Gobierno de El Salvador, 'Chivo Wallet', Chivo Wallet, accessed 26 April 2022, https://chivowallet.com/chivowallet.com.

28 According to the 2022 first business survey of the Chamber of Commerce and Industry of El Salvador 'About the role of bitcoin as a legal tender and its impact on the performance of their businesses, 91.7% of the participants said that the implementation of bitcoin has been indifferent to their business, and 86% report that they have not made sales using cryptoassets. These percentages face only 3.6% of respondents claiming that bitcoin has contributed to increasing its sales, and 13.9% report having made sales in bitcoin': see Chamber of Commerce and Industry of El Salvador, 'Businessmen Plan to Invest in El Salvador despite the Challenges Facing the Country', 10 March 2022, https://camarasal.com/empresarios-proyectan-invertir-en-el-salvador-pese-a-los-retos-que-enfrenta-el-pais/.

official currency in their monetary system. Arts. 8[29] and 14[30] of the Bitcoin Law help us to understand better. The Government established a $150 million fund at the State Development Bank of El Salvador (BANDESAL) called 'FIDEBITCOIN' through a decree issued under Art. 14.[31] The fund aims to guarantee the automatic conversion from Bitcoin to US dollars through Chivo and vice versa.[32] The Central Bank of El Salvador has released the 'Institutions' Participation in the Bitcoin Ecosystem.' The El Salvador Superintendency of the Financial System has published 'Guidelines for the Authorisation of the Operation of the Bitcoin and Dollar Services Technology Platform.' These regulations are necessary due to Bitcoin's status as a digital asset-based payment system legally interpreted as a financial instrument. This creates a complex situation where a decentralised payment system is re-centralised by the presence of an intermediary like Chivo or BANDESAL through FIDEBITCOIN.

When Bitcoin is recognised as a legal tender and can be circulated within a legal system with an alternative payment or value circulation, it loses the unique characteristics that the Bitcoin blockchain provides. If the Salvadoran government complains about the measures required for virtual currencies, it will inevitably intervene. Furthermore, if this happens, we will be faced with a payment instrument that no longer has the characteristics of cash. Art. 7 of the regulation for the operation of FIDEBITCOIN ensures the confidentiality of functions like those provided by Salvadoran banking law. However, this confidentiality should not be detrimental to non-confidential information regulated by specific laws such as the BANDESAL, Bitcoin, and FIDEBITCOIN.

There has been some discussion regarding the monetary policy currently employed by El Salvador. One question is what would happen if a legal system allowed multiple currencies to be considered legal tender. Although it may be legally permissible, there are concerns about such a move's potential economic and monetary implications. Our current economic model, based on agents, only permits one currency to be issued and governed by a central bank.

29 'Without prejudice to the actions of the private sector, the State will provide alternatives that allow users to carry out bitcoin transactions, as well as automatic and instant bitcoin-to-dollar convertibility if desired. The State will promote the necessary training and mechanisms for the population to access bitcoin transactions.'

30 'Before the entry into force of this law, the State shall guarantee, through the creation of a trust in the Banco de Desarrollo de El Salvador BANDESAL, the automatic and instantaneous convertibility of bitcoin to dollars of the alternatives provided by the State mentioned in article 8 of this law.'

31 'Ley De Creación Del Fideicomiso Bitcoin', Decree No. 137, published in the Official Gazette No. 165, volume No. 432 (August 31, 2021). See also BANDESAL, 'Reglamento Para El Funcionamiento Del Fidebitcoin', accessed 26 April 2022, https://www.bandesal.gob.sv/reglamento/.

32 Art. 1, 'Ley De Creación Del Fideicomiso Bitcoin' under the rules established by the Comité de Normas del Banco Central de Reserva de El Salvador, 'Normas Técnicas Para Facilitar La Aplicación de La Ley Bitcoin', 17 August 2021, https://www.bcr.gob.sv/regulaciones/upload/Normas_Tecnicas_para_Facilitar_la_Aplicacion_de_la_Ley_Bitcoin.pdf.

Currency creation is a matter of government monopoly, a crucial point. Legal tender was established for economic systems that rely on financial intermediation, and the monetary authority ensures that the currency can function as a unit of account, store of value, and means of payment, guaranteeing its value and ensuring creditors. The state, the most crucial creditor in the tax system, is thus linked to public finances and monetary sovereignty, and they are two sides of the same coin.

The monetary experiment in El Salvador demonstrates how DLT and blockchain technology can potentially lead to a revision of the economic-legal framework of money, despite any concerns surrounding its reasoning and implementation.[33] From a theoretical perspective, it is essential to note that empirical research data on the macro-drivers of crypto-assets has yet to be definitive. The current understanding is that crypto-assets are not commonly used as a medium of exchange, particularly when compared with alternatives to Bitcoin. Instead, they are often perceived as a risk asset with investment potential.[34] The latter is the most relevant crypto-asset feature when considering where and why transactions occur.[35] Crypto-assets are a preferred store of value due to their ability to reach people without intermediaries and ease of storage, transport, and access. This is particularly evident in the survival story of individuals living under the threat of harm from their families, communities, or repressive governments.[36] The analysis of empirical data on digital currencies finds counterevidence in the analysis of coins based on DLT but issued by governments directly or through central banks. Reference is made to the issuance of a cryptocurrency by the Marshall Islands and digital currency by CBoB, the sand dollar. The former attempt was, however, nipped in the bud, while the latter is still ongoing.

12.1.2 The need for digital currency issued by a central bank to be recognised as legal tender

Unlike Bitcoin in El Salvador, we are not under a mandated legal tender. However, in the case of the Marshall Islands, there is a partial overlap with the Salvadoran legal framework, with the national currency being added as legal tender to the US dollar, although the Marshall Islands has no monetary

33 'El Salvador's Experiment with Bitcoin as Legal Tender', NBER, accessed 8 October 2022, https://www.nber.org/digest/202207/el-salvadors-experiment-bitcoin-legal-tender.

34 Erik HB Feyen, Yusaku Kawashima, and Raunak Mittal, *Crypto-Assets Activity around the World: Evolution and Macro-Financial Drivers*, Policy Research Working Papers (The World Bank, 2022), https://doi.org/10.1596/1813-9450-9962.

35 Clemens Graf von Luckne, Carmen M Reinhart, and Kenneth S Rogoff, 'Decrypting New Age International Capital Flows' (NBER Working Paper Series, October 2021), http://www.nber.org/papers/w29337.

36 'SEC.Gov | Paper, Plastic, Peer-to-Peer', accessed 8 October 2022, https://www.sec.gov/news/speech/peirce-paper-plastic-peer-to-peer-031521.

authority. It may explain why the parliament of the island republic approved an act on 'sovereign currency' (named as 'SOV') to be issued as decentralised, being based on blockchain technology,[37] via an initial currency offering,[38] by the Ministry of Finance[39] in a sale of 24 mln units.[40] However, SOV features are mixed between those that are properly of a legal tender currency (for 'all debts, public charges, taxes, and dues'[41] and a 'non-redeemable'[42] nature) and those that are securities or financial instruments. It emerged by the involvement of the provisions of the Marshallese Banking Act as well as digital currency exchange regarding AML and the proxy to the Ministry of Finance to promulgate regulations to guarantee the monitoring of the ICO process and SOV trading.[43] And even more, from the reserved destination to predefined fund trusts, to serve national targeted needs,[44] also counting on the 40 per cent offering exclusively for non-Marshallese citizens.[45] As stated in the SOV Foundation whitepaper, the Marshallese government views the issuance of SOV as serving a political economy purpose rather than solely monetary.[46] Operating a small country's central banking and financial market regulatory frameworks can be costly due to administrative requirements. The SOV whitepaper explains that blockchain technology can govern a monetary measure, with an algorithmic protocol setting its yearly growth at 4 per cent. This allows for adopting a 'State' legal tender currency linked to the national economy.[47] The IMF has repeatedly warned the small island republic of the risks of such a project. In particular, according to the IMF, SOV would raise risks to macroeconomic and financial stability as well as financial integrity.[48]

37 Republic of the Marshall Islands, 'Declaration and Issuance of the Sovereign Currency Act 2018', Pub. L. No. 125ND2 P.L. 2018-53 (2018), para. 102, https://sov.foundation/law.pdf.
38 Ibidem, para. 104 (4).
39 Ibidem, para. 103 (a).
40 Ibidem, para. 105 (2).
41 Ibidem, para. 104 (1).
42 Ibidem, para. 104 (5).
43 Ibidem, para. 110 (2).
44 Such as budget and other national causes, mitigation of damages caused by global warming and climate change, protection of the fisheries and marine resources to ensure sustainable harvesting of tuna and other specialities in the territorial waters, implementation of solar and other renewable energy facilities to reach 100 per cent sustainable energy resources, management and recycling of waste, investment into ecotourism projects, special needs of the people as a consequence of the US Nuclear Test Program, and distribution of SOV to Marshallese residents-citizens.
45 Declaration and Issuance of the Sovereign Currency Act 2018, para. 106.
46 SOV Foundation, 'The Marshallese Sovereign (SOV): Fair, Sustainable, Money', 10 September 2019, https://perma.cc/XX2Y-MZ4X.
47 SOV Foundation, 20.
48 'IMF Executive Board Concludes 2021 Article IV Consultation with the Republic of the Marshall Islands', IMF, accessed 9 October 2022, https://www.imf.org/en/News/Articles

Moreover, the SOV issuance could jeopardise the country's last US corresponding banking relationship with First Hawaiian Bank, exacerbating the Republic of Marshall Island's access to global financial networks.[49] Regardless of which theory of money is invoked, whether it be the state theory as discussed in Annex A of the SOV whitepaper, the institutional theory, the functional theory, or even the modern theory of money, it is essential to remember that

> issuing, managing and sustainably maintaining a cryptoasset designated as legal tender is a complex endeavour and requires important prerequisites such as an adequate legal and regulatory framework, sufficient capacity to supervise and regulate the SOV as well as the security of the underlying system and a viable digital infrastructure.[50]

Moreover, we cannot ignore what is stated in the SOV whitepaper regarding international law. It claims legitimacy for an independent nation to exercise sovereignty and issue its own currency.[51] Is it possible to create a decentralised monetary authority that does not rely on a central bank? This would align with Knapp's state or chartalist money theory, which advocates for a legal tender monopoly. Despite the possibility of the US dollar and SOV coexisting under the state theory of money, another crucial consideration is specific to the Marshallese crypto-asset, which remains untested. While the coexistence of legal tender currencies may be economically justifiable, we cannot overlook the significance of money's 'social technology' aspect—its adoption beyond the formal legal system.

The Bahamian central bank's issuance of the sand dollar provides an opportunity to test the significance of a government-issued digital currency being embraced by its own populace. The sand dollar digital currency is distinct from those of El Salvador and the Marshall Islands because a state central bank issues it. Citizens of the Bahamas can use traditional paper and digital currencies made possible by blockchain technology. This is all done under a standard monetary policy. Although the sand dollar has been available since 2000, and the government has released all the needed regulatory rules to embrace the new potential of a CBDC, it makes up less than 0.1% of the currency in circulation, being still limited avenues to use it even if the Bahamas central bank already completed the initial integration of the sand dollar with the Automated

/2021/05/27/pr21142-marshall-islands-imf-executive-board-concludes-2021-article-iv-consultation.

49 Sonja Davidovic, 'The Marshall Islands SOV Deconstructed', *The Global Fintech Intelligencer* (blog), 8 June 2021, https://theglobalfintechintelligencer.com/2021/06/08/the-marshall-islands-sov-deconstructed/.

50 Davidovic.

51 SOV Foundation, 'The Marshallese Sovereign (SOV): Fair, Sustainable, Money', 22.

Clearing House system.[52] Around the same time the IMF published its Article IV Consultation, the Bahamas government issued a policy white paper regarding the future of digital assets in the Bahamas. Para. 7 is concerned about the 'Bahamian's Access to Digital Assets.' It is a short paragraph, but it is interesting—in the aims of this chapter—with the following statement:

> We will work with the SCB,[53] CBoB, and the private sector on ways to enable Bahamians to access digital assets with B$, and for Bahamians to pay taxes using Sand Dollars. We will also seek to promote wider use of Sand Dollars in commerce on the islands.[54]

Even CBDCs remind us that of the three defining functions of money, only one is steadily in the hands of the government: a unit of account. The unit-of-account function remains the way to guarantee the nominal value of a currency for paying taxes and ensure its legal tender role.[55] It is worth considering the potential of CBDCs to fulfil all the functions associated with traditional currencies. One could speculate whether the emergence of various payment instruments as stores of value and mediums of exchange is a reaction against the government monopoly on money. If this is the case, it begs the question of why there has been such a proliferation of payment options. Perhaps we should examine how these instruments are produced and the underlying reasons for their production.

12.2 The role of digital currency in shaping a new banking and payment system

Consider CBDCs: there are two primary models for their design, token-based and account-based models. If the token-based model gains prevalence over the account-based model, it would result in the reintegration of all three functions of public money. How should this choice affect the financial system, namely the banking sector? What would be the impact on the institutional framework addressing the monetary policy? Will the proliferation of new shapes of digital money affect geopolitics and lead us to a reform of the international monetary

52 *The Bahamas: 2022 Article IV Consultation-Press Release; Staff Report; and Statement by the Executive Director for The Bahamas* (International Monetary Fund, 2022), para. 27, https://www.imf.org/en/Publications/CR/Issues/2022/05/06/The-Bahamas-2022-Article-IV-Consultation-Press-Release-Staff-Report-and-Statement-by-the-517631. For updated data see The Central Bank of The Bahamas, 'Press Release: Public Update on The Bahamas Digital Currency Sand Dollar', accessed 23 July 2023, https://www.centralbankbahamas.com/news/press-releases/press-release-public-update-on-the-bahamas-digital-currency-sanddollar-3.

53 The Securities Commission of the Bahamas.

54 'The Future of Digital Assets in The Bahamas - Office of the Prime Minister', 20 April 2022, https://opm.gov.bs/the-future-of-digital-assets/.

55 Co-Pierre Georg and Katharina Pistor, 'The Right Response to the Libra Threat', Project Syndicate, 5 August 2019, perma.cc/3WJW-FJ4K.

system? Finally, would it mean the end of fiat currencies? Answering these questions is not easy because they are predictions. It brings further difficulty that underlies the analysis method typical of economic law. Namely, it should first establish the overall design on which the future monetary system will be permeated. The design aims to determine if there is a viable legal framework for supporting economic systems that are not tied to monetary policy.

The temptation could be to nationalise the 'production' of money that now is in the power of the banks: 'banks would become only brokers of money they have on deposit, not creators of money, as is the case now.'[56] If, as a study of the US financial system has shown, CBDCs can replace a significant portion of outstanding bank deposits, they appear to have no impact on the cost of credit due to the credit system's ability to raise capital in wholesale markets.[57] Implementing CBDCs can impact banks in terms of operations and business models. The design of CBDCs is closely tied to the lending function of banks, which could affect the universal bank model. However, before implementing CBDCs, a legal issue regarding the definition of banking at the EU level must be addressed. A second aspect concerns the governance of money. While promoting the production of money can help regulate liquidity, it is worth considering the evolving structure of the payment system. Digital currencies allow for the adoption of new forms of payment and new kinds of money, such as stablecoins. There has been some progress in resolving a regulatory issue related to asset-referenced tokens in the MiCA system in Europe. The market for stablecoins is currently uncertain and may be shaped by regulations from other jurisdictions.

Additionally, the design model for CBDCs will impact the monetary policy framework and the authority responsible for it. While discussing central bank governance, it is worth considering the influence of technology on the future of finance. As we shift towards a more digital economy, it is essential to evaluate how technological progress will affect the regulation and governance of central banks. Obtaining non-specific fiat currencies for those residing in a particular jurisdiction is easier. It is important to take into account how this could affect the currency's ability to handle financial emergencies and the global monetary system. The digital dollar's influence may decrease compared with digital currencies, such as the digital euro and digital yuan.[58]

56 Daniel Pinchbeck and Ken Jordan, What Comes After Money? Essays from Reality Sandwich on Transforming Currency & Community (Berkeley, California: Evolver Editions, 2011), 127.

57 Toni M Whited, Yufeng Wu, and Kairong Xiao, 'Central Bank Digital Currency and Banks', *SSRN Electronic Journal*, 2022, 33, https://doi.org/10.2139/ssrn.4112644.

58 'Digital Currencies: The US, China, and the World at a Crossroads' (Stanford, California: Hoover Institution Press, 2022), 55 ff., https://www.hoover.org/research/digital-currencies-us-china-and-world-crossroads.

12.3 The legal dimension of digital monies issued (or not) by a central bank

Although there has been extensive economic issues analysis, more legal studies must be done.[59] One of the first papers concerning the legal aspect of CBDC from an international perspective was published by a group of researchers at the legal department of the IMF in 2020.[60] Their legal analysis is centred on two primary issues. The first issue involves determining if the central bank has the appropriate mandate to issue a digital currency and if it qualifies as legal tender. The second issue pertains to monetary law and the currency system. The first issue is significant as it determines whether digital currency falls under the legal framework of legal tender.

Additionally, there is consideration for creating a separate regulatory regime for CBDCs. When choosing the status of a CBDC, it is essential to consider whether it is a digital version of physical currency with legal tender status or a distinct currency backed by central bank money. These are crucial factors in defining a CBDC nature. It could be helpful to pause and analyse a specific aspect of the present circumstances, which is the foundation of the financial system infrastructure. If a digital currency is created using DLT, the most likely option, the currency is essentially a token dependent on that particular infrastructure. This is a neutral technological decision, as it not only alters the mechanism for circulating currency but also its legally established nature. That is to say that in a fiat monetary system coming from a physical space, such as the current one, dematerialisation serves to perform the tasks required by the needs of a global economy, i.e., to facilitate the exchange of money. Still, the legislator with jurisdiction does not need to define what the paper with which banknotes are minted or the metal alloy that gives life to coins is from a private law perspective. These structures are made of materials and only become legally recognised through fiat acts. The infrastructure is the law. But a DLT or blockchain infrastructure also brings with it rules. It does not need the law to define them. And even if it did, it could escape it.

To sum up, the significant rise of cryptocurrencies since 2009 and stablecoins since the mid-2010s demonstrate that central bank infrastructures must be updated and revised, irrespective of our individual opinions. Although we do not want to go to such an extreme, central banks could also be redundant from an issuing standpoint. It is a point that relates to the issue of 'moneyness'

59 See for more details Toni Ahnert et al., *The Economics of Central Bank Digital Currency* (Frankfurt am Main: European Central Bank, 2022); Ratikant Bhaskar et al., 'Central Bank Digital Currencies: Agendas for Future Research', *Research in International Business and Finance* 62 (December 2022): 101737, https://doi.org/10.1016/j.ribaf.2022.101737.

60 Wouter Bossu et al., 'Legal Aspects of Central Bank Digital Currency: Central Bank and Monetary Law Considerations', *IMF*, IMF Working Paper, 20, no. 254 (November 2020), https://www.imf.org/en/Publications/WP/Issues/2020/11/20/Legal-Aspects-of-Central-Bank-Digital-Currency-Central-Bank-and-Monetary-Law-Considerations-49827.

and is still only debated by scholars and central bankers.[61] When it comes to the absence of inherent value in fiat currency, analysing the issue becomes far more complicated with digital currencies on DLT. Does the form of currency impact its legal tender status? Legal tender will only be granted to a currency that shares a single technical characteristic with physical money—fiat money issued by a central bank. The additional technical features differentiate it from a traditional cryptocurrency. We would not deal with a physical coin issued on a specific blockchain. However, we would still encounter legal issues similar to those associated with digital currency rather than physical money. Wholesale CBDCs operate similarly to current regulation systems like RTGS. The topic changes significantly in the case of a retail CBDC.

Are these distinct types of public funds, or are they the same? An excellent example of focusing better on the point is what happens to Scotland's banknotes. The Scottish pound is also issued by commercial banks but is fully backed by the BoE. However, in the case of a digital Scottish pound, it would be different from what it is now. The difference between public and private money may vary in terms of their digital representation using tokens based on DLT technology. They enable us to go beyond simply digitising money (like with e-money) and push the boundaries towards removing its ties to a specific government or authority. The edge in Europe can be traced back to the first interaction between sovereign and bankers' money during the 16th century.[62] The unique features of DLT are challenging the validity of the current system. With the ability to establish robust networks that can be enforced at a jurisdictional level, DLT raises questions about the effectiveness of the existing system. DLT, especially blockchains, tend to eliminate central control, which leads to a shift in the boundary between public and private money. This has a range of structural effects.

The idea behind stablecoins can be traced back to reasons that extend beyond the common goal of improving financial inclusion. Stablecoins act as a connection point between the conventional finance system and decentralised finance. At this stage, their pseudo-crypto structure makes them an ideal payment system for those looking for a disintermediated payment system. The story of Libra/Diem and the Terra-Luna crash demonstrates the challenges of ensuring currency stability in a centralised monetary system, even with fiat collateral. In monetary contexts, the effects that can occur are often complex and systemic. Rules are in place to balance the protection of constitutional interests rather than just monetary objectives. Although the balance may vary based on different legal systems, the overall synthesis relies on the monetary system established by the Bretton Woods agreements.

61 See for a definition and analysis Simon Gleeson, *The Legal Concept of Money*, First edition (Oxford: Oxford University Press, 2018), 7, 8, and 50.

62 Marie-Thérèse Boyer-Xambeu, Ghislain Deleplace, and Lucien Gillard, *Private Money & Public Currencies: The 16th Century Challenge* (Armonk, NY: ME Sharpe, 1994).

The key to interpreting this becomes clear when considering the dual nature of economic law institutions. The operativity of digital currencies has a private law dimension that determines whether they can evade regulatory control. For example, privacy comes to mind. On the contrary, the ubiquity feature of blockchain infrastructure can significantly reduce the role of the intermediated financial system. Consequently, as the power of individual central banks decreases, so does their ability to effectively manage the monetary system and achieve their monetary policy goals. Central banks and the BIS have thoroughly analysed these factors and initiated studies and pilot projects before introducing CBDCs. There needs to be more consideration given to how implementing a CBDC will impact the use of public money as legal tender. Instead, the focus is on whether the legal system needs to be modified to accommodate a digital currency. However, this issue extends beyond its theoretical and nominal significance.

12.4 Some final considerations

Since fiat currency introduction, legal tender has always been associated with physical cash. However, it is commonly accepted that legal tender can also refer to deposits. It is essential for any digital solution meant for the public to take this issue seriously. Money is a crucial public good, as it ensures the certainty of economic transactions through its related economic and legal function as a unit of account. The transfer of legal tender currency, both as paper money issued by central banks and by commercial banks' private money, is a piece of note of the legal system to guarantee the transfer of value. Electronic payment systems have recently made it possible to settle financial obligations without physically tendering currency. This has become a common practice.[63] As DLT evolves, it will likely replace physical cash and even transform how we view demand deposits. This innovation has the potential to revolutionise the payment system. In the meantime, there may be two separate popes, each with their own unique characteristics. This applies to their use as a currency (with a focus on privacy) and their effects on the banking system, followed by the monetary system.

Cash is primarily managed through the banking system and various payment systems. However, with the issuance of a CBDC, the circulation of currencies beyond national boundaries will become more effortless. As a result, there will be increased competition between payment methods, including legal tender digital coins issued by central banks and stablecoins, which will

63 Kazuaki Sono, 'Legal Tender: A Notion Associated with Payment', in *Current Developments in Monetary and Financial Law, Vol. 2* (International Monetary Fund, 2003), 679 ff., https://doi.org/10.5089/9781589061767.072. On this specific point see also Vincenzo De Stasio, 'Verso un concetto europeo di moneta legale: valute virtuali, monete complementari e regole di adempimento', *Banca, Borsa e Titoli Di Credito* 6 (2018): 749 ff., 747-761.

likely play a significant role. This will necessitate integrating payment systems to facilitate the smooth transfer of funds between different currencies and payment methods.[64]

Central banks typically address many issues (especially at the BIS level), which are now being reconsidered due to the increasing likelihood of CBDCs becoming a reality. Based on the limited use cases analysed, it is essential to consider that even if CBDCs become legal tender, consumers may use them infrequently due to concerns about privacy and surveillance. Cash may still be preferred for these reasons. Let us return to the initial idea that money is not just another public good. Users' trust and confidence must be maintained regarding public money. Encouraging confidence and enhancing marketability is crucial. This involves market factors and creating a network of merchants who accept and promote CBDC usage, achieving interoperability with and enlisting participation from the traditional banking sector. However, the main challenge lies in redefining the role of public powers in effectively controlling the liquidity and soundness of a 'national' economic system. It is not a coincidence that the discussion around the issuance of CBDC has prompted countries to revisit their regulations on the authority to issue money as legal tender. Issuing a digital currency as legal tender involves analysing its private law aspects and its relationship to traditional legal tender and monetary law. The analysis also considers the elements of public and international law, closely connected to the earlier mentioned progressive desovereignisation. The introduction of CBDC would provide a legal tender-based cross-border payment option, simplifying the process of retaining funds in incoming foreign legal tender currency.[65] Establishing statutory restrictions on the use of digital legal tender could turn out to be a viable strategy. This approach could be especially impactful in poverty relief and public assistance projects. Issuing it would go against the intended process and ultimately result in it being seen more as a payment option rather than significantly impacting monetary policy.

It would be insightful to examine the progress made by economically advanced countries in developing their CBDC projects, particularly that of the e-CYN. It has come to our attention that the draft amendment of the law on the PBoC extends legal tender recognition to the e-CYN. Furthermore, a provision in the civil code has been enforced, starting in 2021, which states that 'where an obligation is the payment of money unless otherwise provided by

64 This is especially so if a decentralised financial ecosystem (DeFi) is developed. Moreover, what is happening in the payment system is emblematic of the changing needs and objectives of economic policy in the EU. The announcement of a European sovereign wealth fund can no longer be read in terms of cooperative regulation or regulatory competition. Still, a single public policy and policy design sounded on resilience. It is to wonder if monetary policy would be neutral in the long term.

65 FinTech Department, 'Concept Note on Central Bank Digital Currency' (Reserve Bank of India, October 2022), 14, https://rbidocs.rbi.org.in/rdocs/PublicationReport/Pdfs/CONCEPTNOTEACB531172E0B4DFC9A6E506C2C24FFB6.PDF.

law or agreed by the parties, the creditor may request the debtor to perform in the legal tender of the place of actual performance.'[66] When the codified rule is read alongside the one that pertains solely to the renminbi and its digital counterpart, it may seem to contradict the idea of monetary sovereignty. However, in practice, this acknowledges the impact of a digital currency recognised as legal tender on matters related to solvency law. Maintaining the legal value of money is vital in ensuring the smooth operation of a multi-level monetary payment system centred around the national currency. However, the provision in question does not seem like the '*datio in solutum*' concept, as it applies explicitly to transactions crossing international borders. To guarantee the '*best choice status*' of the national currency or the '*finality*' of the settlement of debts, the state can use market instruments to improve its own currency management in an environment that allows competition from other currencies, or it can use compulsory legal tools to make the national currency legally solvent. It is worth noting that Art. 65 of the PBoC gives the Chinese central bank the authority to stop the production and circulation of digital tokens that are not the digital renminbi. If such tokens are produced or sold, the central bank can order them to be destroyed, confiscate any illegal profits, and impose a fine for unlawful activity.[67] Therefore, legal tender is interpreted as a function of a modern payment system but does not go so far as to recognise all the possible issuance of tokens linked to legal tender.

Until now, the US and UK did not view the creation of CBDCs as essential. They understood the libertarian implications but underestimated the importance of monetary sovereignty. As a result, EU countries are considering issuing a digital euro, and the proposed regulation for its legal tender is the first step to face. Legal scholars and national policymakers play an essential role in ensuring the stability of the international monetary system in the face of CBDC concerns. If we collaborate and tackle these concerns, we can prevent CBDCs from becoming dangerous. Instead, they could serve as a chance to establish a stable overhaul of a future digital monetary system.

66 'Civil Code of the People's Republic of China' (2020), art. 514, http://www.npc.gov.cn/englishnpc/c23934/202012/f627aa3a4651475db936899d69419d1e/files/47c16489e186437eab3244495cb47d66.pdf.

67 It does not exceed five times the illegal amount; if the illegal amount cannot be determined, a fine of not less than 100,000 yuan but not exceeding 500,000 yuan shall be imposed. If the circumstances are serious, a penalty shall be imposed in accordance with the provisions of Article 61(2) of the Law on the People's Bank of China.

13 A European Central Bank Digital Currency under German Law[1]

Sebastian Omlor and Aurelia Birne

13.1 Status quo

The debate on CBDCs in the euro area and many other jurisdictions is moving forward.[2] Fundamental legal issues arise with the potential introduction of a new and, above all, digital form of money. For this reason, the German legal framework for a digital euro will be examined in this section, focusing on currency and monetary law and general provisions of civil law and payment services.

13.1.1 Access types to CBDC

Regarding the concrete implementation of CBDC, the scope of accessibility of a digital form of currency is particularly important regarding its legal, commercial, and social effects. The decision on which legal persons will have access to a digital euro is strongly linked to potential impacts on the financial system and risks for users. For instance, concerns are raised that the introduction of CBDC will lead to the gradual abolition of cash and, consequently, to the impossibility of anonymous payments.[3] Economists also see the danger

1 It should be noted that this chapter was made available for publishing prior to the approval of the draft of the 'Regulation of the European Parliament and of the Council on the establishment of the digital euro' by the European Commission. Nevertheless, the Authors' insights on this particular issue addressed in the text still hold relevance and significance.

2 According to a survey by the Bank for International Settlements, the majority of the 63 central banks surveyed are looking into the potential impact of digital central bank money. See, Christian Barontini and Henry Holden, *Proceeding with Caution: A Survey on Central Bank Digital Currency*, BIS Papers, No 101 (Basel: Bank for International Settlements, 2019). Concerning the digital euro, see *Towards a Legislative Framework for a Digital Euro* (Brussels, 2022), https://www.ecb.europa.eu/pub/conferences/html/20221107_joint_ECB_EUC_conference.en.html.

3 Maximilian Foster et al., 'Digitaler Euro auf der Blockchain' (bitkom, 2020), https://www.bitkom.org/sites/default/files/2020-04/200423_infopapier_digitaler-euro-auf-der-blockchain.pdf. Emphasises that the digital euro cannot fully replace cash with all its functionalities: Deutsche Bundesbank, 'Monatsbericht: Chancen und Risiken von digitalem Geld', April 2021, https://www.bundesbank.de/de/aufgaben/themen/monatsbericht-chancen-und-risiken-von-digitalem-geld-826314.

DOI: 10.4324/9781003258261-17

of 'bank runs,' in which many customers of commercial banks transfer their money to central bank accounts within a short period, thus triggering a liquidity crisis for commercial banks.[4] By withdrawing deposits, banks would have to refinance themselves via the capital market, and a disintermediation of the banking sector could occur.[5] This implementation debate discusses two conceivable access models to digital central bank money. These two access models describe digital currency issuance as wholesale CBDC or retail CBDC.[6]

13.1.1.1 Wholesale CBDC

A digital currency issued as wholesale CBDC would only be accessible for commercial banks and is therefore designed as currency for interbank and securities trading. Consequently, consumers and non-banks would be excluded from

4 Federal Association of German Banks, 'Europas Antwort auf Libra', 17 June 2020, https://bankenverband.de/themen/europas-antwort-libra/.

5 See, Bank of Canada et al., 'Central Bank Digital Currencies: Foundational Principles and Core Features Report No. 1 in a Series of Collaborations from a Group of Central Banks', 2020, https://www.bis.org/publ/othp33.pdf; Federal Association of German Banks, 'Europas Antwort auf Libra'; Ulrich Bindseil, 'Tiered CBDC and the Financial System', *ECB Working Paper Series* No 2351 (January 2020): 8 ff.; Manuel Klein, Jonas Groß, and Philipp Sandner, 'Der digitale Blockchain-Euro: Sind Central Bank Digital Currencies die Zukunft?', *ifo Schnelldienst* 73, no. 3 (2020): 44.

6 Bank of Canada et al., 'Central Bank Digital Currencies'; FinTechRat beim Bundesministerium der Finanzen, 'Der digitale, programmierbare Euro', January 2020, 8 ff., https://annaelbe.net/bilder_datenschutz/200708-fintechrat-digitaler-euro.pdf; European Union Blockchain Observatory & Forum, 'Central Bank Digital Currencies and a Euro for the Future', June 2021, 7, https://www.eublockchainforum.eu/sites/default/files/reports/CBDC%20Report%20Final.pdf; Wouter Bossu et al., 'Legal Aspects of Central Bank Digital Currency: Central Bank and Monetary Law Considerations', *IMF*, IMF Working Paper, 20, no. 254 (November 2020): 9 ff., https://www.imf.org/en/Publications/WP/Issues/2020/11/20/Legal-Aspects-of-Central-Bank-Digital-Currency-Central-Bank-and-Monetary-Law-Considerations-49827; Tony Richards, Chris Thompson, and Cameron Dark, 'Retail Central Bank Digital Currency: Design Considerations, Rationales and Implications', September 2020, 31–32; Sebastian Omlor, 'Blockchain-Basierte Zahlungsmittel Im Geld- Und Währungsrecht', in *Fin-Tech-Handbuch: Digitalisierung, Recht, Finanzen*, ed. Florian Möslein and Sebastian Omlor (Munich: CH Beck, 2nd ed. 2021), para. 33; Sebastian Omlor, Mathias Link, and Lutz Auffenberg, eds., *Kryptowährungen Und Token*, Recht, Wirtschaft, Steuern. Handbuch (Frankfurt am Main: Fachmedien Recht und Wirtschaft, dfv Mediengruppe, 2nd ed. 2023), chap. 9; Foster et al., 'Digitaler Euro auf der Blockchain', 8; Sebastian Omlor and Aurelia Birne, 'Digitales Zentralbankgeld im Euroraum', *Recht Digital* 1 (20 November 2020): 2 ff.; Cornelia Manger-Nestler, 'Digitales Zentralbankgeld aus währungsrechtlicher Sicht', *Recht der Zahlungsdienste* 2, no. 1 (2021): 5; 'Der digitale Blockchain-Euro: Sind Central Bank Digital Currencies die Zukunft?', 43; Benoît Cœuré and Jacqueline Loh, 'Central Bank Digital Currencies' (BIS, March 2018), 7 ff.; Aurelia Birne, Mirjam Eggen and Christian Sillaber, 'Prinzipien zur Übertragung von Retail CBDC', *Recht Digital* 6 (6 June 2022): 3 ff., English version: https://dx.doi.org/10.2139/ssrn.4303955; for cross-border payments with Wholesale or Retail CBDC see Sebastian Omlor and Aurelia Birne, 'Digitales Zentralbankgeld im Grenzüberschreitenden Zahlungsverkehr', *Zeitschrift für Wirtschaftsrecht* 2022, 1785; Aurelia Birne, Das Allgemeine Privatrecht der Blockchain-Token, 2023, 209 ff.

using a digital euro.[7] The aim is to promote cross-border payments between financial institutions and the settlement of securities transactions. By introducing wholesale CBDC, the existing two-tier monetary system would be maintained while establishing a more efficient interbank payment system.[8] For example, the Association of German Banks calls for the digital euro to be issued only through the central bank issuing to commercial banks.[9]

13.1.1.2 Retail CBDC

In the case of retail CBDC, consumers and non-banks should have access to CBDC directly, indirectly, or hybridly.[10] It would be used for payment alongside cash and deposit money.[11] The aim is to increase the efficiency of payment transactions and compensate for the decline in cash. In addition, access to risk-free money without dependence on the solvency of a commercial bank would be ensured, as well as competitiveness against privately issued money, for example, cryptocurrencies.[12]

In December 2019, the ECB published a report presenting a retail CBDC model based on DLT.[13] With this approach, the digital euro is to be issued to the public as a means of payment, but through intermediaries with two-tiered interest rates. Instead of directly servicing the digital euro users, the central bank uses intermediaries to provide and manage the CBDC. They process transactions on behalf of their customers and provide them with custodial services. Intermediaries hold users' private keys to initiate payments, as they do not have direct access to the network. The two-fold interest rate is intended to counteract a bank run, or disintermediation of the banking sector, to the extent that large sums of digital euros are not held. The ECB has the exclusive right to issue and redeem the digital euro.

In a report published in October 2020,[14] the ECB fleshed out its vision for a digital euro and presented various design options for a retail CBDC. In contrast to the previous report, the approaches are not focused on a specific tech-

7 See Omlor and Birne, 'Digitales Zentralbankgeld im Euroraum', 2 ff.; Klein, Groß, and Sandner, 'Der digitale Blockchain-Euro: Sind Central Bank Digital Currencies die Zukunft? ', 44.

8 Foster et al., 'Digitaler Euro auf der Blockchain', 8; Klein, Groß, and Sandner, 'Der digitale Blockchain-Euro: Sind Central Bank Digital Currencies die Zukunft? ', 43.

9 Federal Association of German Banks, 'Europas Antwort auf Libra'.

10 Omlor and Birne, 'Digitales Zentralbankgeld im Euroraum', 3 ff.; FinTechRat beim Bundesministerium der Finanzen, 'Der digitale, programmierbare Euro', 10 ff.

11 Detailed at Raphael Auer and Rainer Boehme, 'The Technology of Retail Central Bank Digital Currency', 2020, 86 ff.; Richards, Thompson, and Dark, 'Retail Central Bank Digital Currency: Design Considerations, Rationales and Implications', 32.

12 Foster et al., 'Digitaler Euro auf der Blockchain', 8.

13 ECB, 'Exploring Anonymity in Central Bank Digital Currencies', *In Focus* Issue no 4 (December 2019).

14 ECB, 'Report on a Digital Euro', October 2020, https://www.ecb.europa.eu/pub/pdf/other/Report_on_a_digital_euro~4d7268b458.en.pdf.

nology and include direct access options for end users. The potential back-end infrastructure of the digital euro assumes that the responsibility for issuing and managing a digital euro remains with the Eurosystem.[15] Concerning this back-end infrastructure, a distinction is made between a centralised and a decentralised system.[16] In a centralised system, all transactions are recorded via a Eurosystem infrastructure provided by the central bank. The central bank would issue the digital euro and execute the transactions via its own infrastructure. Users hold their own accounts directly with the central bank and can initiate payments. Either the user gets complete and direct access to this account, or intermediaries step in as custodians. In contrast, with a decentralised infrastructure, users or intermediaries would verify the transactions themselves. In this case, the central bank would have to set technical standards for verification to guarantee a certain level of security.

In addition to the design features of the back-end infrastructure, end-user access solutions to the central bank's infrastructure are discussed.[17] A concrete access solution strongly depends on the chosen Eurosystem's infrastructure and, thus, on whether the user is granted intermediary or direct access to the digital euro. Access to euro services can be enabled either via hardware or software applications. Both require strong customer authentication and identification. In any case, the ECB must integrate various end-user access solutions to allow wide accessibility. Whether DLT will be used for the infrastructure of a digital euro has not been decided yet. Decentralised and centralised technologies are part of the testing phase of the Eurosystem for the issuance of CBDC.[18]

In July 2021, the Eurosystem introduced the investigation phase of its digital euro project, including the clarification of design options and distribution issues for a Retail CBDC.[19] In October 2023, the ECB announced the start of a two years preparation phase of the digital euro project, following the completion of the investigation phase and including the finalization of the digital euro rulebook.[20] The ECB has, however, clarified that the preparation phase is no final decision on the issuance of a digital euro.

The European Commission's Proposal for a Regulation of the European Parliament and of the Council on the establishment of the digital euro published in June 2023[21] also provides rules for a retail CBDC with the status of

15 ECB, 36.

16 ECB, 37.

17 ECB, 41.

18 ECB, 'FAQs on the Digital Euro', 14 April 2021, no. 4, https://www.ecb.europa.eu/paym/digital_euro/faqs/html/ecb.faq_digital_euro.en.html.

19 ECB, no. 8.

20 ECB Press Release, Eurosystem proceeds to next phase of digital euro project, 18 October 2023.

21 European Commission's Proposal for a Regulation of the European Parliament and of the Council on the establishment of the digital euro, Brussels, 28.6.2023, COM(2023) 369 final;

legal tender, issued by the ECB and managed by payment service providers offering digital euro payment services for the access, use and transfer of the currency units.

13.2 The legal nature of CBDC under German law

The issue of CBDC, its legal nature, and applicable private law standards are in question, especially with a focus on currency law and monetary law, as well as on general civil law provisions and the law on payment services.

13.2.1 CBDC as a form of currency

The concept of currency defines the scope of a sovereign monetary constitution of a state and ensures a uniform monetary system.[22] The currency thus consists of two components, the abstract and the concrete concept of currency, which form a necessary unit.[23] In the abstract, the currency creates a united monetary system; in the concrete, it reflects the monetary constitution of a State and is thus legitimised and geographically determined. Consequently, a digital euro could only fall under the concept of currency if included in the European Monetary Union Member States' monetary constitution. The monetary body of the European Monetary Union recognises the euro as the sole currency, Art. 3 para. IV TFEU. Art. 128 TFEU provides for issuing euros only as banknotes and coins. These are considered the only legal tender of the Union and establish a legal obligation to accept payment.[24] Therefore, the European monetary constitution must be extended to the issuance of the euro as currency in a digital form.[25]

13.2.2 CBDC as money in a legal sense

The legal nature of the digital euro in terms of private monetary law must be considered concerning the classification of the digital euro as a form of

for details see Sebastian Omlor/Alexander Schneider, 'Der Kommissionsentwurf zur Einführung des digitalen Euros', Zeitschrift für Bank- und Kapitalmarktrecht, 10 (2023): 649.

22 Hugo J Hahn and Ulrich Häde, *Währungsrecht*, 2., vollst. überarb. Aufl (Munich: Beck, 2010) § 2 para. 2; Omlor, 'Blockchain-Basierte Zahlungsmittel Im Geld- Und Währungsrecht'§ 33 para. 12; 'Kryptowährungen im Geldrecht', Zeitschrift für das gesamte Handels- und Wirtschaftsrecht, 183, no. 2–03 (2019): 307.

23 Sebastian Omlor, *Geldprivatrecht: Entmaterialisierung, Europäisierung, Entwertung*, Jus privatum 184 (Tübingen: Mohr Siebeck, 2014); 'Geld und Währung als Digitalisate', *JuristenZeitung* 72, no. 15–16 (2017): 758 ff., https://doi.org/10.1628/002268817X14990888646265; Alexandra Spiegel, *Blockchain-basiertes virtuelles Geld* (Mohr Siebeck, 2020), 49, https://doi.org/10.1628/978-3-16-159396-3.

24 Stefan Grundmann, 'Comment on BGB § 245', in *Münchener Kommentar zum Bürgerlichen Gesetzbuch*, ed. Franz Jürgen Säcker et al., 9. Auflage (Munich: CH Beck, 2022), para. 50.

25 Omlor and Birne, 'Digitales Zentralbankgeld im Euroraum', 5 ff.

currency. Classification as money within the meaning of German civil law is an essential prerequisite for applying monetary private law standards.[26] This is because monetary debts within the purpose of the private law provisions will be fulfilled with such means of payment that qualify as money within the meaning of the German Civil Code.[27] The qualification as money in the legal sense, therefore, opens up the scope of application of private monetary law norms of the general part of the German Civil Code, the law on monetary debts or property law regulations relating to money. Numerous provisions of the German Civil Code use the concept of money or require a monetary debt as the object of performance. Therefore, if the digital euro were to fall under the concept of money under the German Civil Code, private money law standards would apply. In this context, it is therefore questionable which prerequisites a means of payment must fulfil to fall under the legal concept of money. In the absence of a uniform legal definition of money in a legal sense,[28] a two-tier concept of money in a legal sense has developed, consisting of both an abstract and a concrete idea of money.[29]

13.2.2.1 Concrete concept of money

The concrete concept of money refers to cash.[30] Therefore, the prerequisites for classification as money in the concrete sense are its recognition as legal tender, its general recognition as a medium of exchange, and its embodiment.[31] In the euro area, banknotes denominated in euros are the only unrestricted legal tender, see Art. 128 para. I sentence 3 TFEU.[32] However, mainly retail

26 See for use cases of the concept of money: Sebastian Omlor, 'Comment on §§ 244-248 BGB', in *J von Staudingers Kommentar zum Bürgerlichen Gesetzbuch mit Einführungsgesetz und Nebengesetzen*, by Julius von Staudinger, Sebastian Omlor, and Volker Rieble, Neubearbeitung 2021 (Berlin: Otto Schmidt - de Gruyter, 2021), paras A93, B2 ff.

27 Cf. Christian Berger, 'Comment on §§ 244, 245 BGB', in *Bürgerliches Gesetzbuch: Mit Rom-I-VO, Rom-II-VO, Rom-III-VO, EG-UnthVO/HUntProt Und EuErbVO: Kommentar*, ed. Germany, Rolf Stürner, and Christian Berger, 19. Auflage (Munich: CH Beck, 2023), para. 1 ff.

28 Omlor, 'Comment on §§ 244-248 BGB', para. A32 ff.; *Geldprivatrecht*, 96; Dietrich Schefold, 'Fremdwährungsschuld', in *Bankrechts-Handbuch*, ed. Jürgen Ellenberger und Hermann-Josef Bunte, 6. Auflage (Munich: CH Beck, 2022), § 98 para. 15, 16. Robert Freitag, 'Comment on § 244 BGB', in beck-online.Grosskommentar BGB, eds. Beate Gsell et al. (Munich: CH Beck, 15.03.2021), para. 11. See for the European Union: Robert Freitag and Sebastian Omlor, eds., *The Euro as Legal Tender: A Comparative Approach to a Uniform Concept* (De Gruyter, 2020), https://doi.org/10.1515/9783110640717.

29 See for more details Omlor, *Geldprivatrecht*, 96; 'Comment on §§ 244-248 BGB', para. A65 ff.

30 Omlor, *Geldprivatrecht*, 100; 'Comment on §§ 244-248 BGB', para. A65 ff.

31 Omlor, *Geldprivatrecht*, 100 ff.

32 Michael Rodi, 'Comment on Art. 128 TFEU', in *Europäisches Unionsrecht: EUV, AEUV, GRCh, EAGV: Handkommentar: Mit Den Vollständigen Texten Der Protokolle Und Erklärungen*, ed. Christoph Wilhelm Vedder and Wolff Heintschel von Heinegg, 2. Auflage (Baden-

CBDC could be recognised as legal tender under European law. First, it should be noted that no provision in the TFEU or the ESCB/ECB Statute can be identified that would explicitly exclude the issuance of any form of currency other than embodied euro banknotes as legal tender.[33] Art. 128 TFEU, in conjunction with Art. 16 ESCB/ECB Statute, could serve as the appropriate legal basis for the issuance of CBDC.[34] This is because the right to issue euro banknotes also implies the right to determine the format of euro banknotes, including a digital form.[35] The ECB believes that recognising the digital euro as a legal tender is desirable; otherwise, it would be accepted as a conventional electronic means of payment.[36] Therefore, in line with the ECB's assessments, a primary law amendment would not be necessary due to an existing legal basis for issuing a digital euro as legal tender.[37] Notwithstanding, an addition of Art. 128 TFEU by a third paragraph or adding to the statute's text would guarantee legal clarity.[38]

Indeed, European secondary law on legal tender is limited to embodied monetary instruments, which do not include the euro in a digital form.[39] To establish a digital euro as legal tender, at least Regulation (EC) No 974/98 on introducing the euro would have to be amended in this respect, and according to the ECB's view, based on Art. 133 TFEU, a secondary law that lays down the conditions for issuing a digital euro as legal tender could be adopted.[40] Therefore, CBDC has to be recognised as legal tender under European law[41] and could thus fulfil the first requirement of the concrete concept of money. General

Baden: Vienna: Nomos: Facultas, 2018), para. 6; Helmut Siekmann, 'Comment on Art. 88 GG', in *Grundgesetz: Kommentar*, ed. Michael Sachs, Ulrich Battis, and Germany, Grundgesetz. Kommentar, 9. Auflage (Munich: CH Beck, 2021), para. 97a.

33 ECB, 'Report on a Digital Euro', 25; Omlor and Birne, 'Digitales Zentralbankgeld im Euroraum', 4.

34 The European Central Bank refers to some potential legal competence norms: ECB, 'Report on a Digital Euro', 25.

35 ECB, 25; Omlor and Birne, 'Digitales Zentralbankgeld im Euroraum', 4; Corinne Zellweger-Gutknecht, Benjamin Geva, and Seraina Neva Grünewald. 'Digital Euro, Monetary Objects, and Price Stability: A Legal Analysis', *Journal of Financial Regulation* 7, no. 2 (1 September 2021): 318 ff., https://doi.org/10.1093/jfr/fjab009.

36 ECB, 'Report on a digital Euro', 33; Omlor, Sebastian, 'Grund Und Grenzen Einer Annahmepflicht von Euro-Bargeld', Europäische Zeitschrift für Wirtschaftsrecht, 32, no. 11 (2021): 485.

37 Omlor, Sebastian, 485; Omlor and Birne, 'Digitales Zentralbankgeld im Euroraum', 5.

38 Omlor, 'Blockchain-Basierte Zahlungsmittel Im Geld- Und Währungsrecht'§ 33 para. 14; Omlor and Birne, 'Digitales Zentralbankgeld im Euroraum', 5.

39 Omlor, 'Blockchain-Basierte Zahlungsmittel Im Geld- Und Währungsrecht'§ 33 para. 13; 'Kryptowährungen im Geldrecht', 338 ff.; Omlor and Birne, 'Digitales Zentralbankgeld im Euroraum', 4 ff.

40 ECB, 'Report on a digital Euro', 24.

41 For a detailed discussion, see Annelieke AM Mooij, 'European Central Bank Digital Currency: The Digital Euro. What Design of the Digital Euro Is Possible within the European Central Bank's Legal Framework?', *SSRN Electronic Journal*, 2021, https://doi.org/10.2139/ssrn.3838729.

recognition as a means of exchange requires the specific means of exchange to be used universally.[42] If the digital euro were recognised as legal tender, it would be used as a universal medium of exchange.[43]

CBDC cannot, however, fulfil the characteristic of embodiment. It is still being determined whether the requirement of embodiment in the traditional sense is still contemporary during the progressive dematerialisation of money. One could think of an extension of the concept of embodiment without adhering to the requirement of a physical extension. An embodiment could also mean the definability of a specific and unique digital unit, which can be allocated to a legal person. The allocation of the digital euro could be ensured via a digital infrastructure.[44] Alternatively, the characteristic of embodiment could be supplemented by non-physical objects. The requirement of embodiment could also be abolished. In this case, the concrete concept of money would only consist of the recognition requirements as legal tender and general means of exchange.[45]

13.2.2.2 Abstract concept of money

On the other hand, the abstract concept of money does not require recognition as legal tender or physical embodiment.[46] However, it does require at least normative recognition in the legal system and its use as a universal medium of exchange with the character of a measure of value.[47] The abstract concept of money is not subject to a sovereign act or a legal obligation to accept it.[48] Based on this definition, cash is to be assigned not only to the concrete but also to the abstract concept of money.[49] The digital euro is likely to fulfil all the characteristics of the abstract concept of money. Its recognition as a sovereign-issued form of money or even as legal tender would go far beyond the required normative legal recognition and constitute its use as a universal medium of exchange.[50] Thus, the digital euro may satisfy the abstract concept of money and is legally characterised as money.[51] Specifically, the digital euro could be subject to two established applications of the abstract concept of money: deposit money or electronic money.

42 Omlor, *Geldprivatrecht*, 102.

43 Omlor and Birne, 'Digitales Zentralbankgeld im Euroraum', 6.

44 Omlor and Birne, 6.

45 Omlor and Birne, 6.

46 For detail, Omlor, *Geldprivatrecht*, 98; 'Comment on §§ 244-248 BGB', para. A66.

47 Omlor, 'Kryptowährungen im Geldrecht', 306; 'Comment on §§ 244-248 BGB', para. A67.

48 Omlor, 'Comment on §§ 244-248 BGB', para. A66.

49 Omlor, Geldprivatrecht, 99; 'Abschied Vom Bargeld? – Überlegungen Aus Geldgeschichtlicher, Währungs- Und Geldprivatrechtlicher Perspektive –', Zeitschrift für Wirtschafts- und Bankrecht, 69, no. 49 (Dezember 2015): 2302.

50 See Sec. 13.3.2.1.

51 Omlor and Birne, 'Digitales Zentralbankgeld im Euroraum', 6.

13.2.2.3 Deposit money

According to the prevailing view, deposit money should be recognised as money in the legal sense.[52] Deposit money is the non-corporeal form of a sum of money that is recorded as credit in a personal account instead of using physical monetary symbols.[53] It is a monetary claim in the form of a credit balance at financial entities and can be used for payment at any time.[54] In the case of the issuance of CBDC, there has to be a claim against an issuer. CBDC would be issued by a central authority, namely the ECB.

Regarding wholesale CBDC, only financial institutions are entitled to maintain an account or wallet with the central bank to use the digital euro. The digital euro could be designed as a liability of the central bank and a claim of the commercial banks. A similar situation applies to retail CBDC with indirect end-user access via intermediaries. In contrast to wholesale CBDC, when issuing direct or hybrid retail CBDC, there must be a direct claim of the end customers against the central bank, which can be asserted either by the end customer himself or via an intermediary. The euro tokens may represent a credit balance that could be used for payment anytime. Under these aspects, CBDC could be qualified as deposit money.[55] Suppose digital central bank money is recognised as legal tender. In that case, it cannot be classified as deposit money in the traditional sense but as an extended version which includes a legal acceptance obligation.[56]

52 Omlor, 'Comment on §§ 244-248 BGB', para. A73; *Geldprivatrecht*, 105; Robert Freitag, 'Comment on § 244 BGB', in beck-online.Grosskommentar BGB, eds. Beate Gsell et al. (Munich: CH Beck, 15.03.2021), para. 11.

53 Stefan Werner, 'Bargeldloser Zahlungsverkehr (Girogeschäft)', in *Bankrecht und Kapitalmarktrecht*, ed. Siegfried Kümpel, 6., neu bearbeitete Auflage (Cologne: Otto Schmidt, 2022), para. 4.4; Hahn and Häde, *Währungsrecht* § 3 para. 23.

54 Ulrich Haug, 'Die Deutsche Bundesbank' in *Bankrechts-Handbuch*, ed. Jürgen Ellenberger und Hermann-Josef Bunte, 6. Auflage (Munich: CH Beck, 2022), § 106 para. 52; Grundmann, 'Comment on BGB § 245', para. 6 ff.

55 See Sebastian Omlor, 'Allgemeines Privatrecht', in *Kryptowährungen Und Token*, ed. Sebastian Omlor, Mathias Link, and Lutz Auffenberg, Recht, Wirtschaft, Steuern. Handbuch (Frankfurt am Main: Fachmedien Recht und Wirtschaft, dfv Mediengruppe, 2nd ed. 2023), chap. 6 para. 29.

56 Omlor and Birne, 'Digitales Zentralbankgeld im Euroraum', 7.

13.2.2.4 Electronic money

Electronic money, as a particular form of deposit money, also falls under the abstract concept of money.[57] According to the legal definition of Sec. 1 of the German Payment Services Supervision Act (ZAG),[58] Electronic money means:

> all monetary values stored electronically, including magnetically, in the form of a claim on the issuer that is issued on payment of funds for the purpose of making payment transactions within the meaning of Section 675f(4) sentence 1 of the Civil Code (Bürgerliches Gesetzbuch), and that is also accepted by natural or legal persons other than the issuer.

It is stored either as a credit on a server operated by the e-money issuer[59] or on a cash card. Like deposit money, e-money represents a claim against the e-money issuer of reconversion into regular deposit money.[60]

The question arises whether the digital euro can be structured as electronic money.[61] The monetary value of the digital euro can already be derived from its function as a means of payment or exchange.[62] Regarding a claim on the issuer, the parties would have to contractually agree that the user is entitled to redeem the digital euro for legal tender.[63] The euro token has to be issued concurrently against payment of a monetary amount. The term '*monetary amount*' includes banknotes and coins, deposit money, or e-money.[64] The

57 Sebastian Omlor, 'Comment on § 675c BGB', in *J von Staudingers Kommentar zum Bürgerlichen Gesetzbuch mit Einführungsgesetz und Nebengesetzen*, by Julius von Staudinger, Sebastian Omlor, and Volker Rieble, Neubearbeitung 2020 (Berlin: Otto Schmidt – de Gruyter, 2020), para. 6. For an overview of the disputed legal nature: Matthias Terlau, 'Comment on § 1 ZAG', in *Zahlungsdiensteaufsichtsgesetz (ZAG): Das Aufsichtsrecht Des Zahlungsverkehrs Und Des E-Geldes: Kommentar*, ed. Matthias Casper and Matthias Terlau (Munich: CH Beck, 2nd ed. 2023), para. 202 ff.

58 This legal definition is based on Art. 2 No. 2 of the Second E-Money Directive (2009/110/EC, originally 2000/46/EC); see Omlor, 'Comment on § 675c BGB', para. 5.

59 Sebastian Omlor, 'Comment on § 675i BGB', in *J von Staudingers Kommentar zum Bürgerlichen Gesetzbuch mit Einführungsgesetz und Nebengesetzen*, by Julius von Staudinger, Sebastian Omlor, and Volker Rieble, Neubearbeitung 2020 (Berlin: Otto Schmidt – de Gruyter, 2020), para. 41.

60 Matthias Casper, 'BGB § 675c Payment Services and E-Money', in *Munich Commentary on the BGB*, 2023, para. 30.

61 Omlor and Birne, 'Digitales Zentralbankgeld im Euroraum', 7 ff.

62 German Federal Financial Supervisory Authority, 'Merkblatt - Hinweise zum Zahlungsdiensteaufsichtsgesetz (ZAG)', BaFin, 29 November 2017, Sec. 4.a) aa)., https://www.bafin.de/SharedDocs/Veroeffentlichungen/DE/Merkblatt/mb_111222_zag.html.

63 Lutz Auffenberg, 'E-Geld auf Blockchain-Basis', *Zeitschrift für Bank- und Kapitalmarktrecht* 19, no. 7 (2019): 343.

64 Christian Foerster, 'Comment on § 675f BGB', in beck-online.Grosskommentar BGB (01.06.2023), para. 70.

electronic storage records the user's claim against the issuer.[65] If CBDC is issued on a decentralised infrastructure, only the information about a specific deposit of a user's address is recorded not the units themselves. For electronic storage, however, it is sufficient that the monetary value of a user's account is registered.[66] This can be derived from any electronic storage medium, regardless of the location and form of storage.[67] Decentralised, multiple and supra-local repositories of the relevant units should also fulfil the requirement of electronic storage.[68] In addition, the digital euro must be used to carry out payment transactions that are any provision, transmission, or withdrawal of a monetary amount. If CBDC is structured as e-money, it thus falls under the concept of the monetary amount and can be used to carry out payment transactions.[69] As soon as the digital euro has been issued and is accepted as a means of payment by any third party for its goods or services instead of cash or deposit money, the characteristic of third-party acceptance is also fulfilled. Consequently, CBDC could well be structured as e-money,[70] especially since the concept of e-money is designed to be open to innovation and development.[71]

However, it is still being determined whether the ECB can issue the digital euro as electronic money within the meaning of the ZAG. The ECB can, at most, act as an e-money issuer if it is not acting in its capacity as a monetary authority (cf. Sec. 1 para. II sentence 1 No. 3 ZAG).[72] If the digital euro were to be issued by the ECB in its sovereign capacity as a monetary authority, it would be excluded from the scope of application of the ZAG from the outset, as the latter only contains a privilege for non-sovereign actions.[73] This would be the case if the digital euro is included in the EU's monetary constitution and issued as legal tender.[74] In this case, the ECB would need statutory authorisation to issue the digital euro as electronic money. It is then up to the legislator to establish different regulations or supervision for this constellation.[75] Regarding direct end-user access to CBDC, the legal

65 German Federal Financial Supervisory Authority, 'Merkblatt – Hinweise zum Zahlungsdiensteaufsichtsgesetz (ZAG)', Sec. 4. a) aa).

66 German Federal Financial Supervisory Authority, Sec. 4. a) aa); Omlor and Birne, 'Digitales Zentralbankgeld im Euroraum', 8.

67 BaFin, Hinweise zum ZAG, 29.11.2017, Sec. 4. a) aa).

68 Auffenberg, 'E-Geld auf Blockchain-Basis', 343; Omlor and Birne, 'Digitales Zentralbankgeld im Euroraum', 8.

69 Omlor and Birne, 'Digitales Zentralbankgeld im Euroraum', 8.

70 Omlor and Birne, 8.

71 Auffenberg, 'E-Geld auf Blockchain-Basis', 343.

72 Sec. 1 para. II sentence 1 No. 3 ZAG literally implements Art. 1 para. 1 lit. d of the Second E-Money Directive (2009/110/EC, originally 2000/46/EC), cf. Terlau, 'Comment on § 1 ZAG', para. 192.

73 Terlau, para. 192.

74 Omlor and Birne, 'Digitales Zentralbankgeld im Euroraum', 7.

75 Terlau, 'Comment on § 1 ZAG', para. 192.

relationship between the ECB and the user cannot fall under the scope of application of the ZAG and German payment services law due to the sovereign action of the ECB. Regarding indirect or hybrid end-user access, payment services law could at least be applicable in the relationship between user and intermediary if the latter is a payment service provider or e-money issuer, as defined by the ZAG.[76]

13.3 Legal regulation of CBDC under German law

13.3.1 Application of German monetary private law

Since the digital euro would be issued with retail access as a sovereign means of payment and as legal tender,[77] it at least satisfies the abstract concept of money. It is, therefore, to be characterised as money in a legal sense.[78] Consequently, German monetary private law applies to digital euro transactions. Indeed, the concept of legal tender has yet to find a precise and binding codification in either German or European law. It has been and still is widely associated with granting a compulsory acceptance right to state-issued legal tender.[79] This means that the debtor of a monetary debt could free himself by providing digital euros as legal tender. The creditor could only refuse this if the parties have agreed to the contrary.[80] Suppose the parties agree that the debtor must pay a certain sum. In that case, the payment with the digital euro as legal tender or money in the legal sense constitutes a fulfilment according to Sec. 362 para. I German Civil Code (BGB).[81] In real life, the introduction of CBDC would likely not result in any changes in the case of monetary debts based on private law, as the parties' power of disposition is based on party autonomy and thus remains unaffected.[82] However, public authorities would at least have to accept digital central bank money as well.[83]

Since the digital euro is considered money in the legal sense, the general rules on monetary debts also apply to liabilities in the digital euro. Under

76 Omlor and Birne, 'Digitales Zentralbankgeld im Euroraum', 7.

77 See Sec. 13.3.2.1.

78 See Sec. 13.3.2.2.

79 Grundmann, 'Comment on BGB § 245', para. 50. In detail Rhona Fetzer, 'Comment on BGB § 362 Erlöschen Durch Leistung', in *Münchener Kommentar Zum BGB*, 2022, para. 19; Freitag, '§ 244 BGB', para. 21 ff.

80 Fetzer, 'Comment on BGB § 362 Erlöschen Durch Leistung', para. 19; Sebastian Omlor, 'Blockchain-basierte Zahlungsmittel', Zeitschrift für Rechtspolitik, 51, no. 3 (2018): 87.

81 Martin Avenarius, 'Comment on § 362', in Kommentar BGB Schuldrecht, eds. Barbara Dauner-Lieb and Werner Langen (Baden-Baden: Nomos, 4th ed. 2021), para. 15; Fetzer, 'Comment on BGB § 362 Erlöschen Durch Leistung', para. 19. Declining for Bitcoin Dirk Looschelders, 'Comment on § 362 BGB', in beck-online.Grosskommentar BGB (01.09.2023), para. 203, 204; Omlor, 'Kryptowährungen im Geldrecht', 324.

82 Omlor, Sebastian, 'Grund Und Grenzen Einer Annahmepflicht von Euro-Bargeld', 485.

83 Omlor, Sebastian, 485.

German private law, monetary debts are debts for creating value.[84] The debtor must provide the creditor with abstract and incorporeal power of assets.[85] The object of performance of the monetary debt is thus not concrete since it is not the individuality of a coin that matters but its value.[86] This would also be the case with the digital euro. The object of performance of the monetary debt in digital euros is not a concrete euro token but the euro value embodied by any euro token. Therefore, monetary debts are also not generic debts according to Sec. 243 BGB,[87] to which a person who owes a thing defined only by a class must supply an item of average kind and quality. This standard does not apply to monetary debts as they are neutral value carriers without an individual character. This also applies to the digital euro. There may be an exception to this rule if a definable credit balance in digital euros has been segregated, for example, if this credit balance is held in a separate wallet. In this case, a generic debt may exist by way of exception.[88] Accordingly, a claim for monetary debts cannot be excluded according to Sec. 275 BGB to the extent that performance is impossible for the obligor or any other person. This is because monetary debts cannot become impossible[89] since the content of a monetary debt represents an abstract creation of value that objectively always remains available.[90]

Legal risk assumption in case of delay, demise, loss, or insolvency is also governed by the law on monetary debts. In this case, the place of performance is decisive, which is highly disputed regarding monetary debts.[91] However, some good arguments exist that the area of performance of the monetary obligation

84 BVerwG BVwZ 2006, 835, 837; Freitag, '§ 244 BGB', para. 67; Sebastian Martens, 'Comment on § 244 BGB', in Bürgerliches Gesetzbuch: Handkommentar Mit AGG, EGBGB, ErbbauRG, LPartG, ProdhaftG, VBVG, VersAusglG, WEG Und Ausgewählten Rechtsquellen Des IPR, ed. Harm Peter Westermann, 17., neu bearbeitete Auflage (Cologne: Otto Schmidt, 2023), para. 9; Omlor, 'Comment on §§ 244-248 BGB', para. B2; Geldprivatrecht, 257.

85 Freitag, '§ 244 BGB', para. 67; Omlor, 'Comment on §§ 244-248 BGB', para. B2; 'Kryptowährungen im Geldrecht', 319.

86 Omlor, 'Kryptowährungen im Geldrecht', 319.

87 Daniel Ulber, 'Comment on § 243 BGB', in Erman BGB (2023), para. 5; Freitag, '§ 244 BGB', para. 67; Gottfried Schiemann, 'Comment on § 243 BGB', in Staudinger BGB: Treu und Glauben (2019), para. 17; Omlor, 324.

88 Omlor, 320 ff.

89 Wolfgang Ernst, 'Comment on § 275 BGB', in Münchener Kommentar BGB (9th ed. 2022), para. 13; Thomas Riehm, 'Comment on § 275 BGB', in beck-online.Grosskommentar BGB (1.8.2023), para. 29; Danile Ulber, 'Comment on § 275 BGB', in Erman BGB (2023), para. 11.

90 Omlor, 'Kryptowährungen im Geldrecht', 323 ff.

91 Omlor, 'Comment on §§ 244-248 BGB', para. B20 ff.; Sandra Schmieder, 'Rechtsbeziehungen im Inlands-Überweisungsverkehr', in Bankrechts-Handbuch, § 28 para. 194; Astrid Stadler, 'Comment on § 270 BGB', in Jauernig BGB (2023), para. 1 ff.; Martin Schwab, 'Geldschulden als Bringschulden? ', Neue Juristische Wochenschrift: NJW, 64, no. 39 (2011): 2833–38.

is at the creditor's domicile.[92] If a debt is discharged at the creditor's domicile, the debtor must perform at the creditor's place.[93] The debtor is, therefore, only released from his obligation to act when he performs the owed performance at the creditor's home. In the case of a monetary debt, this means that either the cash amount must be handed over at the creditor's place[94] or the amount owed must be successfully credited to the creditor's account.[95] Consequently, the debtors' obligation is extinguished if the performance owed is rendered to the creditor, see Sec. 362 para. I BGB. The modified debt to be discharged at the creditor's domicile guarantees an appropriate distribution of risk between the parties, as the debtor is in the best position to assess and control the risks associated with the transportation of money.[96] For the monetary debt in the form of digital central bank money, this means that the debtor is only released from his performance debt when the amount in digital euros is credited to the creditor's account or recipient address.[97] If the amount in digital euros is not credited to the creditor's account or address when performance is due, the debtor may default under Sec. 286 BGB.[98] Default leads to increased liability on the debtor's part and may result in claims for damages.[99] If the creditor's delayed payment receipt is based solely on the fault of the potentially involved intermediary and the debtor has placed the payment on time, the debtor may not be responsible for the delay and is not in default under Sec. 286 para. IV BGB.[100] Accordingly, liabilities in CBDC as money in a legal sense are also subject to statutory interest following Sec. 288 BGB. Sec. 244–248 BGB as regulations on monetary debts would also apply to the digital euro.[101]

92 German Federal Supreme Court (Bundesgerichtshof), VIII ZR 222/15 (05.10.2016) Neue Juristische Wochenschrift, 70, no. 22 (2017), 1596-1600, 1597; Omlor, 'Comment on §§ 244-248 BGB', para. B23 ff.; Omlor, 'Kryptowährungen im Geldrecht', 321.; Freitag, '§ 244 BGB', para. 122 ff.

93 Wolfgang Krüger, 'Comment on § 269 BGB', in Münchener Kommentar BGB (9th ed. 2022), para. 6.

94 Cornelia Feldmann, 'Comment on § 286 BGB', in Staudinger BGB: Leistungsstörungsrecht I (2019), para. 117.

95 Omlor, 'vor §§ 244–248 BGB', para. B23 ff.

96 Omlor, 'Kryptowährungen im Geldrecht', 321.

97 Feldmann, '§ 286 BGB', para. 117.

98 Schmieder, 'Rechtsbeziehungen im Inlands-Überweisungsverkehr', § 28 para. 195 ff.; Reiner Schulze, 'Comment on § 270 BGB, in Handkommentar BGB, ed. Reiner Schulze (Baden-Baden: Nomos, 11th ed. 2021), para. 6.; Feldmann, '§ 286 BGB', para. 117; Omlor, 'Kryptowährungen im Geldrecht', 322.

99 Wolfgang Ernst, 'Comment on § 286 BGB', in Münchener Kommentar BGB (9th ed. 2022), para. 3.

100 Omlor, 'Kryptowährungen im Geldrecht', 322.; in detail Michael Beurskens, 'Comment on § 270 BGB', in beck-online.Grosskommentar BGB, (1.8.2023), para. 40 ff.; Schwab, 'Geldschulden als Bringschulden', 2833 ff.

101 See for Bitcoin, Omlor, 'Blockchain-basierte Zahlungsmittel', 88.

13.3.2 The legal framework of CBDC transfers

The transfer of rights on CBDC strongly depends on its legal nature. The legal nature of crypto tokens, in general, is highly debated.[102] In addition to classifying tokens with payment functions under currency or monetary law,[103] the classification of tokens as legal objects of absolute rights, such as property, is discussed.[104] Regarding CBDC, its legal transfer could be governed by property law, assignment law or payment services law.

13.3.2.1 Transfer under property law

CBDC may be issued as an equivalent to cash as legal tender. The provisions of property law on things under the German Civil Code govern the legal transfer of rights on cash as a corporeal object; see Sec. 90, 903 BGB.[105] Only such corporeal objects can be subject to property ownership rights under the German Civil Code.[106] It is true that digital central bank money and crypto tokens, in general, are not qualified as corporeal objects and, therefore, as things under common understanding.[107] However, CBDC may represent legal tender and

102 Cf. Maute, 'Die Rechtsnatur von Kryptotoken', § 4 para. 13 ff.; Omlor, 'Allgemeines Privatrecht', chap. 6 para. 4 ff.; 'Kryptowährungen im Geldrecht', 306 ff.; Möllenkamp and Shmatenko, 'Verträge mit Usern: Blockchain und Kryptowährungen', Sec. 13.6 para. 29 ff.; see for comparative law examination Sebastian Omlor, 'Digitales Eigentum an Blockchain-Token – rechtsvergleichende EntwicklungslinienInhalt', Zeitschrift für Vergleichende Rechtswissenschaft, 119 (2020): 41, 45 ff.

103 See Sec. 13.3.

104 Cf. Maute, 'Die Rechtsnatur von Kryptotoken', § 4 para. 13 ff.

105 Panajotta Lakkis, 'Comment on § 903 BGB', in beck-online.Grosskommentar BGB, (1.9.2023), para. 1, 13; Gerhard Wagner, 'Comment on § 823 BGB', in Münchener Kommentar (8th ed. 2020), para. 242.

106 Lakkis, '§ 903 BGB', para. 1.

107 Cf. Lena Maute, 'Die Rechtsnatur von Kryptotoken', in Rechtshandbuch Kryptowerte, eds. Philipp Maume et al. (Munich: CH Beck, 2020), § 4 para. 1 ff.; Omlor, 'Allgemeines Privatrecht', chapter 6 para. 30 ff.; Stefan Möllenkamp and Leonid Shmatenko, 'Verträge mit Usern: Blockchain und Kryptowährungen', in Handbuch Multimedia-Recht, eds. Thomas Hoeren et al. (Munich: CH Beck, 59th ed. 2023), Sec. 13.6 para. 32; Omlor, 'Digitales Eigentum an Blockchain-Token – rechtsvergleichende EntwicklungslinienInhalt', 49.; Katja Langenbucher et al., 'Virtuelle Währungen', in Bankrechts-Kommentar, eds. Katja Langenbucher et al. (Munich: CH Beck, 3th ed. 2020) Sec. 11 para. 35; Christina Stresemann, 'Comment on § 90 BGB', in Münchener Kommentar BGB, (9th ed. 2021), para. 21; Markus Kaulartz, 'Die Blockchain-Technologie', Computer und Recht, no. 1 (2016), 474-480, 478; Albert Schlund and Hans Pongratz, 'Distributed-Ledger Technology und Kryptowährungen – eine rechtliche Betrachtung', Deutsches Steuerrecht, 56, No. 12 (2018) 598-604, 600; Andreas Walter, 'Bitcoin, Libra und sonstige Kryptowährungen aus zivilrechtlicher Sicht', Neue Juristische Wochenschrift, 72, No. 50 (2019), 3609-3614, 3611; Christian Engelhardt and Sascha Klein, 'Bitcoins – Geschäfte mit Geld, das keines ist – Technische Grundlagen und zivilrechtliche Betrachtung', Multimedia und Recht, 17, no. 6 (2014), 355-360, 357.

should fulfil the same characteristics and benefits as its physical twin.[108] It may therefore be preferable that a CBDC transfer leads to a change of ownership rights on a specific CBDC amount as soon as a successful transaction occurs. Ownership is usually acquired by the agreement that ownership is to pass on the delivery of the respective thing, see Sec. 929 para. I BGB.

In the case of CBDC, the reference point for ownership may be the assignment of the entry within the CBDC network. When transferring CBDC ownership rights, the allocation of a specific currency unit is changed. The physical handover is thus replaced by the change in the distribution of a particular CBDC amount from one user to another.[109] It is conceivable that sending a transaction to the CBDC network could be regarded as an implied offer regarding the change in the allocation of the CBDC amount to the recipient. The acceptance notification can be inferred via Sec. 151 BGB.[110] According to Sec. 151, sentence 1 BGB, a contract exists through accepting the offer without the offeror needing to be notified of acceptance if such a declaration is not expected according to customary practice or if the offeror has waived it. If one decides to use CBDC, it may be considered a standard practice that an acceptance of ownership rights is not to be expected.

Applying property law to the transfer of CBDC is comparable to the German law on electronic securities (eWpG), which qualifies electronic securities and crypto securities as things according to Sec. 90 BGB (Sec. 2 para. III eWpG). Therefore, the transfer of ownership of electronic securities, also in token form, follows the property law provisions of Sec. 929 ff. BGB. Electronic security is issued by entering an electronic securities register led by a register-keeping body that carries out transactions and other changes within the record, see Sec. 14 eWpG. To transfer ownership of electronic security, it would be necessary for the electronic security to be successfully transferred within the register on the beneficiary's instructions and for both parties to agree that the right should pass. The register has a 'publicity effect', so its content is deemed complete and correct, see Sec. 10, 26 eWpG. Depending on the design of CBDC, the CBDC network could constitute public faith and the ECB or a third party could act as a register-keeping body. It should be noted that the national legislator may only adopt such a regulation if the EU member states have the authority to do so under European law.

108 See Sec. 13.3.2.1.

109 For bonds see Matthias Casper, 'Elektronische Schuldverschreibungen: es ist Zeit für einen grundlegenden gesetzlichen Neustart', Zeitschrift für Bank- und Kapitalmarktrecht, 19, no. 5 (2019), 209-217, 211.

110 Similarly, Omlor, 'Allgemeines Privatrecht', chapter 6 para. 80; Markus Kaulartz and Robin Matzke, 'Die Tokenisierung des Rechts, Neue Juristische Wochenschrift, 71, no. 45 (2018), 3278-3283, 3280.

13.3.2.2 Transfer under assignment law

An alternative to the transfer of rights on CBDC based on property law provisions is the transfer by way of assignment under Sec. 398 ff. BGB. According to this provision, the creditor may transfer a claim or right to another person by contract with that person, see Sec. 398, 413 BGB. To assign a claim, the parties must agree on the disposal of the claim, like the transfer of property. However, in contrast to the disposal of things, the disposal of claims does not require any further act comparable to the physical handover of a thing. This is why the assignment agreement is often implied in the purchase agreement because the disposal of claims does not require further action beyond the agreement.[111] If CBDC were a claim against, for example, the central bank, the transfer of the digital unit may simultaneously transfer the claim against the central bank according to Sec. 398 ff. BGB. According to Sec. 399 BGB, a party agreement could ensure that the assignment only takes place in the event of a successful transaction of the digital unit.[112] The successful assignment of a claim or right to the new creditor also has a binding effect for third parties[113] but, on the other hand, cannot result in a good faith acquisition.[114] Accordingly, applying assignment law would result in a lack of protection for CBDC transactions.

13.3.2.3 Transfer under German payment services law

In the context of CBDC transactions, the German legal framework on payment services might apply as an alternative to the transfer under property or assignment law. German payment services law is based on European legislation on payment services.[115] It is implemented in Sec. 675c–676c BGB, while its supervisory part is realised in the ZAG. In the understanding of German

111 Jan Lieder, 'Comment on § 398 BGB', in beck-online.Grosskommentar BGB (01.09.2022), para. 78.

112 Considered in connection with crypto-tokens, Kaulart and Matzke, 'Die Tokenisierung des Rechts', 3281.

113 Busche, 'Comment on § 398 BGB', in Staudinger BGB: Erlass, Abtretung, Schuldübernahme, Mehrheit von Schuldnern und Gläubigern (2022), para. 29; Sebastian Martens, 'Comment on § 398 BGB', in Erman BGB (2023), para. 3.

114 Michael Jünemann and Johannes Wirtz, 'ICO: Rechtliche Einordnung von Token: Teil 1', Zeitschrift für das gesamte Kreditwesen, 71, no. 21 (2018): 1117.

115 Directive 2007/64/EC of the European Parliament and of the Council of 13 November 2007 on payment services in the internal market amending Directives 97/7/EC, 2002/65/EC, 2005/60/EC, and 2006/48/EC, and repealing Directive 97/5/EC, available at: https://eur-lex.europa.eu/legal-content/EN/TXT/PDF/?uri=CELEX:32007L0064&from=EN; Directive 2015/2366 of the European Parliament and of the Council of 25 November 2015 on payment services in the internal market, amending Directives 2002/65/EC, 2009/110/EC, and 2013/36/EU and Regulation (EU) No 1093/2010, and repealing Directive 2007/64/EC, available at: https://eur-lex.europa.eu/legal-content/EN/TXT/PDF/?uri=CELEX:32015L2366&from=DE.

(and EU) payment services law, payment services refer to all payment procedures of cashless payment transactions, including deposit money or electronic money.[116] The application always requires an intermediary who acts as a payment service provider to support or execute the user's payment transactions.[117] Cashless payment services with deposit money usually consist of accounting processes of bank deposits. Due to a payment service, the payer's claim against his payment service provider expires in the amount of the credited deposit. A new claim of the payee against his payment service provider arises.[118] Neither a claim is assigned, nor property is transferred.[119] The scope of application of German (and EU) law on payment services in connection with CBDC, therefore, requires the existence of payment services carried out by payment service providers.[120] The provisions on payment services also apply to a contract on the issuance and use of electronic money, Sec. 675c para. II BGB.

First, it should be noted that an application between the ECB and end users may not be possible. The ECB can only act as a payment service provider if it is not acting in its capacity as a monetary authority. The application might be ruled out since the ECB would likely issue CBDC in its sovereign capacity as a monetary authority.[121] However, payment services law could be applicable between end users and intermediaries if the intermediary is a payment service provider or an electronic money issuer. For services related to CBDC to be covered by German payment services law, CBDC services must be payment services or e-money businesses. Electronic money business means issuing electronic money, Sec. 1 para. II sentence 2 ZAG. Issuance refers to the provision of monetary units or the transfer of electronic units from the issuing entity to the party wishing to use them for payment purposes.[122] Even if the user himself holds an account at the central bank, this cannot be an e-money business since the ECB would issue the digital euro in a sovereign capacity. At least,

116 Directive 2015/2366 recital 23. See also Draft Law to implement the Consumer Credit Directive, the civil law part of the Payment Services Directive and the reorganisation of the provisions on the right of revocation and the right of return, Federal German Government, Bundesregierung, 'Entwurf Eines Gesetzes Zur Umsetzung Der Verbraucherkreditrichtlinie, Des Zivilrechtlichen Teils Der Zahlungsdiensterichtlinie Sowie Zur Neuordnung Der Vorschriften Über Das Widerrufs- Und Rückgaberecht' (2009), 99, https://dserver.bundestag.de/btd/16/116/1611643.pdf. Detailed at Omlor, '§ 675c BGB', para. 1.

117 Foerster, '§ 675c BGB', para. 9 f.

118 Omlor, 'Comment on §§ 244-248 BGB', para. A158; Katja Langenbucher, 'Kontoführung Und Zahlungsverkehr', in *Bankrechts-Kommentar*, ed. Katja Langenbucher, Dirk H Bliesener, and Gerald Spindler, 3. Auflage (Munich: CH Beck, 2020), Sec. 1 para 202 ff.; Katja Langenbucher et al., 'Kontoführung und Zahlungsverkehr', in Bankrechts-Kommentar (2020), Sec. 1 para. 202 ff.; Sandra Schmieder, 'Girovertrag und Kontokorrent', in Bankrechts-Handbuch, § 26 para. 37 ff.

119 Langenbucher et al., 'Virtuelle Währungen', Sec. 11 para. 34.

120 Friedrich Graf v Westphalen, 'Comment on § 675c BGB', in Erman BGB (2023), para. 1 ff.

121 See Sec. 13.3.3.3.

122 Terlau, '§ 1 ZAG', para. 239.

when applying an indirect retail CBDC model, money could be issued as an intermediary CBDC.

Payment services are, for example, all transactions required to maintain a payment account or the execution of payment transactions on a payment account with the user's payment service provider or with another payment service provider, Sec. 1 para. I sentence 2 ZAG. Payment services mostly require the maintenance of a payment account. A payment account is an account in the name of one or more payment service users that is used for the execution of payment transactions, Sec. 1 para. XVII ZAG. Conventional understanding determines the respective claim against the payment service provider or payment service user and records payment transactions.[123]

What needs to be clarified in this context is whether CBDC would necessarily have to be structured as a claim against a payment service provider. If DLT becomes the basis of CBDC, whether a wallet can be considered a payment account is also questionable.[124] The wallet itself does not store the euro token, which in turn determines the claim against the issuer, nor does it record payment transactions. It merely keeps the private key, which in turn can be used to assign or transfer a token. No value is transferred to the wallet provider, nor can the latter dispose of the respective tokens.[125] The wallet could be linked to a conventional payment account with an intermediary to overcome this problem.[126] It is worth mentioning that according to the recitals of PSD2, the definition of payment services should be technology-neutral to allow the development of new types of payment services,[127] which could indicate an application to CBDC transactions.

13.4 Future questions

With the introduction of a digital form of currency and legal tender to the European and German legal systems, legal and regulatory systems designed for legal tender in a physical form must be rethought. The conventional payment system recognises non-cash payment transactions but not with legal tender. In this context, the legal classification of the transfer of entitlements to CBDC and the associated authorisation needs clarification. An inclusion of CBDC in German property law on things requires the extension of its scope of application. However, the extension of property law, designed for physical objects, could lead to application problems. The transfer of CBDC can indeed be regulated by payment services law, at least in the relationship between intermediary and user. However, payment services law does not guarantee absolute legal

123 Matthias Casper, 'Comment on § 1 ZAG', in Kommentar zum ZAG (2023), para. 35.

124 See for more details Omlor and Birne, 'Digitales Zentralbankgeld im Euroraum', 9 ff.

125 Omlor and Birne, 'Digitales Zentralbankgeld im Euroraum', 9.

126 Cf. Jan Max Wettlaufer and Anika Patz, 'Einordnung von Token und Token-Geschäftsmodellen im Recht der Zahlungsdienste', in Rechtshandbuch Kryptowerte, § 13 para. 67.

127 See EU Directive 2015/2366, recital 21.

authorisation. The legal system must protect the digital euro with an *inter omnes* effect. Therefore, consideration should be given to establishing a closed system with special rules for the legal classification of CBDC that emphasises its legal nature and the absolute protection of authorisation rights. Payment services law may still be applicable in the relationship between the user and intermediary in a supplementary way.

13.5 Conclusion

The legal classification of CBDC depends on who and to what extent is given access to CBDC and whether CBDC is issued as legal tender equivalent to cash.

A digital euro could constitute a form of currency if it were included in the monetary constitution of the European Monetary Union. Under European primary law, CBDC can be introduced without amending the treaties; however, European secondary law, in the form of the Euro Regulation, would have to be adapted.

The digital euro can be established as legal tender and thus as money in the legal sense. Therefore, German monetary private law applies to digital euro transactions.

There are several options for the legal regulation of CBDC transactions. However, already existing legal frameworks on the transfer of legal objects only seem directly applicable with difficulties and modifications.

Transactions with CBDCs may fall under German payment services law, at least in the legal relationship between users and intermediaries, but not between the ECB and the end user, should the latter act as a monetary authority.

14 The Digital Loonie

The Legal Framework for a Central Bank Digital Currency in Canada and Beyond

Poonam Puri and Ilona Larionova[1]

14.1 Introduction

Over the past five years, many countries have recognised and initiated their response to the rise of a new digital economy, akin to a fourth industrial revolution. The Bank of Canada, along with central banks worldwide, has been tasked with developing its own centralised digital currency.

While Canada is not at the forefront of CBDC development, it has considered the implications of the emergence of DLT for banking. In 2016, Canada began researching how DLT could be harnessed to transform the national wholesale interbank payments system. More recently, in early 2020, the Bank of Canada announced its plan to undertake a series of initiatives to prepare for the future of cash. As part of its proposed initiatives, the Bank of Canada is considering the development of a Canadian CBDC. At its core, the Bank of Canada, like many central banks worldwide, must decide whether it should issue a CBDC and, if so, how it will implement it.

The answer to these questions will have widespread political, legal, and economic implications for Canadians. Inaction could see the encroachment of another digital currency, whether private or a foreign CBDC, as a dominant currency of commerce and day-to-day transactions in Canada. Therefore, developing a Canadian CBDC may be necessary to protect Canada's monetary sovereignty and ability to direct the country's monetary and fiscal policies independently.

The balance of this chapter proceeds in four paragraphs. § 14.2 sets out a comprehensive background on the Canadian dollar, the loonie. It covers the dynamic history of the loonie—from periods of foreign currency use, private banknotes, the gold standard, a pegged system, to finally, a floating dollar—which is crucial in understanding the implications of pursuing (or not pursuing) a digital loonie. This paragraph concludes by describing Canada's steps in considering and preparing for a centralised digital currency. § 14.3 covers the

1 The opinions expressed are the author's own and may not necessarily reflect those of the Commission.

DOI: 10.4324/9781003258261-18

challenges and process of implementing a digital loonie, including discussing the key features of a CBDC. It concludes by discussing the 'CBDC Loonie Model,' one of three models that the Bank of Canada has engaged in as part of a 2020 project to design a CBDC model supporting its policy objectives: privacy, universal access, security, resilience, and performance. § 14.4 discusses the threat to Canada's monetary sovereignty and the risk of being a late mover in light of the state of CBDC worldwide and the potential risks of non-digitisation. § 14.5 explores the areas of further consideration in developing a digital loonie from a domestic perspective. § 14.6 concludes.

14.2 Background: The loonie through the years

14.2.1 What is a loonie? A history

The loonie is a colloquial term for Canada's one-dollar coin, named after the common loon, an aquatic bird that appears on the back of the coin. First introduced in 1987 as a cost-saving measure to replace the one-dollar bill, the loonie quickly became an integral part of the Canadian economy and identity. Along with Canada's monetary policy, the loonie has weathered periods of peg and float and emerged on the other side. As the world enters a new era of digital innovation, the loonie faces tremendous challenges and opportunities. To successfully navigate the emerging complexities of digitisation, Canada must learn from past successes and setbacks and adapt to new and rapidly changing circumstances.

To contextualise the modern race to CBDC, examining how traditional currency and Canadian monetary policy developed is vital. Until 1950, Canada's approach to both was often reactive, responding to internal pressures, external events and, usually, the wishes of its major partners, the US and the UK. As we advance, many call on the Bank of Canada to reflect on lessons learned and take a more proactive approach to digitising the loonie.

There was no centralised monetary policy during Canada's early French and British colonial periods. Various currencies were used, from intricate Wampum belts fashioned by First Nations to beaver pelts to money printed on playing cards.[2] For a time, coins from England, France, Portugal, Spain, and other Spanish colonies circulated, with their relative value or 'rating' determined by each territory, which ultimately caused confusion and hindered trade.[3]

Canada's first domestic currency was issued in 1817 by the Montreal Bank (today, the Bank of Montreal), based in Lower Canada.[4] Its initial success led to the establishment of other banks,[5] which issued their own private notes. The

2 James Powell, *A History of the Canadian Dollar* (Ottawa: Bank of Canada, 2005), 1–10.

3 Powell, 11–12.

4 Powell, 3.

5 Powell, 17–18. Including the Bank of Quebec and the Bank of Canada in 1818; the Bank of Upper Canada in 1819; the Bank of New Brunswick in 1820; the Second or Chartered Bank

public generally well-regarded the banknotes, and they became the principal currency in British North America.[6] When the government tried to establish a decimal-based currency[7] and issue paper currency in 1841, its efforts were met with opposition from the banks and the public and were ultimately defeated.[8]

Canada took an essential step towards decimalisation in 1853 when the *Currency Act* was passed as a compromise with the British government, which did not want Canada to adopt the US dollar.[9] Under the new act, British pounds, shillings, pence, and US dollars and cents were officially considered units of Canadian currency.[10] Decimalisation was finally achieved in 1857 with a revision to the *Currency Act,* requiring all provincial government accounts to be kept in dollars. The first Canadian coins were issued in 1858.[11]

In 1866, faced with a shortage of resources and a desperate need for a new funding source, the government passed the *Provincial Notes Act of 1866*, establishing a government-issued paper currency for the first time.[12] Although banks were not forced to give up their power to issue banknotes, they were financially incentivised to do so.[13] Only the Bank of Montreal accepted this offer but later resumed issuing its own notes.[14] As a result, both private notes and government notes circulated in Canada for over 80 years.[15]

One year after Confederation, the various provincial note issues were replaced by 'Dominion notes' issued by the Province of Canada and redeemable in the other provinces.[16] The *Bank Act of 1871* was subsequently passed, bringing chartered banks from the four provinces under common regulation and establishing limits on the issue of private notes, including limiting issues to a minimum denomination of $4.[17] Nevertheless, the public circulation of Dominion notes did not surpass that of banknotes until the late 1930s, following the establishment of the Bank of Canada in 1935 and the subsequent

of Upper Canada in 1822; the Halifax Banking Company in 1825; the Bank of Nova Scotia in 1832; and the Bank of Prince Edward Island in 1855.

6 Powell, 18.

7 Any currency which has sub-units based on a factor of 10.

8 Powell, 21–22.

9 Powell, 22–23.

10 Powell, 23.

11 Powell, 24.

12 Powell, 25–26.

13 Powell, 26.

14 Powell, 26.

15 Ben Fung, Scott Hendry, and Warren E Weber, 'Canadian Bank Notes and Dominion Notes: Lessons for Digital Currencies', *Staff Working Paper/Document de Travail Du Personnel*, no. 5 (2017): 3: though the *Bank of Canada Act* that gave the Bank of Canada the sole right to issue notes was passed in 1935, bank notes did not go out of circulation until 1 January 1950.

16 Powell, 27.

17 Powell, 28. This was later raised to $5 with the passage of the *Bank Act of 1880*.

issue of Bank of Canada notes.[18] This is a testament to the Canadian public's historical resistance to a government monopoly and reliance on banknotes.[19]

Canada's efforts to establish a distinctive Canadian currency parallel its journey to gain and maintain control over its monetary policy. Like many other industrialised nations, Canada started with a gold standard, moved to a fixed exchange rate, and, ultimately, a floating exchange rate. The gold standard and the fixed exchange rate provided relative economic stability while subjugating domestic monetary and fiscal policy to exchange rate stability, leaving Canada's financial system vulnerable to the impacts of international events.[20] The floating exchange rate now allows Canada to conduct its monetary and fiscal policy how it sees fit.

With the proclamation of the *Currency Act* in 1854, Canada adopted a 'gold standard,' which set the value of the Canadian dollar in terms of units of gold.[21] Paper money could be converted into gold on demand—and vice versa. This prevented the government from being able to print new currency without an adequate supply of gold to back it. There were also no restrictions placed on the export and import of gold.[22] This meant that Canada had little control over its monetary policy or the exchange rate under the gold standard.[23] The world markets primarily determined the Canadian dollar's purchasing power and the inflation level; the Canadian economy was vulnerable to external shocks.[24]

Canada was on the gold standard between 1854 and 1929, with a 12-year interruption during World War I when the gold standard was suspended to prevent potential bank runs.[25] The great depression that followed World War I in the 1930s emphasised the dangers of an unfettered market system, paving the path to more significant state intervention.[26] Public trust was shifting away from the private banking system, which was blamed for deflation.[27] Simultaneously, the government faced international pressure to create a central

18 Anna Grodecka-Messi, 'Private Bank Money vs Central Bank Money: A Historical Lesson for CBDC Introduction', SSRN Scholarly Paper (Rochester, NY: Social Science Research Network, 19 February 2021), 4, https://doi.org/10.2139/ssrn.3992359.

19 Grodecka-Messi, 4–5.

20 Michael Bordo et al., 'Canada's Monetary System in Historical Perspective: Two Faces of the Exchange Rate Regime', Department of Economics. The University of British Columbia (Vancouver, Canada, 1999), 31, http://web.arts.ubc.ca/econ/.

21 Bordo et al., 33.

22 Bordo et al., 33.

23 Bordo et al., 33.

24 Bordo et al., 16–17.

25 Powell, A History of the Canadian Dollar, 1–10.

26 Michael D Bordo and Angela Redish, 'Why Did the Bank of Canada Emerge in 1935?', *The Journal of Economic History* 47, no. 2 (1987): 405–17.

27 Bordo et al., 'Canada's Monetary System in Historical Perspective: Two Faces of the Exchange Rate Regime', 22.

bank to facilitate international monetary cooperation.[28] As a result, Canada established the Bank of Canada in 1934, which ironically did little to expand monetary policy in its early years.[29]

As international tensions started to rise in the years leading up to World War II and the value of the Canadian dollar began to fall, Canada introduced exchange controls, fixing the exchange rate of the Canadian dollar to the US dollar.[30] This reflected the growing strength of ties between the Canadian and US economies.[31] It also coincided with the dramatic expansion of the government's role in the economy and the Bank of Canada's role in managing the country's debt.[32] At the end of World War II, Canada was one of the 44 countries that met to design an international financial system, which led to the formation of the IMF, as well as the signing of the Bretton Woods agreement, which fixed international exchange rates to the US dollar.[33]

In 1950, Canada made a highly controversial decision to float the Canadian dollar.[34] By then, the Canadian government had twice tried and failed to establish a sustainable value for the Canadian dollar under Bretton Woods.[35] A floating exchange rate meant the Bank of Canada could direct monetary policy to maintain domestic price stability rather than the fixed rate.[36] Though it strained Canada's relationship with the IMF, the decision to float was lauded by academics for protecting the economy from international shocks that caused deflation or inflation and reducing significant movements of capital.[37]

Ultimately, Canada was forced to abandon the floating experiment in 1962. Though the economy performed well during the first half of the float, the latter half was characterised by a slowing economy and a rising unemployment rate.[38] The Bank of Canada, led by the controversial Governor James Coyne, responded by tightening monetary policy, which was criticised for exacerbating the problems.[39] Ultimately, Canada returned to a fixed exchange

28 Bordo and Redish, 'Why Did the Bank of Canada Emerge in 1935?', 405–17.

29 Bordo et al., 'Canada's Monetary System in Historical Perspective: Two Faces of the Exchange Rate Regime', 22.04/04/202:00.

30 Powell, A History of the Canadian Dollar, 51 and 53.

31 Powell, 54.

32 Bordo et al., 'Canada's Monetary System in Historical Perspective: Two Faces of the Exchange Rate Regime', 23.

33 Powell, A History of the Canadian Dollar, 65.

34 Powell, 61.

35 Gordon Thiessen, 'Can a Bank Change? The Evolution of Monetary Policy at the Bank of Canada 1935–2000', Bank of Canada speeches and appearances, 17 October 2000, https://www.bankofcanada.ca/2000/10/can-a-bank-change/.

36 Powell, A History of the Canadian Dollar, 63.

37 Powell, 63–64.04/04/2023:00.

38 Powell, 66.04/04/2023:00.

39 Powell, 66–67.

rate and maintained its peg at 92.5 cents US for the following eight years.[40] However, the Canadian experiment inspired research into the viability of the Bretton Woods system and, on the whole, was deemed a success.[41] This ultimately helped spur the collapse of fixed exchange rates and move to a flexible exchange regime during the early 1970s.

In 1970, Canada returned to a floating exchange rate, not alone this time. As a result of rising inflation rates in the US and increasing capital mobility, the Bretton Woods system collapsed, and all the major currencies floated.[42] Since then, Canada has been free to set its monetary and fiscal policy to pursue domestic policy objectives—though whether this has always been done successfully is debatable. David Laidler has argued that a floating rate alone is not enough; to succeed, Canada requires a comprehensive monetary order, including clear monetary goals pursued in a broader policy framework, credibility among the public, and political institutions accountable to the public.[43]

14.2.2 The new digital economy

Canadian monetary policy has adapted to several major shifts in monetary history, including the change from coins to banknotes, from banknotes to government currency, from the gold standard to a fixed exchange rate, and finally, to a floating loonie. Another monumental shift looms ahead.

The world has entered the fourth industrial revolution, characterised by 'a fusion of technologies blurring the lines between the physical, digital, and biological spheres.'[44] The revolution drives change exponentially and has transformative effects globally across nearly all industries. At its core, this industrial revolution involves the digitalisation of the global economy.[45] Over the past decade, we have already seen technological advancements transforming Canada's monetary and financial institutions. The COVID-19 pandemic has accelerated these changes.

40 Bordo et al., 'Canada's Monetary System in Historical Perspective: Two Faces of the Exchange Rate Regime', 28.

41 Michael Bordo, Ali Dib, and Lawrence Schembri, 'Canada's Pioneering Experience with a Flexible Exchange Rate in the 1950s:(Hard) Lessons Learned for Monetary Policy in a Small Open Economy' (Cambridge, MA: National Bureau of Economic Research, November 2007), https://doi.org/10.3386/w13605, 5.

42 Powell, A History of the Canadian Dollar, 86.

43 Powell, 86–87. See also David Laidler, '2002-3 Inflation Targets versus International Monetary Integration: A Canadian Perspective', August 2002, 34, 2.

44 'The Fourth Industrial Revolution: What It Means and How to Respond', World Economic Forum, accessed 31 March 2022, https://www.weforum.org/agenda/2016/01/the-fourth-industrial-revolution-what-it-means-and-how-to-respond/.

45 Stephen S Poloz, 'Technological Progress and Monetary Policy: Managing the Fourth Industrial Revolution', *Journal of International Money and Finance* 114 (November 2019): 102373, https://doi.org/10.1016/j.jimonfin.2021.102373, 5.

For example, Canada is becoming an increasingly cashless society, with cash purchases predicted to make up just 10 per cent of spending by 2030.[46] Fintech has transformed the financial services sector, created new services, and fundamentally altered how companies connect and interact with their clients. In fact, in 2020, the collective market cap of fintech companies Square, Visa, PayPal, and MasterCard in the US was more than that of the 'big six' banks in the US put together.[47] The emergence of blockchain and DLT has led to the proliferation of cryptocurrencies and DeFi as an alternative to the traditional financial intermediary model.

Central banks must consider where they will fit in the new monetary order in this context. Many are preparing to introduce a CBDC, a digital form of central bank-issued currency denominated in the national unit of account.[48] The development of CBDC has been described as an international race, as many believe that leadership in the digital space will have long-term implications for political and economic power on the global stage. In this race to digitisation, Canada, like the other nations, effectively has three choices: do nothing, permit the use of existing digital currencies (private or another nation's CBDC), or create its own digital currency. Though digitisation is challenging and fraught with risk, the alternative is getting left behind.

14.2.3 The loonie at a crossroad

Though not typically considered an 'early mover' in digitisation, the Bank of Canada has quietly ramped up its fintech capabilities for years. This work started with Project Jasper—a collaborative research initiative launched in mid-2016 by Payments Canada, the Bank of Canada, financial innovation consortium R3, and six commercial banks that are members of the consortium.[49] Project Jasper explored how DLT—essentially, blockchain—could transform Canada's wholesale interbank payments system.[50] At the time, Canada's interbank payments system was entitled the Large Value Transfer System (LVTS) and was run by Payments Canada; its modernised counterpart, Lynx, recently replaced

46 'Moneris | Canada Pushing toward a Cashless Society with a 70 per Cent Drop in Cash Transactions by 2030', accessed 31 March 2022, https://www.moneris.com/en/About-Moneris/News/Canada-drop-in-cash-transactions-by-2030.

47 Samantha Delouya, 'Market Value of Big Fintech Companies Rises to $1 Trillion, More than the Largest Banks', CNBC, 16 September 2020, https://www.cnbc.com/2020/09/16/market-value-of-big-fintech-companies-rises-to-1-trillion-more-than-the-largest-banks.html.

48 Bank of Canada et al., 'Central Bank Digital Currencies: Foundational Principles and Core Features Report No. 1 in a Series of Collaborations from a Group of Central Banks', 2020, 3, https://www.bis.org/publ/othp33.pdf.

49 Payments Canada, Bank of Canada, and R3, 'Project Jasper: A Canadian Experiment with Distributed Ledger Technology for Domestic Interbank Payments Settlement', 29 September 2017, https://www.payments.ca/sites/default/files/29-Sep-17/jasper_report_eng.pdf.

50 Payments Canada, Bank of Canada, and R3, 3.

the LVTS.[51] Though there was no intention to take the project beyond a proof of concept system, Project Jasper aimed to demonstrate that DLT could be successfully applied to meet international standards for payments system infrastructure[52] and help the Bank of Canada understand the implications for Canadian monetary policy and currency, and financial stability.[53]

In a nutshell, Project Jasper proceeded in four distinct phases. Phase I explored whether DLT (precisely, an Ethereum platform) could settle high-value interbank payments.[54] Phase II addressed some of the issues encountered in Phase I, using the open-source platform Corda instead of Ethereum to focus on clearing and settling high-value interbank payments.[55] Phase III expanded on the scope of the previous work by applying it to the securities settlement process.[56] Finally, Phase IV collaborated with the Monetary Authority of Singapore and the BoE to develop a cross-border, cross-currency settlement system to make these payments more efficient and less costly.[57]

There were many important lessons learned from Project Jasper. Interestingly, Phases I and II showed that while a DLT-based payments system showed promise, it did not have many benefits over the LVTS other than the increased speed of settlement.[58] While Phase III showed that integrating a payment and securities settlement system was possible, the project scope needed to be broadened to conclude that this would result in significant cost savings or efficiency gains.[59] Similarly, a cross-border, cross-currency settlement system without an intermediary was proven feasible in Phase IV of the project. Still, the project's limited scope left many important questions regarding its applicability in a real-world scenario. Perhaps most importantly, Project Jasper demonstrated that the public and private sectors could successfully collaborate domestically and internationally in fintech, laying the groundwork for future

51 'High-Value Payment System – LVTS', Payments Canada, 20 July 2021, https://www.payments.ca/high-value-payments.

52 James Chapman et al., 'Project Jasper: Are Distributed Wholesale Payment Systems Feasible Yet?', *Bank of Canada Financial System Review*, June 2017, 3.

53 Carolyn Wilkins, 'Project Jasper: Lessons from Bank of Canada's First Blockchain Project', 10 February 2017, https://www.coindesk.com/markets/2017/02/10/project-jasper-lessons-from-bank-of-canadas-first-blockchain-project/.

54 Bank of Canada, 'Digital Currencies and Fintech: Projects', Phase 1, accessed 2 April 2022, https://www.bankofcanada.ca/research/digital-currencies-and-fintech/projects/.

55 Bank of Canada, Phase 2.

56 Bank of Canada, Phase 3.

57 Bank of Canada, Phase 4.

58 Bank of Canada et al., 'JASPER Phase III Securities Settlement Using Distributed Ledger Technology', October 2018, 10, https://www.payments.ca/sites/default/files/jasper_phase_iii_whitepaper_final_0.pdf.; Amber Wadsworth, 'Decrypting the Role of Distributed Ledger Technology in Payments Processes', *Reserve Bank of New Zealand Bulletin* 81, no. 5 (2018): 18.

59 Bank of Canada et al., 'JASPER Phase III Securities Settlement Using Distributed Ledger Technology', 29.

collaboration. It also paved the road for the Bank of Canada's preparation to issue a CBDC, should the need ever arise.

After wrapping up Project Jasper in February 2020, the Bank of Canada announced that it was undertaking a few initiatives to prepare for the future of money and payments, including:

- Supporting Payments Canada's Payment Modernization programme to improve the speed, reliability, accessibility, and end-user experience of Canada's payment systems.
- Ensuring banknotes remain available to Canadians who want to use them, including maintaining a distribution model that remains resilient and cost-effective.
- As a contingency, building the capability to issue a cash-like CBDC to the public should the need ever arise.

In March 2020, the Bank of Canada launched a call to action for Canadian universities entitled the Model X Challenge. Three independent project teams were invited to submit a proposed design for a Canadian CBDC. One team included one of the authors of this chapter, Poonam Puri, and submitted a proposed model entitled Central Bank Digital Loonie. The Bank of Canada currently reports that it is continuing to build its capability to issue a CBDC and plans to be prepared should the need for it arise.

14.3 Implementing the digital loonie

14.3.1 The case for a digital loonie

While the Bank of Canada has been working to develop a Canadian digital currency, they have made it clear that the project remains a contingency plan for the time being.[60] A digital loonie is still a question of *if*, not *when*. There are a couple of scenarios when the Bank of Canada would have no choice but to digitise; both involve a challenge to the Bank of Canada's ability to carry out its mandate.[61] The central mandate of the Bank of Canada is to 'promote the economic and financial well-being of Canadians.'[62] It fulfils this mandate through the following:[63]

60 Timothy Lane, 'Payments Innovation beyond the Pandemic', Bank of Canada, February 2021, https://www.bankofcanada.ca/2021/02/payments-innovation-beyond-the-pandemic/.

61 Bank of Canada, 'Contingency Planning for a Central Bank Digital Currency', accessed 2 April 2022, https://www.bankofcanada.ca/2020/02/contingency-planning-central-bank-digital-currency/.

62 'Joint Statement of the Government of Canada and the Bank of Canada on the Renewal of the Monetary Policy Framework', 13 December 2021, 2.

63 Bank of Canada, 'Contingency Planning for a Central Bank Digital Currency'.

- Conducting monetary policy to deliver low, stable, and predictable inflation.
- Promoting the stability and efficiency of the Canadian financial system, including payment systems.
- Providing banknotes that Canadians can use with confidence.
- Providing fiscal-agent services to the Government of Canada.

In the first scenario, if Canadians' hesitancy to transact in banknotes reached a point where cash could no longer be used for a wide range of transactions, the Bank of Canada would consider introducing a CBDC.[64] In the second scenario, if one or more other digital currencies (including cryptocurrencies and stablecoins) became widely used as an alternative to the Canadian dollar, the Bank of Canada would be tasked with defending Canada's monetary sovereignty.[65]

Central banks around the world are considering digitisation for a variety of reasons. Though these reasons vary by jurisdiction and advanced economies like Canada are less motivated to digitise than emerging market economies,[66] common motivations include:[67]

- Public access to central bank money in jurisdictions where cash is in decline.
- Improved operational resilience.
- Increased payment diversity.
- Increased financial inclusion.
- Increased speed and efficiency of cross-border payments.
- More anonymity for electronic payments.
- Increased efficiency of fiscal transfers.

Another important benefit of CBDC is stability. A digital loonie pegged to the Canadian dollar will benefit from the stability of the government currency, which cannot be said of other decentralised currencies, which tend to be highly volatile. While the price of the former is influenced by domestic factors (i.e., monetary policy), the price of the latter is almost exclusively moved by external market forces.

Digitisation is also fraught with risk, which has given banks in many jurisdictions, including Canada and the US, pause. Making any significant change to the monetary system without a sound monetary policy in place to support the changes can be disastrous. When Canada first floated the loonie in 1950, the government learned this lesson the hard way. Although everything ran

64 Bank of Canada as above and see also Lane, 'Payments Innovation beyond the Pandemic'.

65 Bank of Canada, 'Contingency Planning for a Central Bank Digital Currency'.; see also Lane, 'Payments Innovation beyond the Pandemic'.

66 Codruta Boar, Henry Holden, and Amber Wadsworth, Impending Arrival: A Sequel to the Survey on Central Banking Digital Currency, 2020, 4.

67 Bank of Canada et al., 'Central Bank Digital Currencies'.

smoothly initially, once the Bank of Canada hit the first bump in the road in the form of a slowing economy and a rising unemployment rate, a mismanaged monetary policy ended the floating experiment. Similarly, rushing into an emerging asset class without a sound understanding of digital currency and a comprehensive management plan could harm the nation's financial stability.

One crucial risk that monetary policy (and CBDC systems design) would need to account for is the potential disintermediation of commercial banks.[68] Disintermediation refers to cutting out a financial intermediary in a transaction; in this context, Canadians might prefer to store their money in the form of CBDC with the Bank of Canada rather than as bank deposits.[69] Commercial banks rely on bank deposits to provide lending services; an insufficient deposit volume would decrease their lending volume and investment activity.[70] Banks may also depend on wholesale funding from institutional investors to a greater degree, thus restricting credit supply in the economy.[71] A related risk to disintermediation is the increased potential of central bank runs.[72] Because central bank money is typically considered the safest, the public could run into CBDC whenever a real or perceived financial crisis occurs. The accessibility of CBDC could make such runs more frequent and severe.[73]

Recent research shows that while CBDCs do have the capacity to crowd out bank deposits, there are ways to mitigate this effect. For example, the central bank compensates for losses in deposits by providing additional central bank funds or disincentivising the accumulation of CBDCs by decreasing CBDC interest rates.[74] In either case, this is a significant risk that central banks must plan for before implementing a CBDC.

Another potential risk is a lack of uptake or the eventual loss of public interest. The crypto world rushes, and the next big thing is always around the corner. Central banks must ensure that the timing of introducing a CBDC is correct and that the public is incentivised to use it over the alternatives: private digital coins, cryptocurrency, foreign CBDCs, and the next 'big thing.' The Canadian CBDC would have to be carefully crafted to be attractive today and not lose its appeal over time. Monetary policy must be forward-looking and

68 Bank of Canada et al., 8; Adina Popescu, 'Cross-Border Central Bank Digital Currencies, Bank Runs and Capital Flows Volatility', *IMF*, 6 May 2022, https://www.imf.org/en/Publications/WP/Issues/2022/05/06/Cross-Border-Central-Bank-Digital-Currencies-Bank-Runs-and-Capital-Flows-Volatility-517625.

69 Jonas Gross and Jonathan Schiller, 'A Model for Central Bank Digital Currencies: Do CBDCs Disrupt the Financial Sector?', *SSRN Electronic Journal*, 2020, 1, https://doi.org/10.2139/ssrn.3721965.

70 Gross and Schiller, 1.

71 Bank of Canada et al., 'Central Bank Digital Currencies', 8.

72 Alissa Gorelova, Bena Lands, and Maria teNyenhuis, 'Resilience of Bank Liquidity Ratios in the Presence of a Central Bank Digital Currency', Bank of Canada Staff Analytical Note 2022-5 (Bank of Canada, 9 May 2022), https://doi.org/10.34989/san-2022-5.

73 Bank of Canada et al., 'Central Bank Digital Currencies', 8.

74 Gross and Schiller, 'A Model for Central Bank Digital Currencies'.

allow for flexible expansion of CBDC's features to keep in step with any new developments.

Central banks must balance the benefits and risks of digitising based on the unique factors intrinsic to their jurisdiction. Moreover, they must ensure that the CBDC model they choose supports key public policy objectives, including supporting the central bank's mandate, coexisting with cash, and enabling innovation and efficiency for consumers.[75]

To fulfil these foundational principles, 14 key features have been identified in a report published by the BIS as part of a collaboration between the BIS and the Bank of Canada, the European Central Bank, the Bank of Japan, Sveriges Riksbank, Swiss National Bank, BoE, and the Fed Board of Governors.[76] Given the fast-paced and, at times, unpredictable nature of digitisation, central banks will eventually have to balance the desire to create the perfect CBDC model with the need to come up with a workable model quickly. This may mean placing more weight on the digital currency's adaptability to evolve and expand its features to help accelerate timelines.

14.3.2 The central bank digital loonie model

As previously discussed, the Bank of Canada engaged three project teams in 2020 to design a CBDC model that would support the following policy objectives:

- Privacy.
- Universal access.
- Security.
- Resilience.
- Performance.

The joint submission by the University of Toronto and York University team presented the Central Bank Digital Loonie (CBDL) model, which proposed a dual-phased approach to introducing the digital loonie.[77] In the first phase, the Bank of Canada would establish a new centralised platform that would be integrated into the existing payment networks. A narrow bank—a financial institution that would create and maintain quasi-anonymous CBDL wallets, perform eKYC[78] on account opening, process CBDL payments, and keep account balances—would operate this platform. A distributed ledger/permissioned

75 Bank of Canada et al., 'Central Bank Digital Currencies'.

76 Bank of Canada et al.

77 Andreas Veneris et al., 'Central Bank Digital Loonie: Canadian Cash for a New Global Economy', SSRN Scholarly Paper (Rochester, NY: Social Science Research Network, 11 February 2021), https://doi.org/10.2139/ssrn.3770024.

78 Electronic Know-Your-Customer onboarding process.

blockchain with limited validator nodes would be established in the second phase. The narrow bank would be a validating node with supervisory authority. This would allow the system to be opened to private service providers/intermediaries to build decentralised services.

Since privacy is a major attraction of cryptocurrency, it is also an essential consideration for a CBDC. The CBDL model secures its users' privacy by default. After going through a third-party eKYC process, users would be assigned their wallet addresses, represented by a quasi-anonymous identifier. Quasi-anonymous means that anonymity would not be maintained when suspicious transactions must be reported under Canada's AML/CFT regulations or information must be revealed by a court order. During the second phase, the stream of transactions would become visible to the validator nodes, so additional privacy measures like mixers/tumblers or one-time addresses would be required to hide user data from private validators.

Universal access is another crucial policy objective, meaning that a user should have access to the CBDC regardless of the user's means, ability or geographic location.[79] The CBDL model assures universal access through offline cards, which allow users to transact when they are not connected to a cellular network. These offline cards can be loaded only from registered e-wallets, and any transactions would be synced when the CBDC is moved from the offline card back to the e-wallet.

Security of the CBDC is vital for obvious reasons and for maintaining the public's trust in the government's institutions, including the central bank. The CBDL model has some security features built-in, including the maintenance of account balances by the narrow bank/validator network, the biometrics/PIN required to operate the e-wallets, and the option of loading an offline card.

The resilience of the CBDC includes the ability to respond to disaster scenarios and system downtimes. While this discussion was beyond the scope of the CBDL model, these are standard issues that can typically be addressed through existing solutions.

Performance, which involves scaling the CBDC for daily use in Canada, also appears to be quite manageable for the CBDL model. The system would not be overwhelmed if CBDLs were to subsume all cash transactions and a proportion of cash/debit transactions. Moreover, the volume of CBDL messages does not exceed the volume that Payments Canada currently manages.

79 Rosa Giovanna Barresi and Filippo Zatti, 'The Importance of Where Central Bank Digital Currencies Are Custodied: Exploring the Need of a Universal Access Device', *SSRN Electronic Journal*, 2020, https://doi.org/10.2139/ssrn.3691263.

14.4 The potential risk of non-digitisation

14.4.1 Loss of monetary sovereignty

If Canada adopts a non-digitisation or wait-and-see approach, the loonie's role as the exclusive legal tender in the country will be vulnerable. CBDC or no CBDC, Canada has no choice but to be a competitive market on a global stage and allow digital currencies to circulate. Though cryptocurrency is not considered legal tender, Canadians can purchase and use various cryptocurrencies to buy goods and services online and in stores that accept them.[80] According to Chainalysis's 2021 Global Crypto Adoption Index, global cryptocurrency adoption has skyrocketed, growing by over 2300 per cent since the third quarter of 2019.[81] Though Canada was not among the top 20 countries in the index, its cryptocurrency use has increased significantly, from 3 per cent Bitcoin ownership in 2016 to 14 per cent in 2021.[82] One in four Canadians is considering investing in cryptocurrency in the future.[83]

If digital coins—whether cryptocurrency, stablecoins, or foreign CBDCs—eventually achieve widespread acceptance and use in Canada, they may threaten Canada's monetary sovereignty through currency substitution. Currency substitution, also known as dollarisation, is when the citizens of a country switch from using their country's legal tender to a different type of currency.[84] These concerns have been top of mind for central banks worldwide and escalated when Meta (then-Facebook) first announced its plans to launch its own private currency Diem (then-Libra), in 2019.[85] The project was eventually scrapped, but rumours have swelled about other tech giants, including Amazon and Apple, launching their own private coins.

For any private digital currency to achieve widespread acceptance and circulation, it would have to be sheltered from the volatility that has come to characterise cryptocurrency. As was the plan for Diem, a stablecoin pegged to the US dollar would be a likely candidate. In this scenario, Canada would be unwilling to participate in a US dollar-pegged system, with the accompanying loss of control over domestic monetary and fiscal policy. As in the past,

80 Financial Consumer Agency of Canada, 'Digital Currency', education and awareness, 17 June 2016, https://www.canada.ca/en/financial-consumer-agency/services/payment/digital-currency.html.

81 'The 2021 Global Crypto Adoption Index: Worldwide Adoption Jumps Over 880% With P2P Platforms Driving Cryptocurrency Usage in Emerging Markets', Chainalysis, 14 October 2021, https://blog.chainalysis.com/reports/2021-global-crypto-adoption-index/.

82 'Bitcoin Ownership Is on the Rise in Canada', Ipsos, accessed 2 April 2022, https://www.ipsos.com/en-ca/news-polls/Bitcoin-ownership-is-on-the-rise-in-Canada.

83 'Bitcoin Ownership Is on the Rise in Canada'.

84 Skylar Brooks, 'Revisiting the Monetary Sovereignty Rationale for CBDCs', *Staff Discussion Paper/Document d'analyse Du Personnel* —, no. 17 (17 December 2021): 3.

85 Brooks, 4–5; see also Raphael Auer, Giulio Cornelli, and Jon Frost, 'Rise of the Central Bank Digital Currencies: Drivers, Approaches and Technologies', *SSRN Electronic Journal*, 2020, 3, https://doi.org/10.2139/ssrn.3724070.

the Bank of Canada's ability to affect the Canadian economy and promote Canadians' economic and financial well-being through monetary policy will be significantly diminished.

14.4.2 Falling behind in the race to digitisation

The rise and prevalence of private digital currencies are well established. There are currently more than 5000 different cryptocurrencies and blockchain-based tokens in circulation.[86]

The rise of private digital currency has spurred the development of CBDCs. Many central banks have begun to rethink the essence of 'cash' and explore their tokenisation of fiat currencies with central bank-issued digital currencies.[87] Even though significant economies like China, the US, and the EU have the resources, technology, and infrastructure necessary to shape the future of the digital economy,[88] we have seen emerging economies prioritising the implementation of their CBDCs to avoid the risk of local currencies getting displaced by the large foreign economies—as we have seen happen with the US dollar in the past.[89]

Indeed, the world's first CBDC, entitled the Sand Dollar, was launched by the Bahamas in October 2020.[90] The Sand Dollar is the digital version of the Bahamian dollar, which is pegged 1:1 to the US dollar; in a sense, the Sand Dollar can be seen as a pilot for a digital US dollar by proxy.[91] So far, the Sand Dollar has done relatively well, with approximately 20,000 active electronic wallets in a population of 400,000 by late 2021[92] and a number one ranking in the PwC Global CBDC Index for CBDC maturity.[93] Though the Sand Dollar

86 With an aggregate market capitalisation of $2.86 trillion as of November 2021: Aliénor Nina Burghartz, 'Private Digital Currencies and the Promise of Global Financial Inclusion', McGill Business Law Platform, 17 November 2021, https://www.mcgill.ca/business-law/article/private-digital-currencies-global-financial-inclusion.

87 Veneris et al., 'Central Bank Digital Loonie'.

88 Tal Elyashiv VC founder and managing partner, SPiCE, 'Op-Ed: A New Global Arms Race in Digital Finance Is Heating Up', CNBC, 21 January 2021, https://www.cnbc.com/2021/01/21/op-ed-a-new-global-arms-race-in-digital-finance-is-heating-up.html.

89 Veneris et al., 'Central Bank Digital Loonie'.

90 'Digital Bahamian Dollar Sand Dollar', accessed 2 April 2022, https://www.sanddollar.bs.

91 'Central Bank Digital Currency: The First Nationwide CBDC In the World Has Been Launched by The Bahamas', accessed 2 April 2022, https://www.forbes.com/sites/vipinbharathan/2020/10/21/central-bank-digital-currency-the-first-nationwide-cbdc-in-the-world-has-been-launched-by-the-bahamas/?sh=565f24f5506e.

92 'Behind the Scenes of Central Bank Digital Currency', 2, accessed 2 April 2022, https://www.imf.org/en/Publications/fintech-notes/Issues/2022/02/07/Behind-the-Scenes-of-Central-Bank-Digital-Currency-512174.

93 Pauline Adam-Kalfon et al., 'PwC CBDC Global Index' (PwC, April 2021), https://www.pwc.com/gx/en/industries/financial-services/assets/pwc-cbdc-global-index-1st-edition-april-2021.pdf.

can only be used domestically now, the Bahamian central bank is exploring the possibility of future cross-border use.[94]

With the Sand Dollar leading the fray, CBDC initiatives are underway and in various stages of development around the world:[95]

- Nine countries have launched a CBDC, including the Bahamian Sand Dollar, the Nigerian e-Naira and the Eastern Caribbean DCash, currently available in Antigua and Barbuda, Dominica, Grenada, Montserrat, Saint Kitts and Nevis, Saint Lucia, and Saint Vincent and the Grenadines.
- Fifteen countries[96] are piloting a CBDC, including China. In April 2020, China became the world's largest economy to pilot its CBDC, called the digital yuan or e-CNY, in four cities, and then expanded the pilot to 28 cities in August 2020. As of June 2021, more than 20.87 million personal and 3.51 million corporate digital yuan wallets have been opened, with a transaction value totalling around $5.39 billion. China is already testing the use of the digital yuan in cross-border transactions with Hong Kong and has made it available at the 2022 Beijing Olympics. It is aiming for the widespread use of the digital yuan by 2022.
- Sixteen countries[97] are in the process of developing a CBDC, including Canada and the EU.
- Thirty-nine countries[98] are still researching a CBDC, including the US. In January 2022, the Federal Reserve (the American central bank) released a highly anticipated report[99] on CBDC, discussing the potential benefits and risks of a US CBDC and requesting public comment on a broad range of questions. Though no formal commitment to issuing a CBDC has been made, the Federal Reserve aims to initiate a discussion with the public and key stakeholders about CBDC.

Among the four largest central banks, including Japan, the EU, the UK, and the US, the US is the furthest behind in CBDC development.[100] Conversely,

94 'Behind the Scenes of Central Bank Digital Currency', 15.

95 'Central Bank Digital Currency Tracker', *Atlantic Council* (blog), accessed 2 April 2022, https://www.atlanticcouncil.org/cbdctracker/.

96 Anguilla, China, Hong Kong, Jamaica, Lithuania, Malaysia, Russia, Saudi Arabia, Singapore, South Africa, South Korea, Sweden, Thailand, Ukraine, and the United Arab Emirates.

97 Australia, Bahrain, Cambodia, Canada, Brazil, the EU, Haiti, India, Israel, Japan, Lebanon, Mauritius, Palau, Switzerland, Turkey, and Venezuela.

98 Austria, Belarus, Belize, Bhutan, Chile, Czech Republic, Estonia, Eswatini, France, Georgia, Germany, Ghana, Guatemala, Honduras, Iceland, Indonesia, Iran, Italy, Kazakhstan, Kenya, Kuwait, Laos, Madagascar, Mexico, Morocco, Netherlands, New Zealand, Norway, Pakistan, Palestine, Peru, Philippines, Rwanda, Spain, Taiwan, Trinidad and Tobago, Tunisia, the United Kingdom, and the United States.

99 Board of Governors of the Federal Reserve System, 'Money and Payments: The U.S. Dollar in the Age of Digital Transformation', January 2022, 40.

100 'Central Bank Digital Currency Tracker'.

China will be the world's first major economy to issue a CBDC. This may have significant consequences for the US dollar and, in turn, economies that are impacted by the US dollar, including Canada. While some believe that there is a 'first mover' advantage that the early issuers of a CBDC will enjoy, there is also a possibility that a 'second mover' can learn from, and improve upon, the first mover's experience.[101] Creating and sustaining a first-mover advantage may be more challenging when markets and technology develop as quickly as they do in the digital currency space.[102]

One way that China could gain a first-mover advantage in CBDC would be the internationalisation of the digital yuan at the expense of the US dollar.[103] This could undermine the US dollar's de facto currency status and influence in world trade.[104] Moreover, it could impact the US's ability to monitor cross-border payment flows.[105] The exchange of payments without US knowledge would weaken the power of the US to issue sanctions by eroding its ability to freeze assets and penalise companies and individuals transacting in the digital yuan.

However, China's internationalisation of the yuan through early digitisation is not a given. To become a reserve currency, three factors must be present: (i) economic weight, (ii) openness and depth of financial markets, and (iii) credibility of economic and legal systems.[106] China is the second-largest economy globally; however, it prioritises capital controls over capital account liberalisation.[107] The credibility of China's economic and legal systems is also lacking in some respects—including an independent central bank and monetary policy, a fair and transparent legal system, and a more transparent and representative political system.[108] Moreover, the digital yuan is a retail-facing CBDC. In contrast, other central banks, including the Bank of Canada, have focused their efforts on wholesale CBDCs that can be used for large-scale cross-border payments.[109]

101 Martin Chorzempa, 'China, the United States, and Central Bank Digital Currencies: How Important Is It to Be First?', *China Economic Journal*, 5 January 2021, 111, https://www.tandfonline.com/doi/full/10.1080/17538963.2020.1870278.

102 Chorzempa, 111; also Fernando F Suarez and Gianvito Lanzolla, 'The Half-Truth of First-Mover Advantage', *Harvard Business Review*, 1 April 2005, https://hbr.org/2005/04/the-half-truth-of-first-mover-advantage.

103 Chorzempa, 'China, the United States, and Central Bank Digital Currencies', 111.

104 'China Seeking First-Mover Advantage in Building Digital Currency: Senior Japan Official', *Reuters*, 8 October 2020, sec. Business News, https://www.reuters.com/article/us-cen-banks-digital-idINKBN26T2MF.

105 'Central Bank Digital Currency Tracker'.

106 Yiping Huang, Daili Wang, and Gang Fan, 'Paths to a Reserve Currency: Internationalization of the Renminbi and Its Implications', *SSRN Electronic Journal*, 2014, 16, https://doi.org/10.2139/ssrn.2441821.

107 Huang, Wang, and Fan, 20.

108 Huang, Wang, and Fan, 22.

109 Chorzempa, 'China, the United States, and Central Bank Digital Currencies', 17.

The strategy of the US Federal Reserve may well be to minimise risk by standing by and learning from the experiences of the first movers.[110] It is unclear whether Canada would benefit from doing the same. On the one hand, rushing to issue a CBDC without understanding the risks and emerging global dynamics may be foolhardy. On the other hand, Canada is unlikely to be able to compete with the US as a second mover. Given the proximity and close relationship between Canada and the US, including commerce and trade, the possibility of the Canadian public widely adopting a retail US CBDC is relatively high.

A mass convergence to a US CBDC throws Canada back to the US dollar-pegged system. An encroachment of foreign CBDCs as the common currency of everyday Canadians exposes citizens to the actions of a foreign government responsible for protecting its economy and its citizens. Canadians' economic and financial well-being would depend on and be under the control of another nation's monetary policies.

14.5 Considerations for a digital loonie

If or when Canada chooses to implement a digital loonie, there will be important legislative and regulatory questions to address. To issue a digital currency, the Canadian government must implement a comprehensive legislative regime that empowers the Bank of Canada to issue a CBDC and addresses the role of other entities involved in the digital currency settlement.

One important consideration is whether the Bank of Canada has the statutory authority to oversee a digital payments system. The Bank of Canada's central mandate is to 'regulate credit and currency in the best interests of the economic life of the nation' and to 'promote the economic and financial welfare of Canada.' The *Payment Clearing and Settlement Act* further confirms that the Bank of Canada is mandated to 'promote the efficiency and stability of the Canadian financial system' by 'providing the means of settlement of Canadian dollar payments.' The definition of a 'clearing and settlement system' in this Act also states that 'the clearing or settlement' must be 'wholly or partly in Canadian dollars.' To prevent any future issues, it would be prudent to update the language in the *Payment Clearing and Settlement Act* to include 'Canadian digital dollars.'

The Bank of Canada must also have the statutory authority to issue a CBDC. Currently, the *Bank of Canada Act* grants the Bank of Canada the sole right to issue 'notes' as a 'first charge on the assets of the Bank.' Though 'notes' is defined broadly as 'notes intended for circulation in Canada,' sections in the Act require that the notes be printed. The *Royal Canadian Mint Act* defines a circulation coin as 'a coin composed of base metal.' Therefore, it

110 Chorzempa, 19.

would also be prudent to update the language in these acts to refer to digital currency and digital coins explicitly.

Intermediaries between individual account holders and the Bank of Canada will likely be used as part of the Canadian CBDC landscape so that the Bank of Canada is not required to open and operate accounts for the public directly. Currently, the Bank of Canada has the authority to accept deposits from

> any bank, an authorised foreign bank that is not subject to the restrictions and requirements referred to in subsection 524(2) of the Bank Act or other member of the Canadian Payments Association, the government of any province or from any corporation or agency of the Government of Canada… [or as] authorised or required by an Act of Parliament.[111]

To ensure that the intermediaries can accept and issue CBDCs, it will be essential to ensure that the intermediaries fit into one of these categories.[112] Furthermore, to ensure that the intermediaries can provide for the custody of CBDC, the *Bank of Canada Act* will require amendments that authorise the Bank of Canada to issue CBDC to the intermediaries and for the intermediaries to hold reserve accounts with the Bank of Canada.[113]

In addition to these statutory considerations, Canada must be prepared to address critical privacy concerns concerning CBDC. It is essential to ensure that the CBDC system complies with Canadian privacy laws and that each individual's data is sufficiently protected from the government. All privacy safeguards must be built into the CBDC system at the outset and implemented throughout the design process.[114] Any data leaks that occur once the CBDC launches will likely affect the uptake and ultimately determine the viability of the CBDC.

14.6 Conclusions

The Canadian loonie has had a rich and unique history. As a former colony of the world's largest empire and current neighbour to its largest economy, Canada has navigated complex relationships and adjusted its monetary policy to weather periods of boom and bust, the gold standard, peg and float, and other events. Given the monumental shift to a digital economy that looms ahead, Canada has some critical decisions to make about the future of the loonie. It is essential to remember that history tends to repeat itself.

111 Bank of Canada Act, s. 18(l, l.1, l.3, o).

112 Veneris et al., 'Central Bank Digital Loonie', 43.

113 Veneris et al., 17.

114 Sriram Darbha and Rakesh Arora, 'Privacy in CBDC Technology' (Bank of Canada, 19 June 2020), https://doi.org/10.34989/san-2020-9.

Canada's first major domestic currency did not start as government-issued notes but as private banknotes. The public trusted the banknotes so much that there was an initial reluctance to use a government currency once one became available. Banknotes went entirely out of circulation only once the government took steps to prohibit their issuance.[115] As private digital currencies continue to proliferate and slowly gain a broader user base, it will be interesting to see whether public opinion swings back in favour of private over public, especially given digital currencies' promise of speed, ease of access, and anonymity. Moreover, if a CBDC is issued after private digital currencies have gained widespread acceptance, it may struggle to replace them.

Canada has also historically fluctuated between pegged and floating exchange rates. Since 1970, Canada has floated the loonie and enjoyed relative independence over its monetary and fiscal policy. The emergence of private digital currencies and foreign CBDCs may present a new challenge to this independence. However, there may also be an opportunity for collaboration with other jurisdictions and the private sector to build a new digital global market and develop the future of banking. In either case, careful research and planning will be essential.

Canada has important decisions to make as it looks ahead to digitisation. While it may be tempting to get ahead in the so-called race to a CBDC, Canada's methodical approach throughout this process has so far focused on prioritising the needs of its citizens over any perceived first-mover advantage. After all, unlike private currencies, there is no room for error regarding a national CBDC.

115 Fung et al., 32.

15 The Evolution of the Finality of Payment or 'How RTGSs, Instant Payment Systems, and DLT Platforms Change the Concept of Money'

Rosa Giovanna Barresi

15.1 The concept of finality and its historical evolution

Developing new forms of money has never been an ordered process, but the last few years have been quite disruptive. The initial privilege given to the technical issues has now given way to a more balanced analysis, focusing on the economic and legal aspects of the digital asset revolution. The new waves of innovation mitigate the problems raised by inadequate solutions developed in the early days. Digital assets, indeed, are a marked improvement over the traditional practice of correspondent banking.

Still, new developments are required to cover the features offered by present-day payment systems. The analysis of the various forms of finality leads to a review of the legal framework for digital assets and a comparison between what digital assets offer and payment systems.

15.1.1 Payment finality in the modern age

Historically, the concept of payment finality was developed alongside the invention of money.[1] Since then, money transfers have been deemed irrevocable and have the power of discharging debtor-creditor obligations: 'although discharge and payments cannot be regarded as synonyms, any controversy about terminology differences is not justified.'[2]

The evolution of finality from a single concept into a family group has constantly followed the history of insolvency proceedings. The latter has always been the most common opportunity to assess the limits of finality in court.

In ancient Greece, insolvent debtors (and their families) ended up as slaves of their creditors, losing all their personal properties and becoming personal

1 Charles M Kahn and William Roberds, 'The Economics of Payment Finality', *Economic Review (Federal Reserve Bank of Atlanta)* 87, no. 2 (2002): 1–12.

2 Rosario Nicolò, 'Adempimento (Dir. Civ.)', in *Enciclopedia Del Diritto* (Giuffrè Francis Lefebvre, 1958), 554.

DOI: 10.4324/9781003258261-19

property themselves.[3] However, the Roman law of the Twelve Tables (449 BC) already prohibited bankruptcy proceedings from ending in slavery: debtors pledged their own bodies as pawns, even though they maintained the right to own property.[4]

After the Christian era, insolvency proceedings were finally restricted to selling the debtor's assets. The Code Napoléon marked the first modern approach to the finality of payments and insolvency. After the Battle of Austerlitz (1805), Napoleon discovered that several army contractors went bankrupt, creating provisioning problems.[5] Out of spite, he participated in all legal experts' meetings on insolvency proceedings and reinstated a relationship between bankruptcy and social stigma that lasted almost two centuries. At the same time, the intermediation function of the banking system became so popular that the concept of *finality by transfer of credit* had to be developed, creating a new problem. Insolvency proceedings being debated in courts led to the common practice of recording the day the sentence had been passed. This then developed into the zero-hour rule, which voids all banking transactions carried out by insolvent participants from the zero-hours period on which their insolvency was declared in court. Its formulation can be found in Art. 23 of the Dutch Bankruptcy Code:

> As a result of the declaration of bankruptcy, the bankrupt debtor loses the right to dispose of and to administer his assets (property) as far as these belong to the liquidation estate, this with effect from and including the day on which the bankruptcy order is rendered.[6]

The zero-hour rule is slowly being suppressed everywhere. Since 2001, Italian insolvency law has required the court clerk to register the exact timestamp (day, hour, and minute) of the instant filing.[7] However, as an unwritten law,

3 Alberto Maffi, 'Family and Property Law', in *The Cambridge Companion to Ancient Greek Law*, ed. Michael Gagarin and David Cohen, 1st ed. (Cambridge University Press, 2005), 254–66, https://doi.org/10.1017/CCOL0521818400.014.

4 Louis Edward Levinthal, 'The Early History of Bankruptcy Law', *University of Pennsylvania Law Review and American Law Register* 66, no. 5/6 (April 1918): 231, https://doi.org/10.2307/3314078.

5 Jérôme Sgard, 'Bankruptcy Law, Creditors' Rights and Contractual Exchange in Europe, 1808–1914', *Working Papers*, Working Papers, 1 May 2006, 8, https://ideas.repec.org//p/onb/oenbwp/109.html.

6 'No Right of Disposition; No Right of Administration', Bankruptcy § 2 (2012), http://www.dutchcivillaw.com/bankruptcyact.htm.

7 'Attuazione della Direttiva 98/26/CE sulla definitività degli ordini immessi in un sistema di pagamento o di regolamento titoli', Pub. L. No. 210, D.Lgs. (2001), art. 3.3; Filippo Murino, 'La Corte di Giustizia UE si pronuncia sulla Direttiva collateral', *Rivista Di Diritto Bancario* I (2017): 26, https://rivista.dirittobancario.it/la-corte-di-giustizia-ue-si-pronuncia-sulla-direttiva-collateral. In Europe, art. 3(1) of the Settlement Finality Directive (SFD) disapplies the zero-hour rule: See 'Settlement Finality in Payment and Securities Settlement Systems', Pub.

the zero-hour rule[8] is still raised in the courts of states with solid commercial traditions with the Netherlands (Indonesia, Netherlands Antilles).[9]

The concept of legal finality creates a disparity between a cash-based and a bank-based payment. The former is final as soon as the cash is delivered, while the latter may still be subjected to claw-back until midnight of the day it has been settled. However, any analogy between these two types of payments misses the fact that a bank-based payment is not only a transfer of money but also requires the exchange of all the data contained in the payment order.[10] With the diffusion of correspondent banking,[11] the concept of finality began to widen from its initial meaning of ***discharge of an obligation*** to the new aspect of the *exchange of data*.

15.1.2 Settlement in correspondent banking

Finality is a multifaceted construct. From an economist's outlook, the degree of finality in payment results from a trade-off between the benefits of indisputability versus the costs of recovering an erroneous or fraudulent transfer. From a legal perspective, the law governing interbank payment infrastructure determines the finality of a given transfer, that is, the criteria for judging when the transfer of an amount of money becomes irrevocable and discharges an obligation.[12]

Correspondent banking can be defined as 'an arrangement under which one bank (correspondent) holds deposits owned by other banks (respondents) and provides payment and other services to those respondent banks.'[13] In correspondent banking, legal finality is reached through a series of steps with general criteria defining each.

Focusing on the US framework, this discussion follows Uniform Commercial Code (UCC) Article 4A, which governs fund transfers in the US.[14] Under

L. No. 98/26/EC, Directive (1998), art. 3 (1), https://eur-lex.europa.eu/legal-content/EN/TXT/HTML/?uri=CELEX:01998L0026-20190627&from=EN.

8 M Hadi Shubhan, 'The Utilization of Unwritten Laws in Bankruptcy Disputes', *Jurnal Rechts Vinding* 8, no. 1 (April 2019): 94.

9 Massimo Cirasino et al., *Reforming Payments and Securities Settlement Systems in Latin America and the Caribbean* (The World Bank, 2006), 38, https://doi.org/10.1596/978-0-8213-6635-6.

10 Vincenzo De Stasio, 'Riparto di responsabilità e restituzioni nei pagamenti non autorizzati', in *Innovazione e regole nei pagamenti digitali*, ed. Maria Cecilia Paglietti and Maria Iride Vangelisti, Consumatori e Mercato 9 (Roma: Roma Tre-Press, 2020), 26.

11 Basel Committee on Banking Supervision, ed., *Regulatory Consistency Assessment Programme (RCAP): Assessment of Basel III Regulations - Australia*, March 2014 (Basel: Bank for International Settlements, 2014), 16.

12 Kahn and Roberds, 'The Economics of Payment Finality', 1.

13 Committee on Payment and Settlement Systems, 'A Glossary of Terms Used in Payments and Settlement Systems' (BIS, 2003), 16, https://www.bis.org/cpmi/glossary_030301.pdf.

14 As amended in 2012 to comply with the federal Electronic Funds Transfer Act. After the latter came into force, the UCC had to acknowledge the supremacy of federal law. See Uniform Commercial Code—Funds Transfers. (68 Del. Laws, c. 430, § 1.)

4A-402 UCC, when a sender issues a payment order to the beneficiary's bank, the moment the order is accepted marks the incurrence of an obligation to pay between the sender and the bank. The arising obligation is then discharged under the conditions listed in 4A-403. This approach has been criticised as it leaves the beneficiary's bank much freedom to accept the transfer order.[15] As specified in 4A-404, when it accepts the payment order, the beneficiary's bank incurs the obligation to pay the beneficiary and notify the same about the order received. This obligation is discharged in the ways described under 4A-405.

Finally, the obligation that originated the sender's payment to the beneficiary is discharged as described under 4A-406. In principle, *operational settlement* is reached after all the actions needed to confirm the payment have been taken. Under 4A-403 UCC, the sender reaches an operational settlement with the beneficiary's bank after the latter has taken control of the funds. *A legal settlement* is reached after operational settlement, after the beneficiary has actually taken control of the funds. Under 4A-405 UCC, legal settlement happens when the beneficiary's bank has credited the funds, netted it against a pre-existing debt, or notified the beneficiary about their availability.[16] *Final settlement* is reached after legal settlement when the relevant insolvency framework establishes that such payment cannot be void or reversed. That is the hardest to achieve, as some bankruptcy provisions are retroactive, voiding all the transactions acted by a person even before she was declared insolvent. Banking practice is inherently complicated, and there cannot be a simple definition of the events triggering a transition from one step to the next. Also, its provisions had to be altered to follow the progress in the payments industry.

15.2 The principle of settlement finality

15.2.1 Settlement finality for RTGS

The culmination of the traditional doctrine based on the approach of the discharge of an obligation is the principle of settlement finality that defines once and for all in which contexts (on which payment systems) legal finality and settlement finality are instantly achieved by the successful emission of an order of payment.[17] Originated by several notable insolvencies (Herstatt risk), this principle states that if a fund transfer is executed on the special class of *desig-*

15 Dianna Kyles, 'The Concept of Payment: Wire Transfer Orders, the Common Law and Article 4A', *Dalhousie Journal of Legal Studies* 11 (2002): 229.

16 For the operational and legal aspects of finality see Hossein Nabilou, 'Probabilistic Settlement Finality in Proof-of-Work Blockchains: Legal Considerations', SSRN Electronic Journal, 2022, 16 ff., https://doi.org/10.2139/ssrn.4022676.

17 Nancy Liao, 'On Settlement Finality and Distributed Ledger Technology, by Nancy Liao', *Yale Journal on Regulation* (blog), 9 June 2017, https://www.yalejreg.com/nc/on-settlement-finality-and-distributed-ledger-technology-by-nancy-liao/.

nated systems, it is irrevocable, instantly settled, and protected against insolvency proceedings.[18] Settlement finality prevents a single operator's default from compromising the designated system's overall operation.[19]

RTGSs were introduced in the early 1990s to allow real-time payments among central and commercial banks.[20] On such systems, all payment orders are processed in the exact order they have been validated. This requires all partners to advance large amounts of liquidity to ensure that their payments are adequately funded. For this reason, RTGSs are mainly used for large-amount transactions between institutional operators.[21] According to the European Settlement Finality Directive (SFD), the instant a designated system has validated an order of payment marks the discharge of its sender's obligation. Moreover, the transfer is made irrevocable, unconditional, and enforceable. Even in the event of a technical malfunction, a designated system must guarantee that all validated payments will be completed (in the appropriate order) as soon as the system is restarted.

All advanced economies have a *designating authority* empowered to define which systems can reliably operate according to the principle of settlement finality. According to the UK legal framework, the designating authority is the BoE.[22] The SFD requires Member States to notify the ESMA, which organisation is their national designating authority.[23]

18 Settlement finality in payment and securities settlement systems, art. 4; Jess Cheng, 'How to Build a Stablecoin: Certainty, Finality, and Stability Through Commercial Law Principles', *Berkeley Business Law Journal* 17, no. 2 (2020): 329, 331 ff., https://doi.org/10.15779/Z38736M287.

19 Henri F Pages and David B Humphrey, 'Settlement Finality as a Public Good in Large-Value Payment Systems', *SSRN Electronic Journal*, 2005, 6, https://doi.org/10.2139/ssrn.750786.

20 Mauro Arcese, Domenico Di Giulio, and Vitangelo Lasorella, 'Real-Time Gross Settlement Systems: Breaking the Wall of Scalability and High Availability', *Banca d'Italia Research Papers*, Markets, Infrastructures, Payment Systems, no. 2 (2021): 7, https://www.bancaditalia.it/pubblicazioni/mercati-infrastrutture-e-sistemi-di-pagamento/approfondimenti/2021-002/N.2-MISP.pdf?language_id=.

21 To regulate them, the European Commission issued Directive 98/26/EC on settlement finality in payment and securities settlement systems. See Paolo Bramini et al., 'TARGET2-Il Sistema Europeo per il Regolamento dei pagamenti di importo rilevante', *Banca d'Italia*, Markets, Infrastructures, Payment Systems, no. 9 (July 2021): 10, https://www.bancaditalia.it/pubblicazioni/mercati-infrastrutture-e-sistemi-di-pagamento/questioni-istituzionali/2021-009/N.9-MISP.pdf.

22 'The Financial Markets and Insolvency (Settlement Finality) Regulations 1999', Pub. L. No. 2979 (1999), 2, https://www.legislation.gov.uk/uksi/1999/2979/made/data.htm?wrap=true. Under part I, 2 of this regulation, the designating authority was either the Financial Service Authority (FSA) or the Bank of England. In April 2013, the FSA was dissolved, so it no longer is a designating authority.

23 Settlement finality in payment and securities settlement systems, art. 2; 'Amending Delegated Regulation (EU) 2018/1229 Concerning the Regulatory Technical Standards on Settlement Discipline, as Regards Its Entry into Force', Pub. L. No. EU/2021/70, Commission Delegated Regulation (2020), https://eur-lex.europa.eu/eli/reg_del/2021/70/oj/eng.

In Europe, the development of the TARGET RTGS (1999-2007) was essential in supporting the introduction of the Single European Currency. In 2008/2009, the EC first consulted about the SFD. During the same years, the new RTGS TARGET2[24] was launched as a collaboration between the Bank of Italy, the Deutsche Bundesbank, and the Banque de France.[25] In 2010, after the financial crisis, a new system of European supervision was introduced, and the European Central Bank's TARGET2 RTGS reached full availability. Technical evolution led to five amendments to the Directive, the latest in 2019. TARGET2 links the ECB and the 20 European member states of the eurozone. In addition to its primary function (real-time protected payments in central bank money), it implements the ECB monetary policy, allowing commercial banks to lend or borrow money at a controlled rate. As for the ECB Guideline, all bilateral liabilities and claims are transferred to the ECB by novation at the end of the business day. This original netting method requires each Eurosystem's central bank (including the ECB itself) to have an account in the Central Liquidity Management Facility. It leaves each partner with a single position (claim or liability) against the ECB itself.[26] As this is an automatic process necessary for the operation of the RTGS, these TARGET2 balances should not be considered debt instruments in the legal sense.[27] The decision to novate all existing obligations to the ECB just means that the ECB is the sole controller of the expansion of the balance sheet of a member state central bank. This corroborates the fact that:

> [the] role of the European Central Bank cannot be categorised as a control-by-administrative act under a superior political decision. At the same time, we cannot identify it with control-as-management, as the decisions of the ECB have only an indirect impact over the national economies through the actions of the national central banks.[28]

24 Rosa Giovanna Barresi, 'The Impact of Monetary Union and the Euro on European Capital Markets: What May Be Achieved in Capital Market Integration', *Fordham International Law Journal* 28, no. 4 (1 January 2004): 1282 ff.

25 Bramini et al., 'TARGET2-Il Sistema Europeo per il Regolamento dei pagamenti di importo rilevante', 13 ff.

26 Guideline of the European Central Bank of 5 December 2012 on a Trans-European Automated Real-time Gross settlement Express Transfer system (TARGET2), art. 6.2.

27 Steffen Murau and Matteo Giordano, 'European Monetary Unification through Novation. The Political Economy of the TARGET System', preprint (SocArXiv, 9 July 2022), 19 ff., https://doi.org/10.31235/osf.io/k3nbh.

28 Filippo Zatti, 'Il controllo della BCE sulle economie nazionali', in *A 150 anni dall'unificazione amministrativa italiana. L'intervento pubblico nell'economia*, ed. Maurizio Cafagno and Francesco Manganaro, vol. V (Firenze: FUP, 2015), 500–501, http://rgdoi.net/10.13140/RG.2.1.3499.8482.

15.2.2 The international dimension of settlement finality

As soon as an EU member state recognises a designated system, this designation is valid for all other member states under the current SFD. However, there is no provision for third-country systems, a *lacuna* that first came to light during the Brexit negotiations.[29] The advent of new financial tools, like Instant Payments systems and DLT systems, has made it necessary to open a new consultation in February 2021.[30] In June 2021, the EC completed a review of how member states implement the finality directive to institutions participating in systems governed by the law of a third country.[31] Interesting to note that EBA Clearing's response to EC consultation on SFD underlined that:

> First, the protection of the SFD should only be extended to third country systems in countries that also protect SFD-designated systems. In other words, the protection should be reciprocal...Second, the relevant EU authorities (be it at the EU or Member State level) should defer to the competent authority of the third country in question...Third, the new EU framework is to defer to the law that governs the third-country system. If the principle of reciprocity is respected, this will ensure that the SFD always applies to payment systems governed by EU law and that the SFD cannot be overridden by the courts of a third country in which the EU-based payment system has participants [32]

15.2.3 Settlement finality as data ownership

The GFC led to the definition of a set of 24 principles for financial market infrastructures (FMI) targeted at evaluating and mitigating liquidity risk.[33] The principles describe settlement finality according to the traditional obligation-based approach. In particular, Principle 8—settlement finality—states that an FMI should provide a clear and specific final settlement, at a minimum, by the end of the value date. An FMI should provide a final settlement intraday or

29 Financial Markets Law Committee, 'Targeted Consultation on the Review of the Settlement Finality Directive in Payment and Securities Settlement Systems', 7 May 2021, 1 ff., http://fmlc.org/wp-content/uploads/2021/05/FMLC-Response-to-SFD-Review.pdf.

30 '2021 - Settlement Finality Review', accessed 3 January 2023, https://finance.ec.europa.eu/regulation-and-supervision/consultations/2021-settlement-finality-review_en.

31 Settlement finality in payment and securities settlement systems, art. 12a.

32 EBA Clearing, 'Response to the European Commission's Public Consultation on the Directive on Settlement Finality in Payment and Securities Settlement Systems', May 2021, 2–3, https://www.ebaclearing.eu/media/azure/production/2759/ebacl_sfd-consultation_summary-for-website_final.pdf.

33 Ouarda Merrouche and Erlend Nier, 'What Caused the Global Financial Crisis? Evidence on the Drivers of Financial Imbalances 1999–2007', IMF Working Paper, 10, no. 265 (December 2010).

in real-time where necessary or preferable.[34] Instead, Principle 12—Exchange-of-value settlement systems—addresses that if an FMI settles transactions that involve the settlement of two linked obligations (for example, securities or foreign exchange transactions), it should eliminate principal risk by conditioning the final settlement of one obligation upon the final settlement of the other.[35]

On the contrary, SFD is probably one of the first cases of *Lex Algorithmica*. The SFD states in articles 3, 4, and 5 the general principle of settlement finality according to which transfer orders are legally enforceable and binding on third parties 'provided that transfer orders were entered into the system before the moment of opening of such insolvency proceedings.'[36] That formulation is based on data-related events, and the actual definitions of the two essential events—when a transfer order enters the system and when it becomes irrevocable—are left to 'the rules of the system.'[37] The first reason is the plurality of systems presently in operation. However, it is clear that the sheer mass of transactions means that only the system itself can document the timeline of these events. The Target2-Securities (T2S) system,[38] designated by the Eurosystem to provide the basic functions required for core settlement purposes, provides an excellent example of this algorithmic definition of finality *as an exchange of data*.[39]

Although not a complete settlement system, T2S defines the three primary events in a transaction lifecycle by describing its operational workflow for validation, clearing and settlement.[40] Describing these three events as SF1, SF2, and SF3 has become a standard in the language of European payment

34 Committee on Payment and Settlement Systems and Technical Committee of the International Organization of Securities Commissions, 'Principles for Financial Market Infrastructures' (BIS & OICV-IOSCO, April 2012), 64, https://www.bis.org/cpmi/publ/d101a.pdf.

35 Committee on Payment and Settlement Systems and Technical Committee of the International Organization of Securities Commissions, 76.

36 Settlement finality in payment and securities settlement systems, art. 3.

37 Settlement finality in payment and securities settlement systems, art. 3; Primavera De Filippi and Samer Hassan, 'Blockchain Technology as a Regulatory Technology: From Code Is Law to Law Is Code', *First Monday*, 14 November 2016, 7, https://doi.org/10.5210/fm.v21i12.7113.

38 Cristina Mastropasqua et al., 'T2S - TARGET2-Securities the Pan-European Platform for the Settlement of Securities in Central Bank Money', *Banca d'Italia Markets, Infrastructures, Payment Systems*, Institutional Issues, no. 4 (September 2021): 10 ff., https://www.bancaditalia.it/pubblicazioni/mercati-infrastrutture-e-sistemi-di-pagamento/questioni-istituzionali/2021-004/MISP-n-4-ENG.pdf?language_id=1.

39 ECB and T2S, 'General Principles of T2S', n.d., 1, https://www.ecb.europa.eu/paym/target/t2s/profuse/shared/pdf/2011_t2s_general_principles.pdf.

40 ECB and T2S, 3.

systems.[41] These definitions translate into precise procedures (and flow charts) to be followed in the case of insolvency of a T2S participant.[42]

15.2.4 Settlement finality for instant payment systems

Instant payment systems are the next step in evolving payment services, allowing instant and direct person-to-person payments. These new systems operate 24/7/365 and ensure service availability thanks to their distributed nature.[43] In Europe, this has been made possible by the introduction of a standard scheme for identifying any banking account in the Single Euro Payments Area (SEPA): the SEPA credit transfer (SCT) scheme and SEPA Instant Credit Transfer (SCT Inst).[44] Over these addressing schemes, two systems have been built: RT1, launched by the Euro Banking Association and managed by EBA Clearing,[45] and Target Instant Payments Service (TIPS), managed by the Eurosystem.[46]

In the US, the Fed announced FedNow, the new interbank RTGS service with integrated clearing functionality, supporting instant payments and settling in central bank money using master accounts. FedNow was then launched on

41 Being SF1: the moment an order has entered the system is defined as the successful *end of the validation process*; SF2: the moment an order becomes irrevocable is defined as the successful *end of the clearing process*, that is when a match has been achieved between sell and buy orders; and SF3: unconditionality and enforceability of the trade are achieved at the *end of the settlement process*.

42 Interbolsa, 'Insolvency of an Interbolsa Participant—Manual of Procedures', 2019, 5–7.

43 Arcese, Giulio, and Lasorella, 'Real-Time Gross Settlement Systems: Breaking the Wall of Scalability and High Availability', 16.

44 Massimiliano Renzetti et al., 'TIPS: TARGET Instant Payment Settlement The Pan-European Infrastructure for the Settlement of Instant Payments', *Banca d'Italia Markets, Infrastructures, Payment Systems*, no. 1 (January 2021): 8, https://www.bancaditalia.it/pubblicazioni/mercati-infrastrutture-e-sistemi-di-pagamento/questioni-istituzionali/2021-001/en-MIS-20210129.pdf?language_id=1. All Payment Service Providers adhering to the SCTInst scheme ensure the maximum execution time for each individual transaction will not exceed ten seconds, the service is guaranteed all year round, 24 hours a day, with a maximum limit of €100,000 per transaction. Considering that at the beginning of 2022, only 11% of all euro credit transfers in the EU were instant, the European Commission issued a proposal to make instant payments more affordable, secure, and widespread, see European Commission, Proposal for a Regulation of the European Parliament and of the Council amending Regulation (EU) No 260/2012 and (EU) 2021/1230 as regards instant credits transfer in euro, COM(2022) 546 final, 26 October 2022.

45 EBA Clearing, 'Overview', n.d., https://www.ebaclearing.eu/services/rt1/overview/; EBA Clearing, 'New RT1 Specifications to Help Users Benefit from Future TIPS Set-Up', 23 April 2021, https://www.ebaclearing.eu/news-and-events/media/press-releases/23-april-2021-new-rt1-specifications-to-help-users-benefit-from-future-tips-set-up/.

46 Renzetti et al., 'TIPS: TARGET Instant Payment Settlement the Pan-European Infrastructure for the Settlement of Instant Payments', 31.

20 July 2023.[47] Contrary to TIPS, built over the TARGET2 RTGS, FedNow does not rely on the FedWire RTGS and operates directly over institutional accounts with the twelve US Reserve Banks.[48]

It is helpful to compare the transaction lifecycle on the T2S system with that of a payment order in FedNow. Here, when the payment order is validated, it is called the 'moment of entry.' It has the same properties as what is called SF1 in T2S. The named 'moment of irrevocability,' which is equivalent to SF2 in T2S, happens after the amount to be paid has been 'reserved' on the payer's account. After that, a payment order is forwarded to the receiver's bank, which could reject the payment only if the order contains some invalid account information for the receiver. The instant this last validation has been successful is called the 'moment of finality' (equivalent to SF3 in T2S), and after that, the payment is protected from any insolvency process.[49] In May 2022, the Fed Board finalised Regulation J, the rule governing payments and funds transfers over the Federal Reserve Banks' FedNow Service.[50] Universal Commercial Code Article 4A has been incorporated into Regulation J to ensure a consistent law application to all transfers over the FedNow Service.

Moreover, suppose a transfer over the new service would meet the definition of 'electronic fund transfer' under the Electronic Fund Transfer Act (EFTA), in that case, the new provisions will also prevail over those stated in

47 In January 2021, the Federal Reserve Banks announced that more than 110 organisations would be part of the FedNow Pilot Program: Federal Reserve Financial Services, 'Federal Reserve Announces FedNowSM Pilot Program Participants', 25 January 2021, https://www.frbservices.org/news/press-releases/012521-federal-reserve-announces-fednow-pilot-program-participants. See Board of Governors of the Federal Reserve System, 'Federal Reserve announces that its new system for instant payments, the FedNow Service, is now live', press release, 20 July 2023, https://www.federalreserve.gov/newsevents/pressreleases/other20230720a.htm.

48 Federal Register, 'Federal Reserve Actions to Support Interbank Settlement of Faster Payments', 9 August 2019, https://www.federalregister.gov/documents/2019/08/09/2019-17027/federal-reserve-actions-to-support-interbank-settlement-of-faster-payments. On 20 March 2023, T2 replaced TARGET2 as the new RTGS system, ECB, Successful launch of the new T2 wholesale payment system, https://www.ecb.europa.eu/press/pr/date/2023/html/ecb.pr230321~f5c7bddf6d.en.html.

49 Federal Reserve System, 'Service Details on Federal Reserve Actions to Support Interbank Settlement of Instant Payments', Federal Register, 11 August 2020, https://www.federalregister.gov/documents/2020/08/11/2020-17539/service-details-on-federal-reserve-actions-to-support-interbank-settlement-of-instant-payments; Renzetti et al., 'TIPS: TARGET Instant Payment Settlement The Pan-European Infrastructure for the Settlement of Instant Payments', 28.

50 Federal Reserve System, 'Collection of Checks and Other Items by Federal Reserve Banks and Funds Transfers through Fedwire – Press Release', Federal Register, 6 June 2022, https://www.federalregister.gov/documents/2022/06/06/2022-11090/collection-of-checks-and-other-items-by-federal-reserve-banks-and-funds-transfers-through-fedwire; Board of Governors of the Federal Reserve System, 'Federal Reserve Board Finalizes Rule That Governs Funds Transfers over the Federal Reserve Banks' FedNow Service - Press Release', 19 May 2022, https://www.federalreserve.gov/newsevents/pressreleases/other20220519a.htm.

the EFTA in the case of any inconsistency.[51] The general principle is that if a payment is made to satisfy an obligation, it is considered discharged to the same extent it would result from a money payment: in an amount equal to the amount of the order accepted by the beneficiary's bank, but not more than the amount of the originator's order at the instant the payment order is accepted by the beneficiary's bank.[52] If payment by the originator does not result in discharge, the originator is subrogated to the rights of the beneficiary to receive payment from the beneficiary's bank under section 4A-404 (a). Under section 4A-404 (b), for a payment not to result in discharge, all the following four conditions need to be met:

i) The payment was made by means explicitly prohibited by the contract between the originator and beneficiary.
ii) The beneficiary notified the originator of their refusal of the payment after receiving a notification of it.
iii) The funds involved in the payment were not withdrawn by the beneficiary or applied to a debt of theirs.
iv) The beneficiary had suffered a loss that might have been avoided if the payment had been made by means of complying with the contract.[53]

Suppose the amount of the payment received by the beneficiary has been decreased by applying payment charges. In that case, that payment is considered in the original amount unless the beneficiary explicitly demands the amount of the deducted charges to the originator.[54]

15.3 Frameworks and legislations about digital assets

15.3.1 The Liechtenstein Token and TT Service Provider Act

This Act was issued in 2019 and was one of the first consistent attempts to regulate the matter.[55] The Act's foundation is the token's definition as a new legal object,[56] solving in this way the issue of recognising an intangible object

51 Federal Reserve System, 'Part 210—Collection of Checks and Other Items by Federal Reserve Banks and Funds Transfers through the Fedwire Funds Service and the FedNow Service (Regulation J)', 108 12 CFR 210 § (2022), 34353, https://www.govinfo.gov/content/pkg/FR-2022-06-06/pdf/2022-11090.pdf#page=8.

52 Federal Reserve System, 34375.

53 Federal Reserve System, 34375.

54 Federal Reserve System, 34375.

55 'Law of 3 October 2019 on Tokens and TT Service Providers (Token and TT Service Provider Act; TVTG)', Pub. L. No. 950.6 (2020), https://www.regierung.li/files/medienarchiv/950-6-01-09-2021-en.pdf.

56 'Unofficial Translation of the Report and Application of the Government to the Parliament of the Principality of Liechtenstein Concerning the Creation of a Law on Tokens and TT Service Providers (Tokens and TT Service Provider Act; TVTG) (Blockchain Act)' (Vaduz: Liechten-

as a property, a typical problem of German law. According to this 'Token Container Model,' a token is defined by the environment hosting it as 'a piece of information on a TT System which can represent claims or rights of memberships against a person, rights to property or other absolute or relative rights; and is assigned to one or more TT Identifiers.'[57] Trustworthy technology systems (TT) are the environment where tokens are registered and traded.[58] This definition covers any type of digital ledger (either distributed or centralised) granting a person the power of disposal over one or more tokens: 'The person holding a Private Key not only has the power to dispose of the Token to which it relates but is also assumed to have the right to dispose of said Token.'[59] Moreover, all parties must agree that the disposer is entitled to transfer the token and the transfer itself.[60] When tokens represent property rights,[61] the 'Physical Validator'[62] is also needed to validate the transfer as a trusted third party who guarantees that those rights still exist and are enforceable. Tokens can be acquired *bona fide*, even if the token disposer was not entitled to rightfully dispose of them.[63] In the case of the loss of a token or access to it, its owner can request the administrator of the TT to separate the token from its content to dispose of the underlying right traditionally.[64]

Virtual currencies are defined as digital monetary units, which can be exchanged for legal tender, used to purchase goods or services or to preserve value and thus assume the function of legal tender (even if they cannot be considered as such). By a similar line of reasoning, the rights and obligations that can be built over a security token are the same as those of the underlying asset. Security tokens are considered to be transferable securities (financial instruments).

Utility tokens are treated similarly to commodities and are subject to EU Consumer Protection.[65] The Act primarily addresses the case of the TT service

---

stein Government, 2019), https://impuls-liechtenstein.li/wp-content/uploads/2021/02/Report-and-Application-TVTG-extract.pdf.

57 Law of 3 October 2019 on Tokens and TT Service Providers (Token and TT Service Provider Act; TVTG), art. 2(1)(c).

58 Law of 3 October 2019 on Tokens and TT Service Providers (Token and TT Service Provider Act; TVTG), art. 2(1)(a).

59 Law of 3 October 2019 on Tokens and TT Service Providers (Token and TT Service Provider Act; TVTG), art. 6.

60 Law of 3 October 2019 on Tokens and TT Service Providers (Token and TT Service Provider Act; TVTG), art. 6.

61 Meaning rights to real objects that have an existence outside the TT.

62 Law of 3 October 2019 on Tokens and TT Service Providers (Token and TT Service Provider Act; TVTG), art. 2(1)(p).

63 Law of 3 October 2019 on Tokens and TT Service Providers (Token and TT Service Provider Act; TVTG), art. 9.

64 Law of 3 October 2019 on Tokens and TT Service Providers (Token and TT Service Provider Act; TVTG), art. 10.

65 'DIRECTIVE 2011/83/EU OF THE EUROPEAN PARLIAMENT AND OF THE COUNCIL of 25 October 2011 on Consumer Rights, Amending Council Directive 93/13/

provider's insolvency stating that 'Tokens must be protected against claims of the TT service provider's other creditors.'[66] To comply with this requirement, the TT must ensure that user tokens are stored separately from those of the TT service provider.[67] From a technical viewpoint, the requirement that all parties agree before transferring a token[68] is challenging to reach on a non-permissioned pseudonymous DL like Ethereum. The Liechtenstein Act looks to be targeted mainly at centralised or permissioned ledgers from this point of view.

15.3.2 The UNIDROIT and UCC 2022

UNIDROIT published a set of general principles on digital assets targeted to facilitate transactions among states, whatever the foundations of their property laws. States are recommended to adopt legislation consistent with these principles, which are also intended to guide the legal profession.[69]

The concept of a *controllable digital asset* is introduced as the basis of the framework.[70] That distinction is necessary as some digital registrations are called 'digital assets' even if they are not subject to *control*. The concept of *control* refers to a relationship between a digital asset and a person where the latter has (i) the exclusive ability to assign control of the digital asset to another

---

EEC and Directive 1999/44/EC of the European Parliament and of the Council and Repealing Council Directive 85/577/EEC and Directive 97/7/EC of the European Parliament and of the Council' (2019), art. 3, https://eur-lex.europa.eu/legal-content/EN/TXT/HTML/?uri=CELEX:02011L0083-20220528&from=EN.

66 Law of 3 October 2019 on Tokens and TT Service Providers (Token and TT Service Provider Act; TVTG), art. 25(1).

67 Law of 3 October 2019 on Tokens and TT Service Providers (Token and TT Service Provider Act; TVTG), art. 25(1).

68 Matthias Lehmann, 'National Blockchain Laws as a Threat to Capital Markets Integration', *SSRN Electronic Journal*, 2021, 13, https://doi.org/10.2139/ssrn.3861519.

69 UNIDROIT, 'Digital Assets and Private Law Working Group', 7 March 2022, 5, https://www.unidroit.org/wp-content/uploads/2022/03/W.G.5.-Doc.-3-Master-Copy-Principles-plus-Comments-with-Questions.pdf. On 10 January 2023, UNIDROIT launched a public consultation related to a set of draft Principles and Commentary on Digital Assets and Private Law, see UNIDROIT, 'Draft UNIDROIT Principles on Digital Assets and Private Law', January 2023, https://www.unidroit.org/wp-content/uploads/2023/01/Draft-Principles-and-Commentary-Public-Consultation.pdf. While the 2023 Draft restated and renumbered some Principles, the changes made did not affect the analysis proposed in this essay. On 10 May 2023, the Governing Council adopted the UNIDROIT Principles on Digital Assets and Private Law, see UNIDROIT, 'Adoption of Draft Unidroit Instruments Principles on Digital Assets and Private Law, 10 May 2023, https://www.unidroit.org/wp-content/uploads/2023/04/C.D.-102-6-Principles-on-Digital-Assets-and-Private-Law.pdf; in September 2023 it was published, see UNIDROIT, Principles Digital Assets and Private Law, Principle 2(2), September 2023, ISBN: 978-88-86449-49-6, https://media.licdn.com/dms/document/media/D4E1FAQHtT-reGlKK7Q/feedshare-document-pdf-analyzed/0/1697349959836?e=1698278400&v=beta&t=fTLLxmXUsCTiFnvwWtFHg87OhZs-v-jb5IldTs2M_cg

70 Principle 6, UNIDROIT, 'Digital Assets and Private Law Working Group', 19.

person; (ii) the exclusive ability to prevent others from obtaining any of the benefits from the digital asset; and (iii) the ability to obtain some benefits from the digital asset.[71] The agreed goal of the framework is to define and protect *any proprietary right* in a *controllable digital asset*. That means not only the proprietary rights acquired through an ordinary sale-purchase but also rights with proprietary effects, such as those acquired during insolvency proceedings. This issue has already raised controversy in some jurisdictions.[72] Again, a rule has been stated for the protection of a *bona fide* acquirer, who receives a digital asset as nominally free of other claims. That acquirer is qualified as innocent even if the transfer of control of the digital asset is made by 'a person that is acting wrongfully and has no proprietary right in the digital asset' (i.e., a thief or a hacker). In such a case, the burden of proof rests on the plaintiff, who needs to prove the bad faith of the acquirer.[73] The general principle is that insolvency laws should not impair a security right because it is a digital asset.[74] That guarantees that no party might subtract digital assets from an insolvency estate because they are not property. However, the still unsolved issue remains whether security rights in a digital asset may have seniority against other claims under the applicable secured transactions law.

Another issue left open is the value of a digital asset inside the estate. Should it be taken as the going concern value (book value) or as its liquidation value, that is, after its conversion into fiat money? The UCC is a set of state laws governing commercial transactions targeted at adopting a uniform framework in the US. In July 2022, Article 12 was proposed for state adoption in order to protect property rights over digital assets.[75] The proposal is based on the concept of 'Controllable Electronic Record' or CER, stated in Section 12-105, describing any information stored in electronic form and susceptible to control.[76] This concept is similar to the 'controllable digital asset' defined in the UNIDROIT Framework. Also, the definition of control is, apart from the ordering of the criteria, very similar to what is stated at UNIDROIT. From this point onwards, the UCC proposal assumes the concept of control as the decisive criterion for solving the issues left open by the UNIDROIT framework. To do this, the proposal lists entities that may be considered 'digital

71 Principle 6, UNIDROIT, 19.

72 Principle 3(2), UNIDROIT, 11: 'in the context of insolvency, where a liquidator or insolvency administrator might assert rights or interests in digital assets on behalf of the insolvent debtor's estate and/or its creditors against third parties, and vice versa.'

73 Principle 9, UNIDROIT, 23–24. The Principle of 'innocent acquisition' is restated under Principle 8, UNIDROIT, 2023 Draft.

74 Principle 20, UNIDROIT, 42. The Principle of 'Effect of insolvency on proprietary rights in digital assets' is restated under Principle 19, UNIDROIT, 2023 Draft.

75 Uniform Law Commission, 'Why Your State Should Adopt the 2022 Amendments to the Uniform Commercial Code', 20 December 2022, https://perma.cc/DEN9-UNW4.

76 Art. 12, Section 12-105, Uniform Law Commission, 'Uniform Commercial Code Amendments (2022)', 30 November 2022, https://perma.cc/7LZ7-F546.

assets' but are not subject to *control* and are already regulated by specific laws, like electronic chattel paper, deposit accounts, and e-money. This clarification is necessary as some definitions of 'digital assets' already put at the state level are unnecessarily inclusive. As an example, in the Wyoming Statute, digital asset *means* 'a representation of economic, proprietary or access rights that is stored in a computer-readable format and is either a digital consumer asset, digital security or virtual currency.'[77] The law envisages three categories of 'digital assets': (i) digital consumer assets; (ii) digital securities; and (iii) virtual currencies.[78] To the extent that the last category encompasses native cryptoassets, this may be accurate. However, the first two categories clearly envisage the digital record as reflecting off-chain enforceable legal rights.

The concept of control is the basis for the definition of a *qualifying purchaser*, describing a person who obtains control of a CER in good faith[79] through a voluntary transaction.[80] A *take-free* rule is posted to protect the qualifying purchaser's rights.[81]

Both UNIDROIT and UCC approaches refer to *control* as the qualifying property of a digital asset. However, it should be stressed that the UCC definition of control is limited to voluntary transactions and excludes rights with proprietary effects, such as those acquired by the administrator of an insolvency estate.

15.3.3 The Law Commission's proposal for digital assets law

The Law Commission of England and Wales intervened in this issue, launching a consultation paper on a law reform aimed at protecting digital assets.[82] In English law and related systems, a digital asset fulfils 'all the indicia of property' but lacks physical existence.[83] To accommodate this, the concept of *intangible things* has been introduced as a *third type of property* in addition to *things in possession* and *things in action*.[84] A thing falls into the new third category of personal property if: (1) it is composed of data represented in an electronic

77 Wyo. Stat. Ann. §34-29-101, Ch. 29, Digital Assets (a)(i), https://wyoleg.gov/statutes/compress/title34.pdf.

78 Wyo. Stat. Ann. §34-29-101, Ch. 29, Digital Assets (a)(ii), (iii), (iv).

79 That is, without knowledge of any prior competing property claim to the asset itself.

80 That is, through a sale-purchase or by enforcing a security interest. Uniform Law Commission, 'Uniform Commercial Code Amendments (2022)', art. 12 Section 12-102.

81 Uniform Law Commission, art. 9 Section 9-317.

82 Law Commission, 'Digital Assets: Consultation Paper 256', 28 July 2022, 4, https://perma.cc/M2WJ-KDC8.

83 Lawrence Akka et al., 'Legal Statement on Cryptoassets and Smart Contracts', ed. UK Jurisdiction Taskforce (The LawTech Delivery Panel, November 2019), 21–22, https://perma.cc/T7B6-PSQL.

84 Johan David Michels and Christopher Millard, 'The New Things: Property Rights in Digital Files?', The Cambridge Law Journal 81, no. 2 (July 2022): 19, https://doi.org/10.1017/S0008197322000228; Law Commission, 'Digital Assets: Consultation Paper 256', 53,57.

medium, including in the form of computer code, electronic, digital, or analogue signals; (2) it exists independently of persons and independently of the legal system; and (3) it is rivalrous.[85] The criterion of *rivalrousness* implies that a person controlling the thing can exclude others from being in control.

As digital assets can attract personal property rights, the Law Commission proposed in the Consultation Paper a third category of personal property, called *data objects*. It includes all intangible things over which control can be exerted.[86] The concept of control is more general than ownership, as it considers the eventuality of the holder and the owner being different persons. Also, the concept of control is more appropriate to deal with how a person may gain control over data. The concept of control is rapidly becoming the universal criteria in recognising digital assets: the UCC's *CER*, the UNIDROIT's *controllable digital asset*, and the *data object* of the Law Commission are defined in a very similar way.[87] Liechtenstein's Token and Trustworthy Technology Service Provider Act prefers an indirect path, leading to the same conclusion. It first defines the class of Trustworthy Technology systems as a way of exercising the power of disposal over digital assets, a concept similar to control.[88]

The Law Commission states the 'innocent acquisition rule' for protecting a *bona fide* acquirer of data objects.[89] This is an important point shared by all the attempts at regulating digital assets and is like the essential property of money, that is, its nature of bearer-asset.

The Law Commission concludes that the legal analysis of digital assets' transfer and settlement finality should be necessarily technology-specific due to the peculiar way they are transferred.[90] This position leads to the issue of producing a technology-specific digital asset taxonomy. The complexity of these tools is constantly growing.[91] In this scenario of continuing technical evolution, the feasibility of a technology-specific taxonomy is questionable. An alternative solution has been proposed based on classifying the *use cases* of digital assets into a conceptual framework that identifies some common legal

85 Law Commission, 'Digital Assets: Consultation Paper 256', 79.

86 Law Commission, 'Digital Assets: Consultation Paper 256', 190, 244. On 28 June 2023, the Law Commission published the Final Report on Digital Assets and the term *data object* was replaced with *digital object* 'to refer to a digital asset within the third category' as crypto-token or an NFT, see Law Commission, 'Digital Assets: Final Report, 28 June 2023, 52, https://s3-eu-west-2.amazonaws.com/lawcom-prod-storage-11jsxou24uy7q/uploads/2023/06/Final-digital-assets-report-FOR-WEBSITE-2.pdf.

87 As discussed, the UCC definition of control is technically limited to voluntary transactions, while the other two are not.

88 Law of 3 October 2019 on Tokens and TT Service Providers (Token and TT Service Provider Act; TVTG), art. 5.

89 Law Commission, 'Digital Assets: Consultation Paper 256', 258.

90 Law Commission, 206.

91 The Digital Assets Taxonomy System (DATS) classifies more than a thousand digital asset technologies. See Wilshire Digital Assets Advisory Group, 'Digital Asset Taxonomy System', December 2021, 3, https://perma.cc/464S-ZYZH.

principles. The framework is based on four hierarchically arranged dimensions (Rights, Representation, Issuance, and Transferability), each representing a specific aspect of the nature of digital assets.[92] As an example, the capability of receiving dividends is one of the several rights that a financial instrument may carry. The framework represents this relationship by three levels of categorisation, locating 'dividends' as a particular case of 'granted interest rights,' which are grouped under 'type of rights' in the 'rights' dimension.[93] This classification process can be conveniently abbreviated as:

Rights → Types of Rights → Granted Interest Rights → Dividends.

15.4 The extension of the doctrine of finality to digital assets

15.4.1 Settlement finality on distributed ledgers

DLT allows multiple parties to keep individual copies of a *shared ledger*, and a *consensus process* leads everyone to agree to a specific update of its contents. However, there is no mathematical guarantee that the consensus process will always reach the desired conclusion. External events beyond the scope of the system (i.e., hard forks, company liquidations, attacks by hackers and impersonators) can retroactively influence the state of the ledger, even after consensus has been reached. On a distributed ledger, settlement finality becomes a probabilistic concept in the sense that the longer a transaction has been considered settled by the ledger participants, the less likely it may be reversed in the future.[94] This *stochastic approach to finality* means that there may be significant impacts on the balance sheets of the involved parties even months after a transaction has been registered on the ledger. On the contrary, the traditional approach to finality is based on defining an unambiguous and transparent moment of finality, after which the transaction acquires legal validity and may be opposed by third parties. The best enunciation of this dilemma is probably in a joint publication by the BIS CPMI and by the IOSCO Board.[95]

When seeking to observe Principle 8, a systemically important Stablecoin Arrangement (SA) should: (i) clearly define the point at which a transfer of a stablecoin through the operational settlement method used becomes irrevocable and unconditional; (ii) ensure that there is a clear legal basis that acknowledges and supports finality of a transfer; and (iii) have robust mechanism(s) for preventing any misalignment between the state of the ledger and legal

92 Jason G Allen et al., 'Legal and Regulatory Considerations for Digital Assets' (Cambridge: Cambridge Centre for Alternative Finance, 2020), 49, https://www.jbs.cam.ac.uk/wp-content/uploads/2020/10/2020-ccaf-legal-regulatory-considerations-report.pdf.

93 Allen et al., 49.

94 Nabilou, 'Probabilistic Settlement Finality in Proof-of-Work Blockchains', 13.

95 Committee on Payments and Market Infrastructures and Board of the International Organization of Securities Commission, 'Application of the Principles for Financial Market Infrastructures to Stablecoin Arrangements', BIS & OICV-IOSCO, July 2022, https://www.bis.org/cpmi/publ/d206.pdf.

finality and ensure that legal finality of a transfer, once it has occurred, is maintained regardless of competing state(s) of the ledger.[96] According to Sir Jon Cunliffe, the BIS Committee on Payments and Market Infrastructures Chair, the technology behind traditional payment systems has evolved so much that a DL-based implementation is not yet competitive.[97]

In order to model the operation of DLs, some alternative theories of finality have been proposed. They focus on describing the exchange of rights on the digital assets hosted on the ledger, leaving the concept of obligation entirely out of the process. In the example of a delivery versus payment (DvP) settlement involving two digital assets hosted on a blockchain, the ***data ownership theory*** describes the process as ***a mutual exchange of property rights*** over the assets. In the current DeFi language, this operation is called a swap because both transfers happen ***simultaneously*** and are registered ***in the same block***. As a result, the swap has the four properties of a transaction: atomicity, consistency, isolation, and durability (ACID).[98] However, regarding the three-events model of a transaction lifecycle, a detailed analysis shows that only the SF3 timestamp can be reliably recorded over a permissionless blockchain.[99]

Also, while the data ownership interpretation requires both assets to be already in token form, there is a well-established opinion that, at present, no money tokenization process can preserve all its essential properties.[100] This is somewhat of a limit for the data ownership theory.

15.4.2 The European pilot regime for DLT-based TSS

The issue of whether the SFD can be applied to a DLT-based security settlement system has been examined by EU regulators. At present, it looks like only a permissioned DLT system can be made compliant with the SFD. The requirement of a 'system operator' as the entity legally responsible for the management and operation of such a system excludes ***designated operations*** over a decentralised, permissionless DLT system. In their Recommendation 21, a group of experts set up by the EU Commission suggested 'to revise the Settlement Finality Directive to allow for the participation in clearing and

96 Committee on Payments and Market Infrastructures and Board of the International Organization of Securities Commission, 64 ff. Principle 8.

97 Jon Cunliffe, 'Some Lessons from the Crypto Winter', 12 July 2022, https://www.bis.org/review/r220713c.pdf.

98 Thomas M Connolly and Carolyn E Begg, Database Systems: A Practical Approach to Design, Implementation, and Management, 6. ed., global ed, Always Learning (Boston, Munich: Pearson, 2015), 671.

99 Advisory Group on Market Infrastructures for Securities and Collateral, 'The Potential Impact of DLTs on Securities Post-Trading Harmonisation and on the Wider EU Financial Market Integration' (ECB, September 2017), 57 ff.

100 President's Working Group on Financial Markets, the Federal Deposit Insurance Corporation, and the Office of the Comptroller of the Currency, 'Report on Stablecoins', November 2021, 13.

settlement and payment systems of any type of regulated financial institution, on the basis of appropriate risk-based criteria.'[101]

While mainstream opinion is that permissionless blockchains should not be deployed in a full-scale large-value payment system,[102] permissioned DLTs are slowly gaining acceptance in trading and settlement. The Project Ion platform (developed by Depository Trust and Clearing Corporation—DTCC) has recently gone live in a parallel production environment for post-trading activities.[103] In the EU, the combination of trading and post-trading activities is presently forbidden in order to encourage risk specialisation and market competition. At the same time, it is a common opinion that using DLT might consolidate trading and settlement into one shared ledger, achieving real-time operation. This order of considerations led the European Parliament to approve a pilot regime for DLT-based market infrastructures.[104]

Besides the traditional concept of having separate multilateral trading facilities and settlement systems, the new regulation allows experimental single-manager operation of DLT-based trading and settlement systems (DLT TSS).[105] Suppose the pilot regime shows substantial benefits in this approach. In that case, splitting the trading and settlement operations into two separate companies will be relatively easy, leaving the blockchain as their unique media for exchanging information.

15.5 Law in the making: Digital assets

15.5.1 On the nature of digital assets

In November 2019, the Bundesrat approved the 'Act on the Implementation of the Amendment Directive to the Fourth EU Money Laundering Directive,'

101 Expert Group on Regulatory Obstacles to Financial Innovation (ROFIEG), 'Thirty Recommendations on Regulation, Innovation and Finance – Final Report to the European Commission' (Bruxelles: EU Commission, December 2019), 19, https://europa.eu/!yu87Xf.

102 Liao, 'On Settlement Finality and Distributed Ledger Technology, by Nancy Liao'.

103 'DTCC | A Fintech & Financial Market Infrastructure Company', accessed 4 January 2023, https://www.dtcc.com/. The new permissioned platform is settling an average of over 100,000 bilateral equity transactions per day. However, this is only a part of the full DTCC flow, which still provides an authoritative record and averages one million transactions per day: 'DTCC's Project Ion | DTCC', accessed 4 January 2023, https://www.dtcc.com/news/2022/august/22/project-ion.

104 This pilot regime offers a regulatory sandbox. 'REGULATION (EU) 2022/858 OF THE EUROPEAN PARLIAMENT AND OF THE COUNCIL of 30 May 2022 on a Pilot Regime for Market Infrastructures Based on Distributed Ledger Technology and Amending Regulations (EU) No 600/2014 and (EU) No 909/2014 and Directive 2014/65/EU' (2022).

105 Recital (14), REGULATION (EU) 2022/858 OF THE EUROPEAN PARLIAMENT AND OF THE COUNCIL of 30 May 2022 on a pilot regime for market infrastructures based on distributed ledger technology and amending Regulations (EU) No 600/2014 and (EU) No 909/2014 and Directive 2014/65/EU.

which entered into force on 1 January 2020.[106] The Act defines *Kryptowerte* (cryptoasset) as digital representations of assets that are neither issued nor guaranteed by any central bank or public entity and do not have the statutory status of a currency or money. These assets are transferred, stored, or traded digitally by persons who freely accept them as a means of payment or as a store of value because of agreements or actual practice.[107] *Ex facto jus oritur*: this is an empirical definition based on the approach followed by the three ESAs for the definition of virtual currencies (VCs).[108] While that definition does not explore the nature of digital assets, it is already defined in German law tradition. As already seen in the Liechtenstein Token and TT Service Provider Act, digital assets lack physical nature and cannot be classified as *Sachen* (objects).[109] This means that Section 90 of the German Civil Code (*Bürgerliches Gesetzbuch—BGB*) does not apply to them.[110]

Consequently, as digital assets cannot have an owner, they cannot be subject to property rights.[111] For the same reason, Section 929 of the BGB cannot be applied to transfer ownership of a digital asset by the usual means of agreement and delivery.[112] In the end, digital assets must be transferred via a *Realakt* (assignment) under Sections 398[113] and 413[114] of the BGB.

On the contrary, the trend in common law and related systems is to introduce the concept of *intangible things* to classify digital assets as a third type of *property*.[115] This allows us to state that digital assets are subject to *control*, but this word assumes a special meaning. In common law, possession is the laxest of the three property-related concepts (possession, right of possession, and ownership). It has been described as a relationship of *intentional control* between a person and a physical object.[116] The concept of *control* is even laxer, as it would be difficult to find and prove the presence of intention on DLT, where many dealings are carried out automatically by *smart contracts*. The UK

106 'Gesetz Zur Umsetzung Der Änderungsrichtlinie Zur Vierten EU-Geldwäscherichtlinie', Pub. L. No. 598 (2019).

107 Gesetz zur Umsetzung der Änderungsrichtlinie zur Vierten EU-Geldwäscherichtlinie, arts. 2, §1 (bb).

108 European Banking Authority. 'ESAs Warn Consumers of Risks in Buying Virtual Currencies', European Banking Authority, 12 February 2018, https://www.eba.europa.eu/esas-warn-consumers-of-risks-in-buying-virtual-currencies.

109 Law of 3 October 2019 on Tokens and TT Service Providers (Token and TT Service Provider Act; TVTG).

110 'German Civil Code BGB' (2013), sec. 90 'Concept of the thing'.

111 German Civil Code BGB, sec. 903 'Powers of the owner'.

112 German Civil Code BGB, sec. 929 'Agreement and delivery'.

113 German Civil Code BGB, sec. 398 'Assignment'.

114 German Civil Code BGB, sec. 413 'Transfer of other rights'.

115 Law Commission, 'Digital Assets: Consultation Paper 256', 53, 57; Michels and Millard, 'The New Things', 19.

116 The City of London Law Society, 'Digital Assets: The Limits of The Concept Of "Possession"', 13 August 2021, 4–7, https://perma.cc/3XGZ-TFHS.

Jurisdiction Task Force suggests that *practical control* of a crypto asset (by analogy with *possession* of a tangible asset) arises when a person (or a group thereof) has acquired knowledge and control of the private key(s) linked to the asset.[117] It should be pointed out that the ledger may identify a different person as the owner of the crypto asset or even hinder this identification.

15.5.2 The genesis of digital rights

Traditional economics defines ownership of an asset as whatever is left after all obligations over it have been accounted for.[118] While adequate from an accountant's perspective, this residual definition of ownership looks incomplete from a legal viewpoint. Most implementations of DLT support only the concept of *control* over a digital asset and leave little or no space for the registration of other rights over it. However, the biggest problem with that definition is that it overlooks the fundamental question of how somebody gained the right to create obligations over that digital asset.[119]

According to Nick Szabo, in 'all cases of property rights, there is a defined space, whether a namespace or physical space and the task is to agree on simple attributes of or rights to control subdivisions of that space.'[120] He proposed three strategies to solve the *genesis question*, as the initial allocation of digital property rights is critical and subjective. The world of digital assets is currently pursuing all three strategies at the same time. After the initial allocation has been carried out, transactions may start, and a digital ledger can be used to track asset history. The first strategy is based on the concept of the *social contract*: existing communities should collectively agree on the boundaries of their respective property rights. Ultimately, this leads to an institutional definition of a digital asset law, enforced by national authorities and coordinated by international organisations. The second strategy is to delegate the process to the digital marketplace. Any benefit of exercising a property right implies a deprivation incurred by someone else (in common law, this concept has been defined as a *rivalry* or *negative control* of the asset). According to the Coase theorem, when information and transaction costs are negligible, market prices will efficiently evaluate the costs and benefits of property rights.[121] Under this somewhat unrealistic hypothesis, the equilibrium solution will be reached wherever civil law places the border between assets and liabilities. The third

117 Akka et al., 'Legal Statement on Cryptoassets and Smart Contracts', 10, § 28.

118 Oliver Hart, Firms, Contracts, and Financial Structure, 1st ed. (Oxford University PressOxford, 1995), 30, https://doi.org/10.1093/0198288816.001.0001.

119 Katharina Pistor, The Code of Capital: How the Law Creates Wealth and Inequality (Princeton: Princeton University Press, 2019), 191.

120 Nick Szabo, 'Secure Property Titles with Owner Authority', 31 March 2016, https://web.archive.org/web/20160331174414/http://szabo.best.vwh.net/securetitle.html.

121 R H Coase, 'The Problem of Social Cost', *The Journal of Law & Economics* 3 (1960): 15, 19.

strategy is to define 'property clubs' delegated explicitly to the 'narrow function' of defining digital property rights on specific domains (i.e., Ethereum).[122] These clubs originate as coder groups and usually evolve into non-profit, management-oriented Foundations. Alternatively, a ***decentralized*** autonomous organisation (DAO) may be set up for that specific purpose.[123]

15.5.3 From the Age of Decodification to 'weak money'

Traditional legal systems were based on the concept of generating whole concepts, abstracting from all the circumstances that might have happened in real life. This requirement for formal closure of the legal system emerged as a solution to the demands for equality of all citizens in front of the law.[124] However, the decision to preclude access to sources external to the judicial system hindered the natural capability of law to solve the social conflicts about the distribution of resources and the protection of cultural identities and values.[125] The Age of Decodification marked a departure from the abstract constructions of XIX-century law.[126] Italian legislators attempted to enhance the legal system by issuing several collections of dispositions targeted at specific aspects of social life. These ***micro-legal systems*** named 'Testi Unici' allowed the use of interpretive methods to understand the ***intentio legis,***[127] leading to a better appreciation of the role of the *concrete case* as a template for judgement. A concrete case is a non-abstract category which keeps only the most relevant parts of the context without drilling down to the detailed level of the

122 'Home', The Ethereum Foundation, accessed 4 January 2023, https://ethereum.foundation.

123 Select Committee on Blockchain, Financial Technology and Digital Innovation Technology, 'Decentralized Autonomous Organizations', Pub. L. No. SF0038 (2021), https://www.wyoleg.gov/Legislation/2021/SF0038.

124 As acknowledged by most constitutional charters where liberalism is deployed. See, for instance, the Art. 3 (1) of the Republic of Italy Constitution.

125 Antonio Gambaro, 'Alcuni problemi in tema di diritto e giustizia nella tradizione giuridica occidentale', in Diritto, giustizia e interpretazione: a cura di Jacques Derrida et Gianni Vattimo, ed. Jacques Derrida, Gianni Vattimo, and Mauro Bussani, Biblioteca di cultura moderna Laterza 1139 (Bari: G Laterza & figli, 1998), 63–77; Claus Offe, '"Homogeneity" and Constitutional Democracy: Coping with Identity Conflicts through Group Rights', Journal of Political Philosophy 6, no. 2 (June 1998): 119–24, https://doi.org/10.1111/1467-9760.00049.

126 Natalino Irti, L'età della decodificazione, 2. ed (Milan: Giuffrè, 1986), 33 ff.

127 Irti, 64; Siro De Flammineis, 'L'età della (apparente) codificazione. Brevi riflessioni sul d.lgs. 1° marzo 2018 n. 21' Diritto Penale Contemporaneo, no. 6/2018 (5 June 2018): 27, https://www.penalecontemporaneo.it/d/6086-l-eta-della-apparente-codificazione-brevi-riflessioni-sul-dlgs-1-marzo-2018-n-21.

circumstance.[128] In non-law terminology, the same approach is often referred to as *use-case*.[129]

It is interesting to recognise a comparable trend in payment legislation. Users are asking for a trustless and convenient means of payment. From their point of view, cash as a means of payment is instantaneously final, traceless, and requires as little trust as possible and no data exchange.[130] No digital form of payment will ever reach these features of cash. Instant finality is never guaranteed, and the exchanged data remains in the participants' knowledge after the payment has been executed, a fact that should mark the proper limit for any juridical analogy between digital payments and cash. According to UCC article 4A,[131] the fund transfer procedure is described as a chain of participants, connected by an *abstract good-faith obligation*, and notifying their will through an *abstract communication channel*. As a result, most interpretations of UCC article 4A need the support of case law for classifying a specific circumstance as a valid acceptance or rejection of a payment order.

The way procedures are referenced in SFD (and the equivalent legislation) marked a real difference from previous attempts. The SFD has been successful precisely because its formulation leaves little space for disputes. However, this *Lex Machina* is still built over a network of trust relationships.

As noted by the EC, the transactions posted by EU participants in an RTGS governed by third-country laws are not protected under the SFD. The reverse is also true: non-EU participants in an EU-designated RTGS are not protected under their own settlement finality legislation.

'In light of the UK's withdrawal from the EU, the UK amended its legislation to enable third-country CCPs, CSDs and payment systems, which are not subject to UK law, to receive settlement finality designation within the UK.'[132]

Also, EBA Clearing has proposed mutual recognition for the designating authorities at the international level.[133] The scenario deriving from the international adoption of the SFD is an example of 'legal space,' *the set of norms considered applicable* to a case, resulting from the superposition of several different legal systems. The operation of a designated system rests on a network of trust relationships, all valid simultaneously. A well-known problem in this context is defining a specific site and time for an international

128 Francesco Viola, 'Il Futuro Del Diritto', Persona y Derecho, no. 79 (December 2019): 19, https://doi.org/10.15581/011.79.9-36.

129 Allen et al., 'Legal and Regulatory Considerations for Digital Assets', 49.

130 De Stasio, 'Riparto di responsabilità e restituzioni nei pagamenti non autorizzati', 26.

131 Uniform Law Commission, 'Uniform Commercial Code Amendments (2022)', art. 4 A, Funds Transfer.

132 Bank of England, 'Approach to the Monitoring of Third Country Systems Designated under the SFR', 14 September 2021, https://www.bankofengland.co.uk/paper/2021/approach-to-the-monitoring-of-third-country-systems-designated-under-the-sfr.

133 See nt. 32.

transaction that spans many jurisdictions and time zones.[134] In the case of a public blockchain like Ethereum, the definition of jurisdiction is left to civil law. In a civil complaint against a crypto influencer, the SEC suggested that the US government has jurisdiction over all transactions on the Ethereum blockchain, as the nodes of that network 'are clustered more densely in the US than in any other country.'[135]

The *Lex Cryptographia* is a drastic attempt at solving this problem by abolishing the network of trust.[136] Many forms of cryptoassets derive their properties from a contract (either wet-ink or implicit) and not from a fiat. This new type of money follows a trend that sees private law as a structuring factor in present-day society and as something that may direct its future evolution (transformative private law). For example, the Payment Service Directive creates an obligation to cooperate between banks and the new PSPs.[137] Such an obligation is not based on a contract, and (at least in common law systems) the principle of the *privity of contract* forbids conferring rights or imposing obligations upon a person who is not a party to the contract itself.[138]

15.6 A temporary conclusion

The innovation process which led to the development of stablecoins is now taking a new direction. After benefiting from the revenues associated with the issuance of stablecoins, the financial sector is coming to appreciate the entire problem of a reliable and safe operation of these products. MiCA[139] sets an example of regulating this market across the different national legislations. However, the US is still the most advanced laboratory for developing stablecoin legislation. The negotiation process has involved a whole cross-section of US society, from politics and foreign affairs to the digital asset industry and

134 Natalino Irti, Norma e luoghi: problemi di geo-diritto, Nuova ed., accresciuta, Sagittari Laterza 150 (Roma: GLF Ed. Laterza, 2006), 83.

135 US Securities and Exchange Commission v. Balina, No. 1:22-CV-950 (United States District Court Western District of Texas Austin Division 19 September 2022).

136 Katrin Becker, 'Blockchain Matters—Lex Cryptographia and the Displacement of Legal Symbolics and Imaginaries', Law and Critique 33, no. 2 (July 2022): 118, https://doi.org/10.1007/s10978-021-09317-8; Filippo Zatti, 'Entangled in Cryptoassets' Legal Nature and Governance: Searching for Clear Boundaries or Working for Their Removal?', SSRN Electronic Journal, 2019, 7, https://doi.org/10.2139/ssrn.3335793.

137 'Directive (EU) 2015/2366 of the European Parliament and of the Council of 25 November 2015 on Payment Services in the Internal Market, Amending Directives 2002/65/EC, 2009/110/EC and 2013/36/EU and Regulation (EU) No 1093/2010, and Repealing Directive 2007/64/EC', OJ L 337 § (2015).

138 Law Commission, 'Privity of Contract: Contracts for The Benefit of Third Parties', July 1996, no. 242, 6.

139 Regulation (EU) 2023/1114 of the European Parliament and of the Council of 31 May 2023 on markets in crypto-assets and amending Regulations (EU) No 1093/2010 and (EU) No 1095/2010 and Directives 2013/36/EU and (EU) 2019/1937 (Text with EEA relevance), https://eur-lex.europa.eu/eli/reg/2023/1114/ojlaw.

traditional finance. For example, John Hsu, Acting Comptroller of the US Comptroller of the Currency (OCC), describes three main areas still needing some regulation: liquidity risk management of deposits, finder activities for crypto trade facilitation, and crypto custody.[140]

The scope of the OCC is clearly limited to banking regulation, and to appreciate the full scope of the problem, the best source is President Joe Biden's executive order[141] and the Digital Asset Framework issued as a Fact Sheet by the White House.[142]

Although they do not rate a specific paragraph, the two concepts of *data privacy* and *national security* are referenced more than four times in the document's body. Apart from these two basic needs, one of the first problems the framework addresses is to define clear limits to the overlapping scopes of intervention of the several federal agencies involved in the issue. Next, the framework asks for bolstering the position of the US in various international organisations and intensifying the efforts against the possible misuse of digital assets.

The last point states the need for exploring a CBDC. It is probably the most important lesson we should draw from all this. Far from being three competing technologies, instant payment systems, stablecoins, and CBDCs need each other to reach maturity. The future of payments leads to a convergence among these three technologies.

140 Michael J Hsu, 'Don't Chase', 11 October 2022, 6, https://www.occ.gov/news-issuances/speeches/2022/pub-speech-2022-126.pdf.

141 Executive Office of the President, 'Ensuring Responsible Development of Digital Assets', 14 March 2022, https://www.federalregister.gov/documents/2022/03/14/2022-05471/ensuring-responsible-development-of-digital-assets.

142 The White House, 'FACT SHEET: White House Releases First-Ever Comprehensive Framework for Responsible Development of Digital Assets', The White House, 16 September 2022, https://www.whitehouse.gov/briefing-room/statements-releases/2022/09/16/fact-sheet-white-house-releases-first-ever-comprehensive-framework-for-responsible-development-of-digital-assets/.

16 Central Bank Digital Currencies and the European Framework for Payments

Friends or Foes?

Gabriella Gimigliano and Maria Cecilia del Barrio Arleo[1]

16.1 Introduction

Technological innovation in payment services is not a novelty and has contributed to developing an integrated and efficient single market for payments at the EU level. However, integrating CBDCs within the current set-up of the payment system has triggered important theoretical and policy questions as well as normative concerns. By focusing on how possible design choices for a digital euro could be coordinated with the current regulatory and oversight architecture for payments and possibly address some open issues, this chapter helps conceptualise the links between the digital euro project and the European payments framework. Therefore, this chapter is structured as follows: § 16.2 provides a primer on plausible digital euro design choices that are still under investigation and advances some considerations regarding its inclusion within the current operational and legal payment framework. Since technical decisions reflect policy-making decisions, § 16.3 describes some of the fundamental policy trade-offs that arise in payments, while §§ 16.4 and 16.5 zoom in on the EU regulatory and oversight frameworks. The European framework for payment has achieved a high degree of harmonisation and infrastructure integration. In this sense, a digital euro should be able to keep pace with the same operational and efficiency standards and eventually fill regulatory and use case gaps. § 16.6 concludes the analysis.

1 This chapter has been written in the context of the Jean Monnet Chair in EU Money Law (2018–2022) held by Dr. Gabriella Gimigliano.

DOI: 10.4324/9781003258261-20

16.2 A primer on digital euro design choices

Before delving into technical design options for the digital euro, it is crucial to consider some foundational principles that run across all CBDC initiatives:[2]

i) Do not interfere with or impede a central bank's mandate.
ii) Coexist with cash and robust private money.
iii) Enable innovation and efficiency in services for end users.

Central banks play a fundamental role in wholesale and retail payment systems by providing a unit of account in the monetary system; ensuring the finality of wholesale payments; providing settlement liquidity; and overseeing the integrity of the payment system.[3]

CBDCs should be designed considering these critical functions in the monetary system, which leads us to the first broad brush distinction between 'wholesale' and 'retail' CBDCs. The former is meant to be used by regulated financial institutions, based upon the current two-tier structure—i.e., a central bank at the core of the payment system that grants accounts to commercial banks and payment service providers (PSPs), who deal directly with the customers. On the contrary, the latter aims to 'make central bank digital money available to the general public just as cash is available to the general public.'[4] In turn, the literature distinguishes between two possible ways of implementing retail CBDCs:

i) The first one is a cash-like design, enabling *token-based* access and payment anonymity.
ii) The second one, *account-based* access, is built on verifying users' identities and would be part of a broader digital identity scheme.

In order to successfully design and implement a retail CBCD, it is crucial to have a proper division of labour between the central bank and the private sector. Maintaining the two-tier structure seems to be the best alternative: 'central banks and PSPs could continue to work together in a complementary way, with each doing what they do best,'[5] the former by providing the foundational infrastructure of the monetary system and the latter by using their creativity and technological capabilities to serve customers better. A one-tier system entirely operated by the central bank (i.e., direct CBDC) would entail

2 Bank of Canada et al., 'Central Bank Digital Currencies: Foundational Principles and Core Features Report No. 1 in a Series of Collaborations from a Group of Central Banks', 2020, 10, https://www.bis.org/publ/othp33.pdf.
3 BIS, 'III. CBDCs: An Opportunity for the Monetary System', BIS Annual Economic Report (Basel: BIS, 23 June 2021), https://www.bis.org/publ/arpdf/ar2021e3.htm.
4 BIS, 72.
5 BIS, 77.

shifting too many tasks, responsibilities, and costs to the central bank, mainly concerning end-users' activities. Central banks can focus on core aspects by delegating operational tasks and consumer-related activities to commercial banks and non-bank PSPs while allowing for better competition and innovation among private actors.

The key differences between the architectural choices put forth by CBDC foundational literature can be summarised as follows:

i) In a *direct* CBDC architecture, the central bank handles all payments in real time and records all retail holdings.
ii) A *hybrid* CBDC architecture incorporates a two-tier structure with direct claims on the central bank, while intermediaries handle real-time payments.
iii) In an *intermediated* CBDC architecture, central banks would only process wholesale payments; in this model, PSPs must be closely supervised to ensure that the wholesale holdings they communicate to the central bank are accurate at all times.

The difference between the hybrid and intermediated models is apparent: the former allows for a combination between, on the one hand, the private sector taking care of client onboarding, compliance, and conducting real-time retail payments, and central banks acting as a backstop to the payment system. Alternatively, in the latter, 'the central bank does not record retail transactions, but only the wholesale balances of individual PSPs,' which means a 'diminished need for centralised data collection and perhaps better data security due to the decentralised nature of record-keeping.'[6]

The kick-off October 2020 report on the digital euro[7] already provided some hints regarding the preferred design choices: it clearly tilted towards a model in which access to the digital currency is intermediated by supervised private intermediaries, while the Eurosystem shall retain control over the issuance.

As former ECB Executive Board member Panetta[8] further illustrates, the digital euro aims to modernise the financial and economic sectors. By design, it should be interoperable with private payment solutions, representing the 'raw material' supervised intermediaries could use to offer pan-European, front-end payment solutions.

Although technical, design issues are essential to understanding the relationship between the digital euro and the current (and future) European

6 BIS, 79.

7 ECB, 'Report on a Digital Euro' (European Central Bank, October 2020), 4.

8 ECB, 'From the Payments Revolution to the Reinvention of Money - Speech by Fabio Panetta, Member of the Executive Board of the ECB, at the Deutsche Bundesbank Conference on the "Future of Payments in Europe"', 27 November 2020, https://www.ecb.europa.eu/press/key/date/2020/html/ecb.sp201127~a781c4e0fc.en.html.

payment system in at least two ways. The EU payments framework has been increasingly electronified and efficient, as described in § 16.4.[9] In this sense, the digital euro represents continuity and will most likely leverage the existing infrastructure. Its adoption—and hence success—relies on market players' incentives to offer front-end solutions to retail users,[10] which shows that private sector involvement remains crucial.

Early experimentations by the Bank of Italy have developed an 'integrated model' as a possible digital euro architecture composed of two features. First, an account-based component, the so-called 'TIPS+,'[11] which, as its name indicates, 'is based on a TIPS-like architecture, where a central platform directly holds individuals' accounts while access to them is provided via third parties (gatekeepers), responsible for the enrolment and identification of the users (KYC principle).' As a multicurrency market infrastructure, TIPS 'combines the scalability of a distributed architecture with the security of a centralised system whose operations leverage the experience of the Eurosystem.'[12] Second, a token-based component was implemented on a DLT platform called 'itCoin,' whose purpose is to complement the cash-like and competitive features of TIPS+. As the report describes[13], itCoin consists of a two-layer payment infrastructure:

> The first layer is the itCoin distributed ledger [...] and the second layer is the itCoin payment channel network (PCN). The first layer is managed by the Eurosystem and can be exploited by intermediaries to build an off-ledger infrastructure [...] The two layers correspond to two different forms of D€ [...] The on-ledger liquidity, i.e., the D€ that circulates on the distributed ledger of the central bank, would constitute a digital euro with many useful features for supervised intermediaries, including programmability.
>
> On the other hand, the off-ledger liquidity, i.e., the D€ that circulates off-ledger in the PCN, would constitute a digital euro that functions online, with many cash-like features, and is available to retail users for their everyday payments.

9 Electronification means the 'migration towards the provision of payment services on a fully electronic and highly automated basis.' See: ECB, 'Electronification of Payments in Europe', Monthly Bulletin, May 2003, 61.

10 Emanuele Urbinati et al., 'A Digital Euro: A Contribution to the Discussion on Technical Design Choices', *Institutional Issues - Bank of Italy*, Markets, Infrastructures, Payment Systems, no. 10 (July 2021), https://www.bancaditalia.it/pubblicazioni/mercati-infrastrutture-e-sistemi-di-pagamento/questioni-istituzionali/2021-010/N.10-MISP.pdf?language_id=1.

11 The acronym TIPS stands for 'TARGET Instant Payment Settlement'; further details are provided in Section 16.4.

12 Urbinati et al., 'A Digital Euro: A Contribution to the Discussion on Technical Design Choices', 21.

13 Urbinati et al., 32.

While this integrated model combining TIPS+ and itCoin is only one among the different possible solutions that the Eurosystem could develop, it illustrates the policy choices underneath technical features. Depending on whether the Eurosystem prioritises higher controllability of the on-ledger liquidity or, on the contrary, market innovation by allowing said on-ledger liquidity to circulate in the retail and unsupervised market, different degrees of central banking control and oversight duties over supervised intermediaries shall emerge.

To conclude, it is essential to recall that design choices are not mere technicalities: they embed policy judgement and fundamental trade-offs, further developed in the section below. Aside from the account or token-based models and the extent to which the digital euro embodies cash-like features, a key aspect concerns, on the one hand, its embeddedness within the current legal framework for payments and alignment with its competition and innovation values and, on the other, the redefinition of central banks' oversight perimeter triggered by these novel arrangements. §§ 16.4 and 16.5 provide an overview of these aspects.

16.3 The digital euro and payments: Trade-offs and policy choices

Before focusing on the novel policy trade-offs triggered by the digital euro project, it is essential to highlight some continuity trends. The intellectual authority exercised by the BIS has contributed to the construction and harmonisation of the regulatory framework for payments, which is also valid for CBDC discussions. However, the internationalisation and harmonisation trends that have emerged in the EU framework for payments are not unique; as a matter of fact, the prudential and banking supervision framework has followed a similar trajectory (in this case, via the BIS Basel Committee on Banking Supervision (BCBS)), which is a direct consequence of an ever-increasing interconnectedness and interdependencies between financial institutions and emerging actors that are now part of the financial ecosystem. One of the early initiatives at the international level in the field of payments was the 2001 BIS Core Principles for Systematically Important Payment Systems, which, as with most of these soft-law principle-based products, aimed at providing high-level guidance on the design and operation of safer and more efficient critical payment systems. These foundational principles call for legal certainty, risk mitigation, and security and operational reliability (or operational 'resilience' in today's parlance), among other aspects, and define central banks' responsibilities and expectations.[14] These principles are still valid as guidance regarding ongoing and future developments in payment systems.

14 In this sense, the principles delineate four key central banks responsibilities: (i) define payment systems objectives and disclose its policies; (ii) ensure their systemically important payment systems abide by the principles; (iii) oversee compliance with the principles by systems they do

The design of the digital euro will reflect fundamental policy trade-offs. As § 16.2 highlights, operational and technological decisions supporting its functioning are underpinned by specific understandings of the nature and role of the digital euro. The bulk of policy and academic literature points to trade-offs and paradoxical features between the digital euro and the existing means of payments: first, the potential effects on private sector innovation; second, the not-so-clear case for a 'public' alternative when it comes to efficient retail payments; and third, the question of whether the digital euro can enhance monetary sovereignty and strategic autonomy in payments, also acting as an antidote against the increasing fragmentation of the monetary system through digitalisation.

Brunnermeier and Landau have accurately summarised the first trade-off embedded in the digital euro project:

> as public money, the digital euro will have to be universally accepted and widely accessible. It should be present everywhere. On the other hand, the Eurosystem may not want to evict private money issuers (the banks) or private payment providers (…) The digital euro will thus be placed into a strange and paradoxical position.[15]

In the same way that, back in the early single currency days, 'the newly established ECB and the Eurosystem were worried that the high costs and low efficiency of cross-border payments might undermine acceptance of the euro by European citizens,'[16] the digital euro poses similar questions. As the Bank of Italy[17] report outlining technical design choices explains, 'the success of a digital euro project will be determined by its adoption by the end users, which in turn depends on the wide participation of the financial industry and, in particular, of the payment service providers,' who can directly encourage or discourage its use. Therefore, one of the paradoxical aspects of the digital euro comes from the need to strike the right balance between being 'ubiquitous' but not dominating;[18] otherwise, such a uniform presence could hamper innovation and competition in the payment services, two policy goals which have been mainly considered in the formulation of the Second Payment Services Directive (PSD2). Regarding the second trade-off, Brunnermeier and

---

not operate; and (iv) promote payments' safety and efficiency. See 'Core principles for systemically important payment systems.'

15 Landau and Brunnermeier, 'The Digital Euro: Policy Implications and Perspectives', 8.

16 Agnieszka Janczuk-Gorywoda, 'The New Transnational Payments Law and Global Consumer Trade: Online Platforms as Providers of Private Legal Orders', *SSRN Electronic Journal*, 2015, 7, https://doi.org/10.2139/ssrn.2694449.

17 Urbinati et al., 'A Digital Euro: A Contribution to the Discussion on Technical Design Choices', 7.

18 Landau and Brunnermeier, 'The Digital Euro: Policy Implications and Perspectives', 11.

Landau[19] claim that from an efficiency point of view, 'there is no obvious case for a "public option" in retail payments,' the same argument brought forward by Federal Reserve member Christopher J Waller in his speech challenging the need for a CBDC.[20] The third fundamental policy choice relates to the digital euro as a way to strengthen a much sought-after sovereignty and strategic autonomy in payments and whether the digital currency can be a way to counteract the ongoing and growing digitalisation-led fragmentation of the monetary system. Despite the efficiency counterargument explained above, former ECB Executive Board member Panetta claimed that the 'digitalisation of payments cannot be ignored by central banks [...]. Central banks cannot escape these transformations, nor should they underestimate the potential for far-reaching shifts that may occur.'[21] This third sovereignty and autonomy-related aspect speaks to a broader and more existential feature underpinning the relationship between the digital euro and the European payment framework: the reinvention of central banks' role in light of the increasing dematerialisation and disintermediation of payments.

Beyond these trade-offs, the digital euro needs to be conceptualised within the idiosyncrasies of the EU payment framework. Since such a project shall be part of the existing regulatory and institutional framework, it is vital to provide the readers with the big picture regarding the state of the harmonisation process for payments and the challenges ahead. These considerations are only an early exploration of the payments-CBDC relationship and are by no means exhaustive. The interaction between CBDCs and payments is, in fact, so vast that it is not possible, within the limits of the chapter, to explore all possible angles; therefore, a subset of elements that were deemed relevant are described below.

16.4 The digital euro and the European regulatory framework for payments

This section takes stock of the European harmonisation process for payments in which the digital euro will be embedded.[22] The ultimate aim of a digital euro should be twofold. First, it should not impair the achievements obtained through the harmonisation process. Second, its design should ideally fill the

19 Landau and Brunnermeier, 12.

20 Christopher Waller, 'CBDC: A Solution in Search of a Problem?', 5 August 2021, https://www.federalreserve.gov/newsevents/speech/files/waller20210805a.pdf.

21 ECB, 'Central Bank Digital Currencies: Defining the Problems, Designing the Solutions - Contribution by Fabio Panetta, Member of the Executive Board of the ECB, to a Panel Discussion on Central Bank Digital Currencies at the US Monetary Policy Forum', 18 February 2022, https://www.ecb.europa.eu/press/key/date/2022/html/ecb.sp220218_1~938e881b13.en.html.

22 Nota bene: this chapter was written before the European Commission's publication of the so-called "payments package", which includes a series of legislative proposals such as the Third Payment Services Directive (PSD3), the Payment Services Regulation, and which was launched in parallel with the digital euro package.

remaining regulatory gaps that have not been addressed during said harmonisation process. This section provides an overview of the state of play of the EU framework for payments representing the legal backbone of the digital euro (§ 16.4.1). A second subsection then zooms in on achievements and shortcomings of three peculiar aspects: the legal status (i.e., rights and obligations) of the European payment service users (§ 16.4.2.1), financial inclusion and the right to access the payment system through a payment account with basic features (§ 16.4.2.2); and antitrust concerns closely linked to the two-sided network externalities exhibited by the provision of payment services (§ 16.4.2.3).

16.4.1 The construction of an internal market for payments

The legal framework for (retail) payments mostly comprises binding rules and regulations.[23] European lawmakers have deemed the provision of payment services as a regulated activity by:

i) Establishing the authorisation and prudential supervision requirements for non-banking payment services providers (payment institutions and electronic money institutions).[24]
ii) Laying down the information requirements in the user-service provider contract relationship with a view to improving consumers' protection and levelling the playing field throughout the Union.[25]
iii) Specifying the duties and obligations in providing payment services to allow for fully automated payment system transactions.[26]

In addition, European lawmakers have tried to complement the antitrust perimeter of action in the payments domain by laying down rules for access to payment systems or setting a ceiling to card-based multilateral interchange fees.[27] Furthermore, it should be recalled that the Markets in Crypto-Assets Regulation (MiCA) has entered into force. This piece of regulation broadly defines crypto-assets as digital assets that may depend on cryptography and exist on a distributed ledger and distinguishes between:

23 Normative and academic references in: Gabriella Gimigliano, 'Title VI "Final Provisions" (Arts 107-117)', in *The Payment Services Directive II*, ed. Gabriella Gimigliano and Marta Božina Beroš (Edward Elgar Publishing, 2021), 231–43, https://doi.org/10.4337/9781839105685.00025.

24 Title II, Directive 2015/2366/EU of the European Parliament, and the Council, of 25 November 2015, on payment services in the internal market, amending Directives 2002/65/EC, 2009/110/EC and 2013/36/EU and Regulation (EU) No 1093/2010, and repealing Directive 2007/64/EC [2015] OJ L337/35 (PSD2).

25 Title III PSD2.

26 Title IV PSD2.

27 Art 35 PSD2; Regulation 2015/751/EU of the European Parliament and the Council, of 29 April 2015, on interchange fees for card-based payment transactions [2015] OJ L123/1.

i) Payment tokens (means of exchange or payment, including money tokens falling beyond the scope of PSD2 and electronic money institutions (EMI) directives).
ii) Investment tokens (which entail rights to future profits).
iii) Utility tokens (which enable access to a product or service).[28]

Within this wide definition of crypto-assets, MiCA pays closer attention to payment tokens, i.e., asset-referenced and e-money tokens. While the former aims to maintain a stable value by referring to the value of several fiat currencies that are legal tender and/or commodities or one or several crypto-assets the latter comprises 'type of crypto-assets whose main purpose is to be used as a means of exchange and that purport to maintain a stable value by being denominated in (units of) a fiat currency.'[29] Like traditional funds, both asset-referenced and e-money tokens confer on the holders a claim over the issuers to reimbursement and, consistently, MiCA compels the issuers to set up a stabilisation and an affirmative asset-partitioning mechanism.[30] Following some leading principles of the European financial and monetary framework, MiCA considers the issuance and marketing of asset-referenced and e-money tokens and the provision of crypto-payment services as regulated businesses, according to the principles of single license and home country control. However, for the purposes of the topic at hand, it should be recalled that CBDCs would be eventually exempted from MiCA application, as the Regulation does not contemplate the cases in which the ECB and/or the NCBs act in their capacity as monetary authorities.[31]

The regulatory harmonisation process described so far aims to improve competition and levelling payment service users' protection throughout EU Member States, regardless of the currency in which the payment transaction is denominated. However, the need to harmonise electronic payment transactions became apparent only after introducing physical euro banknotes and coins in 2002. In this context, the Single Euro Payments Area (SEPA) integration initiative was launched as a joint effort between the European Commission, the European Parliament, the Council of the EU, and the ECB. The aim of SEPA is to enable the possibility 'to make euro payments to anyone located anywhere in Europe as easily, securely and efficiently as within our own

28 See for the latest development, European Parliament, 'Proposal for a Regulation of the European Parliament and of the Council on Markets in Crypto-Assets | Legislative Train Schedule', European Parliament, n.d.

29 See Art 3/ (3), (4), MiCA.

30 Dirk A Zetzsche et al., 'The Markets in Crypto-Assets Regulation (MICA) and the EU Digital Finance Strategy', SSRN Scholarly Paper (Rochester, NY: Social Science Research Network, November 2020), https://doi.org/10.2139/ssrn.3725395.

31 See Rec. 13 and Art. 2(2)c) MiCA.

country —whether that be by direct debit, debit card or bank transfer.[32] The SEPA leading principle is, indeed, the indifference of the country of origin of the payment order with a view to overcoming the different pricing, normative approach, and efficiency level between national and cross-border payment transactions in the euro. This level of integration is mostly achieved thanks to the sharing of regulatory and technical standards, on a voluntary basis, among the financial institutions; these standards indirectly became compelling for the payment services providers thanks to a hybrid—public and private—economic governance arrangement.[33]

As part of the increasing electronification and integration of payments across the EU, it is important to highlight that 'digital central bank money for wholesale transactions is not new, as banks have been able to access central bank money in digital form for decades.'[34] The so-called 'TARGET services'[35] comprise the following infrastructure for digital wholesale money: 'TARGET2 (T2) for wholesale payments, TARGET2 SECURITIES (T2S) for the settlement of securities trading in central bank money, and the TARGET Instant Payment Settlement (TIPS) service for instant payments.'[36] TIPS is indeed one of the latest infrastructure developments within the SEPA integration process and provides for a final and irrevocable settlement of payments in real-time and every day of the year, irrespective of the opening hours of the branches, based on the SEPA Instant Credit Transfer (SCT Inst) Scheme. Currently, TIPS is settling the payments in euros but may also support payments in other currencies (for example, since 2022, in the Swedish krona). Since TIPS settles payments in central bank money and is built up as an extension of TARGET2, the eligible participants are those financial institutions that may join TARGET2. However, as § 16.2 anticipates with regards to possible digital euro design choices, TIPS could 'serve as an environment for the provision of accounts directly to the general public,' thus going beyond its current restrictive access.[37]

32 European Central Bank, 'What Are Instant Payments?', European Central Bank, 28 December 2021, https://www.ecb.europa.eu/ecb/educational/explainers/tell-me-more/html/instant_payments.en.html.

33 More details in Agnieszka Janczuk, 'Sources of EU Payments Law', in *Money, Payment Systems and the European Union: The Regulatory Challenges of Governance*, ed. Gabriella Gimigliano (Newcastle upon Tyne: Cambridge Scholars Publishing, 2016), 2–24.

34 ECB, 'Report on a Digital Euro', 52.

35 The acronym TARGET stands for 'Trans-European Automated Real-time Gross settlement Express Transfer system'.

36 ECB, 'Report on a Digital Euro', 52.

37 ECB, 37.

16.4.2 The framework for retail payments: some research questions under investigation

Like any other EU harmonisation process, the framework for money and payments has lights and shadows, remarkable achievements, and blind spots. It is hence desirable that the launch of a digital euro does not undermine the accomplishments obtained so far and, at the same time, fills in regulatory and use case gaps.

16.4.2.1 The legal status of the European payment service user

When one considers the rights and obligations of Europeans (consumers and businesses) as payment service users, the relationship between PSD2 and the 2005 unfair commercial practices directive[38] cannot be overlooked. Payment service users are entitled to make informed business choices on the main features of the services concerned without being deceived. To this end, payment service users should be provided with information on the normative and economic conditions (i.e., contract terms and conditions in case a framework contract—or the payment account contract is in place) before a contract is concluded. Furthermore, the payment service user is entitled to be informed of the timeline and price of the single payment orders. Whenever the payment service user is a consumer, European lawmakers have established that Member States will set up at least one free-of-charge website, operationally independent from the service providers, which compares the main fees connected to the payment accounts.

Moving to the duties and obligations in the provision of payment services, the payment service users are entitled to (i) see their funds legally shielded against claims of payment service providers' creditors; (ii) make their sensitive payment data protected thanks to GDPR application; (iii) share their data with third-party providers; (iv) make their payment accounts protected against unauthorised or fraudulent initiation of payment transactions unless the payer acted fraudulently. This duty means that PSPs shall be liable for maintaining a security policy. Whenever the payment transaction is denominated in euros, the payment order shall be carried out by the end of the following business day, thanks to the interplay between PSD2 and SEPA regulatory standards. Finally, (v) Member States are compelled to set up an alternative dispute

38 Directive 2005/29/EC of the European Parliament and of the Council of 11 May 2005 concerning unfair business-to-consumer commercial practices in the internal market and amending Council Directive 84/450/EEC, Directives 97/7/EC, 98/27/EC, and 2002/65/EC of the European Parliament and of the Council and Regulation (EC) No 2006/2004 of the European Parliament and of the Council.

resolution (ADR) mechanism for payment service users to submit complaints regarding payment service providers' alleged infringements of PSD2.[39]

European policymakers must contemplate this regulatory context and minimum threshold when considering digital euro features, assuming that the overall system reliability is improved by digital euro issuance. For example, in an 'integrated model' for the digital euro,[40] which combines an account-based (TIPS+) with a token-based mechanism (itCoin), the Eurosystem would be accountable to the users who are unable to access their position (i.e., account) in TIPS+, for example, because the gatekeeper is suddenly unavailable or quit its business. This integrated model combines Eurosystem control over the issuance of the digital currency with a blockchain-based back-end infrastructure based on Bitcoin technology that has been adjusted to address specific digital euro design needs.[41]

Considering that the European harmonisation process for retail payments suffers from some shortcomings, it seems reasonable to consider whether and to what extent the digital euro prototypes may fix them. In fact, inasmuch as PSD2 is a full harmonisation and comprehensive directive, there are at least three key aspects where Member States differ in their regulatory approaches. First, the contract remedies in case PSPs have not properly fulfilled the information requirements; second, the legal statute for monetary obligations; and third, the lack of an efficient cross-border ADR mechanism.[42] To what extent can a digital euro cope with these legal issues? A token-based digital euro might work well when a possessory law regime is applied in such a way that a debtor is deemed to have fulfilled its monetary obligation as soon as it hands over the sum of money owed—in the digital wallet of the creditors. On the contrary, a 'direct' CBDC consisting of account-based access would imply that every European citizen is entitled to hold a TIPS/retail account at the Eurosystem level, which allows him/her to have direct access to digital central bank money, including real-time gross settlement. While such an intermediary-less architecture seems simple, it is unattainable because the ECB cannot manage many clients, not to mention the risks of bypassing private intermediaries.[43]

Turning to the above-mentioned integrated model, the TIPS+ tier does not place any technical constraints on the forms of intermediation such as

39 Benjamin Geva, 'Payment Transactions under the EU Second Payment Services Directive – An Outsider's View', *Texas International Law Journal 54:2 2019*, 1 January 2019, https://digitalcommons.osgoode.yorku.ca/scholarly_works/2718.

40 Urbinati et al., 'A Digital Euro: A Contribution to the Discussion on Technical Design Choices'.

41 Urbinati et al., 25.

42 *Amplius*, G Gimigliano & M Božina Beroš, *The payment services directive II. A commentary*, Elgar Commentaries in Financial Law 2021 (especially, chapters: 6, 8,9, 13).

43 A Bechtel & D Otto-Schleicher, *Possible characteristics of a TIPS-based digital euro*, EU Blockchain Observatory and Forum.

settlement agents or gatekeepers: in the former, 'intermediaries execute transactions on behalf of their customers and possibly, provide storage facilities for digital euro holdings,' [while the latter] 'is in charge only of authenticating end users and provide the technical connectivity between users and the payment system infrastructure.'[44] Intermediaries can thus provide access to the central platform but cannot go beyond the access point role since the digital euro remains a central bank liability. In this mechanism, using pseudonyms allows users to enjoy a high level of privacy: central banks handle only the users' technical identifiers, and intermediaries detect users' identities to the extent needed according to policymakers' choices.[45] It is difficult to conclude whether a proprietary rights/possession-based approach may be applicable. Several questions arise: Who oversees validating the payment transaction? Is a peer-to-peer transfer of digital coins possible? While TIPS+ is described as an account-based system with a centralised infrastructure[46] fully controlled by the Eurosystem, what is the trade-off between them? The proposed integrated model establishes that the Eurosystem controls the digital euro issuance and the core back-end infrastructure; the ownership of the funds is ascertained by proving the knowledge of a specific piece of information, such as a private key, and the transfer of title over the funds is attested by means of cryptographic signature,[47] hence making the possession in law rule applicable.

16.4.2.2 Financial inclusion and the EU law of payments

Financial inclusion was one of the leading policy priorities in constructing an internal market for payment services. To this end, the 2014 Payment Account Directive provided that EU consumers

> should not be discriminated against by reason of their nationality, place of residence or on any other ground referred to in the Charter of Fundamental Rights of the European Union, including the consumers' financial circumstances, when trying to access a payment account in the Union.[48]

44 Urbinati et al., 'A Digital Euro: A Contribution to the Discussion on Technical Design Choices', 17.
45 Urbinati et al., 23.
46 Technically speaking, a centralised infrastructure is built up as a single node in charge of operating the system goal; this will establish a client-server architecture where one or more customers are connected to a central server. Conversely, a distributed infrastructure provides for a set of different and separated autonomous computing elements 'working together to achieve a common goal, in order to appear as a single coherent system and reach the goal, including in the presence of one or more members of the group.' See Urbinati et al., 16.
47 The validity of the cryptographic signature may be ascertained by the parties involved in the transactions, including the ledger operator. See Urbinati et al., 14, 25–26.
48 Preamble (35) Directive 2014/92/EU of the European Parliament and the Council, of 23 July 2014, on the comparability of fees related to payment accounts, payment account switch-

Within this framework, consumers have a right to access the payment system by means of a payment account with basic features. This type of account is a banking account—indeed, only credit institutions can offer them—and provides services enabling account holders to place, withdraw, and transfer funds by means of direct debits, payment cards, and credit transfers free of charge or for a reasonable fee.[49]

However, Jochen Hoffmann emphasised how Member States' transpositions of the payment account directive have not duly considered the obligation to prevent competitive distortions in the banking market, and national laws assume a sort of ***neutral consumer behaviour***; in practice, this means that the burden to provide basic account services lays almost exclusively on the private banking sector.[50]

Financial inclusion is one of the policy priorities that guide the construction of a digital euro.[51] To guarantee an ample degree of inclusion and adoption, however, emotional and functional barriers when it comes to engaging with a digital currency need to be considered and tackled before its issuance.[52] Regarding some of the emotional barriers, such as distrust in banks, a recent study commissioned by the ECB shows that understanding 'the risk-free nature of digital euro as central bank money' is key to its acceptance. Furthermore, according to the digital euro integrated model analysed above, payment service providers will still perform a leading role by providing interoperable services with the existing payment platforms or value-added ones on top of the digital euro. The implementation process of payment accounts with basic features should provide European policymakers with a useful blueprint for constructing a wider digital euro-inclusive strategy.

---

ing and access to payment accounts with basic features [2014] OJ L257/2014 (hereafter, PAD).

49 See Art. 15-20, 25, 2014 Payment Account Directive.

50 J Hoffmann, Implementation of the Payment Accounts Directive, ERA Forum (2019) 237–248 (247). It is also worth noticing that, in the context of the relief measures put in place in favour of Ukrainian refugees fleeing from the war, the EBA has called on financial institutions both to ensure compliance with sanctions against Russia and to facilitate access to basic payment accounts for refugees specifying that 'national competent authorities should ensure that, in line with the Payment Accounts Directive (2014/92/EU), displaced persons from Ukraine have access to open and use payment accounts with basic services' (11 March 2022 press release).

51 Urbinati et al., 'A Digital Euro: A Contribution to the Discussion on Technical Design Choices', 14.

52 Kantar Public, 'Study on Digital Payment Methods', March 2022, 59 ff., https://www.ecb.europa.eu/paym/digital_euro/investigation/profuse/shared/files/dedocs/ecb.dedocs220330_report.en.pdf.

16.4.2.3 Payment service providers and antitrust issues

The harmonisation process for payment is based on a pro-competitive approach. The development of an efficient market for payment services has been a critical pan-European area in which European antitrust principles are applied in full. There are few doubts that the multilateral interchange fees and the price and product access conditions to the payment platforms are critical to the antitrust regulatory framework and action. This is why European lawmakers tried to fill in these gaps, as mentioned in § 16.4.1. European lawmakers have also tried to incentivise the entry of non-financial and non-banking payment service providers into the internal market. However, international credit card issuers still play a leading role. Recently, both the ECB and the EC have prioritised the development of 'homegrown' pan-European payment solutions, benefiting from instant payments to increase the independence of the European payments market.[53] In addition, former ECB Executive Member Panetta has considered the digital euro as one of the operational tools to achieve this policy priority. However, the digital euro will not set aside the traditional platform-based antitrust concerns since the private sector shall oversee the creation of value-added services on top of the digital currency.[54]

16.5 The digital euro and payments oversight function

Further to these regulatory aspects, which are fundamental to the organisation of the EU payment framework, there are supervisory and oversight tasks. These tasks are, however, not the same. Supervision means, in this context, micro-prudential supervision and concerns the financial stability of the single payment service provider. Such prudential supervision tasks, which may or may not be performed by national central banks, comprise not only the assessment and release of the authorisation whenever the applicant meets the legal conditions set in Art. 5 PSD2 but also ascertaining whether these conditions are fulfilled from the beginning to the end of the life of any non-banking payment service provider (either payment institution or electronic money institution). By contrast, central banks' oversight function is typical of institutions acting in their monetary authority capacity. Such oversight function is addressed to payment systems[55] as a whole and their single components too, including

53 It should be noted that the European Commission adopted a legislative proposal on instant payments in euro on 26 October 2022, whose impact and interaction with the digital euro project are still to be understood: https://ec.europa.eu/finance/docs/law/221026-proposal-instant-payments_en.pdf.

54 Urbinati et al., 'A Digital Euro: A Contribution to the Discussion on Technical Design Choices', 23.

55 The payment system may be defined as 'a...set(s) of instruments, intermediaries, rules, procedures, processes and interbank funds transfer systems which facilitate the circulation of money in a country or currency area.' See Tom Kokkola and Europäische Zentralbank, eds., *The Payment System: Payments, Securities and Derivatives, and the Role of the Eurosystem* (Frankfurt

both the subjects, such as service providers or clearing houses and the objects, i.e., payment instruments. In the Eurosystem,[56] Art. 127 TFEU and Art. 22 of Protocol No 4 on the Statute of the European System of Central Banks (ESCB) include the efficiency and soundness of clearing and payment systems, within the Union and with other countries, as the main institutional purposes of the oversight function. This task works according to the principle of decentralisation, by means of which 'the enforcement of common policy stances is entrusted to the NCB of the country where the system is legally incorporated.'[57] *NCBs, in this sense, can act as lead supervisors when necessary while promoting information sharing.*

The Eurosystem's oversight mandate comprises payment, clearing, and settlement systems, while it also includes electronic payment instruments, schemes, and arrangements. Such an oversight mandate aims to ensure the efficiency and stability of financial market infrastructures (FMIs), i.e., the 'backbone of the financial system [...] [which] provide the networks through which financial institutions and financial markets are connected, and financial transactions are cleared and settled.'[58] The oversight mandate goes beyond the payments field to further include securities and clearing.

These multifaceted activities are reflected in the three complementary roles played by the Eurosystem: first, as owner and operator of the real-time gross settlement system called TARGET2, including TARGET Instant Payment Settlement, i.e., TIPS as referred to above, and TARGET2-Securities (T2S); second, as a catalyst, by fostering an increasing harmonisation and supporting the coordination among market participants and other authorities; third, as an overseer, by 'monitoring developments at system and entity level, setting oversight standards for FMI operators, assessing compliance with those standards and inducing change where needed.'[59] For the purpose of this chapter's analysis, the focus is placed on the Eurosystem overseer role in the field of payments (hence excluding the oversight of the clearing and settlement system, which is, for the most part, carried out under national law jurisdiction, and securities).

The Eurosystem payment oversight function covers both (i) payment systems—which comprise, in turn, systemically important payment systems

---

am Main: European Central Bank, 2010), 25. However, the Payment Services Directives laid down a narrower definition as a 'funds transfer system with formal and standardised arrangements and common rules for the processing, clearing and/or settlement of payment transactions' (Art. 4 (7) PSD2).

56 The Eurosystem is formed by the European Central Bank and National Central Banks (NCBs) of those Member States that have adopted the single currency.

57 Marta Božina Beroš, 'Oversight of European Payment Systems: Operational Arrangement and Governance', in *Money, Payment Systems and the European Union: The Regulatory Challenges of Governance*, ed. Gabriella Gimigliano (Newcastle upon Tyne: Cambridge Scholars Publishing, 2016), 130–51.

58 ECB, Eurosystem oversight policy framework, July 2016, 1.

59 ECB, Eurosystem oversight report 2020, April 2021, 7.

(SIPS) and non-systemically important payment systems (non-SIPS) and (ii) payment instruments, schemes, and arrangements. Actually, the former encompasses the latter, as per the definition included in Article 2(1) of the SIPS Regulation:[60] '"payment system" means a formal arrangement between three or more participants [...] with common rules and standardised arrangements for the execution of transfer orders between the participants.' In this sense, one of the most important developments in the payments oversight arena relates to the Eurosystem's framework for electronic payment instruments, schemes, and arrangements (so-called 'PISA'), approved by the ECB's Governing Council in November 2021. As the name indicates, it covers all three elements of the payment system: electronic payment instruments

> *which allow the transfer of value or the discharge of payment obligations between end users [...], schemes defining standardised procedures for such electronic payment instruments, and arrangements providing functionalities supporting the use of electronic payment instruments as well as the services of payment service providers* [emphasis added].[61]

As the PISA framework package explains, technological developments urged the review of the current oversight provisions to include all electronic payment instruments that serve as value transfers between end users. Such transfers comprise not just euro funds as per the definition provided in PSD2,[62] but also 'representations of value backed by claims or assets denominated in euro or redeemable in euro; or other digital assets that are accepted under the rules of a scheme for payment purposes.'[63] This framework complements the activities covered by PSD2 by capturing those actors or entities who might not qualify as payment services providers but whose activities nevertheless fall within the remit of the Eurosystem oversight of payment systems or schemes.

While the PISA framework is meant to capture the increasing complexity of the payment ecosystem considering the proliferation of privately issued payment instruments such as stablecoins, digital euro considerations can still be relevant. As the report on the digital euro recalls,[64] 'although central bank

60 Regulation of the European Central Bank (EU) No 795/2014 of 3 July 2014 on oversight requirements for systemically important payment systems (ECB/2014/28) (OJ L 217, 23.7.2014, p. 16).

61 ECB, 'Eurosystem Oversight Framework for Electronic Payment Instruments, Schemes and Arrangements' (ECB, November 2021), 2, https://www.ecb.europa.eu/paym/pdf/consultations/ecb.PISApublicconsultation202111_1.en.pdf.

62 According to Article 4(25) PSD2, funds mean banknotes and coins, scriptural money, or electronic money as defined in point (2) of Article 2 of EMD2.

63 See nt 60.

64 Urbinati et al., 'A Digital Euro: A Contribution to the Discussion on Technical Design Choices', 8.

liabilities are not subject to regulation and oversight, in issuing the digital euro, the Eurosystem should still aim at complying with regulatory standards, including in the area of payments.’ In fact, as anticipated, depending on the task allocation between the digital euro issuance by the Eurosystem and its distribution by supervised intermediaries, novel schemes and business models can emerge; therefore, it is crucial that the oversight standards remain future-proof.

Before concluding, even if it is possible to draw a distinction between the oversight function, which comprises payment systems, instruments, schemes, and arrangements from a holistic perspective, and the supervisory one, which cares for the financial health of single payment service providers (like the macro- and micro-prudential supervision distinction in banking regulation), overlaps can emerge. Although this section has focused, for the most part, on the former, as an expression of the central banks' role in maintaining the soundness of the payment system, the issuance of the digital euro can also impact the latter. For instance, questions regarding the application of PSD2 strong customer authentication and payment authorisation requirements will acquire a new dimension with the issuance of the digital euro, as the implementation of said requisites will depend upon the interaction between the Eurosystem and the supervised intermediaries, as highlighted in § 16.4. The issuance of a digital euro, therefore, will modify the organisational structure of both payment oversight and supervisory functions.

16.6 Conclusions

Aside from the international central banking trends regarding the exploration and ultimate issuance of a CBDC, the case for a digital euro has been built upon a steady legal harmonisation and parallel electronification of payment methods enabling an increasingly integrated payments infrastructure and landscape. While it is tempting to compare the EU or euro area with other jurisdictions that are ahead in their CBDC project, i.e., China and its well-advanced e-CNY pilots, this chapter shows that—irrespective of the international trends and the 'race to CBDCs'—adopting the digital euro is not so much determined by the technological capabilities or state of the art developments but, rather, the regulatory and socio-economic context upon which its degree of success (i.e., adoption by the general public) depends on.

In a context characterised by an increasing dematerialisation of payments and their integration into everyday life (for instance, paying with your Apple watch), it could be hypothesised that eventually, and provided that it is widely adopted as a means of payment among citizens, the digital euro could contribute to the much sought after 'strategic autonomy' of the EU in the digital world. As summarised by Brunnermeier and Landau, payments lie at the crux of several initiatives and EU policies, having direct links with money, data, and privacy; the European payment landscape is in a state of flux given that core regulatory provisions are currently under review, thus providing policymakers with a chance to make payments fit for the digital era. [65]

While the argument that 'there is no problem to be solved as we already have efficient means of payments' might be compelling, the question surrounding the issuance of a digital euro should go beyond these short-term efficiency and convenience considerations. In fact, digital currencies should aim to provide payment and financial inclusion solutions with a mid-to-long-term view to eventually solve those problems that current market alternatives cannot solve. The Commission's Communication on a Retail Payments Strategy put this very clearly: 'The EU payments market remains, to a significant degree, fragmented along national borders, as most domestic payment solutions based on cards or instant payments do not work cross-border.'[66] Aside from big global players, which manage to capture the whole intra-European cross-border payments market, 'there is virtually no digital payment solution that can be used across Europe.'

These observations by the European Commission are well aligned with central bankers' reasoning behind CBDC issuance; in the case of the digital euro, this approach has been emphasised by former ECB Executive Board member Panetta's speeches and the foundational 2020 digital euro report, specifically when referring to the strategic autonomy embedded underneath the digital euro project. The case for CBDCs, in fact, is not rooted in short-term considerations by which they merely substitute cash or are meant to be one more means of electronic payments. The issuance of central bank digital currencies speaks directly to the role and survival of public institutions, i.e., central banks and public money, in a context increasingly characterised by a full panoply of electronic money but ultimately no fiat currency.

65 Landau and Brunnermeier, 'The Digital Euro: Policy Implications and Perspectives', 45.

66 'Communication from the Commission to the European Parliament, the Council, the European Economic and Social Committee and the Committee of the Regions on a Retail Payments Strategy for the EU' (2020), https://eur-lex.europa.eu/legal-content/EN/TXT/HTML/?uri=CELEX:52020DC0592&from=EN.

17 The Digital Euro, Stablecoins, and the Banking Sector

Reyes Palá Laguna

17.1 Introduction

Although some countries have had real experiences with CDBC (the sand dollar in the Bahamas and the digital Yuan pilot project), the EU has not decided to issue a CDBC.[1] In other words, the debate in developed economies is about how to implement a CBDC rather than whether a digital currency will be implemented.[2] Where this topic is concerned, we have gone from a situation in which finding information about CDBCs was not at all accessible to an 'excess' of information. The discussions focus on designing a European digital legal tender, and several options are on the table.[3] There is, however, considerable agreement on the central role to be played by private banks concerning the implementation and use of the digital euro.

In the EU and other jurisdictions, the approach to introducing a digital euro is via CDBC as a means of payment.[4] Even though it is still too early

1 At the time of sending this writing to the publisher.

2 'Central Bank Digital Currencies: Financial Stability Implications' (BIS, September 2021), 3, https://www.bis.org/publ/othp42_fin_stab.pdf. This report was drafted by seven central banks (Canada, England, Japan, the European Central Bank, Switzerland, Sweden, and the FED) and the Bank for International Settlements (BIS).

3 The vast majority of central banks have published reports or comments about the CBDC, exploring the pros and cons of e-money of this type and different options for its implementation, see Codruta Boar and Andreas Wehrli, 'Ready, Steady, Go? Results of the Third BIS Survey on Central Bank Digital Currency', *BIS Monetary and Economic Department*, BIS Papers, no. 114 (January 2021), https://www.bis.org/publ/bppdf/bispap114.pdf, passim. The proportion of central banks actively engaging in CBDCs in one way or another has increased from one-third in 2018 to almost 90% as of March 2021: see George Giaglis et al., 'Central Bank Digital Currencies and a Euro for the Future', SSRN Scholarly Paper (Rochester, NY: Social Science Research Network, 22 July 2021), https://papers.ssrn.com/abstract=3891861.

4 HM Treasury and Bank of England, 'G7 Finance Ministers and Central Bank Governors' Statement on Central Bank Digital Currencies (CBDCs) and Digital Payments', G7 UK 2021, 13 October 2021, https://assets.publishing.service.gov.uk/government/uploads/system/uploads/attachment_data/file/1025234/FINAL_G7_Statement_on_Digital_Payments_13.10.21.pdf. In their Communique, the G7 Finance Ministers and Central Bank Governors stated that 'any CBDCs, as a form of central bank money, could act as both a liquid, safe settlement asset and as an anchor for the payments system.'

DOI: 10.4324/9781003258261-21

for national central banks to commit to a specific design for a digital euro,[5] it seems that a decision has already been made: a collaboration between the ECB and private banks—at least, this is the foreseeable design supported by the group of central banks in their 2021 report. More specifically, FED Board Governor Lael Brainard has said that

> banks play a critical role in credit intermediation and monetary policy transmission, as well as in payments. Thus, the design of any CDBC would need to include safeguards to protect against disintermediation of banks and to preserve monetary policy transmission more broadly.[6]

It should be borne in mind that issuing a digital euro is not imminent.[7] This is also for the MiCA Regulation entering fully into force in 2025.[8]

This chapter is organised into four main parts. § 17.1 aims to answer why the creation of a digital euro is currently on the table. § 17.2 discusses the digital euro's risks to the banking sector. § 17.3 covers the main topics surrounding the MiCA Regulation, the EU's reaction to the private stablecoins in the pipeline or have already been issued by private actors like Big Tech. § 17.4, by way of a brief conclusion, argues that safeguarding the banking system in a two-tier structure seems to be the most reasonable scenario for implementing a digital euro as a means of payment.

17.2 The digital euro: Why now?

The first question is why the European Union has embarked on the digital euro project. There are several reasons for implementing a digital euro, some linked to specific features of member states' national economies.[9] The assumption is that the digital euro will coexist with cash rather than replace it.

5 ECB, 'Report on a Digital Euro' (European Central Bank, October 2020), 3.

6 Lael Brainard, 'Private Money and Central Bank Money as Payments Go Digital: An Update on CBDCs: A Speech at the Consensus by CoinDesk 2021 Conference, Washington, DC (via Webcast), May 24, 2021', Board of Governors of the Federal Reserve System (US), May 2021, https://ideas.repec.org/p/fip/fedgsq/92030.html.

7 See ECB, 'Eurosystem Launches Digital Euro Project', 14 July 2021, https://www.ecb.europa.eu/press/pr/date/2021/html/ecb.pr210714~d99198ea23.en.html. The investigation phase will examine the use cases for a digital euro and its desired features and functionalities. It will also look at how the digital euro would interact with the European retail payments market and at the business models of public and private participants in the digital euro ecosystem. Finally, it will explore the technical solutions that could best handle these issues: Fabio Panetta, 'Designing a Digital Euro for the Retail Payments Landscape of Tomorrow', ECB, 18 November 2021, https://www.ecb.europa.eu/press/key/date/2021/html/ecb.sp211118~b36013b7c5.en.html.

8 The review of this chapter was completed in January 2023.

9 Pablo Hernández de Cos, 'Avances en la agenda estratégica del euro digital' (Banco de España, 15 November 2021), https://www.bde.es/f/webbde/GAP/Secciones/SalaPrensa/IntervencionesPublicas/Gobernador/Arc/Fic/hdc151121.pdf.

The most obvious reason is the terrible pandemic which started in 2020. One of the consequences of government protection measures and restrictions on the movement of citizens due to the Covid-19 pandemic is the increase in digital payments across Europe and the rest of the world.[10] The fact is that cash usage is declining, although it is still the leading means of payment in retail transactions.[11] The decline of cash payments is not new, however: the use of debit cards began increasing in the early 1990s, and the trend started to accelerate significantly with the introduction of smartphones, mobile banking, and payment apps that made it easier to manage money and conduct cashless transactions. Today, cash transactions in the euro area account for around 10% of GDP. In the UK and the US, it is about 5%; in Sweden, less than 1%.[12] The global pandemic has accelerated this trend. After the pandemic—or after the vaccine—it is uncertain whether this consumer behaviour will change, whether we will return to retail cash payments or whether the trend is permanent. It is a fact that contactless payments are growing in B2C commerce.

In several jurisdictions, tax reasons also contribute to avoiding the use of cash in payments. In Spain, for example, from July 2021, payments to merchants of more than 1000 euros in a single operation cannot be made in cash.[13]

10 See, among many others, Lael Brainard, 'Speech by Governor Brainard on Private Money and Central Bank Money as Payments Go Digital: An Update on CBDCs', Board of Governors of the Federal Reserve System, 24 May 2021, https://www.federalreserve.gov/newsevents/speech/brainard20210524a.htm.

11 In 2019, 73% of retail payments at the physical point of sale and P2P were in cash, and 27% were made using non-cash payment instruments. Cards were the predominant payment instrument for cashless payments (24%). Regarding the value of transactions, cash payments fell from 54% to 48%: ECB, 'Study on the Payment Attitudes of Consumers in the Euro Area (SPACE)', 16 December 2022, https://www.ecb.europa.eu/stats/ecb_surveys/space/html/index.en.html. It is significant that since early 2021, the volume of cash lodged in central banks and commercial banks has fallen by around 20–25% in the euro area. A survey commissioned by the Eurosystem in mid-2020 showed that around 40% of respondents used cash less frequently than before. However, despite the significant drop in the use of cash for payments, there has been a parallel and huge rise in the demand for euro banknotes over the past year: an increase of €190 billion—or €550 per capita—between March 2020 and May 2021. See Fabio Panetta, 'Cash Still King in Times of COVID-19', ECB, 15 June 2021, https://www.ecb.europa.eu/press/key/date/2021/html/ecb.sp210615~05b32c4e55.en.html. According to WorldPay, cash accounted for 27% of in-store transactions in the UK in 2019; in 2020, that had fallen to 13%. In Sweden, Canada, and Australia, less than 10% of physical point-of-sale payments were in cash: WorldPay, 'The Global Payments Report', 2021.

12 Gary Smith, 'China's Winning CBDC Approach', *OMFIF* (blog), 20 November 2020, https://www.omfif.org/2020/11/chinas-winning-cbdc-approach/.

13 Law 11/2021, of 9 July on measures to prevent and combat tax fraud and of transposition of Council Directive (EU) 2016/1164 of 12 July 2016 laying down rules against tax avoidance practices that directly affect the functioning of the internal market. The limit of cash payments increases to EUR2,500 for payments made by individuals not acting as merchants or self-employed professionals. For private individuals who are domiciled outside Spain, the limit for cash payments decreases to EUR10,000: see Diego Martín-Abril Y Calvo and Pilar Álvarez Barbeito, 'The Spanish Anti-Tax Fraud Act Has Been Passed', Analysis GA_P, July

Digitalisation in the payment world would contribute to financial inclusion;[14] this and the spread of smartphones, which is linked to disruptive innovation, should also be considered.

Regarding stablecoins or cryptocurrencies, fear of solid private e-money and its implications for the financial banking payments system and, thus, for financial stability is also a vital issue for central banks. The failed *Libra/Diem* project that caused many central banks to realise that if they did not issue digital currencies, then others would do so needs mentioning here. The strong reaction from governments and banks against Facebook weakened the project—from the initial aim that it would be a real e-coin, it became a stablecoin for payment transactions—but shows that excessive dependency on solely private payment circuits should be avoided.

Almost all these arguments can be summed up in this statement from the ECB:

> A digital euro may even become essential in a number of possible scenarios. For example, if the use of cash were to decline significantly, other electronic payment methods were to become unavailable owing to extreme events, or foreign digital money was to displace existing means of payment largely.'[15]

In the eurozone, the goal of the possible issuance of a digital euro is to create an electronic form of central bank money, a digital legal tender that would be accessible—directly or indirectly—to citizens and merchants. As commented above, this digital euro would not replace cash. Doubts over the Eurosystem's legal capacity for issuing digital euros like banknotes have arisen. According to the most authoritative academic doctrine, Article 128 of the TFEU and Article 16 of the European System of Central Banks (ESCB) Statute permits the issuance of a digital euro as legal tender; the reference to banknotes in these articles does not preclude the physical and non-digital issuance of the Euro.[16] Another argument is the European policy goal of moving forward with true digitalisation of both European financial markets and the economy. The EC adopted a digital finance package on 24 September 2020, including a digital finance strategy and legislative proposals on crypto-assets and digital resilience, to create a competitive EU financial sector that gives consumers

---

2021, 9, https://www.ga-p.com/wp-content/uploads/2021/07/Ley_medidas_prevencion_ENG.pdf.

14 Fabio Panetta, 'A Digital Euro for the Digital Era', ECB, 12 October 2020, https://www.ecb.europa.eu/press/key/date/2020/html/ecb.sp201012_1~1d14637163.en.html.

15 ECB, 'Report on a Digital Euro'.

16 Another subject is the issuance of a retail digital euro to directly serve the ECB's monetary policy, about which several concerns arise. See Seraina Grünewald, Corinne Zellweger-Gutknecht, and Benjamin Geva, 'Digital Euro and ECB Powers', Common Market Law Review 58, no. Issue 4 (1 August 2021): 1029–56, https://doi.org/10.54648/COLA2021066.

access to innovative financial products while ensuring consumer protection and financial stability. According to the EC, the package supports the EU's ambition for a recovery that embraces the digital transition. Digital financial services can help modernise the European economy across different sectors and turn Europe into a global digital player. Implementing the digital euro should be preceded by a transition period with pilot schemes—a DLT is not the only option. It focuses on the digital euro's role as a means of payment. The idea is that the CBDC should perform all the functions of the fiat currency in the payments market.

17.3 The digital euro and risks for the banking system

It is easy to guess the risks of implementing a digital euro to banking activity and financial stability. Private banks are still the dominant source of private money. A CBDC could lead to higher deposit volatility and/or a significant long-term reduction in customer deposits.[17] A credit entity is defined by its role as an indirect intermediary in credit: the bank funds its lending operations through client deposits. Undermining private banks' capacity to receive public deposits could put the entire financial system at risk. One of the central banks' main concerns is that the digital euro must not trigger a rush from cash deposits to digital ones. The possibility of full substitutability between deposits and CDBC should be carefully considered. However, this risk could also emerge if some stablecoins are widely used in one or several jurisdictions.

To return to the issue of the role of credit entities in the implementation of a digital euro, European digital payments in wholesale markets, which is a reality today, could be a good precedent: TARGET 2[18] is the Eurosystem interbank funds' transfer system, technically based on a Single Shared Platform, which is designed to support the Eurosystem objectives of defining and implementing the monetary policy of the euro area and promoting the smooth operation of payment systems, thus contributing to the integration and stability of the euro money market. Linked to TARGET 2 is TIPS (TARGET Instant Payment Settlement), a market infrastructure service launched by the Eurosystem in November 2018 as a response to growing consumer demand for instant payments. It enables payment service providers (credit institutions, payment institutions, and other payment services entities) to offer their customers' fund transfers throughout the European Union in real-time every day of the year. TIPS 2 is a system that provides a harmonised and standardised pan-European Service for settling payments instantly in central bank money.[19]

17 'Central Bank Digital Currencies: Financial Stability Implications', 6.

18 Acronym: Trans-European Automated Real-time Gross settlement Express Transfer system (second-generation).

19 The TIPS service has been developed and is operated on behalf of the Eurosystem by the TIPS platform providing Banca d'Italia, Deutsche Bundesbank, Banque de France, and Banco de España: ECB-PUBLIC, 'Information Guide for TARGET2 Users - Vers. 13', November

In contrast, TIPS currently only settles payment transfers in euros—although other currencies could also be supported if the demand existed. The ECB has announced that TIPS is expected to offer instant payment settlement in Swedish krona as of May 2022, when Sveriges Riksbank will join the platform. Instant payments in Danish krone could also be available by November 2025, when Danmarks Nationalbank is scheduled to join.[20] This will be a significant step forward in consolidating an effective cross-border payments system in Europe and could lead the way for digital euro proof of concept and compatibility with other digital currencies. In TIPS, settlement occurs in central bank money, so participation in TIPS depends on eligibility to access central bank money. For this reason, to open an account in TIPS in euros, an institution must fulfil the same eligibility criteria for participation in TARGET-2.

Spain has Bizum S.L., an app launched by the Spanish banking sector in 2016 that enables immediate bank transfers to a bank account from smartphone to smartphone. Bizum has 19,100,000 active users, and 813,000,000 transactions have been carried out. This instant payment system can be used in 26,700 establishments as a means of e-commerce payment. The banking system has sufficient infrastructure and operational requirements to make instant digital payments safe. For this reason, implementing a digital euro in a two-tier model and maintaining banking intermediation in the financial system would be the best option.

17.4 Stablecoins, MiCA, and the banking sector

In the European Union's case, the digital euro project is at least partially considered a response or reaction to the threats to financial stability that the Union faces with the widespread use of stablecoins or digital currencies.[21] The use of the euro as legal tender and bank deposits are protected by EU regulations (the Eurosystem[22] and deposit guarantee scheme[23]), hence the trust in the EU financial system. The same rationale applies to legal tender and deposit guarantee schemes in the UK, the US, and Canada. To avoid a rush to private stablecoins, central bank initiatives for a digital central currency that

2019, https://www.ecb.europa.eu/paym/target/target2/profuse/nov_2019/shared/pdf/Information_Guide_for_TARGET2_users_v13.0.pdf.

20 European Central Bank, 'Work on Cross-Currency Instant Payments in TIPS Moves Forward', 23 June 2021, https://www.ecb.europa.eu/paym/intro/news/html/ecb.mipnews.210623.en.html.

21 See, Ch. 8 and Philipp Sandner et al., 'The Digital Programmable Euro, Libra and CBDC: Implications for European Banks', *SSRN Electronic Journal*, 2020, 6, https://doi.org/10.2139/ssrn.3663142.

22 See the Treaty on the Functioning of the European Union (TFEU), articles 127 and 282, and the Protocol on the Statute of the European System of Central Banks (ESCB) and of the European Central Bank.

23 Directive 2014/49/EU of the European Parliament and of the Council of 16 April 2014 on deposit guarantee schemes.

allows the same protection level when using CDBC as already exists for legal tender (banknotes) and the risk of widespread use of stablecoins triggers bank deposits. For these reasons, a torpedo has been launched at the European level against SCs that could threaten financial stability in the EU. The missile is MiCA. It seeks to provide legal certainty for crypto-assets not covered by existing EU financial services legislation (mainly MiFID II and Electronic Money Directive[24]) and to establish uniform rules for crypto-asset service providers and issuers at the EU level. The text lays down detailed rules for stablecoins when these are e-money or asset-reference tokens.[25]

Article 3.1 (7) defines 'electronic money token' or 'e-money token' as 'a type of crypto-asset that purports to maintain a stable value by referencing the value of an official currency of a country.' However, some of what is colloquially known as stablecoins might also be subsumed under the definition of 'asset-referenced token' as long as article 3.1 (6) defines an asset-referenced token as

> a type of crypto-asset that is not an electronic money token and that purports to maintain a stable value by reference to any other value or right or a combination thereof, including one or more official currencies of a country.

More clarification of these two definitions is required in the delegated acts that shall be adopted by the European Commission (Art. 139).[26] Based on these

24 Directive 2014/65/EU of the European Parliament and of the Council of 15 May 2014 on markets in financial instruments (MiFID II); Directive 2009/110/EC of the European Parliament and of the Council of 16 September 2009 on the taking up, pursuit and prudential supervision of the business of electronic money institutions.

25 Regulation (EU) 2023/1114 of the European Parliament and of the Council of 31 May 2023, on markets in crypto-assets and amending Regulations (EU) No 1093/2010 and (EU) No 1095/2010 and Directives 2013/36/EU and (EU) 2019/1937. This Regulation clarifies that crypto-assets issued by central banks acting in their monetary authority capacity or by other public authorities will not be subject to the Regulation (Art. 2).

26 The preamble (19) to the MiCA Proposal tries to offer a glimmer of light in the following terms: 'At present, despite their similarities, electronic money and crypto-assets referencing an official currency differ in some important aspects. Holders of electronic money as defined in Directive 2009/110/EC are always provided with a claim against the electronic money issuer and have a contractual right to redeem, at any moment and at par value, the monetary value of the electronic money held. By contrast, some crypto-assets referencing an official currency do not provide their holders with such a claim against the issuers of such crypto-assets and could fall outside the scope of Directive 2009/110/EC. Other crypto-assets referencing an official currency do not provide a claim at par value with the currency they are referencing or they limit the redemption period. The fact that holders of such crypto-assets do not have a claim against the issuers of such crypto-assets, or that such claim is not at par value with the currency those crypto-assets are referencing, could undermine the confidence of holders of those crypto-assets. Accordingly, to avoid circumvention of the rules laid down in Directive 2009/110/EC, any definition of e-money tokens should be as wide as possible to capture

definitions, it can be said that MiCA does not cover Bitcoin (but covers the crypto-assets service providers). The DLT that supports Bitcoin and the characteristics of this crypto-asset lead one to believe that it cannot be included in the definition of an e-money token or asset-referenced token from the time when Bitcoin has no stable value by reference to any other value or right or a combination thereof. However, circumstances change rapidly, and each jurisdiction's situation must be considered: El Salvador adopted Bitcoin as legal tender in September 2021.[27]

As the MiCA's goal is to regulate non-bank issuers of crypto-assets that are not 'unique and not fungible with other crypto-assets' (article 2.3), the text defines the regulatory framework of all crypto-assets that are not covered by existing financial services legislation; for example, if the crypto-asset can be considered a financial instrument, MiFID II, MiFIR, and other level 1 rules will be applicable.

MiCA includes the obligation for the issuer to draft a white paper to provide information about the characteristics and risks of crypto-assets not covered by existing financial services legislation, which present many of the same risks as more familiar financial instruments.[28] The text imposes stricter requirements on stable issuers than on issuers of other crypto-assets, for example, utility tokens.[29]

all types of crypto-assets referencing a single official currency. In addition, strict conditions on the issuance of e-money tokens should be laid down, including an obligation for e-money tokens to be issued either by a credit institution authorised under Directive 2013/36/EU of the European Parliament and of the Council (13), or by an electronic money institution authorised under Directive 2009/110/EC. For the same reason, issuers of e-money tokens should ensure that holders of such tokens can exercise their right to redeem their tokens at any time and at par value against the currency referencing those tokens. Because e-money tokens are crypto-assets and can raise new challenges in terms of protection of retail holders and market integrity that are specific to crypto-assets, they should also be subject to the rules laid down in this Regulation to address those challenges.'

27 In some jurisdictions, the approach taken to Bitcoin and other cryptocurrencies is to oversee the advertising of these assets. This is true in Spain, where Circular 1/2022 of January 17, of the CNMV, defines the rules on the content and format of promotional messages for crypto-asset campaigns when the crypto-assets—other than financial instruments—are considered an investment: CNMV, 'New CNMV Circular on the Advertising of Crypto-Assets for Investment Purposes', 17 January 2022, https://www.cnmv.es/portal/verDoc.axd?t=%7B1cbaf61c-57c2-4830-bd6a-071f806795e2%7D. In our opinion, this is a realistic approach to enhancing investor protection.

28 A critique of MiCA's white paper regulation can be found in Paolo Giudici and Guido Ferrarini, 'Digital Offerings and Mandatory Disclosure: A Market-Based Critique of MiCA', in *Digital Finance in Europe: Law, Regulation, and Governance*, ed. Emilios Avgouleas and Heikki Marjosola (De Gruyter, 2021), 87–108, https://doi.org/10.1515/9783110749472-004.

29 Utility token is defined as 'type of crypto-asset which is only intended to provide access to a good or a service supplied by the issuer of that token' (Art. 3.1(5) of the Proposal, Art, 3.1 (9) of the MiCA).

In order to ensure financial stability, and since the emerging category of stablecoins has the potential to be widely accepted and potentially systemic, MiCA includes measures to address potential risks to financial stability and monetary policy that could arise from significant stablecoins in Title III (asset-referenced tokens) and Title IV (electronic money tokens). The general principle is that e-money tokens can only be offered in the EU or traded on a crypto-asset platform if the issuer is a credit institution under Directive 2013/36/EU or an 'electronic money institution' under Directive 2009/110/EC (Art. 48). In contrast to non-credit institution entities, credit institutions can issue asset-reference tokens without special government authorisation. Non-credit institution entities have to apply for specific permission after meeting certain requirements, mainly that they are established in the EU; that is, the issuer shall have a registered office in the Union (Art. 16).[30] Other legal requirements have to be fulfilled as detailed in Art. 18 of the MiCA.

It is essential to point out that competent national authorities may refuse the authorisation of an asset-referenced token or e-money token issuer if the issuer's business model can pose a serious threat to financial stability, the smooth operation of payment systems, or the integrity of the market. The competent authorities shall also refuse authorisation when the ECB or a central bank, where applicable, expresses a negative opinion on the smooth functioning of payment systems, monetary policy transmission, or monetary sovereignty.[31] This is an essential point of it.

It should also be noted that MiCA introduces restrictions on issuing asset-referenced tokens that are widely used as a means of exchange: when, for a given asset-referenced token, the estimated quarterly average number and value of transactions per day associated with uses as a means of exchange is higher than 1,000,000 transactions and €200 mln, respectively, within a single currency area, the issuer shall stop issuing the asset-referenced token and present a plan to the competent authority, within 40 working days, to ensure that the number and value of transactions per day associated to uses as means of exchange within a single currency area is kept below these thresholds (Art. 23).

More stringent requirements apply when an asset-reference token is classified as significant. To protect financial stability and European monetary sovereignty, EBA can determine that a stablecoin is significant based on several criteria, such as the value of the stablecoins or their market capitalisation, the

30 The authorisation requirement should however not apply where the asset-referenced tokens are only offered to qualified investors, or when the offer to the public of asset-referenced tokens is below € 5,000,000, or the equivalent amount in another currency over a period of 12 months (Art. 16 para. 2).

31 The competent national authority should consult the EBA and ESMA and, where the stablecoin is referencing Union currencies, the European Central Bank (ECB) If the currency is not the euro, the national central bank of issue of such currencies should be consulted before authorisation is granted or refused.

number and value of transactions, size of the reserve of assets, the issuers' cross-border activities, and the interconnectedness with the financial system.[32] Article 45 lists the additional obligations applicable to issuers of significant asset-referenced tokens, such as other own funds requirements, liquidity management policy, and interoperability. The supervisory responsibilities on issuers of meaningful asset-referenced tokens shall be transferred to the EBA.[33]

The Regulation also requires authorisation for providing services related to crypto-assets such as custody (wallet providers), exchange services between fiat currencies and fiat currencies, advice, and so forth. It is important to note that, in line with MiFID II, the Regulation should not affect the possibility for persons established in the Union to crypto-asset services from a third-country firm on their own initiative. Where a third-country firm provides crypto-asset services on the initiative of a person based in the Union, the crypto-asset services should not be deemed as being delivered in the Union. However, suppose a third-country firm solicits clients or potential clients or promotes or advertises crypto-asset services or activities in the Union. This should not be deemed a crypto-asset service provided at the client's own initiative. In such cases, the third-country firm should be authorised as a crypto-asset service provider.

The Regulation sets out several duties and obligations for issuers of stablecoins: they shall act honestly, fairly, and professionally (Art. 27); they are subject to ongoing information obligations (Art. 30);[34] and are required to

32 The EBA shall classify asset-referenced tokens as significant asset-referenced tokens when three of the following criteria are met in at least two consecutive reports from the issuer home competent authority: (a) the size of the customer base of the asset-referenced tokens, including those which do not interact directly with the issuer, is higher than 10 mln; (b) the value of the asset-referenced tokens issued, where applicable, their market capitalisation or the size of the reserve of assets of the issuer of the asset-referenced token, is higher than € 5 billion; (c) the number and value of transactions in those asset-referenced tokens is higher than 2,500,000 transactions and € 500 mln respectively, per day; (f) the interconnectedness with the financial system; (g) the same person or related group of persons issue several e-money tokens, asset-referenced tokens and provide crypto-asset provider services (Art. 43).

33 Chapter 5 of Title VII specifies the EBA's powers and competences on issuers of significant asset-referenced tokens and issuers of significant e-money tokens. Legal privilege (Art. 121), request for information (Art. 122), general investigative powers (Art. 123), on-site inspections (Art. 124), exchange of information (Art. 125), administrative agreements on exchange of information with third countries (Art. 126), disclosure of information from third countries (Art. 127), cooperation with other authorities (Art. 128), supervisory measures by EBA (Art 130), fines (Art. 131), that can be periodic penalty payments (Art. 132). "The Court of Justice shall have unlimited jurisdiction to review decisions whereby EBA has imposed a fine, a periodic penalty payment or any administrative penalty or other administrative measure in accordance with" MICA (Art. 136).

34 Preamble (48): 'In addition to the information provided in the crypto-asset white paper, issuers of asset-referenced tokens should also provide holders of such tokens with information on an ongoing basis. In particular, they should disclose on their website the amount of asset-referenced tokens in circulation and the value and composition of the reserve assets. Issuers of asset-referenced tokens should also disclose any event that has or is likely to have a significant

establish a complaint handling procedure for investors (Art. 31). They shall also comply with other requirements, such as rules on conflicts of interest (Art. 32), notification on changes to their management body or its competent authority (Art. 33), governance arrangements (Art. 34)[35], and own funds and requirements for the custody of the reserve assets (Art. 35). An issuer shall only invest the reserve assets in secure and low-risk assets.[36]

Title VII (Chapter 4) sets out detailed provisions on the EBA's powers and competencies related to the supervision of issuers of significant asset-referenced tokens and significant e-money tokens, including supervisory responsibilities (Art. 117) and rules on supervisory colleges for issuers of significant asset-referenced tokens (Art. 119).[37]

---

impact on the value of the asset-referenced tokens or on the reserve assets, irrespective of whether such crypto-assets are admitted to trading.'

35 These governance arrangements include a clear organisational structure with well-defined, transparent, and consistent lines of responsibility and effective processes to identify, manage, monitor, and report the risks to which they are or might be exposed. The management body of such issuers and their shareholders should have good repute and sufficient expertise and be fit and proper for the purpose of anti-money laundering and combatting the financing of terrorism. Issuers of asset-referenced tokens should also employ resources proportionate to the scale of their activities and should always ensure continuity and regularity in the performance of their activities. For that purpose, issuers of asset-referenced tokens should establish a business continuity policy aimed at ensuring, in the case of an interruption to their systems and procedures, the performance of their core payment activities. Issuers of asset-referenced tokens should also have a strong internal control and risk assessment mechanism, as well as a system that guarantees the integrity and confidentiality of information received (Preamble (51)).

36 As stated in Preamble (54), 'In order to cover their liability against holders of asset-referenced tokens, issuers of asset-referenced tokens should constitute and maintain a reserve of assets matching the risks reflected in such liability. The reserve of assets should be used for the benefit of the holders of the asset-referenced tokens when the issuer is not able to fulfil its obligations towards the holders, such as in insolvency. The reserve of assets should be composed and managed in such a way that market and currency risks are covered. Issuers of asset-referenced tokens should ensure the prudent management of the reserve of assets and should, in particular, ensure that the value of the reserve amounts at least to the corresponding value of tokens in circulation and that changes in the reserve are adequately managed to avoid adverse impacts on the markets of the reserve assets Issuers of asset-referenced tokens should therefore have clear and detailed policies that describe, inter alia, the composition of the reserve of assets, the allocation of assets included therein, a comprehensive assessment of the risks raised by the reserve assets, the procedure for the issuance and redemption of the asset-referenced tokens, the procedure to increase and decrease the reserve assets and, where the reserve assets are invested, the investment policy that is followed by the issuers. Issuers of asset-referenced tokens that are marketed both in the Union and in third countries should ensure that their reserve of assets is available to cover the issuers' liability towards Union holders. The requirement to hold the reserve of assets with firms subject to Union law should therefore apply in proportion to the share of asset-referenced tokens that is expected to be marketed in the Union.'

37 Powers to issue non-binding opinions are conferred to the college in Art. 120 for asset-referenced tokens and e-money tokens. These opinions can be related to require an issuer to hold a higher amount of own funds, an amended crypto-asset white paper, envisaged withdrawal of

17.5 Conclusion

After this brief account of MiCA, it can be concluded that in Europe, a robust private stablecoin will only be issued by credit entities, electronic money institutions, or new entities domiciled in the EU and subject to the supervision of national central banks or, in the case of significant stablecoins, the ECB. This regulation safeguards financial stability and the European banking system. The issue of a digital euro as a means of payment will reduce the importance and use of stablecoins as substitutes for legal tender and enhance their role as investments. Banks currently provide some services for crypto-assets and are likely to continue to do so.

When designing the digital euro, the ECB's most plausible hypothesis would seem to be the two-tier model. This model entails the collaboration of credit entities in the distribution and custody of the digital euro issued by the ECB.

authorisation, envisaged agreement of exchange of information with a third-country supervisory authority, and so on. Competent authorities or the EBA shall duly consider the opinions of the college and where they do not agree with the opinion, including any recommendations, their final decision shall contain explanations for any significant deviation from the opinion or recommendations.

Part V

Towards the Uncharted Times of the Digital Assets Era

18 Decentralised Finance and Capital Markets Regulation

Eugenia Macchiavello

18.1 Decentralised finance, capital markets regulation, and CBDC: The aim of this chapter

'Decentralisation' has been traditionally used in the context of large business organisations and public law to refer to the transfer of some powers from the centre to the perimeter but has recently assumed specific connotations in the financial sector context. In particular, DeFi has been widely used in the financial world without an official definition.[1] It can be found in financial regulation literature to indicate, in a first, broad sense, the provision of financial products or services in a peer-to-peer manner that does not involve conventional financial intermediaries (and their centrally organised processes).[2] In a

1 Angela Walch, 'Blockchain's Treacherous Vocabulary: One More Challenge for Regulators', *Journal of Internet Law* 21, no. 2 (August 2017): 9–16; Angela Walch, 'The Path of Blockchain Lexicon (and the Law)', *Review of Banking & Financial Law* 36 (2017): 713–65; Vitalik Buterin, 'The Meaning of Decentralization', *Medium* (blog), 6 February 2017, https://medium.com/@VitalikButerin/the-meaning-of-decentralization-a0c92b76a274.

2 See Financial Stability Board, 'Decentralised Financial Technologies: Report on Financial Stability, Regulatory and Governance Implications', 6 June 2019, https://www.fsb.org/wp-content/uploads/P060619.pdf: 'The decentralisation of financial services refers to the elimination – or reduction in the role – of one or more intermediaries or centralised processes that have traditionally been involved in the provision of financial services.' The FSB intends to cover such terms as peer-to-peer lending (as decentralised risk-taking), DLT-based systems (decentralised record-keeping), and a broad range of technologies (AI, cloud computing, big data, etc.) used to decentralise the provision of services. See also Dirk A Zetzsche, Douglas W Arner, and Ross P Buckley, 'Decentralized Finance', *Journal of Financial Regulation* 6, no. 2 (20 September 2020): 172, https://doi.org/10.1093/jfr/fjaa010. (identifying decentralised finance as the 'decentralised provision of financial services through a mix of infrastructure, markets, technology, methods, and applications,' where decentralised provision means 'provision by multiple participants, intermediaries, and end-users spread over multiple jurisdictions, with interactions facilitated, and often in fact enabled in the first place, by technology.' Therefore, DeFi is frequently 'based on distributed ledger technology as the basis of token-based ecosystems', but, more generally, can involve the four 'ABCD' technologies at the heart of FinTech/Regtech: AI, Blockchain, Cloud and Data (Zetzsche, Arner, and Buckley, 173–74, 179.). Moreover, Iris H-Y Chiu, 'Regulating Crypto-Finance: A Policy Blueprint', *SSRN Electronic Journal*, 2021, https://doi.org/10.2139/ssrn.3805878. referring to Sid Coelho-Prabhu, 'A Begin-

DOI: 10.4324/9781003258261-23

narrower sense, it refers to providing financial services or creating markets in the context of a blockchain or DLT/blockchain[3] infrastructure.[4] It consists of an electronic database of transactions shared and distributed across some participants—nodes—validating new entries through a 'consensus method.' It is also a digital infrastructure for creating other applications and providing services ('DLT-ecosystems').

The DLT is a technology per se decentralised and characterised by diffused power. It has been conceived in a crypto-anarchist and cypher-punk environment to create a society free from governments, laws, and traditional finance (especially after the financial crisis), only ruled by the code ('The Code is Law'[5]).[6] Consequently, it has the potential (not always realised) to build

---

ner's Guide to Decentralized Finance (DeFi)', *Coinbase* (blog), 6 January 2020, https://www.coinbase.com/blog/a-beginners-guide-to-decentralized-finance-defi.

3 In this chapter, I will use DLT and blockchain interchangeably for convenience. For current definitions of DLT and blockchain and relative differences: Michel Rauchs et al., 'Distributed Ledger Technology Systems: A Conceptual Framework' (Cambridge Center for Alternative Finance, 2018), https://www.jbs.cam.ac.uk/wp-content/uploads/2020/08/2018-10-26-conceptualising-dlt-systems.pdf; European Commission, 'Consultation Document on an EU Framework for Markets in Crypto-Assets', 2019, https://commission.europa.eu/system/files/2020-01/2019-crypto-assets-consultation-document_en.pdf.

4 See Angela Walch, 'Deconstructing "Decentralization": Exploring the Core Claim of Crypto Systems', in *Cryptoassets*, by Angela Walch (Oxford University Press, 2019), 39–68, https://doi.org/10.1093/oso/9780190077310.003.0003; Fabian Schär, 'Decentralized Finance: On Blockchain- and Smart Contract-Based Financial Markets', *Review* 103, no. 2 (2021), https://doi.org/10.20955/r.103.153-74: 'The term decentralized finance (DeFi) refers to an alternative financial infrastructure built on top of the Ethereum blockchain. DeFi uses smart contracts to create protocols that replicate existing financial services in a more open, interoperable, and transparent way.' A recent study commissioned by the European Parliament-ECON refers the term 'decentralised finance' (DeFi) 'to financial activities (lending, arbitraging, derivatives, collateralisation) operated without any intermediaries through automated protocols and smart contracts': Jean-Pierre Landau and Markus K Brunnermeier, 'The Digital Euro: Policy Implications and Perspectives', 2022, 53; Nic Carter and Linda Jeng, 'DeFi Protocol Risks: The Paradox of DeFi', *SSRN Electronic Journal*, 2021, https://doi.org/10.2139/ssrn.3866699; Camila Russo, 'What Is Decentralized Finance?: A Deep Dive by The Defiant | CoinMarketCap', CoinMarketCap Alexandria, February 2022, https://coinmarketcap.com/alexandria/article/what-is-decentralized-finance.

5 The expression is by Lawrence Lessig, *Code and Other Laws of Cyberspace* (New York: Basic Books, 1999). See also Primavera De Filippi and Samer Hassan, 'Blockchain Technology as a Regulatory Technology: From Code Is Law to Law Is Code' (arXiv, 8 January 2018), http://arxiv.org/abs/1801.02507.

6 See Michèle Finck, *Blockchain Regulation and Governance in Europe*, 1st ed. (Cambridge University Press, 2018), 36, https://doi.org/10.1017/9781108609708; Karen Yeung, 'Regulation by Blockchain: The Emerging Battle for Supremacy between the Code *of* Law and Code *as* Law', *The Modern Law Review* 82, no. 2 (March 2019): 207–25, https://doi.org/10.1111/1468-2230.12399; Marcella Atzori, 'Blockchain Technology and Decentralized Governance: Is the State Still Necessary?', *SSRN Electronic Journal*, 2015, 45–49, https://doi.org/10.2139/ssrn.2709713. See also Zetzsche, Arner, and Buckley, 'Decentralized', 172: 'DeFi, however, is more than this: the objective is to develop systems which use technology to eliminate borders, jurisdiction and the necessity of centralized control including governments.'

systems in which essential functions are performed in a distributed way by a network of different entities in terms of nature (for example, natural/legal), roles (for example, users/developers/miners), and incentives (social/spiritual/financial),[7] part of the new 'collaborative economy.'

Therefore, such a form of DeFi challenges the same structure and principles of financial regulation and supervision, conceived with traditional centrally managed intermediaries and markets in mind,[8] raising doubts on the applicability to the same existing laws and legal categories. However, we also witness various forms of 'reintermediation,' ranging from new unregulated operators performing the functions of traditional 'intermediaries'[9] to regulatory approaches forcing disintermediated finance to convert back to intermediated finance (§18.5. about the US and EU) and, finally, to a natural trend towards more centralisation and intermediation. On this latter aspect, we can recognise a trend towards increased centralisation and concentration of power in the evolution of decentralised finance, as previously verified in other sectors such as internet networks, file sharing, and social networks (see §18.3).[10] International, European, and national regulators are evaluating regulatory responses to this phenomenon, still trying to understand its characteristics and implications.

CBDCs, as discussed throughout this book, have often been conceived as a government response to, in particular, crypto-currencies (especially stablecoins) and, in general, to DeFi and crypto-finance in order to exploit the benefit of the same (for example, financial inclusion and client satisfaction also through better accessibility and convenience; easy cross-border payments; more resilience and efficiency) while eliminating the main risks (lack of

7 Juri Mattila and Timo Seppälä, 'Distributed Governance in Multi-Sided Platforms: A Conceptual Framework from Case: Bitcoin', in *Collaborative Value Co-Creation in the Platform Economy*, ed. Anssi Smedlund, Arto Lindblom, and Lasse Mitronen, Translational Systems Sciences (Singapore: Springer, 2018), 183–205, https://doi.org/10.1007/978-981-10-8956-5_10.

8 Phoebus Athanassiou, *Digital Innovation in Financial Services: Legal Challenges and Regulatory Policy Issues*, International Banking and Finance Law Series, volume 34 (Alphen aan den Rijn, the Netherlands: Kluwer Law International BV, 2018), 39, 52–53; Philipp Paech, 'Securities, Intermediation and the Blockchain: An Inevitable Choice between Liquidity and Legal Certainty?', *Uniform Law Review* 21, no. 4 (December 2016): 612–39, https://doi.org/10.1093/ulr/unw040; ESMA, 'Advice: Initial Coin Offerings and Crypto-Assets', 9 January 2009, https://www.esma.europa.eu/sites/default/files/library/esma50-157-1391_crypto_advice.pdf; Emilios Avgouleas and Alexandros Seretakis, 'Governing the Digital Finance Value-Chain in the EU: MIFID II, the Digital Package, and the Large Gaps Between!', in *Digital Finance in Europe: Law, Regulation, and Governance*, ed. Emilios Avgouleas and Heikki Marjosola (De Gruyter, 2021), 1–36, https://doi.org/10.1515/9783110749472-002.

9 See also Iris H-Y Chiu, 'Fintech and Disruptive Business Models in Financial Products, Intermediation and Markets—Policy Implications for Financial Regulators', *Jornal of Technology Law and Policy*, no. 1 (2021): 86–87.

10 See Primavera De Filippi and Xavier Lavayssière, 'Blockchain Technology: Toward a Decentralized Governance of Digital Platforms?', in *The Great Awakening: New Modes of Life amidst Capitalist Ruins*, ed. Anna Grear and David Bollier (Santa Barbara: Punctum Books, 2020).

public money relevance, monetary policy ineffectiveness, banks disintermediation and consequently inability to finance economic activities and families).[11] Nonetheless, the first experiments in this area and current discussions around the digital euro or other CBDCs, when resorting to DLT, tend to exclude the use of genuinely decentralised models (public permissionless systems like Bitcoin or Ethereum) from the design options.[12] The levels of decentralisation, however, are varied, as well as the implications. Among the proposals of CBDCs, we can also find hybrid models (combining centralised issuance of the CBDC and interdependent decentralised networks)[13] and more decentralised ones (to create a global digital currency).[14]

In the present chapter, after analysing some typical aspects of DeFi (in its narrower sense) in the area of capital raising (§18.2 and §18.3) as well as related legal issues (§18.4 to §18.6), I will try to derive lessons and implications also for the different context of CBDCs (§ 18.7).

18.2 Benefits and risks of DeFi and different levels of decentralisation

Decentralised finance might present several benefits, such as financial inclusion (more straightforward and affordable access for all), customer-friendly services (convenient, fast, digital), transparency, increased competition, and diversity in financial markets as well as resilience to cyber-risk and manipulations.[15] Nonetheless, eliminating traditional intermediaries and related financial

11 See ECB, 'Report on a Digital Euro' (European Central Bank, October 2020). Among others, see also Landau and Brunnermeier, 'The Digital Euro: Policy Implications and Perspectives', 11, 20 ff.

12 Some projects do not entail the use of DLT. See Raphael Auer and Rainer Boehme, 'The Technology of Retail Central Bank Digital Currency', *BIS Quarterly Review*, March 2020, https://www.bis.org/publ/qtrpdf/r_qt2003j.pdf; Ross P Buckley et al., 'Sovereign Digital Currencies: Reshaping the Design of Money and Payments Systems', *Journal of Payments Strategy & Systems* 15, no. 1 (2021): 7; Tao Zhang and Zhigang Huang, 'Blockchain and Central Bank Digital Currency', *ICT Express* 8, no. 2 (June 2022): 264–70, https://doi.org/10.1016/j.icte.2021.09.014. See also for the digital euro project: ECB, 'Report on a Digital Euro', 13; Wouter Bossu et al., 'Legal Aspects of Central Bank Digital Currency: Central Bank and Monetary Law Considerations', *IMF*, IMF Working Paper, 20, no. 254 (November 2020): 10 ff., https://www.imf.org/en/Publications/WP/Issues/2020/11/20/Legal-Aspects-of-Central-Bank-Digital-Currency-Central-Bank-and-Monetary-Law-Considerations-49827.

13 See also, regarding the digital euro, ECB, 'Report on a Digital Euro', 39–40.

14 Abdurrahman Arum Rahman, 'A Decentralized Central Bank Digital Currency', *MPRA Paper*, no. 111361 (3 January 2022), https://mpra.ub.uni-muenchen.de/111361/.

15 About decentralised finance's advantages and risks: Don Tapscott and Alex Tapscott, 'Realizing the Potential of Blockchain A Multistakeholder Approach to the Stewardship of Blockchain and Cryptocurrencies', *WEF (White Paper)*, June 2017, https://www3.weforum.org/docs/WEF_Realizing_Potential_Blockchain.pdf; Yan Chen and Cristiano Bellavitis, 'Blockchain Disruption and Decentralized Finance: The Rise of Decentralized Business Models', *SSRN Electronic Journal*, 2019, https://doi.org/10.2139/ssrn.3483608.

regulation conceived to respond to classical risks of the complex structure of financial intermediation creates new risks and eliminates essential functions (for example, pricing by underwriters, transparency of markets) not always provided by the new DLT systems. Further risks also depend on the different levels of decentralisation. In this regard, it is necessary to underline the extreme variety of models in DLT systems.[16] Permissioned and federated private blockchains are closed networks in which data are visible only to a subset of users and, consequently, present a certain level of centralised governance needed to set the rules about who can participate in the network and the consensus process (when meeting specific requirements) as well as to verify the identity of admitted participants.[17] Moreover, they present different preferred consensus methods, such as the practical Byzantine Fault Tolerance (pBFT), Istanbul BFT (iBFT), and federated BFT (fBFT), in which only known nodes with specific rights can validate and add records (no miners) and are faster, compatible with requirements about finality,[18] but less censorship-resistant compared with PoW/PoS (reinstating the importance of a trusted central authority).[19] These 'closed'/private structures have been considered models for implementing the DLT infrastructure

16 The DLT infrastructure has become famous with Bitcoin (conceived as an alternative to the traditional payment system). It was later used to create several other networks with their own native tokens (e.g., Ethereum, Filecoin). These famous DLT 'eco-systems' are examples of public and permissionless blockchains, in which everybody can access and potentially participate in the validation process based on 'consensus,' since it cannot rely on the existence of a central authority. The main consensus methods used in public permissionless networks consist of the Proof-of-Work (PoW) model (Bitcoin and Ethereum) or Proof-of-Stake (PoS) model (Peercoin, BitShares, NXT, and, in the near future, Ethereum 2.0), which show a high level of resistance to attacks but are quite expensive, slow, and high energy-consuming (with PoS reducing such issues compared with PoW). In the PoW method, nodes compete to solve a mathematical puzzle to validate a transaction, receiving a reward in the form of tokens when they win; in the PoS, the identification of the validating nodes is randomised, but the nodes with the highest number of tokens at stake end up validating the transaction and in proportion to the same, although they might decide to outsource to a third party, sharing the reward (Delegated PoS: Rauchs et al., 'Distributed', 68; Parma Bains, 'Blockchain Consensus Mechanisms: A Primer for Supervisors' (IMF, January 2022), 8, https://www.imf.org/en/Publications/fintech-notes/Issues/2022/01/25/Blockchain-Consensus-Mechanisms-511769.

17 Harish Natarajan, Solvej Krause, and Helen Gradstein, 'Distributed Ledger Technology and Blockchain', Working Paper (Washington, DC: World Bank, 2017), https://doi.org/10.1596/29053.

18 In the pBFT and iBFT methods, only a few known nodes validate the entries and reach a consensus through messaging at a certain moment in time; in the fBFT, some nodes might remain unknown and only a subset of nodes are needed to reach a consensus. Other methods, such as the Proof-of-Elapsed-Time (PoET) based on a randomised leader node to validate probabilistic finality, have been developed by companies (e.g., Intel) and might precedent competition and concentration issues: Shijie Zhang and Jong-Hyouk Lee, 'Analysis of the Main Consensus Protocols of Blockchain', *ICT Express* 6, no. 2 (June 2020): 93–97, https://doi.org/10.1016/j.icte.2019.08.001; Bains, 'Blockchain Consensus Mechanisms', 12 ff.

19 Rauchs et al., 'Distributed', 36; Hossein Nabilou, 'Bitcoin Governance as a Decentralized Financial Market Infrastructure', *Stanford Journal of Blockchain Law & Policy*, 30 June 2021, 181, https://stanford-jblp.pubpub.org/pub/bitcoin-governance/release/2.

within the financial system (for example, for the issuance of transferable securities and DLT-based markets)[20] and also through the collaboration of groups of financial institutions.[21] Such types of DLT systems, consisting of closed groups (often of financial institutions), still relying on a central authority and based on an IP-protected code designed by big technological companies (for example, Corda, Hyperledger fabric), represent a clear departure from the original decentralised model and inspiration, which was instead based on an open source structure, freely accessible, democratic system.

This chapter will focus on decentralised public models because of their revolutionary character. Still, at least a part of the analysis will also be shown to be transposable to private DLT systems.

18.3 'Decentralised DLT' systems: Their multi-layered structure and governance implications

The most widespread and advanced model of public and permissionless DLT systems in the financial sector presents a particularly complex structure organised in multiple layers. Taking Ethereum as a model, we can observe a main protocol layer that constitutes the underlying structure of the network and allows the basic functioning and storing of the data as well as the creation, through mining, of native tokens (Ether), which are used to reward miners (and therefore to make the system work through the validation of transactions) and for payments within the network.

Nonetheless, on top of this protocol, many other interlinked structures and applications (D-Apps) have been created with varied functions, all relying on the main infrastructure conceived on purpose as open and interoperable. Among these, in particular, ICOs, i.e., offerings of app-tokens[22] organised (at the app-layer) by companies or individuals (users of the leading blockchain), with the help of app coders, also taking advantage of the simplified and fast

20 Among numerous studies exploring the advantages and risks in deploying DLT for issuance, trading, and clearing of securities: Joseph Lee, 'Distributed Ledger Technologies (Blockchain) in Capital Markets: Risk and Governance', *SSRN Electronic Journal*, 2018, https://doi.org/10.2139/ssrn.3180553; Randy Priem, 'Distributed Ledger Technology for Securities Clearing and Settlement: Benefits, Risks, and Regulatory Implications', *Financial Innovation* 6, no. 1 (December 2020): 11, https://doi.org/10.1186/s40854-019-0169-6.

21 See the R3-Corda project: Richard G Brown, 'R3 Corda: A Distributed Ledger Designed for Financial Services', Fintech, DeFi, Blockchain, Web3 Daily News by Finyear, accessed 25 February 2023, https://www.finyear.com/R3-Corda-A-Distributed-Ledger-Designed-for-Financial-Services_a35855.html. Other financial institutions, such as JP Morgan, have preferred developing their own blockchain: JP Morgan, 'Blockchain and the Decentralization Revolution', 2018, https://www.jpmorgan.com/solutions/cib/investment-banking/corporate-finance-advisory/blockchain.; JP Morgan, 'Onyx by JP Morgan', accessed 25 February 2023, https://jpmorgan.com/onyx/index.htm.

22 Consider, for instance, electronic assets conferring certain rights, including receiving a future service/product or participating in certain decisions, stored, and traded on a blockchain.

process introduced by the protocol ERC20 (i.e., a model of the token with specific minimum characteristics) recently developed by Ethereum.[23] Such tokens can present different functions (payment, digital representations of rights, access to an application or service, hybrid).[24]

Other apps might be created to serve the previous ones, often relying on smart contracts (i.e., complex sets of pre-set electronic inputs) and other automatic systems: bulletin boards (advertising or aggregating buying and selling interests), markets and exchanges of native or app-tokens (for example, Coinbase), liquidity pools and automatic lending platforms of crypto-currencies (for example, Compound, Uniswap),[25] price aggregators or robo-crypto-advisors, or other services allowing the interaction between different crypto-applications and the aggregation of data from the same. Also, decentralised organisations (DO) have developed, consisting of new decentralised business organisations in which electronically enforced rules govern relationships, and even decentralised autonomous organisations (DAO in the narrow sense), i.e., DO entirely run by code/smart contracts.[26]

Despite eliminating traditional intermediaries (for example, IPO underwriters, distributors, venture capital funds) and consequent advantages in terms of costs,[27] speed, liquidity, control-retention, and network effects,[28] we assist

23 Jonathan Rohr and Aaron Wright, 'Blockchain-Based Token Sales, Initial Coin Offerings, and the Democratization of Public Capital Markets', *Hastings Law Journal* 70, no. 2 (1 February 2019): 463.

24 For a renowned classification, see FINMA, 'Guidelines for Enquiries Regarding the Regulatory Framework for Initial Coin Offerings (ICOs)', 16 February 2018, https://www.finma.ch/en/~/media/finma/dokumente/dokumentencenter/myfinma/1bewilligung/fintech/wegleitung-ico.pdf?sc_lang=en&hash=83EE49D77DA54DD079F314D9EDCBDC3D.

25 See Schär, 'Decentralized Finance', 163 ff.

26 The DO typical example is 'TheDAO' conceived as a venture capital fund without a manager (but with 'curators' proposing projects and tokens' holders deciding whether to invest) and became (un-)famous in June 2016 when a hacker took advantage of an (app-code) bug to 'move' around USD50 million from TheDAO to his/her account and the Ethereum community decided, not without criticism, to 'reverse' the operation ('fork'), violating one of the fundamental blockchain's principles: SEC, 'Report of Investigation Pursuant to Section 21(a) of the Securities Exchange Act of 1934: The DAO', 25 July 2017; Walch, 'Deconstructing "Decentralization"'; Primavera De Filippi and Aaron Wright, *Blockchain and the Law: The Rule of Code* (Cambridge, Massachusetts: Harvard University Press, 2018), 136; Malcolm Campbell-Verduyn, *Bitcoin and Beyond: Cryptocurrencies, Blockchains, and Global Governance*, 1st ed. (London: Routledge, 2017), 157, https://doi.org/10.4324/9781315211909; Rohr and Wright, 'Blockchain-Based'; Wulf A Kaal, 'Blockchain-Based Corporate Governance', *Stanford Journal of Blockchain Law & Policy*, 4 January 2021, https://stanford-jblp.pubpub.org/pub/blockchain-corporate-governance/release/1.

27 Costs would only consist of the expenses for setting up the infrastructure and developing the protocol, and in exchange fees: Paech, 'Securities', 3; Iris H-Y Chiu, 'Decoupling Tokens From Trading: Reaching Beyond Investment Regulation for Regulatory Policy in Initial Coin Offerings', *Corporate Finance: Capital Structure & Payout Policies EJournal*, 2018, 6.

28 For blockchain-based ventures: Yokoi-Arai Mamiko and Iota Kaousar Nassr, 'Initial Coin Offerings (ICOs) for SME Financing' (OECD, 2019), 10 ff, 24 ff., https://www.oecd.org

nevertheless to a partial reintermediation. For instance, crypto-exchanges. Although they emerged to exchange tokens with fiat money and/or crypto-currencies (crypto-exchanges in a narrow sense),[29] they have also started to list prices, match demand and offers and execute orders (crypto-trading venues), or buy on their own account (crypto-dealers). To reduce asymmetric information, some crypto-exchanges have also organised 'Initial Exchange Offerings' (IEO), conducting initial screening of projects and due diligence analysis, as well as marketing and promotional activity to attract investors.[30] Other new intermediaries are platforms disseminating pricing indexes, rating platforms, and wallet providers.

The resulting architecture and governance of such DLT networks are very complex, involving varied participants at different levels, and like no other structure previously used in the financial sector. At the protocol level, we have core developers (generally voluntary workers, anonymous or with pseudonyms), who appear to be the only ones authorised to significantly modify the protocol-layer code, and 'ordinary' coders, with only proposing and supporting roles. 'Miners' (again anonymous and geographically distributed) are network nodes contributing to creating each block with transactions' data and receiving a reward in 'native' (protocol) tokens. Finally, users participate in the network to access the services provided through the blockchain and become nodes making available to the network their computers and committing to keeping the software updated without receiving rewards. Such different roles can even be assumed by the same individual (for example, user, node, developer) since there is not necessarily a separation of powers or roles.[31] Internal governance of such a network is opaque. It potentially presents electronic experts with oligarchy and various forms of power concentration, making it difficult to measure the adequate level of decentralisation.[32] As mentioned, core developers are those with true decision-making power. However, in public blockchains, decisions are discussed among the entire network and collectively taken through various informal methods,[33] effectively implemented

/finance/ICOs-for-SME-Financing.pdf; Dmitri Boreiko, Guido Ferrarini, and Paolo Giudici, 'Blockchain Startups and Prospectus Regulation', *European Business Organization Law Review* 20, no. 4 (December 2019): 665, https://doi.org/10.1007/s40804-019-00168-6.

29 Most crypto-to-fiat transactions: Rauchs et al., 'Distributed', 43–46.

30 Boreiko, Ferrarini, and Giudici, 'Blockchain Startups'.

31 For this reason, analogies between, for instance, the Bitcoin network and constitutional systems (embedded in checks and balances, separation of powers) or corporate governance models are misplaced: Nabilou, 'Bitcoin Governance'.

32 Atzori, 'Blockchain Technology and Decentralized Governance', 52 ff.; Rauchs et al., 'Distributed', 36; Walch, 'Deconstructing "Decentralization"', 27; Adem Efe Gencer et al., 'Decentralization in Bitcoin and Ethereum Networks', 2018, https://doi.org/10.48550/ARXIV.1801.03998.

33 Governance forms range from 'benevolent dictators' or foundations ('off-chain governance') to rules embedded in the code and related to the number of tokens possessed ('on-chain governance'): Philipp Hacker et al., 'Regulating Blockchain: Techno-Social and Legal Chal-

through miners' consensus, and 'forks' (i.e. duplications of the same protocol which then continue separately) can be created (or threatened) in case of dissent among participants.[34] History shows that 'hard forks' can be implemented—and the 'immutable' ledger changed—through concerted efforts by core developers and main nodes (representing 51% of the network) to repair incidents/bugs (even if they occurred at the 'app-layer').[35] Miners might present geographic or ownership (for example, poolers[36] or owners of the hashing facilities) concentration, although they tend to maintain power distribution.[37]

Instead, we find less decentralisation at the ICO (D-App) level. For instance, crypto-exchanges/markets generally present centralised structures (especially when holding clients' private keys—clients' accounts—and executing orders off-chain only in their books or having the power to block orders).[38] However, decentralised exchanges (DEXs) have recently emerged, replicating the blockchain structure of a distributed network and automatic execution of orders on-chain through smart contracts.[39] However, centralisation can be realised by retaining or assigning governance rights. Furthermore, several smart contracts and systems rely on external data sources ('oracles'), for instance, to determine

---

lenges—An Introduction', in *Regulating Blockchain*, by Philipp Hacker et al. (Oxford University Press, 2019), chap. 7, https://doi.org/10.1093/oso/9780198842187.003.0001; De Filippi and Lavayssière, 'Blockchain Technology', 8; Rauchs et al., 'Distributed', 55; Campbell-Verduyn, *Bitcoin and Beyond*, 48 ff., 54 ff.; Atzori, 'Blockchain Technology and Decentralized Governance', 57.

34 See Jeffery Atik and J D George Gerro, 'Hard Forks on the Bitcoin Blockchain: Reversible Exit, Continuing Voice', *Stanford Journal of Blockchain Law & Policy*, 23 June 2018, 1, 5, 10, https://stanford-jblp.pubpub.org/pub/hard-forks-bitcoin/release/2; Alex Galea, 'Bitcoin Development: Who Can Change the Core Protocol?', *Medium* (blog), 10 September 2018, https://galea.medium.com/bitcoin-development-who-can-change-the-core-protocol-478b8ac5fe43.

35 BIS, 'V. Cryptocurrencies: Looking beyond the Hype', BIS Annual Economic Report (Basel: BSI, 2018), https://www.bis.org/publ/arpdf/ar2018e5.htm; Walch, 'Deconstructing "Decentralization"'; Nabilou, 'Bitcoin Governance', 179 ff.

36 As for leaders of groups of miners formed to pool together computational power and share rewards.

37 See Rauchs et al., 'Distributed', 20, 68.

38 See IOSCO, 'Issues, Risks and Regulatory Considerations Relating to Crypto-Asset Trading Platforms', May 2019, 4, 13, 35, https://www.iosco.org/library/pubdocs/pdf/IOSCOPD627.pdf; Apolline Blandin et al., 'Global Cryptoasset Regulatory Landscape Study', *SSRN Electronic Journal*, 2019, https://doi.org/10.2139/ssrn.3379219; Rauchs et al., 'Distributed', 22; Hacker et al., 'Regulating Blockchain', 340; Primavera De Filippi and Aaron Wright, *Blockchain and the Law: The Rule of Code* (Cambridge, Massachusetts: Harvard University Press, 2018), 179; Boreiko, Ferrarini, and Giudici, 'Blockchain Startups'; ESMA, 'Advice', 25 and Annex; Robby Houben and Alexander Snyers, 'Cryptocurrencies and Blockchain', *EU Parliament*, July 2018, 27, http://www.europarl.europa.eu/supporting-analyses.

39 Finck, *Blockchain Regulation*, 62; ESMA, 'Advice', 44; Rauchs et al., 'Distributed', 22. (DEXs represent 7% of crypto-exchanges but only a few present decentralisations at all stages, for example, custody, order matching, and clearing/settlement).

prices or amounts. Such sources and data might be manipulated or otherwise controlled ('oracle risk').[40]

Therefore, the types of risks to consider and the risks typically highlighted for investors concerning crypto-assets (volatility and fraud) can vary significantly. While in more centralised structures, we find the typical agency and counter-party risks at high levels of decentralisation, relevant risks related to the complex governance structure described above, concentration risks stemming from the use of similar technologies and technology-experts oligarchy; operational risks related to the multi-layered structure (failure of the infrastructure can severely affect the app level); use of oracles and uncertainty of power/accountability distribution in key financial infrastructures (for example, payments, markets); consequent inefficient management; and risk of frauds and illegal activities.[41]

18.4 DLT networks and EU capital markets regulation: Existing laws

Putting aside the ongoing discussion about the legal classification of certain crypto-currencies and app-tokens, we would like to briefly test the compatibility of existing capital markets regulation with a DLT-ecosystem scenario in this paragraph.

The classification of crypto-assets, for instance, as financial instruments implies the application to DLT systems of an enormous bulk of EU financial regulation, which might not suit decentralised or hybrid systems (starting with the identification of the applicable law and jurisdiction and enforcement)[42] nor address the highlighted risks.[43]

40 Carter and Jeng, 'DeFi Protocol Risks', 23–24; Giulio Caldarelli and Joshua Ellul, 'The Blockchain Oracle Problem in Decentralized Finance—A Multivocal Approach', *Applied Sciences* 11, no. 16 (18 August 2021): 7572, https://doi.org/10.3390/app11167572.

41 Financial Stability Board, 'Decentralised Financial Technologies', 6 ff.; ESMA, 'The Distributed Ledger Technology Applied to Securities Markets', 2 June 2016, 17 ff., https://www.esma.europa.eu/sites/default/files/library/2016-773_dp_dlt_0.pdf; Dirk A Zetzsche, Ross P Buckley, and Douglas W Arner, 'The Distributed Liability of Distributed Ledgers: Legal Risks of Blockchain', *U Illinois LR* 4 (2018): 1361, https://doi.org/10.2139/ssrn.3018214; Carter and Jeng, 'DeFi Protocol Risks', 13 ff.; Cristina Cuervo, Anastasiia Morozova, and Nobuyasu Sugimoto, 'Regulation of Crypto Assets', IMF, n.d., 3 ff., https://www.imf.org/en/Publications/fintech-notes/Issues/2020/01/09/Regulation-of-Crypto-Assets-48810.

42 For its global reach and lack of a point-of-control: Expert Group on Regulatory Obstacles to Financial Innovation (ROFIEG), 'Thirty Recommendations on Regulation, Innovation and Finance', December 2019, 51, 58, https://finance.ec.europa.eu/system/files/2019-12/191113-report-expert-group-regulatory-obstacles-financial-innovation_en.pdf; Zetzsche, Arner, and Buckley, 'Decentralized', 184–89.

43 Expert Group on Regulatory Obstacles to Financial Innovation (ROFIEG), 'Thirty Recommendations', 32; ESMA, 'The Distributed Ledger', 5. See also Avgouleas and Seretakis, 'Governing the Digital Finance Value-Chain in the EU'.

As an example, tokens' issuers and promoters (in less decentralised systems) might be regarded as, respectively, issuers and offerors under the Prospectus Regulation (PR, 2017/1129), with potential implications also under the Transparency Directive (TD, 2004/109) and Market Abuse Regulation (MAR, 596/2014).[44] Nonetheless, the application of such provisions and related duties might require EU law adaptations: for instance, prospectus schedules (Delegated Regulation EU/2019/980, ESMA guidelines and national rules) should include information about the blockchain functioning and related risk factors;[45] MiFIR (600/2014)[46] and TD rules on pre/post-trade information (very detailed and product-specific) would need adaptations (at level 2) to insert specific codes, standard forms, and transparency thresholds for tokens.[47]

Sometimes, instead, the classification under existing laws is itself challenging: some crypto-exchanges and specialised blockchains might be considered operating de facto trading venues (regulated markets or, more arguably, MTFs/OTFs)[48] but only when: a) the system brings together multiple-party buying and selling trading interests based on pre-established rules (even algorithms-based) and executes orders resulting in a contract;[49] b) someone is identifiable as managing/operating the same.[50] The latter condition is crucial: only if a legal entity or team is setting up and monitoring the system and able to solve critical issues should seek authorisation as, depending on the case, the investment firm or market operator[51] respect MiFID II/MiFIR (systems/procedures to ensure transparency and fair, orderly, and efficient trading) and MAR obligations. However, recognising a central operator might be challenging in genuine decentralised exchanges, excluding the qualification as a trading venue or complicating the identification of the rules' addressees.

Similarly, certain crypto-exchanges and blockchain infrastructure[52] might appear similar to settlement securities systems (SSSs)—for realising tokens set-

44 Only when tokens are traded on what can be considered a regulated trading venue (see below).

45 European Commission, 'Consultation Document', 41–42.

46 Articles 3-11, 25-27.

47 Thresholds for transparency waivers are identified based on current trading volumes of each traditional security and data on tokens trading currently lack. European Commission, 'Consultation Document', 37–38.

48 About the notion of trading venue in a DLT context: Securities and Markets Stakeholder Group, 'Advice to ESMA Own Initiative Report on Initial Coin Offerings and Crypto-Assets', 19 October 2018, 16, https://www.esma.europa.eu/sites/default/files/library/esma22-106-1338_smsg_advice_-_report_on_icos_and_crypto-assets.pdf; ESMA, 'The Distributed Ledger'; European Commission, 'Consultation Document', 35.

49 Articles 4(1) No. 19 and 4(1) No. 21-23 MiFID II.

50 See ESMA, 'Questions and Answers on MiFID II and MiFIR Market Structures Topics', 16 December 2022, chap. 5.2, https://www.esma.europa.eu/sites/default/files/library/esma70-872942901-38_qas_markets_structures_issues.pdf, question 10.

51 Art. 1(1) MiFID II. See European Commission, 'Consultation Document', 29–30.

52 In principle, the blockchain makes *per se* superfluous a settling intermediary, since transactions happen simultaneously and automatically, but in the case of tokens considered transferable securities traded on the capital market (in hypothesis, also crypto-exchanges), registration

tlement (payment-versus-tokens delivery) among accounts—central securities depositories (CSDs)—when also recording in book-entry form the issuance and transfer of tokens and/or holding tokens' accounts (for example, clients' private keys) with disposal power—and central counter-parties (CPPs)—when interposing themselves between parties on financial markets, triggering the application of MiFID II/EMIR (648/2012/EU), Settlement Finality Directive (SFD, 98/26) and Central Securities Depositories Regulation (CSDR, 909/2014) (organisational, governance, segregation rules), together with national laws, and relative authorisations.[53] Nonetheless, decentralisation raises issues about how to identify the 'system operator' and ensure its ability, for example, to suspend the orders of an insolvent participant,[54] and, more generally, comply with governance rules, interoperability requirements with other SSDs/CSDs, and the monitoring and management of contractual relationships within the network (the consensus-based validation process potentially looking as outsourcing of core SSD's functions).[55]

However, further potential revisions of SFD/CSDR pertain to conflict of law rules (appearing the existing account location criterion challenging)[56] and the concept of 'finality' (the time when an order is considered irrevocable) concerning consensus-methods and forks (although also dependent on national laws), in addition to the more general issues about smart contracts' validity and enforceability (also towards third parties).[57]

Moreover, considering that both regulated trading venues[58] and SSDs/CSDs[59] are by law accessible only by regulated intermediaries and professional operators (with specific features), we would need either to require

and settlement with an authorised CSD is required by EU law: Art. 3(2) and 18(2) CSDR. Advisory Group on Market Infrastructures for Securities and Collateral, 'The Potential Impact of DLTs on Securities Post-Trading Harmonisation and on the Wider EU Financial Market Integration' (ECB, September 2017), 25 ff., https://www.ecb.europa.eu/paym/intro/governance/shared/pdf/201709_dlt_impact_on_harmonisation_and_integration.pdf; European Commission, 'Consultation Document', 43.

53 About the potential application of the Short Selling Regulation (236/2012), Financial Collateral Directive (2002/47/EC) and EMIR see: European Commission, 'Consultation Document', 40, 46; ESMA, 'The Distributed Ledger', 31; Blandin et al., 'Global', 27; Athanassiou, *Digital Innovation*, 155.

54 ESMA, 'The Distributed Ledger', 32; Expert Group on Regulatory Obstacles to Financial Innovation (ROFIEG), 'Thirty Recommendations', 50; IOSCO, 'Issues', 24; Athanassiou, *Digital Innovation*, 170; Advisory Group on Market Infrastructures for Securities and Collateral, 'The Potential Impact', 27–28.

55 Article 30(1) CSDR. Advisory Group on Market Infrastructures for Securities and Collateral, 'The Potential Impact', 27–28.

56 Advisory Group on Market Infrastructures for Securities and Collateral, 35–36; European Commission, 'Consultation Document', 45–46; Athanassiou, *Digital Innovation*, para. 6.02.B.

57 Paech, 'Securities', 30; Athanassiou, *Digital Innovation*, 105.

58 Article 53(3), 19(2) MiFID II; about direct electronic access: Art. 48(7) MiFID II). See IOSCO, 'Issues', 11 ff.

59 Cf. Art. 2(f) SFD.

crypto-exchanges/blockchains to impose barriers to entry to un-sophisticated investors (contrary to the 'democratic finance' model) or to revise EU law, admitting retail participants while introducing new safeguards (for example, warnings and retail investment limits) in such DLT-markets.

Finally, miners and wallet providers are not considered by existing financial regulation but, because of their role, might potentially obtain relevant information from an insider dealing (if not already covered by Art. 8(4) MAR 'catch-all' provision) and market abuse's perspectives (offering DLT systems new opportunities for market abuse beyond Art. 12 MAR cases).[60]

18.5 The EU regulation of decentralised DLT systems

Regulators around the world have been adopting varied approaches to the highlighted problems. Although highly varied, national regulators' responses to DLT systems tend to force reintermediation through the extension of existing laws to ICOs and certain related activities (for example, US) or only focusing on issuers and intermediaries involved (for example, exchanges and wallet providers), disregarding decentralised structures (decentralised exchanges or the main DLT infrastructure) and specific new figures (for example, developers and miners) and operations (for example, forks).[61]

Within the EU, the EC has clarified that tokens that are categorised, based on MiFID II and national law, as financial instruments and relative services are subject to existing financial regulation (for example, MiFID II, PR)[62]. However, in consideration of possible problems of compatibility between the new system and EU financial regulation, it has introduced a 'DLT pilot regime,'[63] a form of a temporary sandbox, to test the DLT-resilience of the legal framework, with the view of a future review of the same. It covers only

60 European Commission, 'Consultation Document', 39; ESMA, 'The Distributed Ledger', 29; Zetzsche, Buckley, and Arner, 'The Distributed Liability', 1361, 1376.

61 Except Lichtenstein and Malta: Eugenia Macchiavello, 'Digital Platforms, Capital Raising and EU Capital Markets Law: Different Shades of Decentralisation', *European Business Law Review* 33, no. Issue 7 (1 December 2022): 1057, 1075, https://doi.org/10.54648/EULR2022046.

62 European Commission, 'Communication from the Commission to the European Parliament, the Council, the European Economic and Social Committee, and the Committee of the Regions on a Digital Finance Strategy for the EU' (COM(2020) 591 final, 24 September 2020), https://eur-lex.europa.eu/legal-content/EN/TXT/?uri=CELEX:52020DC0591.

63 'REGULATION (EU) 2022/858 OF THE EUROPEAN PARLIAMENT AND OF THE COUNCIL of 30 May 2022 on a Pilot Regime for Market Infrastructures Based on Distributed Ledger Technology, and Amending Regulations (EU) No 600/2014 and (EU) No 909/2014 and Directive 2014/65/EU (Text with EEA Relevance)', Pub. L. No. L 151/1 (2022). For first comments see Paolo Roberto Amendola, Filippo Annunziata, and Anna Chiara Chisari, 'DLT-Based Trading Venues and EU Capital Markets Legislation: State of the Art and Perspectives under the DLT Pilot Regime', *SSRN Electronic Journal*, 1 January 2023, https://doi.org/10.2139/ssrn.4344803; Jonathan McCarthy, 'Distributed Ledger Technology and Financial Market Infrastructures: An EU Pilot Regulatory Regime', *Capital Markets Law Journal* 17 (26 May 2022), https://doi.org/10.1093/cmlj/kmac009; Dirk Andreas

DLT-multilateral trading facilities (MTF) and DLT-securities settlement systems (CSDs) about tokens like UCITS, shares, and bonds issued by companies and up to specific size, managed by authorised MiFID II investment firms or by CSDs subject to CSDR. In the initial proposal, the DLT infrastructure had to be 'proprietary,' excluding permissionless systems.[64] However, the final text requests DLT-MTFs/CSDs participating in the pilot regime—not to establish but—simply 'to document as appropriate' the rules on the functioning of the operated DLT, the rules for accessing it, and the participation of the validating nodes.

DLT-MTFs/CSDs will have the option to request from NCAs, with ESMA issuing a non-binding opinion, an exemption from specific requirements (some corresponding to the most challenging ones discussed above),[65] under the condition of demonstrating difficulties in applying specific rules in a DLT context and of proposing compensatory measures as well as complying with minimum requirements, including, for instance, direct supervisors' access to data on the DLT system. Interestingly, the DLT operator can choose the jurisdiction (having to apply for the exemption to a national authority) and define the governance and accountability structure (to be published online). It might also entail a liability contractually shared among the participants (Art. 6(1)), contrary to the approach of MiFID II and other traditional laws, where the primary responsibility must remain on the operator. Nonetheless, the regime is still designed as operator-centric, with express duties on the same (security, confidentiality, winding-down plan). Moreover, several legal aspects of security tokens and their holding/custody (including insolvency issues) remain surrounded by legal uncertainty and are left to national law.[66]

Zetzsche and Jannik Woxholth, 'The DLT Sandbox under the EU Pilot Regulation', *SSRN Electronic Journal*, 2021, https://doi.org/10.2139/ssrn.3833766.

64 The Commission believed that decentralised structures deserved lower regulatory attention, being 'still in their infancy' (European Commission, 'Consultation Document', 30.), but limiting EU financial regulation's reach to centralised platforms could have actually had the effect of spurring the development of the former.

65 For example, from the CSD requirement of Article 3(2) CSDR (in case of MiFID II firm) being allowed to record and settle itself on the DLT and from the rules governing MTF participants (admitting also retail investors); from a list of specified CSDR provisions (e.g., about securities accounts and book-entry; access to and participants in the SSS; cash settlement and delivery-versus-payment; settlement finality (Articles 5(2)-(6) and 5(8)). See also reporting obligation in the case of a transaction between two private parties under Art. 26 MiFIR (but potential compensatory measure of giving the supervisor access to DLT data).

66 Heikki Marjosola, 'Security Tokens and the Future of EU Securities Law: Rethinking the Harmonisation Project', in *Digital Finance in Europe: Law, Regulation, and Governance*, ed. Emilios Avgouleas and Heikki Marjosola (De Gruyter, 2021), 256–57, https://doi.org/10.1515/9783110749472-009. I will not discuss MiCA nor national regimes covering tokens other than securities but all these show again a provider-centric approach.

18.6 Decentralised networks: A new type of business organisation deserving new rules?

Considering all the above, it has appeared challenging to apply existing laws, which are targeted to companies, hierarchical and centralised organisations governed by strict governance rules (centred around owners and managers),[67] and cooperation by third parties in the form of bilateral relationships (outsourcing or agency),[68] to decentralised systems, especially when the latter appear non-proprietary, collaborative organisations, based on multi-lateral relationships, consensus-based mechanisms, and electronic code: for instance, who should request the authorisations mentioned above and comply with the requirements (for example, the whole network including ordinary participants, developers and miners or only core developers?)[69] and to apply specific rules (for example, governance rules), also considering the opaque and variegated governance structures of blockchains?

Some positions have tried to respond by forcing DLT networks (and DAOs) into the company category. In doing so, they recognise an unincorporated/de facto company (general partnership) for the joint pursuit of a common economic objective and sharing of profits,[70] with potentially harmful consequences for ordinary users considered as general partners (jointly liable).[71] Regarding DLT networks, some authors would prohibit using unincorporated decentralised structures in the securities sector (for example, as SSDs/CSDs or trading venues) for stability/consumer protection.[72] Others see protocol core developers as fiduciaries/agents of participants[73] or otherwise believe that

67 Mark Fenwick, Joseph A McCahery, and Erik PM Vermeulen, 'The End of "Corporate" Governance: Hello "Platform" Governance', *SSRN Electronic Journal*, 2018, https://doi.org/10.2139/ssrn.3232663; Campbell-Verduyn, *Bitcoin and Beyond*, 48 ff.

68 De Filippi and Wright, *Blockchain and the Law*, 2018; Expert Group on Regulatory Obstacles to Financial Innovation (ROFIEG), 'Thirty Recommendations', 47, 58.

69 Rauchs et al., 'Distributed', 25 ff.; Houben and Snyers, 'Cryptocurrencies', 76.

70 In common-law systems (but the sharing of profits might lack in permissionless networks where excluding the mere appreciation in value of original coins or network effects): Zetzsche, Buckley, and Arner, 'The Distributed Liability', 1400. In civil-law countries, would be either required the (objective) intention to carry on a commercial undertaking under a common name (Germany) or the conferral of goods or services—even computational power and time—aimed ('*affectio societatis*') at conducting a business activity and sharing profits (Italy; France): Mads Andenas and Frank Wooldridge, *European Comparative Company Law*, 1st ed. (Cambridge University Press, 2009), 130 ff., https://doi.org/10.1017/CBO9780511770494.

71 De Filippi and Wright, *Blockchain and the Law*, 2018, 142.

72 Philipp Paech, 'The Governance of Blockchain Financial Networks: The Governance of Blockchain Financial Networks', *The Modern Law Review* 80, no. 6 (November 2017): 1073–1110, https://doi.org/10.1111/1468-2230.12303.

73 See Walch, 'Deconstructing "Decentralization"', 20; Nabilou, 'Bitcoin Governance', 181. They correctly underline that the concept of fiduciary duties and other traditional corporate governance arrangements are not easily transposed in a DLT context since principal-agent relationships are substituted by algorithms and consensus and information is generally not asymmetric. See also Raina S Haque et al., 'Blockchain Development and Fiduciary Duty',

from joint control (and common interest in the joint functioning of the network and reliance on joint efforts) follows joint liability of core developers and miners towards other participants and third parties based on their duty of care (in IT, maintenance, update, correction of an algorithm, transparency) and loyalty and, towards other developers and nodes, the duty to cooperate.[74]

However, some aspects need to be underlined: the leading blockchains provide only the infrastructure for others to build Dapps (although Ethereum developers have also provided the ERC20-protocol for ICOs) and are 'product-agnostic' (not just for security-tokens and financial services). Contrary to traditional managers, many core developers contribute for reputational or idealistic reasons without receiving (at least direct) profits.[75] On the other hand, blockchains' functioning (especially core developers and miners' work) significantly affects single Dapps' performance (in terms of cyber-security, speed, and incidents)[76] while presenting uncertain governance and consequent operational risk.[77] Holding protocol developers jointly liable towards the entire network is therefore acceptable only concerning protocol coding errors or infrastructure failures (or failure to block illegal operations) and within their effective control (difficult to measure though) or formal identification,[78] not for any problem at the Dapp level.[79] Nonetheless, long-term solutions should instead look at DLT networks as a new type of business structure. It has peculiar systems of remuneration (tokens as incentives), voting system (consensus, 'flags'), and dissent (forks)[80] as well as responsibilities

Stanford Journal of Blockchain Law & Policy, 28 June 2018, 139, https://stanford-jblp.pubpub.org/pub/blockchain-dev-fiduciary-duty/release/1. Recently, in favour of recognizing special duties on cryptocurrency service providers: Peder Østbye, 'Different Activity, Different Risk, Different Rules? Exploring Cryptocurrency System Service Providers' Duties and Responsibilities', *SSRN Electronic Journal*, 2021, https://doi.org/10.2139/ssrn.3981015.

74 Zetzsche, Buckley, and Arner, 'The Distributed Liability', 1390.

75 EU Observatory Blockchain & Forum, 'Legal and Regulatory Framework of Blockchains and Smart Contracts' (EU Observatory Blockchain & Forum, 27 September 2019), 17, https://www.eublockchainforum.eu/sites/default/files/reports/report_legal_v1.0.pdf; Raina S Haque et al., 'Blockchain Development', 155, 177.

76 ESMA, 'The Distributed Ledger', 14; Expert Group on Regulatory Obstacles to Financial Innovation (ROFIEG), 'Thirty Recommendations', 32.

77 For example, voluntary work and inefficient management, uncertain liabilities, anonymity, and related risk of illegal activities, unclear jurisdiction and related lack of enforcement: Zetzsche, Buckley, and Arner, 'The Distributed Liability' (and hereby references); Financial Stability Board, 'Decentralised Financial Technologies', 6; ESMA, 'The Distributed Ledger', 17.

78 For a parallel with internet creators' liability: Hacker et al., 'Regulating Blockchain', 330–31; Rohr and Wright, 'Blockchain-Based', 484.

79 See also Blandin et al., 'Global', 51.

80 Sinclair Davidson, Primavera De Filippi, and Jason Potts, 'Blockchains and the Economic Institutions of Capitalism', *Journal of Institutional Economics* 14, no. 4 (August 2018): 639, https://doi.org/10.1017/S1744137417000200; Sinclair Davidson, Primavera De Filippi, and Jason Potts, 'Disrupting Governance: The New Institutional Economics of Distributed Ledger Technology', *SSRN Electronic Journal*, 2016, https://doi.org/10.2139/ssrn.2811995; De Filippi and Lavayssière, 'Blockchain Technology', 6.

(for example, recognising differentiated duties and partial self-responsibility of participants and excluding core developers' liability when incidents happen beyond their best efforts' monitoring, also depending on their remuneration's system), partially associated with Ostrom's commons-based peer-production and shared ownership.[81] This requires new theoretical efforts in both business and financial law.[82]

As a mid-term solution, a governance code[83] should be required for DLT networks also used for financial services/products' offerings/markets in order to set fundamental rules (for example, longer chains prevail and cannot be reverted), govern core developers' appointments, decision-making, and reporting, community voting on fundamental decisions and minorities' protection (see hard forks), profit-sharing mechanisms, duties of core developers (loyalty and care), miners (neutrality, cooperation under certain circumstances), and nodes (update the software and cooperate).[84] At the same time, it would help open up financial law to RegTech (i.e., compliance through technology), allowing platforms to rely on the code to regulate platform's access, monitor/stop operations, and ensure KYC-compliance and fairness in trading/order execution;[85] similarly with SupTech (i.e., 'technological' supervision) but avoiding accessible discharges of responsibility and excessive standardisation (risky for stability).

18.7 Conclusions: Decentralisation, regulation, and insights for CBDCs

DLT systems present new features and related new risks. Faced with them, EU and national regulators have tended to deploy traditional categories and regulatory instruments (for example, regulating intermediaries, not infrastructures/networks or new actors), remaining unable to address the issues raised by decentralised governance systems. A rethinking of existing categories

81 See David Rozas et al., 'When Ostrom Meets Blockchain: Exploring the Potentials of Blockchain for Commons Governance', *SSRN Electronic Journal*, 2018, 1–14, https://doi.org/10.2139/ssrn.3272329; De Filippi and Lavayssière, 'Blockchain Technology'.

82 Recently, in the business organization area, Roger M Barker and Iris H-Y Chiu, eds., *The Law and Governance of Decentralised Business Models: Between Hierarchies and Markets* (Routledge, 2021). In the financial regulation area: Emilios Avgouleas and Aggelos Kiayias, 'The Architecture of Decentralised Finance Platforms: A New Open Finance Paradigm', *SSRN Electronic Journal*, 2020, https://doi.org/10.2139/ssrn.3666029. They suggest, for DLT-ecosystems, a mix of self-governance, partnered governance between regulators, the industry, and stakeholders, and a continuous and dynamic co-monitoring of the system.

83 Hacker et al., 'Regulating Blockchain'.

84 About opportunities/risks in setting up a private supervisor/standard-setting body see Finck, *Blockchain Regulation*; Financial Stability Board, 'Decentralised Financial Technologies', 24.

85 Financial Stability Board, 'Decentralised Financial Technologies', 9; De Filippi and Wright, *Blockchain and the Law*, 2018, 193; Chiu, 'Decoupling Tokens', 19; Yeung, 'Regulation by Blockchain', 220; Finck, *Blockchain Regulation*, 178.

and regulatory instruments appears needed since existing financial regulation seems so far not able to cope with the lack of an operator able to control every aspect of the operations or with 'distributed' accountability.

What aspects of the analysis conducted in this chapter might be relevant for CBDC discussions? Some insights pertain to the design of CBDC architecture and the implications of regulatory frictions.

18.7.1 Issues with public blockchains: Stability at the core

The experience of DLT systems in capital raising seems to confirm that the form of public permissionless blockchains, although identified as the best able to ensure cash-like features and global reach (cross-border simplification), does not represent the optimal structure for CBDCs,[86] for various reasons.

Decentralised structures present relevant operational risks, governance problems, and regulatory uncertainty. While such issues and relative costs might look acceptable when trying to create and accommodate within our legal framework an autonomous, open, democratic, and decentralised system in a trustless and lawless environment, this is not the case in the different CBDC contexts. In the latter, we can rely on a trusted and independent central authority (central bank).[87] On the other hand, legal certainty, trust, and stability are essential principles. Some projects have also advanced the idea of having a central infrastructure managed by the central bank and issuing CBDCs plus other separate interoperable ones (also public/decentralised) providing related services.[88] Nonetheless, concerns might otherwise arise from such interconnectivity (in terms of reputation, security, and stability) where, because of the cash-like feature and decentralised nature of interlinked networks, the central bank cannot set minimum standards for such separate networks and verify compliance for validation and similar aspects.[89] Also, energy-consumption issues (although contained under new consensus mechanisms) cannot be ignored, considering recent central banks' commitments to sustainability.[90]

86 Raphael Auer et al., 'Central Bank Digital Currencies: Motives, Economic Implications and the Research Frontier', *Monetary and Economic Department*, BIS Working Papers, no. 976 (November 2021): 13. See also Athanassiou, *Digital Innovation*, para. 7.02.C.

87 Robleh Ali and Neha Narula, 'Redesigning Digital Money: What Can We Learn from a Decade of Cryptocurrencies?' (Digital Currency Initiative, MIT Media Lab, 17 October 2019), 7.

88 Ali and Narula, 8–10.

89 See ECB, 'Report on a Digital Euro', 40: 'Digital euro holdings and transactions could only be managed in a decentralised way if it were possible to ensure that they were processed in line with central bank requirements at all times. The central bank would therefore need to set the standards (for example cryptography and validation methods) that would allow external parties to transfer central bank money in compliance with appropriate safety standards, even outside a central ledger.'

90 Auer et al., 'CBDCs: Motives', 3, 7.

18.7.2 Issues with private blockchains—Still operational risks

Also, in consideration of the above, many blockchain-based CBDC projects envision private/confederated and permissioned systems in order to benefit from increased speed and control over problems, with central banks or another government authority governing the network, sometimes in partnership with private parties to support central banks' new tasks. The more centralised the governance, the more compatible it appears with regulation. On the other hand, the network will also be more prone to attacks, which can have disruptive effects in the case of an official and crucial system such as the monetary one.

Furthermore, the participation of certain private parties might run the risk of capture and manipulation, which are not admissible in monetary policy.[91] In addition, some of the above-mentioned operational risks can also be found in private blockchains: for instance, the centrality of technology and the related relevant role played by developers and nodes and, in a private blockchain, by big technological companies, with related concentration risk and competition issues. This underlines the general inadequacy of existing laws, which assume that financial institutions are in control (see MiFID requirements, rules on outsourcing and agency, holding companies) and supervisors are able to monitor. At the same time, the true power resides with big techs,[92] although relevant reforms have been announced (see in cloud computing, supervision of fintech).

18.7.3 Reintermediation

To simplify those are the central banks' tasks, many CBDC projects envision hybrid systems, with banks or other regulated intermediaries as front-end providers.[93] Therefore, as with DLT systems for capital raising, we witness, despite the disintermediation announcements, 'reintermediation.'[94] Similarly, we expect several new intermediaries to offer CBDC-related services, with, potentially, new long-value chains.

91 Ali and Narula, 'Redesigning', 6–7.

92 See also Avgouleas and Kiayias, 'The Architecture of Decentralised Finance Platforms'.

93 Auer and Boehme, 'The Technology of Retail CBDC'; Buckley et al., 'Sovereign Digital Currencies', 14. The ECB favours a centralised infrastructure (and ECB's only liabilities). Still, the role of financial intermediaries can range from gatekeepers (managing only onboarding procedures and connectivity between users and the system) or settlement agents (executing transactions and providing storage): ECB, 'Report on a Digital Euro', 26–27, 36.

94 'Once we remove the decentralized nature of a cryptocurrency, not much is left of it:' Aleksander Berentsen and Fabian Schar, 'The Case for Central Bank Electronic Money and the Non-Case for Central Bank Cryptocurrencies', *Federal Reserve Bank of St. Louis Review, Second Quarter* 100, no. 2 (2018): 97–106, https://doi.org/10.20955/r.2018.97-106.

18.7.4 Regulatory frictions

DLT systems are still surrounded by legal uncertainty and a lack of regulatory harmonisation. Before implementing a DLT-based CBDC infrastructure, we must clarify several aspects under national and EU law. They pertain, for instance, to the legal validity and treatment of smart contracts and entries, compatibility with privacy rules, the finality concept,[95] liability issues, legal relevance, and treatment of oracles and new actors (see nodes, miners), as well as conflict of law rules[96] and new rules for technology-related services (outsourcing, supervision of tech-fin). Considering the various models, liabilities and duties within such new networks must also be assigned considering the effective roles, powers, and returns. Finally, regulatory and supervisory instruments innovation is needed to confront innovative phenomena. Therefore Regtech/Suptech solutions and rules embedded in the code should be considered.

18.7.5 Final remarks

All this considered, doubts about the need to resort to DLT/blockchain for CBDCs and suggestions to explore the possibility of improving existing payment systems appear reasonable.[97] Despite the hype for DLT systems, these might represent a complex but unavoidable model to accommodate spontaneous forms of sharing and democratic finance into the financial sector at the cost of more self-responsibility of users and less law centrality but not necessarily to create a digital monetary power and fundamental pillar of the payment system.[98]

95 See Athanassiou, *Digital Innovation*, 206–7.

96 In this regard, see Committee on Payments and Market Infrastructures, *Distributed Ledger Technology in Payment, Clearing and Settlement* (BIS, 2017), 16, https://www.bis.org/cpmi/publ/d157.pdf; Marjosola, 'Security Tokens and the Future of EU Securities Law', 265; Rainer Kulms, 'Digital Financial Markets and (Europe's) Private Law – A Case for Regulatory Competition?', in *Digital Finance in Europe: Law, Regulation, and Governance*, ed. Emilios Avgouleas and Heikki Marjosola (De Gruyter, 2021), 213–52, https://doi.org/10.1515/9783110749472-008.

97 See also Buckley et al., 'Sovereign Digital Currencies'.

98 Instead, willing to strictly interconnect CBDCs and DLT-ecosystems, using the former to finance the crypto-economy: Iris H-Y Chiu, 'Central Bank Digital Currency for the Crypto-Economy: An Experi-Mental Proposal Based on the European Single Market and Institution-Building', *California Western International Law Journal* 51, no. 2 (2021). Latest update of this paper: 22 March 2023.

19 Central Bank Digital Currencies

What Future for Banks and Other Financial Intermediaries?

Francesca Mattassoglio

19.1 Introduction

The introduction of a CBDC, especially a retail one, will have an impact on numerous aspects of the financial and banking system, as a CBDC is not simply a digitalisation of cash but has consequences for the central bank's monetary policy functions and the dynamics of the market for payment services. The stability of commercial banks,[1] including their lending capacity, is another issue. This chapter will focus mainly on this latter.

Direct access to a *central bank's* digital currency should reduce commercial banks' activity in the context of payment services, with consequences for their ability to collect savings and related credit business. A CBDC should induce users to prefer the safety and protection of central bank accounts, thus depriving intermediaries of liquidity[2] and forcing them to draw on funding from the wholesale market with higher interest rates.[3] This risk becomes even more acute during a crisis.[4] Moreover, this situation should, in theory, lead to the

1 About this issue, see Michael Kumhof and Clare Noone, 'Central Bank Digital Currencies - Design Principles and Balance Sheet Implications', Bank of England Staff Working Paper, no. 725 (2018), https://doi.org/10.2139/ssrn.3180713.

2 John Barrdear and Michael Kumhof, 'The Macroeconomics of Central Bank Digital Currencies', Journal of Economic Dynamics and Control 142 (September 2022): 9, https://doi.org/10.1016/j.jedc.2021.104148; Seyed Mohammadreza Davoodalhosseini, 'Central Bank Digital Currency and Monetary Policy', Journal of Economic Dynamics and Control 142 (September 2022): 104150, https://doi.org/10.1016/j.jedc.2021.104150.

3 Hossein Nabilou and Alessio M Pacces, 'The Law and Economics of Shadow Banking', in *Research Handbook on Shadow Banking*, by Iris Chiu and Iain MacNeil (Edward Elgar Publishing, 2018), 7–46, https://doi.org/10.4337/9781785362637.00008; Valerio Lemma, 'Banking e Shadow Banking al Tempo Del Covid-19: Riflessioni Nella Prospettiva Del Market in Crypto-Assets (MICA)', *Rivista Di Diritto Bancario*, 21 November 2020, 851, https://rivista.dirittobancario.it/banking-e-shadow-banking-al-tempo-del-covid-19-riflessioni-nella-prospettiva-del-market-crypto.

4 Warren Coats, 'Free Banking in the Digital Age?', Banking & Finance Law Review, 33, no. 3 (September 2018): 415–21; Ben Broadbent et al., 'Ben Broadbent: Central Banks and Digital Currencies' (London School of Economics: Bank of England, 2016), www.bankofengland.co.uk/publications/Pages/speeches/default.aspx; Yves Mersch, 'Virtual or Virtueless? The Evo-

DOI: 10.4324/9781003258261-24

total disintermediation of banks—in their role as money issuers—as well as of the payment institutions that have entered this sector in recent years.

The outcomes of a CBDC depend on the concrete design implemented by the central bankers. In this light, the BIS suggests a 'minimum invasive design'[5] that would preserve the role of the private sector in retail payments and financial intermediation.

To better understand this point, analysing how central and commercial banks create money should be helpful.

19.2 A memo on how central and commercial banks create money

The power of central banks in the basic money supply concerns only a small fraction of the total money stock (cash and deposits). The remainder consists of commercial banking money produced through the so-called currency multiplier. When a central bank subscribes to public securities as well as when it offers money to the banking system, it generates liabilities, in other words, a corresponding monetary basis for the purchase.[6] This monetary basis is introduced into the trading system through expenditures—for example, by the

lution of Money in the Digital Age', European Central Bank, 8 February 2018, https://www.ecb.europa.eu/press/key/date/2018/html/ecb.sp180208.en.html. For an alternative opinion, see David Andolfatto, 'Assessing the Impact of Central Bank Digital Currency on Private Banks', *The Economic Journal* 131, no. 634 (3 March 2021): 525–40, https://doi.org/10.1093/ej/ueaa073; David Andolfatto, 'Fedcoin: On the Desirability of a Government Cryptocurrency', *MacroMania* (blog), 3 February 2015, http://andolfatto.blogspot.com/2015/02/fedcoin-on-desirability-of-government.html. For the author, introducing a CBDC is an element capable, under certain conditions, of improving access to credit provided by banking intermediaries and guaranteeing lower interest rates, thanks to the competition that could animate the system. According to the author, in theory, if the CBDC interest rate were to be set independently of the interest rate the banks receive on reserves (IOR), the introduction of a CBDC should in no way discourage bank lending. If, on the other hand, the CBDC rate were to be set below the IOR rate, the bank would seek to match its own rate with the CBDC rate to preserve deposits. This is because the bank would lend to the central bank at the rate set by the IOR and only pay the CBDC rate to depositors. If the IOR–CBDC spread is positive, it can be advantageous for banks to keep deposits. According to another hypothesis, banks could be driven by competition from the CBDC to introduce more favourable contractual conditions for depositors. Suppose access to the CBDC is possible at no cost. In that case, the demand for physical currency will disappear, but this should not prevent the effectiveness of the monetary policy pursued by the central banker (see page 4).

5 Benoît Cœuré and Jacqueline Loh, 'Central Bank Digital Currencies', March 2018; Morten Bech and Rodney Garratt, 'Central Bank Cryptocurrencies', *BIS Quarterly Review*, 2017, https://EconPapers.repec.org/RePEc:bis:bisqtr:1709f; Christian Barontini and Henry Holden, *Proceeding with Caution - a Survey on Central Bank Digital Currency*, 101 vols, BIS Papers (Bank for International Settlements, 2019), https://www.bis.org/publ/bppdf/bispap101.pdf; Raphael Auer, Giulio Cornelli, and Jon Frost, 'Taking Stock: Ongoing Retail CBDC Projects', 1 March 2020, https://www.bis.org/publ/qtrpdf/r_qt2003z.htm.

6 Cesare Imbriani and Antonio Lopes, *Macroeconomia, un'introduzione: mercati, istituti finanziari e politiche*, 1ª ed (Torino: UTET università, 2016).

public sector through salaries for public employees. These funds, in turn, feed into the deposits and current accounts held by individuals with commercial banks (the so-called collection of public savings), which increase the bank's liabilities and correspond to an equal increase in budget assets. At this point, the banking system can provide credit thanks to the funds collected by surplus entities. The credit provided by banks will then be used for consumption or investment and can be intercepted again by the banking system. Only in the case of cash does one euro require a one-euro monetary basis; in the case of one euro of deposits, only a fraction, equal to the sum of the obligatory and free bank reserves constituted against the deposited amount, is sufficient.[7]

Therefore, all the wealth generated, except cash, requires the intermediation of the banking system. This possibility is not discretionary but subject to binding rules thanks to both the prudential regulation and the action of the central banker, primarily through the determination of mandatory reserves. The dynamic of the 'trust' involved in this case depends on how banks create money and their liquid reserves and other on-balance-sheet assets, which can be quickly converted into cash but can never guarantee prompt and full repayment of all overnight deposits. That is why a bank-run scenario is so frightening. To reduce this risk, all legal systems provide several warranties, such as the deposit guarantee, aimed at protecting depositors' savings at credit institutions up to a fixed amount and compel banks to maintain their reputation, thanks to strict supervisory protocols[8] and requirements to comply with increasingly pervasive capital adequacy criteria. For example, within the European Banking Union,[9] banks must observe strict capital controls in compliance with the various Basel agreements implemented over the years.

Regarding the first constraint, the decision on reserves, which commercial banks must hold at the central bank, is essential in implementing monetary

7 Olivier Blanchard, Alessia Amighini, and Francesco Giavazzi, *Macroeconomia: una prospettiva europea*, Nuova ed (Bologna: Il Mulino, 2020).

8 Michael McLeay, Amar Radia, and Ryland Thomas, 'Money Creation in the Modern Economy', *Quarterly Bulletin* Q1 (2014), https://www.bankofengland.co.uk/-/media/boe/files/quarterly-bulletin/2014/money-creation-in-the-modern-economy.pdf.

9 As is well known, it is based on three pillars. The first, which entered into force in November 2014, consists of the Single Supervisory Mechanism (SSM), a system that has assigned to the European Central Bank the functions of supervision of systemically important institutions (Council Regulation No. 1024/2013 of 15 October 2013). The second is based on the so-called Single Resolution Mechanism, operational since January 2015, which ensures a centralisation regarding the bankruptcy or rescue of a financial institution, supervised by the ECB. Finally, the third pillar is the so-called Single Resolution Found, i.e., a Common Savings Fund, to be established by 2023, on which see Directive 49/2014/EU of the European Parliament and of the Council of 16 April 2014 on deposit guarantee schemes. For a comment, see Franco Tutino, 'Vigilanza Unica Europea e Squilibrio Di Rischiosità Delle Banche: Verso Nuove Regole Di Limitazione Dei Rischi?', *Bancaria*, no. 3 (March 2014): 15, https://bancaria.it/livello-2/archivio-sommari/gli-ultimi-sommari-di-bancaria/bancaria-marzo-2014/vigilanza-unica-europea-e-squilibrio-di-rischiosit-delle-banche-verso-nuove-regole-di-limitazione-dei-rischi/.

policy. Reserves held by banks are divided into reserve requirements and free reserves. The monetary authorities establish the formers as a percentage of the number of bank liabilities in the form of money. They help to ensure economic stability, as they can, for example, be used to move money in real time between financial institutions, ensuring final and risk-free settlement.[10] Reserves are, therefore, essential for achieving the objective of financial stability, allowing liquidity to be provided to the system in both good and bad times. This liquidity helps companies settle payments and protect themselves from liquidity demands. In addition, a central banker who can act as a lender of last resort and provide liquidity to the banking system constitutes a further element of the protection network (safety net) responsible for protecting the resilience and confidence in the banking system.[11]

In this context, most money in circulation is produced by private commercial banks. In the case of a future cashless society, this situation would reach its extreme conclusion, with private commercial banks issuing almost all money in circulation.[12] As a result, private individuals can only request deposits from commercial banks[13] or cash from the central bank. From an accounting point of view, this causes an increase in bank liabilities, as the demand for deposits generates an increase in reserves. Therefore, the basic demand for money is the result of a demand for money from the public and a demand for reserves, both compulsory and discretionary, from the banks. From a macroeconomic point of view, the monetary function is, thus, reflected in the process of creating the total quantity of money available to the public, which can be summarised in the so-called mechanism of the multiplier of money and deposits. This formula makes the currency coincide with the sum of the demand for cash (legal currency) and bank deposits in a bank account. With these considerations in mind, it may be easier to understand the possible impact of a future CBDC.

10 In the United Kingdom, for example, selected commercial banks and financial institutions hold electronic central bank money in their real-time gross settlement (RTGS) accounts with the Central Bank. These balances are known as balances of reserves or liabilities. This RTGS service is the backbone of any electronic payment in the UK.

11 According to the reconstruction of Cullen O Roche, 'Understanding the Modern Monetary System', *SSRN Electronic Journal*, 2011, https://doi.org/10.2139/ssrn.1905625. in the American context, the role of the Fed would be that of an entity specifically created to act as the lender of last resort for the private banking system after the scandals and failures of the late 1800s and early 1900s, thus pursuing an aim in the public interest.

12 'The move towards cashless payments results from a progressive regulatory shift away from the state-based payment system dominated by cash, in which access to a means of payment is universal, towards a private monetary regime. A private regime in which banks, payment firms, and commerce platforms are controlling who is able to access their services.' See Federico Lupo-Pasini, 'Is It a Wonderful Life? Cashless Societies and Monetary Exclusion', Review of Banking & Financial Law, no. 40 (2020): 166, https://dro.dur.ac.uk/30666/1/30666.pdf.

13 On the role of banks as creators of money, see James Tobin, 'Commercial Banks as Creators of "Money"', in *Banking and Monetary Studies*, ed. Deane Carson (Homewood, Ill., RD Irwin, 1963), 408, 408–19, http://archive.org/details/bankingmoneterys0000unse.

19.3 The CBDC and the new monetary theories

A key concern in the design of a CBDC is its potential impact on commercial banks, and there is a general requirement 'that any CBDC must not compromise financial and monetary stability.'[14] For this reason, the BIS[15] stated that all CBDCs should be designed to support the fulfilment of public policy objectives, should not impede the central bank's ability to accomplish its mandate, and should 'do no harm' to monetary and financial stability,[16] with particular attention paid to the potential disintermediation of banks. Indeed, awareness of the many shortcomings of the current system has prompted some scholars to rethink the entire structure of the currency and propose a new theory of money.

In particular, the new monetary theory of 'Sovereign Money'[17] trusts in technological development and considers CBDCs a way to give back to the state a predominant role with respect to money compared with the banking role played by commercial banks.[18] According to this proposal, central banks

14 See F Panetta, 'Designing a digital euro for the retail payments landscape of tomorrow,' introductory remarks by Fabio Panetta, Member of the Executive Board of the ECB, at the ECON Committee of the European Parliament, Brussels, 18 November 2021, https://www.ecb.europa.eu/press/key/date/2021/html/ecb.sp211118~b36013b7c5.en.html, which highlights that 'the digital euro will be designed to be an efficient means of payment, but also to preserve financial stability. We will be careful to ensure the financial sector can adjust in an orderly manner. To prevent excessive and abrupt shifts from commercial to central bank money, we will need to strike a balance between maximizing its appeal as a means of exchange and limiting its use as a form of investment. Different design options and decisions all have a bearing on one another, so making a coherent set of choices will be key. We have a clear timeline that takes these interlinkages into account and will ensure a coherent product.'

15 BIS, 'Central bank digital currencies: financial stability implications,' September 2021, https://www.bis.org/publ/othp42_fin_stab.pdf, which underlines that 'Unlike central banks, issuers of stablecoins are not bound by principles to design products that would co-exist and interoperate with other forms of money or to promote ongoing innovation and efficiency (i.e., the second and third principles outlined in Group of central banks (2020). This could cause fragmentation in a payments ecosystem, just like any other closed-loop payment system (CPMI (2018)). Significant stablecoin adoption and the potential consequent fragmentation could result in excessive market power and the type of deposit disintermediation described as a risk for CBDC issuance, but with lower public benefits.'

16 G7, 'Public Policy Principles for Retail Central Bank Digital Currencies (CBDCs)' (HM Treasury, 14 October 2021), https://assets.publishing.service.gov.uk/government/uploads/system/uploads/attachment_data/file/1025235/G7_Public_Policy_Principles_for_Retail_CBDC_FINAL.pdf.

17 Christian Felber, *Money: The New Rules of the Game* (New York, NY: Springer Berlin Heidelberg, 2017), 29., which considers that 'money should become a public good, a "public service," a modern "common" and a "res publica," as is the case or would desirably be the case for the education sector, internet or public safety.'

18 In this regard, see Joseph Huber, Sovereign Money: Beyond Reserve Banking (Cham: Palgrave Macmillan, 2017), https://doi.org/10.1007/978-3-319-42174-2; A Proposal for Supplying the Nations with the Necessary Means in a Modern Monetary System, vol. 99–3, Der Hallesche Graureiher : Forschungsberichte Des Instituts Für Soziologie (Halle: Univer-

should regain control over the money supply, not just cash, with the consequent abolition of the possibility of the private banking channel creating money in the form of overnight deposits.[19]

In the United States, there has been a strong debate on this issue and a proposal to establish a new 'Fed Account'—in other words, allowing private individuals, especially unbanked people, the possibility of opening an account directly with the Fed.[20] An even more radical position suggests a new 'democratising finance'[21] to respond as a response to the existing 'franchise finance' system, in which the private sector exerts the real power of money issuing is exerted by the private sector. According to this doctrine, it would be necessary to thoroughly review this structure by reactivating the central role of the state and then of the population, allowing it to regain power over the management of money, including deciding which entities are worthy of funding. Such an interpretation is intended to exploit the new potential, including monetary policy functions, of CBDCs, both from the point of view of their 'programmability' and the possibility of their being linked to an interest rate, in addition to enabling actions such as so-called 'helicopter money,' which allows the central banker to bring resources directly into the portfolios of private individuals and businesses without having to go through the banking channel.[22] Such a possibility, of course, would undermine the balance of the whole system, and that is why, now, the consensus is that a minimal CBDC design that would (try to) maintain the status quo and, therefore, leaves the balance between the central bank and private intermediaries unchanged is the preferred approach. In accordance with this opinion, the BIS proposes that CBDCs should be conceived of as part of a two-tier system in which the central bank and the private

sität Halle-Wittenberg, Philosophische Fakultät I Sozialwissenschaften und historische Kulturwissenschaften, Institut für Soziologie, 1999), https://nbn-resolving.org/urn:nbn:de:0168-ssoar-116724.

19 Joseph Huber, 'Digital Currency. Design Principles to Support a Shift from Bankmoney to Central Bank Digital Currency', *Real-World Economics Review*, no. 88 (2019): 76–90.

20 Morgan Ricks, John Crawford, and Lev Menand, 'Central Banking for All: A Public Option for Bank Accounts', *Great Democracy Initiative*, June 2018, 1–16; Mike Konczal, 'A Federal Reserve Reform Agenda: Eight Recommendations', *Rooseveltinstitute.Org*, September 2020, https://rooseveltinstitute.org/wp-content/uploads/2020/09/RI_FedDA_Working-Paper_202009.pdf.

21 Saule Omarova, 'The People's Ledger: How to Democratize Money and Finance the Economy', *Vanderbilt Law Review* 74, no. 5 (1 October 2021), https://scholarship.law.vanderbilt.edu/vlr/vol74/iss5/1.

22 Omarova, 22. From an economic point of view, such an assumption would require a radical change in the Fed's balance sheet itself in view of the enormous growth required of its portfolio, which should allow it to effectively replace the activities of banking intermediaries. In particular, the Author 'advocates the issuance of general-purpose CBDC (the "digital dollar") and concurrent migration of all transaction deposit accounts from private banks to the Federal Reserve. Focusing on the ultimate "end-state" whereby central bank accounts fully replace—rather than uneasily co-exist with—private bank deposits, the Article explores the full range of new monetary policy options the proposed structural shift would enable.'

sector continue to play their respective roles. Commercial banks and payment service providers should still be entrusted with most operational tasks. In contrast, the central banks should be responsible for ensuring the stability of the value of virtual money, guaranteeing the elasticity of the bundled offer, and monitoring the system's overall safety.[23]

To better focus on this issue, it is necessary to say a few words about the different design options for CBDCs.

19.4 Direct, indirect, or hybrid CBDC

A CBDC should be made available to individual users through several different models, summarised as direct, indirect, or hybrid CBDCs. In the simplest model, the so-called direct CBDC, the user opens an account directly with the central bank, which should also manage all transactions with regular updates. This model is undoubtedly very challenging for the central banker from a technical point of view because it requires directly managing all connections, as well as user accounts, and dealing with critical issues related to the payment system, such as ensuring the connectivity and operation of payments, even offline, and taking care of specific risks arising from the direct relationship with the customer, such as controls based on KYC. Moreover, introducing a direct CBDC should lead to the complete disintermediation of traditional banking operators, thanks to the concentration of functions on the central bank. Such a solution might be suitable for small countries but would become substantially unmanageable for larger countries or blocs such as the EU or China.

In a so-called 'indirect' or 'two-tier or tiered system'[24] CBDC, instead, the central bank does not have any direct contact with the users, i.e., it does not need to manage retail transactions or the relationship with private individuals, which would continue to be the responsibility of the intermediaries. In this case, end users would make payments by instructing their supervised intermediaries, who would also manage their accounts with the central bank. In so doing, it would always be the responsibility of the intermediaries to authenticate end users, carry out KYC-related activities, comply with the commitments laid down in the AML and CFT legislation, and ensure technical connectivity between users and infrastructure. However, under this model, the private

23 BIS, 'Annual Economic Report' (Basel: BIS, 2021), 79, https://www.bis.org/publ/arpdf/ar2021e.htm.

24 For this definition, see Michael Kumhof and Clare Noone, 'Central Bank Digital Currencies - Design Principles and Balance Sheet Implications', *Bank of England*, Staff Working Paper, no. 7 (May 2018), https://doi.org/10.2139/ssrn.3180713. It is equivalent to the notion of 'synthetic CBDC.' Along these lines, see Tobias Adrian and Tommaso Mancini-Griffoli, *The Rise of Digital Money*, FinTech Notes 19/01 (International Monetary Fund, 2019); Robleh Ali, 'Cellular Structure for a Digital Fiat Currency', in *Digital Currency Economics and Policy*, by Bernard Yeung (WORLD SCIENTIFIC, 2020), 89–102, https://doi.org/10.1142/9789811223785_0010.

party could not have a direct claim against the central bank but only against the intermediary.

As a result, both models have some critical points, which is why there is a third suggestion regarding a 'hybrid' CBDC. This intermediate solution gives financial intermediaries the task of managing the payment system while ensuring that users have a direct claim against the central bank. In this model, the intermediaries participating in the system would incorporate digital services into their activities and exploit the innovative infrastructure to promote competition in the payment market. According to experts, the choice of such a hybrid model should be accompanied by a great deal of attention to the issue of credit. In particular, the system's stability would imply a strict separation between the situations of individual customers and the positions of each PSP, also ensuring portability. This precaution would become particularly important in the event of bankruptcy by this type of entity when it would allow the CBDC to be kept separate from the assets available to creditors. Any regulation should also consider the possibility of ensuring mass portability, i.e., giving the central bank the power to change its relationship with retail clients in case of problems with an intermediary.

From the central bank's point of view, the indirect CBDC implies duties similar to those of today's system. On the contrary, the direct CBDC model would require more technological capacity. The central bank would have to manage all transactions independently, with a volume of payment traffic comparable to that currently flowing through credit or debit cards.

Finally, hybrid architecture is certainly the most complex one to manage from a technical point of view. The central bank still needs to maintain retail balances while not directly managing the payment system. However, according to the experts, it would have the advantage of being able to be used on a large scale using existing technology and needing a relatively modest infrastructure, even in the largest currency areas of the world.

19.5 Remuneration and limit holdings of CBDCs

Another key element that must be considered in the design of a CBDC concerns its remuneration, as it constitutes a liability to a central bank and presents a lower intrinsic risk than any deposit made at a commercial bank. This provides many advantages but also several problems, especially related to the fact that universal access to central banks' deposits—as already mentioned—can greatly impact bank intermediaries' ability to collect savings, ultimately affecting the system of access to credit.[25] To achieve such a result, it would also be essential to consider the interest rate associated with the CBDC, as well as to distinguish between the CBDC and the other forms of digital money already

25 Kumhof and Noone, 'Central Bank Digital Currencies - Design Principles and Balance Sheet Implications', 2018.

issued by the central bank (reserves). As far as remuneration is concerned, the simplest solution is to set a fixed remuneration of zero, like cash. Otherwise, the provision of remuneration, especially where it is variable, would allow the central bank to exercise more discretion in regulating its rate over time, at the same time or independently of changes in the other rates over which it has control, and even to provide for different scales of remuneration.

A further important element that may impact the relationship between CBDCs and commercial banks is the introduction of a limit on digital currency holding for each user. This solution is not accessible from a technical point of view. As a matter of fact, such a choice would require identifying each holder and then introducing instruments to allow them to hold only up to the threshold that has been set. If a subject exceeded the limits, the excess CBDC could be directly transferred to his account.

One more expedient that could be introduced, always to limit the use of digital money and connected to the previous point, could be to apply more onerous interest rates or service fees as certain thresholds are exceeded. From the central bank's perspective, working on interest rates would allow citizens access to the digital currency in large quantities while guaranteeing others access to it without quantitative restrictions.

For a more detailed overview of the issues, it is helpful to analyse some examples of CBDCs that have already been implemented.

19.6 Some CBDC projects around the world

19.6.1 The Bahamian sand dollar

CBoB introduced a digital version of its currency (Sand Dollar Project)[26] to continue the Bahamian Payments System Modernization Initiative (PSMI) in early 2020.

According to its promoters, this CBDC aims to pursue social inclusion, ensuring access to digital payment and banking services for the whole population, including micro, small, and medium-sized enterprises in the digital space. The fight against money laundering and other illicit ends should also benefit from such a choice. The central bank is responsible for issuing currency, monitoring participation, and sponsoring a centralised KYC infrastructure/identity. Even if the central bank does not directly provide front-end services to customers or even digital portfolios, it is responsible for managing the ledger of all individual transactions relating to digital money. The central bank will also implement a centralised KYC registry to maintain user identification data. Authorised financial intermediaries, whether banks, credit unions,

26 For more detail, see 'Digital Bahamian Dollar Sand Dollar', accessed 2 April 2022, https://www.sanddollar.bs; Central Bank of The Bahamas, 'Project Sand Dollar: A Bahamas Payments System Modernisation Initiative', 24 December 2019, https://www.centralbankbahamas.com/viewPDF/documents/2019-12-25-02-18-11-Project-Sanddollar.pdf.

or new payment service providers, can offer mobile payment portfolios. Banks must also contribute to the customer due diligence regime, facilitating the connectivity of deposit accounts with mobile portfolios and enabling foreign exchange transactions. Moreover, the banks have the duty to share the KYC process with other payment service providers and cooperate with them by allowing direct debiting and withdrawals from deposit accounts of holders of digital money portfolios (with the customer's consent).

The model, which uses blockchain technology, is token-based and can be transferred by smartphone via QR codes. This design pays attention to several risks in preserving traditional bank deposits. In this light, it introduced limits on the amount of B$ instruments that private individuals, supervised financial undertakings, and other financial institutions may hold. In addition, to be able to carry out higher-value transactions, personal digital portfolios must be linked to deposit accounts with national financial institutions, in which any surplus currency will have to be deposited. As the goal of the Sand Dollar Project is financial inclusion, individuals are still allowed to hold mobile portfolios without the need for a bank account. Without exception, however, all portfolios held by companies must be linked to consolidated bank accounts. To further eliminate similarities to deposits, interest will not be paid on any digital currency.

19.6.2 The Cambodian Bakong

In Cambodia, the Bakong project,[27] launched in October 2020, is based on a blockchain developed by the Japanese company Soramitsu. The Bakong, named after one of the temples at Angkor, consists of a mobile application with a digital wallet that allows transactions to be made using QR codes without any bank account.[28] The Cambodian system requires the central bank to operate directly in both retail and wholesale payments. The Bakong provides a new platform based on DLT permissioned technology, with nodes located at the central bank. However, to operate an account, individuals and intermediaries must register in the system. Users can download the application and register with their bank or other payment service provider for a Bakong

27 National Bank of Cambodia, 'Project Bakong Next Generation Payment System', June 2020, https://www.nbc.gov.kh/download_files/research_papers/khmer/NBC_BAKONG_White_Paper.pdf; Ledger Insights, 'Cambodia's Central Bank: Bakong Blockchain Payments May Help de-Dollarization', Ledger Insights - blockchain for enterprise, 9 August 2021, https://www.ledgerinsights.com/cambodias-central-bank-bakong-blockchain-payments-may-help-de-dollarization/.

28 Data show that between April and June 2021, the number of users holding a portfolio doubled to reach 200,000 users for a total of 1.4 million transactions, equivalent to a value of US$500 million. See National Bank of Cambodia, 'Economic and Monetary Statistics', 330, April 2021, https://www.nbc.gov.kh/download_files/publication/eco_mon_sta_eng/Review%20330%20Apr-2021-En.pdf.

account. As a result, intermediaries are also responsible for identifying the customer (both for KYC and AML purposes), storing information, and managing Bakong accounts in this case.

Transactions are validated using a Byzantine Fault Tolerant (BFT) consent algorithm that ensures consistency in the distributed register and resistance to transaction tampering from possible cyberattacks while avoiding double-spending and counterparty risk in the exchange of digital assets. Transactions are made transparent on the validation nodes, which NBC manages, but without revealing the identity of the parties involved in the execution of the transaction. The management of KYC by end users is the responsibility of private institutions alone. This segregated approach strengthens customer privacy and ensures public confidence. Financial institutions must register with the central bank to receive permission to join the network and access the payment gateway so that their customers can create an account under their domain. Thus, the payment system allows financial institutions to monitor transactions and manage user accounts within their institutions. As a result, Bakong does not eliminate the role of banks and payment service institutions, as it still implies that they manage customer information and conduct the KYC procedure.

19.6.3 The Nigerian eNaira

Nigeria announced its eNaira with the slogan 'same Naira, more possibilities.'[29] For all intents and purposes, this will constitute a legal currency, like the physical one, with a 1:1 guaranteed stable exchange rate. The Central Bank of Nigeria (CBN) believes that introducing a CBDC could have a significant impact in many respects in terms of improving payment systems, financial inclusion, and addressing the cost of remittances.

From the point of view of its design, the eNaira is directly inspired by the principle of 'do no harm' or non-interference with the CBN's ability to pursue its objective of monetary and financial stability. In the future, it will also have to co-exist with other forms of money already in use, such as cash, reserves, and bank deposits, to promote innovation and competition in the banking and financial systems. For this purpose, no interest rate will be paid, and limits will be placed on its possession regarding daily traffic volume and overall holding.

The eNaira is a hybrid CBDC, i.e., it has two levels. In this case, the CBN is responsible for issuing the currency but relies on private financial institutions for distribution and, more generally, for the relationship with individual users. In this context, the central entity retains control over the digital currency-based payment system. It is also responsible for issuing currency, managing the portfolio, and maintaining a central register of all transactions. Meanwhile, the role of financial institutions and other payment service providers is to manage and process retail payments while also providing other services based on

29 'eNaira Design Paper | Same Naira. More Possibilities', https://enaira.gov.ng/about/design.

the eNaira system. The platform allows users to be identified and protected against attacks, ensures transactions' speed, and respects the privacy and confidentiality of transactions.

The Nigerian CBDC is account-based, taking advantage of the high banking level achieved over the past few years. In order to implement this model, three elements must be guaranteed: first, a basic register provided by the CBN that acts as the core of the platform and allows the recording of transactions and processing of payments; a set of financial institutions that act as intermediaries to offer payment services to users; and payment service providers that enable the eNaira payment ecosystem to be developed.

According to the CBN, it is predictable that introducing a CBDC could entail a risk of disintermediation, forcing banks to fund on the wholesale market, with higher interest rates and consequent effects on other assets. For this reason, the central bank has chosen to limit the use of digital currency to micropayments and introduce limits on portfolio size. The CBN has also reiterated its focus on the objective of reducing the use of cash, which could further increase the use of commercial banks' currency.

19.6.4 The Swedish e-krona

The Swedish CBDC will be a digital token (e-kronor) issued by the central bank.[30] To gain access and make payments with the token, each user must have a digital wallet that allows interaction with other participants in the network, namely banks and payment service providers. In this case, the system looks like a two-tier system. As is the case with cash, only the Riksbank will be able to issue and redeem the e-kronor, but only intermediaries who are part of its network will have relations with end users. The Riksbank controls the network, consisting of the participating nodes, while the participants manage their nodes, requesting e-kronor in exchange for funds. Participants can then store and transfer tokens to the end users' wallets. The responsibility for identifying and verifying customers lies with the intermediaries. End users can use various e-krona payment methods thanks to the digital wallet app, for example, on a mobile phone or at a merchant's cash register (terminal).

In order to use e-kronor for payments, the digital wallet must first be activated by a participant connected to the e-krona network. After activation, the user can receive e-kronor as payment from another user; pay a reseller with e-kronor; make transfers from their bank account to the digital wallet (and vice versa); and check their e-krona balance.

30 Sveriges Riksbank, 'The Riksbank's e-Krona Pilot', February 2020, https://www.riksbank.se/globalassets/media/rapporter/e-krona/2019/the-riksbanks-e-krona-pilot.pdf; Hanna Armelius et al., 'E-Krona Design Models: Pros, Cons and Trade-Offs', *Sveriges Riksbank Economic Review*, no. 1 (2020): 80–96.

During this phase, the possibility of using the currency offline has not yet been tested. In contrast, the possibility of controlling both supply and demand through a limit on the holdings in the portfolio has already been considered, such as setting an interest rate. The technical solution of bearer tokens would, in fact, be compatible with both the introduction of a possible holding limit and the fixing of an interest rate, either positive or negative.

19.6.5 The Chinese digital yuan

In 2019, after a few years of work, China announced its digital currency/electronic payment (DCEP) to create a digital yuan (eCNY).[31]

This initiative aims to introduce a retail CBDC, even if it would be reductive to read the digital yuan only from the perspective of an instrument aimed at building a Chinese cashless society. In fact, it is part of a much broader project that concerns the entire Chinese fintech industry and its regulation.

Thanks to platforms such as WeChat (Tencent) and Alipay, the Chinese payment system has been substantially revolutionised for some years.[32] In this context, traditional banks—mostly publicly owned—have progressively lost their position and have been relegated to the function of guarantor of deposits.

The e-CNY adopts a centralised management model and a two-tier approach. The right to issue e-CNY belongs to the state. The central bank maintains a prominent position within the operating system but only enters direct contact with commercial banks, not with users. The e-CNY appears, from an architectural point of view, to be a hybrid system. The tokens issued by the PBoC to intermediaries are only transferred to the accounts of retail and wholesale customers at a later stage.

The PBoC project provides that banks are the only ones who can participate in issuing digital currency, excluding those who still need a banking license.[33] For this reason, some authors believe introducing this central bank currency could successfully reverse this trend, allowing banks to regain ground concerning the digital giants.[34] The PBoC aims to create a digital currency as similar as possible to the physical currency, thus maintaining its main characteristics. To this end, the e-CNY acts as a token that can also be used without an internet

31 Working Group on E-CNY Research and Development of the People's Bank of China, 'Progress of Research & Development of E-CNY in China', July 2021, http://www.pbc.gov.cn/en/3688110/3688172/4157443/4293696/2021071614584691871.pdf.

32 In this regard, see Richard Turrin, *Cashless: China's Digital Currency Revolution* (Gold River, CA: Authority Publishing, 2021), 30.

33 Turrin, 274.

34 The central bank creates money by transferring funds to commercial banks and, at the same time, withdraws a corresponding amount of RMB from deposits. In turn, the commercial bank will be able to exchange, at the request of its customers, e-CNY with RMB and vice versa. Once inserted in their electronic purse, the user can decide to use them for their payments, alternatively with the other currencies held.

connection; it does not bear any interest and has a 100% reserve obligation,[35] thus preventing banks from using those deposits to provide credit and creating a new currency.

Initially, the intention of the e-CNY was not to replace cash and may be used as an alternative to other national payment systems. Competition between private parties will also be prohibited. Therefore, the future system of Chinese digital retail payments will consist of both e-CNY and funds held in the electronic accounts of authorised operators, which will be considered interoperable, and both will constitute cash in circulation.

19.7 Some final remarks

These central banks' experiences show a preference for a two-tier/hybrid CBDC retail model in which central bankers and private operators—especially banks—play a specific role. First, the right to issue digital currency belongs to the central bank, which maintains a privileged position in the system and does not enter direct contact with end users. In other words, digital currencies are issued by bankers to intermediaries, who then proceed to transfer them to retail accounts.

Central bankers are wary of the possible impact on the banking sector and are attempting to minimise the risk of disintermediation. In this light, some systems have introduced or are considering introducing specific limits on the holdings in portfolios or transactions in the CBDC. It is usually not possible to earn interest on such holdings.

However, at this moment, it is difficult to imagine how, in practical terms, the EBC and other central bankers should act in the future, what type of digital money should be introduced, and, more importantly, what kind of relationships with private subjects (commercial banks and Big Tech) should be designed. However, this latter issue is crucial to introducing a successful CBDC, and all legal systems must address and resolve it.

The solution may be a public-private partnership based on a clear understanding of the transformations that technological innovation is causing in the monetary field.

On this point, however, we must be realistic. Central banks, especially the European ones, need to catch up compared with private competitors and, even more, Big Tech. This should make the central banks more determined to bridge this gap, approaching the phenomenon with new skills and an open mind.

35 Turrin, *Cashless*, 137–38.

20 Beyond Digital Assets

What is Next for Money and Payments?

Filippo Zatti and Rosa Giovanna Barresi[1]

20.1 Introduction: Fiat, legal tender, official currency, what else?

The year 2023 is emblematic of how we experience 'money' in the modern world. One thousand years ago, the first form of banknote appeared in China.[2] However, the concept of *fiat money* first came into light in Roman law.[3] So, *fiat* value existed well before the rise of central banks, as we conceive in modern times, or since the foundation of the BoE. Before central banks, the money function was provided by public banks featured 'for the ability to create a privileged set of claims (ledger money or circulating notes) of a form that purely private institutions could not easily replicate.'[4]

Also, *legal tender* is not a term coined in the central bank era.[5] It should be noted that the indistinct use of various terms to refer to the instrument by which we enable the transfer of value and fulfil the obligation also contributes

1 The editors of this book have diligently reviewed and approved the final draft. Filippo Zatti is here responsible for drafting and the content of §§ 20.1, 20.2, and 20.6, while Rosa Giovanna Barresi is responsible for §§ 20.3, 20.4, and 20.5.

2 According to Barry Eichengreen, 'Thousand Years of Paper Currency, and What Comes Next', in *The Euro at 20: The Future of Our Money*, ed. Johannes Beermann (Munich: Penguin Verlag. Kindle Edition., 2022), 329. However, this recurrence is not commonly accepted, as others date the issuance of the first Chinese banknote called 'Jiaozi' (纸币) or 'paper money' to the Tang Dynasty (618-90/AD). See Udo Milkau and Jürgen Bott, 'Digital Currencies and the Concept of Money as a Social Agreement', *Journal of Payments Strategy & Systems* 12, no. 3 (Autumn/Fall 2018): 217.

3 As Professor Zhang Qinglin suggests. See Ke Da, 'Also on the Legal Tender Nature of Central Bank Digital Currency in China', *Journal of Shanghai University of Finance and Economics* 6, no. 22 (2020): 123.

4 William Roberds and François R Velde, 'Early Public Banks I', in *Money in the Western Legal Tradition*, ed. David Fox and Wolfgang Ernst (Oxford University Press, 2016), 322, https://doi.org/10.1093/acprof:oso/9780198704744.003.0017.

5 In 1526 in Venice, 'Bankers were required to pay depositors on demand and in cash without delay; bank money was made *legal tender* except when specific clauses for payment "out of bank" would be made.' See Roberds and Velde, 332. After a few years, in 1593, 'ostensibly in response to the common problem that bills of exchange were not paid in cash but by assignment of another debt so that creditors had to "pass through fifteen or twenty hands" before being paid, and on the terms of the debtor.' See Roberds and Velde, 335.

DOI 10.4324/9781003258261-25

to clarifying the legal framework of the parties giving rise to the exchange. For instance, Macleod reminds us that the etymological history of the word *currency* is 'final debt settlement by delivery of property.'[6] There is a common thread between the control of money and the nature of monetary transactions. From a legal standpoint, *seigniorage* and settlement *finality* are emblematic of this.

Nowadays, when we talk of *money*, we refer to central bank debt, which enjoys a privileged status as a *transaction medium* (for example, in terms of *legal tender* and *payment finality*), rendering it the most liquid asset in most contemporary economies.[7] A digital currency issued by a central bank is also a liability. Then, what would be the effects on seigniorage from the issuance of CBDC for a central bank? Is seigniorage a helpful indicator for understanding monetary law and policy changes?

The CBDC design model adopted could vary the impact. However, seigniorage would increase through savings on cash handling (meaning printing, storage, and transportation of physical cash)[8] and growing demand for central bank liabilities,[9] even directly in the case of remunerated CBDCs. However, that on seigniorage revenues is one of their possible effects.[10] They would also bring changes in bank size, lending to the economy, and bankruptcy costs.[11]

6 Jens Reich, *Seigniorage: On the Revenue from the Creation of Money*, 1st ed. 2017 (Cham: Springer International Publishing: Imprint: Springer, 2017), 4, https://doi.org/10.1007/978-3-319-63124-0.

7 Roberds and Velde, 'Early Public Banks I', 321.

8 Barry Eichengreen and Ganesh Viswanath-Natraj, 'Stablecoins and Central Bank Digital Currencies: Policy and Regulatory Challenges', *Asian Economic Papers* 21, no. 1 (20 February 2022): 8, https://doi.org/10.1162/asep_a_00843; 'Reserve Bank of India—Speeches', para. 31, accessed 31 January 2023, https://www.rbi.org.in/Scripts/BS_SpeechesView.aspx?Id=1111, according to him 'Introduction of CBDC has the potential to provide significant benefits, such as reduced dependency on cash, higher seigniorage due to lower transaction costs, reduced settlement risk. Introduction of CBDC would possibly lead to a more robust, efficient, trusted, regulated and legal tender-based payments option.'

9 Walter Engert and Ben S C Fung, 'Motivations and Implications of a Central Bank Digital Currency', in *Do We Need Central Bank Digital Currency? Economics, Technology and Institutions*, ed. Ernest Gnan and Donato Masciandaro (Do We Need Central Bank Digital Currency? Economics, Technology and Institutions, Milan: SUERF/BAFFI CAREFIN Centre Conference, 2018), 66 ff. See also Novi Maryaningsih et al., 'Central Bank Digital Currency: What Factors Determine Its Adoption?', *Buletin Ekonomi Moneter Dan Perbankan* 25, no. 1 (20 June 2022): 6, https://doi.org/10.21098/bemp.v25i1.1979. They point out, 'The decline in demand for cash could reduce the central bank's income from seigniorage, forcing the central bank to rely on the government for operational funding.'

10 See Nicola Bilotta and Fabrizio Botti, eds., *The (Near) Future of Central Bank Digital Currencies* (Peter Lang CH, 2021), 42, https://doi.org/10.3726/b18087.

11 See Martina Fraschini, Luciano Somoza, and Tammaro Terracciano, 'Central Bank Digital Currency and Balance Sheet Policy', *SSRN Electronic Journal*, 2021, 4, https://doi.org/10.2139/ssrn.3804966: 'when CBDC deposits are less onerous than bank deposits, seigniorage revenues increase and taxes decrease while the risk exposure of the central bank remains the same.'

These findings are significant as most of the discussion over CBDC design focuses on either the technological aspect of it or on the disintermediation risks.[12] By introducing a CBDC, the role of seigniorage may change, potentially affecting monetary governance's economic and legal aspects and changing monetary policy transmission radically. Additionally, introducing a digital currency issued by central banks may also impact how the money transfer has been ruled until now.

What the digital transformation of money emerges is that the layered solution of a monetary system based on intermediation as the link between public and private power in the exercise of the monetary function is destined to reshape. DLT opportunities have evidenced the relevance of the seigniorage in formatting money. They have created money-like transfer systems that do not require the legal and political infrastructure of the monetary systems known and implemented to date. We can find seigniorage in cryptocurrency or DLT-based digital currency such as stablecoins.

Seigniorage for a cryptocurrency refers to the profit that a cryptocurrency issuer or miner can earn by creating new units of the coin and selling them on the market, making the difference between the cost of production and the market price as seigniorage.

The issuer of a stablecoin can earn seigniorage by distributing new units of the currency and using the funds generated to invest in assets that generate a return. This return can be used to offset any losses incurred because of changes in the value of the underlying collateral or to provide a source of profit for the issuer.[13]

The concept of seigniorage for cryptocurrencies and stablecoins is like that of traditional fiat currencies. However, the mechanics of how seigniorage is earned and how much it can impact the economy can differ. Introducing cryptocurrencies and stablecoins can disrupt the traditional monetary system by removing seigniorage from the exclusivity central banks have had with the banking system.[14] This can change monetary governance dynamics and shift the balance of power away from central banks and towards private actors in the cryptocurrency market. Additionally, the transfer modalities offered by cryptocurrencies and stablecoins can bypass the need for a banking intermediary, benefiting from the inherent legality of the platform on which they

12 Martina Fraschini, Luciano Somoza, and Tammaro Terracciano, 'The Likely Impact of Central Bank Digital Currencies on Quantitative Easing', *LSE Business Review* (blog), 27 April 2021, https://blogs.lse.ac.uk/businessreview/2021/04/27/the-likely-impact-of-central-bank-digital-currencies-on-quantitative-easing/.

13 Robert Sams, 'A Note on Cryptocurrency Stabilisation: Seigniorage Shares', TeX, 16 January 2023, 3–5, https://github.com/rmsams/stablecoins/blob/997b310106a2d99a734cf4bdba9d820b1548bf6e/paper.pdf.

14 Charles M Kahn Alwazir Manmohan Singh, Jihad, 'Digital Money and Central Bank Operations', IMF, May 2022, 7, https://www.imf.org/en/Publications/WP/Issues/2022/05/06/Digital-Money-and-Central-Bank-Operations-517534.

are managed. Two issues arise that are relevant from a legal point of view at the end of the analysis driven by this book. Is the central bank's erosion of financial sovereignty incompatible with maintaining the current institutional structure? What legal reforms are needed for CBDC to guarantee 'final debt settlement by delivery of property?' Or will it also have to share this privilege with private payment providers?[15]

20.2 Sovereignty and seigniorage in the digital currency era

What do sovereignty and seigniorage have in common? And how important are they with digital currency? According to the ECB, *seigniorage* is an 'exotic word' consisting of either earning interest on the money a central bank lends or receiving a return on the assets it acquires.[16] Seigniorage is not just an ancient practice. It is an endless combination of other current techniques and has a feedback effect on these. The idea of seigniorage as merely revenue from the government's monopoly of the issue of coins is, of course, outdated. The income derived from this monopoly contributes only a fraction of the total seigniorage revenues of modern governments,[17] even if it varies depending on the role of central banks and fiscal authorities.

The term seigniorage is usually restricted to the government's revenue from the money supply, but the government does not supply all money. As the GFC suggests, we probably need to rethink seigniorage according to the importance that banking intermediaries have assumed in creating money over time.[18] However, we cannot overlook the possibility that the return to the seigniorage, most in the availability of monetary power, may also contribute in the digital context to fostering phenomena that can be referred to as Gresham's Law.[19] At the same time, we must not neglect that the monetary policy consequences widely differ depending on the structure of private currency markets. Public

15 Aleksander Berentsen and Fabian Schar, 'The Case for Central Bank Electronic Money and the Non-Case for Central Bank Cryptocurrencies', *Review* 100, no. 2 (2018): 104, https://doi.org/10.20955/r.2018.97-106.

16 European Central Bank, 'What Is Seigniorage?', European Central Bank, 18 November 2021, 4, https://www.ecb.europa.eu/ecb/educational/explainers/tell-me/html/seigniorage.en.html; see also Bank of Italy, 'Seignorage', n.d., https://www.bancaditalia.it/compiti/emissione-euro/signoraggio/https%3A%2F%2Fwww.bancaditalia.it%2Fcompiti%2Femissione-euro%2Fsignoraggio%2Findex.html%3Fcom.dotmarketing.htmlpage.language%3D1 quoting Article 32.1 of the Statute of the ESCB and of the ECB according to which is 'The income accruing to the national central banks in the performance of the ESCB's monetary policy function.'

17 Reich, *Seigniorage*, 4.

18 Ole Bjerg, Laurie Macfarlane, and Josh Ryan-Collins, 'Seigniorage in the 21st Century: A Study of the Profits from Money Creation in the United Kingdom and Denmark', *SSRN Electronic Journal*, 2017, 5, https://doi.org/10.2139/ssrn.2921225.

19 Kevin Dowd and Richard H Timberlake, eds., *Money and the Nation State: The Financial Revolution, Government, and the World Monetary System*, Independent Studies in Political Economy (New Brunswick, NJ: Transaction Publishers, 1998), 173.

currency may be more likely to lose its role as a medium of exchange altogether.[20] Economic law analysis would help search for a holistic solution based on the mentioned technical or economic issues. The latter is meaningful, but the former is functional to the constitutional framework of monetary policy and payments system. Extolling the partisan praise of one type of currency or payment system, noting its praises and critical issues, respectively, is only the first step towards a necessary reform of the monetary order. Would we still need a digital revolution if we had never questioned the legal basis of money production, creation, and circulation? The aim is to find a solution that considers the importance of currency within the economic market system and the fundamental liberal values that underpin political systems in many countries. We need to discover the solution within the realm of freedom. Otherwise, we run the risk of leaving it to alternative forms of seigniorage management, which, however brilliant, are unconvincing because of their rigidity and mechanics, which are ill-suited to the goals of social justice that should be given no less attention than those of distributive justice.

The mind clearly goes to the consensus mechanisms introduced by DLT, particularly blockchains, to enable coinage and economic valorisation on the one hand and to secure its circulation and transaction ability on the other. This system is very similar to the commodity money system[21] but seeks ***deinstitutionalisation*** to pursue ***desovereignisation*** rather than ***denationalisation***.[22] The market would therefore be the system to adopt for the choice of currency, also following Von Hayek's beliefs. However, is this system a feasible remedy to regain confidence in a fiat currency/legal tender-based monetary system? Is neutrality—in the sense of independence from politics—comparable to what is guaranteed to monetary authorities in many legal systems?

The analysis of the seigniorage/legal tender binomial reveals how the legal qualification of money cannot be unrelated to the function of government. It is itself an instrument of economic policy. So, from a legal point of view, the system of liquidity governance cannot be neutral. Simplifying, we could say

20 Maxi Guennewig, 'Currency Competition with Firms', 10 November 2022, 28, https://www.dropbox.com/s/r2s3wobsxdlylxy/JMP_Guennewig.pdf?dl=0.

21 Considering 'Clearly there is no need of making coin a legal tender at any specified weight. If governments would confine their legislation to fixing by enactment the fineness of the precious metal and the number of grains that shall constitute each piece of a given name, they may safely leave the maintenance of the coinage in its integrity, and the value of the pieces, to be regulated by individual interest and action.' See Brough, William, *The Natural Law of Money* (New York: G P Putnam's Sons, 1896). 'Bitcoin's design embodies a basic version of monetary policy that does not consider the state of the real economy': see Rainer Böhme et al., 'Bitcoin: Economics, Technology, and Governance', *Journal of Economic Perspectives* 29, no. 2 (1 May 2015): 234, https://doi.org/10.1257/jep.29.2.213.

22 Henrik Karlstrøm, 'Do Libertarians Dream of Electric Coins? The Material Embeddedness of Bitcoin', *Distinktion: Journal of Social Theory* 15, no. 1 (2 January 2014): 29 ff., https://doi.org/10.1080/1600910X.2013.870083.

that a currency that only performed the function of a unit of account would not be such because it would not be able to perfect that which is the final regulation, and which requires the simultaneous exchange with a thing corresponding to the value of the thing sold. CBDCs represent a *de facto* hybrid to cryptocurrencies, stablecoins and fiat currencies. A combination in which the governance of the money remains in the hands of the central bank and the infrastructure for its conveyance shifts to a DLT.

From a legal point of view, the analysis should also extend to alternative scenarios from which a digital currency issued by a central bank is introduced. Clearly, the changes that will have to be introduced in the current legal frameworks cannot fail to consider the existence of parallel monetary phenomena even if a prohibition solution such as the one already adopted in some jurisdictions were to be enacted. It is still being determined whether measures aimed at regulating and improving efficiency in monetary markets and payment systems are effective with the resilience of DLT technology. Similarly, regulating cryptocurrencies and stablecoins as phenomena within financial intermediation will only sharpen the problem. We are not dealing with a solution in search of a problem but with a problem in search of a solution other than compliance. There are times in history when failing to accept the profound changes taking place and the rationales behind them means not only finding fake solutions but, above all, setting the stage for traversing more than uncharted waters. The significance of the stablecoin phenomenon and cryptoassets is now a fact.

The figures provided by international organisations bear witness to this. But it was somewhat expected that this would happen. So why this slowness in realising that a path needs to be re-established in which those aspects that were not willing or able to be addressed after the global financial crisis are defined? Money as digital means realising that it is no longer an electronic currency and is destined to change the physiognomy of how the monetary function has been understood so far. The legal qualification of a digital asset is a narrow passage fraught with difficulties, requiring new solutions to genuinely unique phenomena. And above all, it must be tackled in such a way as to ensure the uniformity that has so far been lacking in the private sphere. This is even if the intervention was limited to payments' settlement, as in the case of finality. The legal qualification of a digital asset is a narrow passage fraught with difficulties, requiring new solutions to genuinely unique phenomena. And above all, it must be tackled in such a way as to ensure the uniformity that has so far been lacking in the private sphere. Even when limiting our analysis to the finality of settlements, we perceive a fundamental incompatibility between the different ways English law and German law describe a transaction involving digital assets. This complication signals that more efforts are required to achieve an operational synthesis between the two approaches. Such activities are well underway on the specific issues of interoperability, finality, and privacy as they are applied to the circulation of digital assets.

20.3 Interoperability, sovereignty, and finality

Whenever new forms of money are developed, several issues at the boundary between economy, politics, and law come to attention. Among those, the most relevant is the universally acknowledged requirement of interoperability.

Since their introduction, currencies have freely circulated outside their jurisdiction. Later, Roman jurists formalised the *fungibility* principle, i.e., allowing the settlement of a debt in silver through an equivalent amount in gold.[23] By the end of the Middle Ages, the monetisation of the European economy was driven by a variety of coins from Italy, Byzantium, and the various Muslim states. The need to support their interoperability led to understanding the three essential functions of money: *moneta effectiva*, *moneta numeraria*, and *moneta di conto*.[24] At the same time, interoperability emphasised the acknowledgement of monetary sovereignty, which is constantly undergoing a circular process of centralisation and devolvement. At the same time, a Roman tradition linked coinage rights to the emperor himself, and the Middle Ages fragmented minting authority into the hands of counts, dukes, bishops, and abbots. After establishing absolute power, French kings centralised the issuance of money and started debasing coinage to increase seigniorage revenues.[25]

At first, absolutist monarchies availed themselves of the services of European banker families. Still, the need for professional public debt management led to the establishment of national central banks such as the Sveriges Riksbank (1668) and the BoE (1694). Since then, monetary history can be described as tuning the delicate balance between the attributions of central and commercial banking. The last significant step was introducing the RTGS system, which ensured payment *finality* for central bank money in its digital form.

However, the expansion of credit and the introduction of new forms of money have created new problems regarding sovereignty and interoperability.[26]

23 Thomas Rüfner, 'Money in the Roman Law Texts', in *Money in the Western Legal Tradition*, ed. David Fox and Wolfgang Ernst (Oxford University Press, 2016), 107, https://doi.org/10.1093/acprof:oso/9780198704744.003.0006.

24 They were roughly equivalent to store of value, medium of exchange, and unit of account. See Philipp Robinson Rössner, 'From the Black Death to the New World (c.1350–1500)', in Money and Coinage in the Middle Ages, ed. Rory Naismith (Leiden, Boston: Brill, 2018), 162.

25 Nicole Oresme ('*De moneta*', 1382), stated for the first time the modern approach to this problem: while the prince issues money for the common good, he is not the owner of it, and cannot debase its value. As money is a measure of natural wealth, it is owned by those who possess such wealth. See Rory Naismith, 'Introduction', in *Money and Coinage in the Middle Ages*, ed. Rory Naismith (Leiden; Boston: Brill, 2018), 8.

26 With the two exceptions of El Salvador and the Central African Republic, which declared Bitcoin an official currency. See Habtamu Fuje, Saad Quayyum, and Tebo Molosiwa, 'Africa's Growing Crypto Market Needs Better Regulations', *IMF* (blog), 22 November 2022, https://www.imf.org/en/Blogs/Articles/2022/11/22/africas-growing-crypto-market-needs-better-regulations.

It has been observed that even if the law defined CBDC as a 'currency,' it would lack the privileged status as traditional currency under private law.[27]

A €100 banknote holds the same nominal value either inside the eurozone or outside it, and independently from the nationality of its holder. Although experiments in CBDC interoperability are underway, there is no uniform approach to the definition of the international circulation of CBDC. Even in the eurozone, the agreement is limited to transferring the ***underlying value*** of notes and coins.[28] According to German law, digital assets have no object quality (*Sache*) and must be transferred only via an assignment (***Realakt***).

However, this may create a problem as, under assignment law, any transfer is successfully terminated as soon as an agreement is reached between the parties, and no registration is necessary. A better solution would be to frame the transfer of value under property law in analogy with the physical transfer of money. Under this alternative model, the transfer is deemed successful only after the payer has surrendered possession and the receiver has established control of the title. This needs legislation and technical change.[29] Moreover, these issues become more relevant as CBDCs extend outside their national dimension and new regional exchanges are being investigated. The BIS suggested three models for interoperability, ranging from the very loose coupling of Model 1 (based on one-to-one adaptors) to the very tight coupling of Model 3, which expects multiple CBDCs to share the same software platform. Model 2, currently the most popular, is based on a set of standard interfaces or a common clearing mechanism.[30]

The Regulated Liability Network (RLN) envisages a form of unified ledger to be shared among sovereign and non-sovereign currencies, exploring the proof-of-concept of a unified settlement network among ten US banks with the collaboration of the Federal Reserve Bank of New York and the SWIFT

27 Wouter Bossu et al., 'Legal Aspects of Central Bank Digital Currency: Central Bank and Monetary Law Considerations', *IMF*, IMF Working Paper, 20, no. 254 (November 2020): 34, https://www.imf.org/en/Publications/WP/Issues/2020/11/20/Legal-Aspects-of-Central-Bank-Digital-Currency-Central-Bank-and-Monetary-Law-Considerations-49827.

28 In Germany, Finland, and The Netherlands, the holder of a note (or of a coin) owns both the object and its value. In the remaining states of the eurozone, notes and coins are considered public goods, and their holder owns only the nominal value represented by them. See European Legal Tender Expert Group (ELTEG), 'Definition, Scope and Effects of Legal Tender of Euro Banknotes and Coins' (Brussels, 22 March 2010), 8, https://ec.europa.eu/economy_finance/articles/euro/2010-03-22-legal-tender-euro_en.htm; European Commission, 'Commission Adopts a Recommendation on the Scope and Effects of Legal Tender of Euro Banknotes and Coins', Text, European Commission - European Commission, 22 March 2010, https://ec.europa.eu/commission/presscorner/detail/en/IP_10_331.

29 Aurelia Philine Birne, Christian Sillaber, and Mirjam Eggen, 'Principles for the Transfer of Retail CBDC', *SSRN Electronic Journal*, 2022, 5, https://doi.org/10.2139/ssrn.4303955.

30 Raphael Auer, Philipp Haene, and Henry Holden, 'Multi-CBDC Arrangements and the Future of Cross-Border Payments', *BIS Papers*, no. 115 (March 2021): 4 ff., https://www.bis.org/publ/bppdf/bispap115.pdf.

consortium.[31] As well as the BIS-sponsored mBridge project for a custom-built blockchain infrastructure allowing CBDC-based international payments between the Hong Kong Monetary Authority, the Bank of Thailand, the PBoC, and the Central Bank of the United Arab Emirates.[32]

Defining the governance of these new regional exchanges requires the cooperation of central banks and within the political framework. Central bankers are careful about expanding their oversight to non-economic issues, as they may overstep their policy objectives, with climate change being a case in point.[33]

20.4 Emission rights as digital assets

Growing sentiment advocates that central bankers should consider energy transition risks provided their other institutional activities are included.[34] After all, central banks own a substantial share of the world economy and its emissions due to their corporate asset purchase programmes.[35] Those advocating a greater involvement in climate issues point to the controversial results of the EU Emissions Trading Scheme (EU ETS).[36] Every year, regulators allocate to

31 The Regulated Liability Network, 'The Regulated Liability Network. Digital Sovereign Currency', 15 November 2022, 18 ff., https://regulatedliabilitynetwork.org/wp-content/uploads/2022/11/The-Regulated-Liability-Network-Whitepaper.pdf. The goal of the RLN is to ensure extensive interoperability among digital assets and all the liabilities presently managed by the banking sector. Such a unified circulation guarantees the fungibility between central bank money and commercial bank money, ensuring a unit of currency is worth the same amount everywhere. The concept of the singleness of money was first introduced by Tommaso Padoa-Schioppa: see European Central Bank, 'Shaping the Payment System: A Central Bank's Role - Speech by Tommaso Padoa-Schioppa Member of the Executive Board of the European Central Bank Delivered at the Bank of Korea's Conference on Payment Systems in Seoul', European Central Bank, 13 May 2004, https://www.ecb.europa.eu/press/key/date/2004/html/sp040513_1.en.html.

32 BIS Innovation Hub, 'Connecting Economies through CBDC', October 2022, https://www.bis.org/publ/othp59.pdf.

33 US Fed chair Jerome Powell has explicitly refused to take any role in it: 'We are not, and will not be a "climate policymaker."' See 'Speech by Chair Powell on Central Bank Independence', Board of Governors of the Federal Reserve System, accessed 5 February 2023, https://www.federalreserve.gov/newsevents/speech/powell20230110a.htm.

34 Isabel Schnabel, 'Climate Change and Monetary Policy', IMF | FD Finance & Development, September 2021, https://www.imf.org/en/Publications/fandd/issues/2021/09/isabel-schnabel-ECB-climate-change.

35 If the ECB offloaded from its portfolio the assets from the 25 top polluters, it could cut 90% of its own carbon footprint and more than 10% of the global one. See Josephine Richardson and Ulf Erlandsson, 'Wind down (of CSPP) Is Coming' (AFII, 8 June 2022), 1, https://img1.wsimg.com/blobby/go/946d6aac-e6cc-430a-8898-520cf90f5d3e/AFII_WindDownIsComing-0002-0001.pdf. The ECB announced more steps to align its activities towards the goals of the Paris Agreement: see 'United Nations Treaty Collection', § 7. d Paris Agreement (2015), https://treaties.un.org/pages/ViewDetails.aspx?src=TREATY&mtdsg_no=XXVII-7-d&chapter=27&clang=_en.

36 Established in 2005 as the world's first international emissions trading system.

each participant a fixed number of EU Allowances (EUAs), entitling its owner to emit one metric ton of carbon dioxide.[37] By the end of the year, emissions are estimated, and participants must cover them by surrendering the equivalent amount of EUAs: those who cannot are subject to heavy penalties.[38] Unused EUAs arising from emission reductions can be carried on to the next year or freely traded on the EU ETS market.[39]

The ECB considers the EU ETS essential in climate change issues. However, it noticed that the system covers only half of EU greenhouse gas emissions, and the extended lifecycle of allowances leaves their market open to speculation.[40] At a basic level, the financial sector still needs to agree on the nature of EUAs and how to assimilate them into present-day corporate accounting standards. An initial interpretation of EUAs as taxes was rejected by the European Court of Justice, as they are not applied at a fixed rate and are not intended to generate revenues.[41] In the present version, the Regulation defines EUAs as fungible, dematerialised assets managed by a centralised database whose registrations are *prima facie* and sufficient evidence of title. The ETS market guarantees the *finality* of the trading, allocation and surrendering processes.[42]

English law has recognised EU (and UK) allowances as a third form of intangible property, according to the criteria of the existence of a statutory framework conferring their holder an exemption from a fine, regulating their

37 'Directive 2003/87/EC of the European Parliament and of the Council of 13 October 2003 Establishing a Scheme for Greenhouse Gas Emission Allowance Trading within the Community and Amending Council Directive 96/61/EC, art. 3(a).

38 Directive 2003/87/EC of the European Parliament and of the Council of 13 October 2003 establishing a scheme for greenhouse gas emission allowance trading within the Community and amending Council Directive 96/61/EC, art. 16.

39 'Commission Delegated Regulation (EU) 2019/1122 of 12 March 2019 Supplementing Directive 2003/87/EC of the European Parliament and of the Council as Regards the Functioning of the Union Registry (Text with EEA Relevance)', art. 5.

40 Christine Lagarde, 'Climate Change and Central Banking', 25 January 2021, 2, https://www.bis.org/review/r210127d.pdf; 'EU Carbon Price Tracker', Ember, accessed 5 February 2023, https://ember-climate.org/data/data-tools/carbon-price-viewer/. In November 2020, the ECB set out its supervisory expectations relating to climate-related and environmental risks. After asking institutions to assess themselves against the guidance received, only 12% of the assessments disclosed metrics on those specific risks of their portfolio: ECB, 'Supervisory Assessment of Institutions' Climate-Related and Environmental Risks Disclosures' (Frankfurt am Main, Germany: ECB, March 2022), 4, https://www.bankingsupervision.europa.eu/ecb/pub/pdf/ssm.ECB_Report_on_climate_and_environmental_disclosures_202203~4ae33f2a70.en.pdf.

41 Air Transport Association of America and Others v Secretary of State for Energy and Climate Change, No. C-366/10 (ECJ 21 December 2011).

42 'Commission Delegated Regulation (EU) 2019/1122 of 12 March 2019 Supplementing Directive 2003/87/EC of the European Parliament and of the Council as Regards the Functioning of the Union Registry (Text with EEA Relevance)', Articles 36 and 74.

transferability, and assigning them a market value.[43] Following the same reasoning, the Law Commission for England and Wales has even proposed classifying all digital assets as intangible properties.[44] However, accountants soon discovered that allowances could not be considered voluntary investments.[45]

The financial sector is coming to appreciate that the risks implied in the energy transition process may be as substantial as those associated with climate change.[46] This will require evolving central banks' financial stability and prudential supervision approaches.

20.5 The digital euro and payment privacy

The offline circulation of CBDC has become a standard feature of the most advanced projects about this new means of payment. As soon as the need for a digital wallet emerged, offline operation was suggested to support financial inclusion and improve resilience to natural calamities. That is, in any event, mobile networks lacked coverage or availability.[47]

It is only a short time before payment privacy is acknowledged as the main reason for supporting offline payments. When the digital euro project entered the investigation phase, the offline operation still needed to be considered among the basic requirements for the prototype.[48] However, there were many indications that payment privacy was the most popular issue among those advocating the centrality of cash.[49] The European Data Protection Board

43 Armstrong DLW GmbH v. Winnington Networks Ltd., No. HC10C00532 (Royal Courts of Justice 11 January 2012), ch. 156, para. 58, 49.

44 'Law Commission, 'Digital Assets: Consultation Paper 256', 28 July 2022, 147-148, https://perma.cc/M2WJ-KDC8.

45 Applying the same accounting standards defined for any other financial instrument creates inconsistencies between the companies who actively trade in them and those who choose not to trade. Accordingly, the IFRIC 3 standard (2004), which defined allowances as variable-price financial instruments, was withdrawn just within a year of its issuance, IASB, 'IASB Withdraws IFRIC 3 "Emission Rights"', 25 June 2005, https://www.iasplus.com/en/news/2005/June/news2147.

46 Romain Hubert et al., 'Scenario Analysis of Transition Risk in Finance' (Paris: Institute for Climate Economics, May 2022), 8, https://www.i4ce.org/wp-content/uploads/I4CE_2022_Scenario-analysis-of-transition-risk-in-finance.pdf.

47 See Rosa Giovanna Barresi and Filippo Zatti, 'The Importance of Where Central Bank Digital Currencies Are Custodied: Exploring the Need of a Universal Access Device', *SSRN Electronic Journal*, 2020, https://doi.org/10.2139/ssrn.3691263; see Proposal for a Regulation of the European Parliament and of the Council on the establishment of the digital euro, COM/2023/369 final.

48 The investigation phase started in October 2021. The so-called 'selective privacy' for low-value payments and offline operations were both earmarked as desirable options, see ECB, 'Progress on the Investigation Phase of a Digital Euro', 8 September 2022, 1, 8, https://www.ecb.europa.eu/paym/digital_euro/investigation/governance/shared/files/ecb.degov220929.en.pdf.

49 The ECB has held surveys and consultations on the digital euro. According to the results published in April 2021, privacy was by far the most popular issue (43% of the answers), followed

(EDPB) adopted a statement underlining its concern with the initial design. Online operation of the digital euro required any transfer to be validated by a third party, which would have access to personal and transaction data.[50] As a result, the EDPB pointed out that this approach was inconsistent with Articles 7 and 8 of the European Charter of Fundamental Rights and with the data protection principles of necessity and proportionality.

EDPB's final recommendation considers the opportunity for a 'privacy threshold' exempted from the AML/CFT obligations of verifications and tracing in force. At the same time, digital wallets should be interconnected with ATM networks.[51] However, consider that the digital wallet could be completely self-sufficient, even more so in the case of UAD.[52] As a result, the offline operation has been selected as one of the five use cases for the digital euro prototype.[53] A holistic analysis suggests that a smart digital wallet should allow the storage of generic digital assets and digital identity artefacts. It should also support software updating as new cryptographic protocols are continuously developed.[54]

This approach is consistent with the guidelines established for the EUropean Digital Identity wallet ecosystem.[55]

Although the market value of payment data continues to increase, privacy and identity issues are just two more aspects in the whole landscape of digital assets.

---

by security (with just 18%). See ECB, 'Eurosystem Report on the Public Consultation on a Digital Euro', April 2021, 10, https://www.ecb.europa.eu/pub/pdf/other/Eurosystem_report_on_the_public_consultation_on_a_digital_euro~539fa8cd8d.en.pdf.

50 See EDPB, 'Statement 04/2022 on the Design Choices for a Digital Euro from the Privacy and Data Protection Perspective', 0ctober 2022, https://edpb.europa.eu/system/files/2022-10/edpb_statement_20221010_digital_euro_en.pdf.

51 EDPB, 3.

52 Rosa Giovanna Barresi and Filippo Zatti, 'From Wallets to Universal Access Device?', in *Cryptoassets, DeFi Regulation and DLT: Proceedings of the II Token World Conference*, ed. Javier Wenceslao Ibáñez Jiménez, 1st ed., Derecho de Blockchain y Digitalización de La Sociedad (Madrid: Editorial Reus, 2023), 132, https://doi.org/10.30462/9788429027044.

53 As described in the documentation supplied to the solution providers. The other four types of payments are person-to-person online payments, e-commerce, and point-of-sale. In this latter case, both payments by the sender and by the receiver will be tested. See ECB, 'The Eurosystem's Technical Onboarding Package for Digital Euro Prototyping', 7 December 2022, 1, https://www.ecb.europa.eu/paym/digital_euro/investigation/profuse/shared/files/dedocs/ecb.dedocs221207_cover_note_digital_euro_front_end_prototyping_publication_of_technical_onboarding_package.en.pdf.

54 Rosa Giovanna Barresi and Filippo Zatti, From Wallets to Universal Access Device?

55 The eIDAS Expert Group has developed the concept and the specifications for the European Digital Identity Framework. See EUDI, 'The Common Union Toolbox for a Coordinated Approach Towards a European Digital Identity Framework', January 2023, https://code.europa.eu/eudi/architecture-and-reference-framework. See also 'EU Digital Identity Wallet Pilot Implementation | Shaping Europe's Digital Future', 15 June 2023, https://digital-strategy.ec.europa.eu/en/policies/eudi-wallet-implementation.

20.6 Some final 'tips'

The long journey we have proposed to the reader ends here. It could only be a long one. Currency is a subject whose perception required complexity long before technology introduced significant payment system innovations. Now that a transformation is also looming for the currency issued by the central banks, the question becomes even more evocative and, simultaneously, the bearer of more significant changes than scholars have grasped and with which practitioners have grappled.

What is the reason for transforming the currency issued by the central bank from physical to digital while leaving the underlying regulatory framework untouched? Can it be explained by financial inclusion or the need to maintain the role of money as a public good? Why bother to move the handling of payments through digital money issued by central banks to a DLT platform when that same money can be transferred effectively and even efficiently with payment systems that rely on account-based electronic and mobile payment systems?

Reconstructing this passage takes much work. Indeed, two elements have fostered the focus on digital currencies over time. On the one hand, the possibility of freeing oneself from fiat money by initiating a process of transferring sovereignty from authority to individuals. On the other, the idea that counteracting this phenomenon would avoid the disappearance of the jurisdictional dimension as we have known it since the Peace of Westphalia. Already in 2016, a Reserve Bank of India Report stated:

> Several benefits of digital currency (issued by a central bank, A/N), including the instantaneous settlement of transactions, reduction of cash costs, and ability to provide a more comprehensive and unified source of credit history and reduction in instances of tax avoidance. The most significant benefit, however, is that the technology makes it extremely difficult to counterfeit and, more importantly, enables the central bank to detect the existence of counterfeit currency on a real-time basis.[56]

This is crucial: a DLT-based digital currency lets you know transactions in real time. In the case of DLT-based digital coins, real-time tracking of transactions is an effect due to the aim to ensure their verification without relying on a central authority. When digital currencies are issued by an authority, as for central banks, real-time monitoring of transactions could be an aim itself. Those who oppose the issuance of a fiat digital currency that is also a legal tender do so

56 It is the Watal Report: see Committee on Digital Payments, 'Medium Term Recommendations to Strengthen Digital Payments Ecosystem' (Ministry of Finance, Government of India, December 2016), 51–52.

because of duality, which the proliferation of DLT-based payment systems in the last decade has made concrete. DLT made it possible to issue and circulate forms of money without recognising the monopoly of legitimate force. In 1997, a book titled 'The Sovereign Individual. Mastering the Transition to the Information Age' suggested a reading of the possible evolution of money as a currency:

> During the Industrial Age, we became so accustomed to thinking of the provision of currency as a service for which one does not pay directly that it was easy to forget that the issuers of the dollars, pesos, pounds, and francs, namely governments, did require that we pay, and pay dearly—through inflation.

We are experiencing the intertwining of two distinct conceptual frameworks of the role of law in the economy, to which is added the ability of technology to emulate alternative regulatory solutions to law. While the former phenomenon repeats itself over time, the latter manifests its potential far beyond the payment system. This world should not be frightening a priori, but neither can its impact on our societies be underestimated. The lengthy constituent phase that the central banks of most countries are considering issuing a CBDC can be explained in various ways, but certainly among these must only be with the realisation that this is much more than a digital version of the legal tender fiat currency. Indeed, any development of money in the digital age must consider the need to guarantee its users the perception of stability, security, convenience, freedom of choice, and trust in its 'reusability.'[57] Undoubtedly, various kinds of monies will continue to coexist through competition in an institutional ecosystem. Therefore, one can expect money to leave behind reliance on quantitative competition and move towards competition over quality.[58] That will inevitably affect the idea of 'legal tender,' as we have conceived until now and its correlation with tax payment.[59] On the other hand, the idea that there is a unique breakpoint for trust in fiat money, which is more likely to be reached in a severe shock when central bank equity turns profoundly negative and fiscal backing is lacking, must be revisited.[60]

The search for the Holy Grail would be a system that could somehow reconcile the domestic benefits of monetary autonomy with the international coordination achieved by fixed but adjustable exchange rates: in other words,

57 Milkau and Bott, 'Digital Currencies and the Concept of Money as a Social Agreement'.

58 Makoto Nishibe, 'The Crisis of Capitalism and the "Quality" of Money', in *The Enigma of Money*, by Makoto Nishibe (Singapore: Springer Singapore, 2016), 87–92, https://doi.org/10.1007/978-981-10-1819-0_6.

59 Stefan Eich, The Currency of Politics: The Political Theory of Money from Aristotle to Keynes (Princeton: Princeton University Press, 2022).

60 Wilko Bolt et al., 'The Bank of Amsterdam and the Limits of Fiat Money', *SSRN Electronic Journal*, 2023, 29, https://doi.org/10.2139/ssrn.4346056.

a system that could square domestic social and economic experimentation with peace and international cooperation.[61] This book contributes to focusing the analysis on the long-term perspective. This legacy of those in the past has allowed us to find a way to live in peace and prosper. This is the hope of all who value what is invaluable from what is not.

61 Eich, The Currency of Politics.

Index

Note: Page numbers in *italics* indicate figures, **bold** indicate tables in the text, and references following "n" refer notes.

Made in the USA
Las Vegas, NV
19 September 2026

13e5343e-5108-4b94-8ebf-b7000ec58a06R01